Second Edition

Dynamic Alignment Through Imagery

Eric Franklin

Human Kinetics

Library of Congress Cataloging-in-Publication Data

Franklin, Eric N.
  Dynamic alignment through imagery / Eric Franklin. -- 2nd ed.
      p. cm.
  Includes bibliographical references and index.
  ISBN-13: 978-0-7360-6789-8 (soft cover)
  ISBN-10: 0-7360-6789-2 (soft cover)
  1. Dance--Physiological aspects. 2. Posture. 3. Body image. 4. Mind and body. I. Title.
  RC1220.D35F73 2012
  615.8'5155--dc23

                              2011037066

  ISBN-10: 0-7360-6789-2 (print)
  ISBN-13: 978-0-7360-6789-8 (print)

The web addresses cited in this text were current as of November 2011, unless otherwise noted.

Acquisitions Editors: Judy Patterson Wright, PhD, and Gayle Kassing, PhD; **Developmental Editor:** Ray Vallese; **Assistant Editor:** Derek Campbell; **Copyeditor:** Jan Feeney; **Indexer:** Marie Rizzo; **Permissions Manager:** Martha Gullo; **Graphic Designer:** Joe Buck; **Graphic Artist:** Denise Lowry; **Cover Designer:** Keith Blomberg; **Photographer (cover):** © Alexander Yakovlev/fotolia.com (top), © PhotoDisc (right), © Eyewire (bottom); **Photographer (interior):** Eric Franklin, unless otherwise noted; **Photo Asset Manager:** Laura Fitch; **Visual Production Assistant:** Joyce Brumfield; **Photo Production Manager:** Jason Allen; **Art Manager:** Kelly Hendren; **Associate Art Manager:** Alan L. Wilborn; **Illustrations:** © Eric Franklin; **Printer:** Sheridan Books

Printed in the United States of America   10

The paper in this book is certified under a sustainable forestry program.

Human Kinetics
Website: www.HumanKinetics.com

United States: Human Kinetics
P.O. Box 5076
Champaign, IL 61825-5076
800-747-4457
e-mail: info@hkusa.com

Canada: Human Kinetics
475 Devonshire Road, Unit 100
Windsor, ON N8Y 2L5
800-465-7301 (in Canada only)
e-mail: info@hkcanada.com

Europe: Human Kinetics
107 Bradford Road
Stanningley
Leeds LS28 6AT, United Kingdom
+44 (0)113 255 5665
e-mail: hk@hkeurope.com

For information about Human Kinetics' coverage in other areas of the world, please visit our website: www.HumanKinetics.com

E4014

Contents

Acknowledgments

I would like to thank my teachers Zvi Gotheiner, Martha Myers, Bonnie Cohen, Cathy Ward, the late André Bernard, and many others who have inspired me over the last 30 years of working with dynamic alignment and imagery.

I would also like to thank my editors at Human Kinetics, Gayle Kassing and Ray Vallese, for their excellent work on this book. They were always responsive to my questions and generously offered their expert guidance.

The book's copious illustrations would not have come into being without the help of the gifted artist Sonja Burger with whom I was able to create many of the drawings. Several drawings were also designed by Katharina Hartmann.

Introduction: How I Came to Use Imagery

At the Gymnasium Freudenberg (Mountain of Joy), the Swiss Latin preparatory school in Zurich that I attended for six and a half years, I learned many valuable things. My back, however, acquired the skill of stooping over Latin verse for hours on end. The school's rigorous class schedule, which started at 7:10 a.m., was hardly what you might expect in a gymnasium, a place where physical activity takes place. At the Gymnasium Freudenberg, little emphasis was placed on sports: There was no football team, no track team—or any team for that matter. But I loved to dance, and in the evenings I danced and exercised in the cellar at home, alone or with my brother. When I graduated from school, therefore, my posture was not as bad as it might have been, although it took years to reverse the "Latin-verse effect."

When the school put on its first theatrical production, to my surprise I was selected to play the lead. I knew nothing about auditioning, but I had apparently struck the right note. I remember being told that I didn't have to do much to be funny. I wasn't sure what the director meant by this statement until I rolled onto the stage for the first time. We were producing Molière's *Le Bourgeois Gentilhomme,* and I played a rather simple-minded, rich bourgeois trying to learn to dance. As I bounced about the stage with great enthusiasm during rehearsal, the fellow playing the dance teacher was very perturbed. His dancing was, of course, supposed to look totally superior to mine. Finally, I learned to look clumsy. I believe my trick in achieving this awkwardness was to imagine my legs wiggling like rubber and my neck stiff as an oak. (You are welcome to try it.)

When I first attended a ballet class, the teacher told me that my back was crooked as a banana. This correction was given in the strict Swiss manner of teaching: First teachers told you how sorry you looked and then they yanked you into the right shape. The remark was delivered with an undertone of "How dare you show up in class with that kind of back!" I can still see the outraged look on the teacher's face, which naturally made me feel sad and self-conscious. I wondered how to straighten my back. I was taught the pulling-up method, which seemed to be the standard procedure. My navel was supposed to stick to my lumbar spine, my buttocks needed to "tuck under" somehow, and my chin had to recede. The question was how anyone could enjoy dancing in this position. Breathing seemed out of the question. My back didn't actually *feel* like a banana, so I kept trying to imagine what the teacher was seeing. I tried to imagine my back in a position that would justify such a cry of indignation. But this didn't bring me closer to solving the problem.

REINFORCING WHAT YOU WANT

I now know that I was actually reinforcing the opposite of what I wanted. If you don't want your back to look crooked, you shouldn't focus on it *not* being crooked as a banana. Instead you need to replace the image of a banana with that of something straight yet flexible—a waterspout, for example. Put simply, your mind is a large screen filled with the images you have absorbed throughout the day. Your mind is instructed by these images and the thoughts that accompany them. The problem is that most of your 20,000 or so thoughts, flashing images, notions, and so on are similar to those of the previous day. As the images and thoughts repeat, they slowly but steadily bring about a change in the direction the images suggest. According to Indian Ayurvedic medicine, if you want to know what thoughts you have had in your life so far, you should look at your body (Chopra 1990a). To help clarify the connection between thought process and posture, try the following experiment:

Sit on a chair in a slumped position and think, *I feel great, fantastic . . . never better. I am having the time of my life.* Notice the discrepancy between your posture and your thoughts. Now reposition yourself in a vibrant, upright sitting posture and think, *I feel awful, sad, dejected.* Again, your thoughts do not match your posture. In a good posture, it is more difficult, albeit not impossible, to have depressing thoughts. Conversely, in a bad posture, it is challenging to think positively. Posture reflects thoughts; thoughts mold the physical being.

If posture and thought process are intimately connected, then, in a sense, your thoughts are constantly sculpting your posture, changing your alignment. The reverse holds true as well: Your posture influences your thinking. Your thoughts are part of a powerful matrix that influences your posture. The flood of words and images around you affects the way you sit, stand, and walk. Notice how comforting, encouraging words of praise from a parent or trusted teacher can immediately improve your posture: "Good! Well done! Perfect! Beautiful! Excellent job!" Conversely, observe the tension stifling all movement in students that are told they are not good enough.

Both the pictures and the words in your mind influence the feelings in your body, which in turn feed your thoughts and mental pictures. To create powerful and dynamic alignment, you can use this roundabout cycle to your technical advantage if you fertilize your mind and body with constructive information and weed out destructive thoughts.

PURPOSE AND WILL

To accomplish something, you must first have a clear purpose and the will to fulfill it. In sports and dance the purpose is reflected in the mental plan for executing a new movement with the specific imagery to help in solving technical problems. To do this intelligently, you need to increase your ability to observe what is going on inside your body. The key to improvement is the ability to compare your feelings with the knowledge you have of the correct functioning of your body. If there is a discrepancy between your awareness and your knowledge of good function, you have the tool to improve your movement. This process will succeed only if you have learned imagery that corresponds to the anatomical function of the body.

After graduating from the Gymnasium in Zurich, I went to New York because I was convinced it was the place to learn how to dance properly. I enrolled at New York University's Tisch School of the Arts where, ingrained with the Swiss work ethic, I pushed myself very hard. This resulted in a great deal of emotional pressure, so I was not the most relaxed person. I remember lying in bed and tensing my muscles, just to see how much strength I might have gained; obviously my sleep wasn't very restful.

I found the first part of my anatomy class with André Bernard very interesting. We learned about bones and posture, and I eagerly took notes. The second part of class was a bit unusual, though. We would lie on our backs and imagine our anatomical parts or a symbolic representation of our bodies changing in various ways. It was nice to lie down in any case, just to get some rest. The class was at the end of the day, and it was difficult to stay awake after an intense schedule of dance. However, if I could stay alert and concentrate on the images, I seemed to be more rested and my body less achy than if I simply dozed off for a half hour.

We were instructed to practice daily because it would take time for the images to change our posture and movement habits. My habits were obviously lacking because I had a recurring backache and knee problems. I had seen several doctors, but none of them could figure out what was wrong. (I now know that my problems were due to bad alignment in my legs and back.) At one point I was even told that I had only two or three months of dancing left in my knees. Swimming gave me some relief and brought my muscles back to normal for a while. However, if I didn't swim for a week, the pain would recur.

One day as I practiced imagining my legs hanging over a clothes hanger and watching my back spread on the floor (see figure I.1), I suddenly experienced an incredible release of muscle tension. It was a tremendous relief and brought tears to my eyes. From then on, I practiced imagery with increased motivation, and my back tension and knee problems receded. It had taken a year to bring about this release, but the experience taught me several valuable lessons in the use of imagery.

I had no way of knowing that using imagery would release my back tension in such a marvelous way. Nevertheless, I practiced purely on faith that it could work as nothing else had. The result was better than I had anticipated. I learned to trust the image and that there was no limit to what can be accomplished with imagery. I discovered that a postural change initiated as an image creates and reflects a psychological change. Being centered is not just a biomechanical event.

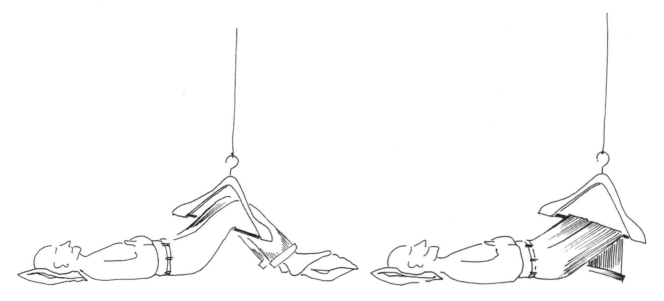

Figure I.1 Imagining legs collapsing over a clothes hanger.

Adapted from L.E. Sweigard, 1974, *Human movement potential: Its ideokinetic facilitation* (New York: Dodd, Mead), 233.

Improving my posture eliminated my emotional pressure, reducing my mental stress. Some people unconsciously shy away from using imagery precisely because of its power. Their fear of the emotional release associated with a physical release is simply too great. Through years of teaching I have found that some people are tremendously attached to their physical and mental tension; it has become so familiar that it seems essential to their identities. Those who profess their willingness to improve their alignment are often not ready to do so on an emotional level.

Changing alignment in a dynamic way, not just altering your external shape, changes your relationship with the whole world and the people in it. A static change is just a momentary forcing of your body into a more upright position. It lasts about as long as you pay attention to it. As soon as you continue your activities, you collapse into your previous posture. Alignment is dynamic when it respects the rules of biomechanical efficiency. Dynamic alignment is the most effortless and energy-saving organization of your structure as it transitions from one position to the next. This sense of effortlessness is reflected in your motivational state. A dynamic change, therefore, includes your whole being, your entire identity. To improve your alignment, you must be willing to embrace all the consequences to your personality, a transformation that may be overwhelming. You are an integrated being; you need to change the whole as you change a part, or improved alignment is merely a cosmetic adjustment that crumbles under the slightest test in the real world. I have often watched dancers who have good posture while doing an exercise reveal their true (slouched) identity as soon as the teacher explains the next exercise.

Dynamic alignment needs to withstand the influence of your surroundings. This is not easy because much of what is socially nurtured in postural imagery, particularly in advertisements, is highly static, tense, and slouched.

My pelvis had been habitually misaligned and tilted forward (as is obvious in photos I have from that period). The resultant lumbar lordosis (forward curvature of the lumbar spine) was excessive, shortening the back muscles in that area and putting strain on my ligaments and joints. Imagining my back spread out on the floor helped my lumbar spine to settle down (aided by gravity) toward the floor, lengthening the lumbar curve (although by no means do you want to straighten out the curve!). Letting my legs hang over the clothes hanger released the excessive (rocklike) tension in my legs, allowing my pelvis to balance easily on top of my legs, finding its perfect, nonrigid alignment.

But why did it take so long for anything to happen? Well, first of all, my scientific background made the whole idea of imagery seem a bit suspect, even esoteric. I believed that only hard work with plenty of sweat dripping from my brow could improve movement skills. Initially it is difficult to grasp that such purely mental training will greatly improve your progress because it usually takes a while to develop enough mental power to have a noticeable effect on the body. In a society looking for immediate results, this lag time is one of the reasons why people give up on using imagery.

Science, however, is catching up with imagery, and today there is an abundance of evidence supporting the benefits of imagery in its many forms. Nevertheless, there is a lingering doubt with many people about its efficacy. One of the skills, therefore, of imagery educators is to provide early successes to students learning about imagery. This will increase motivation to stick with the process until the power of imagery comes to its full fruition.

Learning imagery is akin to learning a language. Who would complain about not being able to read a French newspaper after only two weeks of French lessons? It can take years of consistent practice to learn a language well enough to read a newspaper with some fluency, just as it took me a year of practice at using imagery to bring about a release of tension in my back. I learned to stick with an image, even if it did not produce results initially.

As I became more and more aware of the impact that my imagery and thinking has on the body, I began to study with every teacher I could find who used imagery and to read every book I could find on the topic. To my great joy, my dance movement skills in general improved rapidly, and five years after being called banana back, I was dancing in a New York dance company.

Using imagery is not very effective without personal desire and intention, and even with clear intention, imagery is a subtle process that requires patience. However, if used systematically, imagery can work long-term miracles, eliminating the roots of your alignment and coordination problems. Forcing changes in your body may yield short-term gains, but it greatly increases the chance of injury. So never give up on imagery; in time you will discover its amazing potential.

USING IMAGERY FOR ALIGNMENT

This book is divided into four parts. Part I discusses the origins and uses of imagery (which I have already touched on in the introduction) and provides a first taste of dynamic imagery in practice. Part II lays out the biomechanical and anatomical foundation for understanding complex imagery based on physics and kinesiology. Part III provides anatomical imagery to help you fine-tune your alignment and increase awareness of your body. Part IV further discusses posture and provides summarizing imagery. In a related book titled *Dance Imagery for Technique and Performance* (1996), I discuss imagery in dance education; improvisational imagery; and imagery in dance technique, choreography, and performance. In another book, *Conditioning for Dance* (2004), I focus on exercises to enhance strength, flexibility, and balance using rolling balls, exercise bands, and imagery.

Many additions and changes have been made for this second edition. Chapter 3 introduces the concept of neuroplasticity, the fact that using imagery creates biological changes in the brain that relate to the improvements of alignment and movement skills in general. Chapter 4 introduces the Franklin method four-step process of creating change. Chapter 5 contains an overview of the uses and types of imagery. The anatomical imagery exercises are extensively revised, and imagery related to muscle and organs are added. Many new imagery exercises can be found in chapters 10 (Pelvis, Hip Joint, and Company), 11 (Knee, Lower Leg, and Foot), 12 (Spine and Body Wall), and 13 (Shoulders, Arms, and Hands). The imagery is based on the most recent findings in biomechanics, and research evidence and more variety in the types of imagery applied have been added to all chapters.

I have chosen to illustrate some of the images in this book. This edition contains updated and revised as well as many new illustrations. I am aware that an illustration is always done from a specific point of view and that the same image could look different if drawn by someone else. Most of these illustrations have gone through numerous stages and changes and are, in a sense, momentary pictures of an unfolding process. Therefore, they should serve as concrete and inspirational starting points for your own exploration.

You can use this book as a general reference or as a guide for systematic study. If you are an instructor using this text, most likely you will reorganize the material to suit your preferred mode of presentation. If you are practicing without a teacher, the following suggestions might help you in exploring imagery.

First, read through the introductory material in parts I and II and practice the exercises. Continue practicing as you proceed to the anatomical section, even if you do not fully understand all of the material. Your understanding will grow with your experience in using imagery.

The material presented in part III, anatomical imagery, can be approached in two ways. In a class situation, with a teacher's supervision, it may be preferable to proceed in the sequence presented in the book. If you are practicing on your own, select some material from each of chapters 10 through 15 for daily study as well as holistic imagery from chapter 17. Select imagery that appeals to you, and stick with your selection until you feel you are ready for something new. This could mean working on the same image for a day, for several weeks, or for months. For example, you may choose to use a different image for the pelvis every day while sticking with the same holistic image for a longer period.

Several times a week, practice in the supine (lying faceup) position. Throughout the day, take every opportunity to practice while sitting, standing, walking, and exercising. Vary your approach to imagery, using it before, during, and after movement in many sensory modalities. Stop your desk work for a moment and focus on a sitting exercise. Work on standing and walking images when you go shopping (but continue to pay attention to traffic lights). Do not limit your practice to the time you spend in training or exercising. Although class time is conducive to intense concentration on alignment, limiting your effort in this way will create the notion that improving your alignment is something that is done only in movement classes. It is equally important to practice during your daily chores, when you normally would not be thinking about your alignment. This is an essential part of integration and will speed your progress immeasurably.

I have frequently observed people entering movement classes in their "this is me" (body image) alignment and, as class begins, adjusting their bodies into their "class" alignment. That class alignment, always sprinkled with tension, looks unnatural. Because it does not conform to your body image, it cannot be effortless, making it difficult to achieve your highest level of coordination. There is a constant battle going on in your nervous system between your body-image alignment and your class alignment. Also, your class alignment is less reliable than your body-image alignment because it requires more effort to reestablish.

Remember, even after you have decided to improve your alignment, you are still mainly reinforcing your old alignment; your old habits are still 90 percent effective. The goal is to reduce this percentage as quickly as possible, to integrate new information rapidly. Your most important allies in this effort are practicing in the supine position and using imagery during daily activities.

USING THE AUDIO FILES

With the new edition of this book you have the opportunity to listen to audio recordings of imagery processes. The four audio recordings are available online at **www. humankinetics.com/franklinaudio**. Following are the names of the audio recordings, their approximate run times, and brief descriptions:

◆ Dynamic Alignment (12:30) uses imagery exercises to introduce you to some core concepts of dynamic alignment, including postural sway, counterbalancing, anatomical planes, and the central axis.

◆ Focusing On Space (8:00) walks you through imagery exercises that ask you to imagine different spaces as vividly as possible, using multiple senses.

◆ Practicing Sensory Imagery (8:37) continues the exploration of the senses (visual, kinesthetic, tactile, auditory, gustatory, and olfactory) to produce more vivid images, which enhances the effectiveness of using imagery.

◆ The Inner Flashlight (10:47) is an imagery exercise that allows you to view the space within your body three-dimensionally and also to appreciate the distances between and relationships among these spaces.

I have created and recorded these personally to help increase the understanding of how imagery is used effectively and assist in embodying dynamic alignment.

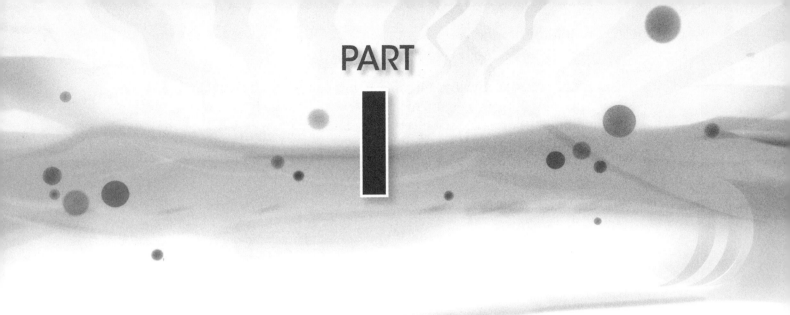

PART

I

Posture and Dynamic Alignment

The purpose of good alignment is to create efficient, coordinated, and healthy movement. The obvious conclusion is to improve alignment dynamically through movement practices rather than static positioning of the body.

Static positioning involves putting yourself or your student in a position that conforms to the laws of biomechanical efficient alignment. The ability to do this requires knowledge of force transfer through the joints in the neutral standing position, a minimum level of self-awareness, and, in the case of the educator, tactile skill. There are two fundamental problems with the positioning method as the exclusive path to improving alignment: A nonmoving position does not inform the body about how to move better, no matter how good the position looks from a geometric, aesthetic, or biomechanical point of view. Also, telling someone to place herself in a certain position commonly increases tension and gripping, which will reduce the availability of those muscles to produce movement. Instructions like "lift your pelvis," "pull in your abdominals," and "close your rib angle" may produce better alignment from a visual perspective. However, in most cases, these instructions lead to increased muscle tension and gripping as the person engages muscles to arrange the skeleton in a place that her former postural habits have not produced. The result is that movement is less efficient because movement requires the contraction of muscles; and if muscles are already occupied with the job of holding a correct position, less contractile power is available for producing movement. This may seem counterintuitive at first because someone positioning herself may feel strong even though the net available force for movement has been reduced. This raises the question of how to proceed if positioning is not always a sensible option. Moving functionally—that is, moving with awareness of the anatomical changes happening in the body—is one of the more elegant pathways. This book provides the knowledge and procedures for creating efficient movement through a dynamic and multiperspective approach.

A distinct advantage of the dynamic approach over an exclusively static approach is the fact that muscles gain more strength and flexibility through moving than through maintaining a position. The static perfect picture of alignment will serve more as a goal than as a direct procedure. The process of improving alignment through movement will lend to balanced muscle tone by increasing effort where it is needed and reducing it where it is not needed.

At the risk of sounding like an advertisement, I can tell you that the benefits of creating dynamic alignment are numerous. Better alignment improves the efficiency of your body, reducing strain on both a physical and a psychological level because physical strain and exhaustion tend to dampen your mood and general outlook on life. Problems that may seem insurmountable in the depleted state become manageable when you are physically prepared.

The energized body exudes confidence. Improved coordination and observation skills enable you to progress faster in sports or dance. Your mind is trained to grasp three-dimensional movement sequences and perform them more accurately. You feel new connections and relationships within your body that continuously help you find improved solutions to your movement problems.

Better biomechanical transfer of forces through the joints and body systems reduces the likelihood of injury. Even nutrition is enhanced, because the increased flexibility and reduced strain improve circulation of body fluids such as lymph, blood, and synovial fluids. Finally, it is an excellent method for resting and regenerating your body after physical activity. Best of all, you do not need a suitcase to improve your dynamic alignment on the road; your mind is capable of training you anytime, anyplace.

In the following chapters, I use the term *posture* to denote the overall picture presented by your body when you are standing, sitting, or lying down. Alignment emphasizes the aspect of posture that is concerned with the geometric and biomechanical relationships of the parts of the body.

Chapter 1 covers how posture and alignment have been important objects of contemplation throughout cultural history, as evidenced by Egyptian, Roman, and Greek statues. We will see that the origin of using imagery for alignment as it relates to movement efficiency neither originated in the psychological tradition of imagery nor in the arena of sport psychology but rather in the somatic disciplines. Chapter 2 discusses the different ways in which alignment can be approached. Rather than having one model of alignment and trying to make the science and practice fit a singular model, we discover a great variety of seemingly contradictory pathways to creating a balanced alignment. This chapter also serves as an opportunity to notice which model seems to conform best to our current concept of alignment. Chapter 3 discusses the brain and consciousness and the basic structure of the nervous system, while chapter 4 introduces the Franklin method four-step process to create change. Chapter 4 also introduces the concept of body image and nature of developmental movement patterns. Chapter 5 introduces the uses and types of imagery. We will learn about the many positive results that can be achieved through the use of imagery and what types of imagery can best be used to serve these various purposes. We will also look at different ways of delivering an image and what makes an image more effective. Chapter 6 looks at what makes imagery effective, such as vividness and the ability to generate, modulate, and maintain an image. In this chapter, we will also learn how to improve our imagery skills, which will lead to faster and more effective results.

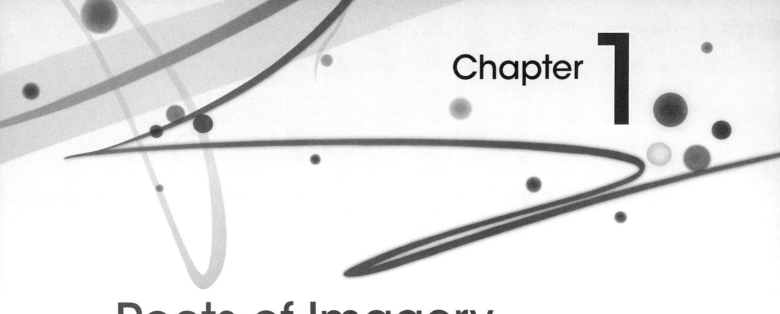

Chapter 1

Roots of Imagery for Alignment

Posture is as individual as a fingerprint.

Approximately 35,000 years ago, there appears to have been a sudden expansion in the creation of body ornamentation and the use of visual imagery. This flowering of the visual sense did not coincide with an expansion in brain mass, which had been stable in Homo sapiens for at least 90,000 years (White 1989). Visual thinking pervaded all areas of human cultural evolution. It became the basis of rituals as humans imagistically transformed into other animals and elements for various purposes such as healing or hunting. Both the healing and the performing arts grew out of the rituals engendered by imagining.

According to Jeanne Achterberg (1985), imagery as a healing tool has its roots in the 20,000-year-old tradition of shamanism: "The shaman's work is conducted in the realm of the imagination and their expertise in using that terrain for the benefit of the community has been recognized throughout recorded history" (p. 11). Magician and curer, the shaman is also both dramatist and performer. Julius E. Lips (1956) contends that modern drama developed from cultic-religious performances and mimic dances, in which actors initially impersonated gods and eventually took on the roles of jesters, clowns, and storytellers:

> *The very good time enjoyed in the "theater" by peoples even of the most primitive cultures shows that the deepest roots of theatrical effect have nothing to do with complicated stage mechanisms, individual stardom, or fashionable playwrights. Imagination is the magic cue. (p. 181)*

Our perspective on the origins of alignment as it relates to the human body cannot be complete without a glance at the civilization of ancient Egypt more than 4,000 years ago. Posture was paramount, as can be surmised from the depiction of the pharaohs: They were the image of perfect alignment (although a teenage pharaoh probably slouched as much as his not-so-kingly counterparts). Why, then, these serene and magnificently aligned pharaohs? Why were the Egyptian people presented with this kind of image and not a naturalistic one, which the highly skilled artists of the time could have easily produced?

In the Egyptian culture, alignment seems to have been a basic necessity of life. Once a year, the landscape turned into a black, muddy quagmire, thanks to the Nile, whose profuse swelling obliterated all boundaries. An Egyptian farmer, on discovering that his parcel of land had shrunk due to poor alignment of the ropes used by the alignment corps (or whatever they were called), would have complained. For the Egyptians, this loss of land had to be avoided at all cost—there wasn't much time to grow crops. Order, and with it perfect alignment, was truth. Therefore, the pharaohs were (or should have been) the image of perfect alignment. To depict the

Figure 1.1 An example of good Egyptian alignment.

pharaoh in any other position, such as gnawing on a chicken bone while sprawled out on a couch, was scandalous. (There was such a revolutionary period, but it lasted only 20 years out of 3,000.) Sitting or standing, the pharaohs had to be models of good posture—strong, yet calm and in control, ready to create order out of chaos (figure 1.1).

The pyramids, too, were aligned with uncanny perfection, quite a feat without modern measuring tools. The following is a wonderful image from my notes on a lecture by Robert Thomas on March 13, 1995: Only twice a year, at the temple of Abu-Simbel, formerly on the banks of the Nile, a streak of sunlight passes precisely over the eyes of four figures (situated 60 meters within the mountainside!). To create such stunning architecture, you *must* have great imagination and visualization skills.

Moving to the other side of the Mediterranean basin, we find that memory techniques involving mental imagery (or mnemonics, named after Mnemosyne, the Greek goddess of memory) seem to have been invented by the Greek poet Simonides (556-468 BC), at least according to the roman orator Cicero (16-43 BC). The Greeks and Romans seemed to have used imagery to remember their speeches. Posture and bodily attitude played an important role in ancient Greece and Rome and were signs of societal status. The uffici galleries in Florence contain row upon row of Greek and Roman busts and sculptures in which posture is a key component. The Renaissance elaborated on many of these themes. Michelangelo's (1475-1564) sculpture *David* (1504), on view at the Academia in Florence, is a superb example of relaxed, centered, and expressive alignment.

Moving southward while carrying loads on their heads has been a means of transport for African and Indian women for thousands of years. Contrary to popular notions, this is not necessarily more efficient than carrying loads on the back, nor is it effortless. Unless alignment is near perfect, it can harm the cervical spine (Lloyd et al. 2010). But I will never forget watching Indian women effortlessly climb a fairly slippery embankment with their freshly washed clothes packed in metal containers on their heads. Surely, this can be done only with fine-tuned control of alignment, which seems entirely natural to these women (figure 1.2).

Thus, we investigate the power of the imagination, which seems so inextricably linked with the performing arts. The following provides more background on the evolution of the science linking imagery and movement, a sort of who's who in ideokinesiology (imagery as related to movement).

IN SEARCH OF IDEAL POSTURE

The following section explores some of the varied approaches to improving posture and defining ideal alignment. It is not about finding the one and only right method of gaining ideal posture but discovering how a multitude of ideas can inform our sense of alignment. The richer the sources we can draw from, the more dynamic the resulting alignment.

Heinrich Kosnick and Mabel Todd

At the turn of the 20th century, Heinrich Kosnick, a pianist in Munich, developed a system of mental imagery to enhance the skills of his students. Calling his method psycho-physiological, Kosnick recommended using imagery while in a supine position. He found the images

Figure 1.2 Indian women demonstrating good alignment by carrying loads of clean clothes on their heads.

he created to be so effective that he wrote two books, *Lebensteigerung* (*Life-Enhancement*, 1927) and *Busoni: Gestaltung durch Gestalt* (*Shaping Through Form*, 1971). Busoni was a respected pianist and teacher who was trying to establish a scientific foundation for his work. Kosnick (1971) suggested in-depth knowledge of anatomy as a prerequisite for experiencing the correct functioning of the body and claimed that the directed will leads to the movement goal. Margrit Bäumlein-Schurter, a pupil of Kosnick's, wrote a book of exercises called *Übungen zur Konzentration* (*Exercises for Concentration*, 1966).

Around the same time that Kosnick was developing his ideas, American Mabel Todd, author of *The Thinking Body* (1972), used her great skill and insight into the functioning of the human body to create astonishing changes in herself and in her students. If her profound writing is any reflection of her teaching, it must have been a transforming experience to witness her work, which she referred to as "structural hygiene." Her books, which also include *Early Writings: 1920-1934* (1977) and *The Hidden You* (1953), emphasize the elegant construction of the body and its ability to change in response to will. Todd, who taught at Columbia University Teachers College, had movement difficulties caused by a serious accident. Although it seems the doctors of her day were unable to help her much, by using imagery, she was able to fully regain her ability to move. She is credited with proposing hook lying, or the constructive rest position, as a training position for mental imagery (see "Constructive Rest Position" in chapter 6).

Lulu Sweigard and Ideokinesis

Working with dancers, Lulu Sweigard (1974) researched and developed Todd's ideas, defining ideokinesis as "repeated ideation of a movement without volitional physical effort" (p. 187). In 1929, she initiated one of the few studies available on the effects of imagery on alignment to "determine whether ideokinesis . . . could recoordinate muscle action enough to produce measurable changes in skeletal alignment" (1939 doctoral thesis). In meeting with students for weekly 30-minute sessions over 15 weeks, Sweigard discovered nine lines of movement along which most postural changes take place.

Nine Lines of Movement

The following descriptions of the lines of movement and their effects are accompanied by occasional references to imagery used in this book.

1. Line of movement to lengthen the spine downward (see chapter 12, figure 12.36) releases tightness in the back muscles, especially in the lumbar region.

2. Line of movement to shorten the distance between the midfront of the pelvis and the 12th thoracic vertebra activates the deep and superficial muscles in front of the pelvis that counterbalance the erector spinae group. Activating this line releases tension in the erector spinae.

3. Line of movement from the top of the sternum to the top of the spine can either lengthen or shorten, depending on alignment needs. It improves the alignment of the upper spine in relation to the pelvis, allowing the head to balance on an axis in a manner that releases tension in the neck and shoulder muscles.

4. Line of movement to narrow the rib cage improves the flexibility of the rib cage, thereby improving spinal alignment and diaphragmatic action. (It is important to note that these images are not voluntary actions. You are not actively narrowing your rib cage; you are only imagining this line of movement.)

5. Line of movement to widen the back of the pelvis releases tension across the back of the pelvis, allowing the femur heads to center in their sockets. Weight transfer from the legs to the pelvis, and vice versa, is greatly improved by this line (chapter 10, figure 10.23).

6. Line of movement to narrow the front of the pelvis balances the widening across the back of the pelvis. It increases the stability of the front pelvic arch and activates the muscles in the front of the pelvis. Figure 1.3 shows the Sweigardian zipper.

7. Line of movement from the center of the knee to the center of the femoral joint brings the whole leg into alignment, greatly benefiting the knee. This movement balances the muscular action around the femur and allows greater control of the leg (chapter 8, figure 8.5, the resultant force).

8. Line of movement from the big toe to the heel centers the weight thrust through the ankle joint by allowing the longitudinal arch of the foot to be "resurrected."

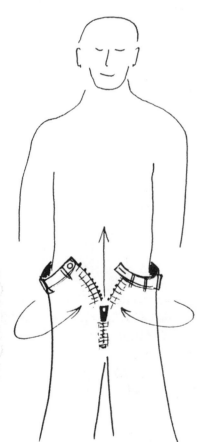

Figure 1.3 An imagined zipper closing up the front of the pelvis.

9. Line of movement along the central axis of the body lengthens the body upward. The summation of all the other lines, this movement allows you to attain your ideal height and, by creating a stronger axial core, release superficial muscle tension (see figure 2.4*a*).

For more information on the nine lines, I recommend Sweigard's *Human Movement Potential: Its Ideokinetic Facilitation* (1974).

Sweigard's Goal

Using a direct, one-to-one approach, Sweigard hoped to raise the standard of what was considered normal movement ability. She called her method an education rather than a cure. To Sweigard, ideokinesis was not a relaxation technique but a way to balance muscle action around the joints.

It is important to understand that relaxation and tension are related. Although balancing muscle action requires the release of tension in certain muscle groups, it also entails an increase in tension in other muscle groups. In many instances, people with shoulder tension do not just need to relax their shoulders. They also need to increase the tone in the central supporting muscles and organs as a foundation for permanently reducing shoulder tension. Muscles often become tense to compensate for inefficiency in another area of the body. Although some images seem geared to either increasing or reducing tension, the result of visualizing an image is usually a complex redistribution of muscular tension, edging toward the desired balance around the joints. Sweigard (1974) notes the following:

> *The all-important voluntary contribution from the central nervous system is the idea of the movement. Concentration on the image of the movement will let the central nervous system choose the most efficient neuromuscular coordination for its performance, namely innate reflexes and feedback mechanisms. (p. 6)*

Ideokinesis Versus Releasing Work

According to Bäumlein-Schurter (1966), the process of realignment begins with releasing work, which is followed by the creation of "life-carrying tone." This notion differs from Sweigard's, at least in theory. From the very beginning, the ideokinetic method sets out to activate flaccid muscles and release tense muscles simultaneously. The aim is to move toward balanced muscle action from the outset of the training. In practice, most beginners can apply releasing imagery (the shoulders melt like ice cream, the back spreads out on the floor) better than activating imagery (the central axis lengthens upward). For the experienced imager, however, releasing and activating imagery are opposite sides of the same coin: The effect of a releasing image is also experienced through the concomitant activation of flaccid musculature; the effect of an activating image is also experienced through the concomitant release of tense musculature. Therefore, there is more similarity in the practical application of ideokinesis and the work of Kosnick/Bäumlein-Schurter than is apparent from the underlying theories.

Barbara Clark

Barbara Clark, first a client and then a student of Todd's, wrote three manuals titled *Let's Enjoy Sitting-Standing-Walking* (1963), *How to Live in Your Axis—Your Vertical Line* (1968), and *Body Proportion Needs Depth—Front to Back* (1975). Several of Clark's students, among them André Bernard, participated in the creation of *Let's Enjoy Sitting-Standing-Walking*. Most recently, Pamela Matt of the dance faculty at Arizona State University wrote *A Kinesthetic Legacy: The Life and Works of Barbara Clark* (1993), an in-depth look at Clark's great contribution to this field. Clark created some exercises for increasing awareness of the central axis, paramount to any improvement in alignment.

Clark's student, André Bernard, began teaching at the dance department of New York University School of the Arts in 1965. Bernard, whom I first encountered at NYU

Circling Your Axis

Stand in a comfortable position with your arms hanging at your sides. Imagine a vertical line or force beam originating on the floor between your feet and moving up through the center of your body. This line must be re-created at every moment. You cannot take it for granted; you need to infuse power into it continuously. Your body seeks to orient itself around this line, which is your central axis. (It is as if the individual cells of your body find this axis a convenient line of orientation.)

Lift your feet off the floor alternately by flexing easily in your hip sockets. Feel your central axis between your shifting legs. Begin to rotate around this axis. The axis does not move through space. Like a merry-go-round, your body revolves slowly about its central post. Once you have completed a 360-degree circle, try turning to the other side. Notice the difference between turning to the left and turning to the right.

Find a reference point just in front of your toes, perhaps a division between two tiles or a scratch on the floor. It should be something that you cannot feel with your toes (so you cannot cheat). Rotate again to the first side, maintaining your focus on the horizon. After you have finished your revolution, check your reference point to see if you have moved forward, sideways, or to the back. Repeat to the other side and check your reference point.

Now do the exercise with your eyes closed. When you believe you have completed a 360-degree revolution, open your eyes and check your position. Repeat the exercise to the other side.

By now you should have discovered which is your easier turning side (usually the side where you deviate less from your central axis).

The point of this exercise is to discover the precise difference in sensation between turning to one side and turning to the other. What small chunk of sensation is missing on one side but not the other? How exactly does the axis change from one side to the other? Does the axis look different, or have a different quality, when you turn to one side versus the other? Can you interchange sensation or quality between the sides to balance them?

Now you are ready to circle your axis by doing small quarter-turn hops. After every quarter-turn hop, do one hop in place. The sequence is as follows: quarter-turn hop, hop in place, quarter-turn hop, hop in place, quarter-turn hop, hop in place, quarter-turn hop, hop in place; repeat the exercise one more time to the same side.

Again, practice to both sides. Then try the same exercise with half turns and finally whole turns (even double turns, if you are an experienced dancer or gymnast). (Exercise adapted and expanded from Barbara Clark and André Bernard.)

in 1979, is very skilled at using his hands to help in visualizing anatomy, a process called tactile aid. The images seem to pour out of his hands. His deep, resonant voice, especially valuable during constructive rest sessions, contributes to the overall impression of an image. Bernard once described Clark as "a primitive abstractionist, using basic, earthy thinking; her imagery is like a Picasso painting" (lecture notes 1982). Both Clark and Bernard gave sessions to dancers and actors, among them Marilyn Monroe, who was supportive of Clark's writing effort (Matt 1993).

Many other excellent teachers were trained by Barbara Clark, including John Rolland, who wrote *Inside Motion: An Ideokinetic Basis for Movement Education* (1984). Rolland taught alignment at the Vermont Movement Workshop and in 1981 was invited to teach in the modern dance department of the State Theater School in Amsterdam (now called the School for New Dance Development).

I practiced the Circling Your Axis sequence (on p. 8) frequently with the Swiss national gymnastics team. It showed clearly that jumping power alone (of which they had plenty) will not create successful double turns in the air. A clear concept of your axis will use less random power and improve your turns.

Joan Skinner

During her dance training, Joan Skinner, who performed with the Martha Graham Dance Company, the Cunningham Dance Company, and many others, discovered that many of the things she was taught created a forced style of movement, causing tension and pain. Working on her own for several years studying the Alexander technique, she discovered a new method of training based on the body's own knowledge. In a radical departure from traditional dance training, Skinner's classes might involve lying on the floor immersed in an image or improvising to a haikulike totality image. (Haiku are short Japanese poems that evoke a certain mood.) Skinner's method, which she called releasing, uses poetic imagery and provides a profound base for effortless movement and control. Stephanie Skura, choreographer and teacher of the technique, said the following in a July 1993 personal interview:

> *Letting go is a crucial preparation for allowing an image to truly move you. Releasing does not have to do with moving softly; it has to do with a constant flux without grabbing onto anything. You get your orientation not by holding onto some center, but by letting the energy flow within you, through you, and around you. This is not an industrial age, mechanistic view of energy; it is not something finite that you can manufacture, store, and use up. You feel yourself as part of a greater energy.*

The concepts inherent in Skinner releasing remind me of Heracleitus, Greek philosopher of Ephesus (around 500 BC), who maintained that all things are in a state of flux. He said that unity persists through constant change and used the analogy of the river to explain: "Upon those who step into the same rivers different and ever different waters flow down" (*Encyclopædia Brittanica*, 1966 ed., "Heracleitus," 386). Not all things need to be changing at all times. Rocks and mountains can be temporarily stable, but they will eventually change as well.

The concept of flow is crucial to creating dynamic alignment. Just as your mind can sculpt your body into a certain posture, your mind can also help your body flow into better alignment. And here is the good news: A flow cannot be held because it then ceases to be a flow; therefore, alignment based on this notion cannot become rigid. If you begin to realize that your alignment is flowing, constantly changing, even if on a cellular or molecular level, you are able to take charge of this flow. Using imagery, you can constantly guide your alignment toward increased efficiency without ever holding on to it. If you were to stop the flow, even in what appears to be a biomechanically well-aligned position, tension would ensue. The building blocks of the body, the cells, are both filled and surrounded by fluids. Therefore fluid motion is inherent in our very structure.

SOMATIC DISCIPLINES

Dancers, Pilates and yoga educators, and, more recently, athletes have found various somatic disciplines to be very useful in improving their skills. Not necessarily based on the use of imagery such as ideokinesis and Skinner releasing, the following techniques apply imagery (usually nonmetaphorical) in certain contexts.

Alexander Technique

Donald Weed (1990), a teacher of the Alexander technique, writes that all of the work can be distilled down to two discoveries:

> (1) In every movement you make, there is a change in the relationship of your head with your body that precedes and accompanies that movement, and which either helps you or gets in your way. (2) The conscious mind has the capacity to override every system, including the natural ones. (p. 26)

The Alexander instructions, which allow the head to go up and forward and the back to widen, seem to harmonize well with the imagery used by Todd and Sweigard. The Alexander concept of inhibition, of saying no to the habitual mental and physical reactions, is very relevant to imagery work as well.

To use an image effectively, you first need to clear your mind. You cannot be in a nervous state, your mind filled with a jumble of thoughts, and then pile images on top of all that. It simply does not work. You must be open and receptive to new possibilities in your body. Nor should it be necessary to act on every impulse that comes to mind or muscle. (A muscle impulse is one that you feel in your body before you realize in your mind what you want to do.) In fact, you need to learn how to react as little as possible to any irrational urge to *do* something. In this way, you can become selective about how you perform a movement, choosing the most efficient of the many movement patterns available. The proper pattern can be found only in a peaceful state—a state in which impulsive movement patterns can be ignored, overridden, or inhibited.

Autogenic Training

The purpose of autogenic training (AT), a technique developed by the German I.H. Schultz (1982), is to release tension, lower your heart rate, and change other physiological conditions of your body. The imagery used here relaxes and calms the body and mind, suggesting heavy limbs, a cool forehead, and a quiet heart. AT also uses self-talk in the form of positive affirmations. It is interesting to compare images used by Schultz, Kosnick, and Sweigard to reduce overall body tension: Schultz (AT) directs students to experience the limbs becoming heavy, Sweigard suggests the body as a suit of clothes collapsing front to back, and Kosnick (as related by his student Bäumlein-Schurter) has the body sink downward into the ground.

Functional Relaxation

Functional relaxation (FR), or Funktionelle Entspannung, is a somatic movement therapy developed in Germany by Marianne Fuchs, who was trained in the German Mensendieck method. The goals of FR are to experience weight, inner rhythm, and movement in the expirational phase of breathing to promote an economical use of the body. Fuchs uses imagery in a variety of ways. For example, a series of exercises in FR "remembers" the 15 inner spaces by clearly visualizing them. These inner spaces, together with skeletal awareness, are important to the upright posture. Fuchs (1984) also points out that faulty movement and postural patterns created by negative emotions can be remedied only through the use of positive feelings and images.

Feldenkrais Technique

With Feldenkrais technique, developed by Moshé Feldenkrais, there is no right or wrong posture. The technique asks questions such as these: What is your structure? Where are you? What are you doing? What is your intention? Feldenkrais uses movement exercises, some of them deceptively simple, to create changes in flexibility and movement patterns. It sometimes requests the student to perform a movement on one side of the body and only visualize it on the other side, or to imagine a movement several times before actually doing it. Layna Verin (1980) states that Feldenkrais accomplishes its results by

> enabling you to become more sensitive to differences. By devising a configuration of movements that cannot be performed without this refinement. By making you aware of the minute interval between the time your body mobilizes for movement and you actually do that movement—the minute interval that allows you to exercise that capacity for differentiation and to change. (p. 84)

Body-Mind Centering

Founded by Bonnie Cohen and associates in 1973, the School for Body-Mind Centering (BMC) teaches movement through anatomical, physiological, and developmental principles. Cohen, whose background is in the fine arts, dance, and theater, was licensed as an occupational therapist and a neurodevelopmental therapist by the Bobaths in England. She also studied neuromuscular reeducation (another name for Todd's imagery work) with André Bernard, and she studied zero balancing, a bodywork method developed by Fritz Smith and Katsugen Endo ("the art of training the nervous system"), with Haruchi Noguchi in Japan.

Imagery is intrinsic to BMC and is applied to the musculoskeletal, respiratory, digestive, circulatory, nervous, and hormonal systems. Child development is explored in detail; early movements such as creeping, crawling, and rolling are related to the evolutionary stages of the animal kingdom. Bonnie Cohen has published *Sensing, Feeling, and Action: The Experiential Anatomy of Body-Mind Centering* (1994), a collection of articles that had formerly appeared in *Contact Quarterly.*

From Crawling to Standing

Get onto all fours and prowl around the floor like a child who is pretending to be a tiger in the jungle. Occasionally the tiger decides to become playful and rolls onto its side and back, or it may do a complete roll. Next the tiger practices crawling backward, as if retreating from a threat, only to recoil off its powerful hind legs and increase the speed of its forward motion.

Begin to crawl forward at an ever-faster pace, and finally, change as harmoniously as possible to an upright walk. As you continue to walk, imagine that you are still crawling. (It is particularly important just to think the image, not to do it.) Notice how this affects your alignment. Now begin to run, and imagine that you are a tiger bounding across the grasslands with a flexible spine and soft paws.

Yoga

Yoga is Sanskrit denoting "yoking" or "union," similar to the Latin *yugum* and the German *Joch*. It means the linking (yoking) or union of the human consciousness with something higher, something transcendent, something eternal (Rishabhchand 1953). The most popular of all yoga scriptures is the Bhagavad-Gita (*Lord's Song*), written 2,500 years ago. At that time yoga was already considered an ancient tradition. Yogic beliefs and practices are also evident in the Rig-Veda dating back to the third millennium BC, making it the oldest literary document in any Indo-European language (Feuerstein 1996). Yoga is of particular interest because it is the oldest literary source for both the practice of alignment and imagery. Mental imagery is used in hatha yoga but also in vajrana (tantric) Buddhism of Tibet to achieve heightened states of concentration or meditation (Feuerstein 1996, p. 86). In one stage of this spiritual practice, the deities are visualized together with their respective environments known as mandalas (circles). Details of the visualization are drawn from oral instructions and special manuals. Many of the instructions bear similarities to modern approaches found in sport psychology as it pertains to improving the concentration of athletes.

In the United States, the most recognized and practiced form of yoga is hatha yoga. (*Hatha* is Sanskrit for "force" or "forceful.") Hatha yoga is founded on the notion that the human body is not a mass of living matter but a mystic bridge between the spiritual and physical being (Rishabhchand 1953). Certain positions called asanas serve to activate and conserve the currents of vitality, or prana, and improve strength, stamina, and flexibility. Breathing exercises called pranayama purify and strengthen the nervous system and calm the mind by directing and stabilizing the circulation of life energy. The basic texts of hatha yoga are the *Yoga Sutras of Patanjali* (circa second century BC). These texts describe relaxation as the very essence of the postures, which should be steady and comfortable and should be accompanied by the loosening of tension. The alignment of the body should be achieved with freedom from tension, or to word it positively, with effortlessness, which is always a sign of good alignment.

Finally, the notions proposed by the Rig-Veda are similar to modern theories of imagery function: "The Vedantic position was that the mind itself (as well as the senses) is limited power making its own representations, constructions, formations and imposing them on reality" (Aurobindo 1970, p. 211). An image is a mental representation of a physical action, emotional state, or future or past scenario. Our representations are subjective and not absolute; otherwise everyone would see the world in the same way and have the same opinion and emotional reaction to things, which is obviously not the case. The first step in mastering imagery is to realize the relativity of one's representations with the resulting freedom to change the image (mental representation) to make it more suitable for achieving goals (postural, movement, or otherwise).

Pilates

Joseph Pilates (1881-1967) was born in Germany, where he began to develop an exercise system in the 1920s. He was resolved to strengthen his body and improve his health after a sickly childhood. He had a background in yoga, Zen meditation, and martial arts, and his exercises were innovative because they emphasized the harmony of mind and muscle. He used mental imagery to properly inform and initiate the movements. In 1926 Pilates opened up a studio in New York City, and in 1945 he published *Return to Life Through Contrology*, which described his philosophy of exercise. Some of his students began opening studios of their own—making subtle adaptations to the method—and word of Pilates spread among the movement professions. In the 1990s, the mind-body fitness movement took off and Pilates became very popular.

Alignment and imagery are key components of Pilates, which emphasizes a strong core. Sweigard's zipper imagery is used in activating the transversus abdominis muscle to this aim. Sweigard herself may not have agreed with this use of her image, because the effort is voluntary and not purely imagistic. Pilates is a highly sophisticated form of exercise and uses imagery to create a clear focus, modulate the level of effort, and initiate movement during exercise.

Franklin Method

All of the previously mentioned methods are strikingly original and creative. They are linked by their use of imagery—in some form or another—as a catalyst for change. I finish this chapter with some words on the approach to alignment that I have been teaching for the past 20 years, called the Franklin method. This is the philosophy on which this book is founded.

The goal of dynamic alignment is overall health and efficiency of movement. In my 30 years of teaching, I have come to the conclusion that placing people in what are deemed "correct" positions rarely improves movement skills and often enough impedes them. Your whole body is part of a symphony of coordinated movement. As you move, minute adjustments and shifts are taking place, some of which are apparent while others are invisible to the naked eye. Any part of the body that does not take part or resists this complex coordination though a fixed idea of posture will negatively influence the efficiency of the whole system.

In a sense, your ideal posture is reinvented at every instant. In every moment, the ideal combination of limbs, joints, gravity, moving parts, connective tissue, and muscle must be found and directed by your brain and nervous system. If your concept of alignment is static, it will impede the subtle adjustments needed for coordinated movement. The complex matrix of your support system is shifting from one position to the next. In other words, the set and timing of muscles used for position A are not the perfect set and timing for position B.

Correcting posture by instructing which muscles to activate is based on the idea that everyone uses the same set of muscles and with similar timing to achieve alignment. This has been shown to be scientifically unsound (see chapters 11, 12, and 13). Instead of teaching positions, you need to train alignment with movement in mind. Similarities exist, but posture is like a fingerprint. The aim of focusing on an individual muscle or joint is to integrate a localized improvement of efficiency into the entire movement experience.

Dynamic alignment is movement. To create stability in movement, you must have oscillations—subtle movements to dampen the effect of the forces that you are dealing with, such as gravity and muscles. In other words, the elastic body has more stillness.

In the following chapter we explore how a variety of postural models can contribute to your understanding of dynamic alignment.

SUMMARY

The importance of posture can be dated to the ancient Greek, Roman, and Egyptian cultures. In modern times, Mabel Todd and other somatic technicians have emphasized the importance of alignment for efficient movement and health. Mabel Todd's student Lulu Sweigard initiated an early study on the effects of imagery on alignment. Her aim was to determine whether imagery could recoordinate muscles in order to produce measurable changes in alignment. Her study resulted in the formulation of nine lines of movement aiming at improving posture.

Chapter 2

Postural Models and Dynamic Alignment

Your movement is only as good as your alignment permits.
Your alignment is only as good as your economy of movement.

The purpose of this chapter is not to create a limited or static definition of posture and alignment but to broaden your sense of posture and open up many possible dynamic routes to improving alignment. There are numerous approaches to aligning your body, and you can gain insight from each of them, rather like putting on different-colored glasses. One moment you perceive your alignment as a string of pearls, the next moment as a pendant mobile. Soon you notice how your bones are moving in three-dimensional counterbalance to create healthy efficiency of motion. Your habits are just what they are—mostly unconscious ways of holding and positioning yourself. Once you realize they are only one version of your posture, and perhaps not the most efficient, you become open to changing them. By understanding postural models, you become more adept at noticing your postural and movement habits and deciding whether they are serving the purpose of healthy movement and well-being.

But go back in history for a moment and think about posture from a historic and anthropological perspective. The earliest evidence for systematic training of the body through exercise and reference to posture stems from ancient Greece, specifically the Olympic Games.

Every muscle you have in your body exists only because it is functionally valid; it was and is needed as a part of the whole to provide movement. This has been true long before any encoded systems for the training of the body existed. People were not out of shape just because gyms did not exist. Standing, walking, running, sitting, getting up and sitting down, running, climbing, carrying, pushing, and pulling were plenty of exercise for every muscle and sinew in the body. Walking is probably the most common form of movement that activates your complete musculoskeletal system. Viewed from this perspective, all the systems you have for training the body today are opinions on how to achieve the same results that these common movements have done for thousands of years.

The historical perspective seems to be forgotten when you are admonished to hold or tighten certain muscles simply to stand up correctly. If nature would have not endowed you with a way to activate all the muscles in your body without special voluntary involvement, these muscles would not exist in the first place. Evolution, which is driven by function, would have eliminated them.

As you perform the imagery and exercises in this book, you will find out that simple daily movement, when performed functionally, will improve your posture. In other words, there are thousands of ways to align your body, not just one. Just about any movement performed in a functional way will improve your alignment. Functional means economical; the movement is done efficiently with a high output-to-input ratio. Little effort is going a long way. But what has gone wrong and why is exercise necessary for most of us these days? Our jobs and lifestyles do not usually contain hours of walking or climbing or running as a natural part of daily activities. Also, the ground we walk on is usually even and paved, eliminating much of the counterbalancing activities that train the muscles and postural system. The arrival of structured modern exercise is welcomed and needed, but it comes with a challenge: Which is the right thing to do for each individual, based on which evidence? A confusing array of constantly changing ideas and suggestions bombard the person involved in the world of fitness, exercise, and postural training. To be effective, your awareness of your body and function must be involved in postural training.

WHAT YOUR POSTURE REVEALS

Posture reveals your genetic and social heritage as well as the sum of your mental and physical habits. There are as many types of posture as there are human beings. Your posture is constantly and imperceptibly changing, reflecting your psychological state. If you took full-length photos of yourself from the front and side every morning and looked at them in sequence, you would see that your posture is in constant flux. Your posture for the day depends on what you did the previous day, your psychological state and body tone when you went to bed, the position you slept in, and changes in your body image, among other factors. In a photo taken in the evening, you would likely be shorter and your body would have rearranged itself in the direction suggested by your movement habits and tasks of that day.

A skilled dancer, athlete, or yoga educator can detect daily postural changes and factor them into his or her alignment in both dynamic (moving) and static (still) states. Larry Rhodes, who was the department chair of New York University when I was a student there, once noted the following: One of the first things that needs to be done in a dancing day is feeling the subtle adjustments that must be made to gain full functionality.

Daily changes accumulate so that postural habits become more visible with age. Many people shrink with the passing of time, partly because the body contains less and less water as it ages. Also, the body must resist gravity, the tendency to be pulled toward the earth's center. Todd's term *postural pattern* implies that the outward manifestation of body shape is the result of an inner network of forces. Postural controls depend on the functioning of the central nervous system, the visual system, the vestibular system, and the various receptors located in the musculoskeletal system. According to Todd (1972): "The postural pattern is that of many small parts moving definite distances in space, in a scheme perfectly timed, and with the exact amount of effort necessary to support the individual weights, and to cover the time-space-movement" (p. 22). Sweigard (1974) defines the upright posture in relation to a physical parameter:

> *The consistent and persistent alignment of the parts of the skeletal structure in relation to the line of gravity when the subject assumes an easy standing position with the weight evenly distributed—according to his or her own judgment—on the feet, with the ankles in the sagittal plane of the femoral joints and with the arms hanging freely at the side. (p. 173)*

Every human has a certain upright posture that yields the most efficient use of his or her body. In dance, it is often the aesthetic requirements; in daily life it is the social setting that influences posture, sometimes interfering with efficiency.

When you are standing, you have constant postural sway. In other words, you are falling just slightly and are reflexively rebalanced. Postural sway distributes the effort of standing over a constantly changing set of muscles and joints, which is efficient. This is another good reason not to instruct posture as something that does not move or is fixed in a position in space. A more rigid posture is commonly adopted by people in pain—back pain, for example. Why, then, should it be adopted as a model for healthy alignment?

POSTURAL HABITS

Partly developed in utero, movement habits are reflected in how you manage each of your daily tasks. After birth, you go through a complex set of developmental stages at a rate determined by genetic, social, and other cultural forces (Piaget 1993). Once a baby is able to sit, we marvel at its ability to balance its head perfectly over its torso. Despite having a considerably larger head relative to the rest of her body than an adult, a baby will sit in good alignment according to the rules of efficient mechanics, even if the parents and older siblings slouch at the dinner table. If the parents continue to be bad examples of alignment, however, the child will most likely model that behavior and allow her efficient posture to deteriorate.

Of course, myriad other factors influence the development of movement habits—the games you play, immediate environment, climate, innate interests and talents, the way in which you explore your environment, and how you imitate your play-mates. I remember meeting the father of one of the young gymnasts I was coaching in Zurich in 1989 and recognizing him as soon as he walked into the gym by the way he carried his shoulder blades—his posture was very similar to the patterns I knew so well in his son.

Cultures with lifestyles that foster good alignment usually entail varied movement tasks in everyday life: sitting on floors, carrying baskets on the head, and running (even adults) to greet visitors to the village. Such cultures lack comfortable furniture that promotes flaccid "hanging out." The Xhosa women of the Transkeian Territories of eastern South Africa rarely walk but *dance* home from their work in the fields. I

Figure 2.1 A child using a deep-knee crouched position during play.

haven't seen many people dancing home from their office work, although they probably need the exercise more than the Xhosa.

It is difficult to carry something on your head while slouched. The deep pelvic and leg muscles maintain power, and the hip joints remain flexible in a deep-knee crouch position, the working posture in many Eastern countries. This seems to be a universal position in childhood, because it is used by young children across all cultures (figure 2.1). On the other hand, it is easy to get accustomed to lying (you can hardly call it sitting) on soft living-room furniture. This kind of posture reduces body tone needed for good alignment. The hip joints lose their flexibility because they are not exercised over their full range, which in turn increases the strain on other body structures in an effort to compensate for this lack of flexibility.

RICH SOURCES FOR DYNAMIC ALIGNMENT

The purpose of this section is to explore some of the varied approaches to improving posture and defining ideal alignment. It is not about finding the one and only correct method of gaining ideal posture, but discovering how a multitude of ideas can inform your sense of alignment. The richer the sources you can draw from, the more dynamic the resulting alignment.

Metaphors of Bodily Efficiency

There are many theories on how to maximize the efficiency of the body to keep it healthy and injury free. One approach suggests that the body is a machine that can be perfected by improving its mechanical functioning. In this scenario, you are dealing with an intricate combination of pumps, pipelines, pulleys, levers, and power stations controlled by a grand computer. If you oil, trim, and adjust this machine so that everything is in place, mechanical force transfers efficiently through the entire system.

A somewhat different approach comes from the East: The body is thought to be an interconnected field of energy, known as qui (energy flow) or prana (Sanskrit, vital force). The flow of energy through designated pathways determines the body's state of health. Freeing and balancing these pathways, as is done in Chinese acupuncture and acupressure, for example, allows for optimal functioning.

Since ancient times, mental balance has been recognized cross-culturally as the basis of the well-functioning body. As the ancient Romans said, "Mens sana in corpore sano," meaning "A healthy mind will be found in a healthy body." Many ancient and some very recent healing traditions try to create a state of mind that optimizes bodily function. French psychotherapist Émile Coué (1857-1926) contributed substantially to the reemergence in the West of the notion that the mind holds great power over the body. Famous for his formula, "Every day in every way, I am feeling better and better," he based his method on the power of the imagination.

We seem unable to envision an outside object that does not exist within us in some form. Architecture, arches, domes, walls, canals, chemical factories, and computers can all be found within us. Even if a discovery seems like a revelation, entirely new, sooner or later the sciences come up with something similar in the body. Plato even states in the *Phaedo* that everything we can conceive of preexists as a so-called form or idea. We take this one step further by saying that everything we can conceive of preexists in our human form.

Each society takes its metaphors for bodily function from its most prevalent machines. In ancient Rome, for example, the heart was an oven because an oven was a standard household item. The notion of the heart as a pump didn't arise until the industrial age made pumps commonplace (Miller 1982). Later, a more refined knowledge of body chemistry revealed that the heart is also a gland. Once the cell was discovered as the basic building block of tissue, science began to divide and subdivide the body into ever-smaller units. The future surely holds new models in store for the body.

Postural Models

A model is an image that attempts to clarify dominant structural and functional aspects. Close to the scientific norm, or apparently completely removed from it, a model may be the first glimpse of a new insight, a fresh look at things that should not be immediately discarded if they are off the beaten track. The history of science is full of correct ideas that were initially rejected. For example, Watson and Crick's model of the DNA structure, the double helix, wasn't an exact representation, but rather a first look at a structure presented in such a way that the human mind could readily visualize it. Some models share notions, while others seem to be completely at odds with each other. Sometimes parts of one model can be added to another one, creating a mixed model.

Is there a comprehensive metaphorical model that embodies the complete structural and functional nature of erect human posture? If defined, will it help you find your ideal alignment? The following sidebar exercise describes three models for focusing attention on particular aspects of posture, thereby forming the basis of better understanding that can lead to a deeper experience of posture. I have found that spontaneously varying the models creates a more dynamic sense of alignment.

Switching Among Models

Now practice switching from one model to another. By doing this, you can approach the same issues from several angles. Finally, you will mix the models. The following models emphasize the relationship between the head and the rest of the body:

Your head floats up and your body dangles easily from your head (figure 2.2*a*). If you prefer to use a metaphor, you can think of your head as a balloon and your body as the string hanging down from it (see also figure 14.3). Practice this image while standing, walking, sitting down, and getting up.

Think of the body providing support for the head. The head balances easily on top of the spine (figure 2.2*b*). Metaphorically, you could think of the body as an upward surging energy that culminates at the top of the spine. The head floats on this energy. Another metaphor for this model is that of a waterspout (the body) buoying the head on top. Practice this image while standing, walking, sitting down, and getting up. (See also figure 17.7.)

After you have familiarized yourself with both models individually, try switching from one to the other in your mind's eye. Which of the models appeals to you? Is the experience you derive from the models the same or different?

Now let's create a mixed model as in figure 2.2c. You will transfer the dangling aspect from model A to the arms and legs only. Use the upward energy from *b*. but limit it to the core of the body and the spine. You will also use the concept of the head sitting on the top of the spine from *b*. Practice this mixed image while standing, walking, sitting down, and getting up. Feel free to create other mixtures

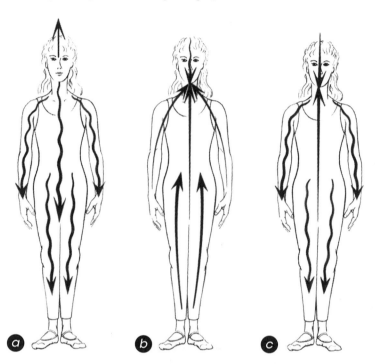

Figure 2.2 Different perspectives: *(a)* Your head floats up and your body hangs from it. *(b)* The body supports the head. *(c)* Mixed postural model.

The following sections describe some of the basic postural models that will be useful in creating dynamic alignment.

Atomary and Planetary

Coined by the Greek physical philosopher Democritus, the word *atomon* means "indivisible." According to his theory, the only things that exist are the atoms and the void. Everything we know of consists of different configurations of these atoms. Between the atoms is emptiness. After death, we disintegrate into these small, indivisible particles, a reassuring notion for the ancient Greeks to whom life after death was not necessarily an enticing prospect.

In the atomary, or planetary, postural model, the human body is seen as a miniature solar system, with all the parts oriented to and arranged around a common center, maintaining specific relationships within the whole (figure 2.3). Orientation toward a common center is, of course, an important image in dance. The parts may be seen to circle, loop, draw an ellipse, or spiral around the center. In the ideal arrangement, the

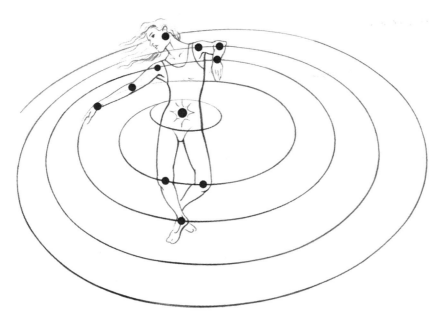

Figure 2.3 The human body as a miniature solar system.

relationship of the parts to the center creates the most efficient posture and movement. Function is impeded if the parts are too bunched or too spread apart. Depending on the individual, this may mean moving the parts lower, higher, nearer, or farther in relation to the center. Ultimately, center can be a point in space, a line, or even a plane.

As can be surmised from his famous drawing of a man in a circle, Leonardo da Vinci believed man's center to be at his navel. Da Vinci most likely got this idea from reading *De architectura* by the Roman builder Vitruv (33-14 BC), in the following:

> *The natural center of the human body is the navel. If a human being outstretches his hands and feet and one puts a compass on the navel as center, both the tips of the fingers and the tips of the toes are touched by the resulting circle. If the circle is connected to the human shape, so is the square. If one measures from the soles of the feet to the top of the head and compares the result with the distance between the outstretched arms one finds the same size in width as in height. (Translated from Tages Anzeiger Magazin 1993, p. 39)*

Building Blocks or Centers of Gravity

Used by Mabel Todd and Ida Rolf, among others, this model visualizes the main units of the body, such as the head, torso, and pelvis, as building blocks. Todd (1972, p. 59) writes the following: "If the median line of the structure passes directly through the center of the weight of each block, gravity will exercise an equal pull on all alike, and the structure will stand." More units can be added to differentiate between the head, neck and shoulders, abdomen and pelvis, thighs, knees, and feet. The parts can be pictured as square blocks, cylindrical spools, or spheres. They may consist of wood, stone, or bales of hay; they can be hollow or dense. In correct alignment, the line connecting centers of weight is perpendicular to the ground (see figure 2.4*a*). If centers are not aligned, muscular imbalance, strain, and inefficiency result (see figure 2.4*b*). As Rolf points out, the three axes passing through each of the blocks—the vertical, sagittal, and transverse—need to be aligned with each other.

Suzanne Klein-Vogelbach (1990), a German movement therapist, compares the body systems in motion to a chain but substitutes the picture of a block pyramid or cone for static analysis. If the lower block is larger than the one immediately above it, the connecting structures are subject to the least strain, as exemplified by the spine.

Looking down on a seated 12-month-old, one can clearly see the alignment of the main blocks, head over pelvis (figure 2.5). A child playing with blocks intuitively applies these

Figure 2.4 *(a)* Correct alignment of the building blocks model. *(b)* Incorrect alignment leads to muscular imbalance, strain, and inefficiency.

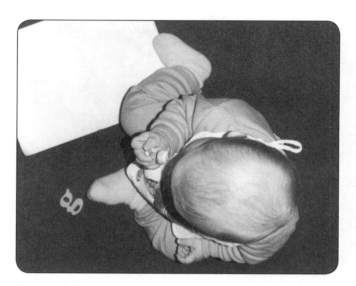

Figure 2.5 Looking down on a sitting 12-month-old whose head is aligned over the pelvis.

Building Blocks

Focus on your spine and imagine it composed of wooden building blocks arranged in a somewhat imperfect fashion atop each other as viewed from the front. Allow a magic force (or magic fingers) to move these blocks into excellent alignment with each other. Think of this force as coming equally from both sides (figure 2.6).

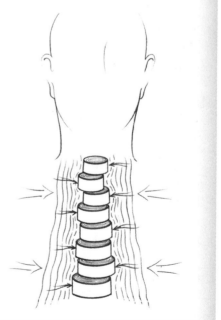

Figure 2.6 A magic force aligns the spine.

principles, sometimes with astonishing dexterity. When my daughter and I used to build high towers of blocks, she could casually plunk another block on top of a tower without disturbing the fragile structure. These childhood experiences of structural balance can be called on to help fine-tune the sense of alignment.

Tensile Compression

A refinement of the building-block model, a tensile-compression model, holds the structure upright by creating a balance between elements that resist being compressed and those that resist being elongated. Figure 2.7 shows a playground tree, as they are called in Switzerland. Vaguely reminiscent of the human form, it features all the elements of a tensile-compression model. Its central compression member, a wooden pole, can be likened to the spine. Arranged circularly around this axis are the tensile parts, the hanging ropes and girders. The top loop corresponds to the shoulder girdle hanging from the apex of the spine, the middle loop to the rib cage hanging from the thoracic spine, and the final loop, rather low and small, to the

Figure 2.7 A playground tree, in Switzerland, is an example of a tensile-compression structure.

pelvis. Unlike the tensegrity model described later, this structure depends very much on the central pole for its integrity. To turn the playground tree into a tensegrity model, you could attach the ropes firmly on the top and bottom and take the slack out of them so that the structure would be maintained even if the tree were uprooted. The fundamental problem of both the building-block and tensile-compression model is that many structural elements of your body, such as collagen and bone, start to deform and change their shape under persistent pressure or even lack of pressure. In other words, we are not like a beam of wood or a block at all but slowly change shape, depending on the nature of the forces pressuring the system. That is why we need a nervous system and brain that perform a never-ending dance of subtle changes to make sure that no area of the body is exposed to a constant pressure.

To Be a Tree

Imagine yourself to be a tree. Your arms are the branches and your upper body and legs are the trunk. Be aware of the upward force of the trunk and of the downward pull of the hanging branches. Now imagine being covered with snow. Watch the snow slide off the branches.

Mabel Todd (1972) further differentiated the tensile-compression model, writing about three primary planes in the body that determine balanced alignment. A tensile plane created by the axes of the legs extends upward through the thigh joints. A compression plane created by the axis of the spine extends sideways and downward through the lower border of the sacrum. The third plane is produced by the laterally extended line of gravity. Todd found that the best balanced upright position is that in which these three planes are parallel to each other and their forces are in balanced action.

> *The balancing power between the compression members in the back and the tensile members in front is like the bicycle chain. Should something happen to make either portion of the chain relax or contract more than the other, it could not be moved forward, around, back, and up over the little wheel, and forward again smoothly. . . . Power, in the form of compression force, comes down the back and turns forward through the pelvis, and as tensile force it travels upward again from the pelvis to the top of the chain, through sternum, hyoid, mandible, to the base of the skull, and down the spine again. (p. 215)*

The expression "up the front and down the back" originates from this model.

Chain of Action

Go for a stroll and imagine that your walking movement powers a bicycle chain that moves up the front of the body and down the back (as described previously). You can also use the image of an energy flow or a conveyor belt. Now try imagining yourself running to power the bicycle chain. Keep the chain moving smoothly up the front and down the back.

Force Closure Model

The human body is a place where force is produced on the inside of the body, and forces may also be experienced on the body originating on the outside. These energies need to be dealt with efficiently and in a safe way. Form closure denotes joints that are stabilized by the nature of their shape. Joints that are stabilized by muscular power are force closed. In the ideal posture, force closure is always perfectly matched to the task at hand. Either too much or too little will slowly degrade the body. Force closure needs to be focused perpendicularly to the joint in need of stabilization to prevent shear. This mechanism has been called self-bracing (Vleeming et al. 1990). The body deals with incoming energy by adjusting the amount of force closure absorbing it into the myofascial system.

If you shift your weight to one leg, the joints of that one-leg pelvic half need to carry twice as much weight, because previously the same weight was distributed on both legs. This means the muscles will engage more to force close the joints. When you shift back to both legs, the muscles in each leg and pelvic half will be less active. This is easy to feel. If you shift your weight to the right leg only, for example, and notice the amount of effort (force closure) you are using in your muscles and maintain that effort as you move back, you will notice that the effort is not too much in that leg; it is not matched. In postural teaching the effort needs to be matched to the task at hand. If you are instructed to contract a muscle more than is necessary for optimal force closure, such a situation has just occurred.

Bone Rhythms and Fractal Force Absorption

In 1995 I created the term *bone rhythms* to describe how the bones and joints of the body relate three dimensionally to create optimal efficiency of movement (see figure 2.8). Using all three dimensions is the most economical way to generate and absorb force. A baseball throw is a three-dimensional event because more force can be generated, just as the movement of the pelvic half when landing from a jump. This three-dimensional movement is powered by the shape and structure of the joints, muscle slings, the ligaments, and connective tissue. (See chapter 10 on the pelvis.) In good posture, the bone rhythms are balanced in all three planes.

Force is distributed three-dimensionally through the bone rhythms. No single attachment site of muscle to bone needs to carry excessive force, which would be the case if the spine's construction were based exclusively on a uniplanar fulcrum, force, and lever system. Finally, the body can be seen as a three-dimensional fractal damping system. A fractal is a reduced-size copy of a larger shape. Many objects in nature but also the organs and connective tissue of the body are fractally organized. A tree and the lungs—an inverted tree, so to speak—are fractally structured.

Water-Filled Balloon

Bones and muscles alone are not responsible for posture. The connective tissue and the organs are also involved. The organs are not just passive weights that need to be carried around by the bony framework and muscles; they can contract and even move around a

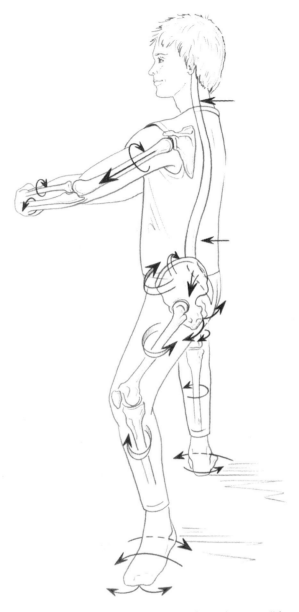

Figure 2.8   The bone rhythms in a dance plié.

bit. Muscles depend on the organs for their fuel. Humans consist mostly of water contained in and between the cells and in the connective tissue, rather like water-filled balloons stacked on top of each other and bound together with large rubber bands (the connective tissue) to create a balloon tower. Deane Juhan (1987), instructor at the Trager Institute and author of *Job's Body*, describes a model of the human body as a water-filled balloon tightened by circular cords and shaped into a cylinder:

> *At this point, our cylinder does not really need an internal skeleton in order to remain upright; in fact, a skeleton could even be suspended inside the cylinder from the top, without its toes touching the bottom, supported solely by the tension of the pressurized walls of the bag. (p. 81)*

This view is similar to the Noguchi exercise system described in *Zen Imagery Exercises*, by Shizuto Masunaga (1991), in which the body is viewed as organs and bones suspended in an aqueous solution, contained in a large bag of skin. If you cradle a baby in your arms, the baby feels like a little balloon filled with warm water, not like a structure that is primarily maintained by bony girders.

You can, of course, carry out the image ad infinitum: If the organs are water-filled balloons in their own right, then the master balloon would contain smaller balloons, which again would contain even smaller ones, the cells. In reality, the cells are not impermeable, as are latex balloons, but allow fluids to pass through their membranes by osmosis, permitting two adjoining compartments to balance their concentration of salts.

Whether corded or stacked, the balloon structure is capable of bearing weight yet is flexible and resilient enough to adapt to many situations. The same alignment principles used with the building-block model apply here. The importance of this model lies in the fact that it appreciates the supportive function of each individual cell, the connective tissue, the fluids, and organs of the body. It allows you to feel fluid inside the body while maintaining a clearly delineated structure outside. The bones can be seen as spacers that help maintain the overall shape. The ideal water-filled balloon model can bear and move weight without losing elasticity. Weight bearing actually helps distribute the nutrients within the balloon. Figure 2.9a shows a balloon-type model with spacers, and figure 2.9b a compression-type model.

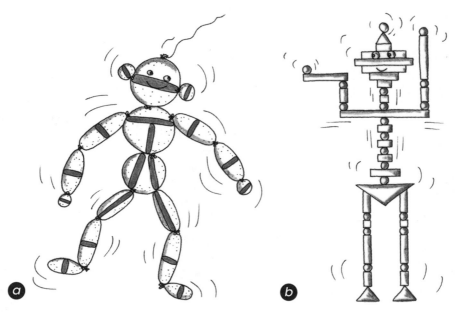

Figure 2.9 (a) The bones can be seen as spacers that aid in maintaining the overall shape of the balloons. (b) In the compression model, weights rest on each other like building blocks.

Tensegrity

Buckminster Fuller invented the word *tensegrity*. Its definition is found in the 1975 book *Synergetics*: "The word tensegrity is an invention: it is a contraction of tensional integrity. Tensegrity describes a structural-relationship principle in which structural shape is guaranteed by the finitely closed, comprehensively continuous, tensional behaviors of the system and not by the discontinuous and exclusively local compressional member behaviors" (p. 372). Tensegrity provides the ability to yield increasingly without ultimately breaking or coming asunder. A model of a tensegrity structure consists of beams/spacers and wires/tensile elements.

In the human body the beams are represented as bones, and the wire elements are the muscles and connective tissue such as tendons, ligaments, and fascia. Bones are very good at resisting compression and muscles; tendons and ligaments are good at resisting pull. The great tensile strength of the wires absorbs the force created by weight and impact and thereby prevents the beams from being overly compressed. The building-block model requires heavier materials because the compression elements carry all the weight locally. The tensegrity model can carry larger loads than a building-block model of equal weight and remain resilient because impacting forces are distributed throughout the structure. If you compress a tensegrity model, you will notice that all the tensile elements, not just one or two, will stretch. The force is being distributed to the whole system for absorption. Also, when you release your compression, it will rebound immediately (figure 2.10).

Figure 2.10 If you (*a*) compress a tensegrity model, (*b*) it will rebound immediately.

Alexandra and Roger Pierce (1989) contend that the body is more like a "tensegrity mast" than a single spherical structure: "A tensegrity mast is a vertical interweaving of individual tensegrity cells. The spine, with its tapestry of soft tissues built up around the out-thrusting bony processes of each vertebra, bears a striking resemblance" (p. 39). Imagine your spine as a stack of building blocks. As soon as you bend over, the blocks fall down, never to recover. The tensegrity system actually can use the fact of bending to store elastic energy in its tensile components. This force will help the spine extend again and regain its shape.

Rubber-Band Tensegrity

1. **Spinal rebound:** Seat yourself in an upright position without leaning against the back of your chair. Think of your spine as a tensegrity mast. Imagine the connections between the individual vertebrae (spacers) to be numerous small rubber bands. These rubber bands maintain the upright integrity of the spine by keeping the vertebrae aligned on top of each other. Allow your spine to bend in any direction, stretching some of the rubber bands. As they contract, the

rubber bands restore the spine to its original alignment. The spine is not rigid but bobs back and forth for a while until coming back to its full upright resting position. Repeat the exercise in another direction, maintaining awareness of the reboundlike quality of the return to center.

2. **Tensegrity stroll:** Go for walk while imagining yourself to be a tensegrity system. With every step you take, your whole body will absorb some of the impact through minute stretching and give of its tensile elements. Imagine that your whole spine, rib cage, and shoulder girdle allow a minute amount of give with every stride. Compare that feeling to walking with a compression or a lever model. In the latter, the impact of a step is absorbed by the leg and hip joints compressively through the bone, and the rest of the body does not participate in absorbing the incoming forces. You will probably notice that the first way of walking feels more elastic and comfortable.

Tubular

Stanley Keleman (1985), bodyworker and author of *Emotional Anatomy,* refers to the body as an organization of tubes and pouches. "Uprightness is the ability to structure and coordinate tubes, layers and pouches in the field of gravity" (p. 18). He describes three basic layers of the body. Digestion and breathing take place in the innermost layer; the middle layer provides support and movement; and the outer layer, the skin, separates us from the outside world. The layering aspect of the tubular model is very valuable in creating a three-dimensional feeling of movement and alignment. Using the planes and axes to improve your alignment may limit your perspective to the notion of two-dimensionality. Tubes add depth.

Layers

1. **Three discrete layers:** Visualize the three basic layers of the body. The innermost is organ (or the marrow of a bone on a limb), the middle layer is muscles, and the outer layer is skin. Imagine initiating movement from the different layers. What is it like to initiate movement from the innermost layer? From the middle layer? From the outermost layer? Once you have gained a sense of the layers, try to switch your awareness rapidly from one layer to another. Notice how this affects your movement.

2. **Interconnected layers:** So far you have been focusing on the depth of the three separate layers: deep to superficial, superficial to deep. Now focus on the concept of one layer interconnected throughout the body. Begin with the skin. Become aware of how it covers the whole body. Notice how stretchable and strong it is. Notice that it is constantly interfacing with the environment. Once you are attuned to your skin layer, move down to the muscle envelope and feel that layer throughout the body. Notice the inherent strength of the muscle, its potential for movement, its elasticity, its power. Now move to the next-deepest level, organ and bone. Concentrate on that layer throughout the body. Notice the stability of the bone and the plump, resilient volume of the organs. Next, go to an even deeper layer, focusing your awareness inside the marrow of the bone and the core of the organs. Finally, head back up to the surface of the body. Guide your awareness back through the consecutive layers like a submarine coming up from a deep dive.

SUMMARY

Dynamic alignment is neither static nor a finite state; you are not working toward the day when you finally attain perfect alignment. Static postural teaching is valid only for a structure that has no intention to move. Even if your alignment is already good, there is always room for improvement. You are constantly moving to a deeper level of experience, an even subtler adjustment, a new perception. Posture is adaptive; the amount of effort you use should be geared to the task at hand, not to a fixed concept of muscle contraction. The same posture can be achieved with a changing combination of muscles, which makes sure that no single muscle or bony point is overly compressed, stretched, or stressed in any way. To improve your alignment, therefore, requires the ability to tune in to your body and sense how much effort is just right. In this process it is important to become aware of your postural habits, persistent ways in which you hold and position yourself. Notice whether they serve your aim of efficient movement.

Each model discussed in this chapter brings us closer to the concept of dynamic alignment—the clear-cut shapes of the building block, the bounciness of the balloon, the depth of the tubular layer, the self-contained resilience of the tensegrity model, the loops and circles of the atomic model. Shape and motion are intertwined; motion creates shape, and the shape contains the motion that created it. The bone rhythms describe the way in which bones and joints of your body move three-dimensionally to create efficient force absorption and generation.

In a good posture all the forces of movement are balanced in such a fashion as to produce maximum safety and adaptability for your muscles and joints. Alignment needs to be taught through movement, imagery, and awareness, by aiding in embodying optimal function.

Chapter 3

Foundations of Mental Imagery

You get better at what you practice, including your thoughts, images, and emotions.

In a sense, you are surrounded by a sea of information, impressions, and events, and you are constantly choosing to react or not react to the environment. You also have an inner sea of thoughts, images, and emotions that influence your actions. This chapter investigates several theories on how imagery affects the body. But before considering them, try to better understand the concept of body-mind interaction by comparing the body to a ship at sea.

The captain (the brain) looks out for danger and makes sure that the ship is on course. If danger arises, the captain needs to evaluate the situation and decide how to act. Fortunately, the ship's systems can function independently of the captain's conscious awareness, or he would not be free to steer the ship. He is assisted by information from his radar mate and lookouts (touch, eyes, ears, nose) and his navigational charts (memory). The ship has a gyroscope (vestibular system, proprioception, postural reflexes) that automatically keeps it upright. Experienced at sea, the captain has mastered many difficult skills (developmental memory, sensory memory). Once he makes a decision about what action to take, he does not need to run down to the machine room (muscles, organs) himself to change the speed and the direction of the ship. Instead, he sends his command through an intercom (nervous and hormonal systems) that communicates with the machine room. If the machine room operators (lower-brain functions) have received clear orders, they perform all the necessary tasks independently of the captain. They make sure that the angle of the rudder and the rotations of the propeller (bones as levers) conform to the captain's orders. Occasionally, they will need to inform the captain of a problem with the machinery (uneasiness, pain). The captain may choose to go to a harbor (doctor, therapist) for repairs or to ignore the problem for the moment if there is imminent danger.

The ship, of course, will maneuver only as well as the skill of the captain permits. To improve his skills, the captain might take some additional training (body therapies, anatomical studies, imagery training). It is said that a good captain identifies with and becomes one with his ship (physicality, sensory awareness, embodiment). He might find ways to become more aware of the special behavior of his ship at sea. He might also ask the mechanics to inform him about inherent problems with the rudder and motor (sensory acuity). The more he knows about his ship and its behavior in all kinds of weather, the better he will master difficult situations.

Obviously, you need to train your captain-brain to guide your ship-body with greater skill. Perhaps less obviously, the reverse holds true as well—your body teaches your brain. Once trained to be fully conscious, the sensory abilities inherent in your anatomy are a source of tremendous information. You must train yourself to process and react to that information as soon as it is sensed.

Everyday thinking is not sufficient training for complex changes in your mind-body organization. Like muscles, your brain gets stronger at whatever it does regularly. If you practice imagery techniques, your brain gets better at doing that. Conversely, if your mind regularly wanders off into a jumble of random thought, it gets better at that. To understand how best to train your thought process, you need to know more about the nature of consciousness.

BRAIN AS THE BASIS FOR IMAGERY

The human brain consists of some 100 billion neurons, which is roughly equivalent to the number of stars in the Milky Way (Flanagan 1991). These neurons make about 1,000 connections on average with other neurons. The brain therefore has about 1,000 trillion connections, a quite unimaginable number. The main portion of the brain, the cerebrum (Latin for brain), is divided into lobes that relate to the overlying cranial bones. If you take a look at the brain from the outside, you will see a convoluted array of thick bundles called the neocortex, which is only a few millimeters thick. The evolutionarily older part of the brain is invisibly buried deep beneath. You may also observe that there is a fissure between the two halves, creating a right and a left brain.

Most functions that you need and use from day to day are not being controlled by the part that you see (figure 3.1). Actions like breathing, regulating blood pressure and chemistry, and reflexes are done by the forebrain and midbrain. Surprisingly the whole of the neocortex is involved in imagery and planning; the former is more associated with the posterior neocortex, and the latter is more associated with the anterior. There are some subsystem areas, related to speech production, vision, and movement, but they are heavily associated and rely on a great amount of dialogue to produce their amazing feats of sensation and action. The frontal lobes are important for planning, movement, and social behavior; the parietal lobes receive and process data from the senses; the temporal lobes hear and interpret music and language; and the occipital lobes specialize in vision. But as mentioned earlier, other areas of the brain will be needed for the completeness of these functions.

Other brain structures include the limbic system, the "emotional" brain, which is intimately connected to the forebrain. Among the structures of the limbic system we find the amygdala, which is involved in fear and related anger responses; the hippocampus, which acts to reduce the stress response and helps in establishing long-

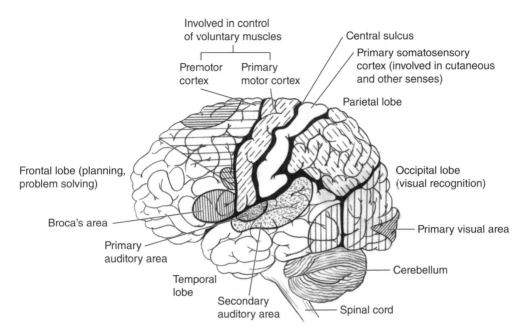

Figure 3.1 Structures of the brain.

term memory for facts and events; the thalamus, which relays sensory information to the cortex; and the brain stem, which controls automatic body functions such as breathing. These systems react plastically to our behavior by growing or shrinking.

The cerebellum, located just below the cerebrum, is responsible for skilled movement. The cerebellum is involved in the retention of coordinated movement sequences you have learned, storing them in the brain to be recalled when necessary. When I was a student at New York University, my fellow students and I asked Larry Rhodes to demonstrate multiple pirouettes. Although he hadn't pirouetted in a long time, he astounded us with an astronomical (so it seemed to us) six or seven perfect turns. He explained that once the correct feeling for a movement has been firmly established, you only need to recall the sensation and the body will automatically (with the help of the cerebellum) reproduce even complex movement sequences. Even after many years pass without practicing a certain skill, the neurons that once stored or represented a movement in your brain can be reactivated much faster than if you were to learn the movement for the very first time.

BRAIN AND CONSCIOUSNESS

Our understanding of the brain's function has increased exponentially in the past few years. The MRI has allowed us to watch the brain in real time and to see activity that is related to our images and thinking. A lot is known about the function of individual neurons, the cells of the nervous system, and fundamental relationships within the brain. However, the wiring in the brain is so complicated and there are so many interconnections that so far no complete map of the brain exists. The brain's relationship to consciousness remains unanswered. Are we conscious and therefore our brains are active, or does the activity of our brains create our consciousness? We know that a relationship exists and that mental experiences can create changes in the brain, but the nature of consciousness has not been explained. Are we simply a set of functions and behaviors represented by the brain? As early as 1974, Lulu Sweigard, quoting Mabel Todd from a privately published book and from *The Thinking Body* (1972), explained that the image changes the patterning of the nervous system:

> *Change is possible only through the enormous task of recoordinating the neuro-muscular pathways responsible for the habitual balance and movement patterns. It can be accomplished only if the method of teaching informs, stimulates, and challenges the student. . . . The idea of the movement alone suffices to start all movement along its most suitable path. This concept as a method of teaching was first proposed by Todd. Her basic premise was that "concentration upon a picture involving movement results in responses in the neuromusculature as necessary to carry out specific movements with the least effort." She derived this theory empirically, through extensive experimentation. (p. 6)*

The previous statements are based on the premise that the mind and the brain are identical. Having a thought or holding a picture in the mind sends a message through the nervous system because thoughts and the nervous system are related, even though it is not totally clear how. Magazines and articles show brain areas that are highlighted in certain colors with captions marking them as "the area for X" or "the psychological state of Y." In reality we know only that these areas become relatively more active than surrounding areas when we exhibit certain behaviors, movements, and psychological states. However, there may be many other areas of the brain necessary for any psychological or movement function.

Scientific studies and advances in physics have spawned fierce controversy over this premise of the inseparability of mind and body. The machinists explain consciousness as a pure function of the brain, which is a supercomputer whose functions they cannot explain. The mysterians, who contend that there is an aspect to the mind that we just do not understand, counter that there is no way to scientifically evaluate an individual's way of experiencing.

Damasio, the famous neurologist, states, "Core consciousness is conceived as the imaged relationship of the interaction between an object and the changed organism state it causes." As we can see, Damasio uses imaging in his explanation and states that the "somato-sensing structures" are necessary for core consciousness to emerge (Parivzi and Damasio 2001).

Children cannot use imagery or conceive of a new object until they have sensed and therefore experienced its various components. The accumulation of sensory perceptions of an object leads to the ability to imagine it: "I feel heavy like a sack of sand." With children, you first have to establish these concepts by playing with a sack filled with sand—or a tin soldier, which is heavy and metallic, or a cloth doll, which is light and malleable. The process begins with the baby taking objects into her mouth. Using this sensory method, the baby soon learns to distinguish the feel of wood from the feel of cloth and the round shape of a teething ring from the square shape of a building block. Later, a doughnut can be appreciated as something that is round as well as soft; still later, one can also recognize the letter O in the doughnut. This is why an important part of imagery training is sensory stimulation.

The limbic-hypothalamic system of the brain could play an important role in connecting mind and body. The limbic system is known for its function in human emotions. But the cortical "thinking and planning" part of the brain and the limbic system are in a constant dialogue through a great number of neural connections. Thoughts, emotions, and images are certainly interconnected on the level of the brain. The hypothalamus is the major regulator of the body's basic systems, such as hunger, thirst, temperature, heart rate, and blood pressure. The brain uses virtually identical pathways for seeing objects and for imagining them—only it uses these pathways in reverse. In the process of human vision, a stimulus in the outside world is passed from the retina to the primary visual cortex and then to higher centers until an object or event is recognized.

Although we may have pathways from mind to body and from body to mind, questions remain. How did the mind get into the body? Is the body the only outlet for the activities of the mind? In attempting to solve these problems, are we trying to make bread without dough? There are several schools of thought.

Physicists Bohr, Heisenberg, and Margenau agree that "consciousness cannot be fully accounted for by the physical sciences as they are currently understood" (Dossey 1985, p. 163). Experiments in quantum optics show that events can influence each other faster than any signal can travel between them (Chiao, Kwiat, and Steinberg 1993). Perhaps images are not bound exclusively to the nervous pathways. "In quantum mechanics, the irrational has indeed come to pass: Interactions between the nonmaterial and material are commonplace" (Dossey 1985, p. 163).

There is mounting evidence that the mind's influence can be found outside the body. If you divide a colony of worms with identical genetic material into two groups and give them to two separate groups of experimenters, the following occurs: If the experimenters are told that the worms are especially intelligent, they will do better than the other group, whose "trainers" are told that the worms are especially stupid. Since you cannot coax a worm with sweet talk or caresses, perhaps the attitude of the trainers influences the worms' ability to learn. Does this imply that the mind has effects outside of the brain? Thomas Nagel (Gelman et al. 1992), professor of philosophy at Rutgers University, explains:

> Imagine you come across a wiggly, crawly creature. You put it in a box and leave it awhile. When you open the box, a butterfly flies out, and you say, "Gee, that's got to be the wiggly, crawly creature." Nothing else went in, it has to be the same; but you can't imagine how it could be. That's the problem with consciousness, the butterfly that emerges almost magically from the brain. (p. 46)

Can the thinking mind affect things and people directly? Could it be that the mind of the teacher influences the student directly, not just through the use of words or touch? I have known dance teachers with this attitude: "Very few people were made to dance, and certainly not most of the people here." Watching the students in such a class, I see tension, sullenness, self-distrust, and a failure to achieve. I am sure we have all experienced the benefits of receiving encouragement, or what is often referred to as positive vibrations. It seems that the more deeply an image is held in the teacher's mind, the better he can convey it, and the more likely the student will react to it. Sometimes the presence of a certain teacher makes a student perform better. Perhaps the student's ability reflects the teacher's attitude. Perhaps the student feels more confident or simply wants to do better. Mabel Todd (1972) writes the following:

> When doing exercises under instruction we are apt to think that we move or direct the moving of the muscles. What actually happens is that we get a picture

from the teacher's words or his movements, and the appropriate action takes place within our own bodies to reproduce this picture. The result is successful in proportion to our power of interpretation and amount of experience, but most of all perhaps to the desire to do. (p. 33)

Bending Your Arm

Ask a friend to extend one arm straight to the side and tell him that you are going to try to bend the arm. Notice how much your friend can resist your effort. Then tell your friend to think of a river of energy flowing through the arm and out into space. He should keep the image of energy flow alive as you again try to bend the arm. You will notice that the arm is harder to bend, even though your friend has not suddenly become stronger. Certain ways of thinking increase the body's force without altering the structure.

NERVOUS SYSTEM

Let's take a closer look at the intercom—the brain-body network called the nervous system. The sensory part of this network reminds of me of an enormous market. Like a messenger sent out from the brain to get specific information (for example, about the position of a limb), the nerve cell, or neuron, can be thought of as the brain's personal shopper. Amid the jumble of voices touting oranges, apples, broccoli, and turnips (information about limb positions), it needs to find lettuce only.

Neurons consist of a cell body with a nucleus, dendrites, and an axon. There are three types of neurons: sensory neuron, motor neuron, and interneuron.

- Sensory neurons gather information and provide stimuli for reflex activity, then bring the information to the attention of the central processing unit, the brain.
- Motor neurons carry commands to their attached muscles. If enough motor neurons are firing, the muscle will contract.
- Interneurons allow communication between sensory and motor neurons, among other higher tasks.

There is, in fact, a strong similarity between firing a gun and stimulating a muscle. Instead of gunpowder, electrochemical activity is shot down the axon, the neuron's lengthy arm (Miller 1982). Because a single muscle fiber always releases the same amount of work at the same time, the motor neurons need to fire many shots at many fibers to activate an entire muscle.

However, the metaphor fails to incorporate the whole class of operations in the nervous system that are not excitations but inhibitions. Is it possible to fire a shot that inhibits? Instead of stimulating a process, an inhibitory signal restrains or stops a process. Compare this concept to how a dam regulates the flow of water through a river. The amount of water arriving at the dam cannot be regulated, but what can be regulated is how much water is retained and how much is allowed to continue its flow down the river basin.

Muscles receive excitatory and inhibitory messages all the time. If excitation dominates, the dam is not functioning and the river banks of the structure are overwhelmed. The result is loss of coordination and spasticity. As in the case of the ancient Nile, the whole country, or anything resembling conscious movement, may be lost. Good alignment, like water control, is a balance between sufficient stimulation of muscle activity to create an upright stance and sufficient restraint of muscular activity for this stance to be as effortless as possible.

The nervous system is divided into the central nervous system and the peripheral nervous system. The central nervous system consists of the brain and the spinal cord. The cord transfers information to and from the brain and is encased within the spine and the dura, an extra-strong covering of connective tissue. The peripheral nervous system can be subdivided into the somatic and the autonomic systems. The somatic nervous system maintains contact with the outside world and sends impulses to the striated muscles used in gross and subtle movement. The autonomic nervous system controls the internal organs, which generally are not consciously controlled (although, with practice, such control can be exercised to a limited degree).

NEUROPLASTICITY AND IMAGERY

In the past two decades the notion that the brain is fixed and unchangeable has finally been relegated to the history of science. Interestingly enough, it has been known for quite a long time that the brain is changeable. William James (1842-1910) was probably the first to suggest that the brain can change. Any animal or human that learns or changes its behavior is also changing the biology of the brain. Young squids have been shown to be good learners (Stewart 1997). Even sponges, a very primitive animal, are plastic. Reflexes, which have the image of being fixed in their nature, have some plasticity; in other words, they can change depending on the nature of input or even inhibited by a higher brain function. There are of course some behaviors, so-called fixed action patterns, that display little plasticity. It would be quite unwise to be able to unlearn blinking or swallowing.

Generally speaking, though, your human brain, just like your body, responds to your behavior and actions with adaptive change. The neural circuits are constantly being shaped by your behavior and the environment. This shaping can happen at the level of the synapse, the interface between two neurons. This term was coined by Sherrington as early as 1897. Plasticity involves changes in the sensitivity at the synapse. No fewer than 1,461 proteins, or 7 percent of the human genome, are involved in the information processing of the synapse in laying down memories (Bayés et al. 2010). Neuronal plasticity may also create additional connections, sprout dendrites in the amygdala, and increase the number of cells in the hippocampus. Large behavioral changes may even cause the remapping of whole areas of the cortex. Plastic changes in synaptic activation levels can happen in seconds, whereas a change in the mapping of the brain may take several months or longer. In this case, the neurons have switched their roles in what function they are representing. Remapping may take place if someone loses the function of an area of the body due to an accident. The area of the brain that was responsible for a lost function is slowly occupied by other functions. But what if you have not lost function but are simply practicing a lot of movement skills or imagery? In this case weak, or dormant, connections are called on and strengthened.

You can use the metaphor of trail hiking. Some trails look like they are being used a lot—the ground is flat and well trodden. Other trails display overgrowth—they have not lately been frequented by hikers. New paths can open up, too. If you choose to hike straight through a field, you do not create a path on your own. But if more and more hikers decide to follow your footsteps, eventually this will become a usable trail. To return to your nervous system, neural circuits are strengthened by what you experience and choose to do. If you dance ballet and then take up tango, the circuitry that relates to ballet will slowly weaken while you build up the neural representation for tango. Some skill transfer will take place and your sense for ballet will never vanish, because the path once trodden will stay visible for a long time.

Therefore, if your alignment is less than ideal, slouched perhaps, not only are you influencing your muscles, joints, organs, and connective tissue in an adverse way, but you are also shaping the neural pathways that support slouched posture. In your brain you are creating the representation for slouching. When you decide to improve your alignment, it will also require a biological change in your brain, which takes time and depends on your motivation. If you are motivated and energized at the prospect of improving your posture, it will happen a lot faster than if you are doing it because someone told you that it would be a good idea. You improve at what you do at the level of your motivation to improve. And doing in this case includes thinking, imagining, emoting, and moving.

The World in the Brain

One of the responsibilities of the brain is to create an image of the world within which you can function optimally. This image is plastic—it is constantly changed by input from the environment. When you are dreaming, you are often absorbing, balancing, and resetting the image you have of the world. C.G. Jung (1875-1961) created a whole type of imagery in psychotherapy called active imagination to continue the thread of a dream in waking and help to explain or resolve issues related to such dreams. In a dream it may happen that what you see appears to be entirely real. This proves that your brain is able to generate your whole imaginary environment and reality. Another way to prove this inner world is the ability to close your eyes and imagine you are walking, cooking, or talking to someone. This ability of the brain is the basis of using imagery in sports, dance, and exercises.

To create change in your brain's biology, you need to change the quality and frequency of input you are providing to your brain. If you have been performing a movement with excess tension, for example, the brain region representing that movement also represents the tension. This has important consequences for teaching imagery. You cannot just tell a student to relax, because she does not have the sufficient representation for that experience. She feels normal in her tension. The more the student practices without creating the desired changes, the more the brain is laying down the representation that is not the desired one, making it even harder to change. Therefore I suggest a step-by-step strategy (the Franklin method, APAC; see chapter 4) for creating such changes. In all the steps, imagery is used but in a different manner. In the first stage, you may use biological or metaphorical imagery combined with self-touch and small movements to create the relaxed shoulders. In the second state, you may use mental rehearsal without involving any movement to practice the desired skill. In the third stage, you can call on intuitive or spontaneous imagery to help anchor the experience in your biology from a personal perspective.

The movement is first practiced with this new experience in the mind and in the body as a feeling (kinesthetically). In this way, you can experience the desired type of coordination as soon as possible and create the brain representations for optimal movement and posture.

Changeable Brain Imagery

Imagine your brain to be responsive to your actions and behavior, ready to change and improve its connections. Your brain is ready to make you happier and more confident and improve your posture and movement. Now think of all the synaptic and neuronal changes happening to bring you toward your goals of better function and happier emotional states. As you imagine this, do you feel a change? What about trying the opposite: the image of a decaying brain? Does it make you cringe? Move back to the positive image and embellish it with maximal creativity and bathe in the knowledge that your brain is improving in every instant.

Move Your Brain

Imagine your brain floating in cerebrospinal fluid within your skull. Move your head right and left, front and back, and imagine the brain responding. Now imagine that your brain is initiating the movement. Does it feel different when you imagine the brain creating the movement as opposed to thinking of the skull moving the brain?

Left Brain, Right Brain

Some areas seem to be predominantly involved in a certain function, but neat compartmentalization does not exist. The left hemisphere is traditionally seen to be more involved in language and grammar as well as exact numerical computations. As early as 1861 an area key to language production located in the left frontal lobe of the cortex was named after its discoverer, Broca. The right hemisphere seems to be more creatively involved in language and numerical estimations. Therefore, linguistic function is located in both hemispheres, and patterns or organizations of language ability have been found to be as unique as fingerprints. The whole cortex is involved to a greater or lesser degree in the formation of mental images and significant overlap between the areas activated during visual perception and visual imagery. If you imagine seeing something and you actually see something, similar areas of the brain are active (Ganis, Thompson, and Kosslyn 2004). Knowledge of words and mental concepts is found to be spread widely throughout the brain. A third-party mediator, the convergence zone, is required to join the knowledge.

Imagery Exercise for Left Brain and Right Brain

Imagine the two halves of your brain as balanced. You may think of them leaning against each other and having equal weight. When you imagine the two hemispheres, do you visualize them as the same size? Imagine a horizontally configured figure eight in your brain, the center of which is between the hemispheres. Mentally move through this figure eight from one side to the other and back. Notice if the image also affects your posture. Imagine that the hemispheres are in a fluid interchange of information enabling the whole cortex to create the imagery that is most relevant to your current needs.

DEVELOPING MIND: THE ROLE OF IMAGERY

A baby's capacity to use imagery can begin very early. The baby understands that an object exists, even if part of it is hidden, as early as 5 months of age. At this age, the baby realizes that the toy has a life of its own; it doesn't just exist when the baby looks at it. At about 12 months, the baby can purposely imitate other people by using a memory or an image of something he has seen. At about two years of age, the child can think ahead and solve simple logistical problems by imagining their outcomes. Before building a tower of blocks, the child can decide that he wants the tower to be very high and realize that he will need to collect blocks from all over the playroom to achieve this. The child is using his visual memory to plan ahead. He can imagine stories he has been told and can begin to play roles and imitate the contents of these stories. In the next stage, the child begins to practice social skills such as imaginary cooking and shopping, putting objects into new relationships with each other, and endowing them with qualities. As a parent, you know not to pick up the Kleenex (they are bedcovers) and to leave the pencils in place (they are forks and spoons). The child can now also imagine new spaces—the bed is a boat, and beneath the covers is the wolves' den.

At age 3, the imagination turns even more vivid. The child turns into a baby elephant munching on grass (straws) but can instantly change back to being himself if necessary (to drink something). He may go through a ritual of transformation, shaking and wiggling to convert to a crocodile, only to become a lion a minute later. Children love to imagine they are animals and to invent imaginary playmates.

Because children can constantly change themselves and the objects around them, many children's books and games are image based. A book I had when I was a child suggested this: "A bird can fly. So can I. I can squirm like a worm. Swish, I'm a fish. A clam is what I am. Pitter pitter pat, I can walk like a cat" (Krauss 1950). In another, I remember reading the following: "There was the school, so white in the morning sunshine it seemed to sparkle! Peter felt as if there were sparkles running around inside him, too. . . . Peter felt as lonely as a cloud going nowhere" (Kingmann 1953). Both images contain interesting themes for dance improvisation, and it is certainly hard to slouch when you've got sparkles inside your body.

Fantasy rules at this stage of development. Children imbue inanimate objects such as dolls, fluffy animals, even spoons, with consciousness—a notion that lasts until about the age of 8. Hide and seek becomes very interesting. The child may still have difficulty imagining all the spaces to hide in the home, but once she discovers these places, she can remember them and seek them out. Imagery is also tied to movement tasks at this age. Jumping rope, my 3-year-old requested the rope to go higher and said that she was going to jump up to the ceiling. She then jumped "higher than ever."

Magical thinking and fantasy become highly developed. At age 4, children begin to use symbols, which also connect to their increased language skills. They can distinguish among a great variety of animals and even the individual characters of animals of the same kind. A 4-year-old uses imagery in an increasingly adult fashion, relating it more to the adult reality of purpose and achievement. At this age, visualization is approaching the peak of its development (Kavner 1985). Children can now place themselves in unusual and inventive situations, see relationships among imagined situations, develop empathy, imagine what it is like to be a mommy or a daddy or a favorite character from a children's book, and envision all the things that that character has to deal with. Often a child has a favorite imaginary character that he or she likes to play. The child loves to invent stories around this character and will never tire of listening to a parent tell about the imaginary things happening in that character's life. At this age, improved motor control and balance enable more complicated movement sequences and the first signs of ability to learn gymnastics or dancing skills. A child will now begin to imitate even difficult movements that adults are practicing, such as a pirouette (spinning on one foot), and at times quite successfully. The child is not concerned with failure or success, only with having fun.

Because children are natural imagers, even the smallest events are important sensory-image builders: building a snowman, pouring hot applesauce, drawing with gooey finger paints, splashing through puddles, listening to the sounds at the zoo. The good news is that imagery skills seem to remain intact with age, except that the ability to generate imagery may slow down a bit (Dror and Kosslyn 1994).

The more your sensory memory is filled with tactile, visual, and kinesthetic information, the easier it will be to create imagery later in life. Images based on childhood experiences are particularly powerful because everything is so new and fresh. The same image will evoke a different response from each person, because each sensory cupboard is filled with a personal mix of experiences. This holds true for all of the images contained in this book. The ones you respond to most are reinforced by your own sensory memory.

Pendulum

The following exercise is found in Kükelhaus' (1984) book *Urzahl und Gebärde* (*Primal Number and Gesture,* originally published in 1934). Hang a pendulum from your finger. (If you don't have a pendulum, you can create one by hanging a key from a string.) Now look away. Don't pay any attention to the pendulum, but think of it turning in a circle. Concentrate as much as you can on *circle*. Don't do anything else. Try not to consciously move your finger. You will find that the pendulum will begin to move in a circle. Try the same experiment using the image of a straight line or an ellipse. You will find that the pendulum's movement will reflect the image in your mind. Then stop the pendulum and try to re-create the same circle, line, or ellipsoid by intentionally moving your finger. You will find that it is much more difficult to create a delicate regular circle using conscious control. By using imagery, you can often achieve a more fine-tuned motion than with voluntary action.

You may have noticed that if you think about moving to the right and then actually move to the right, the movement will be smoother and easier. However, if you think about turning your head to the left and then turn it to the right, you will feel resistance; it will not be quite as easy. Your nervous system immediately starts creating the muscle setup that supports your imagined action. Many problems in dance and sport can be avoided by recognizing and eliminating "contraindicated" imaging. For example, if you think *lean back* or *hold* while turning, it becomes difficult. Instead, support the action by thinking *turn* or *revolve*. (See the chapter on pirouettes in my 1996 book *Dance Imagery for Technique and Performance*).

SUMMARY

In this chapter you have discovered that the brain is changeable—it is plastic and remains so throughout life. One of the most important tools in generating this change is mental imagery. A child's ability to imagine peaks at an early age, and with practice this ability can be maintained into old age. The brain has some areas that are more specialized than others to perform certain functions, but this is not a neat division of labor. Many areas of the brain work together to create a certain outcome, such as speech production. Finally, visual imagery and visual perception rely to a great degree on the same areas of the brain. In chapter 4 you will learn a four-step system to help you improve your alignment and movement skills.

Change Through Imagery

If you want to change your body, first change your mind.

In the previous chapters we talked about the theories and neural structures underlying mental imagery. Ultimately no theory will help you move better or align unless there is some hands-on experiential learning involved. After many years of teaching imagery, anatomy, and movement, I have developed a four-step model that is easy to remember and at the same time addresses the most important elements that are needed for change. You can use this model to improve your movement and alignment, but you can also apply it to many other areas of your life.

Part of what can change is your body image, which is the sum of your perceptions relating to your body. The body image is subjective, and it develops and changes throughout your lifetime. Developmental patterns relate to how you develop your movement skills, from crawling to walking. The level of integration of these developmental stages influences your body image as well as others' opinions about your body. You can practice and develop your imagery skills and use these skills in forming a holistic image of your body.

FOUR STEPS FOR CHANGE

Recently I started a class session by asking the following question: Is exercise healthy? Surprisingly, the answer was not an unqualified yes. Everyone in the movement profession knows of people who got hurt from exercising or engaging in any variety of sports. Much research shows the health benefits of exercise, but the benefit of any type of movement or exercise depends on the quantity, quality, and safety of its performance. This insight leads to the next question: How do you improve the quality and efficiency of your training? Repetition alone is not the answer. If you are practicing with misalignment or tension, you will simply ingrain that movement pattern more deeply in your brain and body.

I propose the following procedural model called APAC (assess, plan, act, and compare), which has helped thousands of people taking Franklin method classes to create more efficient alignment and movement. Research in Germany (Rieman and Franklin 2010) validates the hypothesis and value of the four-step process of APAC.

1. Assess

The first step in helping your body become more efficient is evaluating your postural status quo. You need to review the current state of your movement and alignment for elements that warrant improvement. You can do this evaluation with the help of an outside expert, such as a coach or trainer, but you could also do much of it yourself. The rationale for this is quite simple. No therapist or teacher, even the most brilliant, can change the circuits and representations of your brain for you. In the end it is always your behavior and your experience that will create that change, so why not start at that point? The person who wants to improve his physical state needs to be empowered, and research points to the importance of involvement on that level even when dealing with back pain (Larsson 2010).

Ample information about the state of your alignment and movement is constantly being relayed to your conscious awareness with the help of your senses. This information is provided by the sense organs of posture and movement, the exteroceptors (eyes and ears) and proprioceptors located in your muscles, tendons, ligaments, inner ear, and joint capsules. If your ability to focus on the state of your body is sufficient, you will be able to discover when alignment and movement feel good and also what areas feel uncomfortable and not coordinated.

There are challenges: You may not be able to feel faulty alignment and movement patterns in the first place because they have become habits. Also, what is wrong actually feels normal. This is why overuse injuries can happen in the first place. Overuse injuries simply indicate that you have used your body for too long in the wrong way. You have been performing movement day in and day out without noticing that you are slowly degrading your physical self. Ultimately the task of the postural and movement educator is to help you to help yourself, to help you feel and notice what you did not notice before so that that aspect of your posture and movement becomes available for change. If the postural educator perceives his job simply as putting you in the right position and fixing you without you being able to participate in the process by noticing why this right position or new way of moving improves your alignment, movement, or enjoyment, the change will not last, and it might even reduce your movement efficiency. In this stage you ask yourself these questions: How am I doing, mentally, physically, emotionally? Am I all OK, or is there room for improvement?

2. Plan

Once you have finished your evaluation, you need to make a plan to implement improvements. The content of this plan is drawn from how the body functions anatomically and how the body receives fresh input from the nervous system to move in the most functionally efficient fashion. The bulk of this book provides content for this plan. In this stage you ask yourself these questions: What tools do I need in order to improve? What resources can I access at this time? Do I need to increase my tools and resources before I begin?

3. Act

Now the plan needs to be implemented or fed forward into your body and mind. This book contains hundreds of ways to do this. This is where imagery and embodied anatomy come into the picture. You are appreciating your physical design and imagining how you would like to experience your alignment, movement, and motivational state. There are many flavors to the action of feeding forward into your body and mind, ranging from self-talk to highly metaphorical and pictorial imagery, which are elucidated in great detail in chapters 7 to 17. Embodied anatomy means that the knowledge of anatomy not only is intellectual but also can be imagined as a function in your own body. The anatomy is felt and seen in action as you move—a physical insight, so to speak.

4. Compare

In the final stage, you notice the result of your practice. Have you improved? If so, what has changed? You are comparing your new state with your original status quo. In this stage it is important to record all positive changes and relate them to how you made the progress. You will then be able to repeat your four steps to improve even further. If you did not improve, you need to review your plan and tools to feed them forward.

Example of the Four-Step Process

In this example of APAC, we focus on the neck. In the first step, notice the state of your neck. Stand in a comfortable position and move your head and neck in a variety of directions and notice how long and relaxed it feels. Lift your right leg and left leg by flexing the hip joints and notice how smooth the action feels. Notice what happens when you actively lengthen your neck: You may actually increase tension in the muscles of the neck and, more surprisingly, the resistance in the hip joint when you repeat your hip flexions. By using voluntary effort to lengthen the neck, you lost the ease of movement (see the chapters on the pelvis, spine, and neck for more explanation). This obviously is not the goal you wanted to achieve.

In the second step, you need to decide on your goals and assemble your tools. You will use self-touch, self-talk, metaphorical imagery, and anatomical imagery while in motion. All the anatomical knowledge you need is that muscles can lengthen and shorten and that there are several layers of muscles in the neck.

In the third step, you act on your plan. Place one hand on your neck and squeeze the muscles as if you are squeezing a sponge. While holding your neck, gently nod your head as if saying yes. Imagine the many layers of the muscles of the neck sliding on top of each other. Discover the most slippery image you can. As you nod your head forward, imagine the muscles lengthening. As you nod your head backward, imagine the muscles shortening. Perform self-talk, such as *flexible, stretchy, soft neck*, to accompany the imagery. If you wish to coordinate your movement with your breathing cycle, exhale on flexion and inhale on the extension phase of your head and neck. After a minute or two, let go of your touch and imagine your neck to be a sponge filling with warm (or cool) water.

Finally, in the fourth step, notice what has changed. Compare your current state to the earlier experience of your neck. How long does your neck feel? Move your head and notice your muscles and joints. Now you will be able to lift your leg without resistance in the hip joint and have a lengthened and flexible feeling in your neck without using any effort for it to be so.

BODY IMAGE AS BASIC FEEDBACK

When you start the process of change and assessing your state of being, the first thing you may encounter is your body image. Your body image is your fundamental feedback, the sum of the conscious and unconscious subjective opinions and ideas you have about your body. You must take this fundamental image into the equation when you start the process of changing your body through a systematic process of imagery.

Achterberg (1985) writes about the neurological basis of the body image:

> . . . body image itself is generally lateralized in the right hemisphere. When damage occurs in the parietal lobe of the right hemisphere through a stroke or injury, the patient may fail to recognize part of his or her own body. (p. 122)

The term *body image* has gone through conceptual changes. It can be thought of as the sum of visual, tactile, gustatory, olfactory, and kinesthetic sensations, but it also includes awareness of posture, intentionality, aims, and inclinations. Heinz Werner (1965), editor of *The Body Percept,* points out another aspect of body image: "The spatiality of the body (unlike that of external objects) is not a spatiality of mere positions but a spatiality of situations" (p. 100). Werner describes an image used by Merlau-Ponty to clarify his point: "If I stand in front of my desk and lean on it with both hands, only my hands are stressed and the whole of my body trails behind them like a tail of a comet" (Merlau-Ponty 1962, p. 100).

Body image is a dynamic phenomenon, not just a sensory image. Every activity continuously modifies it. Body image includes your experience of your body's enclosing surface, the shape and volume contained within this surface, its weight, and closely related state of tension (Naville 1992). You can train yourself to perceive these elements more clearly and distinctly through imagery exercises, thus modifying your overall body image. The detailed and simultaneous perception of many elements of the body image should be an important part of improving your alignment. In dance, the term *physicality* refers to a very complete, moment-to-moment experience of motion based on a highly differentiated body image. In this sense, physicality helps you become aware of your moment-to-moment changes in alignment.

As a child develops, so does her body image. The child must first learn to distinguish between herself and the environment, and only slowly does she become aware of her own body shape, of the individual body parts, and of their names and interrelationships.

Language is a prerequisite for detailed body orientation. Once you can imagine a body part and can see its form and place in space, you can begin to talk and finally write about it. Therefore, your choice of words when speaking about an image is related to the response the image will elicit. Also, the same words can cause a variety of responses based on the individual's body image and sensory memory. If you say, "Imagine your shoulders dropping downward" (strictly speaking, the shoulders keep their shape and surface contours as they move downward), you address a different mix of body image elements than when you say, "Imagine your shoulders melting downward" (the shape and the surface outline of the shoulders change as they move downward). Yet other responses may result from using words such as "Imagine your shoulders hanging . . . falling down . . . sliding downward." Each person's exact response will depend on his or her personal experience of the language and imagery that has been used. Often the only way to find out which choice of words and mental imagery is best—which has evoked the greatest response—is by requesting feedback from the individual.

One of the few ways to gain direct insight into a person's body image and specific alignment problems is by looking at drawings he creates of himself. A drawing can reveal a sense of the relative importance and awareness of one's body parts. Of course, a subject must not be aware that his drawings are being used for this purpose or he may portray himself as having a well-aligned body even if he does not.

The drawing in figure 4.1a was done by a four-year-old child. The head is differentiated from the torso, but there is no neck. There are arms, legs, and a slight indication of feet. The drawing in figure 4.1b was done by the same child at age five. Note that several new components of the body image have arrived: hands with individual fingers, eyebrows, ears, and distinct feet.

Every shape and position you take, especially if it is new, contributes to your personal body image. The relationship between body image, especially its visual and kinesthetic components, and what you actually look like is important in dance, exercise, and sports. Unlike the artist, you cannot step back from your drawing and compare your inner pictures with the outer reality. Looking at videotapes of yourself is often a very surprising experience. You notice that the way you felt, or what you pictured yourself doing, does not necessarily correspond to what you see on the

Figure 4.1   Growing awareness of body image reflected in drawings by (a) a four-year-old and (b) a five-year-old.

Perceiving Your Body Image

1. **Drawing your body image:** Once a week, make a drawing of yourself in standing position as viewed from the front and another as viewed from the side. Put the drawings in a book, date them, and do not look at them for at least three months. (Each time you add a new drawing to the book, do not look at the previous drawings.) After three months, place all the drawings side by side in chronological order. Do you detect a pattern? A shift in your alignment? This exercise is especially interesting if you are working on your alignment during the documented period.

2. **Malleable clay:** Lie on the floor. Think of yourself as a piece of clay that is very malleable. Now think of the most elegant and skilled hands touching your body and beginning to shape it into the ideal, most functional form. Try imagining the hands of Michelangelo or Leonardo da Vinci creating a beautiful work of art out of your body, such as the sculpture *David* in Florence, Italy.

3. **Imaginary sculptor:** You are made entirely of clay. Move your body into a variety of postures and let the imaginary artist create your ideal form. Watch as the artist's imaginary hands improve and perfect each pose you get into. Don't limit yourself to traditional shapes and forms; any position can be perfected by the imaginary sculptor. Do not worry about what "perfect" entails; let the sculptor take care of that.

screen. The awareness of body image holds relevance for movement education. Even if the teacher sees that a student's shoulders are not on the same level, for example, the student may not be perceiving this. One of the tasks of the teacher is to inform the student's body image of relevant aspects to improving his movement and alignment.

Proprioception is an important part of your overall body image. The term is derived from the Latin *proprio* ("self") and *capto* ("to grasp") and was coined by Charles Sherrington (1964). Proprioception denotes the kinesthetic sense (or kinaesthesia), the movement and position of your limbs—the sense of tension and force, the sense of balance, and the sense of heaviness and effort (Brumagne 2010). Muscle spindles are the sensory receptors mainly responsible for the sense of position and movement, the tendon organs for the sense of tension or force, and the vestibular system for the sense of balance and gravity. The sense of effort itself is produced by the brain (Gandevia 1996), which may explain some of the effects of kinetic imagery and imagined effortlessness. Some proprioceptive ability is also located in the skin, especially the sole of the feet and the hands.

Tapping the Position

Move into various positions and let your partner tap you lightly all over your body. Tap more gently over joints and more vigorously over muscles. You may also ask your partner about the appropriate strength of your tapping. Sense your whole position as clearly as possible before you move into another position, where your partner begins tapping you again. Repeat the exercise several times until you can move from position to position and mentally scan your whole body to experience its total shape, surface, weight, and volume. As you gain experience, try to perceive the entire body at once.

Major organs of balance and sensing gravity are located in the vestibular system and macular organs of the inner ear. The latter contain tiny calcite stones called otoliths, which sit on stalks called hair cells that are embedded in a kind of gel. These hair cells are deflected by the weight of the stones when you move your head. Even the slightest movement suffices to elicit a signal down the sensory pathways and inform the brain about gravity and translatory movements of the head. Another type of hair cell floats in a fluid in the ear's semicircular canals. When the fluid moves as you change your head position, the hairs move, once again eliciting a signal that informs the brain about acceleratory movement of the head. The eyes are the important determinants of your position in space, but thanks to all the other assistants of your sensory apparatus, most people can readily close their eyes and still determine where they are in space. However, the position of your eyes even when closed is important for balance because of the large amount of proprioceptive muscle spindles in the muscles that move the eyeball. All of this information is relayed to the brain, where the evidence of motion is interpreted and pieced together.

Balancing With Closed Eyes

In the upright position with your weight equally balanced on both legs, close your eyes. Standing on both legs, it is probably not much of a challenge to stay balanced. Now move your eyes under your eyelids to various positions and notice how this affects your balance: Look up, down, to the right, and to the left, and circle your eyes as well. Notice if the challenge to stay balanced increases.

Now do the same standing on just one leg. First keep the eyes still and looking forward under the eyelids. Now look up, down, to the right, and to the left, and circle your eyes. Most likely this is a much more challenging task.

Influencing Body Image

Use specific images to influence your body image. If your arms are short, imagine them long. If your feet don't point, imagine perfect feet. Think of yourself as perfectly proportioned. If you feel your back is short and tight, create an ideal back for yourself. Think of yourself as having the power contained in Aladdin's lamp, of knowing that your wishes will be granted.

Dancers are trained to perceive shapes, and they usually reproduce shapes better than nondancers, but anyone can learn to improve shape memory. In many instances, it is useful to be fully aware of your own position and simultaneously control an outside activity. While supporting a partner, a dancer maintains his partner's equilibrium as well as his own posture. Inferior alignment in this situation can cause injury. Images increase awareness of position and dynamics, filling the body with new sensory information and enriching the body image.

The richer the body image, the more pathways there are to improving your alignment and movement skills. Concentrating on your movement and body organization provides valuable feedback for fine-tuning your body image and, with it, your alignment. Many movement teachers are skilled at filling in gaps in a student's body image by pointing out parts of the body that seem to be "unfelt" or "unclear." A teacher might say, "See the whole shape of your back. Feel the leg moving through space. See the line of your arabesque." Touch is a powerful way to influence body image because it is one of the first ways you experience the boundary of your body. A dancer's relationship to space can be compared to the painter's relationship to the canvas. You want to be able to paint with very fine strokes, not just broad ones. Many exercises for increasing awareness of body boundary are featured in my previous book *Dance Imagery for Technique and Performance* (1996).

The way a person experiences surrounding space can influence alignment. If the space is experienced as threatening and constricting, the body may shrink away and become tense. If the space is experienced as welcoming and confidence inspiring, the body will tend to open up and release tension. It is interesting to observe passengers leaving a cramped airplane after a long journey from a cold climate. As they emerge into what seems like infinite space and warmth, their alignment changes: Their bodies can finally take the space they need.

Relationship to space is pivotal in improving alignment. Many factors besides size influence how your body responds to a certain space: the people in it, past experiences you have had in the space, the colors, the odors, even the texture of the furniture.

External Space and Alignment

During the course of a day, observe how your body reacts to the various spaces you enter. Try to change the spaces you are in by using your imagination. If you find a room constricting, imagine it to be the most spacious and luxurious room possible.

DEVELOPMENTAL PATTERNS AND MENTAL IMAGERY

As an adult, you have the ability to change because you want to and have a fully developed brain and cognitive skills to do so. At birth, movement repertoire is relatively small. Babies are equipped with only rudimentary movements for survival. Inherent patterns guide the motor development of babies through a great variety of stages that finally lead to walking. Each stage of development needs to be processed to ensure motor coordination in adulthood. These stages are mediated by primitive reflexes that need to be spontaneously activated and inhibited with good timing. If activation of primitive reflexes persists into adulthood, certain movement coordination and cognitive development may be challenged (Gibbons 2010).

Developmental therapies aim to help the patient reintegrate missing or not fully integrated developmental stages. Infant reflexology therapist Vojta (1992) has demonstrated that by stimulating certain reflex points, a patient can rediscover important developmental movements. Vojta attributes some postural problems to the lack of certain movements during development.

Cohen (1994) has found that the more developmental patterns you have experienced, the more avenues of expression are open to you:

if the body is the instrument through which the mind is expressed, then one can just play more kinds of melodies, or different kinds of verse, timbre. (p. 100)

Four basic locomotor movement patterns can be observed in phylogenetic development (evolution of the vertebrate animals) and ontogenetic development (growth of the individual human being): spinal, homologous, homolateral, and contralateral. The first three patterns are the more primitive motor patterns that underlie the more complex patterns seen in the future (Cohen and Mills 1979).

The spinal movement pattern consists of bending the body forward, backward, and sideways, as in a forward or backward arch or a side bend in dance. In homologous movement, the upper or lower limbs move symmetrically at the same time, such as in a sauté (vertical jump) from first position. The homolateral movement pattern is an alternating motion that occurs between one side of the body and the other. The left arm and left leg move together and the right arm and right leg move together, as seen in the crawl of a lizard. Figure 4.2 shows a baby reaching for a toy in a homolateral pattern. In the contralateral pattern, the left arm and the right leg move together, or vice versa. This is the typical crawling pattern of infants before they begin to walk.

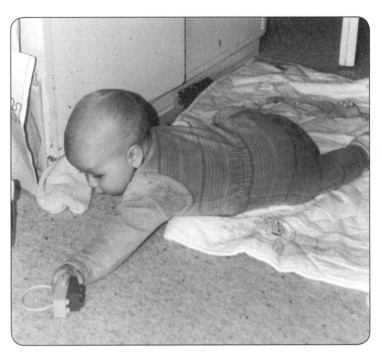

Figure 4.2 A child reaching for a toy with a homolateral movement pattern.

WRONG HABITS THAT FEEL RIGHT

Personal style of movement is formed by genetic background, developmental patterns, and habits acquired continually throughout life. You were born with certain movement patterns, such as walking. A child will learn to walk because it is an inherent movement mediated by a central pattern generator (Crommert 1998). The style of walking, however, may be modified by movement styles observed in parents and siblings and by the lack or abundance of space for exploring movement during childhood. Changing movement habits is not always easy because what you have been doing all along feels normal, and change, even if it is to your advantage, may feel abnormal, at least initially. When you start doing a movement differently, your brain's neural representation for this new movement is still weak and the former still dominant. Unless you evolve into new movement habits carefully and with repeated practice, change can send an alarm through the body: *This is not the way you normally move. This is not your habitual movement and tension level. This is not your habitual alignment.*

I remember working on the hand of a student who had been complaining about it feeling restricted. When I asked, "How does it feel now compared to your other hand?" he said that the hand I had worked on felt very smooth and flexible, whereas the other hand felt like a block of wood. He also said that the smooth and flexible hand did not feel right just yet; he needed to get used to this new sensation as part of himself.

When you begin to change something, you may go through a state of sensory confusion or disorientation. This may be a good sign, signaling that rewiring is truly taking place in your nervous system. Many of the familiar feelings related to how you move are becoming outdated, even though they still feel more comfortable and the new way of moving feels strange. You can probably see that you are doing better, but for a new movement habit to really take hold, it needs to feel natural. However, this does not mean that if you are not feeling confused you are not making progress.

RETAINING YOUR PROGRESS

There is no one specific reaction to progress and change. Some people learn consistently, others learn in spurts and starts, and still others seem to make no progress until virtually overnight their ability moves to a higher level. At times, a certain pressure needs to build up before any great improvement can be made. Therefore, don't feel frustrated if you are doing your best and it doesn't seem to make much difference initially. Your body and mind may be preparing for a big leap forward.

When you do have a breakthrough, there is a terrific new sensation of freedom and ease of motion. Often such experiences have been prepared by workings of the nervous system that are beneath the level of conscious awareness. At times, you may have such an experience and there will be no trace of it the next day, although usually you will regain it with time.

If you want to ensure that you will be able to re-create an experience more readily the next day, tie it to an image that symbolizes the experience. The image can be kinesthetic, visual, or tactile. The idea is to recall the experience by visualizing its symbol.

Perhaps after a training session your shoulders feel free of tension as never before. Create an image to go with the feeling. Don't be satisfied with simply thinking, *Gee, my shoulders feel looser.* Think of an image that describes the looseness more precisely. Is the sensation like having a silk scarf draped around your neck? Is it like fluffy cotton balls falling on your shoulders, or like a stream of warm water being poured over them?

Once you have chosen an image, you only need to think *fluffy cotton* or *silken scarf* to recall the sensation. By practicing calling forth the image regularly until the new sensation has established itself more firmly in your subconscious, you will speed up the process of creating better alignment and movement.

Once you have become more experienced, you can rely less on imagery from external sources and work with images that arise spontaneously out of the vast resources of your mind, out of your movement intuition.

The development of imagery skills can be divided into three phases:

1. Learning the basic concepts and skills of imagery—developing an understanding of the uses, types, and processes of imagery.

2. Drawing imagery from external sources (programmed imagery) and practicing calling it forth repeatedly and consistently.

3. Working with your own intuitive and spontaneous imagery. Although in this phase you may still be using external imagery, you are sufficiently trained to know that an appropriate image will present itself when needed and you are able to evolve your own imagery from a teacher's suggestions.

MOTIVATION AND CHANGE

You must be highly motivated to create the focused imagery necessary for success. You can't be wondering, *Am I there yet?* as you try to achieve a desired movement goal. You must focus on experiencing the process as fully as possible, because it is that heightened awareness that is going to make you succeed in reaching your goal.

Try a little experiment. Take a moment now and raise your arm above your head.

Did you actually do it? Or did you say to yourself, *I'll just imagine it; I don't really feel like lifting my arm.* If you did raise your arm, did you do it with pleasure, or were you apathetic?

The higher the motivational energy, the better the quality of movement. We've all had days when we didn't feel like working out, going to the gym, or taking an exercise class (rarely, of course). On such days it is more difficult to get moving, at least initially, than on a day when you're raring to go. Injuries usually occur on days when you are less than perfectly motivated, providing further evidence of the impact mental state has on movement quality (Mechelen 1996). When you are tired or uninvolved, you feel the effort of each movement. When you are energized or involved, movement is effortless and time flies. Images are crystal clear, your senses are acute, and every fiber of your being seems to be cooperating. The motivation seems to be coming from the cells themselves; your muscles seem to have an intelligence of their own. It is as if they hardly need to be told what to do because they are so involved in the task and ready to perform it.

SUMMARY

In this chapter you were introduced to the APAC four-step process for change. You reviewed factors that influence your ability to change your movement and alignment, such as proprioception, body image, and developmental movement patterns. For some, imagery will create rapid change and it is easy for them to improve their movement patterns, while others are more challenged to do this. Progress depends on the ability to generate and maintain vivid imagery but also on the nature of your body image, which may be resistant to change. Your developmental movement patterns influence your posture and movement efficiency as an adult. You may need to replay some early patterns to be able to move to a higher level of efficiency in your movement and posture. Finally, your imagery skills move through the acquisition of basic concepts and tools and a phase of acquiring programmed imagery to the ability to generate your own personal imagery. In chapter 5 you will look at guidelines for successful use of imagery.

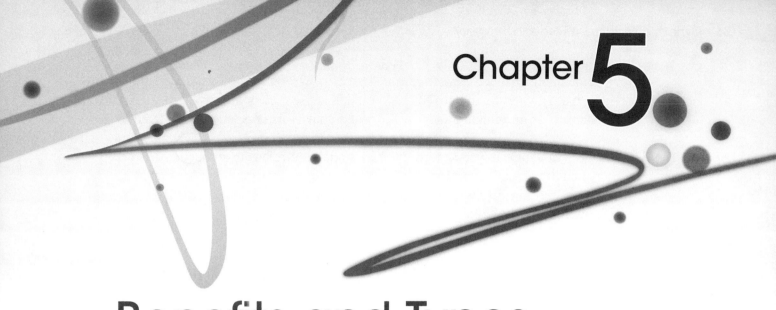

Benefits and Types of Imagery

The best image is the one that discovers you.

Imagery is a varied and multifaceted topic, both in its applications and appearance. It is important to start the exploration of imagery with clarity about these different categories, even though with an increase in sophistication, many of these types of imagery will be used in combination and in relation to each other. We start by putting things in boxes, only to later mix and match the contents of these boxes for the best results.

The function of an image is what it can do for you, the reason why you are imagining in the first place. The results you get from using imagery can range from improving your health to building your confidence or increasing jumping height. The content of your imagery or type of imagery you use to achieve your purpose varies with the desired outcome, your personal style of imagery, and the educational setting. The better you match the goal you have set yourself with the type of imagery you use, the better your results.

Imagery exists in a variety of sensory modalities, such as auditory, visual, and kinesthetic. A good match between the sensory modality and the desired result will enhance the benefit of the imagery. If you are imagining a tree, for example, it is more likely to be a visual image, whereas focusing on your alignment or the timing of your movement would benefit from a kinesthetic component. In art forms such as dance, these modalities intermingle quite often. The kinesthetic image of feeling yourself swaying in the wind like a tree could be employed in the realm of dance and invention of movements.

Imagery can be anatomical or metaphorical and even a combination of the two. An anatomical image is based on biological fact, whereas a metaphor can be as inventive and fanciful as the desired outcome requires. You are employing a metaphor when you are using words to describe something that is usually used for something else. If you are imagining your shoulder to be soft and melting like ice cream, then you took some qualities of ice cream and transferred them to your shoulders. Metaphors come in handy when you do not have an available sense memory for what you desire to create in your movement and body but you do have this sense memory related to another object.

Imagery can come to you intuitively or it can be acquired from an outside source. Quite often these two modalities intermingle as a coach's instruction to use a specific image may lead to your own spontaneous invention.

Following is an exploration of the nature of these concepts, the uses, benefits, types, and delivery styles of imagery.

BENEFITS: WHAT IMAGERY CAN DO FOR YOU

Imagery has functioned as a healing modality for thousands of years. Ancient Greek healing temples called *asklepieia* had dream rooms where patients would imagine themselves back to health in a dreamlike state or with the help of guided imagery. Backed by an increasing amount of scientific evidence, imagery has been rediscovered as a healing modality in recent times. Certain diseases, such as conditions of the heart, seem to respond well to healing, meditative, and relaxation imagery (Ornish 1990; Shah 2004). Currently research is also being done on the effectiveness of imagery for treating asthma and cancer and for boosting immunity (Freeman and Welton 2005).

Detailed healing imagery processes for bones, organs, glands, the nervous system, and even the cells can be found in my book *Beautiful Body, Beautiful Mind* (2009).

Imagery can be used in rehabilitation (for example, in the management of back pain) and for education (to improve teaching skills and solve problems). As another example, visualize cells of your body containing a cell membrane, a nucleus, and numerous organelles. Imagine the cells of your body being washed (figure 5.1). If you like, you can imagine specialized organelles called lysosomes performing this work, removing waste materials and debris and leaving your cells sparkling clean and feeling magnificently healthy.

Figure 5.1 Imagine a cell being scrubbed and cleaned.

From E. Franklin, 2009, *Beautiful body, beautiful mind: The power of positive imagery* (Hightstown, NJ: Princeton Book Company). Reprinted by permission of the author.

Imagery has been shown to be valuable in reducing pain under a variety of circumstances (Fick et al. 1999). A student of mine working in the emergency ward of the university hospital of Zürich reported to me that imagery techniques are most effective for people in pain and in shock. The imagery can be used to directly alleviate or distract from the source of pain. Imagery also functions as a pain reliever in childbirth and can be used to reduce the incidence of injury in dance (Noh, Morris, and Andersen 2007).

Imagery can improve the performance of a specific movement. The type of imagery commonly employed for this aim is motor imagery (Murphy 2002), or cognitive-specific imagery (CS). Cognitive-specific (CS) imagery focuses on improving defined movement skills. This is done through mental rehearsal, also known as mental simulation of movement (MSM). MSM can be used to improve the performance of an athletic routine, exercise methods, or a dance step. Cognitive-general (CG) imagery focuses on rehearsing game plans and has mostly been researched for team sports. Much anecdotal evidence points to the use of CG imagery as part of choreographic creation.

The categorization proposed by Pavio has been refined in the past decade (Hall 1998). Munroe and colleagues (2000) proposed to categorize imagery by asking four questions: the what, where, why, and when of imagery. You can perform imagery during a dance class and while riding on a bus; this is the where of imagery. You can perform imagery before, during, and after a dance or exercise class; this is the when of imagery. You can perform imagery to improve your movement skills, become more confident, and set and reach goals; this is the why of imagery. You can perform imagery from an internal perspective or as if you are watching yourself from the outside. You can use imagery for a certain time, with a certain rhythm, and in a variety of sensory modalities. You can use anatomical and metaphorical imagery; this is the what of imagery. Table 5.1 outlines the benefits of imagery while table 5.2 outlines the types of imagery.

Motor imagery is also valuable for musicians and those rehabilitating from injury. For several years I worked as a guest professor in the music department of the University of Vienna. Motor imagery improved the musicians' expressivity and accuracy when performing (Lotze et al. 2003). The goal of imagery to improve performance includes increasing and maintaining focus, heightening body awareness, and increasing synchronization efficiency. In dance and theater, imagery helps to build character and convey style and emotion.

There is an important distinction to be made here between imagery that focuses on a specific movement and imagery that is aimed at improving biomechanical efficiency in general. A dancer or athlete can mentally rehearse a specific movement to improve the performance of a specific movement or use imagery to improve the body's organization regardless of the skill to be performed. In the latter case, the imagery improves the overall coordination of the muscles, organs, and joints for maximal economy of movement. Improving performance with the latter type of motor imagery is a large focus of this book because it benefits all types of movement. Specifically, targeted motor imagery (CS) may be limited in its benefits to the target movement and also may be limited in its results by the body organization the dancer or athlete exhibits. I propose distinguishing motor imagery with the aim of improving overall efficiency of the body from motor imagery that focuses on a specific movement by adding the words *general* and *specific* to the terms (that is, motor-general imagery and motor-specific imagery). Motor-general imagery denotes imagery that improves efficiency in general. An example of this type is imagining the fluid motion of the hip joints, which could benefit runners, dancers, or yoga teachers. A runner will probably not imagine a pirouette or a plié, while a yoga practitioner will probably not imagine he is running a marathon to improve his yoga asanas (poses), but all groups will benefit from imagining the efficient function of the diaphragm in breathing. Mental simulation of movement, or motor-specific imagery, however, focuses on a clearly delineated outer form of movement.

Motor-general and motor-specific imagery can be combined. If you imagine yourself walking up the stairs, you can visualize the hip joints, specifically the heads of the

Table 5.1 The Why of Imagery: Benefits

Use of imagery	Potential results
Improving motor control for specific movement: motor-specific imagery or cognitive-specific imagery	Mentally rehearsing or mentally simulating a specific type of dance, exercise, or athletic movement can improve motor control, learning, and retention.
Imagery for improving movement efficiency in general: motor-general imagery	Biological imagery or metaphorical imagery is used for improving biomechanical functioning and economy of movement in the body in general. Not tied to a specific movement routine.
Healing imagery	Evidence is increasing about the healing power of imagery for a variety of health issues.
Imagery in pain management	Beliefs, anxieties, and imagery of a negative outcome or positive outcome can influence the pain experience.
Imagery for injury reduction	Mental imagery and related interventions such as autogenic training reduce the occurrence of injury.
Imagery in rehabilitation	Imagery is used for regaining motor control, improving belief in healing potential, and accelerating healing.
Imagery for setting and achieving goals	When used systematically, imagery increases the likelihood of achieving goals. Also used in the business environment.
Imagery that increases arousal (motivational-general arousal)	Imagery creates states of readiness and activation, important before competitions and performances.
Imagery for relaxation	Imagery induces a state of calm and reduces muscle tone while increasing parasympathetic activation.
Imagery for increasing confidence (motivational-general mastery)	Imagery can increase the trust in one's skills and ability to succeed under a variety of circumstances.
Imagery for creating game plans and choreography (cognitive-general imagery)	Focuses on improving game plans or choreographic invention.
Imagery in religious practices and meditation	Imagery has been used in yoga and other religious practices for thousands of years. Meditation with imagery increases the ability to focus and reduces stress.
Imagery in education (cognitive aspect)	Imagery aids understanding, mental creativity, and problem solving (solving challenges in mental imagery).
Imagery in movement education	Imagery assists in learning movement, creativity, and problem solving (dance steps and dance and theatrical improvisation through imagery).
Imagery for improving alignment	Imagery leads to better alignment. This is often done through a series of imagery steps that lead to a final whole-body image of better alignment.
Imagery for improving flexibility	Hundreds of images aid flexibility; the most obvious is imagining flexibility.

femurs, carrying your weight upward, and your motor imagery will gain a layer of precision. Moving from the hip joint is MGI, and walking up the stairs is MSI. MGI is often a combination of biological or metaphorical imagery to improve alignment and movement efficiency. Obviously, the complexity of the imagery will need to relate to the skill of the student.

Several theories explain how motor imagery is supposed to create its effects. Among these are the psychoneuromuscular theory (Carpenter 1894) and functional equivalence. Carpenter's psychoneuromuscular theory suggests that imagined movement activates muscles in way that is similar to real movement, only less so. The theory points to a trickle-down effect, the fact that there are so-called peripheral responses to imagined actions in one's muscles. Edmund Jacobson (1930) showed early on that imagining bending the arm produces small contractions of the muscles used for flexing the arm. Functional equivalence posits that there are similarities to the structures of the brain

Table 5.2 The What of Imagery: Types

Type of imagery	Applications and advantages
Biological imagery (anatomical, biomechanical, physiological): Also called experiential anatomy in somatic body therapies. Excellent for improving motor control.	A very precise use of imagery. Requires an introduction to anatomy. Excellent for learning about the body, increasing awareness, and improving coordination. The teacher must not get lost in factual details but create an experience based on the anatomical knowledge.
Morphing imagery: The image moves between the metaphorical and biological aspect with the aim of retaining the precision of the biological imagery and the quality of the metaphor.	The teacher and students of such imagery must understand anatomy and the metaphorical relevance of the image.
Metaphorical imagery: Metaphors describe something using words that are usually used to describe something else. The image may bear little or no relation to human biology. It can improve movement coordination, motor control, and especially the quality of movement.	Metaphorical imagery must appeal to the student, and it is often useful for the student to discover the image himself. The teacher may be able to elicit metaphors through skilled asking of pertinent questions. Commonly used in dance, Pilates, yoga, aikido, tai chi, and chi gong.
Sensory imagery: The senses traditionally include the visual, auditory, gustatory, olfactory, and tactile. However, the tactile sense does not suffice to encompass all of the possible imagery that relates to movement. In fact, the tactile sense is only a limited aspect of proprioception.	Includes proprioceptive-kinesthetic, tactile, visual, auditory, olfactory, and gustatory imagery as well as timing and rhythmic aspects of imagery. Using a variety of senses can increase image vividness.
Ideokinetic imagery: As developed by Mabel Todd, Lulu Sweigard, Barbara Clark, and André Berrard. Focuses on postural imagery and the nine lines of movement connecting bony landmarks of the skeleton.	The nine lines of movement either lengthen or shorten to improve the overall postural pattern. Performed mostly in the supine constructive rest position.

that process imagined and real movement. Whether using imagined or real movement, you have used the same part of the brain, leading to improvements in performance.

Most recent research seems to point in a new direction for motor imagery that goes beyond functional equivalence. In people whose areas of the brain relating to movement are damaged, it does not seem to impair their ability to imagine alternative creative strategies of mimicking the movement mentally. The mind is creatively involved in finding new solutions to perform the movement (Daprati et al. 2010).

When imagery is related to mood states, arousal, goal achievement, or confidence, it is called motivational imagery. Pavio (1985) distinguishes between cognitive and motivational imagery, which can be used in general and specific manners. Motivational-specific imagery focuses on end states, or goals that you would like to achieve. These goals can be fixed, in the sense of winning a competition, or oriented toward the step-by-step progress you would like to make.

Motivational imagery can be further divided into motivational-general mastery (MGM), with the purpose of increasing confidence, and motivational-general arousal (MGA), with the aim of modulating states of arousal. MGM helps you to cope with challenging situations, stay positive, and increase confidence. Getting excited about an upcoming event and feeling ready to go as well as the opposite, feeling relaxed and in control with the help of imagery, are examples of MGA. This type of imagery is useful before a dance or theater performance and as preparation for teaching or presenting at conferences. When presenting an image in an educational setting, it is helpful to provide the visual picture in conjunction with a kinesthetic response and a meaningful motivation. If you understand the meaning of the process, you will enjoy the imagery more and participate with greater sharpness.

The types of imagery used in achieving the previously discussed goals can be varied and combined in a complex manner. The nature of the task will determine which type of imagery is the most appropriate.

Happy and Sad Arms

Lift your arms over your head and lower them again. Next time you do this, think *My arms are light and happy.* Even if the words feel a bit contrived, practice it regardless and notice how much effort was involved in doing so. Repeat the movement while thinking, *My arms are heavy and depressed.* You may notice that this image immediately makes your arms feel heavier.

Internal and External Perspective

Much of the research stimulus and the development of concepts on motor imagery were derived from observation and anecdotal evidence related by athletes in the 1960s and 1970s. In contrast, the systematic analysis and application of imagery in exercise and dance are much more recent developments. When I started teaching imagery to dancers in the 1980s, I needed to develop dance- and exercise-related imagery resources that suited the refined and highly complex needs of dance movement. Some concepts could be gleaned from somatics, but even those resources were limited in nature and often contradictory. The challenge was to create a coherent system of imagery that united the concepts from sports and somatics with the new ideas that I had evolved for dance, somatics, and exercise. The use of local anatomical imagery and metaphors hardly existed, if at all, in sport at the time, but in dance and exercise they were key to improving technique and expressive skills. First, I will explain the concept of perspective, then I will discuss the possible uses of imagery in space. Finally, we will practice the combination of these two concepts.

In an internal perspective, the performer's attention is focused on the actual bodily movement involving kinesthetic sensation. The performer is imagining himself from the inside out, seeing his surroundings as if he were in action at the time. Internal perspective is a form of self-awareness during movement. While a basketball player may tend to focus on how it should feel to throw the ball with the right force, direction, and spin, a yoga or Pilates practitioner may feel himself doing the exercise on the yoga mat or exercise apparatus.

In an external perspective, you are seeing yourself as an outside observer. You are watching a movie of yourself in action, so to speak. Athletes, exercisers, and performers can use both internal and external perspective and switch between the two. If an exercise teacher prepares a class, she may begin by visualizing herself teaching the class as if observing herself from the outside on a stage. However, the teacher may also use the internal perspective to feel and see herself moving from the vantage point of her body to fit the exercises to the potential skill level of the students.

More evidence is needed to show that all types of imagery, including the varied uses of imagery in space and anatomical and metaphorical imagery, are very useful in sports and the therapeutic setting as well. Dancers and exercisers need to practice switching perspectives and gaining control over their ability to mix and match the imagery perspectives.

The Spatial Location of Imagery

The location of an image in space (both internal and external) needs to be distinguished from *perspective.* Imagery can be used in a variety of locations in space. The spatial aspect of imagery can be subdivided into internal and external; those subcategories can be further divided into local and global. When an image is located in one specific place, it is called local imagery. When it is present everywhere, it is called global imagery. When an image is internal, it is located inside your body; when it is external, it is located outside your body. Imagining your hip joint is an internal and local image. This kind of imagery is commonly used in yoga, Pilates, fitness, and dance coaching. If you imagine your body to be filled with balloons moving you from the inside, you are using an internal global image (one that is inside your body and everywhere; figure 5.2). Visualizing the central axis inside your body is an internal local image. Your axis is not everywhere, only at the center of your body, so it is therefore a local image. Seeing an image moving locally inside of your body may not be related to actual bodily movement. If you can see a soft feather floating between your shoulder blades, relaxing all your local muscles, you are using an internal local image without necessarily moving your body as a whole. If you are feeling your shoulder blades moving, you are also using an internal local image. Both of the above images, the feather moving to relax muscles and the shoulder blades moving, are also visual and kinesthetic in nature.

Figure 5.2 Floating balloons move your body from the inside.

The spatial use of imagery denotes where the image is located, the perspective of the point from where you are representing the image. If you are imagining the space around you—possibly the rehearsal space, stage, or a sports stadium—from the vantage point of your body, you are using the inner perspective, although not necessarily an inner image. The imagery you are seeing is actually external and global because the stadium you are imaging is outside you.

What about the reverse, an inner local image with an outer perspective? Imagining this is possible as well—when you see yourself from the outside and take note of the alignment of your shoulder blades, for example.

All this may seem overly complicated, but the fact is that our minds can and do perform these mental feats frequently, only we are not consciously aware of it. The point is to become aware of what your mind can do and practice imagery in all its variations to turn your mental power into a tool for improving your movement skills. Also, knowing what types of imagery exist can greatly enhance your teaching skills by giving you an expanding tool chest to create positive change for your students.

If you imagine a bird flying over your head, you are using an external and local image. The bird is not filling your whole external space. It is moving through it in a specific location. If you are looking at it from the inside of your body and feeling your body as you watch the bird, you are using the inner perspective. If you see yourself from the outside as a bird flies over your head, the spatial use of the image remains the same, but the perspective has changed to external. When visualizing a snowstorm and watching the flakes blow and swirl all around your body, you are imagining an external global image. If you are in your body as you watch the snowflakes, perhaps feeling the sensation of pressure and wind all around you, then you are in the internal perspective. If you see yourself from the outside in a snowstorm, the image is still global and external while the perspective is now external as well. A child may transform her outer reality by imagining a forest or a beach—another case of an external global image. Children often play in the external perspective with external imagery. They are role playing both with themselves as the actor and with objects on the outside. A dancer may externally place an image on the surface of her body, in the intimate space surrounding her, in the larger personal space, or on the whole stage, even the entire world. If the image is of another dancer or of an object on stage, the image is external and local. Table 5.3 summarizes the types of spatial imagery.

Table 5.3 The Where of Imagery: Spatial Location

Spatial imagery type	Example
Internal local	Imagine your hip joints. Imagine your central axis.
External local	Imagine a tree on a hill. Imagine another dancer on stage with you.
Internal global	Imagine the inner space of your body as interconnected. Imagine all your muscles to be flexible and strong.
External global	Imagine yourself in the falling rain. Imagine yourself surrounded by beautiful flowers.
Growing	Imagine a ship approaching the dock you are standing on.
Shrinking	Watch a balloon float away from you and vanish in the distance.
From the inside out	From your fingers, laser-like beams of light shine into space.
From the outside in	Imagine the warmth of the morning sun penetrating your skin and warming you.

Even though the previously described spatial imagery is not yet common in sports, athletes may use perspective and space to paint a vivid picture of a goal they would like to achieve as if it has already been achieved. These images can have both internal and external components, such as the crowd cheering and how your body feels once you have succeeded. As previously mentioned, images that control the external environment can likewise change the body's alignment and energy. Because you can mentally transport yourself, you suddenly look, feel, and move differently.

Imagery can also become larger or smaller and grow or shrink. When imagining your cells earlier on, you made your cells much larger than they actually are to be able to visualize them. This is an example of greatly increasing actual biological size through imagery. Images can also grow or shrink slowly. If you are having an unwanted thought, watch the worrisome word or image simply shrivel up and vanish! It's great fun, too. I recommend this use of imagery in auditions and at competitions.

Finally, an image can originate in your body and extend out of it and vice versa. If you imagine the rays of sunlight entering your body and warming your every cell, you may be using imagery from outside the body to the inside. If you imagine your central axis lengthening up and out of your body, you are using an image that originates in your body but extends beyond it.

Imagining a Butterfly

A butterfly flies toward you, becoming larger and larger in your vision as it approaches. Something is written in colored letters on its wings. The letters get larger and larger and will soon be clearly visible. It is a message for you. The butterfly comes right up to you so you can read the message. Now the butterfly flies away and becomes smaller and smaller. Eventually all you see is the sky, which fills your whole visual image.

Imagining Large and Small Spaces

Imagine yourself on a vast plane at sunrise. See and feel the sun coming up over the horizon. Then imagine yourself stuck in a small room without any windows. Notice how the images affect your posture, your alignment, even your breathing.

Imagery has been an aspect of religious practices and meditation for thousands of years. Meditation has been shown to reduce stress, increase focus, and improve the ability to discern between relevant and irrelevant content of the mind. The ability to shift attention to something that is more useful or valuable in a chosen moment is a fundamental skill of change. Shifting attention is one of the fastest and simplest ways to help you feel different. If you become aware of your eyes relaxing in their sockets as you read these lines, you may feel different; if you focus on your breathing, your perception of the reading activity will change as well. Meditation has been shown to remodel the brain, shrinking the amygdala (an area responsible for stressful responses to life) and increasing the size of the hippocampus (an area related to memory and learning) (Hölzer et al. 2010).

TYPES OF IMAGERY

In the following section we explore the what of imagery in detail. Imagery comes in many shapes and forms; the more you know about the varieties and flavors, the more you can use what suits you best. Also, you may discover new types of imagery that you did not know existed but will help you improve your alignment, performance, and general well-being.

Lynette Overby (1990) of the faculty of the University of Delaware speaks of direct imagery as a nonverbal representation of an actual movement. You are using direct imagery when you visualize your fingers extending into space. Direct imagery generally remains true to biology, even though it may change some aspects with a specific goal in mind, in this case the lengthening of the fingers. Indirect imagery related to the concept of metaphorical imagery as an external event, sense memory, or object is projected into the body and used to clarify a process or movement and to change its movement quality and sense of effort.

Biological and Metaphorical Imagery

Biological imagery and metaphorical imagery are excellent types of imagery for increasing motor and performance skills, improving dynamic alignment, creating physical awareness, and fostering creative invention. Biological imagery can be subdivided into anatomical, biomechanical, and physiological imagery. Anatomical imagery is a direct anatomical representation of an aspect of your body, such as imagining your lungs. Biomechanical imagery focuses on the movement and forces involved in your body, whereas physiological imagery represents aspects of your chemical, hormonal, and fluid functions.

When you envision your scapula rotating as you elevate your arm, you are using anatomical imagery. Your scapula does in fact rotate when you lift your arm and you are therefore being biologically accurate. When you picture your scapula as a wheel, you are using metaphorical imagery. Imagining your arm cutting through space is direct imagery. Once the arm cuts through space as a sword, the imagery is indirect, or metaphorical. In this book we use the term *metaphorical imagery*.

Biological imagery is precise but often requires a learning phase before it can be used with precision. Metaphors can often be used more rapidly by novices if they are derived from sense memory. Without learning about the design of the scapula and being able to visualize it properly, it may be difficult to see it moving in space. In this case, a metaphor that creates the desired quality, direction, and general idea of movement can be called on. For novices in anatomy, a wheel is most likely easier to visualize than a scapula. The wheel image may create the desired movement trajectory through space but not the correct amount of effort. In this case the wheel may be replaced by a slippery bar of soap or a miniature surfboard.

It is apparent here that metaphors can be very personal. A metaphorical image that works fabulously for one person may not work at all with another person. Also, some metaphors are very close to the actual anatomical reality while others are not. Research conducted at Loyola Marymount University in California on the effect of a variety of metaphorical imagery on the jump height of dancers found that all imagery seemed to improve jump height, but the global metaphors were more effective (Heiland, Franklin, and Rovetti 2010).

Biological imagery can also be changed into a metaphor and returned to biology before, during, or after movement. In other words, the imagery transforms, or morphs, between its anatomical and metaphorical equivalent. Your shoulder blade moving on your back can turn it into a slippery bar of soap, then return to the image of the shoulder blade while retaining qualitative aspects of the bar of soap. In this way the metaphor creates the desired quality of movement, while the biological image retains the precision in visual design. In teaching or coaching situations it is advantageous to present a selection of metaphors so that athletes or students can select what works best for them. Perhaps it is not a slippery bar of soap but a soft lathered sponge that will provide the desired movement quality. If the metaphor is not present in the students' or athletes' sense memory, a prop may help in creating it (figure 5.3).

Physiological, Anatomical, and Biomechanical Imagery

Physiological, chemical, anatomical, and anatomical-biomechanical imagery are all types of biological imagery. Biological imagery can be performed during movement but also without any movement involved. If the purpose of the imagery is to improve movement performance, biological imagery will most likely be performed during movement. If the goal is to promote learning, creativity, or healing, it is often performed without accompanying movement.

Figure 5.3 A prop can help create a metaphor for movement. The photo taken at the Juilliard School in New York shows bone models, an expander model, and a stretchy sponge used to demonstrate bone, joint, and muscle movements.

If you focus on the energy production capacity to increase your endurance in swimming or running, it is a physiological image. If you imagine hormonal balance in your body, you are using a chemical image. If you imagine the flexibility of the alveoli in your lungs as you breathe, you are using anatomical imagery. Biomechanical imagery can be subdivided into kinetic and kinematic imagery. When using kinematic imagery, you are imagining the movements of the bones and joints in space. In the case of kinetic imagery, you are focusing on the forces that are involved. If you feel how the heads of the femurs are pushing up against your hip joints as you stretch your legs, you are using a kinetic image. If you imagine the head of the femur spinning in the socket as you lift your leg, you are performing kinematic imagery. Osteokinematic imagery focuses on the movement of the bones, arthrokinematic imagery on the movement of the joints. There are many examples of this kind of imagery in chapters 10 to 15 of this book.

Imagery Delivery

When teaching the effect of motivational imagery, I use the following process: Ask your students to lift their arms over their heads and lower them again. Notice how much effort was involved in producing the task. Now tell your students this: "If you lift your arms within the next 10 seconds a very happy event will occur in the next three days of your life." The students' arms will fly up before you even realize it.

On the other hand, if you tell students, "Your head is a balloon," not much will happen in the way of postural change, but they may be thinking that the teacher's head is also a balloon. But if you add motivation and a kinesthetic response, you many notice changes starting to happen. "Imagine your head floating up like a balloon, resulting in

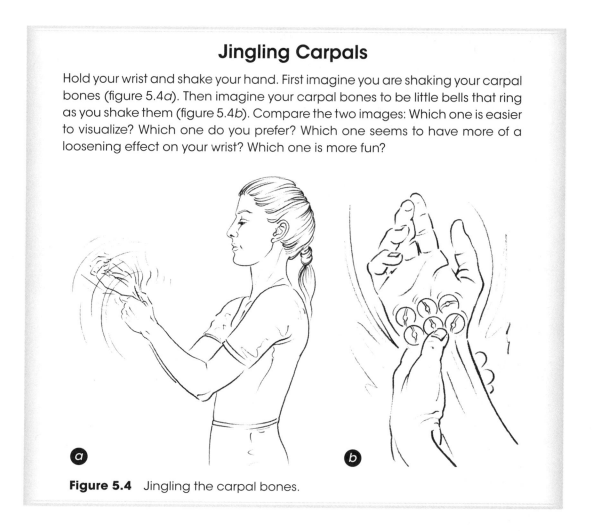

Jingling Carpals

Hold your wrist and shake your hand. First imagine you are shaking your carpal bones (figure 5.4*a*). Then imagine your carpal bones to be little bells that ring as you shake them (figure 5.4*b*). Compare the two images: Which one is easier to visualize? Which one do you prefer? Which one seems to have more of a loosening effect on your wrist? Which one is more fun?

a

b

Figure 5.4 Jingling the carpal bones.

the feeling of a lengthened spine." By adding meaning, you may even reach students who are having trouble experiencing a somatic response. "Imagine your head floating up like a balloon and the resulting feeling of lengthening, which puts you on track for a healthy back." And you can always add more motivational and anatomical imagery: "Just look at those smiling intervertebral discs; they are now getting replenished." Commonly people will attend a class for a healthy back, not for imagining their heads as balloons. To associate balloon head with back health is a far stretch especially for beginners; in fact, they may think it is rather odd and expect more concrete exercises.

Guided Imagery and Imagery Dialogue

In guided imagery, you use imagery for healing. It is guided because the practitioner may be reading a script or listening to a recording of someone leading a series of visualizations to heal an organ or body system. Such imagery can be focused on any body systems, such as the muscles, organs, glands, and connective tissue. Imagery can also focus specifically on the immune system, sensory organs, and bodily fluids, such as blood and lymph. Many examples can be found in my books *Inner Focus, Outer Strength* (2006) and *Beautiful Body, Beautiful Mind* (2009).

In an imagery dialogue, you start by focusing on a body part or area and noticing what imagery spontaneously emerges. You ask the body area for imagery that will promote healing. This imagery is then applied to the area with the goal of creating healing.

Mental Simulation of Movement

Mental simulation of movement (MSM), or motor-specific imagery, is usually performed while not moving with the aim of improving athletic, exercise, or dance performance. It is, however, advantageous to perform MSM while moving slightly or positioning yourself in a way that relates to the target movement. In dance, this is called marking. Lying on the floor while mentally simulating a complex and energetic movement is probably not advisable because your state of arousal in supine position does not match the movement you are practicing.

Two of the first highly acclaimed athletes to apply mental rehearsal imagery were French Alpine skier Jean-Claude Killy and high jumper Dick Fosbury (Dardik and Waitley 1984). Killy would picture himself skiing down the slope, seeing all the bumps and curves, and planning precisely how he would pass through the poles. Fosbury visualized himself clearing the height he had selected. A dancer might imagine going through a dance routine with perfect ease or finding the through-line of an entire dance by running through it mentally. Similarly, a yoga practitioner may visualize his perfect pose form before performing it.

Imagery Strings

Imagery strings is a term I created to describe the process of using imagery to aid in the learning and retention of movement. A series of images is strung together so that the practitioner can better remember a movement sequence. These images are most commonly metaphorical. Imagery strings are very useful for learning and retaining dance steps and complex game plans. Instead of demonstrating steps requiring good visual to kinesthetic transfer of skill in the learners, simply tag an image to each movement. Here is an example of such a sequence: "Pick an apple (reach), open a curtain (arms push open curtain), punch a bag (kick the leg), reach across a table (sweep the arm in the horizontal plane), pull on a band (reach and pull)."

Sensory Modalities

When you hear the term *imagery,* you probably think of pictures in your mind's eye. But an image need not be visual; it can be located in any one of your senses. Traditionally there are five senses: visual (seeing), auditory (hearing), tactile (touch), gustatory (taste), and olfactory (smell). This list is not satisfactory for training alignment and for people involved in exercise, sports, and dance. Proprioception and its subelements must be included in the list as separate sensory modalities. Proprioception consists of the kinesthetic sense (movement), the sense of position, balance, muscle tension, gravity, and effort. These are all perceptions that need to be distinguishable and imaginable if you are to improve your alignment and movement skills. A dancer needs to be an expert at experiencing subtle shifts of weight, as does a gymnast, diver, and many other types of athletes. Other sensory modalities include rhythm and timing. Imagining the rhythm can be very helpful in improving motor control and accelerating the learning movement. A dancer or athlete may be strong and flexible, but if the sense of rhythm is awry, performance will suffer (MacPherson, Collins, and Obhi 2009).

Often the most powerful imagery is composed of several modalities that can occur simultaneously or in rapid order. This does not mean you should always use as many senses as possible when you use imagery; rather, you should use only the ones that create the best results for you. A dancer may rely on auditory and kinesthetic imagery, an athlete on the combination of visual and kinesthetic imagery. A cook will most likely rely mostly on gustatory and olfactory modalities. If you imagine yourself standing under a waterfall, you may have the sensory experiences of seeing and feeling the water pouring down your body, hearing it thundering all around you, smelling its fresh scent, and tasting it in your mouth. By using many senses, you begin to enrich the image, which may make it more effective. This is not always easy, because most of us prefer to use imagery in one or two senses. Notice which type of sensory imagery feels least comfortable to you and gradually add these elements into your practice of imagery.

The brain purposely gives a sense of completeness of your sensory world to make you feel safer. The senses send your brain information about your environment, registering what changes and what doesn't. The nervous system does not supply you with all the information it gathers with its sensors throughout the body. If it did, you would be flooded with information. The sensations go through a filter, a gateway before arriving at the brain, much like the kidneys filter blood. Once the information arrives, the brain completes the picture, makes sense of it, and gives it meaning. An image localized in only one part of the body can powerfully influence the entire body. The image may be just one aspect of what is needed to change the whole. Trying to process all the information needed to make a change may be overwhelming, but give the brain just one hint and it can absorb the other changes below the level of consciousness.

Imagine you are in a dark room with a flashlight in your hand. If you shine the light in one direction, you can see a chair leg; if you shine it in another direction, you see a vase and a telephone. Although you see only parts of these objects, you still recognize them because your brain completes the information. If the flashlight emitted a ray of light as thin as a laser beam, this would be a good representation of how limited the senses are. Also, as you walk through the dark room, you may choose to focus your attention on subtle sounds, on hints of light, and on the texture of the floor under your feet. You are now opening these sensory gateways to increase your perceptions of touch and hearing. Turning up the volume on certain sensory perceptions is one of the keys to improving movement skills and alignment. If you are standing, you may not normally focus on the pressure distribution of your feet on the floor. By turning up the volume on tactile perception, you may be able to use this information to adjust your balance. If you regularly turn up the volume on feeling your body moving, the kinesthetic sense, you will also improve your skill at imagining movement kinesthetically because of the equivalence of the areas representing the perception and actual movement. The more you can develop the richness of your senses, the greater the impact of your images. Like a painter who needs to create the subtlest changes in hue, you need to hone the precision of your sensory images.

As you go through the following exercises, notice which of the senses is easiest for you to imagine. Is it feeling movement (kinesthetic-proprioception), visual, auditory, or other? Decide to practice more sensory imagery in the areas where you feel challenged to empower your imagery facility.

Proprioceptive Imagery

Proprioception (of which kinesthetic imagery is an aspect) involves the physical feel of a movement. It includes the sense of position, muscle tension, balance, gravity, and effort. For example, you may imagine how much muscle tension you are using to push your body into the air as you jump, how your body feels in the air as you jump, or how much effort you are using to plow through the water when you are swimming. Noticing subtle changes in proprioception is an important tool for aligning your body as well as for accomplishing any movement.

Tactile Imagery

Tactile imagery is closely related to kinesthetic imagery. In fact, the two are sometimes combined under the joint heading of tactile-kinesthetic. I like to distinguish between the two because purely kinesthetic imagery need not be elicited by touch, but it is a prerequisite for tactile imagery. You might remember how you were touched by a teacher who coached you in an exercise. In this way, you can reinforce the image until it becomes ingrained in your nervous system. Practicing imagery with a partner is aided by specific tactile imagery of where, how, and when you touch or are touched by your partner. You may also conjure up imaginary massaging hands to release shoulder tension.

Auditory Imagery and Rhythm

Before they perform, musicians often use auditory imagery to hear the sound they want their instruments to produce. Dancers can hear the music in the mind's ear while practicing certain dance sequences. Before a dancer performs a pirouette or an athlete throws a javelin, it is helpful to have the image of the rhythm of these movements. Jaclyn Villamil, former ballet teacher in New York, once suggested the auditory image of hearing an ascending scale as you raise your leg into the air. Perhaps a high jumper can benefit from this image as well. In alignment practice, you can "hear" the strength of your central axis, imagining it to be a powerful geyser. You might also remember the pitch and timbre of a correction you received in class and store it in your auditory memory for future use.

Olfactory Imagery

The sense of smell, very important for animals, is less important for humans than the visual and auditory senses. Yet olfactory images can be powerful because they have the most direct pathway to the brain of all sensory images. A smell can instantly conjure up the distinct ambience of a place visited long ago. Smells attract and repel humans like no other sensory stimulation. Try the olfactory image of moving through a space filled with the scent of a luscious perfume or flower and notice how it affects your posture.

Gustatory Imagery

Gustatory images govern the realm of taste. A good cook can imagine how a sauce will taste before mixing the ingredients, or how the taste of a soup will change depending on what spices are added. An actor might imagine the tastes his or her character encounters during a lunch scene. Clay Taliaferro, original member of the José Limón dance company who is famous for his role in Limón's choreography of *The Moor's Pavane,* directed the dancers at a workshop in France to be involved in the movement as if tasting it, as if chewing on a sweet, succulent carrot.

Examples of Sensory Images

1. **Testing:** Test your sensory preferences and skills:

   - **Visual:** Can you remember sequences from the last movie you saw?

   - **Proprioceptive-kinesthetic:** Can you imagine feeling cycling or swimming? Lifting something and experiencing its weight? The feeling of tensing your muscles? The feeling of relaxing your muscles? The feeling of falling off balance and regaining it again? The difference between running up a hill with a lot of effort and casually walking along the street?

   - **Tactile:** Can you imagine yourself touching a soft piece of cloth, a hard metal surface, and the bristles of a brush?

   - **Auditory:** Can you imagine hearing your favorite music? A bird's song?

   - **Olfactory:** Can you imagine smelling one of your favorite foods? The scent of a flower?

   - **Gustatory:** Can you imagine tasting delicious food?

   - **Timing and rhythm:** Can you imagine the feeling of running rhythmically at a certain speed and then changing that speed and rhythm?

2. **Sensory richness:** Imagine a waterfall in front of you. See the sunlight reflected in it, making it glitter like a fluid diamond; feel the pressure created by the water's force; hear the high and low pitches of a crescendo; taste the water droplets on your lips; smell the pungent, enriched air.

3. **Sensory stimulation:** Carry a sack of rice on your head for a moment. When you remove it, you can readily experience your head floating upward. Walk on all fours with the same sack on your back, moving your back up and down. When you remove the sack, you will find that your back is more flexible and snakelike.

4. **Projection of a sensory experience:** Knead a piece of clay and experience its malleability. Feel the clay in your hand, smell the clay, look at its color. Then focus on a spot in your body that needs to be more malleable and project your experience into that area. Next, hold a piece of wood in one hand and a piece of cotton in the other. Notice the difference in texture and quality. Shift your concentration from the hardness of the wood to the softness of the cotton. Project this experience onto a point in your body that needs to transform from hardness to softness.

5. **Foot motion:** Move one of your feet in many ways. Imagine it to be as malleable as a piece of clay. Wiggle it, shake it, circle it, tap it against the floor, pick up and release an imaginary towel with your toes. Then stand up and compare the feeling in your left foot and right foot and left leg and right leg. You may notice that your legs feel as though they are aligned differently. One leg may seem to have more volume or to be straighter than the other.

6. **Balance:** Stand with your weight equally distributed on both feet. Lift one foot off the floor and balance for a moment. Do the same with the other leg. Lift one leg again and imagine that a clone of that leg is still standing on the floor. Notice the difference between your ability to balance when using and not using this image.

STYLES OF IMAGERY DELIVERY

Imagery can be delivered to your experience in a variety of ways (table 5.4). Someone can provide you with the image or you can discover it yourself. Imagery can be found through an illustration (as in this book), heard in a recording, or read from a script.

Table 5.4　Styles of Imagery Delivery

Imagery delivery style	Applications
Programmed imagery (sometimes called prescriptive imagery)	The teacher or coach provides the image. You have been given the image and are applying it to yourself.
Intuitive imagery (also called receptive imagery)	The opposite of programmed imagery. An image that seemingly self-generates in your mind. May not be as spontaneous as it seems, since the training of imagery and knowledge of metaphors and anatomy improve the frequency of spontaneity.
Imagery dialogue: Addressing a part of the body and requesting images that will help to heal that area	You are talking to your body or areas of your body as if they can respond to your inquiries. Requires patience and repeated inquiry but can be most effective in discovering imagery that is appropriate to the situation.
Guided imagery: Commonly used for learning and healing	Commonly delivered as a monologue or as a recording or script with the specific aim of creating relaxation, healing, or achievement of a goal. It is useful to have theoretical and practical knowledge of symbolism and metaphors to create an effective script of guided imagery.

Programmed and Intuitive Imagery

Programmed imagery is brought to you by external instruction. Intuitive (also called receptive) imagery simply arrives in your mind spontaneously. This book contains hundreds of images for you to practice and hone your imagery skills. These are programmed images. Ultimately, you will have your own intuition about imagery and create your own, or, as I often experience it, you will discover imagery. Many of the images that I use in a class setting or when training myself seem to come to me out of the blue. They suddenly and most appropriately appear on the screen of my mind's eye (or any of the other senses). Obviously, this is a highly intuitive function, but I believe that the years of training with programmed imagery enable the mind and body to understand my training and teaching needs and create an ongoing link between the task at hand and the image that will be most helpful in the specific situation. In this sense, the intuition is trained through the use of many programmed images. As you practice imagery daily, your intuition for imagery improves. It also depends on what kind of programmed imagery you practice. If you learn a lot of anatomical imagery, you will most likely become better at discovering anatomical imagery that works for you, and the same holds true for metaphors. There is much research to be done to determine the relationship between programmed imagery and spontaneous intuitions.

Even when working with an image that you have not discovered yourself, the specific way in which you experience an image is highly individual. No two people experience the same image identically. Therefore, the descriptions of the images in this book, as well as the drawings, should not be considered absolute but as starting points for your individual explorations. In this sense you are always using your own imagery.

Sometimes imagery appears as a spontaneous flow, a free association of images. Sometimes these images seem related; at other times they seem to be jumping from one topic to the other. Here is an example of free-association imagery that I have experienced:

> *Shoulder blades bouncing, as if on a physio ball . . . they are socks filled with sand that now pours out . . . they are fluffy like feather-filled pillows, . . . the eyes are yawning, they seem crooked . . . sending breath into the eye sockets . . . the sockets gently cradle the eyes, like a cherry sitting in pudding . . . pelvic floor expands as I inhale, sit bones widen, parting like curtains in a draft of wind.*

How does such a chain of associations begin? It seems that the mind-body calls you to the right spot, linking the areas that need attention, creating new imagery to keep the input into the mind-body system fresh and stimulating. You can also decide on a starter, or seed, image and see what associations arise from it. This is commonly used in dance improvisation. You can start by thinking, *I am being moved by currents of water*, and notice that as you move, new imagery emerges that relates to things other than water; rather, it relates to your associations with water.

Self-Teaching Imagery

Certain types of imagery can provide feedback on the status of your alignment and body balance. Usually it takes a considerable amount of practice before you can use imagery in this fashion. Examples of this kind of image include the following:

◆ While in a supine position, imagine yourself to be floating on a magic carpet. As the carpet lands on the floor, do both sides of the carpet touch down at the same time? Does the right touch down before the left? Does the front part touch down before the back? The way the carpet lands can inform you of imbalances and preferences in the use of your body halves.

◆ While in a supine position, imagine your pelvis to be a burlap sack filled with rice. There is an open seam on either side of the sack. Let the rice pour out of the left and the right sides of the sack. Does it flow out of both sides equally, or does it seem easier to visualize the flowing on one side? If the latter, it could indicate increased muscular tension on the nonflowing side of your pelvis.

◆ Imagine you can exhale through your sit bones (ischial tuberosity) as if they were straws. Does it feel like you can do this equally on both sides? If a sit bone does not want to exhale, this could indicate tension in the musculature surrounding that bone and most likely the corresponding hip joint.

Image Narrative and Imagery Bundles

An image narrative may act as spontaneous guidance. These thoughts float into your mind, sparked by your movements or by free-floating associations. They may be intuitive or learned self-corrections such as these: *The shoulders are level, as well as the pelvis. The backs of the legs relate to each other. The sit bones move on the same plane.* Or they may be more poetic: *Energy circulates around and through my body. Rays of light shower down and fill me. My eyes gaze over the vast surface of the planet; my vision circles the immense sphere.* These thoughts may occur very quickly and reside quietly on the threshold of awareness.

A dancer may relate the effects of many images that have been practiced over time. All the images pertaining to spatial awareness are bundled under the thought *space.* Other bundles could consist of images related to *flow, align,* or *center.*

SELF-TALK: THE INTERNAL MONOLOGUE

Certain images do not function without thinking about them and vice versa. For example, try to describe to someone how you got out of bed this morning without having any images of that event. You will not be successful. Certain images contain a lot of information and do not need any additional verbal input. When imagining the *Mona Lisa,* most people have an immediate image and they also could say something about the image: "A famous painting made by Leonardo da Vinci of a lady with a very special smile." If, however, I ask people to imagine the movement of the diaphragm during exhalation, many would be challenged to conjure up a clear or even correct picture. This is surprising because it is an activity people perform on average 20,000 times a day. That is where metaphors come in handy. They are able to bring about images that contain much anatomical information in a form that can be readily grasped. "The diaphragm can be compared to a parachute floating in your rib cage. When you exhale, the parachute gently floats upward; when you inhale, it floats back down." To create the metaphor, you use many words. These words can be repeated inwardly until what remains is the feeling of the movement while the words are long gone.

Every day you have about 40,000 thoughts. In that sense, thinking is a constant and ongoing activity. The question is this: How many of these thoughts are beneficial for your state of being, and how many are detrimental? If you ever had thoughts that made you think, *I should not be thinking this,* then you know what it is like to have unwelcome guests in your mind.

When I am teaching, I sometimes say, "There are two classes going on: the one I am teaching and the one going on in your head. The benefit you derive from this class depends not only on my teaching skills but also on your mental contribution. If it is positive, you will tend to benefit more; if negative, the reverse holds true."

The importance of thought control, or having the ability to influence, is an ancient insight and has been used in yogic and other Eastern religious and health practices for thousands of years. One of the terms used is the mantra. In modern athletics the common term is *self-talk.* This can take the form of very short statements done during a movement to create the desired imagery experience such as *explosive, smooth,* or *centered.*

Most people consider the internal monologue to have an immediate effect. If you think, *My breathing is calm and relaxed,* you will notice your breathing patterns responding. If you think, *My breathing is shallow and tense,* you will most likely notice a change. Commonly movement training will be accompanied by a stream of thoughts or in some cases a single thought followed by emptiness. A runner may think, *Faster than ever,* and for the rest of the race his mind is empty. A dancer my think, *Exquisite musicality,* and then just dance away. Someone desiring to maintain herself in a good mood may say, *I feel wonderful and when that is not the case I revert to feeling wonderful.*

One way to look at thoughts is to think of them as guests at a party. The question, then, is this: Are the guests in my head invited and friendly or people who are here to bother me and my activities? If they are bothersome, it is time to ask them to leave.

Thought Watching

Take a moment to watch your thoughts. Once you do this, you may notice times that are free of thoughts and times when you wander off and think of things randomly. Notice whether you can think certain things at will, such as *Shoulders relaxed, breathing deep and free, feet grounded, spine aligned.* Also perform a movement such as slightly flexing and extending your spine. First think, *Flexible, elastic spine,* then perform the same movement thinking, *Rigid, tense spine.* You will notice that the thoughts you have are immediately creating a change in the ease and flexibility of your movement. Your thoughts are a foundational part of your movement training.

SUMMARY

Imagery has numerous benefits. Imagery can improve your ability to perform a specific movement and increase the efficiency at which you perform movement in general. Using imagery can result in increased motivation and confidence and improve your ability to mentally set and reach goals. Imagery can improve focus and concentration as well as expressivity and creativity. Imagery can help reduce pain and foster healing.

To reach these aims, you can use a variety of types of imagery. These include biological and metaphorical imagery and a whole range of sensory modalities. Imagery can be used in various places in space and from an inner or outer perspective. Imagery can be learned from an outside source or be intuitively discovered.

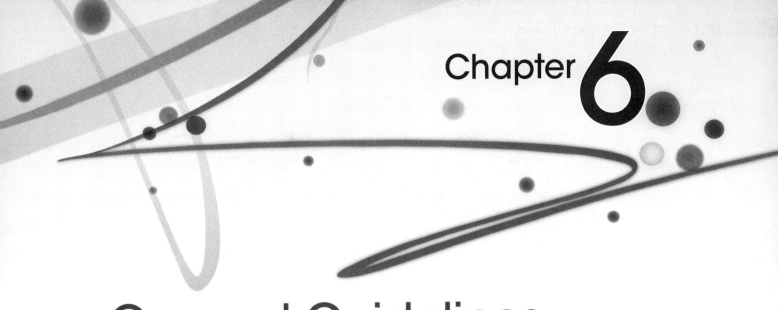

Chapter 6

General Guidelines Before Using Imagery

About 40,000 thoughts and images flash through your mind every day. How many of these are supportive of your goals?

As with any other skill, your ability to use imagery will benefit greatly from systematic practice. To obtain maximum benefit from such practice, you need to approach it with the proper tools. The goal is to have a positive experience early in your practice so that you are highly motivated to continue with practicing mental imagery and to further improve your skills. If you perform imagery ineffectively, you may think that it does not work for you. Research has shown that imagery is useful at all stages of learning, but more so for expert practitioners. Imagery is a way to distinguish skilled from unskilled performers. Simply becoming an expert will improve your performance (Hall 2001; Robin 2007). Start by learning the functions that imagery can serve for you as well as the types of imagery that are available for achieving these goals. As you start applying them, you will get a feeling for the various approaches to imagery and learn how to practice in the most effective way. The functions and types are covered in the previous chapter; this chapter focuses on effective application and positions for imagery work.

FACTORS THAT INFLUENCE SUCCESSFUL IMAGERY

Increasing evidence points to the fact that similar cerebral structures are involved in motor imagery and the actual performance of movement. This means that the more you can make your imagined experience reflect what is happening when you are actually moving, relaxing, or feeling motivated or confident, the better the imagery will work for you. If you can generate strong perceptions of what you would like to achieve, you will be more successful at imagery. Many elements come into play to make this work, including the ability to guide the imagery (sometimes called controllability) and the ability to create vivid imagery. The notion of controllability is referred to in this book as imagery generation, maintenance, and modulation. Other factors are the ability to focus without interruption and its opposite, distraction control. Can you stay with your imagery even when you are being disturbed by outside noise and activity as well as your own thoughts, not relevant to the imagery, that are popping into your mind? This takes practice. In my classes I often start out with an exercise called one-minute focusing. The students are requested to stay focused on the perceptions arising from their bodies—breathing, posture, tension level, and so forth. They are also instructed not to perform "mental time travel"—in other words, to wander off into some past or future event in their imagery and thoughts. After one minute, the students are interviewed for their ability to do this. About 50 percent of the students report having mentally wandered off instead of staying kinesthetically connected to their bodies.

Another important factor for successful imagery is timing. Complicated movement takes more time to mentally simulate, but ideally the time you use to imagine should bear similarity to the timing of the actual performance of the movement you wish to improve (Guillot and Collet 2005). If you are an ice skater or a dancer practicing a turn, it is important to imagine the turn in real time. If you do it too slowly, the imagery may actually disturb the performance of the movement. Individual aspects of the turn may be separated out and practiced individually. This principle can be altered so that certain parameters of the movement are changed. Say you are turning too slowly, or your head spotting (rapid spin of the head to keep the eyes facing forward) is too flaccid. You can mentally practice at an accelerated speed to improve this aspect of the turn.

The ability to switch between imagery modalities is a reported skill of high-level athletes (Holmes and Collins 2001). Following are examples of switching perspectives both spatially and from biological to metaphorical.

GUIDELINES FOR USING IMAGERY

The ability to generate, maintain, and modulate an image is a fundamental skill. If the image is like a flickering light (in other words, it comes and goes), it will not be as effective as if you can keep it alive for a desired period. The length you maintain the image depends on the task at hand. You may spend much of a day using the image of resilient, springy feet as you walk about. On the other hand, you may merely spend a moment focusing on a goal in the form of an image. The ability to transform (modulate) an image is an important tool for movement, motivation, and goal setting. When you visualize a goal and you are not quite happy with the scenario you came up with, you can change things in your mind's eye until you find it to be just how you want. A dancer or athlete may want to run through a variety of images with the aim of improving a skill and notice which one is the most effective in creating the desired change. For this, again, the ability to modulate the image is a necessary skill.

Another factor that is important for effective imagery is vividness. A vivid image usually involves at least two sense modalities and is spatially and dynamically clear and crisp. To create vividness, be excited about your imagery. Even if you have never done it before, start trying new sensory modalities, spatial uses, and perspectives. Think of the saying "the taste of victory, the sense of success." If you are imagining sparkling water bubbles moving up your central axis, hear them crackle and pop, let them tickle the front of your spine, taste the bubbles, smell their freshness. If you are dancing or performing, it may be good to include the external environment in vivid detail. Imagine the stage or stadium and include the sounds and activities surrounding you to aid your realistic preparation for performance.

Allow the image to have movement. The image must have precise location: a place it starts and ends, a force of direction and range. If you imagine your back spreading out like butter, visualize the process of melting, not the result (the molten butter); be clear about where the melting starts and in which direction it is going and at what speed, and include an appropriate movement quality.

Feel the movement. Get kinesthetic and involve many aspects of proprioception such as position, tension, weight, balance, and effort. Feel the quality of movement, feel the metaphor, involve the sense of kinesthetic perception as much as possible. If you believe you are a weak kinesthetic imager, start with simple movement sensations. Take one step and see if you can remember what that felt like. Lift your arms and lower them and see if you can remember the feeling of that performance. Develop your imagery muscle from your sense memory. Then graduate to more complex kinesthetic imagery.

Switch from internal to external and from external to internal perspective and notice which works better for the result you would like to create. If you are using imagery for improved head alignment, you may start by seeing the precise design and biomechanics from an internal perspective, then switch to the external perspective and see yourself with perfect head alignment from the outside. The same can be done for movement and exercise. Mentally perform a jump as if you are feeling it from the inside, then see yourself jump in the desired fashion as a spectator. Or imagine the feel of an exercise, then watch yourself from the external perspective in perfect form.

Practice switching between biological and anatomical imagery. You may have a preference for one or the other, but it is useful to try both possibilities. Do you prefer visualizing the intervertebral discs anatomically or metaphorically as cushiony water beds to improve the sense of dynamic stability in your spine?

Switch spatial perspectives with the aim of maximizing the neuroplastic potential of your brain. Keeping the imagery interesting and stimulating accelerates positive changes. A runner may use the external global image of wind pushing him forward and switch to the internal and local image of elastic rebound in his Achilles and patellar tendons. Attach strings to your knees that are pulling them forward to return to an external and local focus.

Combine programmed imagery and receptive imagery. Start with an image from your memory or a previous coaching, such as *My shoulders are melting like ice cream.* Subsequently self-talk: *Is there a more useful image at this time?* Or talk to the body part: *What metaphor could now help my shoulders to relax?*

Practice controlling negative imagery. When a negative image comes up, acknowledge it and dissolve it. There are many strategies to this aim: Watch the image or words you are thinking dissolve like a sugar cube in water. Place the image you do not like in a balloon and watch it float off with the balloon. Think of the opposite of the negative image. A common negative image in the realm of healing is fear of pain and hurt. Instead of thinking, *I do not want pain,* which is of course imagining pain, conjure its opposite: the sense of well-being and a comfortable soothing experience in your body.

Use your sense memory to recall positive imagery experiences. Keep a journal of your favorite imagery experiences. Make drawings of them as well. This is an excellent strategy for improving your imagery ability.

When using biomechanical or anatomical imagery, accuracy is key. If you visualize your hip joint but the image is not in the proper location, the image may lead to reduced motor control. If you are an exercise teacher, never assume that anatomical imagery is clear to your students. If you instruct students to move flexibly through the joints of their spines, do not assume that students have a clear picture of these joints. The facet joints of the spine, for example, are quite challenging to visualize for a novice. Students, then, could be imagining an incorrect location or design of these joints or nothing at all in the way of joints. Biological imagery may need an introduction before you employ it.

If you are using a metaphorical image to facilitate a biomechanical action, be sure that you can reasonably justify the metaphor. A classic example is to instruct "Imagine lengthening the spine," during spinal rotation. The spine actually becomes slightly shorter in rotation due to ligamentous tensioning, which is protective of the spinal cord. If you are using the image to keep the students from buckling or collapsing their spines, you need to clarify and differentiate it from the idea that the spine actually does lengthen in rotation. Metaphors should be based on function unless you as the instructor are very clear about why you are going against anatomical function.

Be ready to exchange metaphors. Always have another idea handy in case the metaphor you are using is not working for you or your students. Also, a metaphor may have worked wonderfully yesterday but simply does not fulfill its task today. The brain loves variation to keep it fully engaged, and differing mood states often require different metaphors.

Use self-talk to elicit a new metaphor: *I am now going to discover today's most useful metaphor for my lower back.* If intuitive images do not happen spontaneously, they can often be evoked through an inner dialogue.

Spontaneous (intuitive) imagery is just that. It may happen anytime during the day, when the brain has fully formed a mental picture and it can be brought to your consciousness. If the situation allows, stay with the image for as long as possible so it can unfold its benefits fully for positive change. If you are spending a lot of time focusing on a certain area of the body, imagery supporting this area may arise more commonly than from other areas.

It might take a long time before a spontaneous image starts to have meaning for you. In this way, a spontaneous image is like a time capsule—you never know when its contents will be unearthed. Often trying too hard to imagine will prevent a new process from emerging. Open yourself to the image and let it do its work. It is often best to analyze the results when the imagery session is over.

Research has confirmed what we already knew intuitively: An excellent time to use imagery is just before going to sleep (Debarnot et al. 2009). If you mentally rehearse your goals before you go to bed, these images will be stronger and clearer when you wake up. If you think they are keeping you awake, use a relaxation image to help you gain restful sleep.

For nonmovement imagery such as ideokinetic imagery and constructive rest, it is all right to move slightly to adjust your position, but otherwise you should use no further movement to support the imagery. If you are mentally rehearsing an active athletic or dance technique, participatory movement is useful for maintaining the brain's autonomic activation at a level appropriate to the task being imagined. In other words, do not rehearse an explosive jump while lying in a relaxed position on the floor. This will simply create a confusing set of representations in your brain and will not lead to the desired improvements.

Be aware of your evaluation of the imagery as it is happening. Such a meta-imagistic function can improve the quality of the imagery. But the additional mental activity can also disturb the process, decreasing its clarity and effectiveness. All too often critical comments can destroy an image. Often an image cannot be judged superficially.

Look at every image as though you have never seen it before—with a fresh perspective. If you cannot let go of a previous experience, you will not be able to have a new one. Sometimes by letting go of the need to make progress, you progress faster because the body begins to support the evolving experience kinesthetically rather than cognitively. If you are always trying to get it right, you are never arriving, by definition. Just be the result you want to achieve.

A useful practice is to verbalize your images aloud, if the situation permits: "I see my central axis vibrating like the string of a guitar, sending ripples of sound into the surrounding space."

You may use music, clapping, and sound to enhance the image. Play a soundtrack with wave sounds to accompany the visual image of waves during dance improvisation. Switch off the sound, but continue to improvise and hear the wave sound in your mind's ear. Listen to Mozart while using any image. Almost any type of music will have a beneficial effect. Listening to music will allow an image to unfold hidden treasures.

It is helpful to begin an imagery session by focusing on your breathing. Your breathing patterns can tell you a lot about your alignment and muscle tone. Changes in your breathing patterns, such as a deepening and slowing of your breathing rhythm, are often a sign that an image is working. Comparing your breathing patterns before and after an imagery session will help you discover the relationship between your alignment and your breathing.

Combine observation with imagery. If you are a dancer or an athlete, you can watch your own best performance for inspiration or for creating optimal imagery, or you can watch others. This kind of observation and imagery practice can work very fast for you. If you see a performer do something that is still challenging for you, try to model that person's movement with as much kinesthetic astuteness as possible and you will get good results. Match the type of imagery to the task at hand. Mental simulation of movement is more likely to help the performance of a high jump, while physiological imagery is more likely to improve your endurance.

Practice imagery regularly at key points during the day. Motivational imagery and goal-setting imagery are valuable in the morning to get you in a good state of confident arousal for the day. You may review your day imagistically in the evening and sort out what you would like to improve the next day. You can also use imagery during training to improve the performance of a dance or athletic movement. If you discovered a new way of performing an action that is superior to the way you did it before, it is important to review the action in your mind to anchor it in your sense memory.

Finally, you can use imagery at any time of the day to improve movements of daily life such as walking and sitting and breathing. An improvement in a common activity will create a positive substrate for your sport, dance, or exercise performance as well.

TRAINING YOUR ABILITY TO USE IMAGERY

Imagery skills, similar to training a muscle, need to be developed and refined. You cannot be impatient with imagery training—it works differently than most other types of training. If you practice for only two weeks using an intelligent strength-training scheme, you will notice considerable improvement; this is generally not so with imagery. The mind takes more time to adapt, change, and develop its power because you are usually not aware of your specific processes of thinking. It is much easier to characterize someone's walking style than her thinking style. People tend to think that the mind works naturally, forgetting that it is also a part of the body, which can be more or less efficient.

If you use imagery for two weeks without noticing results, don't be discouraged. You should compare the situation to learning any new skill: Could you become a proficient skier after only two weeks of practice? Yet the time and effort necessary for developing imagery skills is well worth it. It is so beneficial that many people wonder how they ever managed without it. Also, imagery improves your mastery not only of sports and dance but also of academic subjects.

The following exercises work on basic imagery skills using the types of imagery described in chapter 5. It is helpful to have someone read the exercises to you so you can practice without having to refer to the book. You can also make a tape of the exercises. Practice in any of the positions described previously.

Flashlight Travels the Body

The purpose of this exercise is to view the space within your body three-dimensionally and also to appreciate the distances between and relationships among these spaces.

Imagine a flashlight traveling through your body. Watch it illuminate every space, nook, and cranny inside you. Start at the center of your head. Shine the light inside the back of your head, then inside the top of your head. Illuminate your chin and forehead from within.

As the flashlight travels downward, watch it casting its light on the inner surface of your neck. Move through your shoulder area into your left arm. Visualize the entire expanse of your left upper arm opening in front of you. Shine the flashlight down to your elbow, and once the light has arrived there, shine it into the palm of your hand, then watch as it lights up each finger all the way to its very tip.

When you have finished exploring your hand, travel back up through your left arm, across your shoulders, and into your right arm. Shine your light down the whole length of your upper arm, down to your elbow, and beyond. When the light has arrived at the elbow, shine it down through your forearm into the palm of your hand, illuminating all the fingers to their tips.

Return up through your arm to the shoulder and begin to explore the vast expanse of your thorax and abdomen. Shine the light in 360-degree arcs and make sure you have covered the whole area, taking note of the placement of each organ. Flood your entire back with light and then shine the light at the back of your navel. Move down to investigate the entire inner space of your pelvis.

Prepare to travel down your right leg. Observe the volume of your thigh from within as you enter, and make sure you cover the whole area with your light before you move into the knee. Investigate the entire inner space of the knee, and then delve into the lower leg. Notice how the shape of your lower leg narrows as you enter the ankle. Explore your foot, peeking into the heel, the midfoot, and every toe. Shine your light onto the underside of your toenails.

Slowly retreat from your foot and leg, giving the inner surfaces a last inspection. Move back through the pelvis, which seems enormous compared to the toes, and then plunge into your left leg. Once again, observe the volume of your thigh from inside, shining the light over the entire inner surface as you move into the knee. Investigate the entire inner space of the knee before you head into your lower leg. Thoroughly inspect the inner shape of the lower leg, then glide through the ankle, brightening its interior surface as you go. Analyze the inner contours of the heel and the middle foot, then shine the light into the tunnels of each toe. Slowly reemerge from the foot and leg, giving the inner surfaces a last 360-degree inspection.

Move the light to the center of your body and turn up the brightness so that it shines into all of your extremities. As you experience the flashlight making the brightest light you can imagine, view the entire inner surface of your body and then the whole inside space of the body illuminated at once.

Turn off the flashlight and rest for a moment. Now turn the flashlight back on and make the light even brighter than before. Let the light illuminate the entire inside of the body to the tips of the fingers and toes.

Quietly turn off the imaginary flashlight and rest.

Roll to one side to get up when you are ready.

Movement Within, Through, and Outside the Body

1. **Floating colorful balloon:** Imagine a colorful balloon. Watch it float up toward the sky. Watch it become smaller and smaller. Imagine another balloon floating down from the sky. Reach out and let it fall into your imaginary hand, bouncing it up and down a few times. Change the color and size of the balloon. Use your imaginary hands to make the balloon spin and turn.

2. **Driving a carriage:** Imagine yourself to be the driver of a 19th-century carriage. Feel the horses pulling on the reins. Restrain the horses and guide them around a curve in the road. Feel the bumpy road beneath you and watch the trees and houses pass in your peripheral vision. Experience the sun shining on your back and the wind blowing against your face. Hear the horses whinny as their hooves pound the cobblestones. Bring the carriage to a sudden stop by pulling hard on the reins. Listen as it becomes so quiet you can hear the horses breathing.

3. **Holding an ice-cream cone:** Imagine yourself holding an ice-cream cone. Feel the weight of the cone. Notice the sun shining on the cone. Watch as the ice cream begins to melt down over your fingers. Taste the ice cream. What flavor is it? What does it feel like gliding down your throat? Feel the ice cream as it arrives in your stomach. Take another lick before it drips on the floor.

4. **Walking through the woods:** Imagine that you are walking in the woods. Smell the trees, the herbs, and the flowers. Feel the soft, spongy earth beneath your feet; hear the leaves and branches crunch as you step on them. Occasionally a ray of light warms your skin. As you arrive at a tree, feel the texture of the tree trunk. Lean against it and feel its sturdiness against your back. Continue walking

through the woods. As you emerge from the woods, feel the sunshine saturate your entire body like a warm bath.

5. **Walking along the beach:** Imagine walking on a beach. Feel your feet sink into the sand; feel the sand between your toes. Hear the waves breaking and the seagulls crying overhead; smell the ocean breeze. Move closer to the water and feel it sweep across your feet and ankles. Feel its refreshing coolness. Notice how the water makes the sand softer, and feel your feet sink farther into it as you walk. Run up into the dry sand and notice how it sticks to your feet.

6. **Shining stained-glass window:** Imagine yourself standing under a red stained-glass window. As the sun shines on you through the window, you are enveloped in its red glow. Change the color of the window to blue, green, yellow, purple, pink, orange, and white. What differences do you feel with each color?

7. **Flashing mixed images:** Feel yourself smoothing a blanket on a bed. Hear the soft sound of a balloon as you let it fly off into space. Float on a water mattress. Hear a steam locomotive pulling out of a train station. Be a leaf falling from a tree. Walk rapidly down a spiral staircase. Feel your feet gliding over a slippery surface. Be a flower opening to the sun's rays. Be a basketball bouncing up and down and then swooping through the basket.

CONCENTRATION AND ATTENTION

The ability to concentrate and focus attention is a key skill for the success of imagery. Mira Alfassa (1982a) writes about concentration: "It is to bring all the scattered threads of consciousness to a single point, a single idea. Those who can attain perfect attention succeed in everything they undertake; they will always make rapid progress" (p. 143).

Concentration is related to attention and perception. At every moment your brain is being bombarded with more information coming in from the senses than you can possibly pay attention to. What does come to your attention has already been preselected by the brain. In addition, a lot of what you become aware of is an interpretation. The brain takes care of a lot of sorting so that you do not need to figure things out from scratch. This comes in handy in emergency situations. You do not need to analyze a threat based on individual sensory properties that need to be assembled to make sense to you: Large, furry, a big mouth full of sharp teeth, stripes, and menacing gestures—must be a tiger! Humanity would have become extinct under these circumstances. But sometimes the brain does not figure things out without people noticing the process. Most people have had the experience of seeing something that first looked like one thing and then suddenly changed to be what it actually is. For a moment the interpretation prepared by the brain was incorrect until more sensory information came online. In summary, what you perceive is only a fraction of what is coming into your sensory system, and at the same time perception may also involve some preinterpretation by the brain.

Concentration is the skill of actively focusing your attention; concentration is total focus. If your thoughts toss about randomly like tumbleweed, using imagery effectively will be difficult, if not impossible. To test your ability to clear your mind, try emptying your mind for one minute. Why would you want to think about nothing? It creates an open space that can be filled at will with specific content. Clearing your mind, focusing on your breath or on a specific point or object, is also very focusing. Many relaxation techniques are based on this ability. Because you take the thoughts flying around in your head for granted, it often feels normal to be in a scattered state. Eminent performing artists and athletes, however, connect their peak experience in physical performance to an elevated level of mental concentration.

Calming the mind allows you to experience the body as a whole. Shunryu Suzuki (1970), who helped popularize Zen meditation in the West with *Zen Mind, Beginner's Mind,* writes, "To stop your mind does not mean to stop the activities of mind. It means your mind pervades your whole body" (p. 41). Zen even uses images to explain concentration: The mind is as quiet as an undisturbed lake. Thoughts are like clouds passing by that want to reflect in the lake. Don't watch the clouds; let them go by. Once you can control what does and does not reflect in the lake, your imagery will become very effective. This is also true for the spontaneous production of imagery. The intellectual analytical mind needs to be calmed so that it becomes receptive to imagery. Cathy Ward, former soloist with the Erick Hawkins Dance Company, teaches, "You lose your concentration and your movement stops." June Balish recounts the teaching of Jennifer Muller, who put it even more simply: "Technique is 99 percent awareness."

Total concentration, therefore, is a prerequisite to good technical skills in sports and dance. Without it, your movement will be like riding on a road full of potholes as you drift in and out of full consciousness. You will be unable to connect movements and create movement flow; you will be unable to feel your whole body in space; as a dancer you will be unable to clearly express the choreographer's intent. Dancers often miss out on the full benefits of dance class because they spend a good part of it just getting focused. Although for most of us, learning how to concentrate is a matter of practice, Larry Rhodes, director of the Julliard School in New York, once recounted to me that he never had trouble concentrating because he was just so interested in dancing.

Concentration is essential in maintaining optimal alignment through a complicated movement sequence. In the time it takes the distracted mind to regain full concentration, an unsupervised body part can slip out of alignment and sabotage your technique. Because posture is maintained by innate reflexes, you won't fall over if you don't concentrate on your body, but in performing difficult movements, maintaining total concentration adds another dimension of control.

According to the May 28, 1993, Zurich edition of the *International Herald Tribune,* conductor Kurt Masur was once more than a minute into leading the New York Philharmonic in a performance of Charles Ives' "The Unanswered Question" when he suddenly signaled the orchestra to stop playing. Turning to the surprised audience of 2,700 people in Avery Fisher Hall, he advised, "Just concentrating makes you healthy, so if you are listening with the same concentration to our music making, you would enjoy it and will forget to cough."

Focus

1. **Think about nothing, and focus on your body:** Sit in a comfortable position and try to think about nothing and focus on the perceptions arising from your body. When you first try this, you will find that your mind wanders and every little noise or itch may distract you. Just keep practicing several times a day. Taking one minute out of your schedule every day is not a major sacrifice. If you find it impossible to keep your mind clear, select a point of focus or keep track of your

breathing, counting each breathing cycle as one count. Focus on an object such as a stone, a shell, or a point on the curtain. Choose something to focus on that is plain rather than thought-provoking.

2. **Area of focus:** One method that is helpful in discovering things about the body is to concentrate on a certain anatomical structure and see what ideas about the area emerge. Choose an area in which you want to create more motion, flexibility, or awareness. Select an area of the body that you would like to concentrate on, such as the connections between the ribs and the spine. Move in any fashion you desire and keep your focus on that area. Notice the images that arise. If your mind wanders off to an irrelevant subject, gently bring it back to that area.

3. **Angle of observation:** Another important factor in imagery is your angle of approach. Watching the spine from the front is not the same as watching it from the back, from above, or from below. Choose an area of the body such as the hip joint, and use your mind's eye to watch it from differing angles as you move. Watch it from in front, in back, below, and above. Certain angles will give you insights that others will not provide.

4. **Subdividing time:** Another important aspect of concentration is the ability to make more time. If you can concentrate intensely on a given action, time seems to lengthen, giving the nervous system an opportunity to learn more about the action and induce necessary corrections. Raise your arms above your head, then lower them. Perform this action again, paying as much attention to every moment of the action as possible. Note how the sensations you experience are totally different.

STAGES OF LEARNING

In an educational setting, the effectiveness of imagery can be compromised by the following:

◆ Providing the goal or result as an image without the students' having the experience or process to apply the image

◆ Using too many images at once, overwhelming the students with imagery

◆ Always using the same image modality, such as only kinesthetic or only visual imagery

◆ Providing anatomical imagery without the students' having the knowledge base to understand the image properly

◆ Not respecting the fact that learning happens in stages

Using imagery in movement education requires precise stages of learning and correct selection, sequencing, and dosage of images. These stages are the cognitive stage, the processing stage, and the application stage.

The first stage of learning is the cognitive stage. In this stage, the student needs to intellectually understand and initiate the sensing of the properties and details of the image, relevant anatomy, and the goal of the imagery process. The student may ask frequent questions and the teacher is actively involved in guiding the student. Diagrams and pictures are used to clarify the details of the image. Touch may be used in this phase to clarify the location, movement, force, and direction of the image. In this phase the student is getting a first sense of the image.

In the second stage of association learning, the student is processing the image involving trial and error. The teacher is still helping the student, but less as the student is actively manipulating and adjusting the image to make it more personal. The student is starting to experience increased flow in movement and posture that is more organized due to the use of the image.

The third stage is the integrated stage. The movement is now automatic, and the function that the image was supposed to create is in place. The image itself is used only occasionally as a reminder of the proper feeling of the desired movement or posture. The fact that the image created the new sensation of alignment of movement may be entirely forgotten, and what remains is the sense of more efficient movement. It is a mistake to think that the goal of imagery training is to be a walking encyclopedia of imagery. The goal is to create economical and healthy movement and posture and to focus on the task at hand with a clear and open mind.

POSITIONS FOR ANATOMICAL IMAGERY WORK

Most of the images described in this book can be practiced in a variety of situations, such as performing sports, lying on the floor, sitting, walking, waiting for a bus, taking a shower, or dancing. When you start using imagery, I recommend practicing 15 minutes a day in one of the supine positions described as follows and spending at least some of your time walking and sitting while focusing on imagery. Some images are specific to standing or seated positions. Generally speaking, a balance among practice in the supine, sitting, standing, and moving positions is advisable.

Yoga Resting Position

The yoga resting position, sometimes called the corpse pose, is suitable for most imagery exercises. However, when the legs are outstretched, their weight tends to pull up the top of the pelvis, increasing the curvature of the spine, especially in the lumbar region. Viewed from the side, the spine is shaped like a double S containing two convex and two concave curves. The concave curves, or hollows, of the back are called lordosis; the convex areas are called kyphosis. The Y ligament, the strongest in the body, connects the femur to the front of the pelvis and causes leverage action of the legs on the pelvis, tilting it forward. This in turn results in an increase in lumbar lordosis. If this position elicits pain or tightness, roll up a towel and place it under your knees. Elevating the knees should be sufficient for allowing the lumbar spine to rest on the floor (figure 6.1). If the lordosis is very pronounced, place a soft towel or plush

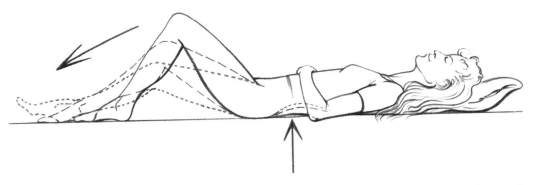

Figure 6.1 When the legs are outstretched, their weight tends to pull the pelvis forward, curving the spine and increasing lumbar lordosis.

ball under the small of your back as well, allowing the lumbar spine to rest on the towel; however, do not let this cushion push the lumbar spine into increased lordosis.

To align your head with your spine, it may be helpful to put a rolled-up towel under your neck and a cushion under your head. Your face should be horizontal to the floor, with your chin neither pointed up toward the ceiling nor pulled into your neck. In some instances, it is desirable to have your head slightly flexed, with your neck subtly lengthened to aid energy flow, but in no case should your neck be extended. You may also use a plush ball or mini-roll for some support under your head.

Finally, placing a small, lightweight pillow or plush ball on your belly may lend a feeling of weight and centeredness and increase your awareness of the breathing process. As you inhale, the abdominal wall rises a little, and the slight resistance afforded by the weight of the pillow increases the tone of the breathing musculature. As you exhale, the abdominals contract, move down, and aid in expelling air from the lungs. The added weight of the pillow slightly increases the expiratory force of the abdominals, making exhalation more complete. The pillow also reflects the give of the organs as they are slightly compressed on inhalation. After practicing a while with a pillow, you can use your sensory memory to place an imaginary pillow on your belly for a similar effect.

Constructive Rest Position

Mabel Todd encouraged a supine position called hook lying to facilitate the imagery process. Lulu Sweigard called it the constructive rest position (CRP) because it is a means of resting that creates more efficient posture. Lying supine changes the orientation toward gravity by spreading the body in a horizontal alignment. Having the floor support the large surface area of the body helps release tension. Because no effort is required to maintain a position, as in standing and sitting, you can concentrate on the images without having to tense any part of your body. This is an important point because in the CRP, you are feeding your body pure imagery signals with the goal of creating improved alignment. While standing or sitting, there is always some competition from the old patterns.

Constructive Rest Position

Ideally, you should lie on a carpet or mat in a quiet area where the floor is not cold. Once on your back, bend your knees at a 90-degree angle, allowing your lumbar spine to rest easily on the floor. For many people, the dominant tone in the external rotators makes the legs fall to either side in this position. If this happens to you, fasten a scarf or a comfortable belt around your legs. Don't fasten it directly at your knees, because this might create a feeling of constriction. As an alternative, lean your legs against each other, knees touching. When tying a belt around your legs, make sure that your ankles, knees, and hip joints are in the same sagittal plane and that both of the leg axes are parallel to the median sagittal plane. It may be more comfortable to have a soft cushion under the balls of your feet, especially if you have high tone in the knee extensors. This will keep your legs from stretching too much. Proper head alignment is achieved in the same manner as described for the yoga resting position. A variation of the classic constructive rest position involves placing the legs on a bed or a chair, ensuring that the lower legs are parallel to the floor. This variation helps prevent cramping in the heels (figure 6.2).

Figure 6.2 A variation on the classic CRP. The lower legs should be parallel to the floor.

When to Use Constructive Rest

◆ Anytime you feel the need to regenerate and revitalize yourself

◆ Before going to bed, to release tension and engender a deeper, more refreshing sleep

◆ In the morning, to enhance energy and coordination throughout the day

◆ Before a performance or competition; however, be sure to allow plenty of time after resting to do a regular warm-up, because constructive rest does not replace cardiovascular revving-up and preparatory warming of musculature and connective tissue

◆ After any strenuous activity, such as morning dance classes, and whenever you feel the need to recharge your batteries during the day

When Not to Use Constructive Rest

◆ When you feel like being physically active

◆ If you plan to use it for longer than 40 minutes, which may actually increase tension

Sitting and Standing

If you have difficulty concentrating or tend to doze off while supine, sitting may be an alternative, although it lacks some of the benefits of the supine position. To practice imagery while seated, you need a good chair. Ideally, the seat should have a level surface and be at such a height that your thighs are approximately parallel to the floor with both feet solidly on the floor (figure 6.3). Detailed sitting exercises can be found in the section on the pelvis in chapter 10. As mentioned earlier, if you are only beginning to use imagery, avoid doing a lot of work in the standing position.

Figure 6.3 The ideal sitting position for practicing imagery.

While standing, you easily lapse into old movement patterns because the center of the body is much higher in relation to the supporting surface and therefore less stable.

USING IMAGERY WHEN IN MOTION

The value of being at rest when using imagery is that you do not reinforce habitual patterns of movement. However, much can be gained by using imagery when standing, walking, or doing other everyday movements. (Specific imagery exercises for walking and running can be found in my book *Dance Imagery for Technique and Performance*.) In this way, you can also make use of any unproductive time you might have, such as while waiting for a bus or train. Skillful use of imagery while moving can give instant feedback about your current alignment, why you have difficulty achieving a movement goal, and which specific image most helps you to correct a problem.

IMAGE NARRATIVE, IMAGE BUNDLES, AND RELATIONAL IMAGERY

An inner image narrative may act as spontaneous guidance while moving. These thoughts float into your mind, sparked by your movements or by free-floating associations. They may be intuitive or learned self-corrections such as *the shoulders are level as well as the pelvis, the backs of the legs relate to each other*, and *the sit bones move on the same plane.* Or they may be more poetic: *Energy circulates around and through my body. Rays of light shower down and fill me. My eyes gaze over the vast surface of the planet and my vision circles the immense sphere.* These thoughts may occur very quickly and reside quietly on the threshold of awareness.

A dancer may bundle the effects of many images that have been practiced over time. All the images pertaining to spatial awareness are bundled under the thought *space.* Other bundles could consist of images related to *flow, align,* or *center.* The imagery may relate to each other and create a synchronization of various areas of the body. Imagining the arches of the foot spreading as the pelvic floor widens when you flex your lower limb is an example of a relational image. Imagining the arm lifting and the shoulder blades swinging outward on your back is yet another. Such imagery is commonly used in this book to create good body organization.

Imagery Checklist: Am I Ready to Use Imagery?

To ensure that you will reap maximum benefit from your imagery sessions, it is a good idea to review some of the factors that make imagery effective. This is especially important when you first begin to use imagery.

❑ Is this image suitable for me and the goal I have in mind?

❑ Is my intention strong? Am I motivated at this time?

❏ Do I like the image I will be using? Does it appeal to me?

❏ Do I think I can benefit from this image? Do I trust the image?

❏ Do I find it easy to involve at least two of my senses in this image?

❏ Does the position I am in or the movement I am doing support the image?

❏ Am I able to focus my mind sufficiently?

❏ Is the image crystal clear in my mind?

SUMMARY

In this chapter you covered the key aspects of successful imagery, such as the ability to maintain and modulate an image and to make it vivid and alive. Other important factors in creating successful imagery include the timing and the clarity of its locus, direction, force, and range. Practice switching from anatomical to metaphorical imagery and changing perspectives. See the imagery in different places, inside and outside the body. Try different positions for performing imagery and perform imagery before, during, and after movement. What would it feel like to focus on your goals while walking versus lying in a relaxed position on the floor? When using metaphors, notice if they are appropriate to your mood. Practice generating receptive imagery using an inner dialogue. Speak an image out loud so you can hear the image as you visualize it.

In this chapter you trained your ability to use imagery with a variety of exercises and learned about the importance of concentration. Focused attention is the gateway to perception. You perceive what you focus on. Finally, you discovered that imagery can appear in bundles or in various areas of the body and relate to each other with the aim of creating better coordination. In the next chapters, you will enter the world of principles of physics and biomechanics to ensure effective biological imagery.

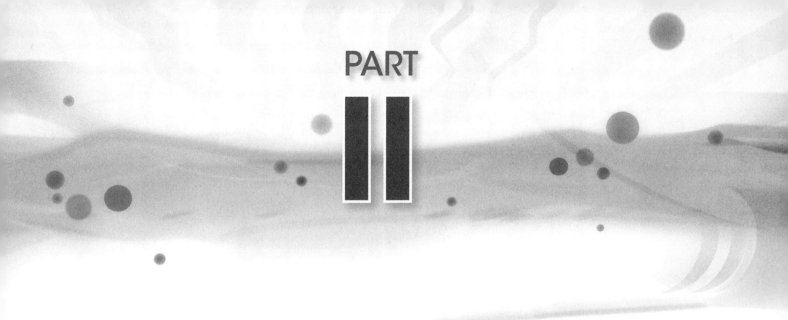

PART II

Biomechanical and Anatomical Principles and Exercises

At times, scientific knowledge enhances art. Many great artists, such as Michelangelo (1475-1564) and Leonardo da Vinci (1452-1519), applied mathematics extensively to make their art more harmonious and expressive. Michelangelo studied anatomy in 1492 in Florence and went on to create the anatomically perfect sculptures *David* (1501-1504) and *Moses* (1515). Leonardo da Vinci started studying the human body because he was fascinated by the fact that the image perceived in the eye is in most cases different than the actual size of objects. At that time it was not known that the brain does much of the work to create the images as we see them. In 1508 he started dissecting and drawing what he saw. His amazing illustrations, valuable learning tools until this day, helped to create more correct imagery of the body. Da Vinci was the first to show the accurate shape of the spine and the orientation of the pelvis. Based on his studies, da Vinci made a glass model of the heart, which demonstrated the most modern understanding of its design to date.

The human body happens to be anatomy, and if you want to understand its movement and alignment, you need to visualize its design and proper function. In a teaching environment, cues or instructions are presented that have been elevated to anatomical fact. This can cause problems in the performance of movement. A common instruction is to imagine lengthening when the spine is rotated. This is a cue, not biomechanics. In fact, the spine slightly shortens to protect the spinal cord. This is mediated by the increased tension in the ligaments and muscles in rotation. By lengthening, the mover creates a conflict between the body's own design to function well and the mental image provided with the aim of improving movement. If you do not know the underlying biomechanics, you might think that the spine actually lengthens. By imagining the movement of the spine as it does occur, you will create more length in a safe way than if you go against the function. In conclusion, effective anatomical imagery requires a basic knowledge of anatomy and biomechanics.

Chapter 7 describes planes and direction in the body and explains the concepts of center of mass, line of gravity, central axis, force, elasticity, and friction. All of these concepts can be valuable when imagined precisely. Chapter 8 discusses Newton's laws of motion, including inertia, acceleration, reaction, levers and mechanical advantage, energy conservation, and dynamic stability. Chapter 9 covers the fundamental design of joints, kinematic chains, and range of motion. We will discover basic muscle and fascia imagery, discuss muscle tone, and visualize continuous chains of muscles connecting areas of the body to integrate us into a cooperative whole.

Chapter 7

Finding Your Center and Befriending Gravity

Posture is a balancing act, not a position.

This chapter introduces fundamental concepts important for dynamic alignment and finding your center. To orient ourselves three dimensionally in our bodies, a common language must be established for detailed mental explorations and imagining the relationships of the body parts to each other and to the whole. A clear mental picture of the planes and axes in our joints will help us create precise anatomical imagery; imagining the central axis gives us a baseline to organize our alignment.

Experiencing gravity is a valuable but often underestimated tool for improving movement skills. Other concepts such as buoyancy will help us float up on our femur heads, while embodying elasticity helps our spine, feet, pelvis, and muscles and connective tissues in general. Understanding these forces will go a long way toward improving your movement proficiency and increasing the health of your musculoskeletal system.

PLANES FOR DIRECTION AND LOCATION

Because our world is three dimensional, we define three planes for the purpose of determining direction and location in the body: the frontal (also known as coronal) plane, the sagittal plane, and the horizontal (also known as transverse) plane. Although there are an infinite number of such planes, only one median plane divides the body in half. Humans are not perfectly symmetrical, however, so the halves are not exactly the same. For example, visualize a cake of homogeneous composition (figure 7.1*a*). The median sagittal plane cuts the cake into equal right and left halves (figure 7.1*b*); the median frontal plane cuts the cake into equal front and back halves (figure 7.1*c*); and the median horizontal plane cuts the cake into equal upper and lower halves (figure 7.1*d*). Two planes crossing create a line; three planes crossing create a point. If you cross the median sagittal with the median frontal plane, you create the cake's central axis (figure 7.1*e*); by crossing all three median planes, you find its geometrical center (figure 7.1*f*).

Instead of cutting up a bunch of cakes, you can also learn about how planes create points and lines by taking two sheets of paper and placing one flat on a table and the other on top at a 90-degree angle to the table. The two sheets of paper meet along a line. If you add another paper at a 90-degree angle to the table that bisects the vertical piece of paper, you will find only one point where all three papers can meet.

The geometric center of an object is not necessarily the same as its center of gravity (COG), which is discussed later.

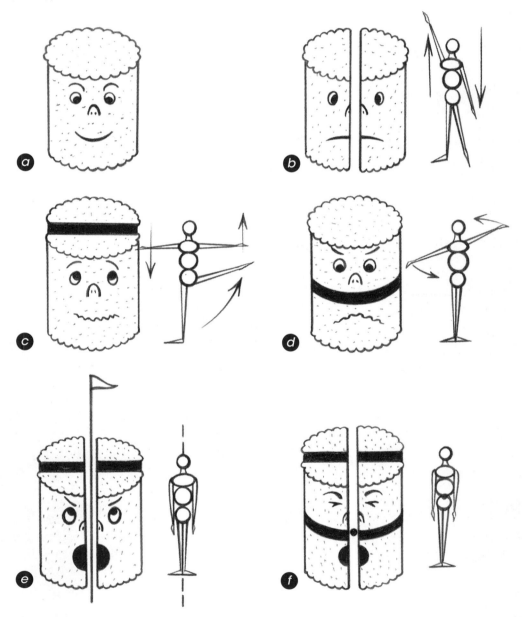

Figure 7.1 A cake can be cut along its median sagittal plane to create two equal left and right halves, along its medial frontal plane to create equal front and back halves, and along its medial horizontal plane to create equal upper and lower halves. If you cut the cake both along its medial frontal and medial sagittal planes, you will create the central axis of the cake. Where all three median planes meet is the center of the cake.

CENTRAL AXIS

Teachers in dance, but also commonly in exercise, Pilates, and yoga, talk about the "center" and being "centered," as well as "moving from the center." I remember when I first started teaching the concept of the central axis. When I asked students, "Where is your center?", "Where do you experience your center?", and "What is the meaning of 'center'?", I would receive all kinds of conflicting answers. There was a vague notion that being centered is important for skill development, technique, and psychological grounding, but how to reliably achieve it seemed evasive.

The purposes of the exercises below are to discover a reliable step-by-step approach for understanding the concept of center, based on scientific fact, and also to develop a kinesthetic image for center that is psychologically grounding and serves as a basis for technical improvement.

As you have seen, the central axis (CA) can be found geometrically by intersecting the median sagittal and median frontal planes. Although the CA is a metaphor that is very helpful for attaining good alignment, it is merely a functional concept.

Planes and the Central Axis

1. **Planes:** Visualize the three median planes through your body. Practice visualizing one plane at a time. Then visualize two planes at a time and the lines created by their intersection. Finally, visualize all three median planes simultaneously (figure 7.2).

2. **Intersections:** Visualize the axis of your arms and legs by intersecting their median sagittal and median frontal planes.

3. **Move in a plane:** Move your body and limbs in only one plane at a time.

4. **Center line:** In the standing position, visualize your center line, the central axis created by the intersection of the median sagittal and median frontal planes. Notice if the line is complete and straight. Do not be concerned if parts of it are fuzzy and even bent. This will improve with practice. Extend the axis out of the body, all the way to the floor between your feet and the ceiling above your head.

5. **Searchlight:** Visualize a miniature searchlight positioned between your feet and shining a bright, contained beam of light up through your central axis. Imagine the light shining out the top of your head. The point where the light touches the ceiling should be directly above the point where it originates on the floor.

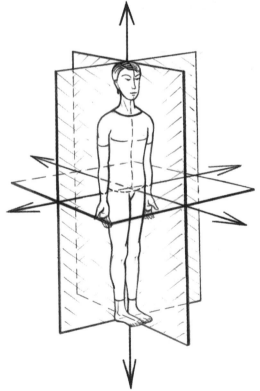

Figure 7.2 Planes through the body.

6. **Guitar string:** Visualize your central axis as a guitar string extending from a point centered between your feet to a point at the center of the top of your head. Give the string an imaginary pluck and see and feel its vibration in the core of your body. Hear the sound of the string as it vibrates. What is its tone?

7. **Rolling:** Lie on your side on the floor. Roll on the floor as if you were a cylinder. Roll to one side, then the other, maintaining your focus on the central axis.

8. **Path of the axis:** To a great extent, the central axis passes through organs rather than bony parts. Its approximate path is up between the sit bones and through the pelvic floor, the bladder area, the small intestine, the right atrium of the heart, the pulmonary trunk, and the esophagus. These organs can be thought of as contributing to the functional axis by virtue of their contractile and hydrostatic properties and weblike fascial interconnectedness along these central areas of the body.

BODY GEOGRAPHY

Anatomists use specific terminology to define direction and location in the body. There are two basic ways of doing this: by describing your absolute position or by describing your relative position. For example, assume that you are in the Empire State Building (ESB) in New York City. To describe your location, you could say that you are in the

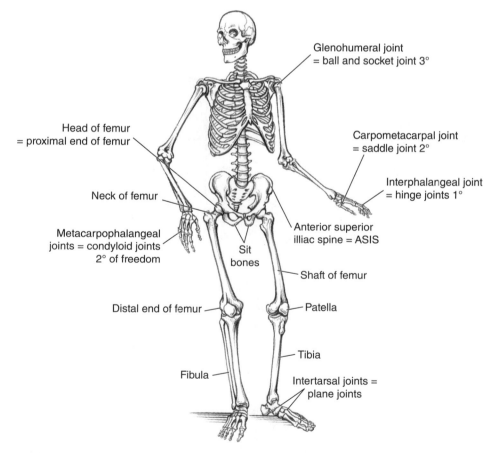

Figure 7.3 Different types of joints in the human skeleton, as well as an example of the proximal and distal end of a long bone.

ESB (absolute location). You could also say that you are in the building on the southeast corner of 34th Street and Park Avenue (relative location). Anatomically, an absolute description of a location would sound like this: "Let's look at the iliac crest (top of the hip bone)." Figure 7.3 shows some absolute skeletal locations. A relative description would be "The pubic bone lies medially (toward the center of the body) to the hip joint." Figure 7.4 depicts the relative locations in the body—superior, or cranial (above); inferior, or caudal (below); anterior, or ventral (to the front); and posterior, or dorsal (to the back).

These terms can be thought of in relation to the three planes discussed previously: In the frontal plane, you can distinguish between a medial (inside) direction and a lateral (outside) direction as well as a cranial (upward) and caudal (downward) direction. In the sagittal plane, you can distinguish between the ventral (front) and dorsal (back) directions as well as between the cranial (upward) and caudal (downward) directions. In the horizontal plane, you can distinguish between the ventral (front) and dorsal (back) directions as well as the medial (inside) and lateral (outside) directions.

Descriptions combining several of these terms are common in anatomy: The anterior superior iliac spine (ASIS) is a prominence located on the forward and upper part of the ilium.

Proximal and distal are another set of relative terms. Proximal means closer to the center of the body; distal means farther from the center of the body. A body part proximal to another is closer to the center of the body. The proximal end of the femur, or thighbone, is the rounded head that sits in the acetabulum, or hip socket. The distal end is the one that forms the upper part of the knee and contacts the shinbone.

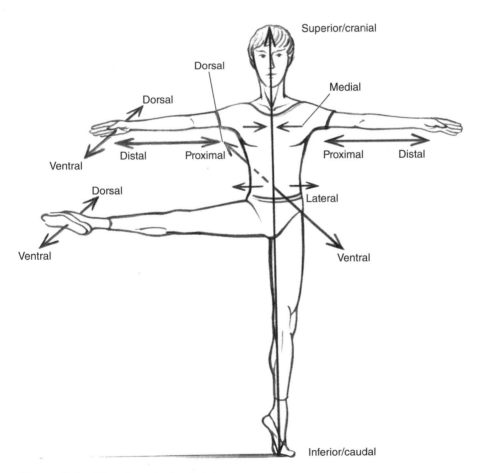

Figure 7.4 Directions in the body.

Now back to the Empire State Building one last time: If I am on the top of the ESB, I am higher than a person on the 12th floor, but the person on the 12th floor is higher than a person on the 1st floor. Therefore, even though the femur head is the proximal part of the femur, the hipbone is proximal in relation to the femur as a whole (see figures 7.3 and 7.4 again).

It is important to be able to distinguish between movement initiated from the proximal and the distal ends of a body part. When you imagine that the tips of your fingers are leading your arm through space, you are initiating distally. You are initiating proximally if you are thinking of the movement of the arm originating in the shoulder joint. Distal initiation tends to lead you out into space; proximal initiation facilitates centered movement. Usually dancers prefer one type of initiation. A mime uses distal initiation to mimic the existence of outside objects, such as an imaginary wall.

JOINT MOVEMENTS

Joints allow the limbs to move in the aforementioned planes. The hip and the shoulder have ball-and-socket joints that permit motion in all three planes (anatomically called three degrees of freedom). The interphalangeal joints of the fingers allow for motion in one plane only. Rather than rely on these planes, anatomy defines joint motion in relation to the body no matter how you stand.

In flexion (to bend), the bones move in the sagittal plane around a transverse joint axis (side-to-side axis), bringing the ventral sides of the limbs closer together. Extension, from the Latin *extendere*, "to pull apart," is the opposite motion in the same plane and around the same joint axis. (See figure 7.1*b*.)

Abduction (to lead away) moves a body part away from the midline of the body in the frontal plane around a sagittal joint axis (front-to-back axis). Adduction (to lead toward), the opposite motion, brings a body part closer to the midline in the same plane and around the same joint axis. (See figure 7.1*c*.)

Medial (or internal) rotation around the longitudinal axis (vertical axis) takes place in the horizontal plane and rotates the body part toward the front midline of the body. Lateral (or external) rotation around the longitudinal axis takes place in the horizontal plane and rotates the body part toward the back midline of the body. (See figure 7.1*d*.)

Circumduction (to lead around) combines all the plane motions. Circumducting your arm will describe a cone shape in space.

Getting used to these terms may be a nuisance initially. However, they are not just an indispensable aid in describing location and direction in the body; they also offer an excellent exercise for training the mind's imagery skills.

FORCE

Force produces, stops, or changes motion; no movement can occur without it. Forces always work in pairs. If you push against a wall (force 1), the wall must be pushing back against your hand (force 2). If this were not the case, your hand would simply go through the wall. Because force is involved continuously throughout every movement, even when you seem to be standing still, understanding force will increase your ability to make intelligent choices for alignment.

Most of the time, you experience force as a push or a pull, such as the pull of gravity. Forces are also at work within the body; for example, a contracting muscle exerts force on the tendons and bones. A force can be visualized as an arrow, called a vector. The vector shows the object of the force, its direction or action line, and its magnitude. The larger the force, the longer the arrow.

Force is also needed in order to stop a moving object. If no external force acts on it, the object will move forever. Here on Earth, of course, friction, gravity, and air resistance prevent objects from moving in the same direction indefinitely. If you would like to improve your dynamic alignment and movement efficiency, become an expert at understanding and dealing kinesthetically with the forces created within your body as well as gravity. The following sections describe various types of force. Contact forces and inertia are discussed in the context of Newton's laws.

Gravity

On Earth, gravity is always present, pulling you toward the center of the planet. Without gravity, you would float away. If Earth did not resist your being pulled toward its center, you would sink through its surface.

Of all the external forces you must contend with, gravity is the most important because it is always there, influencing your alignment. Every time you climb a flight of stairs or get up from a chair, you are overcoming the force of gravity. Since force is defined as mass multiplied by acceleration (Newton's second law), there is no force when an astronaut floats in space (figure 7.5). This means an astronaut can lose significant muscle and even some bony mass and often has difficulty walking after landing. Why is this so? There is no acceleration to speak of when you are floating in space. So even though the astronaut has a mass, because of the lack of acceleration he has no force to contend with. Even if you remained in bed for months, you would not suffer this degree of muscle loss here on Earth, because each movement you make—even the slightest motion of your head or body—is training your musculature. You are accelerating your body, so force comes into play.

Figure 7.5 Gravity is an important, ever-present external force on your body.

The way you sense gravity depends on your relative position. If the bones of your leg are aligned with the vector of the gravitational force, as in standing, you are more likely to experience this force through your bones. If you are lying on the floor with your legs outstretched, you will more readily sense the effect on your muscles.

Gravity keeps you in a permanent weight training room, and your body is the highly articulated barbells. Therefore, the way you move most of the time is the most important part of your alignment training, not your occasional training sessions. Instead of letting gravity bring you down, you need to make it your ally.

Subtle Muscle Response

1. **Noticing gravity in movement:** Stand in a comfortable position. Shift your head slightly forward and notice the reaction in the musculature of your neck. Next, shift your head slightly toward the back and notice any changes in the muscle tone of your neck. Then shift your head slightly to the side and notice how your neck muscles react. Finally, focus on your entire body. Watch for the little movements—the slightest twitching of your fingers, the swaying motion of your body as you stand. Notice how even slight changes in alignment change the activity of your muscles.

2. **Gravity and compression:** If you are standing, notice how shifting your weight from one leg to the other changes how gravity is affecting your body. If you shift to your right leg, the right leg and right side of your body generally will experience more compression, while if you shift to the left, the left leg and left side of your body will experience more compression.

Viscoelasticity

The more you stretch an elastic band, the greater the elastic force pulling the band together again. When you compress a spring, you also feel elastic force. Connective tissue and muscles have a great amount of elasticity, allowing for springiness, bounce, and rebound. Your body is a viscoelastic structure; in other words, it exhibits elements of flow (viscosity) and elements of elasticity (rebound). Viscosity describes the thickness of a fluid. Your body is not a stack of bricks that have a fixed shape and no give. To understand viscoelasticity, think of the flow properties of thick oil combined with the springiness of a rubber band. A rubber band will rebound to its original shape once stretched and released. However, if you heat the rubber band to a certain degree and pull on it for a long time, it will start elongating, flowing into more length; it will not regain its original shape. The heat has made the rubber more viscous.

A ligament or fascia in your body that is put under tension for a long time in the same direction by gravity acting on your structure may viscously flow into more length and lose its ability to rebound to its original length. This means that the way you relate to gravity in movement and your posture will have an effect on how your body shapes itself. An example is the pelvic floor. As the result of a slouched posture or a challenging pregnancy, gravity may push on the pelvic floor, which contains

Imagining Elasticity

Imagine your bones, muscles, and connective tissue are very elastic, making your alignment responsive and adaptable, not rigid or fixed. As you jump, feel your bones and muscles releasing their elastic energy. As you land, imagine yourself rebounding like a bouncing ball and being propelled back up into the air. Now try the opposite and, as you jump, think of your bones as rigid and your muscles as ropes with no elasticity. Compare the difference in height attained with each jump. Practice the elasticity of your body in walking. Notice with each step that your body absorbs the force of each step elastically and uses this energy to power the next step you take.

fascia and ligaments, and cause these to overstretch unless resisted dynamically by the muscles of the pelvic floor. Fortunately, ligaments and fascia are live tissue and have the ability to recover to a certain degree once the pressure is removed. Even better is to take preventive measures through training your dynamic alignment. If you are a dancer or athlete, sensing gravity is beneficial for movement coordination and improves the ability to perform rhythmic movements by sensing the body's ability to rebound and exploit springiness in a safe range.

Buoyancy

For an object to float, an upward force must be exerted on it; otherwise it would sink through the fluid. This upward force is equal to the weight of the fluid displaced by the object. You have submerged a ball in water and felt it pushing upward against your hands. If you let go of the ball, it will surge upward, propelled by the force of buoyancy.

Femur Heads as Buoys

Stand comfortably with your knees aligned in the same sagittal plane as your feet. Visualize the heads of your femurs as buoys, floating on water (figure 7.6). Each buoy pushes up against your pelvis, supporting it. Your pelvis floats easily on the buoys. Float your pelvis down on the buoys as you bend your hip, knee, and ankle joints. Float your pelvis up on the buoys as you stretch your hip, knee, and ankle joints.

Try to think of the buoys initiating the movement. As the water level goes down, so do the buoys, causing your hip, knee, and ankle joints to bend. As the water level rises, the buoys float upward, causing your hip, knee, and ankle joints to stretch. Try to think of the force that moves your pelvis upward as coming from the buoys pushing into your hip sockets.

Imagine the buoys moving up and down equally on both sides; keep them on the same level in your mind's eye. (This exercise will help correct a pelvis that is habitually tilted to one side, provided the condition does not result from one leg being longer than the other.)

Stand on your right leg only and think of the right buoy supporting your pelvis. Next, stand on your left leg only and think of the left buoy supporting your pelvis. Once you have a feeling for this strong yet gentle support of the femur heads in the hip sockets, try walking while imaging the buoys.

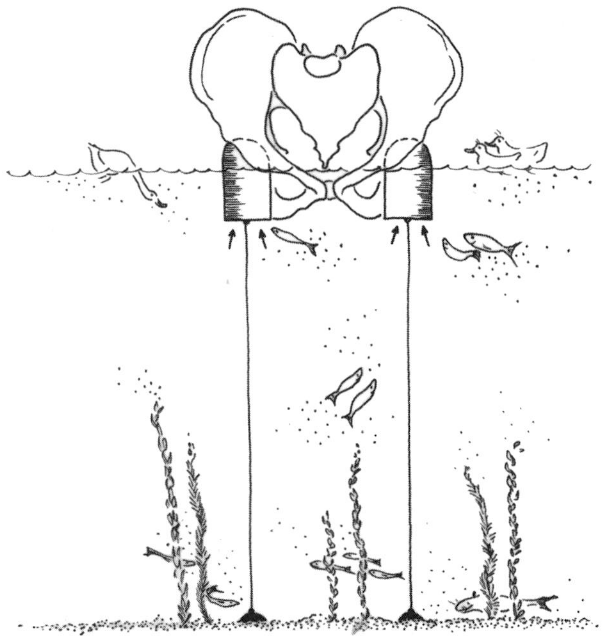

Figure 7.6 Femur heads as buoys supporting the pelvis.

Friction

Friction exists wherever two surfaces touch, glide, or roll over one another. One surface tends to work against or resist any motion of the other surface. This resistance at the contacting surfaces is called frictional force. The magnitude of this force depends on both the roughness of the contacting surfaces and the pressure between them. Friction is important in contact improvisation and partnering.

Walking and running require adequate friction. You have experienced dancing on a floor with too little friction, causing you to slip, slide, and tighten your muscles to create more pressure against the surface. Conversely, a sticky floor has too much friction, preventing turns and causing the knees to twist. A dancer's best friend is a floor with ideal friction. Although imagining a sticky floor to be slippery won't change the floor, it may be very helpful in changing the way you deal with the floor.

Imagining Friction

Imagine that the space surrounding you has varying levels of friction. What is it like to move through a sandstorm, through water, or through the emptiness of outer space with no friction whatsoever?

MATTER AND MASS

Matter is what occupies space. Mass is the quantity of matter an object contains. It is not the same as weight. When you place an object on a scale to weigh it, you are measuring both its matter and the force of gravity on the object. The same object would weigh more on Jupiter and less on the moon. Astronauts (and we're not talking LeBron James) can jump nine feet high (almost three meters) on the moon with all of their equipment on their backs.

A flowerpot will sit on a windowsill until an outside force pushes it in a certain direction. It is stable because the reaction forces of gravity on pot and windowsill on pot cancel each other out. If the flowerpot were pushed off the windowsill by gale-force winds, the combination of its mass and gravity would turn it into a dangerous projectile hurtling toward the ground. If the flowerpot were floating in outer space, without gravity, it would not create any force. If it were to bounce off a passing spaceship, the contact force could provide enough energy to send the pot on an everlasting voyage through space.

Center of Mass

The center of mass is also called the center of gravity (COG). The COG of a geometric object such as a homogeneous sphere is identical to its geometric center. This holds true as long as the mass is equally distributed within the sphere. Figure 7.7a shows a perfect sphere made of homogeneous cork. Here the COG and the geometric center coincide. If the same perfect sphere were made half of cork, half of lead, the COG of the sphere would be within the lead section, but the geometric center would still be in the same place (figure 7.7b).

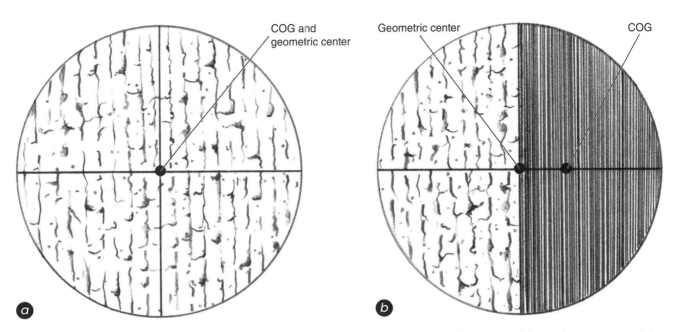

Figure 7.7 (a) A perfect sphere made of homogenous cork. The COG and the geometric center now coincide. (b) A perfect sphere made half of cork, half of lead. The COG is in the lead section, but the geometric center remains in place.

Assuming a human being is a single solid object, its COG lies approximately in front of the second sacral vertebra. However, an individual's COG depends on his or her build and alignment. If a man's torso is very long and muscular in relation to his legs, his COG will be relatively higher.

Gravity acts on the entire mass, although for simplification, it is depicted as acting on the center of gravity, as if all mass were concentrated at that point. Therefore, the COG can lie outside of an object. Strangely enough, the COG of a hoop is in the space in the middle of the hoop. If the pelvis thrusts forward in relation to the rest of the body, the COG may lie within or even behind the sacrum. Bending to the left moves the COG to the left. If you bend far enough, the COG will be situated outside of your body.

Figure 7.8 shows how the COG travels in relation to the body. In figure 7.8a, the COG is identical or close to the geometric center (depending on body build). In figure 7.8b, the arms are being lifted while the upper body is bending to the side; therefore, the COG moves up and to the side. In figure 7.8c, the arms are lifted higher and the upper body is bent farther to the side; thus the COG is even higher and farther to the side, outside the body.

To create good alignment by focusing on the COG, it is helpful to think of the body as composed of individual masses: head, torso, pelvis, and legs. The structure is most stable when the centers of gravity of these masses are located over each other in the same vertical line and when the COG is low (as long as the supporting surface doesn't diminish). Thus, with a lower COG, less effort is required to maintain the balance of an inherently unbalanced system, such as the upright human body. This is the building-block postural model.

Knowing where your center is does not mean that you are centered (that you have control over where your center is placed when you move). Being able to move through connecting steps without constantly recentering is important in dance and gymnastics.

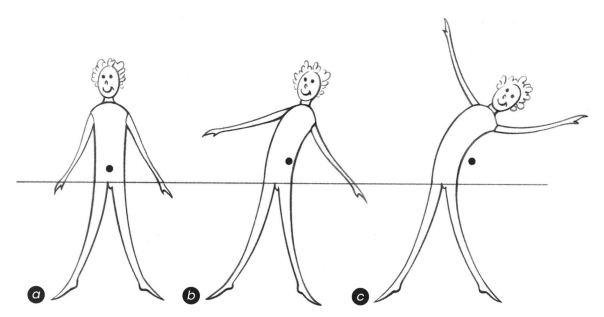

Figure 7.8 *(a)* The COG is identical or close to the geometric center (depending on body build). *(b)* The COG moves up and to the side. *(c)* The COG is outside the body.

A gymnast on a balance beam or ballet dancer performing a piqué arabesque should be able to place her center over the supporting foot in one fluid and direct motion. This can be done only with a secure sense of your body's center.

Working With Your Center of Gravity

1. **Finding the COG:** You can approximate the COG of an object through trial and error. The point where a pencil balances on your finger is just below its center of gravity. If you suspend an object from its center of gravity, there will be no resulting rotation. Try to find the COG of this book.

2. **Changing the location of the COG:** As you move, try to visualize the changing location of your COG. The center of the body is usually in the pelvic area, even if the actual center of gravity is momentarily located elsewhere. Central initiation may "ex-center" the body, sending the COG outside of the body. Think of your center of gravity in normal standing alignment as neutral (figure 7.8*a*). As you move, your center of gravity leaves this neutral point (figures 7.8, *b* and *c*). Visualize the relationship between the neutral point in your body and the actual location of your center of gravity. Merge your COG with the neutral point once again. The interaction between the neutral point and the actual location of COG is similar to the rebound of a yo-yo, with the hand holding it representing the neutral point. The COG moves away from and back to the hand. Improvise with this idea until you become more familiar with the concept of COG.

3. **Concentric growth rings around COG:** Imagine the feeling of centering by visualizing yourself as the core of a tree, surrounded by concentric growth rings. Note how the rings become smaller and smaller as they approach your center. Feel the power concentrated around your center.

Line of Gravity

The action line of the force of gravity, or the line of gravity (LOG), points vertically down toward the center of Earth. If your LOG falls outside your base of support, you will fall over. Daredevil motorcyclists cross deep gorges with ballast attached to their cycles so that it hangs below the rope they are driving on. This ballast causes the COG of the combined driver, cycle, and ballast system to be below the point of support (the wire). It may appear as if the cyclist is delicately balancing the cycle *on* the wire, trying to direct the LOG over the wire, although, in reality, the system as a whole is *hanging* from it. This creates a much more stable balance because the low COG tends to right the cycle.

Lifting the arms overhead is destabilizing because it raises the COG. Rarely do you see a circus artist crossing a wire with the arms overhead. For the same reason, turns with the arms overhead are more difficult to balance.

Working With Your Line of Gravity

1. **Balance on one leg:** After you have tried this with both legs, imagine your body to be filled with sand. Jump up and down a few times and let the sand settle down toward your legs and feet. Now stand on one leg again and see if it is easier to balance while using this image.

2. **Tightrope walking:** If you have the opportunity, try walking over a tightrope or log. Imagine your COG dropping down toward the supporting surface. Notice whether this image makes it easier to balance.

Balancing Your Line of Gravity

In figure 7.9, the pirouetting dancer imagines a heavy ballast beneath the floor attached to her LOG as part of her overall mass. The ballast lowers her imaginary COG, making her more stable and upright. The ballast also helps correct the LOG, making it perpendicular to the floor. The minute changes in alignment that occur in response to the image will suffice in creating the desired effect. Try using this image for any balance or turn. Once the low COG kinesthesia is established, the metaphorical image can be discarded.

Figure 7.9 Imaginary ballast to lower the COG.

SUMMARY

In this chapter you learned about planes and directions in the body. The central axis is an important concept and image for dynamic alignment. To orient yourself in the body, you were introduced to the terms *ventral*, *dorsal*, *cranial*, *caudal*, *lateral*, and *medial*. These terms are useful both in moving your mind's eye inside your body and in comprehending anatomical texts. Bones move in planes around axes formed by their joints. The axes of joints are perpendicular to the planes. If there is movement in the sagittal plane, it is called flexion and extension; if it is in the frontal plane, it is called abduction and adduction; and if it is in the horizontal plane, it is termed medial and lateral rotation. The latter terms are sometimes equated with internal and external rotation. In later chapters you will see that joint axes are rarely fixed but allow for some slight movement and are called instant axes of rotation. This helps protect the joint cartilage as the pressure in the joints moves just slightly from one area to another.

You also learned about forces, including gravity—your permanent weight training machine that constantly pulls you toward the center of Earth. The way you deal with this force on a daily level influences your movement efficiency and alignment more than a few hours spent doing dedicated exercise. The concept of center is commonly used in dance and exercise teaching; therefore it is important to have a clear science-based idea of the center of gravity or the related center of mass.

Finally, you learned that the human body is viscoelastic. It is elastic but also flows in the direction of your postural behavior. A slouched posture may become habitual because of mental habit alone but also because the tissues have slowly stretched to enable this position. This knowledge helps you to conjure up the patience to allow your body the time to flow into a more efficient alignment.

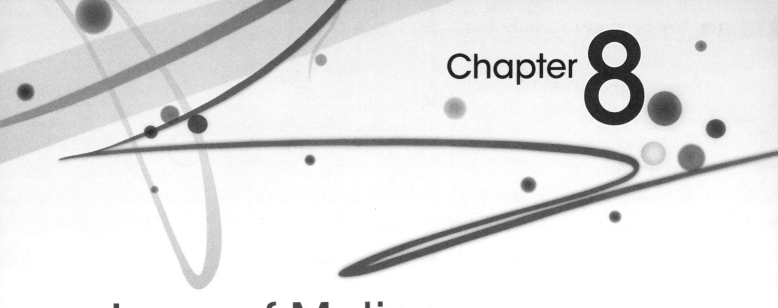

Chapter 8

Laws of Motion and Force Systems

For better posture, befriend gravity.

Motion takes place in accord with three scientific laws discovered by Sir Isaac Newton. Understanding these laws of motion is invaluable for anyone involved in dance, yoga, fitness, or sports because it adds more precise imagery of force, gravity, and reaction to the mental repertoire. These laws will provide a deeper understanding of how the body works and how it deals with inner and outer forces. Successful movement involves dealing efficiently with these forces.

NEWTON'S LAWS OF MOTION

Isaac Newton was born in England in 1643 and formulated the three basic laws of motion in his journal while he was still attending college in Cambridge. These laws are the law of inertia, the law of acceleration, and the law of reaction.

First Law of Motion: Inertia

The tendency of an object to resist changing state, to remain at rest or to keep moving, is called inertia. You experience the effects of inertia when the car you are riding in suddenly accelerates and you are pushed back into your seat. If the car comes to a sudden stop, you are pitched forward because you stay in motion. To move any part of your body, you must overcome inertia. If you are leaping across a dance floor, you must exert force to stop your forward motion. Inertia depends on a body's mass; the larger the mass, the greater the inertia.

Inertia is subjectively experienced as greater under certain conditions. A baby seems heavier when she is sleeping than when she is awake. People who think of themselves as heavy are harder to carry. Efficient movement is smooth and continuous. This is a sign that you are using your inertia, your tendency to keep moving optimally.

Experiencing Inertia

A pendulum is a good learning example for inertia. Theoretically it can stay in motion forever if there were no friction caused by the air slowing it down. Practice this image as you walk. Your arms and legs are pendulums. Imagine them being able to swing effortlessly while retaining their inertia with minimal resistance caused by your muscles, joints, and connective tissue.

Second Law of Motion: Acceleration

Newton's second law was reviewed in the previous chapter in the discussion of force. Newton formulated that acceleration is produced when a force acts on a mass. In other words, an object moves because a force is at work to make it move. In this law, the greater the mass, the greater the amount of force needed, or heavier objects, the ones with more mass, will need more force, should they be moved. The speed of an object with the same mass will depend on the amount of force applied to it. You know this law intuitively. To kick your leg higher and faster, and to jump higher as well, you need to produce more force in your muscles.

Speed is the magnitude of velocity without any specific direction. Velocity is the rate of change of position of an object. Any change in the speed of an object is called acceleration. Acceleration can also induce a change in direction. When the car is accelerating, you feel the seat pushing against your back because a force is being applied to your back. The amount of acceleration you experience depends on the strength of this force and your own mass. The greater the force and the smaller your mass, the more you will accelerate.

It is easier to partner a smaller, lighter dancer because the force you apply has a greater effect. Before executing a lift, you usually practice the step on your own. Obviously, when lifting your partner, increased effort is required. Because the mass of the moving system has increased, you need to exert more force. Acceleration becomes more difficult. Force, mass, and acceleration are always related. If you repeat the same step without your partner, it seems easy because your muscles are attuned to moving a much larger mass.

It is interesting to note that at the cellular level, gravity, and therefore Newton's laws, plays much less of a role. Molecules in the cells are moving through the cellular fluids at a very rapid pace relative to their size and appear to be moving in a random fashion called Brownian motion.

Gravity Exercises

1. **Lifting a briefcase or large book:** For this exercise, use a moderately heavy object such as a briefcase or a large book. Before lifting it, imagine it to be very light, as light as a feather. Then lift the object and put it back down. Now imagine that the briefcase or book is very heavy. When you lift the object again, you may notice that it seems lighter. Because you have prepared your muscles to deal with the increased force, the object seems to have become lighter. Imagining the amount of effort that is to be expected from a task is a good injury-prevention strategy because the body is not surprised by the forces suddenly acting on it.

2. Lifting your dance partner: Imagine the weight of your dance partner just before lifting. By readying your muscles to deal with the increased force, you increase fluidity of motion and reduce the likelihood of injury.

Third Law of Motion: Reaction

Newton's third law states that for every action there is an equal and opposite reaction. Action is another word for force. A reaction is a force that acts in a direction opposite to the action. If forces act on an object without causing it to move, then all the opposing forces add up to zero resulting force.

Forces always come in pairs. As soon as two forces contact each other, reaction force is involved. If you lean two books against each other, each one exerts force against the other. When book 1 applies a force to book 2, book 2 immediately applies a force equal in magnitude and opposite in direction to book 1.

Objects can sit on top of, be braced against, or hang from one another. If you place one hand on the ballet barre, you and the barre exert force against each other. The ropes holding a docked ship exert force on the ship; the ship tugs on the ropes. A chandelier and the ceiling it hangs from exert force on one another.

If you are standing still, the ground reaction force equals your weight. Every step you take elicits a reaction from the ground called the ground reaction force (GRF). If the GRF is insufficient, as on quicksand or on a thin layer of ice, you will sink. If you push rapidly against the ground with a force that is greater than your weight, the ground pushes back with a force greater than your weight, propelling you upward. The moment you leave the ground and cease to exert force against it, the ever-present force of gravity returns you to Earth rather quickly. This is what happens when jumping on a trampoline. For a moment, the surface of the trampoline pushes against your feet with a force greater than your weight. When you come back down, the situation reverses: Now your feet are pushing against the trampoline with a force greater than the reaction of the surface of the trampoline. A rocket is able to escape gravity by continuing to exert force against it after blastoff.

Reaction forces in the form of pulls and pushes are what create balance in partnering (figure 8.1) and are the spice of contact improvisation. Used inventively, reaction forces make apparently gravity-defying movements possible. Reaction force may be imagined at any level in the body.

Figure 8.1   Reaction forces such as pulls and pushes create balance in partnering.

Reaction Force

1. **The atlas as lifesaving ring:** At the level of the hip sockets, you can visualize the reaction force between the heads of the femurs and the hip sockets. At the level of the atlas (the top of the spine), you can visualize the reaction force created by the weight of the head against the atlas. The atlas reacts with an equal force. In figure 8.2, the atlas is depicted as a lifesaving ring to metaphorically clarify the location of this reaction force. By imagining the precise location of a reaction force in the body, you can improve the efficiency of weight transfer and release excess muscular tension.

2. **The floor as being everywhere:** If you lie on the floor and imagine that a part of the body is being supported, you are using reaction force imagery. You can facilitate the release of the shoulder blades by thinking that they are being supported by the floor. The more fully you imagine them contacting the clearly supportive floor, the more that tension drops from the shoulder blades because they are reacting by pushing downward. This technique can be used for any body part and in any position. The Japanese choreographer Komo (of Eiko and Komo) once suggested how one can imagine the floor as being everywhere so that even when you are standing, your arm, cheek, and back rest on the floor. This image creates gentle, easy, effortless movement by giving the body part the feeling of support from the floor.

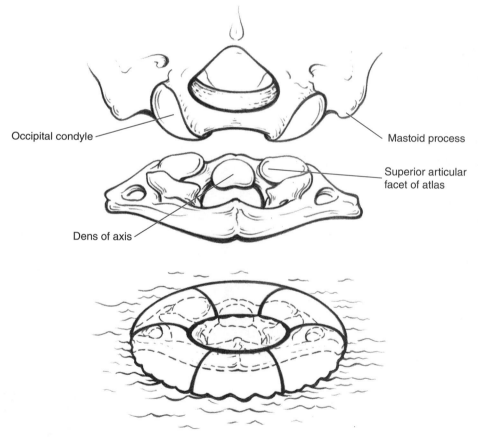

Occipital condyle

Mastoid process

Superior articular facet of atlas

Dens of axis

Figure 8.2 Visualize the atlas as a lifesaving ring to metaphorically clarify the location of this reaction force.

FORCE SYSTEMS

There are three ways in which forces can act on an object: They can be in line with each other in a linear force system (figure 8.3a), they can be at an angle to each other in a concurrent force system (figure 8.3b), or they can be parallel and at a distance from each other in a parallel force system (figure 8.3c). In a complex system, a combination of the above forces is likely to be acting on an object.

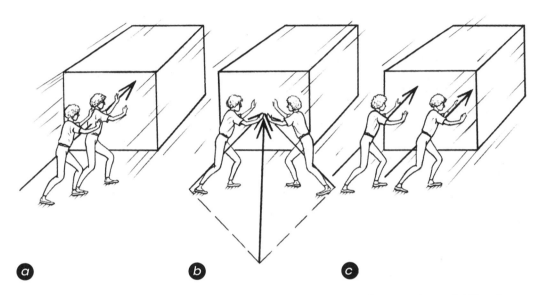

Figure 8.3 (a) Two forces in line with each other—a linear force system. (b) Two forces at an angle to each other—a concurrent force system. (c) Two forces parallel and at a distance to each other—a parallel force system.

Concurrent Force Systems

Two or more forces that act on the same point of an object but are not in line with each other are part of a concurrent force system. When the vectors of two such divergent forces are added to each other, the sum is the resultant force. The action lines of the shaft and the neck of the femur are separate force vectors. Their resultant force is the seventh of Sweigard's (1974) nine lines of action, a line of force from the center of the knee to the center of the hip socket (figure 8.4).

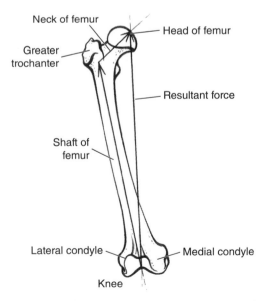

Figure 8.4 Sweigard's seventh line of action, a line of force from the center of the knee to the center of the hip socket.

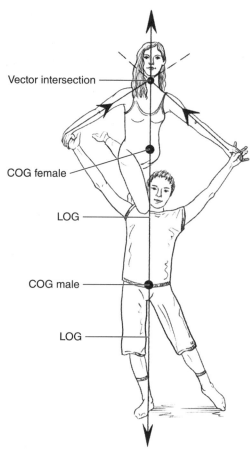

Vector intersection

COG female

LOG

COG male

LOG

Figure 8.5 Three force vectors exerted by a male dancer to stabilize a female dancer on his shoulders.

Adapted from N. Serrebrenikov (author) and J. Lawson (trans.), 1978, *The art of pas de deux* (London: Dance Books Ltd.), 64.

Figure 8.5 shows three force vectors exerted by a male dancer to stabilize a female dancer on his shoulders. The force vectors arise from the contact of hand against hand, knee against shoulder, and shoulder against knee. The male dancer's effort is lowest when the female dancer's center of gravity (COG) is balanced over his COG. This alignment of centers of gravity occurs when the resultant force vector is in line with both dancers' lines of gravity (LOG).

Muscle fibers often point in directions that diverge from the actual resultant pull of the muscle. In pennate muscles, those with fibers arranged like a feather, the individual fibers lie at an angle relative to their tendons. Together, however, the fibers form a concurrent force system with a single resultant force called the total muscle force vector, or the action line of the muscle. When a muscle contracts, at least two force vectors (two pulls) are created: one at its origin (proximal end) and one at its insertion (distal end).

Concurrent Force Systems

1. **Shortening or lengthening the action lines:** The action lines of a muscle can be imagined to shorten or to lengthen. In a stretch, you can imagine the action line of the muscles or muscle group becoming longer. To aid the process, you can imagine the action line of the opposing muscle or muscle group shortening.

2. **Lengthening the back of the leg:** A common image in dance is to visualize the back of the leg lengthening, as in a grand battement. This image helps elevate the leg by aiding the release of the muscles that extend the hip joint and flex the knee. This, in turn, improves the ease of hip flexion and knee extension.

Parallel Force Systems

If the forces acting on an object are parallel to each other and lie in the same plane, they are part of a parallel force system. Levers are examples of parallel force systems.

The closer a weight situated on a lever is to the center, or fulcrum, the less force is needed to counterbalance the weight. Your intuitive understanding of this principle is why you instinctively know not to carry bags away from your body (figure 8.6*a*). The closer the bags are, the less work is needed to counterbalance their weight (figure 8.6*b*).

Figure 8.6 *(a)* If the man carries the bundle on a long stick, he experiences an increased moment force, or torque. *(b)* The closer to the body the weight is carried, the less work is needed to counterbalance it.

If the man in figure 8.6 carries the bundle on a long stick, he experiences an increased moment force, or torque. Moment force is the tendency of a force to cause rotation about an axis. It is equal to the magnitude of a force multiplied by the distance between the force and the fulcrum. In this case, the moment force would be the weight of the bundle multiplied by the distance between the shoulder on which the stick rests and the bundle. To balance this moment force, the man must pull down on the other end of the stick, creating torque with this force. Here the moment arm is found by multiplying the pulling force by the distance between the shoulders and the pulling hand. Because this distance is smaller, the force exerted by the hand must be larger for the two moment arms created by bundle on stick and hand on stick to balance each other. Any force acting on a body outside of its fulcrum will create a moment arm.

LEVER SYSTEMS

The bones and joints of the body are considered lever systems. First described by the Greek mathematician and scientist Archimedes (287-212 BC), a lever is a parallel force system. The purpose of a lever is to create a mechanical advantage or to modulate the distance and speed at the opposite end of the lever. Levers were among the first machines used by humans to haul water and to lift heavy objects. A lever can amplify force, change its direction, or make a force work at a distance from where it is applied. As you know, the way to move a heavy boulder is to place a long rod supported by a smaller stone under it. By exerting force from afar, you amplify its effects and move the boulder more easily. A small mouse can move a large piece of cheese at a great distance from itself using a lever (figure 8.7). The size of the lever matters as well. If you use larger scissors, you can exert more force to cut through thicker cloth, for example. A larger crowbar can do a more forceful job than a shorter one because of the mechanical advantage.

Figure 8.7   Using a lever, a small mouse can move a large piece of cheese at a great distance from itself.

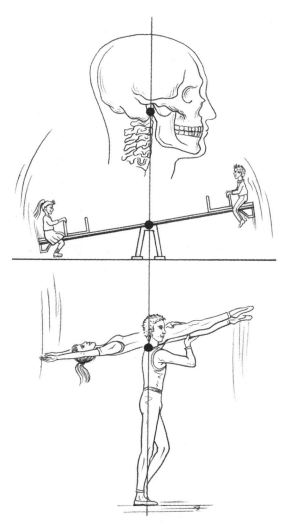

A lever consists of two forces acting around a pivot (also called a fulcrum): the effort force (EF) and the resistance force (RF). The distance from the EF to the fulcrum is the force arm (FA), and the distance from the RF to the fulcrum is the resistance arm (RA). In dancing, muscles are often the EF and gravity is the RF.

First-Class Lever: The Seesaw

In a first-class lever (figure 8.8), two forces are applied on either side of an axis, creating rotation in opposite directions. Pilobolus dance company uses seesaw leverage in their partnering with a dancer in the middle carrying one behind and a dancer in front resting on the outstretched legs of the dancer behind. Besides the obvious forces being generated by the two children in figure 8.8, there are less apparent ones at play. Because contact creates force, the fulcrum touching the seesaw and gravity are also forces to be considered. (Remember that gravity is always acting on an object, even if it is in the air.)

The seesaw is a very versatile lever. It can be used to lift a heavy weight with little force or to move a weight a great distance with just a small movement of the force arm. In figure 8.8, the male dancer uses his hands (effort force) to balance the weight (resistance force) of the female dancer. Above, you can see that the head sitting on the cervical spine is a first-class lever. The atlas, the uppermost vertebra of the spine, serves as a fulcrum. Ideally, only minimal work is required for the muscles to balance the mass of the head equally around the axis of the fulcrum. Because the COG of the head is slightly above and in front of the atlas, a slight muscular effort will be needed to counterbalance this weight. If the head is habitually held forward, the muscles of the neck will need to work harder to maintain balance, causing a muscular imbalance (figure 8.9a). Holding the head over the axis of the fulcrum reduces muscular effort, increasing muscular balance (figure 8.9b). Other first-class levers in the body are the vertebrae balancing on top of each other, the pelvis balancing on the heads of the femurs, the femur balancing on the tibia, and the tibia balancing on the talus. Sweigard (1974) points out the importance of balanced first-class levers for the maintenance of correct alignment.

Figure 8.8   The head sitting on the spine is a first-class lever, similar to a seesaw.

First-Class Levers

Visualize the head as a seesaw balanced on the atlas (the uppermost bone of the spine). Allow the head to balance easily on its fulcrum. Remember what it was like to sit with a friend perfectly counterbalanced on a seesaw. Transfer that feeling to your head.

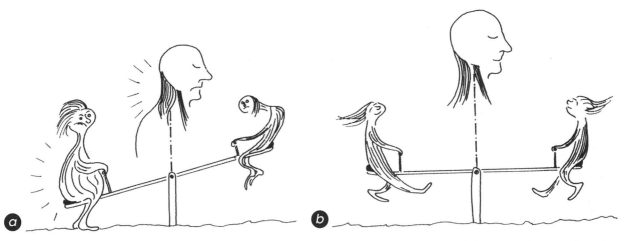

Figure 8.9 *(a)* Muscular imbalance. *(b)* Holding the head over the axis of the fulcrum reduces muscular effort, increasing muscular balance.

Second-Class Lever: The Wheelbarrow

A second-class lever is efficient because the resistance force is between the fulcrum and the effort force, so the length of the effort arm exceeds that of the resistance arm. Although this lever produces efficiency and strength, it has a drawback: The effort force must always move over a greater distance than the resistance force. Also, if the effort force moves upward, the resistance moves upward as well.

The foot can be considered a second-class lever as it pushes off the floor to lift the weight of the body upward, similar to the function of a wheelbarrow (figure 8.10). The second-class lever saves the muscles of the calf a lot of effort. The ball of the foot is the fulcrum; the effort force is applied by the calf muscles via the Achilles tendon at the posterior heelbone. The resistance force is the weight carried on top of the long arch of the foot. When a dancer is in a full relevé and the LOG falls momentarily in front of the ball of the foot, the system can be considered a first-class lever because the weight and force are on opposite sides of the fulcrum. Therefore, from demi-pointe or full pointe, the foot shifts from a second- to a first-class lever. If a dancer's arch does not permit a full toe raise (demi-pointe) that allows for the ankle to be over the ball of the foot, the effort force of the calf muscles increases greatly because the entire weight of the body must be constantly counterbalanced.

Although they are mechanically efficient, second-class levers per se are not commonly found in the human body because they would require lengthy muscles reaching to the distal ends of the bones, transforming the body into a cumbersome mass.

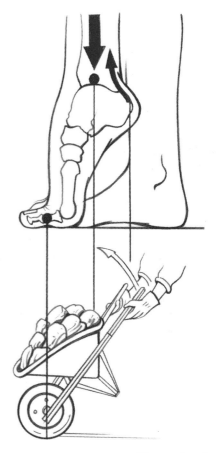

Figure 8.10 As you lift your heel off the ground, the foot turns into an efficient second-class lever, similar to a wheelbarrow.

Demi-Pointe as a Lever

In the toe-raised position on one foot, feel your weight shift slightly in front of, then behind, the fulcrum. Imagine the ankle perfectly aligned over the ball of the foot, creating minimal effort in the muscles of the lower leg.

Third-Class Lever: The Crane

Here the EF is closer to the fulcrum than to the resistance. Although this is not the most efficient configuration, most bony levers in the body are of this type. Therefore, carrying a weight in your hand requires considerable muscular force (figure 8.11). However, the advantages outweigh the loss of force by saving body mass and allowing the distal ends of the bones to move rapidly through space. A small contraction of a

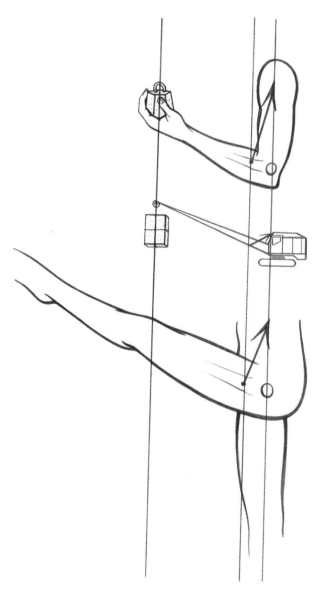

Figure 8.11   Most bony levers in the body are third-class levers, similar to a crane.

muscle at the proximal end of the bone near the fulcrum creates a large arc through space at the distal end of the bone. Efficiency is sacrificed for the ability to proceed through space in an elegant and rapid fashion.

Iliopsoas Flexes the Thigh

Stand in parallel position. Visualize the line of action of the right iliopsoas muscle from the top inside of the femur to the inner surface of the iliac bone and up the side of the spine to the 12th thoracic vertebra. The most important hip flexor, the iliopsoas, inserts very close to the fulcrum of its third-class lever, the hip joint and femur. The advantage of this insertion is speed. Only a small contraction of the iliopsoas causes a large movement at the end of the leg. On the other hand, the iliopsoas must use a lot of effort to lift the leg, several times the weight of the leg. Initiate thigh flexion by seeing this muscle pull up on the femur. Imagine that this muscle can move the knee in space like a crane moving its shovel. Remember that the force for the movement is being applied very close to the hip joint. Once you have experimented with this kind of initiation, imagine making the lever more efficient by visualizing a string attached to your knee. Imagine that this string is the force that lifts the thigh and initiates thigh flexion. In effect, the thigh has become a second-class lever. Let the string move the knee around in space. Once you have experimented with this image, lower the leg and compare the sensations created by the two images. Which image made it easier to lift the thigh? Which image made it easier to move the knee through space? (The iliopsoas is discussed in more detail in chapters 10 and 11.)

Mechanical Advantage

The length (or distance) of the effort arm relative to the length (or distance) of the resistance arm determines the mechanical advantage (or efficiency) of a lever:

M/A = distance over which effort is applied ÷ distance over which force is moved

The larger the ratio of the effort arm to the resistance arm, the larger the mechanical advantage. In second-class levers, the effort arm is longer than the resistance arm, yielding a mechanical advantage greater than 1. Third-class levers have effort arms shorter than their resistance arms, yielding a mechanical advantage less than 1.

The previous formula can be generalized beyond levers:

Mechanical efficiency = work output ÷ work input

A system is efficient relative to the work you have put into it. This is why tension and gripping are not helpful in producing efficient posture and movement. Tension is muscular work that does not contribute to movement. Certainly, when you move, you need to contract muscles to produce such movement, but if you have tight muscles, they are not fully available to move you and may additionally resist your movement rather than support it. Based on mechanical efficiency, postural teaching that advises holding of certain muscle groups is not an advisable strategy in creating efficient alignment.

Imagining the Mechanical Advantage

Try the following images as you perform a high leg kick. Is it possible to change the body's leverage to improve your efficiency? Although you can't move the attachments of the muscles to gain longer effort arms, you can imagine efficiency.

1. **Counterweight:** When your leg is going up, imagine the trochanter (the prominence at the proximal end of the femur) dropping down the back of the leg as a heavy counterweight (figure 8.12). In this way, you transform the third-class lever into a more efficient first-class lever.

2. **Billiard ball:** Think of your leg as hollow and, as it moves upward, imagine a billiard ball starting at your foot and rolling down through your leg toward the socket.

3. **Gust of wind:** Think of your foot being propelled upward by a strong gust of wind.

4. **Imaginary hand:** Think of an imaginary hand pushing your foot upward.

5. **String:** Imagine a string is attached to your foot and is lifting your leg.

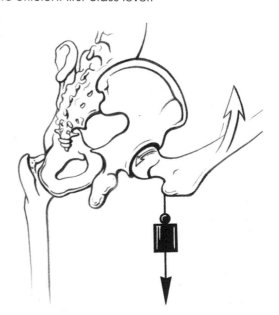

Figure 8.12   The trochanter drops down the back of the leg as a heavy counterweight.

Moment Arm

When two children sit on a seesaw, they exert force against the seesaw at a 90-degree angle. If the muscles in the body were to exert force on the bones, the levers of the body, at such an acute angle, would have to point outward, perpendicular to the bone. The action line of many muscles is actually almost parallel to the bones to which they attach. Because the force is not applied at a 90-degree angle to the lever, the lever arm is the distance between the action line of the muscle and the joint center, or axis of rotation. This distance, called the moment arm (MA), is the shortest distance between the axis of rotation and the line of action of the muscle.

The body uses various mechanisms to create a pulley-like effect, altering the muscle's force vector and therefore the MA. The pulley diverts the action line of the muscle away from the axis of rotation, creating a longer lever on which the muscle can act. The patella (kneecap), for example, forms part of the quadriceps tendon before it inserts into the tibia. This increases the distance between the tendon and the axis of rotation. The longer the lever, the greater the force.

Moment Arm Force

1. **Kneecap float:** Avoid thinking of pulling your kneecap inward or backward as you extend your knees when coming up from a grand plié (deep knee bend). Instead, imagine a widening motion, as if the kneecap were floating perpendicularly away from the femur as you extend the knee (figure 8.13).

2. **Space behind kneecap:** As you extend your leg coming up from a plié, imagine the space behind your kneecap increasing, creating a little cushion of space for the kneecap to glide on. Imagine that the kneecap is being held at a distance from the femur by a balance of forces (see figure 11.7).

3. **Psoas string walk:** Visualize the iliopsoas muscle as two strings inserted at the minor trochanters. The strings detach from their origins on the spine and remain attached at their insertion to the minor trochanters. Watch as the strings drop forward to become horizontal to the floor. The strings are now pointing outward, vertical to the bone. Let the strings pull the femurs forward alternately, leading you out into a walk.

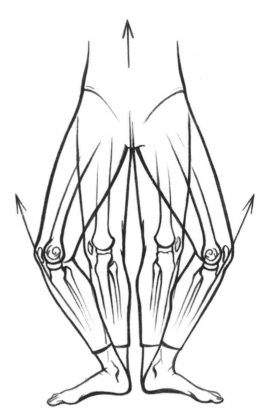

Figure 8.13 The patella gliding on the femur diverts the action line of the muscle away from the axis of rotation, creating a longer lever on which the muscle can act.

ENERGY CONSERVATION

Sometimes it seems as if energy disappears. A bouncing ball goes up and down, the height decreasing with each bounce until it stops. Did the energy vanish? No; it was converted to another form of energy. As the ball moved, some of the energy was used to push the air aside and some was converted into heat as the ball hit the floor. This is known as the law of conservation. A system may undergo many changes, but some measurable quantity of the system never changes.

A seesaw can convert energy from one form to another. When the mass on one end of the seesaw goes up, the mass on the other end comes down. The higher mass has more potential energy. In this case, it is gravitational energy that is being conserved. The mass that rises gains gravitational energy; the mass that falls loses gravitational energy.

In a normal standing position, the head has more potential energy than the hips or the knees because the head has the longest distance to fall to the floor. If it were to fall, it would have the most kinetic energy. In a vertical leap, once you leave the floor against the resistance of gravity, you are moving through space and have kinetic energy. While you are going up, kinetic energy is reconverted into potential energy, and the higher you go, the greater the resulting potential energy. This energy was created by the contraction of your muscles, allowing the bones to leverage against the floor. At the top of your leap, you stop moving for a moment because you have no more kinetic energy—it is now potential energy. The ability to do work is there but is inactive at that moment. As you descend, the energy is reconverted.

When you execute a battement, chemical energy in the muscles transforms into kinetic energy as the muscles contract. This energy is then used to move the bones as levers. The levers gain potential energy as the leg rises into the air. Elastic energy is created as the elastic components in the muscles, tendons, and connective tissue are stretched. As the leg pauses for a moment before going back down, its potential energy peaks. As the leg comes down, it transforms elastic and potential energies into kinetic energy.

These principles of physics indicate how to create efficient movement. When dancing, you usually want to convert a high ratio of your energy into the kinetic form. Of course, there is no way to avoid losing energy in the form of heat and no way to avoid its accompanying and cooling perspiration. But some dancers look like they've just run a marathon after a warm-up or barre work. Feeling very tired after a dance class or training session is not necessarily a measure of success. A good class should leave you feeling flexible and coordinated, not tense and cramped.

Potential Fall and Kinetic Rebound

A fall-and-rebound exercise such as found in the Doris Humphrey dance technique is one possibility for experiencing the change between potential and kinetic energy. You begin the fall with a lot of potential energy and turn it all into kinetic energy as you fall. When you break the fall with your legs, you leverage more energy into the system to move back up and convert your kinetic energy into potential energy as you return to vertical. (See also *Dance Imagery for Technique and Performance,* chapter 8 on swings and arches.)

ABILITY OF MATERIALS TO RESIST FORCE

Whenever a force is applied to a material such as metal, wood, or rubber—or in the human body, bone, muscle, or tendon—the material may change its size or shape. *Strain* is defined as the deformation of a material relative to its original shape; *stress* describes all the reaction forces created within the material when subjected to external forces. The ability of a material to resist force depends on its structure. *Tensile strength* is the degree to which a material can resist being pulled apart. Two equal external forces acting along the same line and in opposition cause tensile stress. The tensile strength of a string is its ability to carry a weight before tearing apart. The opposing forces on the string arise from the weight hanging on the string and the place where the string is attached.

Compressive strength is the degree of resistance to being compressed. Two external forces acting on opposite sides and in the same line against an object cause compressive stress. When you stand up, your bones resist being compressed. If your bones could not resist compression, your body would spread into a sci-fi-like blob on the floor due to the attraction of gravity. This would happen to you on Jupiter, bones or no bones, because the gravitational force there is so much greater than on Earth. In your body, bones are best at resisting compressing forces. Tendons, ligaments, and muscles are built to resist tensile forces. If this were not so, your arms, which are primarily held in place by ligaments, muscles, and tendons, would drop to the ground as the result of the continuous pull of gravity.

Other forces in the human body include shear, torsion, and bending. Experienced at the fulcrum-lever contact area in imbalanced first-class levers, shear causes a body surface to slide over an adjacent surface. Such bending occurs when a load is placed on a supported beam. The magnitude of bending depends on the load's weight and the distance between the load and the supports. Bending is a combination of shear, tensile, and compression stresses. Torsion develops when forces act on a rod or shaft that tend to twist it; again, tensile, compression, and shearing stresses are at work.

Just as the previously mentioned forces are working in the human body, any structure made by humans exemplifies these forces at work. Bricks in a wall resist compression. Cross beams transfer the weight of a floor to the walls. The beams need to resist bending, so if one starts to bend, a brace must be installed. In much the same way, you reduce your risk of injury by refining your alignment and movement patterns to help keep harmful stresses and strains at bay.

Even your inflating lungs provide a certain amount of support. At the gymnasium I attended in Switzerland, we played soccer in a rounded structure called the *balloon*. Based on the principles discussed previously, this sizable outdoor gymnasium without walls or cross beams was supported by slightly increased atmospheric pressure inside the plastic walls. The plastic cover needed to resist being pulled apart; a hole would make the structure collapse. The hull of the balloon was the structure's tensile element. The weight of the cover was resisted by the air, which, if it is contained, resists being compressed like a wall.

Ability to Resist Force

Take a small rubber band and stretch it until it breaks to discover its maximum tensile strength (but watch your fingers!). It reaches maximum at the moment just before it breaks.

DYNAMIC STABILITY

The concept of stability is commonly used in exercise, dance, and athletic conditioning, but sometimes in confusing and contradictory ways. To better understand these concepts, you will imagine a few books stacked up on the coffee table. They are stable because they will not go anywhere unless someone tilts the table or they are carried off. The books can be defined as statically stable. The tilting of the table reveals their robustness, another important term to understand. The robustness of the books shows how much they can resist sliding off the table when you tilt it. If you tilt the table slightly, the books will probably not move, but at a certain point they will start sliding on top of each other as friction is overcome.

I have just described a statically stable system that was disturbed and became unstable. If you see anything that is at rest, it is stable, but this may not necessarily reveal its robustness. Imagine a nice beach where you can see a big stack of towels and also a palm tree. The stack of towels and the tree both are stable. Suddenly a strong wind comes up. The stack of towels is disrupted and collapses. The palm tree is more robust and simply sways with the wind. Both systems were stable, but only the palm tree can move and come back to its original position once the wind has stopped (unless it's a hurricane), making it also dynamically stable. Dynamic stability is the ability to move and be stable at the same time.

The human body obviously needs to be dynamically stable. Imagine that you are running along the beach. As you do this, you are generating forces from within your body and dealing with forces that are arising from outside your body. The ground is pushing against your feet at changing angles with each step. The sand is not even; it has slants and dips that could throw you off and sudden gusts of wind arise, but through ingenious counterbalancing (much of which you are not even consciously thinking about), you remain on your path. Your stability as a dynamic system can be described as staying on your path (trajectory) while dealing with incoming forces with the help of sensory feedback.

If you pick up the stack of towels and run with them, they will rapidly tumble off of your hands, unless you compress them from below and above. The towels are only statically stable; they lack a system that recognizes a disturbance (your hand, wind, acceleration). The stack of towels does not have feedback from a nervous system telling it what is going on and how to react to remain a stack. Such systems can be stabilized by static means; you can push the towels together from above and below as you run. Now your nervous system is taking over the feedback for the towels, which have none. If you transfer this information to alignment, you conclude that dynamic alignment will work best if your feedback is in place—in other words, if you are good at noticing whether your posture is ideal for any given movement or situation. You must process this information rapidly and accurately to be effective. A static model of alignment will not serve this purpose. A person trying to maintain his alignment by the same unchanging strategies through a movement path will actually be using a static model of alignment. Trying to keep your bones stacked in the same alignment or certain muscles contracted as a postural strategy does not take into account that even the slightest shift of body position requires a different set and subset of muscle contractions. This is what happens to people with back pain, in fact—their ability to shift stabilization strategies is reduced (Brumagne, Cordo, and Verschueren 2004). In a healthy individual, the nervous system is adept at sorting out the different alignment avenues that serve the needs of the variable situation. In dynamic alignment you allow your body to find a new equilibrium as an ongoing process. This is where good proprioception (feedback) and effective imagery (feedforward) come into play.

According to Vleeming and colleagues (2004), "Optimal stability is achieved when the balance between performance (the level of optimal stability) and effort is optimized to economize the use of energy" (p. 11). The amount a joint should be compressed should be the minimal amount necessary and tailored to the situation. Any type of cueing, both cognitively and with imagery, should enhance the economy of movement and keep joint pressures at the minimal necessary state for optimal functioning.

If you want to change the shape of a certain structure, it requires force; the amount of force required is the stiffness of the structure. The key when it comes to dynamic alignment is performance, which Reeves defines as "how closely and rapidly the disturbed position of the system tends to the undisturbed position" (Reeves, Narendra, and Cholewicki 2007, p. 270). In other words, what counts is your ability to deal with a disturbance and return to your original posture rapidly. In the following exercise you will practice this and notice which amount of stiffness helps you to achieve this aim.

Dynamic Stability and Variability

1. **Testing dynamic stability:** You can experience the previously described principles in standing alignment with the help of a partner. In this exercise you are going to perturb, or push, your partner (safely) while he tries to stay in place and maintain posture. I suggest varying your pushes and surprising your partner in the way you perturb. Your partner will try several strategies to deal with the situation. First your partner tenses all his muscles while you push him. Then your partner keeps all his muscles relaxed as you do the same. Practice until you find the ideal level of muscle preparedness to stay as quiet as possible as your partner pushes you (little postural sway), and notice how long it takes to return to your original position.

   This experience may show you that too much stiffness, in other words, co-contraction of muscles, is not necessarily the best strategy for maintaining alignment. In my experience, tensing all your muscles makes it more challenging to respond elastically to your partner's pushes. The image I use again is the tree in a storm: The one that bends and sways survives; the one that is stiff is most likely to break.

   People with low back pain, for example, actually have increased stiffness in their muscles, so how could it be a good idea to increase the stiffness in a system that is already stiffer than normal? Hodges (2010) maintains that too much stability may increase joint loading and lead to more problems if maintained. The reason for this is that it reduces the ability of the body to absorb forces through movement. Variability is also reduced by too much stability. In other words, when you perform a movement, you never really do it the same way twice. The best approach to motion seems to be the ever-varying one because then your structures, bones, ligaments, joints, and muscles are always exposed to slightly different forces at different angles, pulls, and tugs, and no one element of the system is overused. Trying to make movement too monotone is not healthy (Angier 2010). This has long been known by dancers as movement improvisation, which is a variability practice and leads to better dance technique.

2. **Testing variability:** Start this exercise the same as the previous one. Gently push your partner and notice how long it takes to get back into the original position. Then allow your partner to move for two minutes on his own with as much variability as possible. Your partner should wiggle, shake, rotate, and gyrate his body. Use music if it helps. Avoid repeating movement. Then push your partner again and notice how long it takes for him to recover. In many instances, the reaction time will be slower.

SUMMARY

In this chapter you explored Isaac Newton's laws of motion to enable you to create imagery based on an understanding of the physics and biomechanics governing the human body. These laws are also a prerequisite to becoming expertly efficient at your posture and movement. The first law tells you that objects tend to keep on moving unless they are stopped by some outside force. This law is exemplified in a variety of movies that have runaway trains as their theme. The second law describes that a heavier object requires more force to move it than a lighter one does. The third law says that if you push on an object, it will push back just as hard. The reason you do not fall through the floor is that the floor is pushing against your feet with a force equal to your weight.

This chapter also discussed levers. The first class is exemplified by the seesaw, the second by the wheelbarrow, and the third by the crane. The head can rock forward and back on the top of the spine, like a first-class lever, but most of the relationships in your body fall under the third-class lever. This is surprising, because it is not the most mechanically advantageous form. What third-class levers do for you is reduce the bulkiness of muscles because a short contraction length can produce a large range of motion. This makes you fast and agile, which is more important than mere mechanical efficiency.

Finally, you found that dynamic alignment is related to the concept of dynamic stability, the concept that human stability functions with the help of feedback control from your brain and nervous system in general. This allows your alignment to be adaptive, to adjust to the situation at hand. Human movement is also variable; in other words, you never perform the same movement in exactly the same manner. This ensures that no muscle fiber, tendon, or joint surface is constantly exposed to the same forces, which would cause them to wear out faster.

In chapter 9 you shall take a closer look at joints and muscles and learn about specific imagery for improving their function.

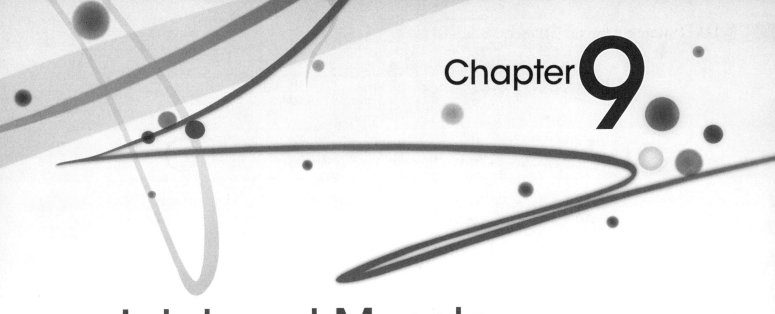

Joint and Muscle Function

Stability is balanced mobility.

A change in the body's alignment is always associated with adjustments in the joints and muscles. The dynamic approach to alignment is not about holding joints or muscles in certain positions, for this would be fixed alignment, quite the opposite of what you are trying to achieve. By understanding how joints and muscles work, you can use imagery to create a balance in them that is strong, yet fluid, ready at any moment to send you into coordinated action. This chapter also introduces fundamental images that pertain to muscles and joints and can be used in all situations to create dynamic alignment and efficient movement.

JOINT TYPES

Joints are divided into two types: synarthrosis (joint without synovial fluid) and diarthrosis (joint with synovial fluid), popularly considered a movable joint. Synarthroses are further divided into fibrous and cartilaginous joints. The sutures of the skull are fibrous joints connected by thin fibrous tissue that allow for only slight motion at birth and in infancy. The joint between the pubic bones, the pubic symphysis, is an example of a cartilaginous synarthrosis.

A diarthrosis enables free movement of the two adjoining bones. The joint is encapsulated in lubricating synovial fluid and covered with cartilage. Joint receptors in the capsule transmit information on the status of the joint to the central nervous system. Hinges and pivots are diarthroses with movement capability in one direction. The interphalangeal joints of the fingers are hinges, and the atlantoaxial joint in the neck is a pivot joint around which the atlas rotates.

Condyloid and saddle joints have two degrees of freedom. The knuckle joints are condyloid; the thumb knuckle is a saddle joint. Ball-and-socket joints (such as the hip) and plane joints (such as the carpals at the base of the hand) have three degrees of freedom.

Joint surfaces are either convex or concave. The ball of the hip joint belongs to the femur (the bone of the upper leg) and is convex. The socket of the hip joint belongs to the pelvis and is concave. If the end of a bone is convex, as in the femur, the shaft of the bone will move in the opposite direction from the surface of the ball (figure 9.1*a*). This means that if you lift your knee, thus lifting the shaft of the femur, the back surface of the ball will move downward. The opposite holds true for the socket of the hip joint. Because the socket is part of the pelvis, it moves in the same direction as the pelvis. If you tilt your pelvis forward (anterior rotation), the socket moves forward as well (figure 9.1*b*). If you move the pelvis back (called posterior rotation), the socket will move back with the pelvis. If the hip joint is stuck or has lost its natural flexibility, the movement of the femur will carry the whole pelvis backward in hip flexion (figure 9.1*c*).

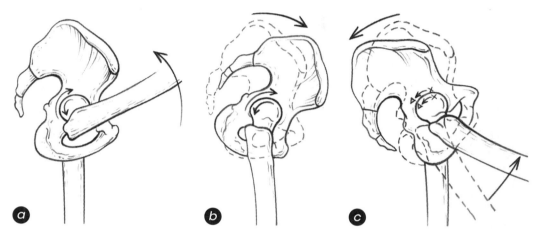

Figure 9.1 *(a)* If the end of a bone is convex, the shaft of the bone will move in the opposite direction from a point on the surface of the ball. *(b)* The hip socket is part of the pelvis and concave. If you tilt the pelvis forward, a point on the socket moves forward as well. *(c)* If the rotation of the head of the femur is insufficient, the pelvis will tuck or posteriorly rotate to accommodate the continuing elevation of the leg.

Imagining Joint Movement

Stand on one leg and lift your knee until your thigh is parallel to the floor. Lower your knee again. Now perform the same motion but focus on the ball in your hip socket moving downward. You may notice that it feels different to lift the leg in this way. Try lifting the knee one more time, but this time visualize an imaginary string attached to your knee, lifting it up as the ball in your hip socket becomes heavy and drops downward (figure 9.2).

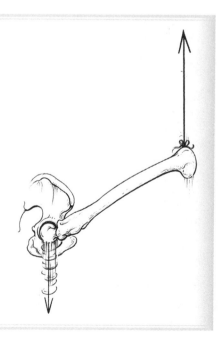

Figure 9.2 An imaginary string lifts your knee; the ball in the socket drops down.

Interaction of Joint Surfaces

Joint surfaces can change their relationship to one another in three distinct ways. The glenohumeral (shoulder) joint exemplifies all three. First, one joint surface can rotate over another, similar to the tires of a car spinning on snow without traction (figure 9.3*a*). Here the contact point of the snow remains constant while the contact point of the tire is constantly changing. Second, a joint surface can roll over another like a tire rolling on a road (figure 9.3*b*), the contact point of each surface changing equally. Third, one joint surface can slide over another as the tires of a car slide over an icy road when the brakes lock up (figure 9.3*c*). The contact point of the tire remains the same while the contact point of the ice changes. Only in the case of the wheels spinning on snow does the axis of the wheel remain in place; in the other cases, the axis moves, creating a so-called instantaneous axis of rotation (IAR). In many cases, joint motion is a combination of gliding and spinning—the IAR moves in an arc through space (see figure 9.4).

Figure 9.3   A joint surface can *(a)* rotate over another, as when the tires of a car spin on snow without traction; *(b)* roll over another like a tire rolling on a road; *(c)* slide over another as the tires of the car slide over an icy road when the brakes lock up. These movements can occur in a combined fashion in a joint. Hip flexion is not a pure spin in flexion, abduction, and adduction. It is accompanied by a slight downward slide in the initial phase of the movement.

Adapted from J.D. Zuckerman and F.A. Matsen, 1989, Biomechanics of the shoulder. In *Basic biomechanics of the musculoskeletal system*, 2nd ed., edited by M. Nordin and V.H. Frankel (Philadelphia: Lea & Febiger), 231.

Lubrication is essential for joint functioning, decreasing wear, and providing nourishment for the cartilage. In figure 9.5, a water fountain designed by Christian Meyer of Munich shows how effective such a system can be in bearing weight. A 1,000-kilogram (2,250-pound) granite ball rests within a perfectly aligned granite socket in a layer of water issuing from a deep underground source. The water creates

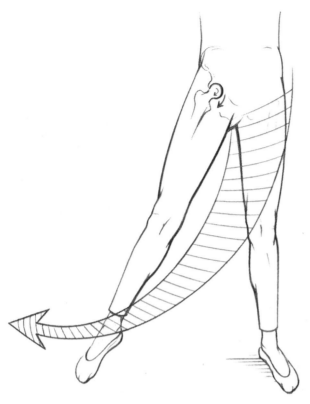

Figure 9.4 Adduction and abduction of the femur in the hip socket trace an arc.

sufficient lubrication and hydrostatic lift so that children can easily set the otherwise heavy ball into rotary motion.

In rotation, the joint surfaces move in opposite directions to each other (counterrotate) . This may be confusing at first because the eye usually sees the movement of only one joint surface, when in reality both joints are moving relative to each other. Figure 9.6 may help in visualizing this phenomenon. The bottom of a ship is depicted as the ball of the joint, and the water surrounding the ball is the socket. As the ship lists to the right, the convex hull glides to the left. The water beneath it rushes to the right, gliding along the hull of the boat. Although the surface of the ocean is still horizontal, the water has changed position relative to the bottom of the boat.

In a high leg kick to the front, the head of the femur drops slightly and spins in its socket. Ideally, the spinning action in the joint suffices for the full extension of the leg. If the rotation is insufficient or gets stuck, the pelvis will posteriorly rotate to accommodate the continuing elevation of the leg,

Figure 9.5 Reminiscent of synovial fluid: A thin layer of water suffices to allow children to move a one-ton granite ball.

which tends to bend the supporting knee (see figure 9.1c). This may cause excessive shear forces in the knee joint.

This situation is comparable to turning a doorknob. If you hold the knob loosely, your hand will simply glide over it without turning the knob. Tightening your grip on the knob will arrest the gliding motion and turn the knob. Likewise, tightening the joints will prevent easy gliding of the leg into high extension. This situation is depicted in figure 9.1c for the hip joint. The two Xs show two opposing points on the head of the femur and the socket of the pelvis. Instead of the Xs moving in opposite directions, or counterrotating as would be the case in a spin, they move in the same direction to the two deltas. Therefore, elevation of the leg has caused the pelvis to tilt backward (rotate poste-

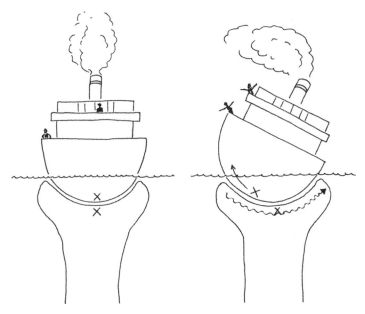

Figure 9.6 As the ship hull glides to the left, the water beneath it rushes to the right, gliding along the bottom of the boat.

riorly). Ease of joint motion can be promoted by imagining the ball spinning easily in the socket and by imagining the counterrotation of the socket.

Joints commonly have instant centers of rotation; in other words, the axis of rotation is not fixed; it moves. In this way, no point of the joint surface receives large pressures over an extended period. The body is good at relaying forces between points so as to minimize impact and maximize the use of available resources.

Imagining Interaction of Joint Surfaces

1. **Counterrotation in the hip socket:** As you lift your knee, focus on the relative motion of the ball and socket. As the knee moves up, visualize the dorsal surface of the ball moving downward (see figure 9.1a). Although the concave surface of the hip socket seems to be stationary, it moves relative to the surface of the ball of the femur. Because the surface of the ball moves downward, the visualized relative motion of the socket is upward. As the knee moves downward, visualize the dorsal surface of the ball moving upward and the surface of the socket moving downward.

2. **Spin, glide, and counterrotation in abduction and adduction of the hip socket:** Move your leg out to the side (abduction) and then move it back in (adduction). In abduction, there is both a downward gliding motion of the ball in the socket and a spin and counterrotation of the socket. The IAR traces a downward and outward arc. Think of this arc on a much larger scale and project it onto the motion of the entire leg (see figure 9.4 again).

To cover all joint possibilities, imagine the upward movement of the concave socket (counterrotation) as occurring slightly before the downward motion of the head of the femur. This imagery syncopation will help stabilize the joint in space.

Kinematic Chains

If you bend your knees (plié), the ankle and hip joints bend as well. Any motion in the ankle joint while standing will result in motion in the knee and hip joints. The bones are linked in a closed kinematic chain—movement in one joint elicits movement in the neighboring joints. With both feet on the floor, the legs are confined by two firm boundaries, the floor and the pelvis, making the legs part of a closed kinematic chain. If the foot is not on the floor, the motion of the knees may or may not involve the hip and ankle joints; this is an open kinematic chain. The same holds true if the hands are fixed in place, such as during push-ups or a downward dog pose in yoga; the movement of the elbow will cause movement at the wrist and shoulder, which is a closed kinematic chain. Once you lift the hand off the ground, you can move the elbow independently of the wrist and shoulder, which is an open chain.

Range of Motion

Every joint has a normal range of motion (ROM). Limitations on ROM may stem from bony deformations or cartilaginous or ligamentous restrictions. In most cases of restricted ROM, the muscles crossing the particular joint are tight. This is why stretching to increase ROM is so prevalent among dancers and gymnasts. Excessive ROM without sufficient strength may result in injury because the joint is not protected by the stabilizing action of the muscles. Dynamic alignment increases ROM by creating balanced muscle action while providing stability. In misaligned standing posture, for example, additional muscle effort will be required to keep the structure from toppling over. Once the body segments are more nearly aligned, these muscles are liberated to move you more freely. Even a slight improvement in alignment may lead to increased flexibility. Your flexibility is as good as your alignment permits.

BONES

Bones are the densest form of connective tissue in the body. In addition to producing white and red blood cells in their marrow, they protect internal organs; for example, the ribs protect the heart and lungs and the skull protects the brain. Stanley Keleman (1985) refers to bones as "inner honeycombs." Although the mineral content of bone is similar to that of marble, it also contains crisscrossing collagen fibrils for elasticity. A demineralized bone can be bent, as if made of rubber, and will rebound into its original shape. Thus, bones can resist high degrees of compression, tensile, and shear forces.

The body contains 206 bones of all shapes. There are short bones in the hands and feet, long bones in the legs and arms, flat bones in the skull, bones with airy compartments in the sinuses, and so on. The long bones are hollow, increasing their resistance to breakage. The sesamoids in the feet act as pulleys and shock absorbers. Some bones (such as vertebrae) do not fit into any of these categories.

Bones consist of several layers that differ significantly from each other in structure and function. Their outer covering is called the periosteum, a tough protective membrane. You can feel this slippery, skinlike covering by placing your finger on the front of your shinbone and moving it around. The next layer of the bone is the dense and compact cortical layer; it is the essence of the bone, its hardest part. Farther toward the center is the cancellous (spongy) layer with a platelike structure called the trabeculae (small beams). The trabeculae are situated along the lines of force through the bones and aid in supporting the joints. The trabeculae arise in response to stresses in the system (figure 9.7), creating force lines similar to the iron girders of the Eiffel Tower or the curving braces in an archway (see figure 11.47).

Similar to coral, the interior of bone consists of many interconnected channels and structures designed to support weight efficiently. Doctors have even been able to use coral in rebuilding bones after injury.

The innermost stratum of the bone is the soft marrow, which is continuously

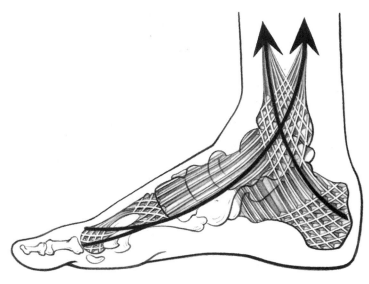

Figure 9.7 The trabeculae are force lines similar to the curving braces in an archway.

producing new blood cells (mostly during childhood, although also in some adult bones). Even as you read this chapter, millions of new blood cells are being born in your vertebrae, sternum, and ilia.

Bones are not at all fixed in shape. Depending on the forces that they are subjected to, they can change in contour and remodel themselves. Just as a wind-blown tree adapts to stresses (figure 9.8), bone will remodel itself according to compression and pulling. A furniture mover's bone mass increases; the bone in a ballerina's second toe thickens. The pull of muscles on bones creates bulges such as those on the major and minor trochanters of the femur.

Most bones can be viewed as spiraled along their long axes. A classic example is the femur, which spirals inward as viewed from the top downward (see figure 10.60). In contrast, the upper arm bone (humerus) spirals outward. The leg bones are actually a stack of counterspirals; the shinbone spirals outward and the foot spirals inward.

Figure 9.8 Just like bone, trees remodel themselves to adapt to stresses, such as wind.

Ribs are interesting because they are both curved and spiraled. These shapes lead to imagery that can help you with spiraling motions such as in the shot put, discus throw, or spiral turns.

Exercising the Bones

1. **Body hangs on bones (walking, standing, sitting):** Place all your weight on your bones by thinking of them as a clothes hanger that the rest of your body can hang on like a well-pressed suit. It is easy for the bones to perform this task; they remain light and buoyant as the body casually drapes over them.

2. **Muscle sleeves:** Think of the bones as arms within their sleeves made of muscles. It may help to think of the muscles as being made of silk or a similar soft material. Wiggle the bones inside their sleeves, imagining that the two can move independently. Allow the sleeves to slide over the bones. It is easiest to begin this exercise by actually moving an arm while using the image. It takes practice to use the image effectively without much movement. Try this image with different parts of the body and notice where it seems more difficult to create the sense of bones being separate from muscles, where it feels like the sleeves are stuck to the bones.

3. **Reach with your bones, reach with your muscles (improvisation):** As you reach out into space, think of your bones leading the way as if they were eager to move out and explore the space. As you experiment with various areas of the body, notice where it is easier to let the bones initiate movement and where it seems more difficult. Is it possible to think of the finger bones moving out into space? The tailbone? The top of the skull? Now practice the opposite: Instead of the bones, which have lost interest in moving out into space, the muscles now lead the way.

4. **Bone core initiation:** Practice initiating movement from the core of your bones. This is the soft part, the marrow. It seems unusual to think of bones as having a soft component, let alone think of this area as moving you through space. However, you may notice that in this softness lies a certain power.

CONNECTIVE TISSUE AND FASCIA

Connective tissue makes a community out of structures placed in each other's vicinity. If you removed everything except the connective tissue, you would still recognize the body's shape. Connective tissue has the seemingly contradictory role of connecting and separating from the most superficial to the deepest layers of your body. Consisting of bones, ligaments, tendons, and fascia, connective tissue creates form, fills space, transfers mechanical force, envelops, and supports. Because it is viscoelastic, it can return to its original shape after deformation and dampen shearing forces. Its structure can be seen both in a macro- and microperspective relating and replicating fractally from large to small.

Bone, the densest form of connective tissue, can withstand the highest compressive loads. Connective tissue is the packaging of all the body surfaces.

There are three kinds of fascia: superficial, deep, and organ related. Fascia related to muscles is like a very tough sheet that separates, connects, and encases. Your muscles would spread out like a glob of honey without fascia. That is why imagery of melting, spreading muscles is not far-fetched. Fascia connects and organizes the spatial arrangement of your organs, hanging them from the ceiling of the diaphragm (as with the liver) or hammocking organs between bony support systems. In this equal partnership, the organs support the surrounding structures with their hydrostatic and muscle properties.

Tendons transfer the force of the muscles to the bones. In most cases, tendons connect the muscles to the bone. They feel firm when the muscles contract and softer when the muscles relax. A tendon may feel hard as bone when the associated muscle is contracted. A flat, broad tendon is called an aponeurosis, such as the central tendon of the diaphragm and the plantar aponeurosis in the sole of the foot. A septum is a thickened fascia separating the muscles and creating compartments. Ligaments are the ropes and pulleys of the body, securing the joints, limiting or guiding joint motion where necessary, and stabilizing structures. Ligaments are really thickened areas of fascia. Commonly they are depicted as individual strands, but often they have connections to muscles and fascial sheaths. Tendons and ligaments have high tensile strength and, in normal activity, have a large reserve of this strength. Like bones, ligaments and tendons can remodel depending on the strains to which they are exposed.

Imagining Separation and Slide in the Fascia

1. **Separate masses of the thigh:** Flex your leg joints, walk a few steps, or perform any type of leg movement. Then imagine the fascia or septi that separate the muscles of the lower leg (figure 9.9). Move with the image of a separation and of clear differentiation between these masses. Mentally note the fact they can be right next to each other and yet perform a different type of contraction. Imagine the muscles sliding and moving within their fascial sheaths.

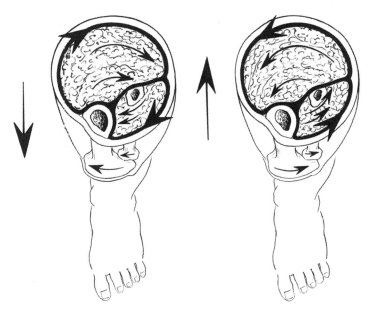

Figure 9.9 Fascia surrounds and separates the muscles of the lower leg.

2. **Iliac fascia and hip flexion:** Perform a hip flexion either by lifting your leg or by flexing the lower limb. Visualize the iliacus muscle located on the inside of the ilium of your pelvis. Now imagine the iliac fascia covering the iliacus from the whole length of the inner lip of the iliac crest to the linea terminalis of the lesser pelvis. Imagine the fascia resting on the muscle like a soft and silky covering that also has some weight. Perform another hip flexion and take note of any changes in sensation.

3. **Stretching with fascia in mind:** Focus on your connective tissue in a stretch. The fascia should not be rigid (figure 9.10*a*). Instead imagine the fascia providing length by being viscous and flowing (figure 9.10*b*).

Figure 9.10 *(a)* Rigid connective tissue; *(b)* viscous connective tissue.

MUSCLES

A muscle is a large bundle of fibers held together by small sheets, which in turn are held together by a larger enveloping sheet. The functional unit of a skeletal muscle, a muscle designed to make you move through space, is a muscle fiber. Every fiber is basically a small contracting machine that can exert force on the bones to which it is attached by shortening itself. Often the function of strength and tone is emphasized in muscle training; however, another important function of muscles is force absorption (damping) to protect joints and other structures. A significant part of force absorption is mediated through the connective tissue.

Connective Tissue of Muscles

Muscles are covered by an interwoven wrapping of connective tissue called the epimysium. The epimysium dives into the muscle belly and forms the septae (separators) dividing it into individual bundles, or fasciculi, whose deeper wrappings are called the perimysium. The perimysium in turn dives yet deeper and surrounds the individual muscle fibers in the form of an endomysium. Tendons, fascia, and aponeuroses also have a connective tissue wrapping called the epitenon. Within a tendon are also fine connective tissue strands called the endotenon. The perimysium of muscle connects to the epitenon of a tendon, which in turn connects the periosteum of the bone. Sharpey's fibers, another form of connective tissue, anchor the periosteum into the bone, which is connective tissue as well. You can see that there is a relationship between each individual muscle fiber, connective tissues, and bones in your body through a near-endless web, or tensegrity grid, of interconnections.

Muscles move connective tissue before they move bone. No muscle fiber runs the whole length of a muscle; the force of a fiber is transferred through the connective tissue to adjoining fibers and finally to the tendon at the end of the muscle (figure 9.11). When you contract a muscle, it pulls on its surrounding connective tissue through many layers that then reach the tendon, which finally pulls on the bone. The reverse is also true. When gravity pulls on a bone, it does not stretch the muscle proteins directly. It first pulls on the tendon, which pulls on the connective tissue of the muscles, which then aids in lengthening the muscle itself.

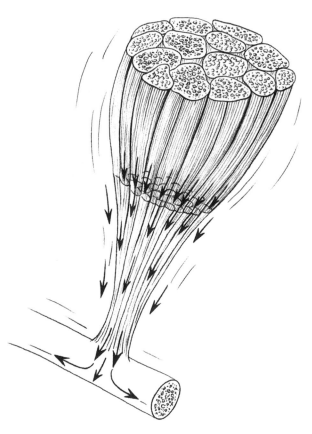

Figure 9.11 Muscle within its connective tissue connecting to the tendon and the bone.

Experiencing Relationships of Muscle-Connective Tissue

When you bend your elbow, imagine the biceps muscle tissue pulling on the surrounding connective tissue through many layers that then pull on the tendon, which pull on the bone. To extend your elbow, imagine gravity pulling on your lower arm, which pulls on your biceps tendon, which pulls on the connective tissue of the muscles, which finally lengthens the muscle. Compare this image to the image of the muscle pulling directly on the bone, without the connective tissue interface or gravity pulling directly on the muscle. You may notice that the image containing the muscle-connective tissue and tendon is more resilient and elastic. I refer to this as muscle-tendon-bone imagery (MTB).

Traditionally muscles are depicted as separate entities that run from bone to bone. This image has been perpetuated by anatomy books that illustrate muscles without their connective tissue wrappings. In reality, muscles are related to bone not only through tendons but also through fascia, aponeuroses, and sometimes ligaments (see chapter 10 on the pelvis and chapter 12 on the spine). The muscles of the rotator cuff

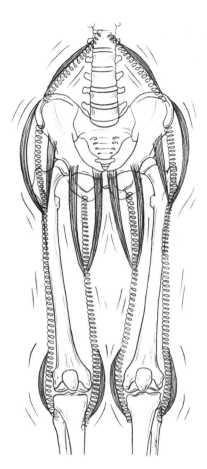

of the shoulder, for example, have insertions into the connective-tissue joint capsule, the gluteal muscles are connected to the sacrotuberous ligament and the tensor fasciae latae, and the latissimus dorsi are connected to the thoracolumbar fascia. Muscles are related to bone and each other through a complex connective matrix. This system allows for three-dimensional force generation and force absorption through muscle-connective tissue dialogue. In figure 9.12, the connective tissue is depicted as coiled springs to which the muscles attach, providing tension.

When muscles contract along their length, they become wider because the same amount of muscle tissue is now concentrated over a smaller distance (figure 9.13). This increase in diameter pushes on the connective tissue, making the muscle more firm. The body uses this system to increase dynamic stability. The increased tension in the fascia is relayed to bones and joints to increase force closure (see "Thoracolumbar Fascia" in chapter 12).

Figure 9.12 Muscles tensing the connective tissue.

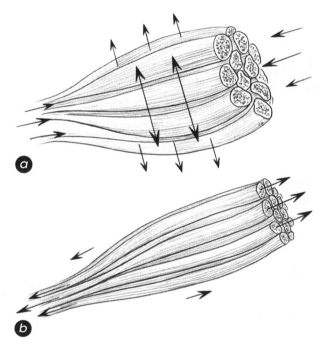

Figure 9.13 *(a)* As the muscle shortens, it becomes wider and pushes on the surrounding connective-tissue wrappings. *(b)* As the muscle lengthens, it becomes narrower and longer.

Widening and Narrowing of Muscle and Connective Tissue

Hold your right biceps and flex and extend your elbow. As the muscles shorten and widen, imagine them pushing against their connective-tissue wrappings. As you extend your elbow, imagine the muscles lengthening within their connective tissue. As you flex your elbow once again, imagine the connective tissue widening in anticipation of the muscle. As you extend your elbow, anticipate the lengthening of the connective tissue. Repeat the bending and stretching of the elbow several times while imagining the muscle action. Finally, compare the ease of motion in the right and left arms. Repeat with the other arm.

Sliding Filament Theory of Muscle Contraction

If you take a microscopic look at a muscle cell, the most obvious thing you can see is a regular arrangement of bands (figures 9.14 and 9.15). These bands are the proteins that cause muscle contraction. Muscles are made of elongated cells containing myofilaments. The myofilaments are arranged within compartments called sarcomeres. There are three types of myofilaments: actin, myosin, and titin.

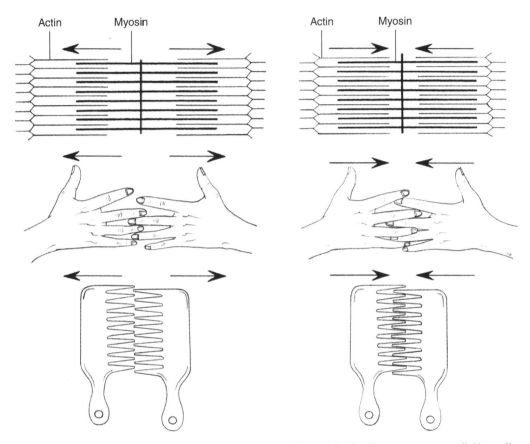

Figure 9.14 The sarcomere slid apart.   **Figure 9.15** The sarcomere slid together.

You can see thicker lines and thinner lines. These are the myofilaments. In striated muscle they are arranged in transverse bands; in smooth muscle the filaments are arranged irregularly. The thicker ones are called the myosin filaments (figure 9.16). The thinner ones are called the actin filaments. The thin ones are attached to what are called the Z-lines and project toward and interlace with the thick ones. So-called titin filaments connect the myosin to the Z-lines functioning as molecular springs to provide passive elasticity. The area with only thin ones is the I-band; the area with thick ones is the A-band. The area with only myosin is the H-zone.

If you increase the magnification of your imaginary microscope, you see that the thicker filaments have little arms that look like the oars of a boat with thick paddles (see figure 9.17). When a muscle fiber (cell) shortens, the filaments slide past each and overlap even more. They remain essentially the same length. Tension in the muscle is produced by cross bridges, which are the myosin heads attaching and reattaching in new positions to the actin as if the oars were repeatedly dipping into

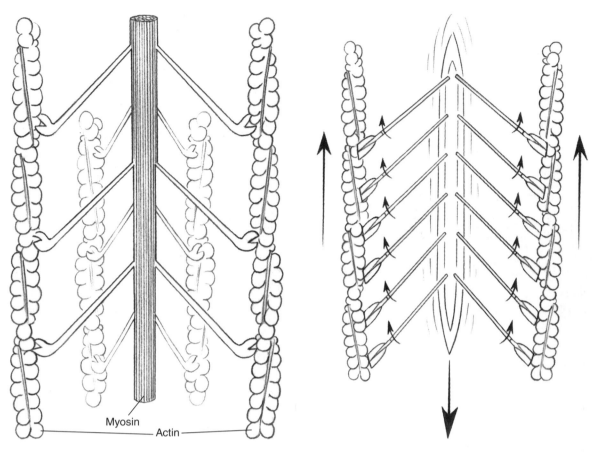

Figure 9.16 Myosin and actin close up.   **Figure 9.17** The rowing-boat image.

water to push the boat forward. (To be accurate, the rowing-boat image would need to be three-dimensional, with oars sticking out to all sides.) Also, the myosin filament pulls the actin toward itself from both sides like a double-sided tug of war. The valuable visual, kinesthetic, and perhaps even auditory imagery that evolves from this anatomical knowledge is that from the point of view of muscle proteins, muscles do not shorten; they slide.

Imagery Exercises for Sliding Filament

1. **Biceps muscle sliding:** Put your left hand on the biceps and slowly bend and stretch the elbow while visualizing the filaments sliding together and apart. Repeat the movement and image 12 times. Stay focused as you do this. When you are finished, drop your arms down at your sides and notice the difference between the two sides. Then also notice the kinesthetic difference between your muscles as you bend and stretch both elbows simultaneously. Commonly the side practiced with imagery feels smoother, more relaxed, and even more flexible.

2. **Pectoralis muscle sliding:** Put your left hand on the right pectoralis. Lift the right arm up until it is parallel to the floor and move it forward until your elbow is

in front of the breastbone. You have now slid the pectoralis filaments together. Move your elbow laterally and slide the pectoralis filaments apart. Move your arm slowly medially and laterally 12 times while imagining muscle sliding in the pectoralis. You may use self-talk such as *Slide together, slide apart* to support this action. Drop your arms down at your sides and notice the difference between the two sides. The practiced side will probably feel more open because the shoulder is more laterally placed and less slouched. Now move both arms at the same time and notice differences in flexibility in a variety of directions. This exercise provides the insight that you can achieve flexibility without forceful stretching of muscles but rather through the combination of touch (tactile proprioception), movement, and imagery.

Innervation

A special type of nerve cell, the alpha motor neuron, signals the muscle fibers to contract. All muscle fibers connect to a single alpha motor neuron, a motor unit, which is the smallest part of the muscle that can contract independently. When the fibers receive a command signal, they can do only one thing—shorten. This doesn't mean that the whole muscle shortens. If only a few muscle fibers receive the command to shorten, no perceptible movement occurs in the muscle. The few fibers that are working may not suffice for contracting the whole muscle. You can compare this situation to a team of husky dogs hooked up to a sled. If only one of the dozen or so dogs attempts to pull the sled while the others are sound asleep, the sled will not move forward. (Note that this is an example of imagery with an educational purpose.)

For a muscle to contract, motor units need to fire repeatedly. The more motor units activated, the stronger the movement. If you are thinking of a movement without doing it, or you are hesitant about doing it, you will activate some motor units but not enough to make you move.

Types of Contraction

Three types of contraction are commonly described: concentric, eccentric, and isometric. Concentric and eccentric contractions are dynamic, involving movement through space of the bony levers to which the muscles are attached. If you hold a weight in your hand and slowly bend your elbow to lift it upward, your biceps and other upper-arm muscles shorten and contract at the same time, as expected. This is a concentric, or shortening, contraction. If you lower the weight, the muscles are still contracting to keep the weight from falling out of control, but they are getting longer in breaking the fall of the weight. This is called an eccentric, or lengthening, contraction. If you simply hold a weight with your elbow bent, the muscles work without lengthening or shortening. This is an isometric, or constant-length, contraction. The term *contraction* can actually be confusing. Literally, an eccentric contraction means away from center, pulling together (in other words, a contradiction in terms). Some authors are therefore replacing the term *muscle contraction* with *muscle action*, which makes more sense.

Slowly Let Go

When your quadriceps muscle straightens your knee, it is performing a shortening, or concentric, contraction. In a squat, this same muscle must break your fall by eccentric action. As your knee bends, the quadriceps lengthens while contracting just enough to break your fall. Visualize the muscle slowly letting go. You can compare the sensation to the notion of carefully lowering a bucket into a deep well. You may also think of the muscle as slowly stretching taffy.

Prime Movers, Synergists, and Stabilizers

For every joint movement, there are muscles that produce this motion, called the movers, or agonists. If you want to bend your elbow, then certain elbow flexor muscles are the so-called prime movers because they are the most important movers. The muscles that oppose this movement are called the antagonists. When flexing your hip, the iliopsoas is the prime mover because it is the strongest hip flexor. Sometimes certain muscles join forces to produce a certain effect; they are called synergists.

The agonist sends an inhibiting signal to the antagonist so that it can perform its function. Just as a ship cannot pull out of the harbor if it is not released from its ropes, an agonist cannot move if it is not released by its antagonist. This process is called reciprocal inhibition, a mutual relaying of tension states so that the muscles can work in harmony.

If joint stability is needed, such as in the standing leg in the high leg kick, then co-contraction may occur, in which both agonist and antagonist contract simultaneously. These muscles are now acting as stabilizers to maintain posture and continuity of motion. Stabilization does not always mean that a part of the body is being fixed in a nonmoving position but may occur dynamically throughout a motion cycle.

Brushed Into Length

Aid the movers by seeing the antagonists as long and released. A dancer extending his arm and leg (or in a leg kick, battement, développé, or any extension) may imagine the underside of the arm and leg being brushed into length (figure 9.18).

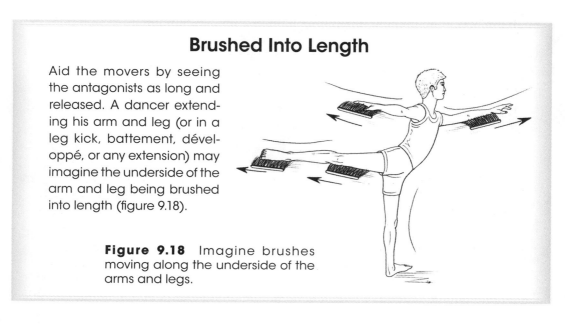

Figure 9.18 Imagine brushes moving along the underside of the arms and legs.

Stretch Reflex

Complex movement would not be possible without an automatic pilot constantly adjusting your posture. This automatic pilot consists of reflexes that underlie your consciously guided movement. Sherrington (1964) writes, "The reflex is independent of consciousness even at first occurrence. It does not emanate from the 'ego'" (p. 156). You have reflexively withdrawn your fingers from a hot plate or flame. The body acts before you can think about it, producing rapid movements to prevent you from injuring yourself. If the doctor's hammer taps the proper point, the knee straightens as the result of the stretch reflex. The so-called muscle spindles monitor the length of a muscle to keep it from being injured by overstretching. To permanently increase muscle length through stretching, this reflex must be circumvented. Reflexes, righting reactions, and equilibrium responses underlie all successful effortless movement. Primitive reflexes are with humans from birth; righting reactions that control alignment come into full bloom at about one year of age. Equilibrium responses maintain balance from the time you first walk (Cohen 1994).

Muscle Tone

Tone (from the Greek *tonos,* meaning tension), the basic level of muscle tension, determines the body's density. Your basic muscle tone is lower when you sleep and higher when you are very active. Without muscle tone, the body would collapse; conversely, excessive tone blocks movement. A baby's muscles feel soft, resilient, and rubbery to the touch because they are free of excessive tension. Some people seem to be in a constant state of high muscle tension, whereas others are in the opposite state—flaccidity. Often you find differing states of tension in the body, such as tense shoulders with high tone and midsection with low tone. Similarly, varying styles of movement require varying degrees of muscle tone. The pre-breakdance robot style of dancing, for example, was definitely a high-tone affair.

The more you can change the level of tone in your body at will, the richer your expressive possibilities. Improvisation is a way of practicing this ability. Balanced tone is one of the goals of dynamic alignment. Most people need to increase tone in the center front of the body, which includes the abdominal and deep pelvic muscles. This in turn helps create the foundation for reducing tension in the shoulder and upper-chest areas.

Exercising Muscle Tone

1. **Changes in tone:** Move like a robot and then like a flowing river. Imagine supporting a heavy weight and then gliding through a silk curtain. Become an oak tree resisting the wind and then a leaf being tossed by the wind. (See also *Dance Imagery for Technique and Performance,* the chapter on improvisation.)

2. **Lying on chestnuts:** Gather a bunch of chestnuts or marbles and spread them on a towel. Lie down with the back of your body on the chestnuts and imagine your back melting down over them. If this hurts, use smooth or plush balls.

Muscles Crossing Joints

Muscles affect only the joints they cross. Some muscles cross one joint, and others cross two joints, often creating opposing actions. Two-joint muscles are most efficient when they can shorten at one joint and lengthen at the other; otherwise they may develop what is called active insufficiency. The rectus femoris muscle, for example, originates at the hip and attaches below the knee. It flexes the hip and extends the knee, making it easier to lift your leg with the knee bent than with the leg straight. If the knee is stretched as you lift the leg, the rectus femoris needs to shorten both at the hip and at the knee, causing an active insufficiency. Simply stated, there is less shortening power left if the knee is extended as you lift the leg. If the knee is bent, the rectus femoris can concentrate its contractile power on the hip.

Extending the leg to the back in arabesque lengthens the rectus femoris at the hip and shortens it at the knee, lending optimal function to this two-joint muscle. When you extend your leg at the hip and bend the knee, the hamstring shortens both over the back of the hip and the knee. If you continue to bend the knee in this position, you will notice that the hamstrings become actively insufficient, sometimes even cramping.

Emphasis on Iliopsoas

In this exercise you will focus your imagery on the deep-lying iliopsoas in hip flexion. This will increase its activity enough to make a perceptible difference in lifting your leg. Lift and lower your knee and notice what this action feels like. To activate the prime mover for hip flexion, the iliopsoas, use an indirect approach, reducing your reliance on the secondary movers such as the rectus femoris. As you lift your knee, imagine the iliopsoas contracting. Visualize the place where you are creasing your hip to be very foldable, soft, and melting. Now lower your knee. Perform the action once again in your mind's eye only, focusing on a very malleable, soft creasing at the hip. Lift your knee again and notice any changes in sensation. Lift your other knee and notice the difference between your legs.

Control Over Individual Muscles

Learning how to control individual muscles is difficult; it can usually be done only with much practice, if at all. Humans would have been extinct long ago if they had to constantly instruct every individual muscle to move (figure 9.19). Body therapies would not exist if you had such control because everyone could optimally adjust every muscle. You would never need massages, but you would spend most of the day organizing your muscles.

Muscle Balance and Posture

Ideally, muscles not required to perform a movement should not be involved. But are there any such isolated movements? Just lifting your arm to the side causes subtle changes throughout the body. Your breathing pattern changes slightly, and even the muscles of the legs need to adjust. Muscles stabilize one part of the body against the movement of another and constantly perform midmovement corrections to maintain balance. All of these actions should happen efficiently without excess strain.

Figure 9.19 Trying to move one muscle at a time would have made us easy prey. Therefore, we have control over the goal of our movement, which subcortically organizes the individual muscles for action. In this case, escape would have been appropriate.

Dynamic alignment helps you achieve this goal by balancing the muscles in your neutral position (easier said than done). I have already pointed out the importance of well-balanced first-class levers for alignment. To simplify for clarity, muscles acting on a bone can be visualized as a tent or drape attached over a central pole. If the muscles are tight, the bone is held rigidly in place (figure 9.20a). If the muscles are flaccid, the bone sways and lacks control (figure 9.20b). If the muscles are imbalanced (tight on one side of the joint and flaccid on the other), the bone loses alignment (figure 9.20c). Ideally, the muscles should be neither too tight nor too flaccid.

Can alignment be corrected by strengthening some muscles and weakening others? To create balance, you could lengthen a habitually shortened muscle and strengthen a weak one. A good knowledge of muscle function is necessary for improving balance with such exercises, and even then success will be limited to creating a temporary and rough balance.

Figure 9.20 (a) If the muscles are tight, the bone is held in place. (b) If the muscles are flaccid, the bone sways. (c) If the muscles are imbalanced, the bone loses its alignment.

Unless you recognize and adjust your basic habits, body image, and movement patterns, you are going to reinforce your old imbalances indefinitely. You do not want your training to improve what you are trying to change. The Franklin method four-step process will help you to create steps in the right direction (see chapter 4).

Minimal Amount of Holding

Hold a ruler in one hand and lower it perpendicularly to the floor. If you grasp it tightly, it will stay in its position. Determine the minimum effort needed in order to keep the stick from falling. Do the same exercise with your left hand and compare the ease with which each hand accomplished the task.

Discovering Muscle Imbalances

There are several ways to begin noticing muscle imbalances in your body. One is simply to palpate an area on one side of the body and compare it in muscle thickness and density to the same area on the other side. The neck is a good place to start because you might hold your head slightly to one side. Put your fingers on both sides of your neck and see if you notice any differences between the muscles on the left and right sides. Compare your findings with your preferred motions of the head: Does it seem more normal to tilt the head slightly to the right or to the left? Does it seem more normal to turn the head to the right or to the left to look behind you? Usually, if you prefer to look to the right, that is also your better turning side in dance, influencing muscle chains all the way down to the feet.

Noticing Differences in Perceived Muscle Effort

Another way to detect muscle imbalances is to stand up from a chair and sit down again. Put your right leg in front and your left in back and stand up and sit down again. Repeat with your left leg in front and your right leg in back. Do this very slowly and notice the differences between the sides. Catch yourself during the day and watch how you stand up and sit down. Most likely you use similar patterns and reinforce them continuously. Also notice differences in muscle effort by altering the position of your legs. What is it like to stand up and sit down with your legs medially rotated, laterally rotated, and in parallel?

How Movement Habits Create Muscle Imbalances

In sports, dance, and exercise, it is important to be equally strong on both sides of the body. Balance of strength may be more important than overall strength when creating optimal movement technique and lifelong musculoskeletal health. You are usually aware of which is your better supporting leg and which leg is better in extension, and you sometimes try to correct the situation. But if your only action is to strengthen and stretch, and you don't attempt to change your movement habits, you will not be entirely successful. Don't work on your alignment only during training. I have observed that when students listen to a teacher's instruction during a movement class, their true alignment patterns often emerge, patterns that are surprisingly different from their exercise alignment. True improvement in alignment is not possible by focusing on and artificially maintaining alignment only during a specific situation.

Muscle Chains

Muscle chains are separate muscles with different origins and insertions but similar lines of action. The left internal oblique abdominal muscles and the right external oblique abdominal muscles form a muscle chain, as do the right internal obliques and the left external obliques. These particular muscle chains support complex rotary and spiral actions throughout the body. Although their connection is not otherwise obvious, muscle chains connect the arm to the pelvis. Anteriorly, the ascending fibers of the pectorals are in line with the internal obliques and the psoas of the opposite side. Posteriorly, the latissimus dorsi connects the arm to the spine and the lumbar fascia. Its fibers are generally in line with the external obliques and the gluteus maximus of the opposite side.

Imagining muscle chains creates strong kinesthetic connections throughout the body, which can manifest in feelings of envelopment, three-dimensionality, and general interconnectedness. This is helpful in spiral turns, but when visualized, these sensations are helpful in many actions, even in standing (see also chapters 10 and 12 on the pelvis and spine).

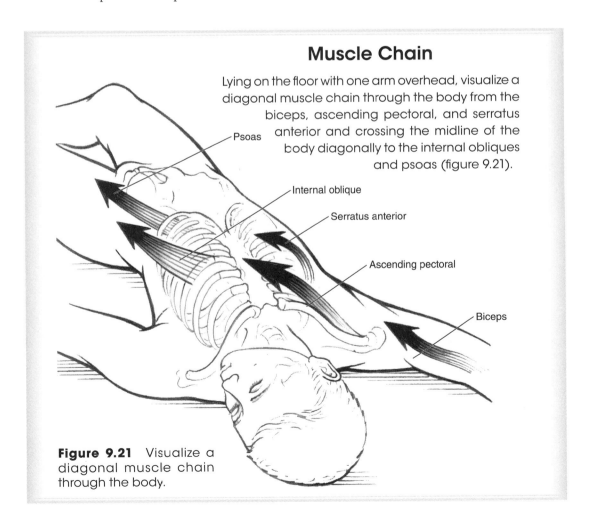

Muscle Chain

Lying on the floor with one arm overhead, visualize a diagonal muscle chain through the body from the biceps, ascending pectoral, and serratus anterior and crossing the midline of the body diagonally to the internal obliques and psoas (figure 9.21).

Psoas

Internal oblique

Serratus anterior

Ascending pectoral

Biceps

Figure 9.21 Visualize a diagonal muscle chain through the body.

SUMMARY

In this chapter you looked at the basic structure and movement of joints, muscles, and connective tissue. A typical joint is encapsulated in lubricating synovial fluid and covered with cartilage. A diarthrosis enables free movement of the two adjoining bones. A synarthrosis does not contain any synovial fluid and has limited motion. You found that the shaft of a bone with a ball at its end will move in opposition to a point on the ball; however, if the bone has a socket, a point of the surface of the socket will move in synchrony with the bone. There are three possible movements in a joint: rolling, sliding, and spinning. In the case of rolling and sliding, the joint axis will move through space, while in the case of spinning it will stay in place.

Connective tissue consists of bones, ligaments, tendons, and fascia; it creates form, fills space, transfers mechanical force, envelops, and supports. Bones are covered by a periosteum and often contain force-transferring trabeculae inside. A muscle is a large bundle of fibers held together by small sheets, which in turn are held together by a larger enveloping sheet. The functional unit of a skeletal muscle, a muscle designed to make you move through space, is the muscle fiber, which is the elongated cells of the muscle. Every fiber is basically a small contracting machine that can exert force on the bones to which it is attached by shortening itself. The contraction consists of a sliding together of myofilaments. When a muscle lengthens, the filaments slide apart. This is an excellent image for creating strong but fluid movement. There are three basic kinds of muscle contraction: concentric, eccentric, and isometric. Concentric and eccentric contractions are dynamic, involving movement through space of the body. If you simply hold a position against gravity or by holding a weight, the muscles work without lengthening or shortening. This is an isometric, or constant-length, contraction. Muscle chains are separate muscles with different origins and insertions but similar lines of action. They are important for transferring forces over large distances throughout the body and assist in dynamic stabilization of the body.

PART
III

Exercises for Anatomical Imagery

Dynamic alignment requires a knowledge of anatomy—the location and status of your joints; the tension states of your muscles and organs; the numerous connections between the muscles, bones, and organs; and the shapes and inner volumes within you—to give the mind options for improving and adjusting alignment and movement efficiency.

A complete survey of anatomy is beyond the scope of this book. In preparing this section, I have focused on the particular needs of dancers, exercise teachers, and movement specialists in relation to proper alignment of the musculoskeletal system. Sports that require a high level of technique and subtle coordination of body systems will also benefit from the imagery.

Although I have subdivided the discussion into the major anatomical groups and their associated imagery exercises, these subdivisions should not be considered absolute because every part of the body is in some way connected to every other part. If you pull on the leg of someone lying in the supine position, the person may feel it in his neck. The connective tissues transfer the mechanical force all the way through the body.

Because of these interconnections, images relate to each other. For example, using an image that influences the sacrum and the joints between the sacrum and the pelvis, the iliosacral joints, creates a reaction on the other side of the pelvis, at the pubic symphysis. The image used for the back of the pelvis may be widening or spreading, whereas the experience at the front of the pelvis may be connecting or integrating. Thus, imagery helps you create a unified experience of the body by heightening awareness of these interactions, bringing you closer to the experience of dynamic alignment.

It always helps to touch the accessible anatomical landmarks. Tracing bony outlines aids the visualization process by creating a tactile map of these parts in your own body. Working with a partner enhances the benefit of many of these exercises. Beyond personality, posture, and fingerprints, every bone and muscle makes you unique.

A person skilled at using imagery creates a synergistic effect, enhancing the effectiveness of each area by visualizing two or more images simultaneously. For example, visualize the shoulders and sacrum widening as the central axis becomes perpendicular to the floor.

I introduce each image with a name suggestive of its purpose and commonly the position or movement in which it may be practiced. These positions are not absolute. You may substitute standing, walking, or improvising if it suits you.

When practicing on one side of the body, take a moment to compare sides before practicing the other side. This has several advantages: You can appreciate the change and remember it better by anchoring it to your whole body's sensation and image. You accelerate the neuroplastic changes in your brain to create permanently improved motor patterns. You start understanding what kind of imagery processes work best for you.

In chapters 10 to 15 you will systematically move through the body and improve your dynamic alignment and movement skills through embodied anatomy. Embodiment can be defined as a physical knowing or a felt insight involving changes in perception and body image. You will start with the center of the body, exploring the pelvis, hip joint, and related structures, then move down the leg to the knee and foot. You return to the pelvis to ascend the spine and discuss the body wall, then move out to the shoulders, arms, and hands. You then reach the head and neck and finally embody the rib cage, breath, and organs. Consider these chapters an adventure in body consciousness.

Chapter 10

Pelvis, Hip Joint, and Company

Embodying function improves function.

Let's start in the center of the body, where life itself begins. The pelvis is the hub of the body, a center of stability and originator of motion. It connects the spine to the legs and functions as a masterful force absorber. "Any large action in space necessitates a weight shift of the pelvis." Because of its large mass relative to the rest of the body, pelvic misalignments cause significant reactions up and down the body chain. The pelvis mediates between the legs and the spine, cushioning excess impact from below before it can reach the delicate spinal cord. The strongest muscle in the body, the gluteus maximus, attaches to the pelvis, and many other large muscles either attach or cross through it. Cradled within, you find your deep abdominal organs lending tone and interconnectedness to the pelvis. Much like a slanted bowl of fruit in a Renaissance painter's still life, the hydrostatic and fluid qualities of the organs mesh with the bony, muscular, and ligamentous elements to create a balanced whole.

PELVIC ARCHES

The pelvis, meaning "basin," is composed of two halves, each containing three bones: ilium, pubis, and ischium (plural *ischia*), or sit bones, from the German *Sitzbeine*, which means "bones to sit on." Until the age of three, these three bones are still separate.

Viewed from the front, the pelvis appears to be an arched structure similar to an ancient Roman, Greek, or Chinese bridge. Arched structures are so stable that many ancient examples remain intact today, including two that the Romans built 19 centuries ago to bring water to Segovia, Spain, and Nimes, France. Competitors entered the ancient Olympic Games, chronicled from 776 BC, through a sacred arched entrance that still stands, a true marvel: naked stone touching naked stone without mortar binding the individual pieces together. The blocks are narrower at their lower ends, forming thick wedges similar in shape to the sacrum. If you stand on such an arch, the wedges push harder against their neighboring stones, increasing the stability of the structure. The central stone, called the keystone, seems to hang in midair, buttressed by the equal forces coming from the adjoining stones (figure 10.1). The effect of the buttressing is enhanced by an interplay of many muscular forces, including the transversus abdominis muscle and the pelvic floor. This active compression is called force closure. The other aspect that allows for the sacrum to remain seemingly suspended between the ilia is called form closure, denoting the interlocking shape of the sacroiliac joint, the junction between ilium and sacrum. In females, the joint surface is more apt to allow movement, important during birth; in males, the surfaces interlock to a greater degree.

The pelvis actually contains two arches: a higher main arch in the rear and a second lower arch in the front. The keystone of the posterior arch is the sacrum, which forms the base of the spine. Its smaller counterpart in front is the pubic symphysis (grown together; see figure 10.46). The adjoining "stones" of the symphysis are the pubic rami; *pubes* (strong) refers to the lower torso (figure 10.2).

Strength in the lower-abdominal area is critical for health and efficient body function. Often the posterior arch is overused while the anterior arch, the strong pubic symphysis, is neglected. By widening across the entire front of the pelvis, instead of isolating the action from the hip socket when externally rotating the legs, you spread the front arch, weakening its coherence.

The arcuate line divides the pelvis into a major and minor part. It runs along a line from the anterior sacroiliac joint to the pubic rami. Above this line is the ala, or wings, of the pelvis, and below is the massive body of the ilia, which forms the roof of the hip joint. This is the area where the force from the legs transfers to the pelvis and where the weight of the pelvis rests on the leg. The arcuate line, together with the arch of the sit bones and iliac crests, give the innominate the look of a figure eight.

If you look at a pelvic half from below or above, you will notice that the orientation of the ischial tuberosities and the ilia are in a different plane (figure 10.3). The

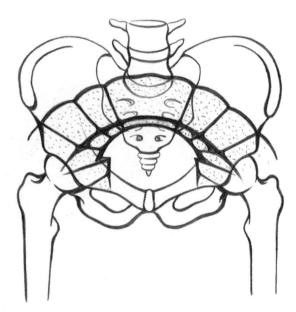

Figure 10.1 The pelvis appears to be an arched structure similar to ancient Roman, Greek, and Chinese bridges.

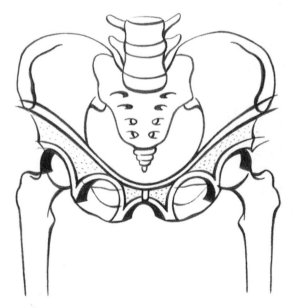

Figure 10.2 The lower arch in front of the pelvis is formed by the pubic bones.

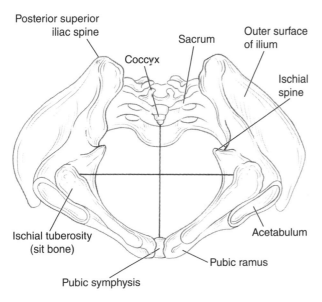

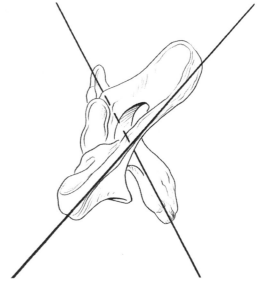

Figure 10.3 Pelvis viewed from below.

Figure 10.4 Orientation of ischia and ilia.

ilia are closer together in back and farther apart in front—in other words, angled outward. The sit bones are farther apart in back and narrower in front—in other words, angled inward (figure 10.4).

If you were to slide your hand over the inner surface of the innominate from top to bottom, you would notice that the motion created is that of an inwardly rotating spiral. The innominate resembles a segment of a spiral (figure 10.5).

Since the pelvic half is also a figure eight (figure 10.6), the combined shapes create a propeller, which is a spiraled figure eight (figure 10.7). Visualizing the design of the pelvis will help you understand the three-dimensional movement of the pelvic halves described later on.

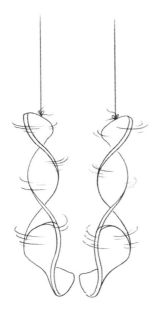

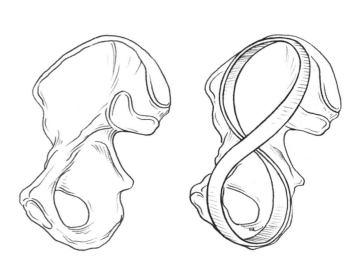

Figure 10.5 The innominate resembles the segment of a spiral, like a spiraled wind chime.

Figure 10.6 The pelvic half resembles a figure eight.

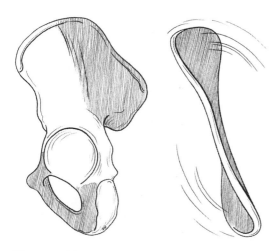

Figure 10.7 Pelvic half resembles a propeller.

If you look at a pelvic half from above, you can also see its archlike design in a variety of dimensions—for example, the inward curve of the ilia and pubic ramus. The sacrum is the keystone of a pelvic arch as seen in the coronal plane, but the hip joint is the keystone of an arch as seen in the horizontosagittal plane.

The trabeculae, structures within bone that transfer the force (internal braces of the bone), reveal the correct path of the weight through the pelvis: from the sacrum to the pubic rami and sit bones, to the dome and central area of the acetabulum (hip socket). This holds true for sitting as well as standing, except that while seated, the force is transferred to the sit bones instead of the hip socket. In sitting, however, there is a tendency to rotate the pelvis posteriorly, thereby rounding the back and putting excessive stress on the back arch and lumbar spine. Allowing weight to travel into the pubic rami invigorates the front arch. Isolating external rotation in the hip sockets allows the pubic arches to direct their force in the opposite direction of the turnout motion toward their keystone.

Imagery Exercises for the Pelvic Arches

1. **Pelvic structures:** The structures of the pelvis that can most easily be contacted are the crests of the ilia. Trace your fingers downward from the lowest ribs to find the iliac crests. The crest itself is arch-shaped and has three lips. The latissimus dorsi, gluteus medius, and external oblique muscles attach to the outermost lip. The internal oblique originates on the central part of the iliac crest; the inner lips are the attachment site of the quadratus lumborum and inferior transversus abdominis. The crests may therefore be sensitive to touch, because you are placing your fingers on a complex area of muscular insertion. Following the arched crest to the front of the body, you reach the anterior superior iliac spines (ASIS). The longest muscle of the body, the sartorius, originates from this bony protuberance. If you glide your fingers down and diagonally toward the front of the pelvis, you arrive at the location of the hip joints, which cannot be directly palpated from above because they are covered by musculature. If, however, you approach the hip joint medially, running your fingers across the pubic rami, you can find the medial rim of the joint. Now move your fingers horizontally toward the center front of the pelvis, where they will encounter the pubic tubercles before meeting above the pubic symphysis.

2. **Imaging balanced muscle slings of the pubic area:** The pubic symphysis has some give; it can move slightly in all directions and acts in conjunction with the iliosacral joint. The pubic rami are fairly active attachment sites for muscles. The rectus abdominis and the internal oblique and transversus abdominis insert above, while the pectineus and adductor longus originate below. The adductor longus tendon is quite prominent and can be easily palpated below the pubic tubercles. These muscle groups relate to each other through the bony bridge of the pubic ramus, forming crossing diagonal slings lining the lower body and upper body. These slings bear importance for the dynamic stabilization of the

pelvis and lower back. To align the body dynamically, imagine balanced slings. Also metaphorically imagine the fan shape of the inner oblique abdominal muscle (figure 10.8; also see figure 12.49).

If you follow the iliac crests to the rear, you encounter the posterior superior iliac spines (PSIS). Below these spines is a shallow depression that is a rough measure for the location of the sacroiliac joint. These are the dimples you can see above the buttocks. The joint is actually situated a bit lateral to the PSIS. Between these points you can feel the small spinous processes of the sacrum. Remember that you are touching through many layers of connective tissue and muscles, the thoracolumbar fascia and multifidi. From there, continue vertically downward, reaching under the buttocks to discover the large bony prominences called the ischial tuberosities, which we call the sit bones. Between the sit bones but slightly higher, you will find the coccyx, commonly known as the tailbone. If you place your thumbs on the iliac crests and reach down the sides of your legs with your fingers, you will find other large bony prominences, the greater trochanters of the femur that sometimes are taken to be part of the pelvis.

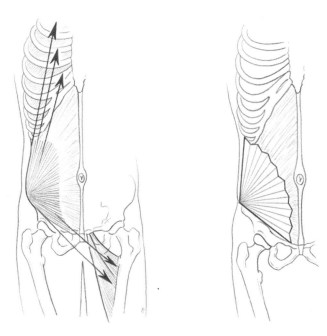

Figure 10.8 Anterior crossed muscle slings and fanlike shape of inner oblique abdominal muscle.

3. **Elastic band buttress (standing, walking):** To experience the effect of the arches on the keystones and force closure, tie an elastic band (a broad rubber band used for conditioning exercises) tightly around your pelvis at the level of the greater trochanters. Both standing and walking, you may notice a lifting sensation through the center of the pelvis as the bracing arches push against their sacral and pubic keystones. If you do this with a partner pushing with his hands, the buttressing person must exert some effort to create the same effect as a band. Tie the band around the top, middle, and lower level of the pelvis and notice where you feel the most supported. This will give you an indication of the bracing effect of your muscles.

BALANCING THE PELVIS

An arch is no better than its foundation; the deeper and more stable the roots of the foundation, the more stable the structure. The choice of materials is the key to success. Where large forces interact, the pelvis is composed of reinforced bone, ligaments, and fascia, whereas other areas are built less solidly. An example is the iliac bone, which is thick and reinforced at its crest and around the hip joint, but its inner portion is thinner. Strong ligamentous ties connect key areas.

The organs are active components in the pelvis. Their weight increases the buttressing effect, making the arches stronger and providing internal hydrostatic support. The organs can also assist in damping forces that are imposed on the pelvis. The water-balloon-like structure of the organs can reduce excess oscillations in conjunction with the fascial system.

If the thrust coming up through the legs is unequal, the keystones will unbalance, causing compensatory strains all the way up the spine. To avoid such imbalances, you need to improve dynamic alignment of the pelvis.

The pelvis can be shifted to the front or back; shifted to the right or left; tilted anteriorly, posteriorly, or laterally; or twisted. In the latter case, the right and the left pelvic halves are not aligned with each other. If the PSIS is higher on the right and the ASIS is higher on the left, the right pelvic half is twisted forward in relation to the left half. Figure 10.9 shows a representation of the twisted pelvis using simple geometric shapes.

Pelvic imbalances can be caused by habitually putting more weight on one leg than the other, which will cause that pelvic half to be pushed upward and rotated posteriorly. Even in a slight imbalance of the bones, the muscular imbalance will become an embedded part of the movement pattern. The sacroiliac joint will not be in an equal position, which may lead to pain and dysfunction. Most people have a preferred standing leg (a leg they prefer to rest body weight on that generally feels more stable) and a gesture leg (the leg they prefer to use when initiating movement in space). This will slowly cause an imbalanced state of the connective tissue and ligaments and inequality in muscular strength. An imbalance can also be caused by unequal leg length.

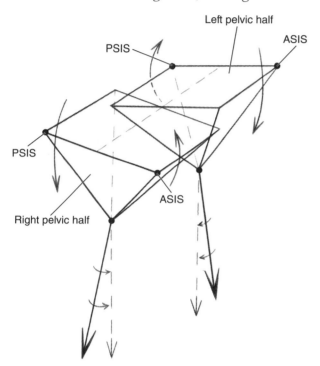

Figure 10.9 Imagine the pelvis to be made of two separate halves in the shape of inverted pyramids.

Imagery Exercises for Balance

1. **Visualizing the pelvic halves:** Make fists with your hands and place them next to each other. Each hand represents a pelvic half. Move your pelvis in accordance with your fists. Remaining side by side, the fists can be shifted forward, backward, or to the right or left or tilted equally forward, backward, or sideways. In the case of the twist, however, one of the fists is rotated forward relative to the other.

2. **Rest toward the pubic symphysis:** Assume a normal standing position and focus on the front of the pelvis. The pubic symphysis is the anterior meeting point of the two pelvic halves. To create a sense of symmetry, feel the two pelvic halves resting against each other at the sacroiliac joint and the pubic symphysis. Perform a variety of movements such as leg lifts and spinal movements while keeping the image of the two pelvic halves resting against each other.

3. **Damping organs:** Perform small hops and imagine how the soft, bouncy weight of the organs reduces perturbations that are happening to the pelvis. The organs are functioning like a gyroscope in a ship to keep the pelvis centered.

4. **Pubic and ischial rami waves:** Imagine the pubic rami and the sit bones as two opposing waves of water clashing against each other. Imagine the energy of the two waves meeting in perfect balance at the pubic symphysis (figure 10.10).

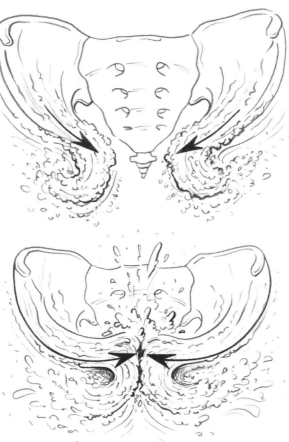

Figure 10.10   Pelvic halves as waves that meet at the pubic symphysis.

5. **Water level (standing position):** Visualize a carpenter's level placed on the top of the iliac crests. Check whether the position of the air bubble in the level is to the left or right of center. Imagine the crests of the ilia leveling off, causing the air bubble to move to center.

6. **Self-check of alignment:** In a standing position, balance your weight equally on both feet. Visualize a horizontal line connecting the ASIS and another horizontal line connecting the hip sockets. The ASIS is fairly easy to palpate at the front of the pelvis. The hip sockets can be visualized behind the midpoint

of the inguinal band, above the sit bones. Notice if these two lines are parallel to each other. Use self-touch to help you feel these points and connect them kinesthetically. If you feel the lines are crooked and not parallel, do not force your pelvis into the right position. The following exercises will start creating more balanced alignment for you.

7. **Buoys floating on water:** Visualize the heads of the femurs as buoys floating on water (see chapter 7, figure 7.6). These buoys support your pelvis. Your legs are the anchor lines, your feet the anchors. Since the water is level, so are the buoys and the pelvis they carry. The pelvis hovers easily suspended on the strong support the buoys provide. If the surface of the water descends (as in bending your legs), the pelvis floats downward equally balanced on both buoys. As the water level rises, the buoys push the pelvis back upward with equal force. If the right side of the pelvis is higher than the left side, visualize the buoy on the left pushing up with increased force, and vice versa. If the pelvis is tilted anteriorly, visualize both buoys pushing up with increased force as your tailbone releases downward.

8. **Sagittal pelvic alignment (standing and walking):** Visualize two spotlights located at the hip sockets. These lights should be directed horizontally to the front. If the lights are shining upward, lower them to horizontal; if they are shining at the floor, raise them to horizontal. The spotlights can be substituted for eyes that are looking forward in a horizontal plane. (This exercise is adapted from Lulu Sweigard.)

9. **Pelvis suspended from axis:** Imagine the pelvis as a bowl. Imagine this bowl hanging from your central axis. Let the rim of the bowl be in the horizontal plane. Bend and stretch your legs and watch the bowl being aligned and suspended from your central axis.

Sit Bones

Prehistoric humans obviously sat on the bottom of the pelvis. Over time, this habit, combined with the pull of the hamstrings on the same spot, produced a significant bulge convenient for sitting—the sit bones. Tribes in New Zealand and Africa naturally sit this way, but people sitting at desks for long periods should learn how to balance on these bones to save their backs and promote breathing and general well-being. A group of people who still spontaneously sit this way are young children (see chapter 6, figure 6.3). The sit bones kept the vital organs of excretion, digestion, and reproduction from being too close to the cold, hard floors of our ancient habitats. Without sit bones, you'd practically be sitting on your bladder.

Padded chairs are a relatively recent phenomenon. On hard surfaces, people were not likely to lean back onto the tailbone (coccyx), as many of us do today when sitting. I once tried sitting on a medieval king's throne for a few minutes and must say that it is one of the fastest ways to appreciate correct sitting alignment on the sit bones.

As mentioned earlier, babies and toddlers sit on their sit bones in perfect alignment, usually until age three, when they may start adopting the postural habits of their not-so-perfect parents. The sit bones can be visualized as miniature legs, their little feet providing an excellent opportunity to learn how to balance the pelvis without creating unnecessary tension farther up along the spine. The sit bones can be likened to the heavy ballast bulbs of sailboats that (one hopes) keep them upright even in the worst of weather. Without its ballast, a sailboat would capsize immediately. The way in which people normally sit affects overall alignment, especially if they spend a lot of time in this position. If the sit bones are pointing downward, the pelvis is perfectly upright and aligned. The fluid concept of a ship's ballast will help you reach this goal in a dynamic, nonrigid fashion.

Activating Your Sit Bones

For the following exercises, choose a chair with a level surface and a height that allows your thighs to be approximately parallel to the floor, creating a 90-degree angle between your thighs and your torso. If the chair slants downward toward the rear, your pelvis will tend to rock backward, making it difficult to sit atop your sit bones.

1. **Visualizing the sit bones (sitting):** Place your hands under your pelvis and feel the weight of the bones on your fingers for a moment. Notice how close together they are. Try to visualize the spatial relationship between the sit bones and the hip sockets, which are only a few inches above. Notice whether you are placing equal weight on both sit bones.

2. **Sit bones as the pelvic base activating musculature of the abdomen, deep pelvis, and pelvic floor (sitting):**

   a. **Rocking sit bones:** Rock forward and backward on your sit bones. Rock very fast and feel the pelvic and abdominal muscles begin to come alive. Slow down until you are barely moving. Finally, sit still and visualize yourself rocking.

   b. **Planting-stick sit bones:** Think of your sit bones as planting sticks. Imagine the sticks pushing into the imaginary soft earth beneath you. Shift your weight back and forth and gently push into the chair with first one and then the other sit bone (planting stick). Notice any differences you feel between the sides.

   c. **Swinging cuckoo-clock weights:** Imagine the sit bones to be the heavy weights that hang from a cuckoo clock. Let them hang down and swing front to back.

   d. **Elevated sit bones:** Repeat the following on both sides. Put your weight on one sit bone and lift the other. Picture the elevated sit bone hanging down like a heavy weight.

   e. **Pelvic floor sit-ups:** Place a smooth ball under the right sit bone or just in front of it. This leaves the left sit bone hanging in space. Lower the left sit bone to the floor and lift it back up again, focusing on the muscles between your sit bones (pelvic floor). Repeat this action about five times and notice the difference between the right and left sides of your body. Repeat on the other side.

   f. **Balancing on balls:** Now place a ball under or just in front of each of your sit bones. Perform small movements with your pelvis and your spine. Rock your pelvis front and back and flex and extend your spine. Stretch your arms up in the air and in a variety of directions. Remove the balls and enjoy balanced sitting posture.

   g. **Melting sit bones:** Imagine your sit bones melting down toward the chair. Flex one leg at the hip socket and lift the knee without lifting your pelvis.

Imagine yourself to be very pliable at the hip joint, perhaps like a folded piece of paper. Repeat several times on both sides.

h. **Dropping head of the femur:** Imagine one sit bone melting down toward the chair while lifting the leg of the same side. Visualize a string attached to one knee and extending vertically upward. Flex at the hip socket and imagine the initiation for the leg lift coming from the string attached to the knee. Visualize the head of the femur centering into the hip socket as the knee rises.

3. **Release tension in the buttocks, lower spine, back of the legs (standing):** Hold your buttocks with both hands and pull them straight up without tilting your pelvis forward. Hold for a minute, then let go slowly. As the buttocks slide down, visualize them and your lower back relaxing.

Sacrum

The sacrum is a three-way transfer point of force wedged between the iliac bones and the spine, a central hub for support and movement. Part of the pelvic girdle and the foundation of the spine, it passes weight from the fifth lumbar vertebra on a slant to the neighboring ilia. Its five fused vertebrae create a solid base for the spine. It is thicker on top than below and has a rather wilted look from the side. At the level of the third sacral vertebrae the sacrum changes direction from a more horizontal orientation above to a more vertical orientation below. The base of the sacrum with the promontory, the top and front edge of the sacrum, seems to be reaching for the center of the body, and your central axis does in fact graze it (figure 10.11, *a* and *c*). This is an important image, because you may initially feel your sacrum to be at the back, but this is true only for the lower part. Lateral to the base of the sacrum are the alae, or wings (see figure 10.11*d*). They can be seen to be widening and reaching for the neighboring ilia. A chimpanzee sacrum is longer and flatter. In the course of evolution, our sacral base moved toward center to form a platform of support underneath the overlying masses of the body. It is always easier to support a weight from underneath than from the side. The curved shape of the sacrum is the initiation of the double-S shape of the spine (figure 10.11*c*). The sacrum supports the lowest intervertebral disc. This fifth lumbar disc resting on the base of the sacrum is a key area for experiencing resilient support. Focusing on this area centers your body; try it while sitting and walking. Improving these fundamental modes of physical existence will go a long way to helping all other movements you perform.

Two large articular facets protrude from the top of the sacrum and connect it to the fifth lumbar vertebra (figure 10.11*b*). They look like large bunny ears and prevent the fifth lumbar vertebra from sliding forward on the promontory. It is interesting that their angle is similar to the diagonal angle of the sit bones, a visual aid that has helped many to embody their sacral facets. The sacrum is somewhat hollow to continue the spinal canal. The dura ends at the level of the second sacral vertebra and nerves exit through eight sacral foramina in the sacrum. Anteriorly to the sacrum you can find the sacral plexus and the rectum. At the apex of the sacrum a small disc forms the connection to the coccyx. On both sides you find the left and right lower edges of the sacrum called cornu, or horns. These can be palpated, as opposed to the anterior aspect of the sacrum, which is helpful when sensing sacral movement.

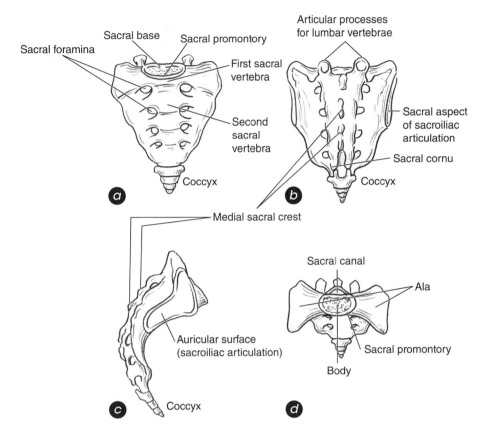

Figure 10.11 Different views of the sacrum: (*a*) anterior, (*b*) posterior, (*c*) lateral, and (*d*) superior.

The sacroiliac joint, formed by the first through third fused sacral vertebrae and the left and right iliac bones (in adults), permits flexion and extension and a slight amount of sliding relative to the iliac bones. This movement is called nutation (figures 10.12*a* and 10.13*a*) and counternutation (figures 10.12*b* and 10.13*b*), derived from the Latin word for nodding.

The range is small, but it is an important movement for force absorption (damping) in the pelvis (about 2 to 3 degrees of rotation and two to four millimeters of translation). In women,

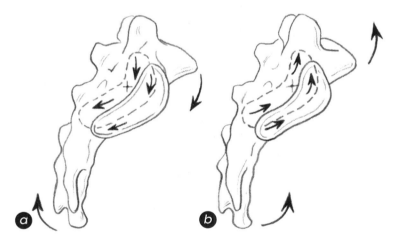

Figure 10.12 (*a*) Movement of sacrum in nutation; (*b*) movement of sacrum in counternutation.

the range is usually larger than in men because of the need for flexibility of the pelvis at birth. The joint is shaped like a boomerang, or C, and the lower part is about one-third longer than the upper, causing the movement to be slightly arc or swinglike. The swing is powered by muscles attaching to the top and back and the bottom of the sacrum. These are the pelvic floor muscles (figure 10.14*a*) and multifidi (figure 10.14*b*), respectively.

In adults, the joint runs from the first to the third sacral vertebrae and is about six to eight centimeters long and two to three centimeters wide. The joint surfaces are

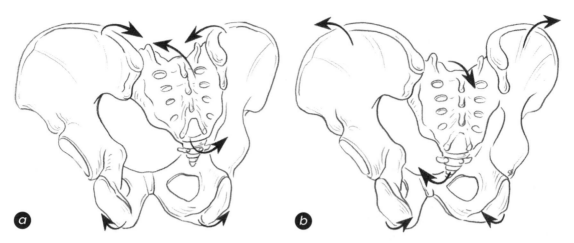

Figure 10.13 (*a*) Nutation and (*b*) counternutation of the sacrum and the movement of the corresponding pelvic halves.

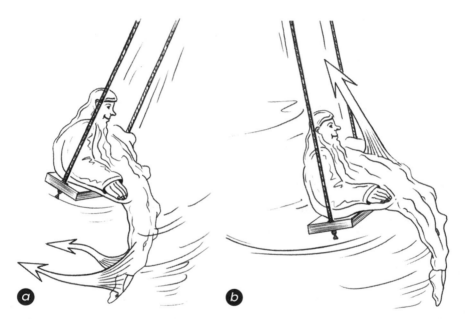

Figure 10.14 Nutation and counternutation as a swinging action of the sacrum (*a*) compelled by the pelvic floor muscles in counternutation; (*b*) compelled by the low back muscles in nutation.

uneven and variable, but the joint is generally a bit wider at the top and narrower at the bottom, creating a somewhat spiraled or propeller-like shape. The sacral surface even has a small socketlike indentation facing a complementary protrusion on the ilium to increase stability and allow for slight rotary movement. The spiraled boomerang is a challenging but rewarding joint to imagine (figure 10.15).

The sacroiliac joint forms a closed kinematic chain with the pubic symphysis, the joint between the two pubic bones. Any motion in the sacroiliac joint is reflected in the pubic symphysis and vice versa. The sacroiliac and pubic symphysis will compensate for lack of hip mobility, differences in leg lengths, and poor postural habits, albeit in potentially detrimental ways. Abnormal pelvic tilting or twisting increases shear stresses at these joints.

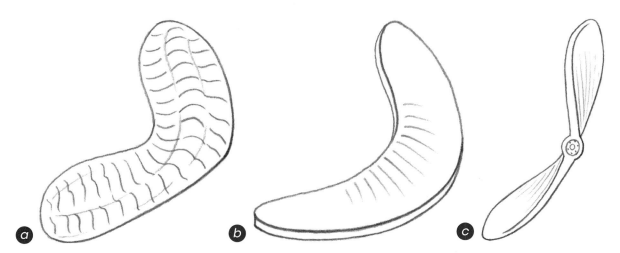

Figure 10.15 The shape of (*a*) the sacroiliac joint is similar to (*b*) a boomerang or (*c*) a propeller.

The weight of the upper body resting on the sacral wedge naturally causes a degree of nutation. If it were not for the strong ligaments counteracting this tendency, the sacrum would simply flop forward and buckle. If you lie on your back, the sacrum will naturally tend to counternutate. Nutation and counternutation should be balanced and not excessive. The ligaments allow the sacrum, pelvis, and legs to function as an integrated arch. The ligaments are key to the self-bracing force-absorbing mechanism of the pelvis (Snijders, Vleeming, and Stoeckart 1993). The ligaments connecting the ilia to the sacrum are the dorsal and ventral iliosacral ligaments and the strong interosseous sacroiliac ligament. The sacrospinal ligament connects the front of the lower sacrum to the ischial spine; the spiraled and triangular sacrotuberous ligament connects the lower part of the sacrum and coccyx to the sit bones. It is also connected to the dorsal sacroiliac ligaments, creating a continuous ligamentous relationship between the PSIS and the sit bones. The biceps femoris, deep gluteus, and deep multifidus have connections into this ligament and create a musculoligamentous relationship from the lower back to the PSIS, sacrum, sit bone, and lower limb. The sacrospinous and sacrotuberous ligaments are important for limiting nutation; the interosseous is the main stabilizer of the joint. Nutation causes the sacrospinous and sacrotuberous ligaments to stretch, whereas the strong interosseous ligament spirals (figure 10.16). What limits counternutation is the long dorsal ligament. Because of its connections to the sacrotuberous ligament and the erector spinae, the long dorsal ligament is a vital point for force transfer between the legs and the spine. Force absorption is assisted by the pelvic floor and anterior longitudinal ligament of the spine (see chapter 12) and the strength of the aforementioned muscles.

By absorbing and storing the incoming forces, the impact on bone, joint, and organs is reduced, creating economy of movement. To better understand this relationship, imagine your arm dropping into an elastic band (figure 10.17*a*). The arm arrives with a certain velocity and has a certain weight that gives it force. The force of your arm is turned into elastic stretch in the band (figure 10.17*b*). The arm is slowed down with the help of the band. To maintain this intelligent design, a co-contraction strategy of holding muscles is not advisable. Lifting your pelvic floor or engaging your gluteus will block force absorption and make you more prone to injury. Co-contraction reduces dynamic stability. This is a logical conclusion, because muscles that are braced are

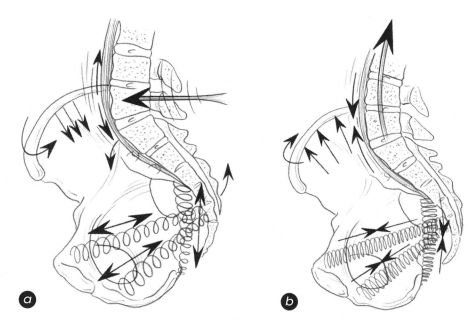

Figure 10.16 Force absorption (damping) by pelvic ligaments, pelvic floor, and anterior longitudinal ligament of the spine. (*a*) In nutation, pelvic ligaments are stretched and lumbar lordosis deepens; (*b*) in counternutation, pelvic ligaments are unloaded and lumbar lordosis lessens.

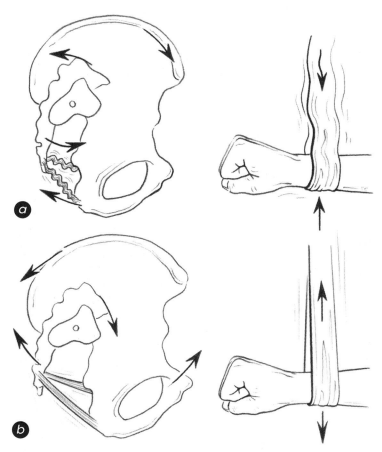

Figure 10.17 Force absorption of sacrotuberous ligaments compared to stretching a band: (*a*) sacrotuberous ligament and band without load; (*b*) ligament and band are loaded.

unable to respond rapidly; they first need to release their holding pattern before they can respond. In dynamic alignment there is no need for bracing. A therapeutic bracing (co-contraction) intervention for the pelvic floor and abdominal muscles may be warranted in case of joint laxity, but it should not become a universal cue for dance or exercise or any type of movement education. In summary, there is no one muscle that holds the key to stability of the pelvis, and too much voluntary activation of the pelvic floor and abdominal muscles is just as problematic as too little. What is needed is balanced and finely tuned control, which can be achieved by increasing proprioceptive and imagery skills.

The dorsal sacroiliac ligament is stretched on counternutation. It is the sole antagonist to the sacrotuberous, sacrospinous, and interosseous ligaments, making the nutated position of the sacrum the safer and more supported one. Counternutating or tucking your sacrum leads to less joint congruity and less ligamentous support.

If you continue the line of the sacrotuberous ligament, you can see that the sit bones, sacrum, and pubic rami act as wheels within the long chain of muscles and ligaments (figure 10.18). The latissimus dorsi relates to the gluteus and biceps femoris through this chain. The gluteus attaches to the whole length of the sacrotuberous ligament connecting the lower back to the iliotibial band. If you continue through the sacrospinous ligament and the fascia of the pelvic floor, you arrive at the pubic symphysis, which in turn leads up the front of the body along the sheath of the rectus abdominis muscle. In this sense the sacrum serves as a hub connecting the upper with the lower and the front with the back of the body.

So far you have evolved the model of the sacrum from a keystone (figure 10.19a) to a vital element in force absorption and dynamic bracing mediated by the ligaments and muscles of the pelvis. The pelvis can be modeled as a tensegrity system (see "Tensegrity" in chapter 2), in which the bones of the pelvis are spacers and the sacrum is merely suspended and not braced between the pelvic bones by myriad tensile ligaments (figure 10.19b).

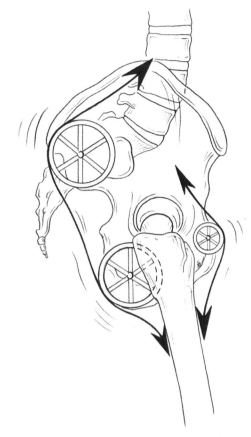

Figure 10.18 Wheels in a chain of muscles and ligaments.

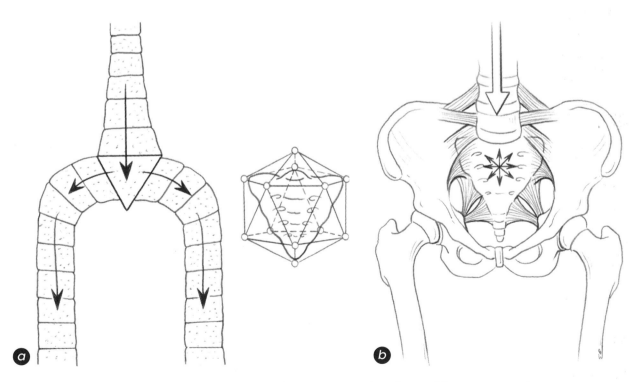

Figure 10.19 (a) Pelvis as a static arch and sacrum as a keystone; (b) sacrum and pelvis as a tensegrity system.

Imagery Exercises for the Sacrum

1. **Experience your weight on the sacral base:** Imagine all the weight of your upper body centering on the sacral base (figure 10.20).

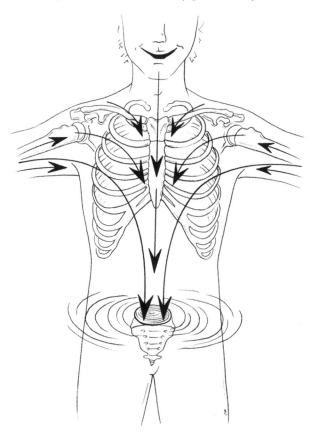

Figure 10.20 Centering your weight on your sacral base.

2. **Path of weight (standing):** Visualize the transfer of weight through the body. The weight of the head transfers to the spine at the atlas, and the weight of the shoulder girdle via the ribs. Then it continues down through the lumbar spine into the sacrum, dividing down into the two ilia, moving forward into the hip joints, down into the legs and feet, and finally to the floor.

3. **Sacral powerhouse:** Visualize the sacrum as the base of the spine, like an inverted pyramid supporting a long, slender column. Imagine the amount of force the sacrum is imparting on the spine. The whole weight of the head, shoulders, torso, and associated organs is resting on the sacrum. Imagine the sacrum impelling the spine from below as if it were a booster rocket. Familiarize your mind with the idea that the sacrum is the first spinal curve creating the wave form of the spine from underneath.

4. **Touching the ligaments:** Touch your PSIS. If it is difficult to locate, note that it lies underneath the top edge of the gluteus maximus muscle. If you rub the area just below the PSIS, you may be able to feel the dorsal sacroiliac ligament. Notice whether they feel the same on the right and the left. If you touch the lower right and left corners of the sacrum (cornu), you will be near the sacrotuberous ligament located beneath the gluteus maximus. Run your fingers between this

point and the sit bone to aid in creating a kinesthetic sense of this ligament. Notice how touching and imagining the ligaments positively affect your pelvic alignment.

5. **Tripod and hub for movement:** The sacral base with the fifth lumbar vertebra (L5) intervertebral disc and the two largest facet joints of the spine are a central area for support and movement. Practice initiating movement from this area and notice how your weight is dynamically supported and guided by the tripod formed by the center of the disc and the two facet joints. Find your sense of support in this area and you will increase your flexible control of the whole body.

6. **Sacral nutation:** Lean forward from your hip joints. This will help move the gluteus maximus muscle away from the sit bone area. Now you can more readily touch your tailbone. Move your fingers slightly to the side and push the fingertips upward, where you will feel the two lower edges of the sacrum. Come back to the upright position and keep your fingers in place as well as you can. As you bend your legs, you will notice that this edge will move back toward your fingers as the sacrum nutates. As you stretch your legs, this edge will seem to vanish forward and upward as the sacrum counternutates. Repeat the flexing and extending of the legs while feeling and visualizing the movement of the sacrum until it becomes clear in your mind's eye: down and back on hip joint flexion, up and forward on hip extension. Remove your hands and shake them a bit to release residual tension. Take a moment to notice the relationship between hip flexion and nutation. Hip flexion and sacral nutation are closely related. It may also be easier to feel your weight supported on the hip joints in the nutated position. When you counternutate by posteriorly rotating the pelvis, it may feel as if your weight is resting more on your lumbar spine and discs. This is why a sense of nutation often makes it easier to balance on your legs.

7. **Sacral nutation through tailbone:** If you cannot find your lower sacral corners, you can also sense nutation via the tailbone. It is not as accurate, because there is a joint between the coccyx and the sacrum, but it generally reflects the movement of the sacrum. Touch the tailbone from underneath, and as you bend your legs you will feel it swing to the rear. The sacrum is now nutating (flexing). As you stretch your legs, you will feel it swing forward again; the sacrum is now counternutating (extending). Repeat the action several times until it becomes clearer in your mind's eye. Notice that if you grip the tailbone, you will not be able to nutate your hip joints properly. This problem may arise in postural instructions that focus on placing the pelvis in the correct position or holding muscles to position the pelvis. You lose hip flexion and force absorption.

8. **Rotate and swing the sacrum:** Place your flat hands on top of each other in front of you in a position that resembles the angle of the upper part of the sacrum (about 45 degrees). As you bend your legs and imagine that the sacrum is nutating, move your hands to demonstrate this action. This will allow you to see the movement as you feel it in your body. You may add self-talk to aid the embodiment: *Sacrum down and back* in nutation, and *Sacrum up and forward* in counternutation. Now compare the following two images: Imagine the sacrum rotating around a fixed axis as you flex your legs and extend your legs. Then try the version with a sense of swing. The sacrum is sliding down the more vertical aspect of the joint surface and then back along the more horizontal part as you flex your legs. As you extend, the sacrum slides forward along the horizontal part and up the more vertical part. You may notice that the swing version may increase your ease and range of hip flexion.

9. **Relative movement of the pelvic half:** If the sacrum moves downward, the pelvic half is relatively moving in the opposite direction (figure 10.21*a*). Were the two joint surfaces to move in the same direction, there would be no movement in the joint. For movement to exist, the adjacent bones must move relatively in opposite directions. Imagining this opposition in the sacroiliac joint (SIJ) very much improves the ability to nutate and counternutate the sacrum. As you flex your legs, imagine the pelvic halves rotating posteriorly on the sacrum. As you stretch your legs, imagine the pelvic halves rotating forward on the sacrum (figure 10.21*b*). Imagine the movement to be equal on both sides.

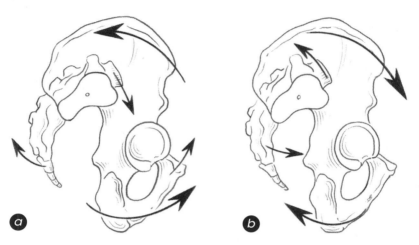

Figure 10.21 Relative movement of the pelvic halves. (*a*) In sacral nutation, the pelvic halves rotate posteriorly (counternutate); (*b*) in sacral counternutation, the pelvic halves rotate anteriorly (nutate).

10. **Innominate and sacral pendulum:** Another way to embody the countering action of the pelvic half and sacrum is to provide them with imaginary pendulums. As you bend your legs and specifically flex your hip joints, imagine the pendulum attached to the sacrum swinging back as the pendulum attached to the innominate swings forward (figure 10.22*a*). When you extend

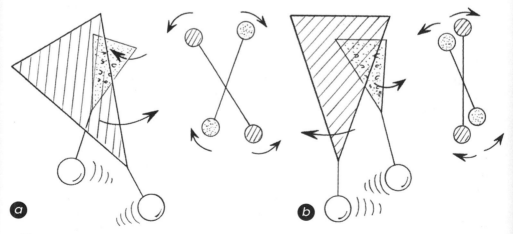

Figure 10.22 Sacrum and innominate as pendulums. (*a*) Sacrum nutates, pelvic half counternutates, sit bone and tailbone pendulums swing apart; (*b*) sacrum counternutates, pelvic half nutates, sit bone and tailbone pendulums swing together.

your leg joints, imagine the pendulum attached to the sacrum swinging forward while the pendulum attached to the innominate swings backward (figure 10.22*b*). Imagine the movement of the pendulums to be balancing each other perfectly. Notice your pelvic posture after this embodiment. Your pelvis may feel effortlessly aligned and centered.

11. **Release your tailbone to stand on heads of the femur:** If you release all tension around the tailbone, you will sense that your weight is more clearly balanced on the heads of the femur. Your shoulders will relax because of the improved pelvic stability.

12. **Sacrum as a Japanese fan (supine):** Imagine the sacrum to be a Japanese fan. As the fan opens and widens, the creases of the fan spread and flatten. As the fan spreads apart, the tail of the fan, the coccyx, also drops down (figure 10.23). (Adapted from André Bernard.)

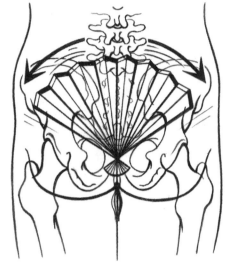

Figure 10.23 The sacrum as a Japanese fan.

13. **Sacrum as the body of an eagle:** Imagine the sacrum to be the body of an eagle and the ilia to be its wings. Feel the strong yet movable connections between the body of the eagle and the wings. Imagine the bird slowly moving its wings. Notice how this affects the pelvis and the entire body (figure 10.24).

Figure 10.24 The sacrum as the body of an eagle and the ilia as its wings.

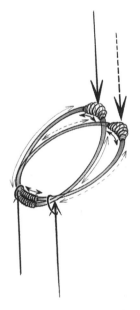

Figure 10.25 Imagine the closed kinematic chain of the pelvic girdle as a circular hoop with two openings for the sacrum and the pubic symphysis.

14. **Pelvic circle (standing, walking, jumping):** Visualize the closed kinematic chain of the pelvic girdle as a circular hoop with two openings for the sacrum and the pubic symphysis. Imagine that these openings contain elastic springs that are able to balance the forces traveling through the circle. If the spring in the rear expands, the one in front compresses and vice versa. The hoop attaches to the legs in front, creating resilient support for the spine in back (figure 10.25).

15. **Suspended sacrum:** Imagine the sacrum suspended from the base of the skull by two elastic bands. Feel the sacrum dangling in the pelvis as it relates to its attachment sites at the base of the skull (occipital condyles). Notice the changes in pelvic alignment resulting from this image.

16. **Refer to center:** As you lift one leg, imagine the weight of the limb traveling through the hip joint and pelvic half and resting on the sacral base. This will allow you to control your movement from a more central place and improve your balance. If you think of lifting the thigh, you will generally use more muscular effort than if you imagine a more central support of the limb.

17. **Sacral spring:** Imagine the sacrum compelling the lumbar spine with a sense of bounciness (figure 10.26). In nutation, the spine lands on the sacrum like a ball. In counternutation, the spine is compelled upward like a ball being tossed from underneath.

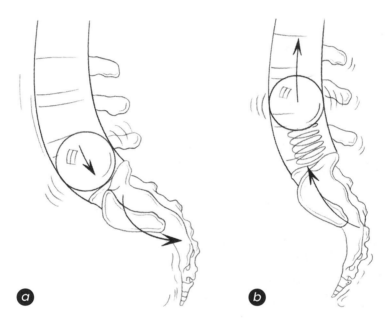

Figure 10.26   Bouncing ball on sacrum: (*a*) nutation, (*b*) counternutation.

18. **Lock and key of the joints:** As the sacrum nutates and moves down and back, imagine it coming to rest with a perfect fit in the opposing joint surface of the innominate bones. Use the image of a key fitting perfectly into a lock to create this feeling of locking into congruence. Sense the sacrum resting against the innominate equally on both sides. Visualize the precise shape, the boomerang-propeller shape of the sacroiliac articulation, for even better control.

19. **Nerve tracts in sacrum:** Feel the nerves slide in the sacrum as the sacrum nutates and counternutates. Feel the nerves initiating nutation. Feel the shape of the spine, the spinal curves existing in the nervous tracts. Feel the cord sliding in the spinal cord as you move.

20. **Buoy base for spine:** Imagine the sacrum to be a buoy in water and being a very resilient and elastic base for the spine.

Imagery Exercises in the Constructive Rest Position (CRP)

The following exercise should be performed in the constructive rest position, as described in chapter 6.

Imagine the shape of the sacrum lodged between the ilia. In your mind's eye, you will be working on creating motion between the ilia and the sacrum. Visualize the sacrum dropping toward the floor; think of it as being heavy. You may want to add an auditory component and imagine hearing it plunk on the floor or hearing it splash as you think of it falling into water. Notice that you are creating motion between the sacrum and the ilia and that there is space between these bones. This image is greatly enhanced by the simultaneous or alternative visualization of the tailbone lengthening downward (see the discussion on the spine in chapter 12).

Coccyx

The coccyx consists of four vertebral remnants attached to the lower end of the sacrum. These remnants form the very end of the spine, composing the vestigial tail. Some animals use the tail as a third leg to improve their balance; others use it to lower their center of gravity (COG), such as when perched on a branch. Several primate species use the tail in swinging from branch to branch. In this case, the tail has prehensile (grasping) qualities similar to those of a hand. In figure 10.27, the lioness is making a right turn (from her point of view). In a sharp turn to the right, the tail stretches and points to the right, shifting the COG toward the inside of the curve and helping the animal change direction. The tail is especially valuable during very fast and very slow movements.

Figure 10.27 Lions and other cats use their tails as a balancing device when running at top speeds.

Imagery Exercises for the Coccyx

1. **Dinosaur tail (standing):** Imagine your tail extending to the floor and becoming strong, like that of a dinosaur or a kangaroo. Use this tail as a third, supporting leg. Imagine your weight balanced equally on your two actual legs and your third tail-leg (figure 10.28). (Exercise adapted from Mabel Todd.)

2. **Trailing your tail (walking):** As you walk, imagine your tail trailing on the floor behind you. (Adapted from André Bernard.)

3. **Tripod:** Imagine you are a standing on a tripod. The legs of the tripod are your legs plus your tail extended downward to the floor. Put equal weight on all points of the tripod and experience their balanced support.

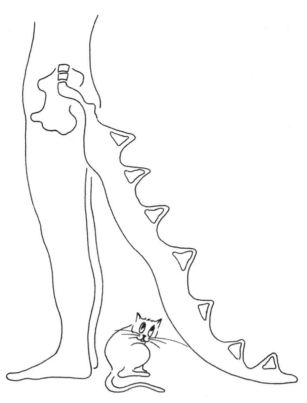

Figure 10.28 Imagine your tail extends to the floor and becomes a strong support, like that of a dinosaur or a kangaroo.

4. **Initiating movement from the coccyx (improvisation):** The coccyx leads you into movement, pulling your whole body with it as it reaches into space.

5. **Head and tail connection:**

   a. **Head and tail initiation (improvisation):** Alternate between initiating movement from your tail and initiating movement from the top of your head.

   b. **Head and tail unified:** Practice initiation from the tail and the head simultaneously to create unified motion of the spine. Remember that the tail forms one corner of the pelvic floor and use the unified feeling of the tail, pelvic floor, and head to stand up and sit down effortlessly. Let the unified spine create powerful movement through space while your legs float effortlessly beneath you.

6. **Tail rudder (walking, improvisation):** Imagine the sacrum to be a ship's stern and the coccyx to be the ship's rudder (figure 10.29). The tail-rudder determines your direction in space. As you move forward, initiate a turn to the right by moving your tail to the right. Initiate a turn to the left by turning your tail to the left. Visualize the whirls and eddies created by the rudder's action. Try turning to the right as the rudder turns to the left. How does this feel?

7. **Primate grasp (supine):** Visualize your tail lengthening and extending toward your feet. Imagine it reaching up and grabbing on to a strong branch so that your body now hangs from your tail. Enjoy the feeling as your entire spine slowly stretches. Swing your body back and forth as you hang from your tail (figure 10.30).

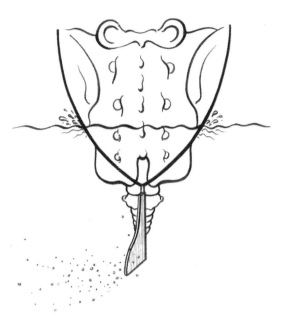

Figure 10.29 The sacrum is the ship's stern and the coccyx is the ship's rudder.

Figure 10.30 Imagine your tail reaching up and grabbing on to a strong branch so that your body now hangs from your tail.

8. **Tail and shoulders:** The sacrococcygeal joint is a small but important planar joint. When this joint is relaxed, when you feel the joint and the whole area as spacious, you may notice your spine lengthening and the shoulders relaxing.

9. **Tail spinal rotation:** Imagine the coccyx as you rotate the spine. If you rotate your spine to the right, think of the coccyx rotating to the opposite side to create core stability. If you rotate your spine to the left, think of your coccyx rotating to the right. You may notice that it is easier to balance (on one leg) and rotate the spine if you imagine the counterrotation of the coccyx.

10. **Tail and spinal flexion:** When you flex your head, it is easier to imagine the tail flexing as well. When you extend your head, it is easier to imagine the tail extending.

11. **Tail lengthening:** Visualize the coccyx as a coiled spring. As you flex your legs, think of the coccyx lengthening. As you extend your legs, think of the coccyx coiling up again.

12. **Tail creasing:** Imagine the joint between the coccyx and the sacrum, the sacrococcygeal articulation. Allow this joint to be very creasable and moveable, reminding you of the foldability of the hip joint. As you flex your lower limbs, causing the sacrum to nutate, imagine this joint flexing so that the tail swings forward as the lower sacrum moves backward. As you extend your lower limbs, imagine this joint to be extending as the lower sacrum moves forward and the tail swings back.

13. **Tail and hip flexion:** The coccyx can be visualized as a spinning top being compelled by a string (figure 10.31). The strings are the pelvic floor muscles attaching to the coccyx. When you flex your right hip joint by lifting that leg, the coccyx is pulled forward by the right pelvic floor muscles (coccygeus, pubococcygeus), rotating it to the left. When you flex your left hip joint, the coccyx is pulled forward by the left pelvic floor muscles and is rotated to the right.

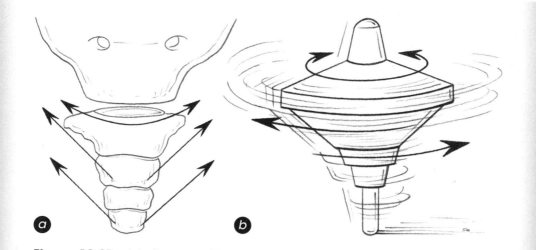

Figure 10.31   (*a*) Coccyx with muscle attachments; (*b*) tail rotating like a spinning top.

MOTION OF THE PELVIC HALVES

The sacrum and innominates, consisting of the ilium, pubic bone, and sit bone, which I shall refer to as pelvic halves, are slightly mobile in humans but not so in a quadruped (four-legged animal). This is due to the movement that is possible in the sacroiliac joint (SIJ) and pubic symphysis, as we have seen previously. There are three fundamental reasons for this with great relevance to human alignment: birth, gait, and force absorption.

First, birth. At birth, the baby's head is about the size of the birth canal, making birthing in humans a challenge at times (figure 10.32). To ease the passage, especially of the baby's head, the bones of the pelvis must allow some motion. In birth, the sacrum nutates, the sit bones widen, and the coccyx moves to the rear. Hip flexion enhances this movement, as midwives know. Giving birth in a crouched or four-legged position aids the birthing process by widening the canal; lying on the back, which counternutates the sacrum, does not. Most likely the male pelvis shares some of this adaptation and has some give, but in general less so than in a woman. This comes in handy when going to the toilet, as you know. If you have ever visited a toilet in southern Europe, you may need to practice your deep crouch and flexibility of the pelvic floor. These toilets have no toilet bowl and require much stability in the pelvic floor and leg strength to reach the target opening located on the floor level, but it is advantageous for healthy evacuation. In humans, hip flexion and a widening of the pelvic outlet are biomechanically coupled motions with major consequences for the training of the pelvic joints and muscles and dynamic alignment.

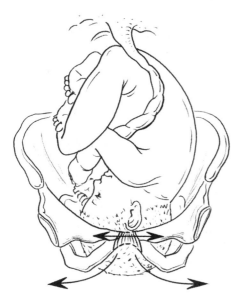

Figure 10.32   The positioning of a baby in the female pelvis.

The second reason is gait. When you walk, the legs are moving in opposition. One leg swings forward, and the stance leg moves back. Because your legs are attached to the pelvis, they impose a twisting force on the pelvis. One innominate rotates forward while the other is rotated backward. This requires some give in the transverse plane of the pelvis, which is afforded by the SIJ. If you did not have this joint, walking would be a rather stiff affair, as you sometimes see in the elderly, whose joints are sometimes frozen. The pelvis can be likened to a twisting plate in walking as seen from above (figure 10.33). The SIJ are the points where the plate is redirected into a differing angle to afford the movement of the swinging legs.

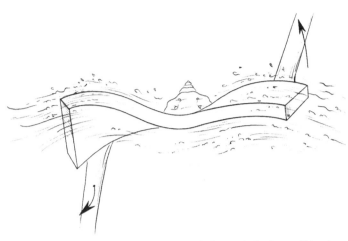

Figure 10.33 The pelvis as a twisting plate in walking as seen from above, with one leg forward and one leg back.

The third reason is force absorption or dynamic bracing, as discussed previously: The pelvis receives large forces with varying velocities from above and below. To maintain safety and efficiency, these kinetic forces need to be absorbed or dissipated but ideally retained to aid in the production of movements that may follow. In mechanics, devices that fulfill this role are called dampers. The human pelvis dampens by turning the kinetic movement imparted to it by the legs and spine into stretch in the muscles, connective tissue, and ligaments. The aponeurosis and the muscles of the sole of the feet act similarly as dampers (figure 10.34).

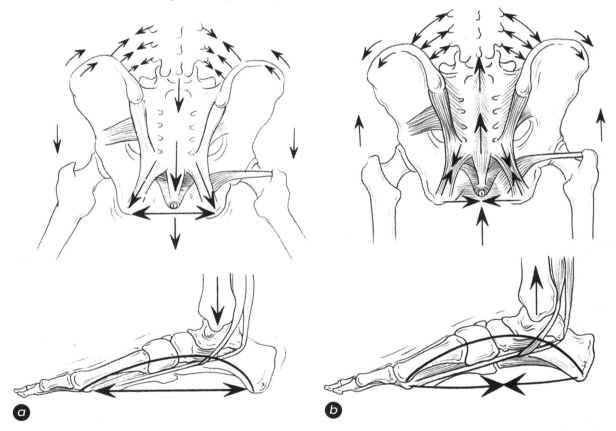

Figure 10.34 Pelvis and feet as force absorbers. (*a*) Foot and pelvis loaded, ligaments stretched; (*b*) foot and pelvis unloaded, ligaments released.

Postural education should enhance force absorption to increase the safety of movement. The pelvic halves move three-dimensionally during nutation and counternutation. This enhances their ability to dissipate forces (see figure 10.13). The movement is a combination of internal rotation and inflare (iliac crests moving inward) during sacral nutation. The movements of the pelvic half are also named nutation and counternutation. In innominate nutation, the pelvic half rotates anteriorly; during innominate counternutation, the pelvic half rotates posteriorly.

The nutating sacrum tends to wedge apart the pelvic halves, especially in the inferior pelvis where it is most needed for birthing and force absorption. The sacroiliac joint is shaped like a C when observed from a lateral view, but following the joint contours reveals a double-wedge configuration reminiscent of a propeller. As the whole sacrum wedges downward in nutation, the upper part of the propeller blade moves forward as the lower part moves back, causing the inferior pelvic halves to be moved sideways as if compelling wind or water (figure 10.35). This causes the forces arriving at the sacrum to be dissipated into stretch in the iliosacral and sacrotuberous ligaments as well as the pelvic floor.

In addition, the bracing effect of the transversus abdominis (TA) and internal oblique muscles comes into play as the ilia inflare and internally rotate. The inferior part of the TA originates from the adjacent inner lip of the iliac crest and runs to the connective-tissue invagination (inward fold) surrounding the rectus abdominis. The nutated position of the sacrum is the better fit (also called closed-pack position) in the SIJ, and most of the ligaments are taut as you flex your hip joints or crouch when you land from a jump, lift a heavy object, or brace for impact. All systems are now working together to absorb force efficiently and safely. If you can imagine this complex but wonderful design in action, it will revolutionize your movement efficiency and create effortless alignment in all movement situations.

The sacrum is tied to the pelvic halves by myriad ligaments, and any movement of the sacrum compels the innominates through these relationships. As the sacrum

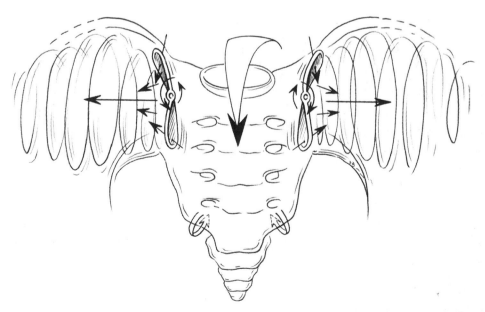

Figure 10.35 Sacroiliac propellers wedge apart the inferior pelvic half during nutation of the sacrum.

moves down and back in nutation, the anterior and posterior iliosacral ligaments pull the ilia inward as the inferior pelvis and sit bones move outward (figure 10.36). The sacrum nutates, the ilia inflare, and the sit bones outflare. When the sacrum counternutates, the sequence reverses: The ilia outflare and the sit bones inflare.

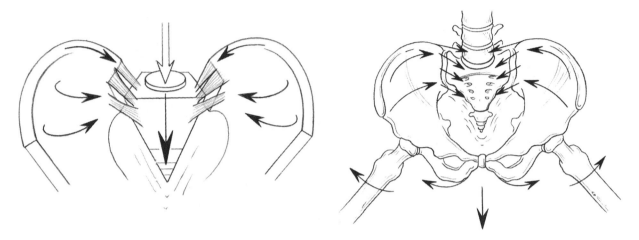

Figure 10.36 Sacroiliac ligaments inflaring the iliac bones and outflaring the sit bones.

Inflare, in a strict sense, is a movement of the pelvic half in the frontal plane around a sagittal axis. But inflare is also coupled with a rotation of the pelvic halves in the horizontal plane. According to Kapandji (1986), this coupled motion happens along an axis running from the SIJ to the pubic symphysis (figure 10.37). The axis is certainly variable, but for imagining the coupled motion, this axis serves as a useful guideline.

The third dimension of movement is the sagittal plane. Even though the movements do not happen in isolation, it is useful to begin your appreciation of pelvic movement by visualizing them as

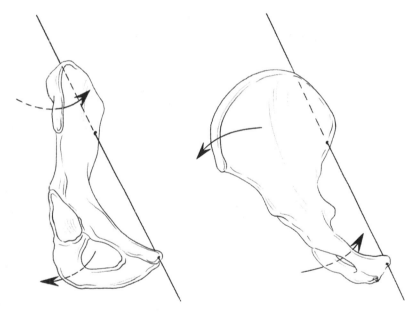

Figure 10.37 Axis for motion (inflare and rotation) of the pelvic half (anterior view).

separate actions (figure 10.38). In the standing position with feet on the floor, the movement of the pelvic halves in the sagittal plane happens only relative to the sacrum.

When you flex your hip joints (bend your legs) in the standing position, your pelvic halves are moving three-dimensionally. Specifically, they do the following:

- Inflare in the frontal plane
- Internally rotate in the horizontal plane
- Posteriorly rotate relative to the sacrum

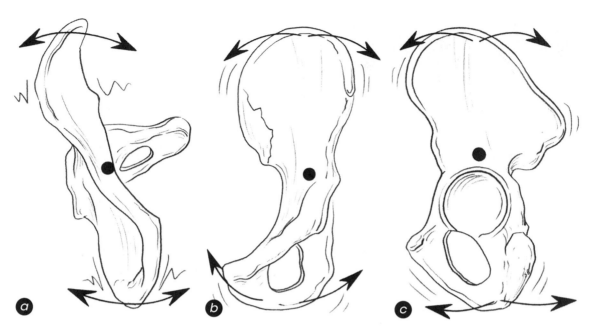

Figure 10.38 Triplanar rotation of the pelvic halves with axes: (*a*) horizontal plane, vertical axis; (*b*) coronal plane, sagittal axis; (*c*) sagittal plane, transverse axis.

When you extend your hip joints (stretch your legs), the pelvic halves do the following:

◆ Outflare in the frontal plane

◆ Externally rotate in the horizontal plane

◆ Anteriorly rotate relative to the sacrum

Imagery Exercises for the Innominates

1. **Widening and narrowing of pelvis:** Stand in a comfortable position and place your hands in front of you to model the movement of the pelvis. As you bend your legs, move your hands apart and self-talk: *Pelvis widens.* As you stretch your legs, move your hands together and self-talk: *Pelvis narrows.*

2. **Movement of sit bones:** Touch your sit bones. As you bend your legs, notice how they move apart and the pelvic floor stretches. As you extend your legs, notice how the sit bones move together and the pelvic floor narrows. If, however, you have been taught to tuck your pelvis for "good posture," you may not feel this at all; you may be doing the opposite as a result of years of practice. In this case, I suggest reviewing the evolutionary and biomechanical logic of movement of the pelvic half and sacrum to begin a new era of pelvic alignment with good force absorption, which is so important for joint health.

3. **Movement of pelvic half, sensing the sit bones:** Place one finger on your ASIS and another finger on the sit bone of the same side. Then shift your weight to that leg. As you bend the leg of that side, you may notice the sit bone moving laterally. As you stretch your leg, you may notice the sit bone moving medially. Repeat this action several times. Also try the reverse: Do not let the sit bone move as you bend your legs. You will notice that you will compensate for a lack of hip flexion by shifting your knee medially (adducting) and flexing your lumbar spine. Then return to the correct imagery and movement. After about

10 repetitions, compare the action of the two legs: Swing your right and left legs forward and notice the flexibility of your hamstrings. Notice how stable you feel on either leg and compare the ease of jumping on either leg. Repeat the exercise on the other leg.

4. **Imaging pelvic half rotation:** Touch the ASIS and sit bone of the same side. Visualize the pelvic half as a spiral or propeller between your points of touch. As you bend your legs, imagine the pelvic half rotating inward; as you stretch your legs, imagine the pelvic half rotating outward. Repeat seven times, then practice the same on the other side.

5. **Combining pelvic halves:** Bend and stretch your legs and imagine the movement of the pelvic half in the horizontal plane. As you flex, imagine internal rotation, and as you extend, imagine external rotation. Use your hands to model the action of the pelvic halves. Place your hands on the back of your pelvis. Slide your hands out to the side and inward along the front of the pelvis as you bend your legs and self-talk: *Widen in back, narrow in front.* As you stretch your legs, slide your hands in the opposite direction. Out in front and together in back: *Wide in front, narrow in back.* Repeat seven times or until you can feel and see the movement.

6. **Inflare and outflare:** Place your thumbs on the outside of the iliac crests and loop the tip of your second finger around the ASIS. As you bend your legs, push the crests inward; as you stretch your legs, pull them sideways with the help of your finger grasping the ASIS. Notice how your pelvis feels to be narrowing on hip flexion and widening on hip extension. Repeat the action several times.

7. **Inflare and outflare with abduction:** Place your thumbs on the outside of the iliac crests and loop your second finger around the ASIS. Abduct your right leg and notice how the ilia of the right side inflares (figure 10.39*a*). Adduct the leg and notice how it outflares (figure 10.39*b*). Repeat the exercise on the other leg to familiarize yourself with action of movement of the pelvic half in the frontal plane.

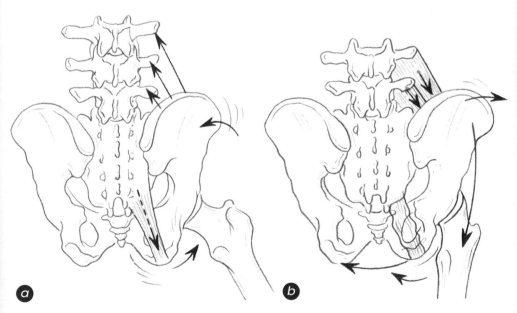

Figure 10.39 (*a*) Inflare and (*b*) outflare in abduction and adduction with sacrotuberous ligament and quadratus lumborum.

8. **Sacrum and flaring:** Visualize the movement of the sacrum in combination with the flaring of the pelvis. As you flex your legs, the sacrum moves down, the ilia inflare, and the sit bones outflare. As you stretch your legs, the sacrum counternutates, the ilia outflare, and the sit bones inflare.

9. **Flower opening:** Repeat the previous action using imagery. Imagine the ilia to be the petals of a flower. As you stretch your legs, imagine the flower petals opening up. As you bend your legs, imagine the flower petals folding together.

10. **Pelvic halves as springs:** Imagine the pelvic halves to be coiled springs (figure 10.40). The sacrum is supported on both sides by these springs. As you bend and stretch your legs or jump, imagine the sacrum rebounding on elastic springy pelvic halves.

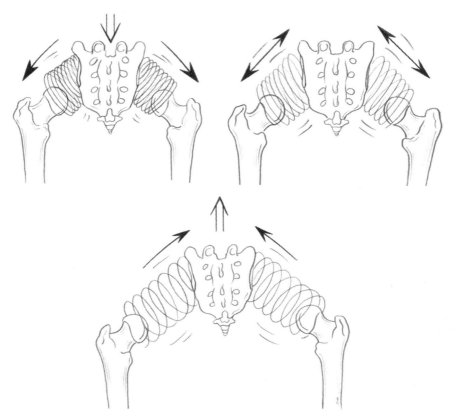

Figure 10.40   Pelvic halves as coiled springs.

11. **Balancing the pelvic halves:** In the standing position, imagine the pelvis to be made of two separate halves in the shape of inverted pyramids. Your sit bones are the points of the pyramids. Shoot a beam of light out of both points. You may find that the beams are pointing in different directions. Ideally, both beams should point vertically downward. Watch the beams adjust until they are both in the same frontal plane. If the beams won't adjust in your imagination, don't force them to. Notice the difference between the beams, and try the exercise again after you have gained more experience working with the pelvis (see figure 10.9).

12. **Beams of light:** As you bend your legs, imagine the beams of light shooting out of the sit bones moving laterally; as you stretch your legs, imagine the beams of light shooting out of your sit bones moving medially.

COUNTERROTATION AND THREE-DIMENSIONAL ALIGNMENT

The femur's display of so-called automatic rotation when you flex and extend was discovered by a German anatomist Meyer (1853). *Automatic* means that it happens without any conscious or voluntary contribution. As you bend your knee, the femur rotates laterally and the tibia medially. When you stretch your knee, the movement reverses and the femur rotates medially and the tibia laterally. Automatic rotation is about 5 degrees of motion, and your proprioceptive system can sense 1/8 of a degree and even less. The shape of the femoral condyles, the cruciates, and the collateral ligaments of the knee drive automatic rotation. When you compare the movement of the femur to the pelvic halves, you notice that they are going in opposite directions. When you bend your legs, the ilia inflare and the pelvic halves rotate inward (figure 10.41), and the femur rotates laterally. As you stretch your legs, the ilia outflare (externally rotate), whereas the femur rotates medially.

The tibia is moving in opposition to the femur and similarly to the pelvic half. If you consider the pelvic half the top of the leg bones and the foot the base of a four-tiered mobile pillar, then segments of the leg counterrotate in flexion and extension (figure 10.42).

What is the purpose of this movement? When you bend and stretch the legs, what you tend to see is that the knees move forward and the pelvis down, but counterrotation is happening as well. There are two fundamental reasons for counterrotation. The first relates to walking efficiency. Humans walk with fairly straightened knees compared to quadrupeds, who locomote with their knees flexed. In humans, the pelvis coasts over the stance leg as if it were a strut or a beam.

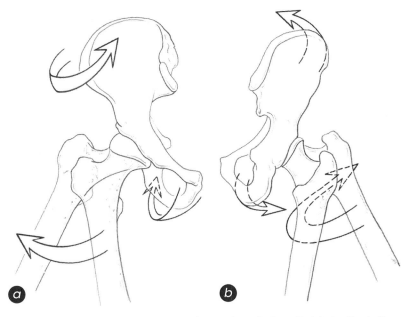

Figure 10.41 Pelvic and femoral counterrotation. Pelvic half rotating inward, femur outward: (*a*) anterior view; (*b*) posterior view.

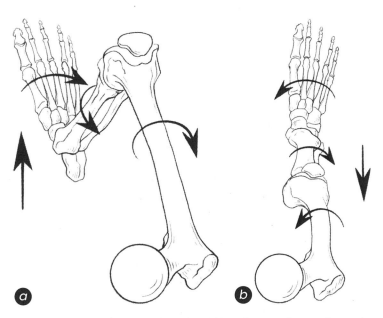

Figure 10.42 Counterrotation of leg bones from above in the right leg. (*a*) Leg in flexion: femur rotates outward, lower leg in, foot relatively out. (*b*) Leg in extension: femur rotates inward, lower leg outward, foot relatively inward.

Figure 10.43 Knee condyles braking like skis.

The action resembles pole vaulting or a gondola in Venice being propelled by a long beam. This saves a lot of energy. If the knee were bent and the heel lifted as with a dog, you would need to engage the quadriceps and hamstring muscles a lot more than you do now. The advantage of a quadruped is that it has four legs connected by a flexible rod, the spine, which greatly increases speed. You can't outrun a cat. However, the human legs exquisitely balance force absorption and a more rigid strut phase in walking to create optimal efficiency.

Another advantage of counterrotation is force absorption and force generation. Efficiency means a high energy-to-output ratio. The human musculoskeletal system engages all three dimensions for this purpose. When you bend your knee as you land from a jump, the knee is not just moving forward; it is also rotating to add another dimension to force absorption. Imagine you are on skis speeding down the slope and need to stop suddenly. You rotate your skis into a lateral position to brake your momentum (figure 10.43). Your knees stay aligned because the tibial plateau is moving exactly in opposition to the femur condyles. The ski slope is moving equal and opposite to you, making it look as if you are staying in place. In good alignment, all counterrotation is balanced.

The knee slows the downward momentum by moving in an arc. The same holds true for force generation. Femoral rotation provides more force than if just one dimension were available. Just think of a baseball pitcher throwing a ball. He uses all three dimensions—sagittal, horizontal, and coronal—to produce force on the ball.

In standing hip flexion, the innominate is therefore moving in opposition to both the femur and the sacrum (figure 10.44).

The traditional way of teaching alignment is to focus on bony landmarks that need to remain in a line or in a certain fixed configuration. However, these landmarks are moving relative to each other as you bend and stretch the legs. Alignment with force absorption is compatible, but it requires a dynamically mobile concept of alignment. The line of gravity through the leg stays aligned while bony landmarks are shifting. Trying to maintain bony points in a fixed position will actually block movement rather than enhance it. In educating dynamic alignment and stability, the problem is often psychological. If you have been taught the positional model of alignment and static stability concepts, it may at first be challenging to grasp these concepts at the outset. But it cannot be denied that the dynamic nature of human alignment is based on maximal efficiency through three-dimensional force absorption and production. And once embodied, rapid progress in movement skills follows.

For the natural three-dimensional movement of the bones and joints throughout the body, I have created the term *bone rhythms*. The bone rhythms show striking parallels to movement in nature (currents of the ocean counterrotating as they meet at the equator, for example).

A dynamically aligned pelvis displays counter-rotation at the SIJ and hip joint and three-dimensional dissipation of forces into the myofascial network. When you flex the legs in a standing position, pelvic alignment is maintained by imagining sacral nutation with equal and relative opposite motion of the innominate (counternutation). This imagery will maintain pelvic alignment (often called neutral) dynamically without increasing tension. The femur rotates outward in lower-limb flexion and inward in lower-limb extension (figure 10.45a). Counterrotating can be imagined and kinesthetically appreciated with the help of sponges. When you twist a sponge, you will feel how you are storing movement energy in its elastic form (figure 10.45b). When you let go of the sponge, it will release its movement energy. Counterrotation allows for the leg to maintain alignment while absorbing and producing more energy than if it could move in only one plane.

In fine-tuned motor control, sacral nutation and pelvic movement initiate simultaneously, while the innominate moves relatively in opposition to both these bones. This is the key to a free hip joint and dynamically aligned pelvic movement. In hip extension the opposite motions take place: The sacrum counternutates, the femurs rotate internally, and the innominates nutate relative to the sacrum.

Figure 10.44 Pelvic half counterrotates both relative to the sacrum and to the femur.

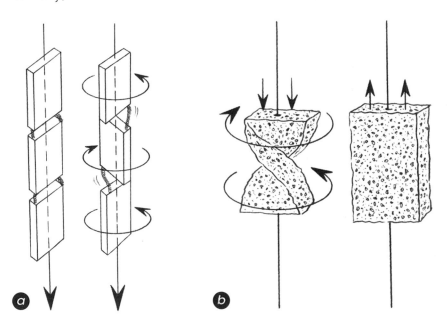

Figure 10.45 (a) Model of counterrotating leg bones; (b) metaphor of twisting sponge.

Imagining Counterrotation

1. **Imagining automatic rotation of femur with touch:** In a standing position with stretched legs, lean forward and place your hands around the middle of your thighs. Your thumbs should be on the inside and the other fingers on the outside to best feel the rotation of the femur. Do not confuse rotation with adduction or abduction, a sideways movement of the femur. Bend your knees and feel the femur rotating outward. Now stretch your knees and feel the femur rotating inward. Repeat the action until you clearly feel the rotation. It will be most obvious in the final degrees of knee extension.

2. **Imagining automatic rotation of femur with the help of the arms:** In a standing position, stretch your arms out in front of you. As you bend your legs, externally rotate your arms to give yourself a visual picture of the movement of the femur. As you bend your legs, do the opposite. If you try to internally rotate your femur as you bend your knees, you will create a lot of tension.

3. **Imagining rotation of pelvic halves and femur, left and right:** As you bend your legs, imagine both pelvic halves rotating inward and the femurs rotating outward. To help you in your imagery, use self-talk: *Pelvic half in, femurs out* as you flex your legs and *Pelvic half out, femurs in* as you extend your legs.

4. **Pelvic half and femur on one side:** Place one hand on your pelvic half, the other on the femur of the same leg just below. As you bend your legs, slide the top hand inward while you slide the hand on the femur out. Your hands should be sliding horizontally around the pelvis and femur. As you extend your legs, do the opposite. Slide the top hand out while the bottom one slides in. Repeat this action 10 times, then compare the legs. You may notice the practiced leg is more stable and flexible.

PELVIC POWERHOUSE

The core of the body has become a major focus in exercise, sports, and dance. In this chapter you explore the dynamic nature of the core. The body's center of gravity is located approximately in front of the second sacral vertebra. As mentioned, the largest muscles of the body attach or pass through the pelvis, your muscular powerhouse. The body is fortunate to have its power so placed: Coordinated muscle action involves the center of the body. The pelvis balances the considerable weight of the upper body on two fairly narrow shafts and must be strong in order to walk. Unless these muscles are perfectly balanced and synchronized with the rest of the body, you cannot make delicate shifts in weight.

Certain invertebrate animals, such as the octopus, move by contracting and shooting water out from their centers, propelling them backward through space like a rocket.

The physical center is crucial for attaining a centered mind. Meditative practices of both Eastern and Western religions imbue the hara, or tanden, located below the navel, with special significance. In *Hara, the Vital Center of Man*, Durkheim (1992) demonstrates the importance of this center both in Eastern and Western thought, quoting some of the teachings of Okada Torajiro, who taught seiza, a practice based on sitting:

> *Pull your strength into one point, your lower abdomen. Your posture is bent, because your mind is bent. Like a five-story Pagoda—this is how immaculate*

your posture should be. Your feet are the firewood, the stomach the oven. Why do your feet hurt? Because you have no strength in your lower abdomen. (p. 205)

Okada says that seiza cured him of his weakness and sickliness as a youth. Ohashi (1991) points this out in *Reading the Body*:

My teacher, Master Shizuto Masanuga, used to tell us that when diagnosing and massaging hara, we must become a mother with a samurai's mind. That means [while] we are eminently gentle, we are at the same time focused, directed and alert. (pp. 116-117)

The pelvic floor is delineated by four bony landmarks: the two sit bones, the pubic symphysis, and the coccyx. Connective tissue and muscle form layers like a lasagna, with strata of connective tissue and muscle. The levator ani muscle forms the internal part of the pelvic floor, attaching to the pubis in front and the obturator internus fascia and the coccyx in back. The pubococcygeus portion of the levator ani attaches to both the tailbone and the pubic symphysis, not unlike a hammock suspended from these two points. These muscles create a safety net, a last supportive resort for the pelvic organs (figure 10.46). The pelvic floor relates functionally to the thoracic diaphragm, iliopsoas, transversus abdominis, rectus abdominis, oblique abdominis, and lumbar multifidus. The pelvic floor can also be related to more distant areas of the body, such as the peritoneum, the first rib circle, and even the tentorium, the connective tissue floor of the cerebrum. The biceps femoris muscle relates to the

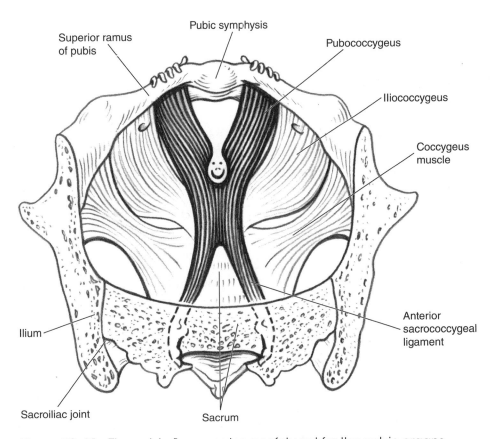

Figure 10.46   The pelvic floor creates a safety net for the pelvic organs.

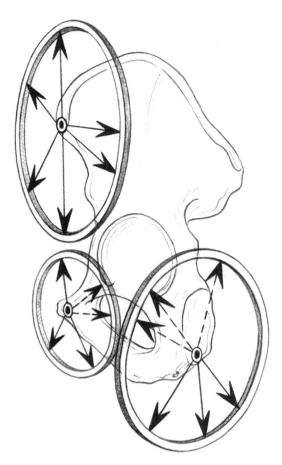

pelvic floor through the sacrotuberal ligament, and the internal obturator relates to the levator ani through the obturator fascia. The adductor muscles relate strongly to the action of the pelvic floor.

The pelvic floor is a psychologically delicate area to work with because of its intimate relationship with the organs of reproduction and excretion; however, the activity of the pelvic floor is important for pelvic alignment, ease of motion of the femur in the hip socket, and balance of the entire spine. An active pelvic floor creates deep support for erect posture, allowing elongation of the spine and freeing the shoulder girdle, neck, and head. Experiencing the pelvic floor also helps improve alignment at a deep level; creating leg and spinal movement and a dynamically strong pelvic floor can help maintain the health of your low back.

The pelvic half and sacrum are the origin and insertion of many muscles. Instead of simply looking at the muscles as singular entities, let us focus on the three-dimensional aligning and force-dissipating nature of the muscles. Most muscles are linked in slings through connective-tissue bridges. These slings meet and interlink at certain hub points.

The pelvis and sacrum have such key areas from which muscles radiate like the spokes of a wheel (figure 10.47). The ASIS is such a hub point; so are the sit bones

Figure 10.47 The pelvis and muscular hub points.

and the coccyx. Such hub points with radiating struts are design features also found in manmade structures such as the London Eye (figure 10.48). The London Eye, or

Figure 10.48 Hubs and struts of the London Eye.

millennium wheel, is a very large Ferris wheel constructed with tensegrity concepts on the river Thames. It is an intelligent structure made of a wheel and a hub with connecting spindles, which can respond to the weather.

The muscles align the pelvis in all three dimensions: sagittal, horizontal, and coronal. The movements in the sagittal plane are nutation and counternutation of the sacrum and anterior or posterior rotation or nutation and counternutation of the innominate. These movements do not happen in isolation from the other planes, but for better understanding you shall imagine the muscles plane by plane.

The muscles that nutate the sacrum are the erector spinae that reach low on the posterior sacrum and pull it up in back. The muscles that counternutate the sacrum are the pelvic floor muscles that attach to the anterior side of the lower sacrum. The erector and pelvic floor muscles are in a tug of war over the sacrum, so to speak (figure 10.49).

There are muscles that cause nutation of the sacrum by posteriorly rotating the innominate. These are rectus abdominis and adductor magnus muscles. The muscles that cause counternutation of the sacrum by rotating the innominate anteriorly are the sartorius, rectus femoris, pectineus, adductor longus, adductor brevis, and latissimus dorsi (figure 10.50).

The muscles that internally rotate and inflare the pelvis mostly act in conjunction, as do the muscles that externally rotate and outflare the pelvis. The transversus abdominis is an internal rotator of the innominate; together with the inner and outer oblique, it also inflares the iliac crest. The quadratus lumborum together with the pectineus, adductor longus, and adductor brevis assist in the inflare action of the iliac crests. Many of the deep rotators are able to assist the inflare of the iliac crests by pulling the sit bones and pubic bones laterally. Among these are the internal and external obturators.

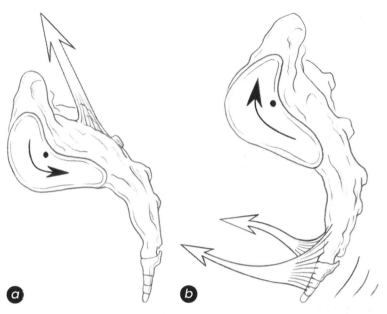

Figure 10.49 (*a*) Lumbar erector spinae nutate the sacrum; (*b*) pelvic floor muscles counternutate the sacrum.

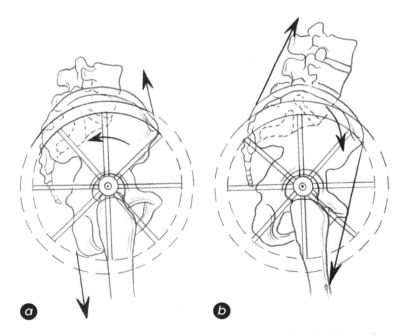

Figure 10.50 Pelvic half depicted as a wheel: (*a*) rectus abdominis and adductor magnus causing the pelvic half (wheel) to rotate posteriorly; (*b*) latissimus dorsi, rectus femoris, and sartorius rotating the wheel forward.

The muscles of the pelvic floor draw the sit bones and pubic bones together with the aid of the quadratus lumborum. They outflare the pelvic halves, and the muscles posterior to the hip joint also aid in external rotation. For dynamic pelvic alignment, it is very helpful to embody the eccentric contraction of the transversus abdominis in outflare (figure 10.51).

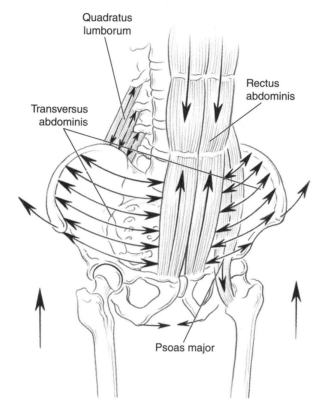

Figure 10.51 Lower-leg extension includes outflaring of the pelvic halves, involving eccentric action of the transversus abdominis and quadratus lumborum; concentric action of the pelvic floor muscles; and rectus abdominis supporting the anterior rim of the pelvis. This illustration also shows the psoas lengthening.

Imagery Exercises for the Pelvic Powerhouse

1. **Internal and external rotation:** Place your hands on the iliac crests. Slide your hands toward the midline of your body as you imagine the transversus abdominis and oblique abdominals inflaring and internally rotating the pelvis. Slide your hands back out to the crests as you stretch your legs. Imagine the pelvic halves rotating externally (outflaring) and the transversus abdominis and oblique abdominals lengthening.

2. **Nutation and counternutation:** Anteriorly and posteriorly rotate the pelvis and focus on the muscles moving the sacrum. As you posteriorly rotate the pelvis, visualize the muscles of the pelvic floor engaging the coccygeus and levator ani. As you anteriorly rotate the pelvis, focus on the lumbar erector spinae moving the sacrum into nutation.

3. **Rotation of innominates:** Stand in a comfortable position. As you flex your legs, imagine the rectus abdominis lifting the front of the pelvis, causing the

sacrum to nutate. It is very important that you allow nutation of the sacrum, or the result will simply be extension at your hip joints. This is a very common issue. As you stretch your legs, imagine the adductor magnus pulling the sit bones down to aid in the movement of the sacrum toward counternutation. You can imagine the innominates as wheels rotating in the opposite direction of the sacrum.

4. **Biceps femoris:** As you bend your legs, imagine the biceps femoris pulling the sit bones outward. As you stretch your legs, imagine the biceps femoris releasing the sit bones inward again. Through its connection to the sacrotuberous ligament, the biceps femoris acts as a dynamic limit to nutation, aiding in force absorption (figure 10.52). Slide your hands from the sacrum down to the fibular head to create a clear image of this important relationship.

5. **Adductors and pelvic floor:** Imagine the adductors to be the anterior continuation of the pelvic floor. As you flex your lower limb in the upright position, imagine and feel coordinated action of the pelvic floor and adductors.

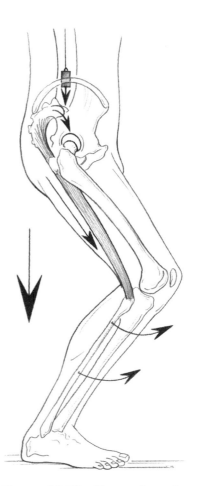

Figure 10.52 Biceps femoris as a dynamic limit to nutation.

6. **Layers of the body wall:** Visualize the layers of the anterior body wall: the transversus abdominis and the inner and outer oblique muscles. As you bend your legs, imagine the layers sliding on top of each other to inflare and internally rotate the pelvic halves. As you stretch your legs, imagine the layers moving outward, one after the other, starting with the innermost transversus abdominis.

7. **Body wall to pelvic floor:** Imagine the oblique abdominals relating to the opposite pelvic half through the midline connections from ribs to the rectus sheath to the ilium. Slide your hands from the superior and lateral ribs across the body to the opposite pelvic half to imagine this relationship. Practice this with both sides at the same time, hands crossing below the navel to reach the opposite pelvic half. Continue the image through the pelvis and into the pelvic floor.

8. **Pelvic geyser (sitting, standing, improvising):** Imagine the pelvis to be the source of a powerful geyser. Feel its profound energy potential. Visualize an eruption of the geyser—first bubbling, then shooting upward through the body (figure 10.53).

9. **Teeterbabe (in motion):** Imagine your pelvis suspended in a teeterbabe, which is a bouncy chair designed to support the pelvis of a baby. The legs dangle; all the weight is controlled at the pelvis (this image is used in the Erick Hawkins technique). I would like to point out that children need to learn to walk in their own time and should not be put into walkers or teeterbabes to make them walk sooner; however, this does not mean that this image is not useful for adults.

10. **Climbing harness (in motion):** Those who have done mountain climbing can imagine the pelvis suspended in a climbing harness. This image is similar to the teeterbabe imagery on the previous page. Your pelvic support is now hanging from ropes, and there is a firm seat under the sit bones and pelvic floor lifting you up.

11. **Increase tone (sitting):** Imagine the four points that delineate the pelvic floor: sit bones, pubic symphysis, and coccyx. See them extend away from each other as you inhale and move closer together as you exhale.

12. **Trampoline:** Visualize the four bony landmarks that delineate the pelvic floor. Imagine a trampoline suspended from these four points. Picture a large ball or any object of your choice bouncing up and down on this trampoline. Do some small jumps without fully leaving the floor, and imagine your pelvic floor to be bouncing up with the ball on top of it. Discover what you must do to make the ball rebound vertically from the trampoline.

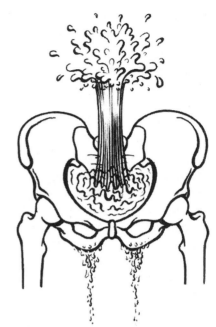

Figure 10.53 Imagine the pelvis to be the source of a powerful geyser.

13. **Drum:** Imagine that the pelvic floor is the surface of a drum (figure 10.54). Feel it vibrate and resonate. (If you wish, you can play drumming music, ideally with a deep bass drum, to enhance the image of the resounding pelvic floor. African drums are usually suitable.) Initiate your motion through space from the vibrating pelvic floor. Experiment with leaps and turns as well. See the lift in the leap as a reaction against the striking of the pelvic floor.

14. **Flying carpet:** Imagine the pelvic floor to be a flying carpet that lifts and supports the pelvis and torso as you move. The flying carpet gently supports the pelvis and the legs.

15. **Angle of the pelvic floor and rib:** Visualize the angle of the rib below the sternum and the posterior pelvic floor between the coccyx and sit bones. As you flex your lower limbs, both these structures will tend to widen; as you extend your lower limbs, both these structures will tend to narrow. This is a good tool for integrating the front and back diagonal of your body.

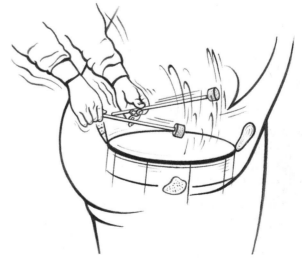

Figure 10.54 Imagine that the pelvic floor is the surface of a drum.

16. Pelvic floor fans: As you in- hale, visualize the pelvic floor opening like a fan. You can visualize multiple fans, one at the coccyx and one at the perineum, opening synchro- nously on inhalation and closing on exhalation (figure 10.55).

17. Architecture of the pelvic floor: Imagine three layers of the pelvic floor from top to bottom or from the inside to the outside of the body (figure 10.56). The deepest layer originates from the tail and sacrum and is fanlike (levator

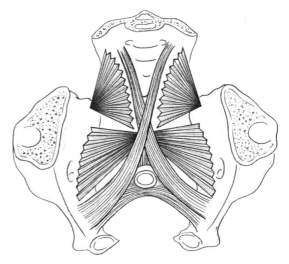

Figure 10.55 Pelvic floor fans.

ani and coccygeus). The anterior part of the pelvic floor stretches between the sit bone and pubic bones like a triangular sail. The most superficial layer forms a figure eight around the anal and urethral sphincter, or penis if you are a male.

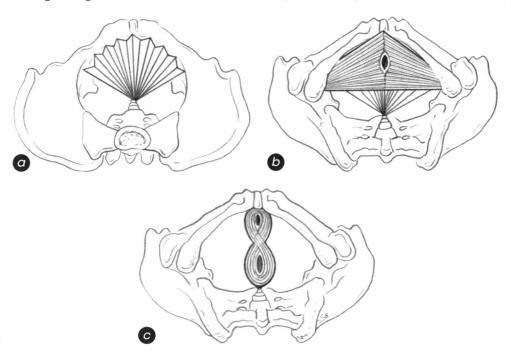

Figure 10.56 Three-layered architecture of the pelvic floor: (*a*) levator ani; (*b*) transversus perineum; (*c*) figure eight of superficial sphincters.

18. Pelvic floor cylinder:

a. Relate the pelvic floor to first rib circle (standing, vertical-level changes of body): Visualize the pelvic floor circle. Visualize the first rib circle. Imagine a cylinder connecting the two circles. Picture this cylinder as vertical. Together the pelvic bowl and the ribs create an oval shape that surrounds this cylinder. Imagine the three-dimensionality of the cylinder and the oval shape (figure 10.57).

b. **Ascending and descending vibration:** Remembering the previous drumming exercise, you can think of the upper and lower circles as two opposing surfaces of a cylindrical drum. Imagine the upper and lower drum circles vibrating in unison. It may be helpful to make a humming sound. Think of the lower drum surface (pelvic floor) sending its vibrations up through the body to the upper circle (first rib circle). Imagine the upper drum surface sending its vibrations down through the body to the lower drum surface.

19. **Activating thoracic and pelvic diaphragms using sound:** Perform gentle hops without fully leaving the floor. Allow a deep "huh" sound to emerge from the air passing through your throat without straining your vocal cords. Visualize the thoracic diaphragm bouncing up and down, creating sufficient air flow through the vocal cords to create a deep, wide sound. Imagine this sound reverberating with the pelvic floor. Let your shoulders and arms hang; do not tense your abdominal muscles. As you continue to bounce, add the image of shaking your tail down to the floor. The

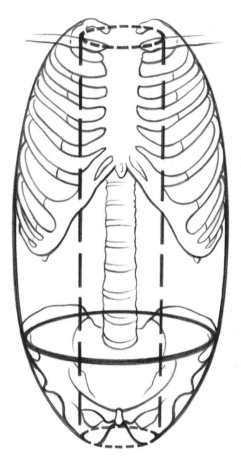

Figure 10.57 Imagine the cylinder created by connecting the pelvic floor circle and the rib circle.

feeling is similar to shaking an old-fashioned mercury thermometer down to zero.

20. **Adductors as fans:** Stand in a comfortable upright position with your feet in a parallel position. Visualize the adductors as fans. You may include the magnus, brevis, and longus in the image. The tip of the fan is located at the sit bone. The long edge is on the inside of the femur along the shaft. As you bend your legs, imagine the fan spreading out. Imagine the lower rim of the fan moving toward the knees. As you stretch your legs, imagine the fan narrowing once again. Repeat the exercise several times and notice any changes in leg and pelvic alignment.

21. **Deltoid-gluteus homologies:** Imagine the deltoids and the gluteus medialis as you perform lower-limb flexion. Imagine the muscles working equally on both sides. Imagine them both melting down and feel this create a balanced sense of alignment.

22. **Adductors as sails:** Stand in a comfortable upright position. Imagine the adductors to be broad sails billowing in the wind. As you bend your legs, imagine the wind blowing from the back of the body between your legs to the front. As you stretch your legs, imagine the wind blowing from the front to the back. Imagine the force of the wind against the adductor sails to power your movement. Notice how the previous exercise improves your stability and pelvic alignment in standing.

23. Organs and bone rhythms: Visualize the organs of the pelvis as two soft balls resting within each pelvic half. As you bend your legs, the pelvic halves rotate inward. Imagine the organs, specifically the colon moving in exact opposition to the bones, balancing the forces in the pelvis. As you stretch your legs, imagine the pelvic halves rotating outward and the organs rotating inward.

HIP JOINT AND FEMUR

The hip joints, which are of the ball-and-socket variety, are responsible for transferring the thrust of the legs to the pelvis. The hip joint has three degrees of freedom: flexion and extension, abduction and adduction, and internal and external rotation. More stable and less mobile than the shoulder joint, the hip joint is pushed to its maximum in many athletic endeavors, dance, and gymnastics.

The hip sockets are located at the front of the pelvis and are angled forward, sideways, and downward, whereas the shoulder sockets are located at the sides of the upper torso. This is an important distinction, because we usually think of the hip sockets as being farther apart than they are and the shoulder sockets as being closer together (to the front, hunched shoulders) than they are. The fastest animals on earth (such as the cheetah) are slender as viewed from the front or back, with acetabulae (hip sockets) very close to each other.

Men's acetabulae are generally closer together than women's, giving men a biomechanical advantage for the transfer of force from the legs to the pelvis (but from the point of view of energy consumption, women are more efficient). The greater distance between the hip sockets in women creates a wider birth canal between the iliac, sit bones, and pubic bones. The depth of the hip socket is enhanced by the acetabular labrum made of dense connective tissue. As opposed to the bony socket, the labrum is somewhat elastic.

The weight of the spine rests in a vertical plane that is behind a vertical plane through the hip sockets, forming a cartlike structure in the torso. The legs can be visualized as horses pulling the cart, with the cart hinged to the backs of the horses. The strap connecting the cart to the horses (the pelvis to the upper legs) is the iliofemoral ligament. Also called the Y-ligament, because it is shaped like an inverted Y, this ligament prevents you from falling straight backward off your horse. When you pick up an articulated skeleton, forgetting that it lacks a Y-ligament, the torso and head tumble to the rear. The point of the Y is located just below the anterior inferior iliac spine, the origin of the rectus femoris muscle. The Y-ligament is connected to this muscle and is therefore made dynamic by such muscular influence. The lateral part is the strongest ligament in the body and can carry about 770 pounds (350 kg) of weight. The medial part is thinner with medially spiraled fibers. The pubofemoral ligament is the most medial, and together with the lateral and medial Y-ligament it creates the Z-like arrangement supporting the hip joint anteriorly.

At the rear of the hip joint is the ischiofemoral ligament, which spirals upward from the lateral edge of the sit bone and posterior edge of the hip socket to the inside of the major trochanter at the same location as the origin of the external obturator muscle. Together with the orbicular zone, a ligament running around the femoral

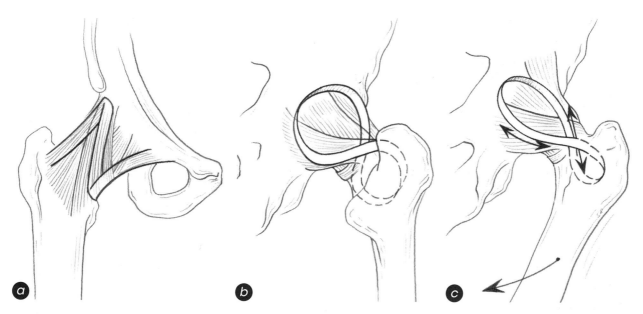

Figure 10.58 Ligaments of the hip joint creating a figure eight. (*a*) Anteriorly the iliofemoral (Y-ligament) and pubofemoral ligament, (*b*) posteriorly the ischiofemoral ligament; (*c*) hip extension tightens the ligament, winding up the figure eight.

neck, the Y- and ischiofemoral ligament create a figure eight enveloping the hip socket and femoral neck (figure 10.58).

The iliofemoral and ischiofemoral ligaments stretch on hip extension and internal rotation and limit this movement. The pubofemoral ligament stretches with abduction and internal rotation. Why does the body have such strong ligaments preventing extension? Because the ligaments are acting as springs to effortlessly support elasticity in standing and walking posture (figure 10.59). The line of gravity runs just slightly behind the hip joints, causing a posterior rotation force on the pelvis. Your pelvis is literally falling backward unless it is restrained. If you did not have the ligaments at the hip, you would strain to contract your hip flexors to stand upright. The body's design does not allow such inefficiency. This leads to the conclusion that you do not need to contract the large gluteus muscle in standing posture, because gravity is taking care of extension and the hip flexors can rest assured of the power of the elastic support of the ligament preventing the pelvis from dropping backward. It is all the more surprising that "butt gripping" and soreness in hip flexors from straining to stand up are so common.

The largest bone in the body, the femur, receives the body's weight on its two ball-shaped heads. Rather than being straight, the femur has a short neck leading to the greater trochanter. This angulation of the neck on the shaft increases the but-

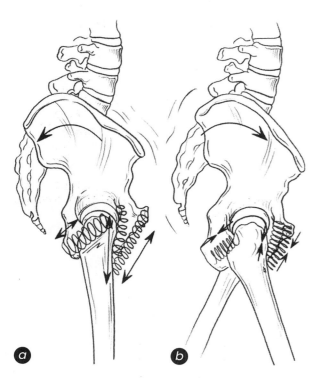

Figure 10.59 Y- and ischiofemoral ligaments as springs. (*a*) Hip extension, posterior rotation of the pelvis; (*b*) hip flexion, anterior rotation of pelvis.

tressing effect on the pelvic arch and enhances range of motion. At birth, this angle is 150 degrees and reduces to an average of 130 degrees in an adult. If the femur were constructed without a neck, this would greatly reduce the range of motion in the hip joint and make it challenging to effectively position the numerous muscles of the hip. The femoral neck is also angled forward in the horizontal plane, called anteversion, the forward torsion of the femoral neck relative to the transverse axis through the knee. It is quite large at birth (30 to 40 degrees). It comes as no surprise that some children tend to walk pigeon-toed to keep their femur heads centered in their sockets. As you age, the angle reduces to the average adult measure of 12 degrees. A small angle of torsion makes it easier to externally rotate your legs, an advantage if you are a ballet dancer. The humerus of the arm is also torsioned, but in the opposite direction.

The minor trochanter is located on the inside of the femur below the greater trochanter and is the area of insertion for the iliopsoas muscle. The trochanters are connected by the intertrochanteric line. Medial to the greater trochanter is a deep grove, the trochanteric fossa, a busy area of muscle attachment.

The femur slants toward the midline of the body as it runs down toward the knees. The generally wider pelvis of women causes them to have a greater inward slant. If you imagine the shaft and neck of the femur as a two-force vector, you can determine the resultant mechanical axis of the femur (see chapter 8, figure 8.5), which you may visualize to achieve correct leg alignment. Looking down the length of the femur from above, you see the angle formed by an axis through the femoral neck and an axis through the femoral condyles (figure 10.60).

In leg flexion and extension, the movement of the femoral head within the acetabulum can be visualized as rotation, but all movement in the hip socket involves some gliding of the femur head in the acetabulum. In hip flexion, as the leg moves upward, the femoral head spins backward (if it were to roll, it would roll toward you) and slides downward a bit. In extension, as the leg comes down, the head spins forward (and would roll away from you).

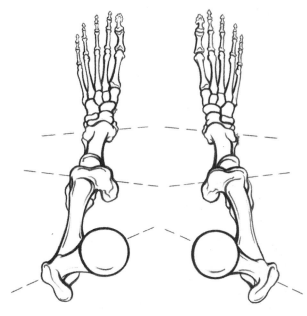

Figure 10.60   The angle of torsion formed by an axis through the femoral neck and an axis through the femoral condyles.

Imagining Leg Alignment

1. **Leg alignment (standing):** Put your finger on your second toe. As though your finger had paint on it, brush up the front of your leg and create an imaginary colored line extending from your second toe, through the center of your ankle, up the front of your lower leg, over the kneecap, over the thigh, and into the hip socket. Repeat the action and visualize the central axis of your leg passing through the center of the ankle bone, lower leg, knee, thigh, and into the

hip socket. Finally, imagine your pelvis balanced equally on both heads of the femurs (figures 10.60 and 10.61).

2. **Locating the hip joint:** There are several ways to locate the hip joint.

   a. **Center of crease:** The fastest way is to flex your hips and notice the crease between the leg and the pelvis. Just above this crease runs the inguinal ligament that connects the ASIS to the pubic tubercle. Place your fingers on the center of that crease and your touch will be located more or less in front of the hip joints.

   b. **Thumb-middle finger spread:** A second method is as follows. The distance between your hip joints is approximately the same as between your thumb and middle finger. Place your spread hand on the front of your pelvis on the inguinal line and your thumb and middle finger will be landing in front on the respective hip articulations.

   c. **Line up from sit bone:** A third way to dis-cover the hip joint is to take a close look at the relationship between the sit bone and the hip socket. The hip joint is located just above the sit bone. Flex your hip joints and lean your upper body forward. This will slide the large gluteus muscle off of your sit bone. With your fingers, touch the sit bone on one side of the pelvis and come back to an upright position. Imagine a line vertically up from your point of touch. This line will run through the hip joint. If you visualize a line from the center of the hip crease of the same side, your hip joint will be where the two lines cross. Repeat with the other sit bone.

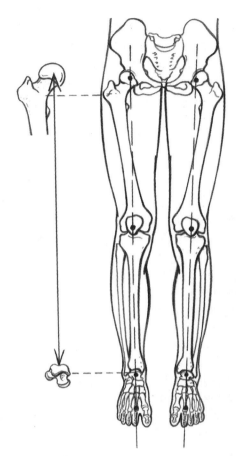

Figure 10.61 The central axis of your leg passing through the second toe, center of the ankle bone, lower leg, knee, thigh, and into the hip socket.

3. **Hip creasing (sitting):**

   a. **Piece of paper:** Place one foot, or at least the heel portion of the foot, onto the chair on which you are sitting. Visualize the crease at the front of your hip socket becoming very deep. Think of the fold occurring as easily as a fold in a piece of paper. Facilitate this image by imagining the sit bones melting down and laterally and the low back widening like a big fan stretching. Repeat the exercise with the other leg. (Adapted from André Bernard.)

   b. **Cloth doll:** Imagine yourself to be a cloth doll with your legs attached to your torso merely by a thin seam. From a sitting position, fold your upper body down over your legs and let your torso rest on them. Visualize deep, foldable hip creases. Remain in this position for a moment. Slowly roll back up through each vertebra of your spine. Initiate the action from the end of your spine, letting the coccyx drop down toward the floor.

4. **Isolation of hip joint action in turnout:**

   a. **Pubic rami:** In the supine position, with your knees bent at a 90-degree angle and feet flat on the floor, let your knees slowly drop to the sides. Visualize the head of the femur rotating in the hip socket and watch the pubic rami push in the opposite direction toward the pubic symphysis. As the right femur externally rotates, visualize the right pubic rami pushing in the opposite direction toward the pubic symphysis. As the left femur externally rotates, visualize the left pubic rami moving in the opposite direction toward the pubic symphysis. Once you have arrived in your maximum turnout, internally rotate your legs and bring them back to the parallel position.

   b. **Standing:** As you externally rotate your legs, imagine the pubic rami moving in the opposite direction toward each other.

5. **Acetabulum and labrum controlling the femur:** Imagine the hip socket including the elastic labrum to be like a hand holding the head of the femur. This hand moves the femur with gentle pushes and tugs to initiate leg movement.

6. **Pelvic ball on heads of the femurs (standing, improvisation):** Imagine the pelvis to be an air-filled ball supported by the heads of the femurs. Visualize the ball bouncing easily on the heads of the femurs. Practice this image also in walking. Visualize the heads pushing gently against the ball, balancing it (figure 10.62).

7. **Femoral head spin:** Imagine that you are looking at the head of the femur from the rear as you lift your leg. Visualize the motion of the head in the hip socket as the leg elevates. Watch the head spinning backward. As the leg reaches its highest point, see the head of the femur glide or drop downward within its socket. (See also chapter 8, figure 8.12.)

8. **Countering the socket:** As the leg elevates, focus on the rear surface of the hip socket. Watch this surface move up in relation to the head of the femur spinning back and sliding down. Watch the back surface of the socket move down in relation to the head of the femur as your leg lowers down again. Imagining the oppositional movement of joint surfaces often contributes to flexibility.

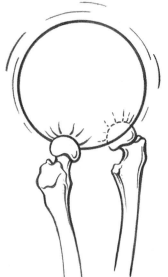

Figure 10.62 The pelvis is a ball bouncing easily on the heads of the femurs.

9. **External perspective:** Imagine that you are looking at yourself from the outside, as if watching a movie or theater performance. Watch yourself move your leg at the hip joint and notice how flexibly you are able to move at the hip. Admire your own fluidity, excellent control, and balance. Notice the resistor as well if it is challenging to see yourself moving well from the outside. Now return to the inner perspective and imagine yourself (mentally simulate) moving your hip joint. Switch between the inner and outer perspectives several times. Notice which perspective you prefer, if at all, and how your pelvis, hip joints, and whole body feel after this exercise.

10. **Ligamentous support:** Visualize your pelvis being elastically suspended by the iliofemoral and ischiofemoral ligaments (see figure 10.59). Bend and stretch

your legs and take a few steps while imagining the pelvis rebounding elastically from these ligaments. Anteriorly rotate your pelvis and shift the axis of your spine squarely over the heads of your femur. Notice how this impedes the sense of elasticity because now the ligaments are slackened and the center of gravity of the pelvis is too far forward. Allow your pelvis to rotate posteriorly and imagine the line of gravity located once again behind the hip joints. Reduce all muscular effort to a minimum and trust in the strength of the ligaments.

11. **Ligamentous stretch in walking:** When you extend your leg to the back in walking, the iliofemoral, pubofemoral, and ischiofemoral ligaments wind up and tighten. Imagine how this action pulls the head of the femur into the socket. As the leg swings forward, the ligaments slacken. Now the head moves slightly out of the socket. You can also imagine the heads spiraling into the sockets on the stance leg and spiraling out of the socket on swing side as you walk.

ILIOPSOAS AND PIRIFORMIS

The iliopsoas can be considered as three muscles: psoas major, psoas minor, and iliacus. The deep part of the psoas major originates at the transverse processes of the first to fifth lumbar vertebrae. The more superficial part arises from the bodies and discs of the 12th thoracic vertebra and the bodies and discs of the 1st to 5th lumbar vertebrae. The psoas lies snugly on both sides of the massive lumbar vertebrae, containing a deeper and more superficial layer that encompasses the lumbar nerve plexus. Although it does not attach directly to the pelvis, it joins forces with the iliacus, a flat triangular muscle that arises from the inner surface of the ilium up to the inner lip of the crest, the sacroiliac and ilio-lumbar ligaments and the base of the sacrum. Via a common tendon, these muscles reach down to the minor trochanter on the medial side of the proximal femur (figure 10.63). Since the psoas and iliacus work in conjunction with each other, they are referred to as the iliopsoas. The psoas minor is a long slender muscle located in front of the psoas major. It runs from T12 to the front of the pelvis and is absent in about 40 percent of people.

The iliopsoas is the primary mover for hip flexion, and its function is crucial for deep hip flexibility. To achieve hip flex-

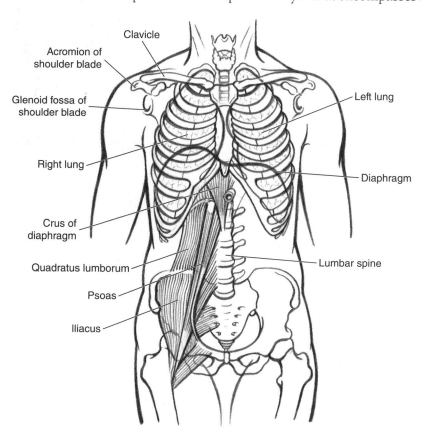

Figure 10.63 The psoas major attaches to the 12th thoracic and 5th lumbar vertebrae.

Clavicle

Acromion of shoulder blade

Glenoid fossa of shoulder blade

Right lung

Crus of diaphragm

Quadratus lumborum

Psoas

Iliacus

Left lung

Diaphragm

Lumbar spine

ion above 90 degrees, the power of the iliopsoas must be exploited, since the more superficial and less powerful hip flexors, such as the rectus femoris and sartorius, are not able to provide this motion. It can powerfully anteriorly rotate the pelvis on the femurs, a useful action when getting up from a supine position. Proper training of the iliopsoas can eliminate excessive tension of the superficial flexors. This function is facilitated by a good balance of the rotators of the femur, the obturator and piriformis muscles.

Why should we need a hip flexor that reaches up all the way to T12? Because of its large size, the iliacus would probably suffice as a hip flexor. But once you lift your leg, a large load is suspended from your lower spine, tending to buckle it. This is where the psoas comes in and contracts in coordination with the iliacus to stabilize the lumbar spine. This function is especially pronounced in the deeper fibers (figure 10.64a), while the anterior and lower fibers as well as the psoas minor tend to flex the lumbar spine (figure 10.64b).

You can imagine a stack of letters that you keep from flying off a desk through the use of a paper weight. The psoas is the compressive bilateral paper weight of the lumbar spine, only its function is mediated through feedback from the nervous system. Once your imagery practice enhances and coordinates the stabilizing ability of the deep psoas, your ability to flex your hip with ease and coordination will increase.

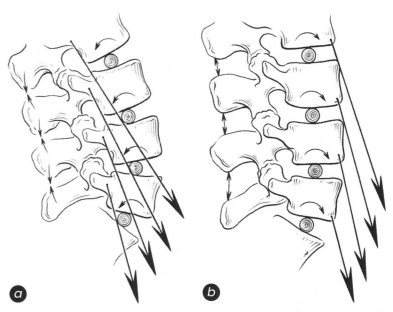

Other muscles also serve to dynamically stabilize the pelvis and lumbar spine, including the transversus abdominis, multifidi, pelvic floor, and muscles reaching all the way to the shoulders and legs.

Figure 10.64 (a) Deeper fibers of the psoas major extend; (b) superficial fibers flex the lumbar spine.

The key is not just strength or the focus on a single muscle as the magic bullet, but balanced action, which starts with good proprioception and a clear image of your design and function. Clinical experience has shown that it may be useful to start the process toward better organization in the lumbopelvic area by embodying the psoas major as the most deep-lying muscle. It is not advisable to habitually engage the rectus abdominis or the gluteus maximus as a strategy to lift the front of the pelvis to improve alignment. The rectus abdominis needs to remain mobile during spinal movements and breathing, while the gluteal muscles need to lengthen during hip flexion.

The deep rotator muscles also relate to the function of the iliopsoas. The internal and external obturators connect the greater trochanter to the pubic and ischial rami and the obturator foramen at a point above the psoas. The external obturator together with the psoas form what is best described as a muscular joint capsule for the hip joint (figure 10.65).

The piriformis connects the ventral surface of the sacrum with the greater trochanter near the internal obturator (figure 10.66). In other words, it connects the sacrum

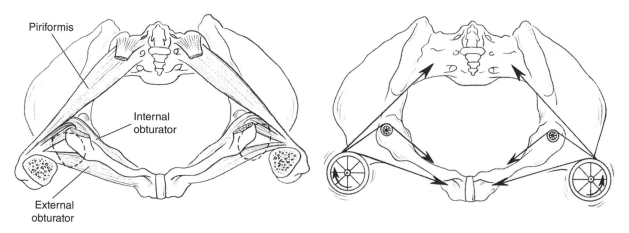

Figure 10.65 The piriformis and internal and external obturators as seen from below.

to the top of the femur like the iliacus, only along a more external route through the larger sciatic foramen. The piriformis also originates from the sacrotuberous ligament and the SIJ capsule, making its influence on the sacrum and SIJ apparent. This is a further example of a muscle that is involved in dynamic tensioning of a joint capsule and ligament.

The gluteus and piriformis relate to each other through the sacrotuberous ligament to which they both insert. The piriformis is a reversing muscle; in other words, it changes from being an external rotator to being an internal rotator at 60 degrees of flexion. It also acts as an abductor and can assist in counternutating the sacrum. Balanced action of the left and right piriformis muscles is essential to efficient standing, walking, and spinal function, because the sacrum forms the base of the spine and inequality of tension between them would eventually produce a change in sacral alignment. If your posture emphasizes loading one leg more than the other, you will be moving toward imbalance in the piriformis. A tight piriformis can cause a dancer's leg to turn in as it extends beyond 60 degrees. The psoas and piriformis are the bridges between the spine and the leg.

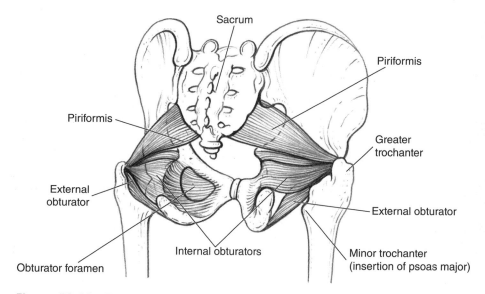

Figure 10.66 The internal and external obturators and the piriformis.

You come full circle if you consider the diaphragm's downward extending crura and the medial arcuate ligament as related to the psoas. The psoas can also be followed upward through the muscle groups on the dorsal aspect of the spine. The inferior fibers of the trapezius muscle attach to the spine of the 12th thoracic vertebra, whereas the superior fibers of the psoas major attach to the body of the 12th thoracic vertebra on the ventral side. In other words, the two muscles are tugging on the opposite side of the same vertebrae. The latissimus can be considered the iliopsoas of the back. The iliopsoas connects the spine and pelvis to the minor trochanter of the femur, while the latissimus dorsi relates the pelvis and spine to the minor tubercle of the humerus.

Snapping hip syndrome may relate to the iliopsoas muscle. In this case, a snapping sound and sensation occur as the leg moves from flexion to extension. The snapping sound may be caused by the iliopsoas tendon rubbing on a variety of prominences, such as the iliopectineal ridge during hip extension. The syndrome is common in dancers and gymnasts. If you have snapping hip syndrome, you should consult a qualified professional, such as a sports medicine specialist, and evaluate your dance technique, especially in the plié. You should also practice the bone rhythms of the pelvis described previously and eliminate tucking of the pelvis in lower-limb flexion.

Rather than simply stretch or strengthen the iliopsoas muscle group, you must balance the entire pelvis and its related structures. Even the condition of the closely allied organs, such as the kidneys and colon, may influence the iliopsoas, and vice versa. Relationships of organ and muscle occur via the fascia. The transversalis fascia covers the iliopsoas and can be considered the continuation of the iliac fascia that relates to the fatty covering of the kidneys superiorly to the diaphragm and anteriorly to the transversus abdominis.

If the iliopsoas is very tight, it tends to pull the pelvis and the lumbar spine anteriorly in the closed-chain standing position, and the increased lumbar lordosis may predispose you to low back pain. In this case, a correctly executed deep psoas stretch usually brings some relief.

Once the psoas is awakened, the flattened abdominal wall coveted by so many fitness enthusiasts and dancers happens all on its own. The all-important sensation of lift of the pelvis is also gained through efficient coordination of the iliopsoas. Once the iliopsoas regains its role as a dual stabilizer and mover, less artificial holding of the abdominals is required. The following exercises focus on the deep external rotators and iliopsoas, one of several paths to efficient use of the iliopsoas group.

Imagery Exercises for the Iliopsoas

1. **Visualizing the iliopsoas:** Visualize your pelvis, hip joint, femur, and minor trochanter, the insertion of the iliopsoas. The minor trochanter is located at the top and back of the femur lateral to the sit bones. Imagine the iliac fossa and the anterior inferior iliac spine, the origins of the iliacus. Imagine the vertebral bodies and discs of T12 and L1 to L4 and the transverse processes of L1 to L5, the origin of the superficial and deep psoas.

2. **Hip creasing:**

   a. **Fishing pole (CRP, legs not tied together):** Imagine the leg to be a fishing pole. The lower leg is the string and the foot is a fish. The handle of the fishing rod is located in the area of the hip joint and extends to the minor trochanter.

Pull the fish (foot) out of the water by initiating the action from the handle. As you perform this action, think of your back and especially the lumbar area spread on the floor (figure 10.67). (Exercise adapted from Lulu Sweigard.)

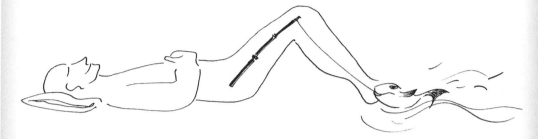

Figure 10.67 Pull the fish (the foot) out of the water by initiating the action from the handle.

Adapted from L.E. Sweigard, 1974, *Human movement potential: Its ideokinetic facilitation* (New York: Dodd, Mead), 290.

b. **Minor trochanter string (supine, standing):** Imagine a string attached to the minor trochanter. Initiate the hip-folding action by pulling the string toward the head in a direction that is perpendicular to the floor. (See chapter 8, figure 8.12.) Don't grip the abdominal muscles. Melt your back (especially the lumbar area) and neck to the floor like honey. Watch for any tension in your trapezius and allow your shoulder blades to sink into the floor. If the upper body can remain relaxed, it is a sign that the psoas major is sufficiently active.

c. **Knee string (supine):** Imagine a string attached to the knee. Pull the string horizontally toward the head to make the leg flex at the hip socket. Feel very foldable at your hip. When the leg returns, let the string lower the foot to the floor very slowly. While you perform these actions, imagine the psoas flowing down next to the spine like a river. The deeper you can imagine the river, the more effective the image.

d. **Spreading iliacus (supine):** In your mind's eye, picture the iliacus muscle located on the ventral, concave surface of the iliac bone. As you flex the leg at the hip socket, imagine the iliacus spreading out and widening across this inner surface. Feel the spreading as a movement, like cake batter spreading, and keep it alive at all times.

3. **Obturator foramen breath circle (supine, sitting, standing):** Visualize the rounded opening between the pubic and sit bones (called the obturator foramen). As you exhale, imagine your breath passing through this opening, allowing it to become soft and permeable. As you inhale, picture the breath circling around the sit bones (figure 10.68). During exhalation, imagine that the opening is the ring of a soap bubble blower. Blow through the ring from inside to out and visualize a bubble expanding outward until it pops.

4. **Obturator melt (sitting, standing):** Visualize the obturator internus as it emerges through the lesser sciatic foramen and turns the corner to meet the back of the greater trochanter. Imagine the obturators and other deep rotators hanging and melting down over the ischial bone (figure 10.68).

5. **Imagining a piriformis stretch (standing):** Visualize the broad origins of the piriformis on the sacrum. Watch the sacrum drop down toward the floor, suspended from the piriformis. Imagine both the left and the right piriformis stretching to equal length like taffy or bubble gum.

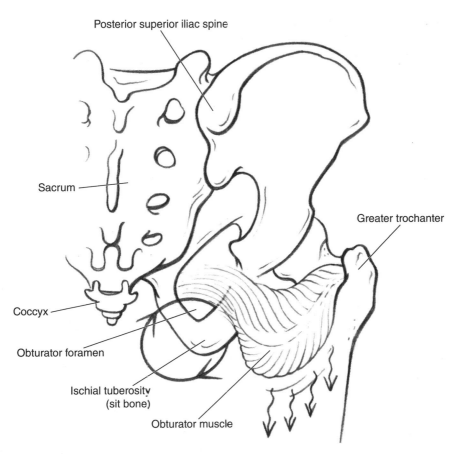

Posterior superior iliac spine

Sacrum

Coccyx

Obturator foramen

Ischial tuberosity
(sit bone)

Obturator muscle

Greater trochanter

Figure 10.68 Visualize the breath circling around the sit bones. Imagine the obturators and other deep rotators hanging and melting down over the ischial bone.

6. **Piriformis lengthening like taffy:** Visualize the piriformis stretched out between the sacrum and the top of the greater trochanter. Touch the greater trochanter with one hand and the lower lateral edge of the sacrum of the same side with the other hand. To find the lower lateral edge of the sacrum, the gluteus maximus must be somewhat relaxed. Imagine the piriformis connecting these two points. Visualize the breadth of the origin of the piriformis on the sacrum. Imagine the muscle stretching like taffy or bubble gum as you flex and slightly adduct your hip joint. Repeat the action several times before comparing hip flexion on both sides. Most likely the hip on the imagined side will feel more flexible and the hip joint more centered.

7. **Piriformis flowing:** Imagine a flow, like a river, from the greater trochanter to the sacrum. Energize the image with the metaphor of water flowing. Imagine water gushing from the trochanter to sacrum. As you practice, you may notice the heads of the femurs feeling more centered in your sockets and the front rim of the pelvis lifting upward.

8. **Head of the femur sinks into hip sockets:**

   a. **Supine (any movement):** Visualize the heads sinking into the hip sockets. (Exercise adapted from Lulu Sweigard.)

   b. **Supine:** Imagine the femur to be a cylindrical wooden pole, such as a broomstick. Visualize the pelvis as soft clay. Imagine the broomstick sinking deep into the clay. (Exercise adapted from André Bernard.)

9. **Hip flexion with release of the low back:** As you flex your hip joint, imagine the muscles of your lower back releasing, relaxing, and widening. Visualize the low back muscles melting to assist in deepening the crease between thigh and pelvis.

10. **Iliacus flow with geyser:** Imagine the iliacus flowing down the insides of the ilia and forming a geyser at the base of the pelvic floor that gushes up the front of the spine to support it (figure 10.69).

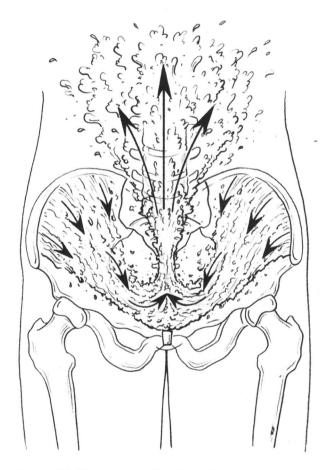

Figure 10.69   Imagine the iliacus forming a geyser.

11. **Hip flexion with psoas flow (supine):** Imagine the layers of the iliopsoas muscle from ventral to dorsal: psoas minor, superficial major, and deep major. Imagine the minor or superficial psoas flowing up toward T12 while the deep layer flows downward toward the pelvis and over the front of the pelvis like a waterfall. Maintain this image as you alternately flex and extend your right and left hip joints. Keep your knees relaxed and flexed to avoid contraction of the quadriceps. A sign of successful activation of the psoas major is the feeling that your abdominal wall is falling toward your spine and your waist is slimming without voluntary effort on your part. This exercise is best performed with two smooth balls beneath the pelvis, providing more range of motion for your legs.

12. **Leg swings from psoas:** Stand with one leg on an elevated surface so that the other leg can hang down easily. Imagine the hanging leg to be the downward

extension of the psoas muscle. Swing the leg back and forth, initiating from the psoas. Imagine you are swinging from the superior fibers, then move posteriorly with your mind's senses and imagine you are swinging from the fibers originating from the transverse processes. After practicing with one leg, take a few steps and compare the feeling between your legs. Then reverse sides and notice which leg feels more like a downward extension of the psoas, more connected to the psoas.

13. **Walking from psoas:** As you walk or run, picture the psoas swinging your leg forward. As the leg moves backward in walking, imagine the psoas being stretched over the front rim of the pelvis like a long piece of taffy.

14. **Lengthening the psoas:** Stand with one leg on an elevated surface and gently swing your other leg back and forth or simply let it dangle. Imagine the weight of your leg pulling the psoas into length. As you swing the leg, imagine the filaments sliding. A minutes of practice will allow the weight of the leg to cause the psoas to stretch longer. After you have completed the exercise on both sides, practice walking with this image. Especially during the swing phase, visualize length through the psoas (figure 10.70).

15. **Melting the iliacus and psoas fascia:** Imagine the fascia of the iliacus and psoas melting or flowing down the respective muscle bellies. Notice how this sensation increases the ease of hip flexion. Allow the iliacus filaments to slide underneath the fascia while the fascia rests on the muscle like a silk garment.

16. **Stretching the iliacus and psoas fascia:** As you contract the iliopsoas during hip flexion, imagine the muscle belly expanding and stretching the surrounding fascia. Compare the image to a stocking or sock being stretched and widened. Imagine the elasticity of the fascia as being part of the muscular changes as you move.

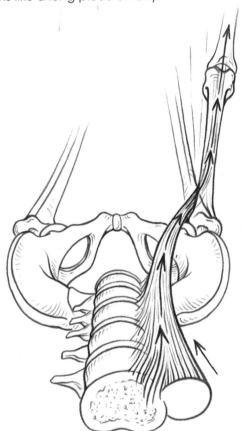

Figure 10.70 Imagine the hanging leg is the downward extension of the psoas muscle; imagine the weight of the leg pulling the psoas into length.

SUMMARY

The pelvis is the intermediary between the upper and lower body. It serves as a relay station for the forces traveling up from the legs and for the weight of the upper body traveling in the opposite direction. It is therefore a center of coordination and movement initiation while absorbing excess force and providing protection for the lower-abdominal organs. The sacrum is the mediator between the spine, innominate bones, and legs. Its movement is called nutation, which is slight but key to dissipate forces. The sacrum can be imagined to be a keystone or as part of the pelvis visualized as a tensegrity system. The hip joint can move three-dimensionally, and its powerful ligaments add springiness to walking and running and absorb force.

The pelvic half and legs can be visualized as a four-story force-absorption system. The counterrotation of the bones in lower-limb flexion and extension allows for force absorption and generation in three dimensions, which is called the bone rhythm. As a consequence, alignment is dynamic and not static as in fixing certain bony points in the right position. The pelvic floor is an active support system that requires the ability to lengthen in lower-limb flexion and contract in lower-limb extension. Hip flexion and an active lengthening of the pelvic floor muscles are dynamically coupled.

The iliopsoas is a muscle of all trades, the most powerful hip flexor and the only one that can elevate the leg above 90 degrees. The iliopsoas can powerfully lift the trunk toward the legs from a supine position and is involved in stabilizing the lumbar spine through the co-contraction of the psoas major.

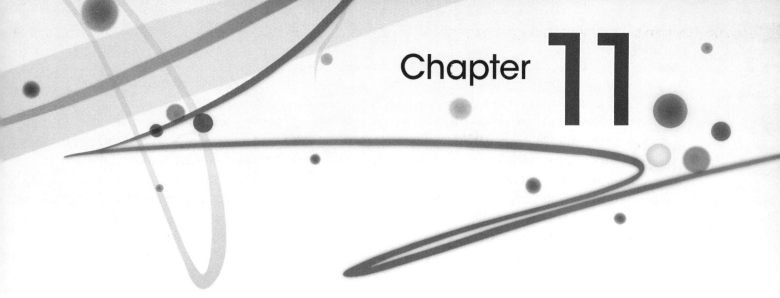

Chapter 11

Knee, Lower Leg, and Foot

You take about 8,000 steps a day, each one an opportunity for improving function.

Try the following experiment: Hold two pencils near their pointed ends and place the flat ends (the erasers) against each other. Now push the pencils together. It is rather difficult not to allow the pencils to slip away from their joint contact. Now hold the pencils farther in so that your grip is much closer to the contact point of the pencils. If you push the pencils together now, you notice that it is much easier to keep them joined because you have reduced the leverage. This is what the knees are faced with: They are placed between the two longest bones, or levers, of the body, which amplify the forces arriving from above and below and are nevertheless required to be very stable and flexible for a lifetime.

The knee solves its dilemma in several ways; one is sheer size and another is rather ingenious. Deep sockets provide stability, as can be seen at the hip, but they ultimately limit flexibility. Therefore, the knee has devised sockets (menisci) that add depth but above all can distort and move to another spot during flexion and extension to increase the range of motion of the joint.

The fibula and tibia of the lower leg have a sort of David-and-Goliath relationship, at least from the point of view of sheer bulk and strength. The tibia transfers 90 percent of the weight from the knee to the foot; its proximal end provides the lower articulating surface of the knee, which the fibula is not part of, and its distal end provides most of the upper articulating surface of the ankle joint. Why do we need the rather delicate fibula? While the tibia is occupied with transferring weight, the fibula is free to make delicate and rapid adjustments at the ankle joint without jeopardizing the transfer of weight, which is essential for maintaining integrity.

Try the following experiment: Cross your right leg over your left so that your right foot is dangling in the air. Place the fingers of your left hand on your inner anklebone and the fingers of your right hand on the outer anklebone of your right foot. The inner anklebone is the distal end of the tibia, and the outer anklebone is the distal end of the fibula. While moving your foot in a variety of ways, you will notice that the inner anklebone moves less than the outer. Especially when your foot performs rapid gyrations, the outer anklebone seems to dance around in comparison to the calmer inner anklebone. Now place your finger on the upper end of the fibula, a bony protuberance located to the outside and below the knee. This is the location of the proximal tibiofibular joint. Place the fingers of your left hand on the proximal end of the tibia just below the inner border of the knee. This time, as you move your foot at the ankle joint, you will feel the motion of the fibula while the tibia remains nearly motionless. Repeat the experiment on the left side.

KNEE

The knee joint is called a double condyloid joint because of the two rounded bulbs called condyles at the lower end of the femur. The condyles, which resemble two adjacent halves of a tire, face the two shallow convex surfaces of the tibial plateau (figure 11.1). The knee joint has two degrees of freedom: flexion and extension around a transverse axis and rotation around a vertical axis. The latter movement is possible only when the knee is flexed sufficiently, ideally about 90 degrees, due to ligamentous restrictions in the extended position. That is why as a dancer you can screw your knees into a better fifth position when you are in plié and then incur a career-ending injury when you straighten.

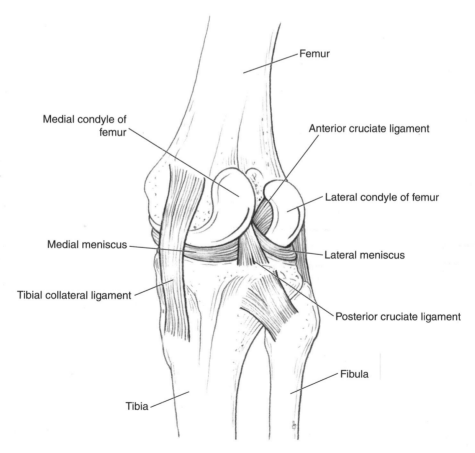

Figure 11.1 A right knee viewed medially and posteriorly.

The knee needs to remain flexible while supporting most of the body's weight. Theoretically, stability could be achieved through rigidity and flexibility through remaining lax, but both are out of the question for the knee. The solution is a large joint with adjustable surfaces. This means that the axis of flexion and extension, which passes transversely through the center of the femoral condyles, is mobile. It moves forward over the tibial plateau in extension and backward in flexion. Were the axis to remain in place, the femoral condyles would be landlocked in the center of the tibial plateau and the shaft of the femur would knock against the edge of the plateau, restricting motion.

Femoral Condyles

As ingenious as this system may seem, it requires some intricate reshuffling in the joint during motion. In flexion, the femoral condyles need to glide anteriorly over their tibial counterparts, or they will roll off the tibial plateau to the rear. The reverse holds true in extension. Here is what happens in lower-limb flexion: As the knees bend, the femoral condyles roll backward on the tibial plateau. So that the condyles can continue to rotate within their grooves on the tibial plateau, they glide forward (figure 11.2). If they were to roll back without this forward gliding component, they would simply roll off the tibial plateau. The forward gliding motion is powered by the anterior cruciate ligament with some help from the menisci (see next paragraph). In extension, the femoral condyles reverse their action: They roll forward and glide backward.

Remember that the condyles are like two adjoining tires. To better visualize the events in the knee joint as you descend in lower-leg flexion, imagine that as the tires begin to roll toward you, they lose their traction and slip forward on the floor (figure 11.3*a*). The surface of the tibia moves backward in relation to the condyles of the femur. As you straighten your legs, the opposite occurs—the tires begin to roll forward and away from you. If they were to continue in this fashion, they would roll off the front of the tibia, so they slip backward on the tibia (figure 11.3*b*). Therefore, the center of rotation of the knee is mobile; it has a so-called instant center of rotation moving back on flexion and forward on extension. Here the tibia moves forward in relation to the femoral condyles to support the anterior portion of the femoral condyles. The forward sliding of the condyles is made possible by the posterior cruciate ligament and the menisci.

Imperfect function of the gliding actions in the knee results in increased compression and shear. Recall the discussion of the slippery doorknob in chapter 9. Tightening the grip on the knob will

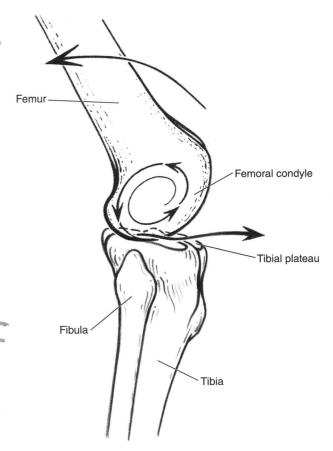

Figure 11.2 As the right knee bends in plié, the condyles of the femur glide forward so they can continue to rotate within their grooves on the tibial plateau.

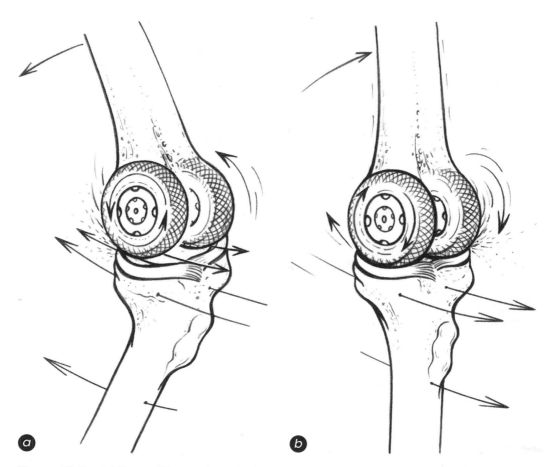

Figure 11.3 *(a)* Tires roll toward you but lose their traction and slip forward on the floor and spin. The surface of the tibia moves backward in relation to the condyles. *(b)* Tires roll away from you, slip backward on the tibia, and spin. The tibia moves forward in relation to the femoral condyles.

prevent motion between your hand and the knob. Similarly, if one joint surface cannot glide easily on top of another, they become stuck to each other. Neighboring joints attempt to compensate for the lack of motion, but there is still an increased chance of injury. In the weight-bearing position, the knee is part of a closed kinematic chain involving the hip and ankle joints. Therefore, improving one joint action increases the efficiency of the entire chain.

The two condyles of the knee reveal themselves to be more complex than they may appear on superficial inspection. The medial condyle is generally larger than the lateral. The frontal view reveals that the medial condyle is longer than the lateral. The view from the side shows that the lateral condyle is shorter and wider than the medial. The trochlea femoris, the area between the upper condyles that serves as a groove for the patella, is somewhat heart shaped. With some imagination you can see the face of an elephant, too (figure 11.4).

Since the tibial plateau is horizontal, the differing length of the medial condyle compensates for the inwardly angled path of the femur from the pelvis to the knee. The Q angle of normally 170 to 175 degrees describes the relative orientation of the shaft of the femur to the tibia. If this angle is larger, it is called *genu varum* (also known as being bow legged); if it is smaller, it is called *genu valgum* (also known as being knock kneed).

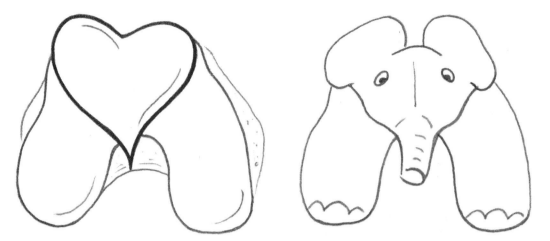

Figure 11.4 You can visualize the trochlea femoris as a heart or elephant.

Between the lower condyles is a tunnel called the fossa intercondylaris, which houses attachment sites of the cruciate ligaments. The image of wheel-shaped condyles is a simplification and a good place to start an exploration of imagery. In reality, the radius of the wheels greatly reduces from front to back, which is not the case for a normal round wheel. In the case of the medial wheel, the anterior radius measures 38 millimeters, while the posterior is only 17 millimeters. In the lateral condyle, the change is more drastic, changing from an anterior radius of 60 millimeters to a posterior of 12 millimeters. The design of the femoral condyles is therefore a spiral—but with several centers. The ratios found in the condyles resemble the Fibonacci spirals found in uncurling ferns, sea shells, and waves (figure 11.5).

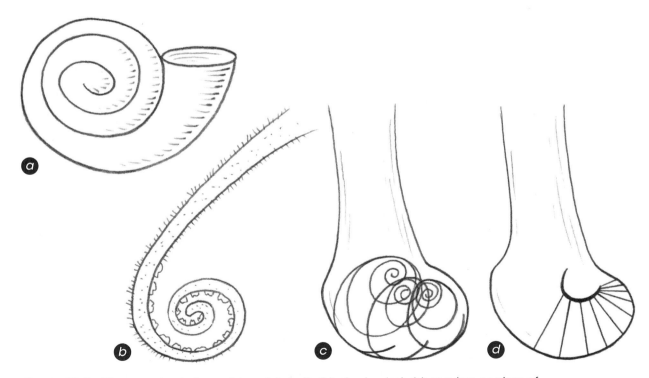

Figure 11.5 Fibonacci spiral condyles: (a) shell; (b) plant spiral; (c) moving centers of the spirals; (d) changing distance of joint axis to surface.

In knee extension, the tibia rotates externally about 5 degrees relative to the femoral condyles; in flexion the action is reversed. The movement is not voluntary; that is, you can't decide whether you will or won't do it. Therefore, it is called *automatic*. Automatic rotation should not be confused with axial rotation of the tibia, which happens only in the flexed position of the knee. The specific curvature of the medial femoral condyle, the difference in shape of the two condyles, and the tension of the anterior cruciate ligament (anteromedial part, which pulls the tibia into rotation under the femoral condyles) are factors involved in the automatic rotation at the knee. The posterior cruciate ligament also plays a part in this movement with regard to alignment. Automatic rotation is reversed by the medial collateral ligament. In contrast to the notion of fixing the knee along the central axis of the leg, you may imagine alignment being created by balanced counterrotation of the femur and tibia. This is the dynamic way to embody alignment because it involves balancing movement and forces rather the linear or static notion of posture.

Menisci

Two wedge-shaped menisci (joint discs) located on the tibial condyles increase the area of contact between the joint surfaces and reduce friction (see figure 11.1). Without the menisci, the area of contact between the condyles of the femur and the tibial plateau would be tiny, producing extreme forces that could disrupt the joint surfaces. The menisci are able to improve load transmission by distributing compression forces around their circumference and turning them into more easily absorbed tensile forces (hoop stress theory). The menisci aid in distributing synovial fluid throughout the joint and contain ample proprioceptors that help in creating balanced muscle tone during knee movement. The menisci divide the knee joint into two compartments: meniscotibial and meniscofemoral. Movement may happen in either compartment. The medial meniscus is shaped like a C; the lateral is more circular because its attachment sites at the center of the tibial plateau are closer together.

The nature of their attachment affords the menisci a degree of adaptive motion. The menisci actually remodel (change their shape) somewhat to fulfill their function of increasing the contact area of the joint surfaces. You may think of them as clay with the resilient properties of rubber and an adhesiveness that keeps them beneath the femoral condyles. They distort like a piece of clay that is being modeled yet rebound to their original shape like a rubber band. When the knee flexes, the femoral condyles roll backward on the tibial plateau, pushing the menisci ahead of them and moving and distorting them to the rear of the knee. When the knee extends, the opposite occurs: The femoral condyles roll forward, moving and distorting the menisci to the front of the knee. The medial meniscus actually moves about 6 millimeters, and the lateral twice as far, because the medial meniscus is attached to the medial collateral ligament, which limits its motion.

If the menisci don't move fast enough, they may get stuck beneath the condyles and tear. This can happen if the surfaces of the femoral condyles roll "uphill" on the menisci instead of "downhill" like a snowboarder in a half pipe. We can also use the metaphor of the car tire on slippery ground. If the ground is slippery, the femoral condyles will glide easily on the menisci as they push them forward (figure 11.6). If the surfaces are dry, the femoral condyles will roll up the menisci and compress them. Thus it is important to maintain sufficient lubrication of the knee joint by regularly moving it in both its planes of motion, actions which should be included as part of a warm-up for dancing, running, and most physical activities.

By providing a barrier to the femoral condyles, the menisci also aid the condyles in their gliding motion on the tibial plateau by pushing them back toward the center of the plateau. The two posterior and anterior horns tie the menisci to the central area of the tibial plateau, which serve as wedge-shaped wheel blocks for the condyles. The medial meniscus, which is attached more firmly, is more vulnerable to being crushed or torn by the femur head because it cannot distort as much as the lateral meniscus. Also, the outer rims of the menisci are less firmly attached so that they distort more than the inner portion. In rotation as well, the menisci reduce friction by distorting to remain beneath the femoral condyles.

Patella

The patella acts as a pulley, increasing the force that the quadriceps muscle exerts on the tibia (figure 11.7). As the body's largest sesamoid bone (a bone that attaches to a tendon of a muscle the way that clay attaches to a string), the patella is part of the tendon of the quadriceps muscle. It increases the distance between the axis of rotation of the joint and the force vector of the quadriceps (see figure 8.13). By reducing the friction between the quadriceps tendon and the femoral condyles, the patella serves as a built-in kneepad to protect the joint from direct outside pressure.

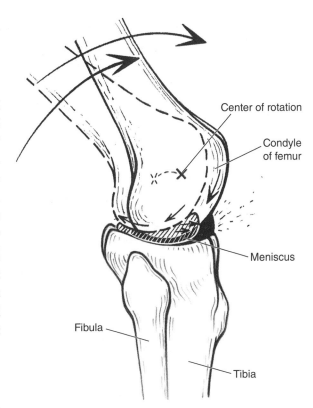

Figure 11.6 If the surfaces are slippery, the femoral condyles can glide on the menisci as they push them forward.

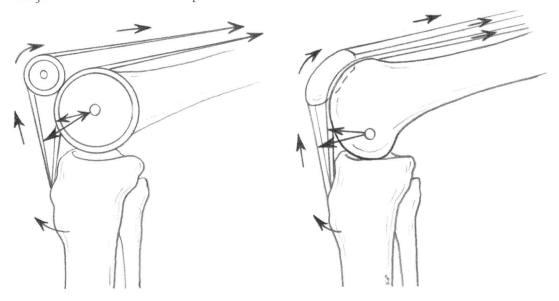

Figure 11.7 The patella as a pulley that increases the distance between the tendon and the joint center.

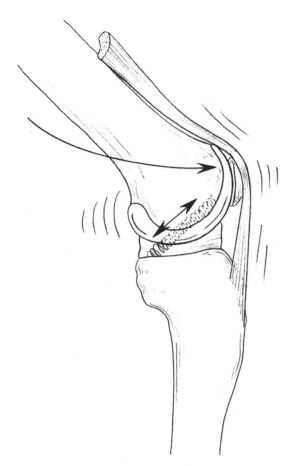

Figure 11.8 Patella-ligament-quadriceps mechanism resisting the forward slide of the femoral condyles.

When you bend your knees, the tibial plateau forms a forward slanted surface over which the femoral condyles are compelled downward by gravity. As your knee flexes, the femoral condyles are kept from moving beyond the tibial plateau through a joint effort of muscles, connective tissue, ligaments, and the patella. Figure 11.8 depicts how the posterior cruciate ligament, quadriceps, patellar ligament, and patella are involved in keeping the femur from sliding forward. As you bend your knees, imagine your femur rebounding off these structures.

Needless to say, bending your knees causes an increase of pressure in the patellofemoral joint, which is why the patellar cartilage on its dorsal surface is the thickest in the whole body. In squatting or performing a dance plié, this pressure can be very large indeed—in fact, the equivalent of several times the body's weight for a squat involving a 50-degree angle of the knee. Alignment greatly influences the amount of pressure; the most deleterious is leaning back as you flex your lower limbs. This is commonly the case if the hip and pelvic floor bone rhythms have not been properly embodied (see "Motion of the Pelvic Halves" in chapter 10).

The patella glides within an intercondylar groove between the upper-femoral condyles. This gliding motion is much like cross-country skiing—it's much easier if you can ski in a good track. You ruin the track by applying too much pressure, skiing on its edges, or crossing it. If the track has been distorted, the increased friction slows you down, making you work harder. Likewise, the patella must move within its groove, because if its track is disrupted, it could cause damage to both the cartilage covering the intercondylar groove and the posterior surface of the patella. To help center the patella, its dorsal surface is shaped like a flat pyramid. The tip of the pyramid points to the center of the intercondylar groove like the keel of a boat.

In the standing position, the patella, its tendon, and the lower leg are rooted to the floor (closed chain). Knee flexion and extension are a rotation of the condyles underneath the patella (figure 11.9). You can imagine the situation by rotating the fist of one hand in the hollow of the other hand. The hollow hand represents the patella and its tendon, the fist the condyles. You can now feel how the fist (simulating the femoral condyles) is rotating beneath the patella.

When you lift your foot off the floor, the situation reverses. Now the patella is gliding on top of the femur. Returning to the hand modeling, the hand now slides over the fist. When you imagine the patella going up and down in the following exercises, you are really imagining relative motion.

As you descend in plié, the patella moves down in its groove with the lengthening of the quadriceps muscle. As you ascend, it glides up in its groove. Because the quadriceps consists of four muscles, their combined pull must allow the patella to glide in a centered fashion in its groove in flexion and extension (figure 11.10a). If, for example, the outside quadriceps, the vastus lateralis, exerts more force than the

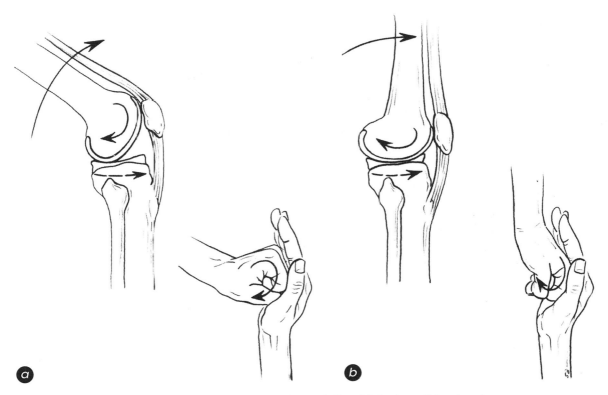

Figure 11.9   Condyles spinning underneath the patella: (a) flexion; (b) extension.

inside quadriceps, the vastus medialis, the patella is pulled medially (figure 11.10b). Similarly, if three rows of reindeer are pulling a sled and the left row veers off to the side, the sled is pulled out of its straight course. The lowest nearly horizontal portion of the vastus medialis is particularly important in keeping the patella tracking in its groove. Keeping the muscles, especially on the outside of the leg, flexible and the bones in good dynamic alignment are key factors to the health of the patellofemoral joint.

The patella is involved in a tug of war between the femur and tibial motions. Since automatic rotation causes the tibia to move out on knee extension, the patellar tendon pulls the inferior tip of the patella laterally while the femoral groove will tend to compel the top of the patella medially. This causes the patella to rotate, or swing inward, in knee flexion and swing outward on knee extension (figure 11.11).

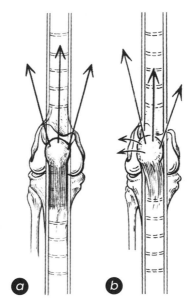

Figure 11.10   (a) The combined pull of the quadriceps must allow the patella to glide in its groove. (b) If the inside quadriceps muscle exerts more force than the outside quadriceps, the patella is pulled medially.

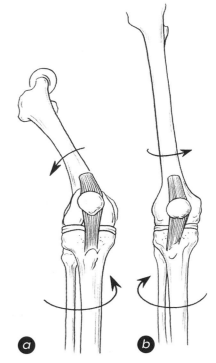

Figure 11.11   Patella rotated by the patellar tendon: (a) flexion; (b) extension.

The posterior surface of the patella that is actually contacting the femoral condyles depends on the position of the knee (figure 11.12). In extension, only the very bottom of the patella is touching the intercondylar groove. In 90 degrees of flexion, the top part of the patella is in contact with the groove. In other words, the patellar contact area moves along the back of the patella similar to a rocking chair or a boat dipping waves.

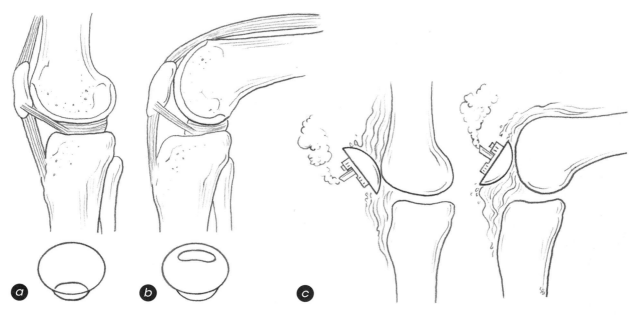

Figure 11.12 *(a)* In extension, the bottom of the patella is touching the intercondylar groove. *(b)* In 90 degrees of flexion the top part of the patella contacts the groove. *(c)* The patella rocks like a boat on the ocean.

Touch Exploration of the Knee

Increasing the proprioception of your knee, your ability to delicately sense where the structures are located, is valuable for improving the function of this joint. In the following section we will draw a detailed mental and sensory map of our knee.

Bend your knee and place your finger on the sharp, bony edge at the front of your lower leg. This is your tibia. Follow the tibia upward until you reach a bony prominence. This is the tibial tuberosity where the patellar ligament attaches, the insertion of the quadriceps muscle into the tibia. If you place your finger on the area just above the tuberosity and stretch your leg, you will notice that the ligament becomes taut as the quadriceps pulls on the patella and the patella pulls on the patellar ligament.

Go back to the tuberosity and place one finger of each hand on top of it. Now move one finger to the left and the other to the right and slightly upward to feel the edge of the tibial plateau, the overhang at the top of the tibia. As you move your fingers farther and pass the ridge of the plateau, you will feel the joint space next to the patella. This space is easier to feel when the knee is flexed, because the menisci are now at the back of the knee situated under the femoral condyles. If you stretch your knee while keeping your fingers in the same place, you may feel the menisci as they fill in this space. The menisci faithfully follow the condyles because they're mobile joint sockets. Finally, move your fingers upward to the patella. Touch the outer edge of the patella to create an image of its general shape. There is much variation, but in general there is a flattish base on top and a tip at the bottom. If you touch the top edge of the patella with your legs stretched and then bend your knee while keeping your fingers in place, you will feel the base of the patella move down and away from your touch as it descends into the intercondylar groove. Now move your touch to lateral joint space. This is where the collateral ligaments are located. When the knee is flexed, the collateral ligaments are not fully tensed. There are two ways to discover them through touch. Externally rotating your knee in the flexed position will make them become taut, because one of their jobs is to limit this action. This will make them easier to palpate. You can also flex your hip and knee and cross one leg over the other in external rotation. This puts the lateral collateral ligament under maximal tension and you can now feel it as a taut string on the lateral side of the joint space of that leg.

Now move your touch upward across the joint space. On each side of the knee you will feel the epicondyles of the knee. This area delineates the center of rotation of the knee. On the medial side of the knee just above the condyle, you may be able to touch the adductor tubercle, where the adductor tendon inserts. The stringy flattish tendon on the outside of the lower thigh at about the same level is the ilictibial band connecting the pelvis with the fascia surrounding the thigh and extending to the fibula. You can easily feel the hamstring tendons at the back of the knee, especially if you flex your knee.

Imagery Exercises for the Femoral Condyles

Familiarizing yourself with your femoral condyles, the fact that you have two balls and sockets in your knee, will aid in improving coordinated movement and alignment of your entire legs. A variety of metaphors, each expressing a different quality and aspect of your femoral condyles, will help to enrich your body image of the knee, leading to smoother and more enjoyable movement and control in the largest joint of your body.

1. **Condylar balance:**
    a. **Standing:** Distribute your weight equally on both legs. Visualize the femoral condyles of both femurs sitting on their respective menisci and tibial condyles with equal weight. From the vantage point of the knees, you are standing on four points of support. At the hip, you are standing on two only: the femoral heads. Visualize ground reaction force pushing upward between the condyles to center your balance (figure 11.13).

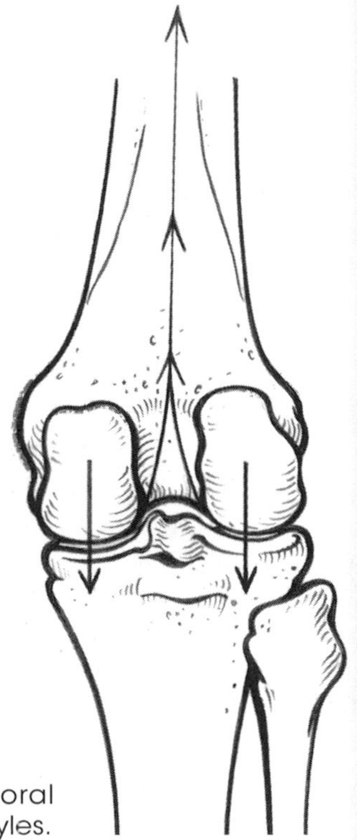

Figure 11.13 Imagine that both femoral condyles rest equally on their tibial condyles.

b. **Balancing condylar tire pressure (standing):** If you sense that there is too much weight on the lateral condyles, visualize them as tires that are being inflated. This will move your legs from a knock-kneed (genu valgum) position to a more centered position. Inflate the lateral tire until it feels like more weight has been shifted to the medial condyle. If it feels like there is too much weight on the medial condyles, the bow-legged position (genu varum), inflate that tire and visualize the weight shifting over to the lateral condyles.

2. **Visualizing movement of the condyles on the tibial plateau (lower-limb flexion and extension):** As the knees flex, the femoral condyles roll backward on the tibial plateau. So that the condyles can continue to rotate within their grooves on the tibial plateau, they glide forward (figure 11.2). As the knees stretch, the femoral condyles roll forward on the tibial plateau. So the condyles can continue to rotate within their grooves on the tibial plateau, they glide to the rear (figure 11.6).

3. **Visualizing movement of the tibia beneath the femoral condyles:** Visualize the tibia gliding in the opposite direction of the femoral condyles. As you flex your knee, the tibia glides backward under the femoral condyles. As you extend your knee, the tibia glides forward under the condyles (figure 11.3).

4. **Tibial-polishing condyles:** The tibia swings around the femur as you flex and extend the knee. Imagine the menisci gliding around the femoral condyles as if they were polishing them. As the lower leg continues to swing, imagine the space between the tibia and femoral condyles increasing, allowing for more synovial joint fluid to enter the joint. Figure 11.14 shows the knee extending.

5. **Visualizing the condyles as spirals:** Visualize the femoral condyles as spirals. As you flex your knees, visualize the tibia sliding along the surface of the spiral, moving closer to the center of the spiral. As you extend your knees, visualize the tibia gliding along the surface of the spiral, moving farther away from the center of the spiral. How does this image compare to the feeling created by imagining the condyles to be regular round wheels?

6. **Visualizing and touching automatic rotation:** This exercise is best done with a partner. Have your partner assume a comfortable standing position. Sit in a comfortable position next to his knee and place one hand on

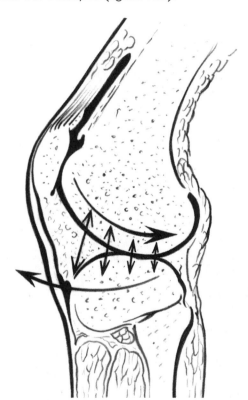

Figure 11.14 The tibia swings around the femur as you flex and extend the knee. As the lower leg continues to swing, the space in the knee joint increases.

the top end of the tibial shaft and the other on the lower end of the femoral shaft. As your partner bends his knees, gently support automatic rotation with your hands. The femur rotates out and the tibia rotates in on flexion; the femur rotates in and the tibia rotates out on extension. Your touch should be very light to assist the image. Do not force any movement. Repeat the action about 10 times, visualizing the movement of the femur and tibia. Before switching to the other knee, take a moment to compare your alignment, stability, and flexibility in the knee you touched and imagined.

7. **Imagining automatic femoral rotation:** Start in a comfortable standing position with your arms stretched out in front of you on a diagonally downward angle. Your arms will serve as a visual model of automatic femoral rotation. Bend your legs, externally rotate your arms, and imagine the external rotation of the femur. Extend your legs, internally rotate your arms, and imagine the internal rotation of the femur. Repeat until you can visualize the movement clearly and you can relax your arms at your sides.

Imagery Exercises for the Menisci

In this section, we will improve the movement and coordination of our menisci using imagery, but even more fundamentally we will develop a positive image and attitude toward these ingenious structures. Many areas of the body are only discussed when a negative condition occurs. Imagine if this were the case with a person—only to be mentioned in a negative context! Developing a positively functional image of the menisci will give your legs and whole body a sense of fluidity and natural flow.

1. **Flow of forces:** Visualize the menisci while you are in a comfortable standing position. Imagine how the vertical downward force of your weight arrives at the four condyles of the knee. Imagine the menisci distributing this axial force into a radial stretching force all around the circumference of the menisci. Bounce gently with your knees and imagine the menisci stretching and giving slightly in response to this action as if they were little inner tubes that were being stretched outward. Imagine the weight and stretch distributed equally to all four inner tubes. Imagine the shape of the inner tubes changing from higher during knee flexion to wider during knee extension.

2. **Lifesaving rings:** Visualize the same action as the previous one, only now try to capture the sensation of the menisci providing lift under the femoral condyles.

3. **Lower-limb flexion:** As you bend your knees and move downward, imagine the menisci sliding and remodeling posteriorly to remain beneath the femoral condyles (figure 11.15a). As you move up, watch the menisci reverse direction and remodel and slide anteriorly to remain beneath the femoral condyles (figure 11.15b). Visualize this action as very smooth and slippery.

4. **Meniscal independence:** This time, try to imagine the menisci initiating the motion of the knee. To initiate flexion, the menisci move posteriorly; to initiate extension, they move anteriorly. (Exercise adapted from Bonnie Cohen.)

5. **Axial rotation with the right knee:** In a sitting position, bend your knee to a 90-degree angle and use your hands to aid in axially rotating your knee. You can do this can by placing your fingers on the front of the tibia and moving it back and forth. Visualize the menisci remodeling beneath the femoral condyles.

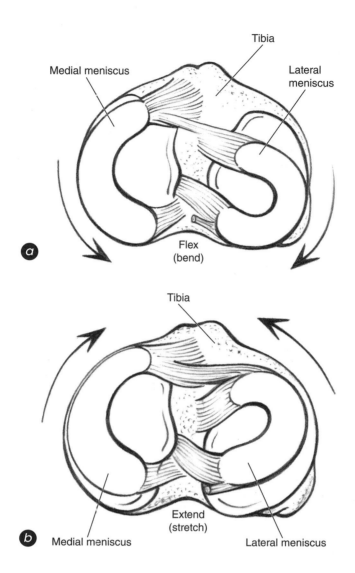

Figure 11.15 Menisci remodeling in the right knee (*a*) posteriorly and (*b*) anteriorly.

When you externally rotate the tibia, the lateral femoral condyle moves forward on the tibial plateau, remodeling the lateral meniscus to the front. The medial femoral condyle moves backward on the tibial plateau, remodeling the medial meniscus to the rear. If you place your finger in the space of the medial joints, you can feel it becoming empty as you externally rotate the tibia, since the meniscus is moving posteriorly (figure 11.16*a*). When you internally rotate the lower leg, the medial femoral condyle moves forward relative to the tibial plateau, remodeling the medial meniscus forward. You can now feel the medial joint space filling out underneath your fingertips. The lateral femoral condyle, however, is moving backward on the tibial plateau, remodeling the lateral meniscus to the rear on that side (figure 11.16*b*). Repeat this action until you have a clear image of the movements. Stand up and compare your stance on your right and left legs. The side you practiced with will feel more stable and centered and the muscles will allow lower-limb flexion and extension to happen more effortlessly. Jumping will be easier as well. Repeat the exploration and imagery on the left side.

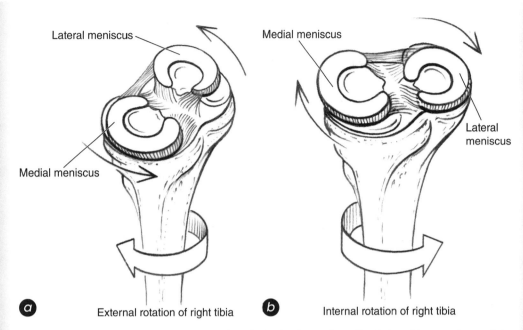

Lateral meniscus

Medial meniscus

External rotation of right tibia

Medial meniscus

Lateral meniscus

Internal rotation of right tibia

Figure 11.16 *(a)* When you externally rotate the lower leg, the lateral femoral condyle moves forward relative to the tibial plateau, remodeling the lateral meniscus forward and the medial meniscus backward. *(b)* When you internally rotate the lower leg, the medial femoral condyle moves forward relative to the tibial plateau, remodeling the lateral meniscus backward and the medial meniscus forward.

6. **Meniscocondylar rhythm:** In lower-limb flexion, imagine the femoral condyles rotating and moving or distorting the menisci, which then move on the tibial plateau; then feel the tibial plateau moving. Imagine this as a one-two-three rhythm: condyles-menisci-tibial plateau. Reverse the image when you extend the lower limb: Think tibial plateau-menisci-condyles. Imagine this as an upward driving or spiraling force. This imagery is useful, even though the movements happen practically at the same time.

7. **Meniscal pendulum:** As you flex and extend your knees, imagine the menisci swinging around the femoral condyles. In repeated rhythmic knee bends, imagine this action to be like a pendulum swinging back and forth under the condyles (figure 11.17).

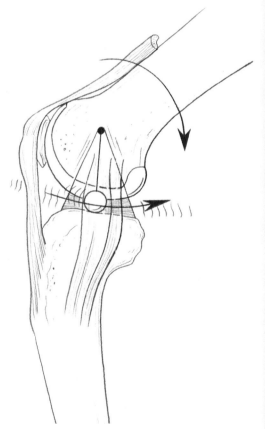

Figure 11.17 Imagine the menisci swinging like a pendulum.

Imagery Exercises for the Patella

The patella is of the rare sesamoid type of bone riding on the tendon connecting the quadriceps and tibia. It leads you through space as you walk, and even though it is not of great size, it makes a big difference for the power you can produce with your legs. Sadly, it is a common place of pain, but good dynamic alignment as well as balanced strength and use will keep your patella healthy. The coordinated functioning of the patella must also be seen in the context of whole-leg bone rhythms and dynamic alignment of your feet, as discussed below.

1. **Wet bar of soap:** As you flex and extend your knees, visualize the patellae gliding easily in their well-lubricated grooves like wet bars of soap slipping in smooth grooves.

2. **Down-and-up movement:** Stand in a comfortable position. In lower-limb flexion, imagine the kneecap sliding down in its intercondylar groove. As you extend your lower limbs, imagine the patella moving upward in the intercondylar groove. Use your hands with wrists flexed and fingers pointing down in front of you to model the movement of the patella. As you flex, move your hands down; as you extend, move your hands up as a visual reminder of the correct image.

3. **Heavy weight and floating balloon:** As you flex your lower limbs, imagine the patellae having a certain amount of weight to help them in sliding downward. As you extend your lower limbs, imagine the kneecaps as little balloons floating upward effortlessly. Also reverse the image and notice how the incorrect embodiment blocks the movement. Note that pulling up your patella has been used as a movement cue in dance and exercise. If you truly pull up your patella, you will contract your quadriceps, making lower-limb flexion impossible—surely not the intention of training. Always end your practice with the correct image of floating on extension and having a heavy patella on flexion.

4. **Pouring sand:** Imagine sand pouring out of your knees as you flex and extend your legs. Visualize your hip sockets and knee in the same sagittal plane as the second toes. This will allow the sand to fall on your second toe.

5. **Bilateral reins:** Visualize reins attached to both sides of the patella and reaching upward along the femur. The reins represent the pull of the quadriceps muscle. The inner and outer reins should pull with equal force in balanced patellar action. If the patella rides too far laterally, the medial reins (vastus medialis) need to pull harder to bring the patella back into line.

6. **Patellar pendulum:** Use your hands as a visual model of the patella with fingers pointing down and wrists flexed. As you bend your knees, the patella swings inward (point your fingertips in). As you stretch your knees, the patella swings outward (point your fingertips out). Imagine the patellae to be swinging pendulums in rhythmic knee flexion and extension.

7. **Kneecaps as little bells:** Imagine the patella to be a little bell swinging back and forth. The bells swing inward to the side on knee flexion and outward on knee extension. Repeat the action several times until it becomes familiar. Also try the wrong action and notice how it increases movement tension. Always finish your practice with the correct image.

8. **Patellar contact surfaces:** Sit comfortably with your knees bent at a 90-degree angle and imagine the contact surface between the patella and femur. It is now at the top of the posterior surface of the patella. Extend one knee at a time and

imagine the contact surface gliding down the back of the patella. When your lower leg is aligned with the thigh, the contact area has reversed and is now at the bottom of the patella. Practice flexing and extending your legs while visualizing the change in contact area until you can imagine a continuous rocking motion of the patella, reminding you of a rocking chair (see figure 11.12).

The knees are an important part of your propulsion system. They aid you in lowering and raising your center of gravity (COG) when required. They fulfill the dual functions of providing flexibility and providing stability with the help of adjustable joint surfaces, increasing the surface area of the joint while maintaining its mobility.

TIBIA, FIBULA, AND ANKLE

The bones of the lower leg, the tibia (shinbone) and fibula (calf bone), form a working unit. The Latin word *tibia* (flute) elicits an image of air streaming through the bone, vibrating it and loosening the surrounding muscles. As the most vertical bone of the body in upright stance and the primary weight bearer, the tibia transfers the force from the femur down to the talus, the keystone of the foot's long arch. The fibula gets its name from a pin used to fasten the toga, the loose outer garment worn by ancient Romans. The fibula does not articulate with the femur. Besides being firmly connected at both ends, the tibia and fibula are bound together by a strong interosseous (between-bone) membrane along their entire parallel length. The interosseous membrane improves the stability of the lower leg and, together with the tibia and fibula, serves as an attachment site for many muscles that move the ankle, tarsal, and toe joints. It is important to maintain the balanced strength and elasticity of these muscles through massage, stretching, and the upcoming imagery. Two joints connect the fibula to the tibia: the proximal tibiofibular joint and the distal tibiofibular joint. The proximal joint is synovial with plane surfaces. The distal tibiofibular joint is a synarthrosis filled with dense irregular connective tissue.

Three bones are involved in the ankle joint that is located between the talus and the tibia and the talus and the fibula. On superficial viewing, the movement of the ankle is flexion and extension (pointing); however, as with the knee, the axis for flexion and extension does not remain in place, providing extra mobility for the joint. Also, the axis for flexion and extension is rather crooked. It runs from a point 5 millimeters below the inner malleolus to 3 millimeters below and 8 millimeters in front of the tip of the fibula. Place your fingers approximately at these points and draw a mental line between touches to visualize the joint axis. Holding a pencil with the correct axial alignment in front of the ankle will help you visualize the axis. You will see a line that runs from ventral-medial-proximal to dorsal-lateral-distal. This means that plantar flexion (pointing) and dorsiflexion (lifting the top of the foot up) do not occur purely in the sagittal plane; there is also some accompanying supination and pronation. In standing lower-limb flexion and extension, the movement of the foot reflects the automatic rotation of the femur. This fact is key to understanding the dynamic alignment of the leg.

The body of the talus is 0.5 millimeters wider in front than in back. Two-thirds of the top joint surface of the ankle is formed by the tibia, and the fibula provides the

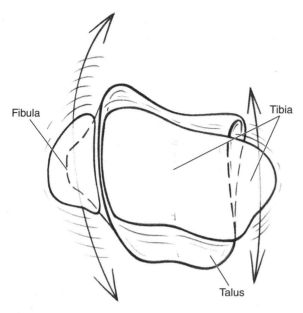

Figure 11.18 The fibula, located on the larger lateral facet of the talus, glides farther than the tibia on the medial facet (bones of the left foot are shown).

outer edge, creating a cavity. Together they firmly embrace the talus, allowing them to swing in the sagittal plane as if working together as an adjustable wrench (figure 11.18). The top of the talus, the talar dome (talar trochlea), boasts three joint surfaces. The topmost surface articulates with the tibia and has a small central ridge that serves as an extra guide rail for the tibia in motion. The lateral edge is curved and longer than the medial one, which is flat and articulates with the inner surface of the tibial malleolus. The lateral joint surface, which articulates with the fibula, is concave and triangular. The lower part of this lateral joint surface is nearly horizontal, an important detail for understanding the motion of the fibula in ankle flexion and extension (see the following paragraphs).

You would expect the joint surfaces just described should fit neatly with the ones offered from above from the tibia and fibula. The ankle joint is in fact the most congruent in the body, but the mortise (such as a carpenter's mortise) is too small to cover the talar dome. The squarish inferior facet of the tibia is only one-third the size of the dome. Ankle flexion and extension must therefore involve a sliding of the tibia over the talar trochlea (figure 11.19).

During dorsiflexion, the talus rolls forward and simultaneously slides its superior surface backward under the mortise. In plantar flexion, the talus rolls backward as its superior surface slides forward under the mortise.

The lateral talar facet for the fibula is longer than the medial facet offered by the tibia, a design feature that forebodes an element of rotational movement in the ankle. Viewing the talus from the side, it appears to be the segment of a wave (figure 11.20).

Rather than bear much weight, the fibula takes part in the pincerlike action of the ankle joint and gives it mobility. The tibial portion is like the weight-bearing palm of one hand, whereas the fibula is like the fingers of another hand making subtle adjustments, depending on the ankle joint's exact positioning (figure 11.21).

When you flex your lower limbs in the standing position, the wider anterior section of the talus becomes lodged between the fibula and tibia,

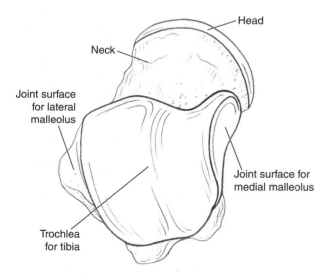

Figure 11.19 Talar trochlea (the left talus viewed from above).

Figure 11.20 Talus from lateral view as the segment of a wave.

creating a more stable position than when you lift up on to the balls of your feet. In this case, the fibula and tibia embrace the narrower part of the trochlea. Since the fibula is located on the longer lateral side of the talus, a greater distance needs to be traveled for the same effect because its movement is greater than that of the tibia. Were you to extend the surface contour of the lateral facet into space, you would create a large circle, the center of which would be on the medial side of the foot. The talus can be visualized as a segment of a cone with its point on the medial side of the ankle. If you were to cut the middle segment out of a party hat or ice cream cone, it would resemble the talus in shape. Therefore, the talus rotates 5 degrees in dorsiflexion relative to the lower leg, the same amount the femur moves in automatic rotation. In lower-limb flexion the femur and talus (taking the foot with it in the non-weight-bearing position) will both rotate 5 degrees externally relative to the lower leg. A major key to creating dynamic alignment is balancing these motions, which will result in the proper alignment of the leg. Maintaining the leg in alignment with a positional image as reflected in the cue "keep your knees over the second toe" does not reflect the oscillatory nature of leg movement (figure 11.22).

The image of knees over the second toe can be likened to a photograph taken of alignment at the midpoint of the oscillation (a regular fluctuation of position around a mean) of the leg bone in flexion and extension. If the knee does not appear to be over the second toe, then the leg is in need of alignment with strategies that maintain its dynamic stability and force absorption through counterrotation. Coercing the knee over the second toe may create the outer appearance of good alignment, but only from a static point of view. This will lead to reduced efficiency and perhaps injury. Placing the knee over the second toe can be used as an emergency remedy but not as a complete strategy of leg alignment. If you are used to thinking or teaching in terms of fixed-point alignment, it may take a moment to adjust to the fact that alignment is a balanced movement and not a position. Using self-awareness, touch, and imagery may seem more time consuming at the outset, but in the long term it is the economical way to go and is based on the nature of human biology.

Both the fibula and tibia glide forward and backward along their talar facets in dorsi- and plantar flexion of the ankle. The amount of flexion and extension is normally 20 degrees of dorsal and 40 degrees of plantar flexion. In weight bearing, the amount may increase by 10 degrees in both directions.

During dorsiflexion the fibula performs many motions. It moves laterally, compelled by the shape of the talus, which is wider in front than in back. This in turn stretches the interosseous membrane and tibiofibular ligaments, turning compression forces that occur in running or landing from a jump into their tensile counterpart. You can use this knowledge to your advantage by imagining the interosseus ligament stretching in moments of impact. This stores elastic energy

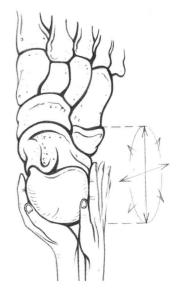

Figure 11.21 If the tibia and fibula were hands, the tibia would bear weight on the palm while the fibula-fingers would make subtle adjustments.

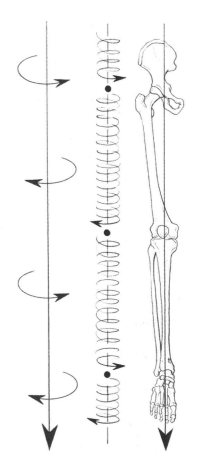

Figure 11.22 Oscillatory nature of leg flexion and extension: counterrotation of leg bones.

in the ligaments and interosseus membrane and reduces wear and tear on your joints and muscles (Weinert, McMaster, and Ferguson 1973).

The fibula also moves upward (cranially) compelled by the slightly higher lateral portion of the talar dome. This would cause the fibular head to compress against its facet under the lateral condyle of the tibial plateau. The fibula prefers to move back (posteriorly) to avoid collision. Because this is not sufficient, the fibula also rotates internally compelled by the anterior and posterior tibiofibular ligaments. Since they are attached on the outside and inside of the fibula, respectively, they produce a cranklike rotary action of the fibula.

With each step you take, you plant a foot on the ground, causing dorsiflexion as the tibia and fibula move forward and the trochlea of the talus slides relatively backward toward the heel. The fibula moves laterally upward and back and rotates inward during this phase. As the foot plantar-flexes in the push-off, the trochlea slides forward toward the front of the foot and the fibula reverses its action. The motions are small (1 to 2 mm) but are very important in balancing the action of the ankle. Imagining them will greatly improve ankle, foot, and leg coordination and dynamic alignment.

The ankle is richly endowed with ligaments that are key to dynamically stabilizing and guiding the actions of the foot. The anterior talofibular ligament runs (as its name reveals) from the talus to the fibula and is particularly important when lifting your weight up onto the balls of your feet (called relevé in dance). This ligament keeps the talus from dropping inward and stabilizes the fibula, which is key to maintaining balance. Since most ligaments are related to muscular dynamics, visualizing their action in movement can noticeably improve coordination. Imagine a strong connection between the fibula and talus on the outside of the foot to help stabilize yourself as you lift your weight up on your toes. Touching the ligament before you perform the action will stimulate proprioceptive feedback, improve the vividness of the imagery, and increase the stabilizing effect of the process. The calcaneofibular ligament running from the heelbone to the fibula stabilizes both the ankle and subtalar joint. It tightens in dorsiflexion, which helps to stabilize the ankle when landing from a jump. If the top of the heelbone drops inward, which is called the valgus position, both the calcaneofibular ligament and its partner on the other side of the ankle, the tibiocalcaneal ligament, become taut to keep the heel aligned. The ligaments need to be assisted in their action by muscles. If this is not the case, they tend to overstretch or, in extreme cases, tear.

Imagery Exercises for the Tibia, Fibula, and Ankle

1. **Ankle pincers:** Hold one foot in a non-weight-bearing position and visualize the talus suspended between the tibial and fibular mortise (figure 11.23). Let the foot swing in the sagittal plane between the pincers. Imagine the pincers widening on dorsiflexion, permitting an easy swinging motion.

2. **Imagining the roll and slide of the talus:** Sit comfortably and lift your feet off the floor. You are now in a position to visualize the movements of the ankle: As you point your foot, visualize the rolling backward of the talus and the sliding forward of its top surface under the mortise. As you flex your foot, visualize the rolling forward and sliding backward of the talus. Repeat the action until you

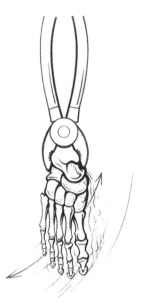

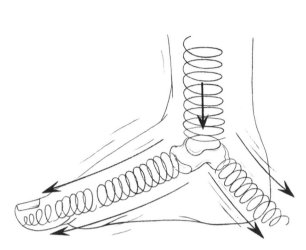

Figure 11.23 The tibia and fibula firmly embrace the talus, allowing the foot to swing in the sagittal plane.

Figure 11.24 Coiled springs converging on the talus.

can feel and see it clearly. Then stand upright on your feet and notice improvements and changes in your sense of balance.

3. **Standing on the talus:** In the standing position, imagine the weight of the body standing squarely on the talus and being distributed to the heel and forefoot by this bone. Imagine your lower leg and foot to be coiled springs converging on the talus and creating a balanced and springy elasticity (figure 11.24).

4. **Lower-leg talus counter-rotation:** Start your imagery practice in the standing position. Bend your legs and imagine the feet sliding or pivoting out on the floor like windshield wipers. Stretch your legs and imagine the feet sliding in on the floor like windshield wipers. Try the opposite image as well: the feet sliding or pivoting inward as you bend your legs. What works better?

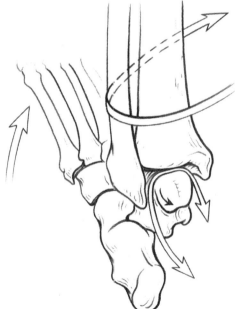

Because the fibula travels farther on the outside of the talus, the lower leg will turn slightly inward with this action or, in reverse, the talus and the foot can be felt as rotating or sliding outward to use a metaphor (figure 11.25). As you stretch your legs, watch the tibia and fibula skim backward over the mound of the talus. Because the fibula travels farther on the

Figure 11.25 The lower leg turns slightly inward; the talus rotates out in dorsiflexion and downward in plié (left foot shown).

outside of the talus, the lower leg turns slightly outward with this action and the talus rotates relatively inward. The balance of these two actions, talus moving in opposition to the lower leg, will allow you to maintain dynamic leg alignment.

5. **Talus through the tunnel of the tibia and fibula:** Now perform the same action, but concentrate on the motion of the trochlea of the talus under the tibia and fibula. As you move downward in leg flexion, focus on how the trochlea slips backward beneath the tunnel created by the tibia and fibula (figure 11.26). As you stretch, watch the trochlea slip forward under the tunnel formed by the tibia and fibula.

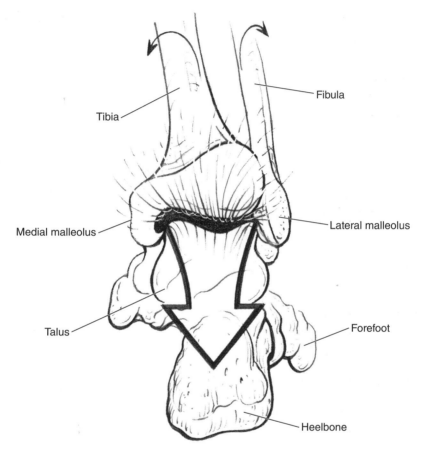

Figure 11.26 As you move downward in lower-limb flexion, focus on how the trochlea of the talus slips backward beneath the tunnel formed by the distal ends of the tibia and fibula.

6. **Talus through saloon doors (plantar flexion and dorsiflexion):** As you point your foot, visualize the tibia and fibula as two saloon doors opening in front (anteriorly), allowing the talus to move forward. As you flex your foot, visualize the tibia and fibula as saloon doors opening to the rear (posteriorly) and allowing the talus to slide (figure 11.27).

7. **Hands adjusting the talus (non-weight bearing):** Visualize the lower end of the tibia as the palm of a hand and the distal end of the fibula as fingers. The tibial palm supports the talus; the fibular fingers are in charge of subtle adjustments. Imagine the fibular fingers initiating movement of the foot at the ankle in a variety of directions (see figure 11.21).

8. **Membrane sail:** Imagine the interosseous membrane to be a sail located between the tibia and fibula. As the wind blows between the tibia and fibula, the sail billows. Visualize the wind blowing from back to front, then imagine it reversing and making the sail billow in the opposite direction. Imagine several changes of direction in the wind. Sense this flapping back and forth of the sail loosening the area. It is helpful to have a partner touch the area between the tibia and fibula as you visualize this action (figure 11.28).

9. **Interosseus membrane jumping:** Stand in a comfortable position. Start with flexing and extending your legs slowly and rhythmically. Increase your speed at a gradual pace as you visualize the interosseous membrane stretching and the fibula and tibia moving away from each other during ankle dorsiflexion (lower-limb flexion). Use the most elastic mental image for this action: rubber bands, taffy, chewing gum, exercise band being stretched. Increase your speed until you feel ready to hop or jump. Feel the widening happening in the precise moment of landing. You may also exaggerate the image of widening. See if you can also walk and run with the sense that compression (downward) forces are being turned into widening tensile (horizontal elastic) forces with each step.

10. **Fibular dance:** Stand in a comfortable position and visualize your fibula. As you flex your legs, imagine the fibula moving up, back, and rotating medially. Feel the fibula as free and mobile, not weight bearing. It is the adjusting rudder, so to speak, while the tibia carries the load. As you extend your legs, visualize the fibula moving in the opposite direction: down, forward, and rotating laterally. See if you can imagine the action during rhythmic

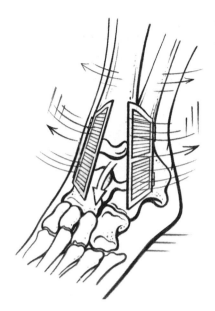

Figure 11.27 As you point your foot, visualize the fibula and tibia widening slightly and creating space as if two saloon doors were opening up.

Figure 11.28 Imagine the interosseous membrane to be a billowing sail located between the tibia and fibula.

leg bending. When you feel that you have a clear image of fibular action, also try jumping. See if you can power your jump by imagining the fibula rapidly moving down and turning out. Stretch your arms out at your sides to model the action of the fibula. As you jump, move the arms in tandem with the fibula. Also reverse the image to see how it impedes your movement. Notice once again how imagining correct function improves function.

11. **Fibular boost:** When jumping, imagine the fibula shooting toward the floor as if it were an arrow. For the more technical minded, you can think of the tibia as a rocket and the fibula the powerful exhaust pushing downward.

12. **Energetic pointing:** As you point your ankle in plantar flexion, visualize a flow of energy down the front of the leg, circling the tarsal bone and continuing over the top of the foot and out through the toes. When dorsiflexing the foot, imagine the energy flowing down the back of the leg, circling the tarsal bone and continuing out the heel (figure 11.29).

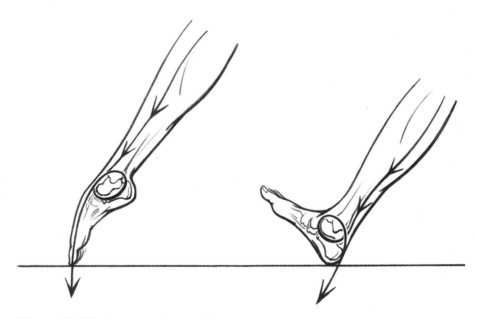

Figure 11.29   As you point and flex your ankle, visualize the flow of energy.

FOOT

Most feet spend their time enclosed in leathery, bodicelike containers. For some athletes, taking off their shoes in a movement class is a novel experience. Quite a few "ahs" and "ohs" are heard as the foot is revealed to be a complex, multijointed entity and not just a lever that assists the legs in walking and jumping. Dancers are usually aware of the technical and aesthetic importance of their feet, but sadly, dance injuries commonly involve the foot. Increased awareness of alignment and balanced strength and flexibility will go a long way in preventing foot problems and increasing the foot's expressive potential.

The foot consists of 26 bones that form 25 component joints. Its duties are numerous and even contradictory in nature. The foot serves as a stable foundation, carrying and cushioning the entire weight of the body. It also propels you through space while adapting to changes in the terrain. The image of a twisted and untwisted chain explains the seemingly instantaneous transformation of the foot from a weight-bearing foundation mechanism to a lever. If you twist a jointed chain, it becomes rigid, much like the foot in its position as a lever. Untwist the chain and it becomes loose, spreading to better carry weight.

The foot can be subdivided in a variety of ways. Three functional sections can be described from front to back (figure 11.30). The hindfoot, or tarsus, consists of comparatively large bones: the talus (cube; the ancient Romans used to play dice with *tali*) and the calcaneus (heel). As you learned earlier, the talus (anklebone) is the transfer point of the body's weight to the foot. The midfoot, or tarsal bones, consist of the navicular (little boat), cuboid (squarelike), and three cuneiforms (wedge formed). The forefoot consists of the metatarsals and the phalanges (toe bones). The joints between the tarsal bones can move in all planes—up and down, sideways, and around. The joints' surfaces can glide on each other, distributing the impact in a multitude of planes.

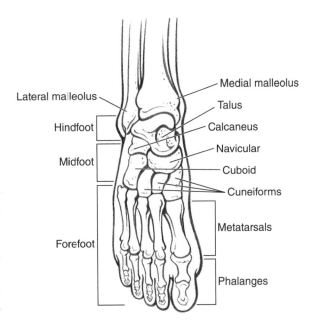

Figure 11.30 The hindfoot (tarsus) consists of the talus and the calcaneus. The midfoot consists of the navicular, cuboid, and three cuneiforms. The forefoot consists of the metatarsals and phalanges.

The foot may be compared to springs in a sack (figure 11.31). Drop the sack on the floor and the springs will rebound slightly, transferring shock to each other, equalizing any excess forces. Most likely, no individual spring is overly stressed and will break. If, however, the springs are replaced with rigid blocks, eliminating the ability to move in relationship to each other, some of them would break if the sack were dropped. The tarsal bones are perfectly fitted to each other to absorb and transfer forces and create a stable and enduring whole.

The foot has two basic functions: support and locomotion. These can be considered separately by dividing the foot into a heel foot and an ankle foot. The heel foot, consisting of the fourth and fifth phalanges and metatarsals, cuboid, and calcaneus, contacts the ground more readily and relates to the fibula and the support function. The ankle foot consists of the first three phalanges and metatarsals, cuneiforms,

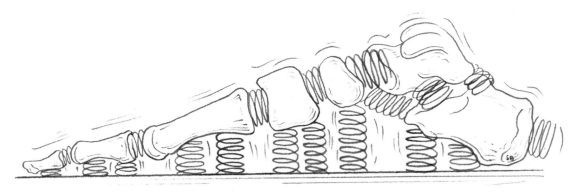

Figure 11.31 The springy foot is able to transfer force from one bone to the other to absorb shock.

navicular, and talus and relates to the tibia. This springy part of the foot transfers the ground reaction force to the tibia, which relates it more to locomotion. The foot also functions to adapt to uneven surfaces and absorb impact. Since it is the part of the body that is most often in direct contact with the environment, it serves proprioceptive functions related to balance, support, and locomotion.

Guided Foot Massage

Fortunately, feet are very accessible to the hands. Most people have at some point massaged their tired, aching feet. The following is a guide to foot massage that will help you identify the many landmarks in this remarkably complex structure.

The inner anklebone, or medial malleolus, is an enlargement of the lower (distal) end of the tibia. The outer ankle, or lateral malleolus, is an enlargement of the distal end of the fibula. Notice that the lateral malleolus is farther down and farther to the rear than the inner malleolus. Stand with your feet parallel and notice how the lateral malleolus is farther back than the medial malleolus.

The talus (anklebone) is much harder to touch. In full plantar flexion, you can usually touch the head of the talus, located on top of the foot between the malleoli, but it recedes when the foot is dorsiflexed. Another place where the head of the talus can be touched is just below and to the front of the medial malleolus. (Anatomically, flexion refers to extreme states. Plantar flexion is toward the sole of the foot, dorsiflexion toward the top of the foot. The term *flex* is really dancers' slang for one type of flexion—dorsiflexion.)

In front of and below the medial anklebone (talus) and distal to the point you just touched, locate the tuberosity (bulge) of the navicular bone. Continue moving toward the toes and locate the base of the first metatarsal bone. Just below the medial malleolus, feel the small, ledge-shaped sustentaculum tali (supporter of the talus), which is part of the calcaneus (heelbone).

Touch the calcaneus on both the medial and lateral sides. Besides its large, smooth posterior portion, you can feel a protrusion of the calcaneus below and in front of the lateral malleolus called the peroneal trochlea. Touch the Achilles tendon above the posterior part of the calcaneus. Glide your fingers along the outer rim of the foot toward the toes, where you will encounter a bony knob, which is the base of the fifth metatarsal bone. It is located just behind the midpoint of the outside rim of the foot. Palpate the cuboid bone between the calcaneus and the base of the fifth metatarsal. The cuneiforms form the arched instep of the foot and are best massaged with relaxed toes so that the extensor tendons do not protrude. Touch the heads of the metatarsal bones on both the dorsal and plantar sides of the foot. (This will be more difficult on the plantar side because of the many layers of muscle.) Below the head of the first metatarsal bone, palpate the part of the flexor hallucis tendon (the tendon that flexes the big toe) known as the sesamoid bones. Finally, manipulate the toe bones (phalanges) and the interphalangeal joints.

Subtalar Joint

The subtalar joint is of prime importance to the adaptability of the foot. If you take a lunge to the side and keep your feet planted on the floor, you will have activated your subtalar joints to do so. If you step on the edge of a rock with resulting twists of your foot, you do not necessarily fall over because the ankle and leg can remain upright as the result of adjustments performed in the subtalar joints. Its dynamic alignment is key to maintaining safety in all kinds of sports, dance, and exercise.

The talus has three articulations with the underlying heelbone. The posterior joint between the talus and the calcaneus is saddlelike; the calcaneus provides the convex saddle and the talus rides on top of it. In the anterior compartment are three meeting points of the bones: a medial joint and an anterior joint between the talus and the calcaneus and a joint between the talus and the navicular. In the latter case, the head of the talus is convex and the surface of the navicular is concave. The subtalar joint also has an elastic joint formed by the so-called spring ligament running from the sustentaculum tali to the navicular. The triangular ligament provides a trampoline-like elastic support for the talus on the inside of the foot. Imagining the spring ligament during walking and jumping creates a welcome sense of rebound.

The motions of the subtalar joints are called supination and pronation and involve a sliding of the joint surfaces on top of each other. The motion can be visualized as a curvilinear, screwlike, or spiraling motion. In subtalar supination (rolling on the outside of the foot), the calcaneus inverts and adducts, moving toward the midline of the body. In subtalar pronation (rolling on the inside of the foot), the calcaneus everts and abducts, moving away from the midline of the body. Some plantar flexion is involved in supination, and dorsiflexion is involved in pronation. The axis of supination and pronation is oblique, inclined upward about 42 degrees and medially about 16 degrees. The relationship between the lower leg and the midfoot can be visualized as a mitered hinge (Norkin and Levangie 1992). In figure 11.32, the foot is depicted in a neutral position. Internal rotation of the lower leg causes pronation of the foot; external rotation of the lower leg causes supination. Supination and pronation allow you to walk

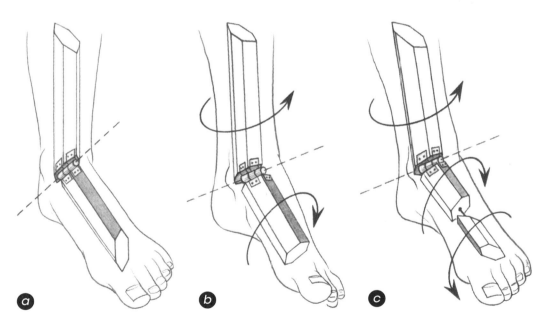

Figure 11.32 *(a)* The relationship between the lower leg and the midfoot can be visualized as a mitered hinge. *(b)* External rotation of the lower leg causes supination. *(c)* If the heel slips and rolls into a supinated position, the forefoot compensates by pronating.

Adapted from P.K. Levangie and C.C. Norkin, 2001, *Joint structure and function: A comprehensive analysis*, 3rd ed. (Philadelphia: F.A. Davis), 379, 385.

along a slope with relative ease. If the hillside is to your right, your right subtalar joint will be pronated and your left subtalar joint supinated, allowing your legs to remain fairly vertical. The action of the subtalar joint is also important in maintaining balance.

In a neutral standing position, a line drawn down the back of the leg should not veer inside or outside as it passes down over the calcaneus. In other words, the portion of the body's weight passing down through the heel can be visualized directly at its center. In standing with the legs extended in alignment, the plane through the Achilles tendon and center of the heel is perpendicular to the floor. But this neutral position, as in the whole leg, is only a moment of time in the movement of the bones as you bend and stretch your legs. The bones of the foot are not a stack of cubes but have the ability to counterbalance each other in movement, absorbing force while maintaining a combined aligned plumb line (figure 11.33).

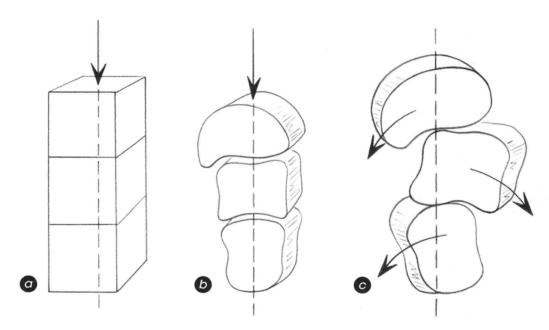

Figure 11.33 *(a)* Immobile stack of bricks; *(b)* mobile stack of foot bones; *(c)* counterbalancing bones absorbing force while maintaining alignment.

The talus is firmly lodged in its tibiofibular mortise. During weight-bearing supination and pronation, the talus abducts and adducts, respectively, and is forced to move the mortise along with it. This means that supination externally rotates the lower leg, and pronation internally rotates it. These relationships are rather easy to feel and have important consequences for exercise, sports, and dance training. If someone is instructed to lift the arches of their feet, it will tend to supinate the foot and externally rotate the lower leg, causing the pelvic floor to tighten and the sacrum to counternutate. Hip flexion will now be more challenging and the lumbar spine more flexed, increasing pressure on the lumbar discs. Posturally instructed supination will also increase the obliquity of the patellar tendon, which is not a favorable position for the health of patellar movement over time. This is another example of the consequences of positioning as the only solution for improving alignment. The alternative solution is to learn how to move with functional awareness, which will allow the body to find its best balance and unrestricted flexibility in all positions.

Imagery Exercises for the Subtalar Joint

1. **Touching the subtalar joint:** Touch the sustentaculum tali on the medial side of the foot below the medial malleolus. It juts out like a little supporting balcony under the medial talus. Just above the sustentaculum you can feel joint space between the sustentaculum, which is part of the heelbone and the talus. If you move the heelbone, you can feel the heel and talus moving relative to each other, the calcaneus moving around a more fixed talus. On the lateral side of the foot you can find the sinus tarsi just in front of the lateral malleolus and next to the corner of the talar neck. If you have trouble finding the neck, dorsiflex your foot until the tendon of the long toe extensor sticks out from the front of the ankle. Medially you will detect a snuffbox-like space inhabited by the talar neck, which you can feel best in plantar flexion and supination of the foot. Below and in front of the sinus tarsi is the cuboid bone; below and behind you can touch the calcaneus. This is an ideal place for improving your mental orientation of the joints of the foot. Wag your heel back and forth and feel the joint space between the more fixed talus and the heelbone swinging around it. The joint movement is a sliding of the calcaneus in a curvilinear arc. You can also imagine the right heel performing a clockwise screwlike (spiraled) motion on supination and a counterclockwise screwlike motion on pronation. For the left heel, the directions reverse.

2. **Weight distribution:** Stand in a comfortable position. Imagine the flow of weight through the talus to the foot. Experience your body weight resting on your two tali. The tali in turn distribute the weight they received to the front and the back. You may imagine the talus having two feet pushing front and back (figure 11.34). Seventy percent of its weight is resting on the calcaneus; the remainder is distributed forward to the midfoot (navicular).

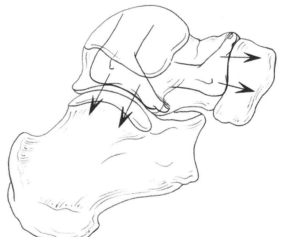

Figure 11.34 The talus has two feet, the anterior one transferring weight to the navicular, the posterior inferior foot transferring weight to the calcaneus.

3. **Imagining subtalar motion in the open chain:** With your foot off the floor, perform supination and pronation (swing your foot back and forth). Imagine the calcaneus sliding around the talus. The mid- and forefoot are moving and only the talus remains in place. Visualize the navicular spinning on the head of the talus while the calcaneus slides underneath the talus.

4. **Ground-reaction-force geyser:** In the standing position, imagine the ground-reaction force surging through the foot and joining at the talus to travel up the leg to the rest of the body.

5. **Imagining movement of calcaneus and talus in standing supination and pronation:** As you supinate, the heelbone inverts and the talus abducts and dorsiflexes. The foot becomes taller. As you pronate, the heelbone everts and the

talus adducts and plantar-flexes. The foot becomes wider. It may help to imagine the relationship between the two bones as counterrotating cogwheels.

6. **Imagining subtalar motion in standing supination and its effect on the leg and pelvis:** Stand in a comfortable position. Your calcaneus now is more fixed to the floor by the weight of your body. Supinate the foot and notice the effect on your whole leg. The abduction of the talus is now moving the mortise externally; therefore supination will cause your leg to rotate externally and your knees to extend slightly. The sit bones will tend to approximate and the pelvis will rotate posteriorly. The calcaneus will now invert (varus heel).

7. **Imagining subtalar motion in standing pronation and its effect on the leg and pelvis:** When you pronate your foot, the leg will tend to rotate inward and the knees will flex while the calcaneus will evert (valgus heel). The adduction of the talus is moving the mortise and rotating the leg inward. The sit bones will tend to move apart and the pelvis will rotate anteriorly. In exercises 6 and 7 you notice that your leg and pelvis are a functional whole, and a change in one part has consequences for the whole system.

8. **Lower-leg rotation—deep roots (balance on one leg):** Ask a friend to balance on one leg and observe the supination and pronation activity. If your friend closes his or her eyes, this motion will be even more evident because without the use of the optical righting mechanisms, balancing is more difficult. Now ask your friend to imagine his or her standing foot to have roots extending deep into the floor. Notice any changes in your friend's ability to balance.

9. **Heavy weight (standing, balancing on one leg):** Practice as previously with a partner but now suggest the following image: The talus is a heavy weight suspended by a plumb line from the hip joint. Allow the weight and plumb line to become very still.

10. **Counterbalance (standing):** Imagine the relationship between the heelbone and talus to be that of circus balance artists. The two bones stay on top of each other by balancing each other's motion. Imagine the two bones to be very sensitive to each other's movement and aiming to stay well balanced.

11. **Subtalar counterrotation:** The heel and the anklebone are two counterrotating cylinders. If the two cylinders move equally and opposite, the lower leg will stay aligned. As you bend your legs, the talus cylinder rolls outward and the heel cylinder rolls inward (figure 11.35). As you stretch your legs, the talus rolls inward and the heel rolls outward.

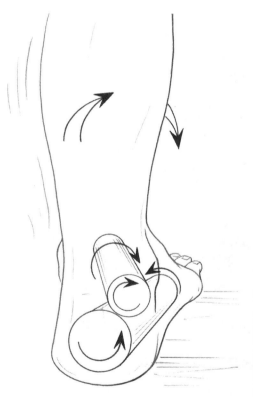

Figure 11.35 Talus and calcaneus are two counterrotating cylinders. The illustration shows the right foot while legs are bent in the standing position.

Repeat the movement with imagery until clear. Notice if the image improves the resiliency and balance of your whole leg.

12. **Abduction and adduction fan:** Starting from a standing position, focus on the movement of the talus in the horizontal plane. This is the abduction-adduction component of supination and pronation. As you bend your legs in the standing position, the talus will adduct and the calcaneus relatively abducts. Imagine the movement to be like a fan widening; as you stretch your legs the action reverses (figure 11.36). The talus abducts and the calcaneus relatively adducts, the fan closes, and the foot becomes slightly taller. Repeat the action several times using the following self-talk. As you bend your legs, *Fan opens, foot widens;* as you stretch your legs, *Fan narrows and the foot becomes slightly taller.*

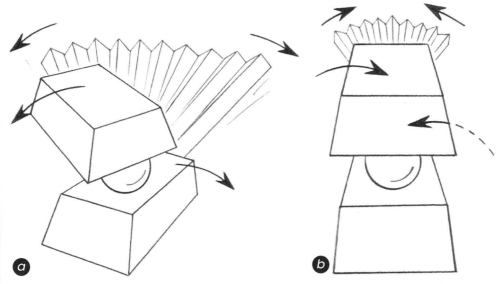

Figure 11.36 Fanlike movement of talus and calcaneus in the right foot in standing position: *(a)* lower-limb flexion (dorsiflexion of the foot); *(b)* lower-limb extension (plantar flexion).

13. **Heel pendulum (standing, balancing on one leg):** Feel the contact surface between your heel and the floor. Imagine the heel to be a pendulum. Visualize the pendulum swinging in and out as you supinate and pronate. The pendulum's swing decreases until it hangs down toward the center of the earth. The heel is now in line with the Achilles tendon (figure 11.37).

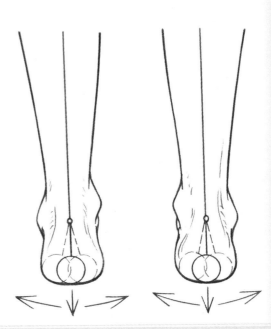

Figure 11.37 Imagine the heel to be a swinging pendulum.

Transverse Tarsal Joint

The transverse tarsal joint (the midtarsal joint) is composed of the talonavicular and the calcaneocuboid articulations (figure 11.38). Together with the subtalar joint, the transverse tarsal joint creates most of the supination and pronation action of the foot. The two joints can work together to create a large degree of supination and pronation or in opposition to each other, allowing the forefoot and hindfoot to twist in opposite directions.

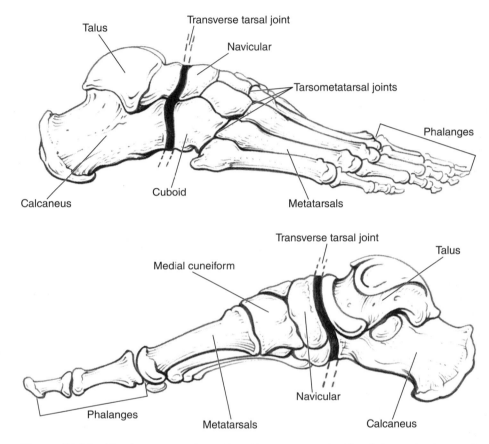

Figure 11.38 The transverse tarsal joint is composed of the talonavicular and calcaneocuboid joints.

Working together to create full supination, the subtalar and transverse tarsal joints cause the foot to become more rigid, which is called the closed-pack position and increases the stability of the foot. The foot is now in lever mode and is able to push against the ground with great force. If the foot is fully pronated, the bones unwind and the foot becomes more flexible. This can be described as the foundation mode where the foot is wider on the ground than in the air. The foot should not spend all its time fixated in either one of these positions but be able to change between the two modes depending on the necessities of movement and the terrain.

Without the transverse tarsal joint, it would be difficult to walk across uneven ground because this joint mediates between the forefoot and the hindfoot (figure 11.39). If the forefoot is forced to supinate, the hindfoot need not follow suit because the transverse tarsal joint can counter this action, allowing the heel to remain vertical. The reverse holds true as well: If the heel slips and rolls into a pronated position, for example, the forefoot can remain flat on the ground.

If the forefoot is made to pronate, the hindfoot counters by supinating. If the heel slips and rolls into a supinated position, the forefoot compensates by pronating (see figure 11.32c). This is essential if you like to walk in moccasins or barefoot, but otherwise the rigid shoes worn today all but eliminate the action of the transverse tarsal joint. This is not necessarily advantageous, because it places additional strain on the ankle and knee joints. Also, certain muscles and joints of the foot lose strength because they are not being exercised.

The transverse tarsal joint, also called Chopart's joint, has a wavelike contour. The lateral part of the wave is formed by the articulation between the calcaneus and the cuboid. The cuboid is somewhat triangular in shape and its joint surface facing the calcaneus is shaped like a saddle. The ventral calcaneus is somewhat funnel shaped and faces the cuboid with its matching convex saddle-shaped joint surface. The joints interlock rather firmly, helping to stabilize the heel side of the foot. The medial part of the transverse tarsal joint is between the tarsal bone and the navicular. The navicular offers an oval concave joint surface that is smaller than the opposing facet from the talus,

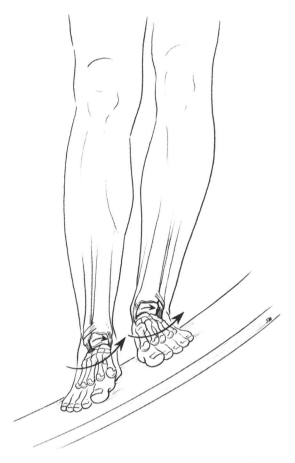

Figure 11.39 Subtalar and transverse tarsal joint adapting to an oblique surface.

which is convex. Here ample movement is possible. You can imagine an Earth-to-Moon relationship as the flexible navicular swings around its more stable neighbor in supination and pronation.

Two joint axes can be visualized in the transverse tarsal joint, creating supination and pronation with a spiraling feeling in the midfoot and forefoot. The longitudinal axis runs in a slightly oblique fashion through the calcaneus and the nose of the cuboid. Around this axis the forefoot spirals in an inversion-and-eversion fashion. The oblique axis runs from craniomedial to caudolateral and is angled 50 degrees to horizontal. The spiral created by this axis contains adduction and plantar flexion in supination and abduction and dorsiflexion in pronation.

Imagery Exercises for the Transverse Tarsal Joint

1. **Long-axis tarsal twist:** Firmly hold your heel with one hand. With the other hand, twist (supinate and pronate) the forefoot along the long axis of the foot. Imagine you are wringing a towel while keeping it in a straight line. Visualize the facet of the navicular spinning on the head of the talus. Notice that the medial aspect of the transverse tarsal joint is moving more than the lateral. After twisting one foot, compare the feel and balance of both feet in a standing position.

2. **Oblique-axis tarsal twist:** Firmly hold your heel with one hand. With the other hand, twist (supinate and pronate) the forefoot along an oblique axis through the foot. Supinating the foot will now involve some plantar flexion and adduction; pronating the foot will involve some dorsiflexion and abduction. Your imaginary towel is now twisting and flexing at the same time. After twisting one foot, compare the feeling of both feet in a standing position.

3. **Imagining the transverse tarsal action in the standing leg in flexion and extension:** Stand in a comfortable position. Flex our lower limbs while visualizing the subtalar and transverse tarsal joints. Imagine a slight unwinding of the foot spiral as you bend your legs. Imagine a slight amount of foot spiraling as you stretch your legs. If you prefer anatomical imagery, imagine a slight amount of supination in the transverse tarsal joint as you bend your legs and a slight amount of pronation in your transverse tarsal joint as you stretch your legs. Notice what happens if you perform the opposite action: pronation of the transverse tarsal joint during lower-limb flexion. Your foot as a whole will tend to overpronate and may feel like it is collapsing inward.

4. **Heel as a boat on the waves:** Supinate and pronate your feet while in a standing position. Imagine the heel to be a boat rocking on the waves (figure 11.40). As you pronate your foot, the top of the heel-ship will rock inward; however, the transverse tarsal joint allows the midfoot and forefoot to counterbalance in the opposite direction of supination. As you supinate your foot, the heel-ship rocks outward and the transverse tarsal joint and forefoot oppose the action by pronating.

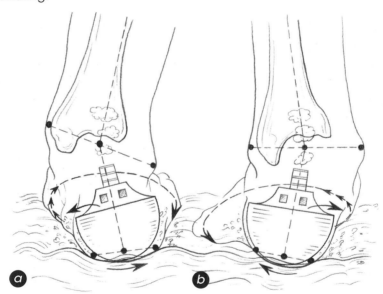

Figure 11.40 Heels as ships rocking in the water. *(a)* Pronation of the heel is counterbalanced by supination at the transverse tarsal joint; *(b)* supination of the heel is counterbalanced by pronation at the transverse tarsal joint.

5. **Forefoot and hindfoot twist:** Take an object such as this book (you may walk along the outer edge of this book; it's included in the price) and place it under the lateral side of your forefoot. Notice how the forefoot pronates and the hindfoot relatively supinates to keep your talus upright. Now place the book under the medial forefoot. In this case, the forefoot is supinating while the hindfoot is relatively pronating to keep you from losing your balance.

6. **Uneven ground:** Take a walk over imaginary uneven ground. Visualize a variety of odd shapes to step on and watch how your foot adapts. Now collect some real objects that cannot harm your feet, such as small stones. After experimenting for a while with walking on real objects, try walking over the imaginary uneven ground again.

7. **Rubber raft:** Imagine your foot to be an inflatable rubber raft. Such a raft can readily adapt to all kinds of waves because it is able to twist along its longitudinal axis. Watch the twisting adjustments of the raft as you walk along a rocky road (figure 11.41).

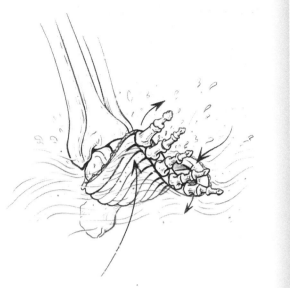

Figure 11.41 Comparing the twisting adjustments of the foot to the movement of a rubber raft.

Tarsals and Metatarsals

The foot contains five tarsal bones. Three of them are called cuneiforms, which is also the name of one of the earliest forms of writing invented by the Sumerians in 3000 BC. The wedge shape of the bones resemble the Sumerian letters. The other two bones are the navicular (boatlike) and the cuboid (cubelike). A transverse section through the intercuneiform and cuneocuboid joints reveals a Roman-style arch and a shape that resembles a cresting wave. The tarsal bones are able to supinate, pronate, flex, and extend relative to each other. Even though the movements are small, they contribute significantly to force absorption and balance.

The five metatarsals are the longest bones of the foot and are therefore an important part of its leverage system. The tarsometatarsal joints also aid the transverse tarsal joint in compensatory motions of the foot. Since it is firmly wedged between the tips of the second and third cuneiforms, the second ray is both the most stable and longest of the five metatarsals. The distal surfaces of the first and fifth tarsometatarsal joints are perpendicular to each other, enabling folding and doming actions of the forefoot. The midtarsal and tarsometatarsal joints work together to create a degree of supination and pronation with their elements of adduction and flexion and abduction and extension. Following are visualizations of the movement as a twisting and untwisting spiral.

Imagery Exercises for the Transverse Tarsal and Metatarsal Joints

1. **Moving the tarsals:** Firmly hold your heelbone with both hands so it cannot move. See how much you can supinate and pronate the forefoot. Do not move the knee or ankle, and keep toe movement to a minimum. You will then be able

to discover how much transverse tarsal, intertarsal, and metatarsophalangeal twisting is available to you.

2. **Heel pendulum while rising on toes:** As you rise on your toes, the foot twists slightly to become more rigid. The heel of the right foot swings slightly inward while the forefoot relatively counterrotates. This causes the bones of the foot to lock and the foot to be more stable. The movement is reflected in the swing of the heel when you rise up on your toes; as you lower, the foot untwists again. As you rise, imagine the heel swinging inward and the forefoot swinging relatively outward (figure 11.42a). As you lower again, imagine the heel swinging outward and the forefoot swinging relatively outward (figure 11.42b). This image will give you a much firmer support as you rise on the balls of your feet.

3. **Sit bone heel pendulum (standing):** Extend the strings of the heel pendulums upward and attach them to your sit bones. Imagine the heel pendulums hanging from your sit bones. As you rise up, feel the heels and the sit bones go inward; as you lower, imagine the heels and the sit bones go outward.

4. **Metatarsals as river logs (standing and walking):** The metatarsal bones can be visualized as logs in a river, touching each other along their entire lengths (figure 11.43). As seen from above, the logs can rotate in two directions: toward each other and away from each other. If they rotate outward, water is pushed upward between them. If they rotate toward each other, they push the water to the side. Visualize the movement of the logs as you walk. When you place weight on your foot, watch the logs spread apart. As you lift your foot, watch them move closer.

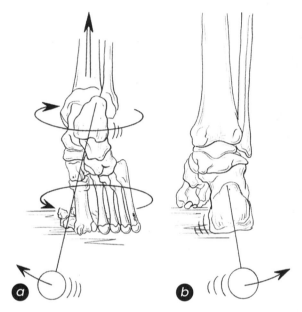

Figure 11.42 Heel pendulum while rising on the toes of the right foot. *(a)* Heel swings in (supination) while rising on the right foot. *(b)* Heel swings out (pronation) during flexion of the right foot.

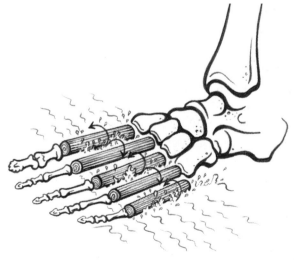

Figure 11.43 Visualize the metatarsal bones as logs in a river.

Toes

Moving in a natural environment seems to create wonderfully aligned toes and feet. The muscles, bones, and joints of the feet thrive among variability of demand, as you can see when observing the aligned toes of the woman in figure 11.44, who washes every day in the mountain streams of India.

There are 14 phalanges in the 5 toes—2 in the big toe and 3 in each of the smaller toes. Rather than carry weight, the toes should be free to make subtle weight adjustments to readily maintain balance. The joints between the metatarsals and phalanges have two active degrees of freedom: extension and flexion and abduction and adduction. The axes for these movements are transverse and vertical,

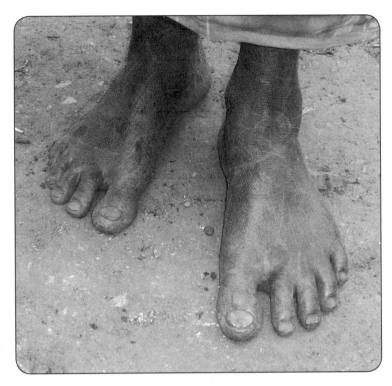

Figure 11.44 Aligned toes of an Indian woman.

respectively. You can also rotate them somewhat around a longitudinal axis, but since there are no muscles that can perform this action, you can do it only with the help of your hands. The interphalangeal joints can only flex and extend. All movements of the metatarsophalangeal and interphalangeal joints contribute to the balance, adaptation, and leverage of the foot.

The rounded wheel-like joint heads of the metatarsals fit into the sockets offered by the phalanges. The base of the socket is reinforced by a cartilaginous plate. During flexion and extension, the joint heads of the metatarsals spin in the convex sockets offered by the cartilage plates and the phalanges.

Two sesamoid bones are located beneath the head of the first and stoutest metatarsal bone. These sesamoids function as impact absorbers and guiding rails for the flexor hallucis longus tendon, the important flexor of the big toe. The sesamoids are attached to muscular reins like a horse and bridle furnished by the flexor hallucis brevis. Some sideways movement is provided by the abductor hallucis attaching to the lateral sesamoid and the adductor hallucis attaching to the medial sesamoid. These muscles also serve to create stronger support for the foot at its edge.

As you go up on the balls of your feet, the toes crease along the heads of the metatarsals, creating the metatarsal break, which lies along the second to fifth metatarsal heads. It is slightly oblique, allowing the weight of the body to be more evenly distributed among the toes. The plantar surfaces of these heads constitute the ball of the foot, the standing surface in demi-pointe.

The foot is at once a foundation—a stable base of support—and a flexible, adaptable lever that can maneuver you through irregular terrain. Its multiple-arch system and the strong ties that reinforce these vaults add flexibility and bounce. Its numerous joints support you and enable you to maintain balance.

Imagery Exercises for the Toes

1. **Spinning metatarsal heads:** As you rise up on the balls of your feet, observe the heads of the metatarsals spinning in the sockets formed by the phalanges and cartilage base plate.

2. **Spreading toes (rising on the balls of the feet):** Imagine the toes spreading out over the floor, creating a large base of support.

3. **Sesamoid movement (rising on the balls of the feet):** Imagine the sesamoids being pulled backward about half an inch (a little more than 1.25 cm) as you rise up. Imagine the sesamoids moving forward a half an inch as you lower down.

4. **Metatarsal break sinking downward (rising up on the balls of the feet):** As you rise onto the balls of your feet, imagine the toes lengthening and the metatarsal break sinking into the floor. Watch the metatarsal break sink downward evenly (figure 11.45).

5. **Toes as dandelion parachutes (supine improvisation):** Imagine the toes to be dandelion parachutes. Watch them float off the end of your feet (figure 11.46).

6. **Toes as feelers (movement improvisation):** Imagine the toes to be sensitive feelers, testing and exploring the space in front of them.

7. **Aligning toes:** Grasp one toe at a time, pull on it, and rotate it gently. Imagine the joints becoming more spacious and the bones aligning. Compare how your feet feel before repeating on the other side.

8. **Weight of the toes:** In the standing position, imagine you can feel the weight of each toe. Bend and stretch your legs, and notice the effect of this image on your whole-leg flexibility.

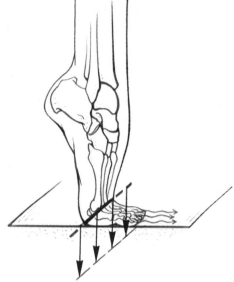

Figure 11.45 As you rise on the balls of your feet, imagine that the toes lengthen and the metatarsal break sinks into the floor.

Figure 11.46 Imagine the toes to be dandelion parachutes.

Arches of the Feet

A multiple-arch system, much like the multiple vaults of the medieval Kloster in Kreuzlingen, Switzerland (figure 11.47), enables the foot to support and distribute the considerable weight of the body. The longitudinal arch begins at the far (distal) end of the heelbone and ends at the far ends of the first and fifth metatarsal bones, respectively (the toes are not part of the arch). The talus is the keystone of the longitudinal arch (figure 11.48a). The keystone of the diagonal arch is the navicular and the cuboid is the keystone of the lateral arch (figure 11.48, b and c).

The middle cuneiform and the second metatarsal bones are the keystones of the transverse arches. The middle cuneiform also serves as the keystone of the diagonal arch. The Romans seemed to have been aware of the importance of the talus as a

Figure 11.47 The medieval Kloster in Kreuzlingen, Switzerland, features multiple arches, like those in the foot, to support and distribute weight.

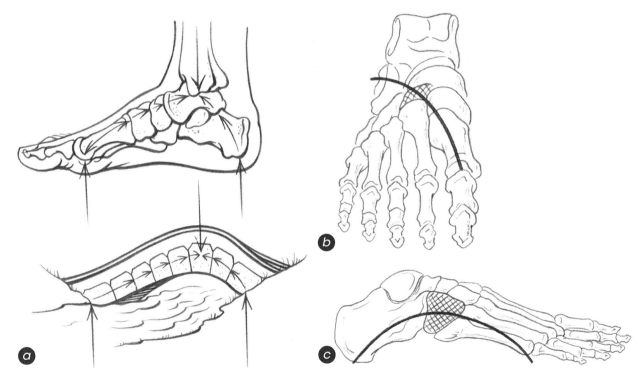

Figure 11.48 (a) The talus is the keystone of the longitudinal arch, (b) the navicular is the keystone of the diagonal arch, and (c) the cuboid is the keystone of the lateral arch.

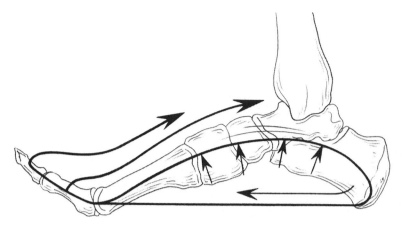

Figure 11.49 Toe extension elevates the arch of foot by tensing the plantar aponeurosis.

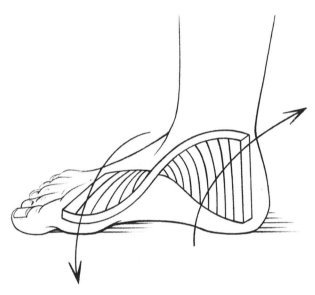

Figure 11.50 The foot can be visualized as a twisted rectangular plane.

keystone, in the physical sense as well as the psychological. In reminding someone not to fall or fail, they would say, *"Recto talo stare"* ("Stand upright on your talus").

The distal ends of the first and usually the fifth metatarsals rest on the buffering sesamoid bones. In this respect, the foot is like an elongated tripod with three main contact points for weight support.

The plantar aponeurosis (neither a foot fetishist nor an obsessed home gardener) is a tough sheet of connective tissue that maintains the arches by tying together both ends of the arch, creating a bowlike tension. Compression of the bow will increase tension in the bowstring, keeping it stable and preventing excessive spreading. The dorsally located toe extensor can contribute to the height of the plantar arch by tensing the aponeurosis in a windlass-like mechanism (figure 11.49).

Earlier you explored the metaphor of a twisted chain to learn how the foot transforms from a rigid lever to a spreadable foundation. Similarly, the foot can be seen as a twisted rectangular plane made of fitted bones and their ligamentous ties. This metaphor helps in understanding the relationship between the longitudinal and transverse arches of the foot. The front of the plane consists of the metatarsal heads, which are close to horizontal and in contact with the floor. The back of the plane, the posterior calcaneus, is vertical (figure 11.50). When you place weight on the foot, it untwists, flattening the arches, which involves pronation; when you push off the floor, as in a leap, the plane twists (supinates) to act as a lever.

Imagery Exercises for the Arches of the Feet

1. **Mediating talus (standing, walking, leaping):** Imagine the talus to be the mediator among the tibia, calcaneus, and navicular. It efficiently manages all incoming and outgoing forces. Like a springy rubber ball with cushioning springs attached to it, the talus receives and distributes forces. To maintain elasticity, no one side of the ball may be subject to constant extremes of pressure (figure 11.51).

2. **Foot as clay:**

   a. **Rolling your clay foot:** Imagine your foot to be a piece of clay. Roll it over a baseball or rubber ball and watch it spread in all directions. The heel spreads to the back and the metatarsals to the front and sides.

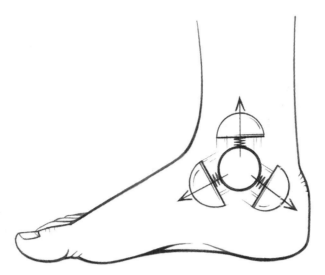

Figure 11.51   The talus is like a mediator among the tibia, calcaneus, and navicular.

   b. **Perfecting your clay foot:** As you point and flex your foot, visualize imaginary hands remodeling your clay foot to perfection.

3. **Foot tripod (standing):**

   a. **Spreading your base:** Visualize the three contact points of the foot—the heel, the distal head of the first-toe metatarsal, and the distal head of the fifth-toe metatarsal as a tripod. Distribute the weight evenly on these three points. Imagine them to be energy centers radiating into space. Imagine the points of the tripod forming a triangle. Watch them move away from each other into space, making an ever-larger triangle (figure 11.52).

   b. **Sci-fi tripod:** Visualize the tripod of the foot. Imagine luminous energy originating at each corner of the tripod, merging at the apex of the vault and streaming up the center of your leg.

   c. **Dynamic tripod:** Stand in a comfortable upright position and focus on the tripods of both feet. Bend your legs and imagine the three footprints of the tripod moving away from each other, spreading the sole of the foot and widening the tripod. Stretch your legs and imagine the tripod becoming smaller, the footprints coming closer to each other. Repeat this action a few times. For comparison you may try to bend and stretch your legs with a nondynamic tripod. You will notice that your legs are more rigid.

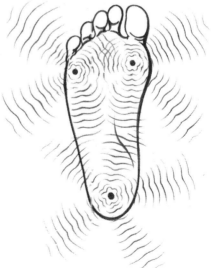

Figure 11.52   Visualize the three main contact points of the foot with the floor as a tripod.

4. **Wave underfoot:** Imagine a geyser lifting the arches of the foot from underneath (figure 11.53).

5. **Transverse arch lift:** Imagine the transverse arch of the foot through the cuneiforms and navicular. Imagine the transverse arch lifting and lowering like a bird flapping its wings (figure 11.54). Every time you step on your foot, the bird's wings flap upward as the arch widens; every time your foot lifts off the floor, the wings flap downward as the arch lifts and domes. Practice this image in walking to activate the transverse arch of your foot.

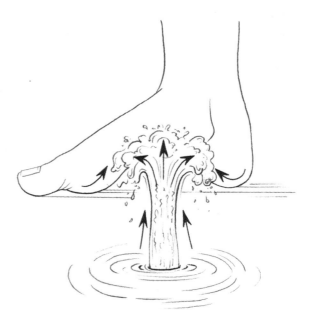

Figure 11.53 A geyser lifts the arch from underneath.

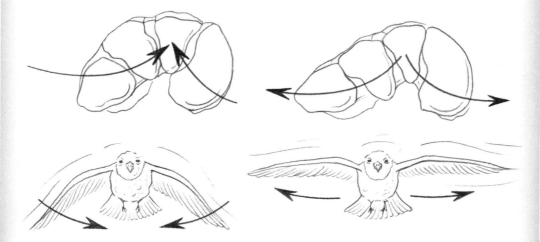

Figure 11.54 Imagine the transverse arch as a bird flapping its wings.

6. **Bow and arrow:**

   a. **Stand on both feet:** Imagine your feet to be bows with the bowstrings toward the floor. Shift your weight from one foot to the other and visualize the bow spreading and the bowstring becoming taut as you place your weight on it. Visualize the bow arching and the bowstring releasing as you take your weight off the foot.

   b. **Foot as a bow with the bowstring toward the floor:** In lower-limb flexion, notice the increasing tension in the string as the bow spreads. In lower-limb flexion, notice the decreasing tension in the string as the bow arches. Now imagine that spreading the bow initiates the downward movement. Finally, imagine the arching of the bow initiating the upward movement.

7. **Three keystones (second position):** Focus on the tali of both feet and the sacrum. Visualize these three keystones simultaneously. Imagine how all three keystones are buttressed equally from both sides. Note that the pelvic arch lies perpendicular to the long arches of the feet.

8. **Foot dome (standing, feet touching in parallel position):** The adjoining arches of the foot create a vaulted structure like a cupola or the Roman pantheon (the oldest domed structure still intact today). The combined tripods of the feet create six major weight-bearing points for the body. There is a small opening between the feet, just in front of the medial anklebone. Imagine a waterspout shooting upward from the ground through the center of this cupola and continuing up between the legs. As the water falls back down, it pours down the outside of the foot, releasing the toes and outer rim of the foot into the ground (figure 11.55).

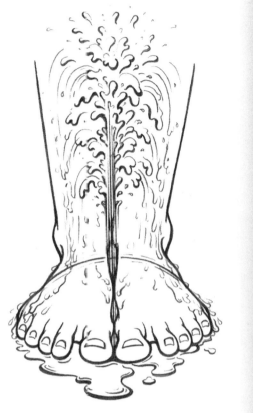

Figure 11.55 Visualize a waterspout spraying upward from between the ankles.

Muscles of the Foot

The foot evolved from the hand. For training the feet, it is therefore helpful to use the foot as if it were a hand to train its muscles. Try grasping a pencil with your toes. Slide a piece of cloth along the floor with your toes. You can divide the muscles of the lower limb according to the muscles' position relative to the fascia in the lower leg.

The dorsal muscles, for example, are arranged in three layers: The gastrocnemius is the most superficial; the soleus is the middle layer; and the tibialis posterior, flexor hallucis longus, and digitorum longus make up the deepest layer. The main mass consists of the soleus. The aforementioned muscles produce flexion and supination. The extensors are not on front where they would ideally be located, but on the side and front of the lower limb. It would not be a good idea to have such a vulnerable mass of muscle available for pumping against rocky outcrops and other obstacles. Even though it hurts to knock your shinbone against an object, it will not immobilize a portion of the muscles of the lower limb. Instead of learning all the functions together with the origin and attachment, visualize the two axes through the ankle. Muscles that run in front of the transverse axis, which runs more or less through the inferior malleoli, will dorsally flex the foot; all muscles behind the transverse axis through the ankle will plantar-flex the foot. All muscles on the lateral side of the (diagonal) axis for supination and pronation will pronate the foot; the ones on the medial side will supinate the foot.

However, most muscles have combined functions. In humans, the gastrocnemius, the soleus, and the plantaris are key muscles for locomotion. They act eccentrically to decelerate your leg with each step. Four-legged animals use their hamstrings concentrically to push themselves forward; humans coast over the legs and these muscles eccentrically, which is very efficient.

The tibialis posterior is a very strong supinator (figure 11.56). It originates deeply at the interosseus membrane and the tibia and fibula. It crosses under the flexor digitorum longus and runs behind the medial malleolus, where you can touch it. It continues above the sustentaculum tali toward the navicular, where you can touch it once again.

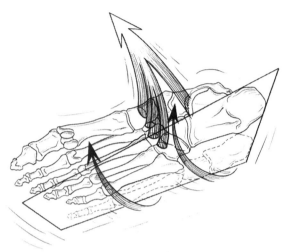

Figure 11.56 Tibialis posterior with its insertions supinating the foot.

The tibialis posterior is the psoas of the foot. It has a very large fanlike area of attachment, a sign of its great power in stabilizing the foot. The strongest fibers run to the tuberosity of the navicular and to the plantar side of the first cuneiform continuing the tibialis posterior's line of action. The middle fibers run to the second and third cuneiforms and with a few fibers to the cuboid and to the bases of the fourth and fifth metatarsal bones. The most dorsal part of the tibialis posterior attaches to the cuboid and the sustentaculum tali. The tibialis posterior attaches to the navicular, which is the highest bone in the foot (not counting the talus, which has no muscle attachments). The tibialis posterior therefore qualifies as the classic stabilizer of the keystone of the arches of the foot. The tibialis posterior even more powerfully elevates the midfoot if you consider its action together with the peroneus longus (PL). They integrate (pull together and lift) both the longitudinal and transverse arches of the foot. The two muscles form a dynamic sling around the sole of the foot.

You have two flexors of the toes: one for the big toe and one for all the other toes. They are called the flexor hallucis longus (FHL) and the flexor digitorum longus (FDL), respectively. The FDL runs behind the medial malleolus. Its tendon can be felt there quite clearly if you flex and extend the large toe. The FDL runs over the sustentaculum tali and then over the flexor hallucis longus. The tendons are connected, coupling their action.

The FHL runs most posteriorly behind the medial malleolus and stays medially on the sole of the foot as it runs to the big toe. It courses underneath the sustentaculum tali providing support. Both the FDL and the FHL aid in stabilizing the longitudinal arch of the foot. Both of these muscles need an occasional stretch as modern shoes do not permit this action. To stretch them: Extend your toes (lift them up vigorously) and dorsiflex your ankle at the same time with your foot firmly planted on the floor. The FHL stabilizes the long arch of the foot also when elevated on the ball of the foot (demi-pointe). It runs underneath the sustentaculum tali. Imagine the FHL elevating the sustentaculum tali as you go up on the ball of your feet. (See also chapter 7 in my 2004 book *Conditioning for Dance*.)

The peroneus brevis (PB) originates on the front and outside of the lower leg and runs behind the lateral malleolus in a common tendon sheath with the peroneus longus (PL). It actually forms a guiderail for the PL. It inserts at the base of the fifth metatarsal. The PB abducts the forefoot and lifts the fifth metatarsal, the outer edge of the foot. It activates a lateral posterior bone rhythm as the fifth metatarsal pushes back the cuboid, which pushes the navicular and heel dorsally. Imagine this event in pronation and the reverse in supination. The PB ensures the fifth metatarsal stays with the cuboid in situations of heavy impact, such as running or jumping.

The PL originates on the lateral lower leg. It runs through a common tunnel with the PB, the floor of which is the lateral malleolus. This is a tight space for two tendons. At this point the tendons practically make a right angle and redirect ventrally. The PL redirects a second time through a special groove in the cuboid underneath the foot. The groove is covered with cartilage, a good anatomical image for smooth PL action. The PL inserts very medially to the first cuneiform and to the bases of the first and second metatarsals. There is also a connection to the first interosseus muscle (and laterally to the flexor digitorum minimi). The PL lifts the lateral side of the forefoot and depresses the medial side of the foot through its insertions on the cuneiforms and the first and second metatarsals. If you feel like climbing a tree with the help of your feet, this muscle will allow you to push the medial side of your foot downward and propel you upward, a function that is pronounced in primates. The classic action of the peroneals is pronation and eversion of the foot. Because they run behind the lateral malleolus on the way to the foot, they can also flex the ankle. As on the other side of the foot, the tendons are held back against the foot by retinaculi. The PB and PL aid in the push-off phase of walking. They help to lift the outside of the foot and to keep your weight over the largest lever for waking, which is the big toe. Extension of the toes in supination is a sign of a weak PL. The extensor digitorum longus is a strong pronator and will compensate for a weak PL. In the flat-footed position the PL's ability to lift the cuboid and therefore stabilize the lateral foot is reduced.

The tibialis group is located at the side and front of the lower leg. They are the tibialis anterior, the extensor digitorum longus (EDL), and the extensor hallucis longus (EHL). They all run in front of the malleoli. The tibialis anterior runs under the superior and inferior extensor retinaculi. If this were not so, the tendons would tend to snap forward like in a bow and arrow. About 1 to 2 centimeters before the tarsometatarsal joint, its tendon divides into two smaller tendons. The first inserts in the medial and plantar side of the first metatarsal base; the other attaches to the medial side of the first cuneiform. The tibialis anterior adducts the foot and lifts the inner rim of the foot; the forefoot follows along. Both the tibialis anterior and the PL tug on the base of the first metatarsal but from opposite sides. The tibialis anterior is a vital muscle in slowing the descent of the foot in the loading response of the foot in walking. It inserts to the first metatarsal head and the first cuneiform.

The EDL runs under the same retinaculi and divides into four tendons thereafter. These insert into the dorsal aponeurosis of the base phalanx. A middle portion of the tendon runs to the middle phalanx while two lateral tendon segments run to the distal phalanx where these two reunite. Through the dorsal aponeurosis is a connection to the interossei. The function of the extensors is manifold. They dorsally extend the ankle and toes in the open chain. In the closed chain they draw the lower leg over the foot. Most of the EDL has the capacity to pronate. The EDL and EHL stabilize the arch of the foot because toe extension increases the tension in plantar aponeurosis. This in turn stabilizes (compresses and lifts) the fundamental arch of the foot.

Imagery Exercises for the Muscles of the Foot

1. **Sliding in their compartments:** As you move your foot, imagine the various muscles of the calf sliding smoothly in their separate compartments.

2. **Flow of gastrocnemius and soleus:** Imagine the gastrocnemius sliding or melting downward and the soleus flowing upward. Notice changes in the flexibility and perceived strength of the ankle.

3. **Navicular support:** With each step, feel the tibialis posterior supporting the navicular and the whole arch of the foot. Imagine the tibialis posterior tugging on the navicular to keep it high and resilient. Imagine the navicular bobbing upward whenever you take the weight off your foot.

4. **Sucking through a straw:** Imagine a straw placed at what you perceive to be the sole of your foot. Imagine sucking water up that straw. You can dome your foot as if it were a mouth gripping a straw. This will center your foot and activate all the muscles that support your arches. You may also want to try the image of eating a long strand of spaghetti.

5. **Lifting hand:** Imagine the tibialis posterior to be a hand reaching around to the sole of the foot and lifting the tarsal bones from below (figure 11.57).

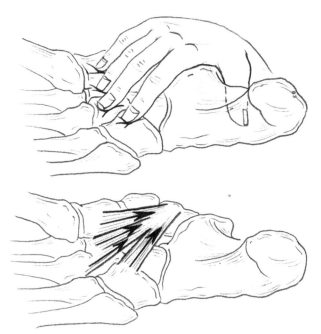

Figure 11.57 Tibialis posterior lifting the foot like a hand (inferior view).

6. **Foot grasp:** Todd (1972) describes the tibialis posterior muscle, with its origins below the knee, as crucial in organizing and maintaining the arch of the foot because of its attachments to the tarsal bones. The following exercises activate the tibialis posterior.

   a. **Massage your claylike, malleable foot:** With your finger, touch the spot on the sole of your foot that you experience as its center. Try to grasp the finger with your whole foot. Enfolding the finger will help activate the muscles that maintain the arch of the foot. Imagine the finger being sucked up by the foot, all the way up between the malleoli.

b. **Fingers coming up from the ground (standing, walking):** As you stand, imagine a finger coming up from the ground under each foot. Imagine your feet grasping the fingers. Each time you take a step, grasp an imaginary finger with your foot.

c. **Acetabular grasp (supine, improvisation):** Simultaneously visualize the center of the foot grasping a finger and the acetabulum grasping the femur head.

d. **Spaghetti through the leg (supine, improvisation):** Imagine a long thread of spaghetti being sucked up through the center of your foot, up the center of your leg, and into the vacuumlike acetabulum.

7. **Lateral bone rhythm of the foot:** Imagine the PB activating a lateral posterior bone rhythm as the fifth metatarsal pushes back the cuboid, which pushes the navicular and heel dorsally. Imagine this event in pronation and reverse the direction in supination.

8. **Climbing a tree:** The PL adducts the big toe, the "thumb" of the foot. Imagine you are climbing a tree with bare feet and using the big toe to push downward to lift you up. Grasping, tree climbing, and pushing the inside of the foot against and down the surface of a tree are good images for this muscle. Imagine a buoyant cuboid in walking.

9. **In the supine position with the feet flat on the floor:** Imagine lifting the cuboid from underneath with help from the PL. Notice whether you can perform this movement and where you feel the muscle activation. Imagine the cuboid to be on an elastic tendon-trampoline. As you land from a jump, imagine the cuboid rebounding in this trampoline situated perfectly beneath it.

10. **PL supports lateral arch:** Imagine the PL supporting the lateral longitudinal arch of the foot. As you walk, imagine the PL pushing the cuboid and the lateral arch forward. If you are a dancer, imagine the PL keeping your weight over the center of the foot by lifting the lateral arch and pronating your foot.

11. **Melting tendons:** To deepen ankle dorsiflexion, imagine the tendons melting and softening in front of the ankle. Think *deep crease* at the front of the ankle.

12. **EDL and EHL pulling lower leg:** At the moment the foot is planted on the floor in walking, imagine the EDL and EHL pulling the lower leg forward over the foot.

13. **Upward and downward flow:** Stand in a comfortable position with equal weight on both feet. Bend your legs slowly and focus on the muscles of the lower limb. As the ankle dorsiflexes, imagine a flow upward along the tibialis anterior and the muscles of the anterior and lateral compartment and down along the posterior muscles of the lower limb. You may bring more precision into the image by sensing the downward flow taking place behind the interosseus membrane, as if the muscles were melting off of the membrane similar to snow sliding down a smooth surface. Notice how these images deepen your leg bend and improve your stability.

14. **Tibialis anterior and PL sling:** Imagine the tibialis anterior and PL forming a sling that connects at the medial cuneiform and base of the first metatarsal. Imagine this sling absorbing force with each step. The tibialis anterior and PL are tugging on the opposite ends of the first cuneiform and base of the first metatarsal. Imagine their forces to be balanced and coordinated as you move.

15. Tibialis posterior and PL sling: Imagine the tibialis posterior and PL forming a sling under the foot comparable to a stirrup (figure 11.58). As you lift up on the ball of your foot, feel the sling lifting your foot from underneath. With each step, imagine the stirrup gently lowering the bones. If you are a dancer performing a plié, allow this sling to gently spread as you go down and lift as you come up again.

16. Support is high: Imagine the tibialis posterior, PL, and tibialis anterior muscles supporting the arches and movement of your foot from high in the lower leg. This is where the actual muscle bellies are located; from here they are acting springlike to absorb and guide the force as you move.

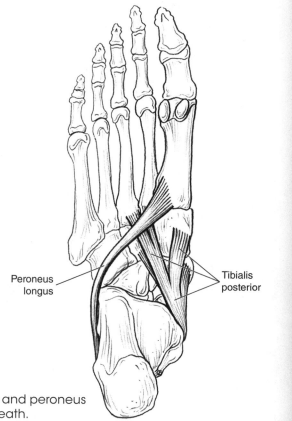

Peroneus longus

Tibialis posterior

Figure 11.58 Tibialis posterior and peroneus longus sling seen from underneath.

SUMMARY

The knee is in the demanding position between the two longest levers in the body. It deals with the challenge elegantly through sheer size and by having two femoral condyles per knee. The meniscal sockets are mobile, providing more flexibility while maintaining stability.

At the ankle, the weight of the leg is transferred to the foot. The tibia is the main bearer of the weight of the body, while the fibula provides mobilizing functions. An interosseus membrane between the two bones can absorb force and provide additional safety from impact. The tibia rotates several degrees in plantar flexion and dorsiflexion, opposing the rotary movement of the femur at the knee. The bone rhythms of the ankle and knee counterbalance each other to create three-dimensional dynamic alignment.

The foot consists of 26 bones and many muscles and ligaments that interact in an ingenious manner to serve the multipurpose tasks of propulsion, foundation, balance, force absorption, sensation, and adaptation. The fundamental design of the foot is the twisted plate, or a spiral segment involving a set of arches. Through adjustments in this spiraled arch, the foot can at once become a more rigid propulsive lever or a wider and stable foundation. Through imagery exercises, this awareness can be improved and the ensuing embodiment benefits whole-body efficiency.

Supination and pronation of the foot influence the leg, pelvis, and whole body in standing. With the help of imagery, these relationships can become felt and seen by the mind's senses, and this knowledge can be used to balance and organize the body for optimal function.

Chapter 12

Spine and Body Wall

Thoughts are generators of being.

Spinal patterns reveal much about cultural heritage and stylistic preferences. In classical ballet, the spine is held in a very slight extension (arched); in classical Spanish dance, it is even more extended (arched); in Native American dance, it is fairly erect; and in traditional Japanese styles, it is slightly flexed (curved forward) (Barba and Savarese 1991). Modern dance employs a great variety of spinal patterns, lumbar initiations, thoracic over- and undercurves, side bends, spirals, and swings.

In typical mammals, the vertebral column is slung like a suspension bridge between the hind legs and forelegs. In humans, this orientation of the spine has been changed to an upright column with many consequences for optimal function. Good alignment is key because a small deviation from the ideal suffices to create constant bending and shearing stresses on the spine. To deal with upright posture, humans have strong abdominal walls, especially in the lower area; the organs are contained within a supportive visceral skeleton. The heart is firmly attached to the diaphragm and connected to the spine with ligaments, and the pelvic floor is reinforced with muscles and fascia. Surprisingly, spinal muscles are less developed in humans than in primates. A human spine is constructed as an upright wave-shaped spring and not configured to be constantly bending forward as may occur in the common desk-bound occupations. In this chapter you will understand how the spine and related muscles work optimally and discover imagery for furthering that functioning in dance, exercise, and sports.

FUNCTIONING SPINE

To fulfill its varied functions, the spine needs to be both stable and mobile. This stability must be dynamic because the spine needs to respond to ever-changing demands of movement and support. Attempts to use static ideas to explain its function will not succeed. The goal is stability during movement—not postural fixation, but dynamic adaptation.

The spine also supports various internal organs and protects the spinal cord while providing outlets for nerves fanning out into the entire body. Composed of many joints, the spine is designed for infinite combinations of movements. If the spine's potential is not fully explored regularly, its muscles, especially the short intrinsic ones, weaken.

As the intermediary between the upper and lower body, the spine carries the weight of the head, organs, and limbs and protects the spinal cord. It does this during complex positions and movements. The spine serves as an attachment site for a multitude of muscles, ligaments, and organs. Through its unique design features, it is able to absorb forces in all dimensions. The intervertebral discs are mostly fluid; the spinal cord is surrounded by the cerebrospinal fluid, and even bone, with its marrow core, is fluid-like at its center. Fluidity should not be equated with weakness, however. If you ever have been knocked down by a breaking wave at the beach, you can appreciate this.

The vertebral column consists of 24 separate vertebrae, composite vertebrae, the sacrum, and the coccyx. The cervical spine, the highest and most mobile part of the vertebral column, consists of seven vertebrae. The thoracic spine consists of 12 vertebrae that support the rib cage. The lumbar spine consists of five large vertebral bodies whose anterior aspects touch or even pass the midline of the body (figure 12.1). The base of the spine is called the sacrum and is composed of five fused vertebrae. The coccyx, the tail of the spine, consists of four vertebral remnants. From the back, the spine down to the lowest lumbar vertebrae looks like a long, slender pyramid, while the sacrum appears to be an inverted pyramid. The broad base of a long pyramid sits on the broad base of a short and wide pyramid, being the most stable static structure. From the side, the spine has four opposing curves in the sagittal plane, which add to its strength and resiliency.

All humans are born with a basic convex curvature, the primary curve, of which the thoracic and the sacrococcygeal remain intact in adulthood. Opposing curves, necessary for sitting and walking, are developed by a baby's exemplary movement efforts. As a baby learns to lift her head, the cervical concavity develops. As she kicks, pushes, pulls, rolls, creeps, and crawls her way through babyhood, the lumbar concavity develops.

Fully understanding the unique spinal design with opposing spinal curves requires a review of human evolution and efficient biomechanical design. In quadrupeds, the spine has only one curve, supported by two pairs of legs in front and in back. Seen from the side, such a spine resembles a suspension bridge similar to the Golden Gate Bridge in San Francisco. In this design the cars are supported by a suspended roadway, just as the organs are supported by the abdominal wall and rib cage in the quadruped. If you were to position such a bridge upright, the singly curved spine would sag forward and buckle unless resisted by powerful posterior muscles. Such is the situation in gorillas or chimpanzees. These animals can walk upright but with much more effort than humans need to put forth.

An apparent solution would be to make the spine straight, like a slender pyramid or a Greek column. This is somewhat the shape of the spine when you look at it from the front.

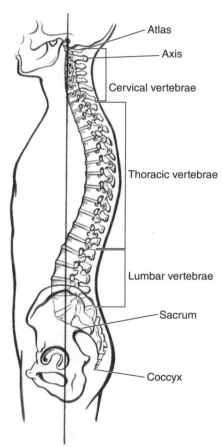

Atlas

Axis

Cervical vertebrae

Thoracic vertebrae

Lumbar vertebrae

Sacrum

Coccyx

Figure 12.1 The vertebral column consists of 24 separate vertebrae, composite vertebrae, the sacrum, and the coccyx.

However, two challenges arise if the spine were a straight column in the sagittal plane: Where do you place the organs and the baby during pregnancy, and how do you absorb forces through a straight spine? A flexible straight column would buckle under strain, and a rigid column would not be able to absorb force, causing shockwaves to reach the spinal cord and brain. The evolution of the two concavities of the spine allowed for a more axially centered structure. The cervical lordosis contributes the necessary dorsal movement of the head back over the sacral base, while the lumbar lordosis contributes a dorsal movement for the thorax. The curves enable the masses of the body, including the viscera (and baby during pregnancy), to be poised over their base of support. If you visualize the spine as a stack of four arches, each one inverted relative to the other, the line of gravity runs behind the apex of the convexity of the arches, thus maintaining the arches' ideal shape. The curves then contribute to force absorption by allowing axial compression to be turned into stretch in the muscles and connective tissue on the convex side of the curves (figure 12.2).

If the spine were straight, the connective tissue and muscles would not be stretched but buckled and shortened. Muscles are much stronger, acting eccentrically; it is easier to support a load through stretch than through compression. The curves intelligently reduce impact on any individual part of the spine by shunting the energy from impact to stretch. Spinal curves need to be adaptive and resilient. In walking, dancing, or jumping, the spine subtly changes the degree of curvature to absorb and release force. An increase in the curve of the arch allows for compression forces to be transferred into stretch, where they can be stored and released to aid further movement. The spine can therefore be likened to a spring or an upright stack of trussed arches. Figure 12.3 exaggerates the changes in the spinal curvature for the purpose of clarity of the action.

Due to differing angles of the spinous processes (projections of the spine), the spinal curves feel flatter to the touch than they actually are. The lumbar spinous processes are nearly horizontal where the spine is concave; in the thoracic concavity, they point downward. The gutters between the spinous processes and the ribs contain powerful

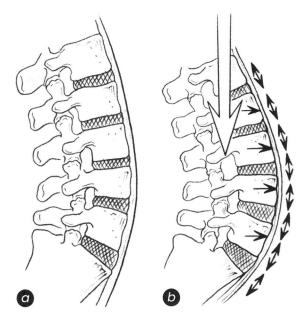

Figure 12.2 (a) Decompression and (b) compression forces in the lumbar spine being converted into stretch in the anterior longitudinal ligament.

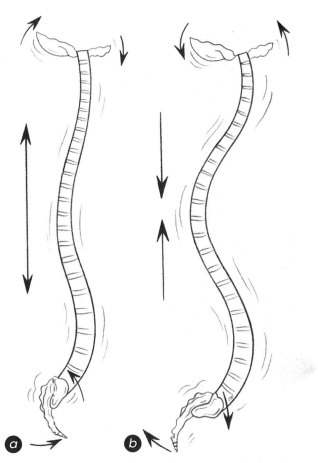

Figure 12.3 Spinal curves (a) lengthening and (b) deepening.

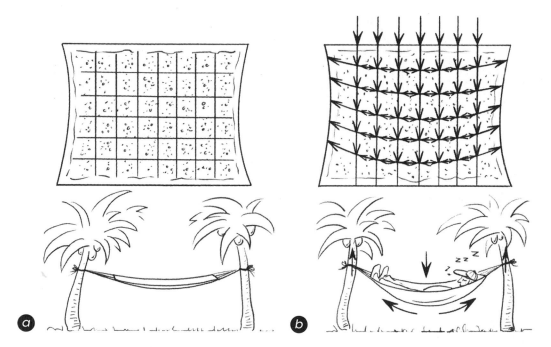

Figure 12.4   Force absorption in the vertebrae compared to stretching a hammock: *(a)* decompression; *(b)* compression.

strands of musculature, evening out the contour of the back so that it serves as a broad resting surface for the body.

As a further line of defense, the vertebrae contain trabeculae (Latin for "small beams"), a latticework of bone that directs forces through the interior of the bone and increases its ability to bear load. The trabeculae within each vertebra allow compression forces to be turned into tensile forces within the bony structure (Bogduk 1997). In this case, the vertically arranged trabeculae transfer the force to the horizontal system and from there to the cortical bone located at the rim of the vertebrae (figure 12.4).

The trabeculae can also be considered spokes of a wheel or a tensegrity system that transfers force away from the intervertebral disc with the help of the deep stabilizing muscles of the spine (Sohier 1991). In this case, the pull of the deep spinal muscles is able to decompress the vertebral end plates through the force lines of the trabeculae (figure 12.5).

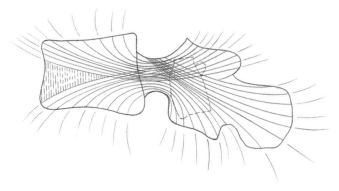

Figure 12.5   Trabecular lines of force relaying forces spokelike through the vertebrae.

Imagery Exercises for Spinal Design

1. **Visualizing the spine:** Visualize the design of your spine. In the sagittal plane, it resembles a tapering column; from the side, it resembles a vertical wave. Experience your spine as a motion-based structure. Imagine the curves as waves in water flowing upward.

2. **Painting your spine:** Using an imaginary paintbrush, color your spine in a variety of shades. Give each part of the spine an individual color: the bodies, discs, processes, and facet joints.

3. **Dynamic curves:** Stand in a comfortable position. Imagine the curves of the spine being perfectly counterbalanced. In your mind's senses travel up along the front of the spine and embody the four curves. Travel down the back of your spine and notice how the curves are slightly less pronounced. As you bend your legs, feel the curves of the spine deepen, which slightly shortens the overall length of the spine. The lumbar and cervical convexities will deepen forward; the thoracic and sacral curvature will deepen backward to counterbalance. As you bend your legs, imagine the spine lengthening and the curves becoming shallower. Repeat the action several times with the following self-talk: *Deeper curves* as you bend your legs and *longer curves* as you stretch them.

4. **Static curves:** Notice what happens if you think of the spinal curves as fixed. In other words, there is one position that is right, and the spine should remain in that position as you bend and stretch your legs. You may notice that the static image of the spine creates tension in your whole body and makes flexing and extending your limbs more difficult.

5. **Springy spine with self-touch:** Stand in a comfortable position. Place one hand on your neck and one hand on your lumbar spine (either the palm or the back of your hand). Bend your legs and experience a slight softening of the lumbar spine and neck as the curves deepen. This softening should not be equated with a sense of weakening; it is simply the fact that the spine is moving forward under your touch. Stretch your legs and feel the spinal curves moving back toward your hands and lengthening. Repeat this action 12 times, remove your hands, and notice the lengthened feeling in your spine. This is a prime example of how moving with an image that corresponds to function creates dynamic alignment. If you were to simply think, *Lengthen your spine*, the result could be static and reduce force absorption.

6. **Springy spine with arms:** Stand in a comfortable parallel position with your arms stretched out in front of you. At this point, your spinal curves are maximally lengthened. Bend your arms and legs and imagine the spinal curves deepening. Feel this as balanced movement forward and back of all the convexities of your spine. Stretch your arms and legs and feel the spinal curves lengthening. Repeat the action 10 times or until you can clearly feel the relationship of stretched limbs to longer curves and flexed limbs to deeper curves. Now relax your arms at your sides and enjoy the effortless lengthened and centered sense of your spine.

7. **Hammocking curves:** As you bend your spine, imagine the lumbar and cervical curves resting into the surrounding and supporting structures, muscle, ligaments, and connective tissue. Imagine the tissue to be like vertically oriented hammocks that support your spinal curves. Allow this image to create a resilient

feeling in your spine. Bend your legs and feel the stretch in the hammock; stretch your legs and feel it rebound again.

8. **Rebounding curves:** As you bend your spine, imagine the lumbar, thoracic, and cervical curves resting against springs located at their apexes. As you bend your legs, the springs are compressed; as you stretch your legs, the springs rebound and push the curves into length (figure 12.6).

9. **Moving with resilient curves:** As you move, imagine your spinal curves adjusting and rebounding off the ligaments and connective tissue surrounding them.

10. **Melting butter (supine position):** Imagine the back to be a chunk of butter. Watch as it melts and spreads. Depending on your personal preference, substitute ice cream, honey, soft snow, milk chocolate. . . .

11. **Smoothing sand (supine position):** Imagine your back to be made of chunky sand arranged in mounds. Visualize the wind blowing down your back, smoothing, leveling, and softening the sand.

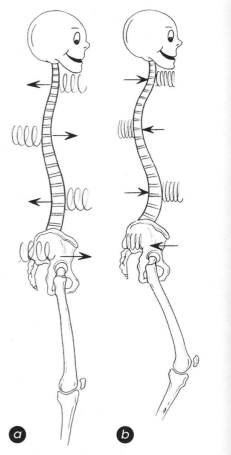

Figure 12.6 Spinal curves rebounding against springs: *(a)* lengthening curves compelled by springs; *(b)* deepening curves compressing springs.

PELVIS

The curves of the spine are influenced by the position of the pelvis. The fifth lumbar vertebra rests on the slanted sacral table, producing intrinsic shear forces in the lower lumbar area. These forces are counteracted by bony, ligamentous, and muscular restraints as well as by the hydrostatic pressure and tone of the abdominal organs and musculature. A line crossing the sacral table intersects with horizontal to determine the lumbosacral angle (figure 12.7a).

In the case of an anteriorly rotated pelvis, a plane defined by the ASIS and the PSIS will be slanted anteriorly (figure 12.8b). If the pelvis is rotated posteriorly, the plane defined by the ASIS and PSIS will be slanted posteriorly (figure 12.8c).

Excessive forward rotation of the top of the pelvis increases the lumbosacral angle, deepening the lumbar curves, which will tend to increase the other curvatures of the spine or cause compensatory reactions (figures 12.7b and 12.8b). Therefore, the COGs of the individual vertebrae will be less well aligned on top of each other, increasing the shear stresses at the lumbosacral joint and other joints of the spinal column. Anterior rotation also increases the stresses on the hip joint. Posterior rotation of the pelvis, commonly called lifting the pelvis, reduces these stresses but increases the stress on the lumbar discs and reduces the ability of the pelvis and spine to absorb force. In addition, the pelvic outlet is narrowed and the muscles of the pelvic floor shortened, reducing flexibility in the hip joint. Posterior rotation of the pelvis and sacrum (tucking the pelvis) tends to flatten the curves (figure 12.8c) and is not a beneficial approach to lengthening the spine. In addition, there are cultural differences. People of African origin generally have deeper spinal curves, which studies have shown decrease the incidence of back pain (Carey et al. 1996). It seems that not the degree of curvature but the dynamic balance and force-absorbing ability of the spinal curves are the key to spinal health.

Overemphasizing the posterior rotation of the pelvis is especially problematic in sports, dance, and certain forms of exercise. In the turned-out dance position, tucking the pelvis distorts the alignment of the legs by forcing the knees forward, increasing tension in the pelvic musculature, and straining the medial aspect of the knees. This reduces the efficiency of hip flexion and leg extension. If you try to eliminate an established tucking habit, you will feel as if your buttocks are protruding to the rear. Since this feels wrong, it is often challenging to repattern. A balanced pelvis is based on good

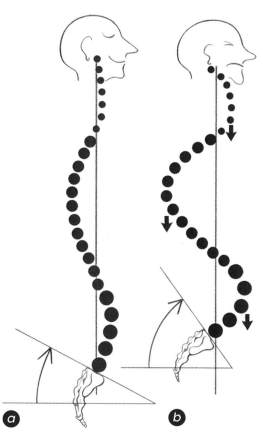

Figure 12.7 *(a)* The lumbosacral angle. *(b)* A larger lumbosacral angle means vertebrae will be less well aligned on top of each other, increasing shear stresses at joints throughout the spinal column.

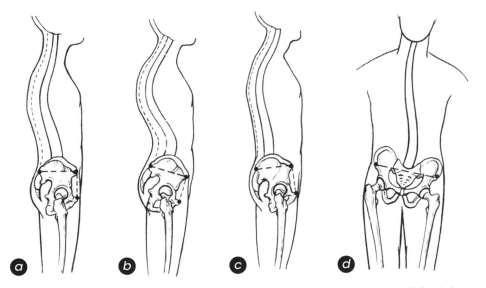

Figure 12.8 *(a)* The ASIS and PSIS in the same plane. *(b)* The PSIS higher than the ASIS. *(c)* The PSIS lower than the ASIS. *(d)* The ASIS not on the same horizontal plane.

movement patterns and dynamic stability, not on the constant tensing of certain muscle groups, which reduces the adaptability of the system.

If the pelvic crests and the ASIS are not level in the horizontal plane, the lumbar spine will deviate to the lower side of the pelvis. This forces the spine into a corrective bend to recapture its vertical alignment. Such curves of the spine in the frontal plane are called scoliotic (figure 12.8*d*). If the pelvic halves are twisted, the spine twists uncomfortably at its very base—certainly not the foundation of good spinal alignment.

If the pelvis is in good static alignment, three points delineated by the ASIS and the front of the pubic symphysis (the joint between the two pubic bones) form a vertical plane. In this case, the ASIS and the PSIS are approximately on the same horizontal plane (figure 12.8*a*). This has been called neutral pelvis. In dynamic alignment, your pelvis should oscillate around this neutral position and certainly not be held there by voluntary muscular contraction. The question is always about performance and well-being. If you place a person in the "correct" position and his ability to move suffers and he feels uncomfortable, this cannot be called a success. Other factors must be considered. (See "Motion of the Pelvic Halves" in chapter 10.)

Therefore, although achieving a visually ideal position may be an important element of efficient functioning, it is no guarantee. An improvement in spinal alignment must be dynamic and centered on motion interrelationships of bones, muscles, and organs, and it must include changes in the person's body image, in which the pelvis and head play a significant part.

The spine and pelvis interrelate in a complex manner. In bilateral hip flexion, the sacrum nutates, increasing the lumbar lordosis. The pelvic halves inflare and internally rotate and the sit bones move laterally. These movements are all small but need to be coordinated with the spinal adjustments. Since the body's intelligence is aiming to absorb and store force, any one part of the body that is held in tension will cause all the other areas to reduce their movement. (See "Motion of the Pelvic Halves" in chapter 10.)

Imagery Exercises for the Pelvis and Spine

1. **String lifting pubic symphysis (standing, walking):** Imagine a string attached to the pubic symphysis. Watch the string pulling up and forward on a slight diagonal to lift the front rim of the pelvis. Imagine this string pulling you into a walk.

2. **Lighting designer aligns the spine (supine, sitting, or standing):** Visualize the spine as a chain of spotlights. Turn on the lights and observe their focal directions. In a relaxed upright posture, they should be illuminating the median sagittal plane. If they shine in many confused directions, adjust them so that they all focus in the sagittal plane. Now adjust them so that they shine with equal brightness.

3. **Aligning your spinal lights (supine, sitting, or standing):** Concentrate on the spotlight at the center of the cervical spine. Its light should shine in the horizontal direction (perpendicular to the central axis). Focus on the spotlight at the center of the thoracic spine. Allow its light to become perpendicular to

the central axis. Finally, focus on the spotlight at the level of the fourth lumbar vertebra; adjust its light so that it too is directed perpendicularly to the central axis. Focus on these three spotlights simultaneously. Watch them become parallel, horizontally aligned in the sagittal plane (figure 12.9).

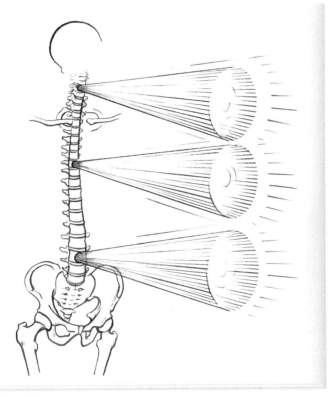

Figure 12.9 Visualize the spine as a chain of spotlights.

VERTEBRAE

Each vertebra consists of two main parts: a cylindrical body in front, mainly responsible for resisting compression forces, and a vertebral arch in back. The arch is formed by two pedicles and the laminae with four articular joint and three nonarticular projections; the nonarticular processes are the spinous and the transverse (figures 12.10 and 12.11). Only the spinous processes can be seen and palpated as the posterior part of the spine. These processes should form a line that divides the back into two equal halves. Because the spinous and transverse processes are interconnected by many short muscles, you have the ability to move the spine in a snakelike manner.

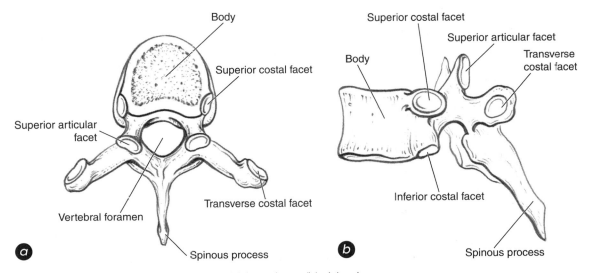

Figure 12.10 A thoracic vertebra: (a) top view; (b) side view.

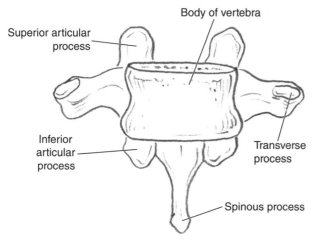

Figure 12.11 Thoracic vertebra from the front.

Because the spinous processes are the visible part of the spine, people tend to think of the spine as being far back, when in fact the weight-bearing bodies of the vertebrae, as well as the intervertebral discs, are more centrally located. The facets are estimated to carry 18 to 20 percent of the load, while the discs carry the remainder. Maintaining such balance is important for spinal health. The body and facets form a triangle, or tripod, which increases stability in balance.

The spine has more depth than you may imagine. If you place your finger in your navel, the bodies of the lumbar spine are only about two to four inches (5 to 10 cm) from the tip of your finger.

Imagery Exercises for the Vertebrae

1. **Weight bearing and articulating (standing, sitting):** Imagine the vertebrae and discs. This is the predominantly weight-bearing part of the spine. Now imagine the arch and the facet joints and processes. This is the more mobile part of the spine. Perform small movements with your spine and imagine the anterior part of the vertebrae carrying more weight while the posterior part guides and mobilizes.

2. **Releasing the spinous processes (standing, sitting, or supine):** Visualize the dorsal spinous processes as little flags or ribbons. Imagine the wind blowing through your body from front to back, unfurling these flags. Watch the flags fluttering in the wind. Picture all the flags aligned one above the other (figure 12.12).

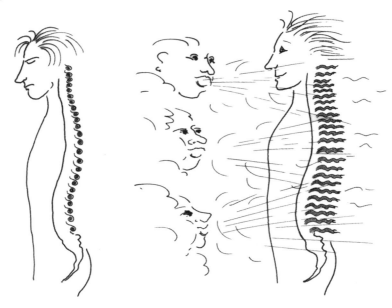

Figure 12.12 Visualize the dorsal spinous processes as little ribbons.

3. Spinous process as an elephant's trunk: Imagine the spinous process is the trunk of an elephant (figure 12.13). Allow this image to create a flexible feeling in the posterior spine.

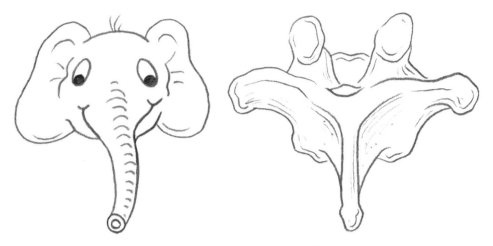

Figure 12.13   The spinous process as an elephant's trunk.

4. A variety of images for the spinous process: Imagine the spinous process to be a kite tail, or a shower head, or a paintbrush, or a pump handle (figure 12.14). Choose the image that works best for you in creating a sense of length and release in your back.

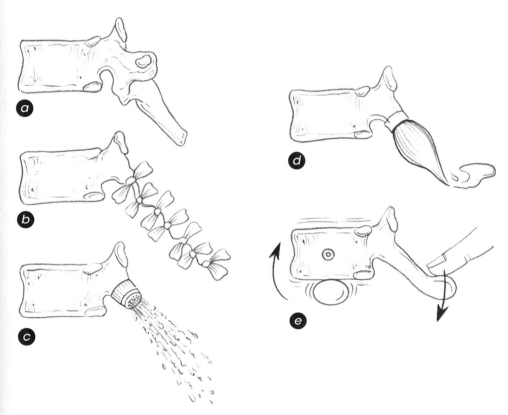

Figure 12.14   Imagery for the *(a)* spinous process: *(b)* kite tail, *(c)* shower head, *(d)* paint brush, *(e)* pump handle.

5. **Fluidity and subtlety of spinal movements (any position in improvisation; music optional):** Imagine the spinal processes as the tongues of a vibraphone. Each process creates its own distinct sound. Hear the spine-vibraphone playing. Feel the vibration of each vertebra (figure 12.15).

6. **Fluttering transverse processes:** Imagine the transverse processes of the spine stretching sideways. Now watch as they begin to move gently, creating a downward current along the sides of the spine. This motion is similar to that of the soft, tiny hairs called cilia used by one-celled animals to move through the water (figure 12.16).

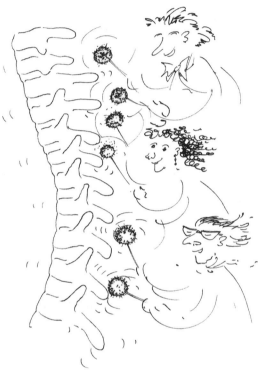

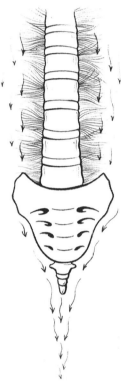

Figure 12.15 Imagine the spinal processes as the tongues of a vibraphone.

Figure 12.16 Imagine the transverse processes of the spine stretching sideways; the movement is similar to that of cilia, used by one-celled animals to move through the water.

7. **Spine as a chain of spheres or pearls:**

   a. **Awakening chain (supine, improvisation):** Lie on the floor and imagine the spine to be an interconnected chain of spheres. Watch as a single sphere comes alive with motion. At first, there is only a gentle stirring, a small rocking motion. The movement of the vertebra intensifies until it inspires its neighbors to move as well. The inspiration spreads along the entire spine until the whole chain is in motion.

   b. **Releasing pearls (supine, sitting, standing, walking):** Imagine the spine to be a string of pearls fastened by a knot at the bottom end. Visualize the knot opening and the pearls gliding off the string. As the pearls drop, watch the space between adjacent pearls widen.

c. **Pearl dance (improvisation):** Visualize the spine as a polished, glistening chain of pearls. Watch how the pearls catch the myriad colors of light. Hear the sounds the pearls make as they roll against each other.

8. **Imagining the tripod:** Imagine the tripod nature of the vertebrae and facet joints. Visualize balanced tripods throughout the spine (figure 12.17).

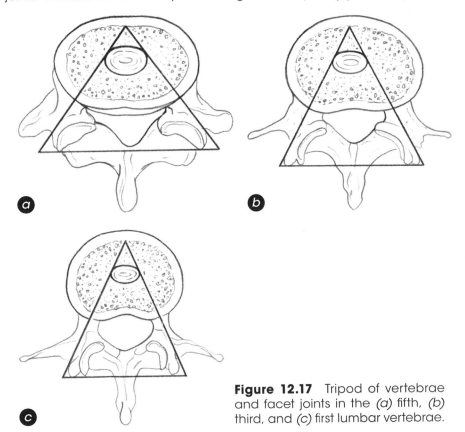

Ⓐ　　　　　　　　　　　Ⓑ

Ⓒ

Figure 12.17 Tripod of vertebrae and facet joints in the (a) fifth, (b) third, and (c) first lumbar vertebrae.

FACET JOINTS

In addition to the main weight-bearing intervertebral joints, the apophyseal, or facet, joints connect two adjoining vertebrae. They are fairly flat and are depicted in figure 12.18 as interlinking hands. The hands are also ensuring that the neural foramen stays open for the nerves exiting the spinal cord.

They permit movement in a variety of directions, depending on their angle, while preventing excessive sliding of one vertebra in relation to another. The inferior articular facet of each vertebra stabilizes it by preventing the vertebra from sliding

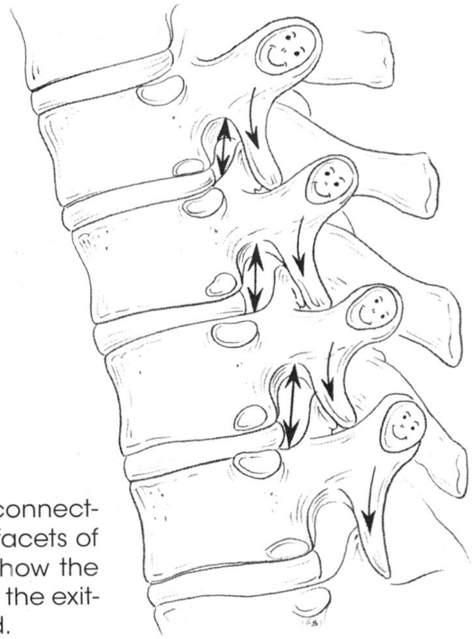

Figure 12.18 The facet joints as interconnecting links of hands; the faces are the facets of the transverse process. The arrows show the importance of maintaining space for the exiting of the nerves from the spinal cord.

forward. The right and left superior articulating facets of each vertebra connect with the right and left inferior facets of the superior vertebrae, like a necklace with two double links between stones. In flexion the facets slide apart (figures 12.19*a*, 12.20); in extension, they slide more closely together (figures 12.19*b*, 12.21).

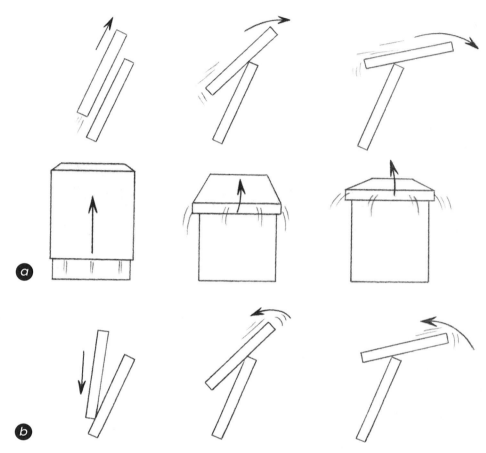

Figure 12.19 Facets sliding: *(a)* flexion, lateral and posterior views; *(b)* extension, lateral view .

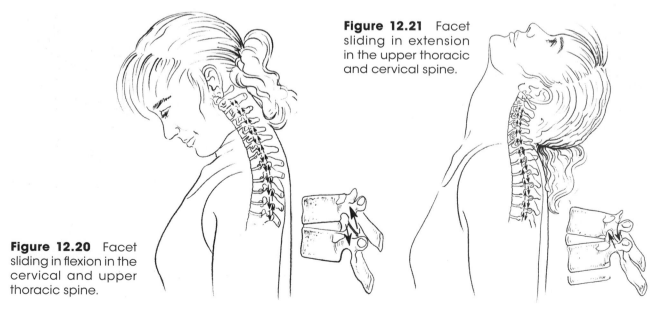

Figure 12.21 Facet sliding in extension in the upper thoracic and cervical spine.

Figure 12.20 Facet sliding in flexion in the cervical and upper thoracic spine.

The facet joints lie approximately in the sagittal plane in the lumbar area; in the frontal plane in the thoracic spine, where they look like shingles on a roof; and at a 45-degree angle in the cervical spine (figure 12.22).

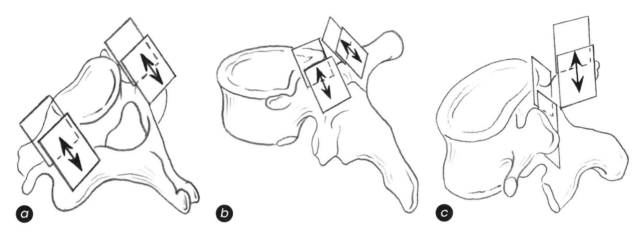

Figure 12.22   Angles of facet joints: (a) cervical vertebra; (b) thoracic vertebra; and (c) lumbar vertebra.

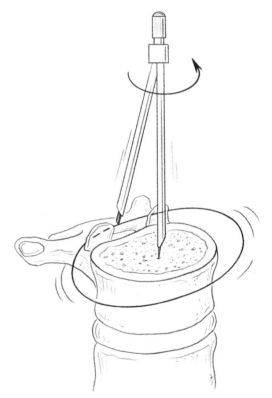

Figure 12.23   Thoracic facets are part of a circle.

This arrangement favors flexion and extension in the lumbar spine, rotation and lateral flexion in the thoracic spine, and fairly unrestricted movement in any direction in the cervical spine. Just above the lumbar vertebrae, the 12th thoracic vertebra bridges the two sections. Its upper-facet joints, like those of the rest of the thoracic spine, are in the frontal plane, whereas its lower-facet joints are closer to the sagittal plane, like those of the lumbar vertebrae. This transition is important to be aware of because of the sudden change in directional mobility. Observing the orientation of the lumbar facets from L1 to the sacrum, you can see that the angle moves from more sagittal orientation toward the frontal plane, creating two outward spirals from top to bottom. The surface of the thoracic facets is part of a circle whose center coincides with the center of the vertebrae, favoring rotation (figure 12.23).

In lateral flexion, the thoracic facets on the ipsilateral side slide down and slightly back, while the facets on the contralateral side slide up and slightly forward (figure 12.24). In other words, on the ipsilateral side, the facets are behaving as in extension; on the contralateral side, they are behaving as in flexion.

Lateral flexion in the thoracic spine may be accompanied by a modicum of rotation to the same side, which differs in amount from person to person. This combination of rotation and flexion is called coupling (Willems, Jull, and Ng 1996). Coupled motion was first proposed by Lovett in 1903. Later research confirmed this finding (Panjabi and White 1995). In an educational situation it is easy to demonstrate coupled motion by bending a

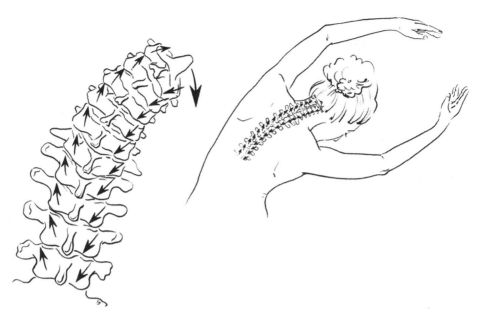

Figure 12.24 Lateral flexion in the thoracic spine.

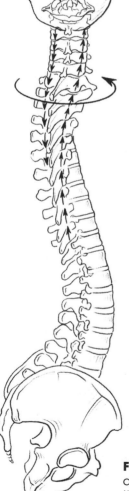

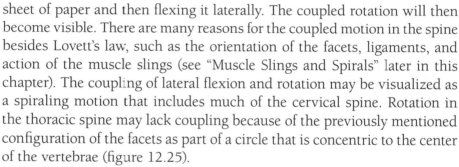

sheet of paper and then flexing it laterally. The coupled rotation will then become visible. There are many reasons for the coupled motion in the spine besides Lovett's law, such as the orientation of the facets, ligaments, and action of the muscle slings (see "Muscle Slings and Spirals" later in this chapter). The coupling of lateral flexion and rotation may be visualized as a spiraling motion that includes much of the cervical spine. Rotation in the thoracic spine may lack coupling because of the previously mentioned configuration of the facets as part of a circle that is concentric to the center of the vertebrae (figure 12.25).

The lumbar spine has about 40 degrees of possible flexion and extension; this motion is its main flexibility asset. During flexion, the inferior facets of the superior vertebrae slide up and out of the superior facets of the inferior vertebrae. During extension, the inferior facets of the superior vertebrae slide down and in between the superior facets of the inferior vertebrae. The downward-sliding facets can reach far down and touch the pars interarticularis, the bony mass between the facets.

The lumbar spine can laterally flex about 30 degrees, during which the facets on the ipsilateral side slide together and on the contralateral side slide apart. Lateral flexion is made easier by spinal flexion. In rotation, the lumbar spine displays coupled motions both in the ipsilateral and contralateral directions. L1 to L4 flex to the opposite side, while L4 to S1 flex to the same side during rotation.

Figure 12.25 Rotation and facet movement in the spine.

Imagery Exercises for the Facet Joints

1. **Visualizing facet sliding in the thoracic spine:** Stand in a comfortable position and visualize facet joints of the thoracic spine and cervical spine. As you flex your spine, imagine the inferior facet of the superior vertebrae slide up and forward. As you extend your spine, imagine the inferior facet of the superior vertebrae slide down and back. Repeat at least five times and notice changes in your sense of thoracic alignment.

2. **Facets are playing cards:** Imagine the facet joints to be playing cards that can slide on top of each other when you flex and extend your spine (figure 12.26).

3. **Balanced motion:** As you slide your facets in flexion and extension, imagine the motion happening to an equal extent in the right and left facet joints.

4. **Rolling out the carpet:** Another image for facilitating the kinesthetic experience of the facets is carpets sliding over each other. Imagine facet carpet being unrolled when you extend your spine.

Figure 12.26 Imagine the facet joints as slippery playing cards.

5. **Imagining orientation of the lumbar facets:** Visualize the orientation of the facets of the lumbar spine. They are angled 90 degrees to the horizontal plane and at L1 15 degrees from the sagittal plane. As you go down toward the sacrum in your mind's eye, visualize the lumbar facets increasing angulation toward the frontal plane. If they were interconnected, they would spiral outward from sagittal to frontal from top to bottom.

6. **Imagining facet sliding in the lumbar facets:** Bend your knees to flex and extend your lumbar spine. As you flex, imagine the inferior facets of superior vertebrae slide up and out of superior facets of inferior vertebrae. The up and out is accompanied by a slight forward motion. As you extend, imagine the inferior facets of the lumbar spine sliding back and down and in between the superior facets of the inferior vertebrae. Repeat the action at least five times, then notice changes in your sense of lumbar alignment and ease of motion.

7. **Lumbar facets as earmuffs:** Imagine the inferior facets of superior vertebrae to be ears and the superior facets of inferior vertebrae to be earmuffs. As you flex your spine, imagine the ears sliding out of the earmuffs. As you extend your spine, imagine the ears sliding back in between the earmuffs. Imagine warm, soft, and cozy earmuffs that the inferior facets must slide out of on flexion and return to on extension. Repeat this action at least five times. You can also place your fingers on your lumbar spine as you do the imagery. Notice changes in alignment of your lumbar spine and pelvis after you have finished. Commonly the lumbar spine will feel more relaxed and lengthened.

8. **Sacral facet sliding:** Visualize the orientation of the facets of the sacral base (S1). Note that they are similarly oriented as the sit bones. They are large and

resemble bunny ears. There is a large range of motion at the L5 and S1 junction, and imagining balanced facet sliding here can be very beneficial for your low back. Place your fingers at the top of the sacrum as you flex and extend your lumbar spine. Imagine the inferior facets of L5 sliding up on the S1 facets. As you extend, imagine the facets going down and behind the bunny ears again. Repeat at least five times and notice changes in your pelvic alignment.

DISCS, SPINE, AND PSYCHOLOGY OF PAIN

The intervertebral discs are a good representation of the psychology of mental imagery as it relates to health. Discs are known to function as shock absorbers between adjacent vertebrae. Since the word *shock* may carry negative connotations and negative belief systems are associated with back pain, I have changed the term to more positive wording: *force absorption* or *force transduction*.

There is mounting evidence of numerous psychological factors that influence back pain, such as imagining negative outcomes (catastrophizing), anxiety regarding pain, fear of movement (kinesophobia), and avoidance behavior. Depression is a better predictor of back pain than an MRI (Linton 2000). People with back pain are four times more likely to be depressed than those without back pain (Sullivan et al. 1992). The back and the intervertebral discs commonly have negative associations. If you ask people about their backs, the response is often in negative imagery, such as stiff, pinched, cramped, and slipped. Discs are usually only talked about when they are causing trouble. Rarely will you hear anyone praise their intervertebral discs and the wonderful condition of their spines with positive imagery. There is evidence that changing the psychological outlook will have an effect on pain generation and the health of your back (Woby et al. 2004). The purpose of biomechanical and metaphorical imagery is therefore not only to improve function on a biomechanical level but also to build and reinforce a positive imagery toward your back and discs.

The 23 discs of the back are ingenious devices that are able to transduce force and allow the spine to have increased mobility. Girded by the strong annulus fibrosus, the central unit of the disc, the nucleus pulposus, resembles a springy water-filled ball. In German, the intervertebral discs are called *Bandscheiben*, literally "ligament circles." Nucleus and annulus contain collagen and water-binding proteins in different proportions to boost either tensile or compression properties.

The discs are girded on both sides by vertebral end plates. Even though the end plates belong to the vertebrae, they are functionally more strongly related to the discs. During compression of the discs from above or below, the pressure moves from the nucleus to the annulus and from there to the end plates and cortical bone of vertebrae, providing lift. This takes time and reduces the pressure on any structure per time unit. The discs are more flexible when unloaded and strong when loaded. The annulus can therefore be compared to an instantly inflatable wall. The wall is strong when needed—that is, under high-pressure situations.

The approximately 25 layers of annular fibers are arranged relative to each other in a diagonal fashion. The fibers of each layer cross each other at angles of 120 degrees similar to a woven basket, allowing the annulus to resist shear in all directions. The deeper fibers become more nearly horizontal and better at resisting translation shear.

Because it's resilient, the nucleus can store energy like a ball compressed and then released. By wrapping bands (the annulus fibrosus) around the ball, you lose some mobility but improve carrying ability. The compressed ball pushes against the surrounding bands, stretching them so that they help in resisting the load. The intervertebral discs convert some of the compression stress into tensile stress through the stretching bands. Discs provide more resistance to large loads and less to small loads. You can compare the situation to a tire. When the tire is loaded, the air within gets pushed against the whole inner surface of the tire, allowing for much more carrying capacity than a wooden wheel of similar size. You may imagine the annulus to be an adjustable spring, depending on the amount of loading the disc is experiencing (figure 12.27).

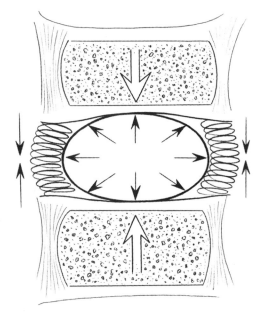

Figure 12.27 Compression in the nucleus converts into stretch and springlike elastic resistance in the annulus.

When you rotate the spine, the annular fibers are stretched, which causes the disc to be slightly compressed as well (figure 12.28). This is an inherent safeguard against stretching the spinal cord. If the spine lengthened during rotation, the cord would be exposed to dangerous shearing. The image of *lengthen your spine in rotation* is an exercise cue that goes against function, which comes as a great surprise. The spine has its maximal length when it is centered and slightly lowered down in rotation. To understand the principle, all you need to do is wring a towel. As it twists, it shortens.

The vertebral end plates are important for the nutrition of the discs. Since the discs contain blood vessels only at their edges, nutrition must come by diffusion through the end plates. As the disc gets compressed, fluids leave the discs and move into the end plates where they are "recycled" and replenished with fresh nutrients. These can enter

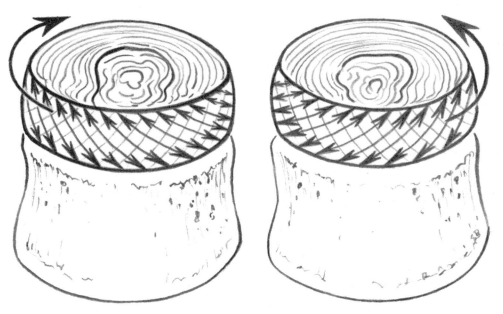

Figure 12.28 Rotation of the spine causes a stretch of the annulus and a slight lowering of the disc.

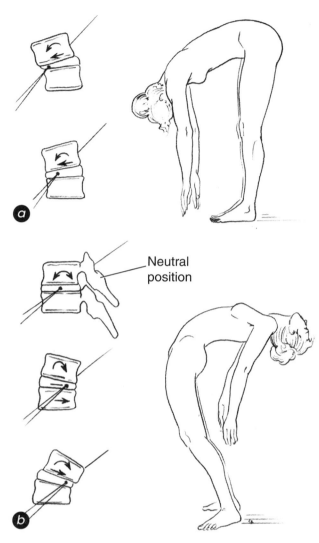

Neutral position

Figure 12.29 The axis of rotation moves (a) forward in flexion and (b) backward in extension.

the disc again during decompression. Movement and a regular cycle of compression and decompression are key to the health of the discs. Bad posture is deleterious for discs because the cycle of compression and decompression is jeopardized. It is interesting to note that sitting compresses the discs more than standing. After sitting for a long time, you should do some gentle stretching motions or perhaps even lie down on the floor and perform some exercises with rolling balls.

When you flex your spine, the anterior wedging action of the vertebrae pushes the fluid in the discs to the rear. The posterior annulus now becomes taut and resists this motion, pushing it back in the other direction. When you extend your spine, the fluid is moved anteriorly. Now the anterior annular fibers will resist this motion. In flexion and extension, the fluid of the disc is being compelled forward and back. A similar situation occurs in lateral flexion, where the fluid moves toward the opposite side of the side-bending action.

The axis of rotation in flexion and extension is not fixed. It moves slightly forward in flexion (figure 12.29a) and to the back in extension (figure 12.29b). In lateral flexion, it moves to the side of flexion. The vertebrae not only dip but also slide in flexion and extension, resembling a surfer dipping his board on top of a wave.

It is interesting to note that one method of earthquake-proofing a building is to place it on four spinelike segments: alternating metal cylinders (vertebrae) with more resilient rubber cylinders (intervertebral discs). Tremors are absorbed by these pillars so that the building barely trembles. Every step you take is a miniature earthquake. Part of the impact is absorbed by the legs and pelvis before it reaches the spine, but the spine buffers the residual quake before it reaches the head and the delicate brain. The motion of a dancer's head, especially when landing from a jump, reveals much about the state of his or her spine. If the dancer glides through space and lands without movement in either the neck or head, the shock has been absorbed before reaching the head. If the spine is rigid, the dancer's head will quiver.

Imagery Exercises for the Intervertebral Discs

1. **Balance board:** Imagine the vertebrae riding on the discs like balancing boards on rubber balls.

2. **Water bed:** Imagine the discs to be water beds. As you move, and even when walking, imagine the vertebrae bouncing on the resilient beds.

3. **Expanding nucleus:** Select a segment of the spine and imagine the nucleus to be a small ball. Observe the ball filling with liquid, pushing against the constricting bands of the annulus to expand the entire intervertebral disc. Watch as the intervertebral disc creates more space for itself by pushing the adjoining vertebrae apart (figure 12.30).

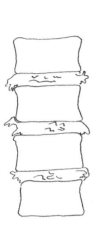

Figure 12.30 The intervertebral disc creates more space for itself by pushing the adjoining vertebrae apart.

4. **Breathing into discs:** As you inhale, imagine that you are inflating your discs. With every inhalation, imagine your discs getting taller and stronger as if you were inflating a balloon or a strong rubber ball (figure 12.31).

5. **Moving from the intervertebral discs:** Once you're finished inflating the intervertebral discs, imagine that the spine finds its support in this soft, fluid column. Try initiating movement from the intervertebral discs. How does this compare to initiating movement from the bodies of the vertebrae?

6. **Discs respond to whole-body movement:** As you bend and stretch your legs, feel the discs gently responding. As you bend, they slightly widen circumferentially; as you stretch your legs, they narrow. You can think of the expansion beginning at the center of the discs and expanding outward as you bend your legs, reversing the action as you stretch them.

7. **Moving the fluid:** As you flex your spine, imagine the fluid moving backward in your discs. As you

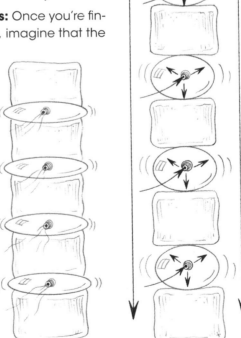

Figure 12.31 Discs inflating like balloons or balls.

extend your spine, imagine the fluid moving forward in your discs. Repeat this image 12 times and notice any changes in your spinal alignment.

8. **Moving the axis of rotation:** As you flex your spine, imagine the superior vertebrae not only dipping but also sliding forward just a bit on the inferior discs. As you extend your spine, imagine the superior vertebrae not only dipping but also sliding backward a bit on the inferior discs. You may notice that this image, which is more functional, increases your range of motion as opposed to the idea of a fixed axis of rotation (see figure 12.29).

9. **Spinal curves and discs:** Place one hand on your neck and one hand on your low back. In a standing position, flex and extend your legs. Review the image of spinal curves deepening and lengthening. Now add the image of the discs becoming slightly wider in leg flexion and slightly taller in leg extension. As you flex your legs, think *Wide discs*. As you stretch your legs, think *Tall discs*. Repeat this image and movement 12 times, and you may notice your spine feels longer and more resilient.

10. **Lumbar vertebrae as corks floating in water:** Imagine the sacrum hanging just beneath the fifth lumbar vertebra, increasing the space between them and giving the disc more space to expand. The coccyx is anchored in the ocean bed. Now see the fourth lumbar vertebra as a cork floating in water, and let both the fifth lumbar vertebra and the sacrum hang downward, increasing the space between the fourth and fifth lumbar vertebrae. Progress up the spine until every vertebra has played the role of the cork (figure 12.32). Watch the discs sigh with relief and fresh nourishment as they are allowed more space.

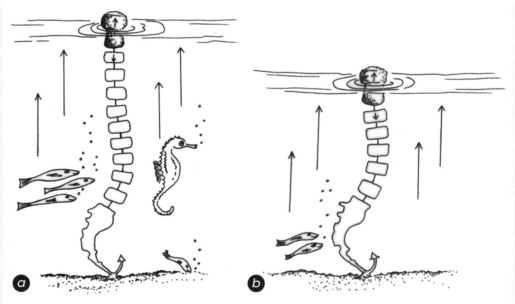

Figure 12.32 Vertebrae as a cork floating on water: *(a)* middle thoracic vertebrae; *(b)* lower thoracic vertebrae.

11. **Opening the intervertebral spaces (supine):** In the supine position, bend your knees and bring your legs back over your head until your toes touch the floor behind you. As you slowly roll back down, imagine each vertebra being placed on the floor individually and at a distance from the vertebrae that are

already on the floor (figure 12.33). Watch as the spaces between the vertebrae increase. Let the distance between them become as large as possible and imagine the discs expanding to receive fresh nourishment.

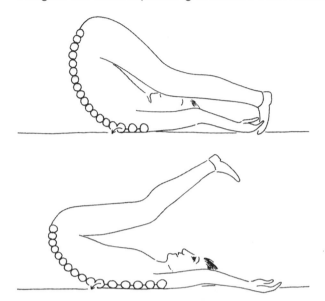

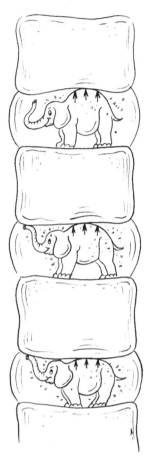

Figure 12.33 Place each vertebra on the floor individually and at a distance from the vertebrae that are already on the floor.

12. **Discs are strong as elephants:** Imagine your intervertebral discs to have the strength and resilience of elephants (figure 12.34). Imagine them expanding upward with great power, providing your spine with more length and juicy plump discs.

Figure 12.34 Imagine your discs as strong as elephants.

SPINAL LIGAMENTS

Many ligaments help stabilize the spine and are important for guiding movement and force transduction. Ligaments are not isolated structures as one may believe from looking at some anatomical books. They are commonly connected and related to the whole fascial system, organs, and muscles. Muscular connections of ligaments provide the ligaments with a dynamic nature. The fundamental imagery of ligaments is focused on providing direction, guiding movement, and absorbing force. The ligaments are richly endowed with proprioceptors. The *intra*segmental system of spinal ligaments binds together adjacent vertebrae; the *inter*segmental system unifies groups of vertebrae. The spinal ligaments can be considered the ligamentous core (figure 12.35).

The capsular ligaments surround the facet joint capsule. The anterior longitudinal ligament (ALL), a very strong ligament, runs along the entire length of the anterior surface of the spine from the sacrum to the second cervical vertebra. Its function in quadrupeds is to prevent the anterior spine from sagging downward. It has two

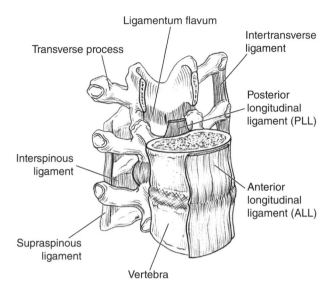

Figure 12.35 Ligaments of the spine.

layers, the deeper of which runs from vertebra to vertebra and is connected with some fibers to the intervertebral discs, whereas the superficial layer is intersegmental. The layering of this ligament allows it to have some slide, which is advantageous in flexing and extending motions. The ligamentum flavum is an elastic intrasegmental ligament on the posterior surface of the vertebral canal connecting lamina to lamina. It is very thick (3 to 10 mm) and contains many elastic fibers, making it look somewhat yellow. It protects the posterior vertebral canal and stretches when the spine is flexed. Thus it helps the spine move from any forward-bending position into a neutral position. One of the functions of the ligamentum flavum is to maintain tension on the disc, aiding its integrity. The ligamentum flavum keeps the discs loaded in preparation for movement and also relates to the facet joint capsule. Through the interspinous ligaments, the ligamentum flavum is connected to the thoracolumbar fascia and all the muscles connected to this broad expanse of connective tissue. The body maintains a broad interconnected dialogue that can relate muscular activity in the low back, shoulders, and pelvis to the spinal joints and discs.

The posterior longitudinal ligament (PLL) contains a significant amount of elastic fibers and runs along the back of the vertebrae and discs. Its deeper layer runs from disc to disc where it broadens and supports the discs' posterior surface. The superior part is thicker and more intersegmental in nature. As you flex your spine, the PLL lengthens. The supraspinous ligament runs along the tips of the spinous processes and is connected to the thoracolumbar fascia. It limits flexion of the spine as well as rotation. The interspinous ligament relays forces from the ligamentum flavum to the supraspinous ligament. Finally, the ligamentum intertransversarium connects adjacent transverse processes. It limits lateral flexion and rotation.

Imagery Exercises for the Spinal Ligaments

1. **Rubber band ligaments:** Imagine the spine as a long spring with interconnecting rubber bands. Move in a variety of directions and imagine the bands stretching and rebounding your spine to neutral.

2. **Tensegrity stretch, no stack:** Imagine your spine to be a tower of tensegrity systems (see "Tensegrity" in chapter 2). Move in a variety of directions and notice how the spine can easily regain its original position. Imagine the nature of your stability to be stretching rather than stacking.

3. **Spinal elastic rod:** Imagine the spine to be an elastic rod that can rebound effortlessly to neutral from any movement.

4. **Crinkling the ligaments:** As you flex your spine, imagine the anterior ligaments crinkling while the posterior ligaments are becoming taut. You can use the image of a tablecloth making small folds as you push it from both ends across the surface. As you extend your spine, imagine the posterior ligaments crinkling

as the anterior ones are becoming taut and lengthened. Repeat this action five times and notice the changes in spinal sensation.

5. **Ligaments alive:** Imagine you could initiate movement from the ligaments. As you flex your spine, imagine the ALL actively supporting this movement, while the PLL, ligamentum flavum, and interspinous and supraspinous ligaments actively resist. As you extend your spine, imagine the actions reversing.

6. **Carpet rolling:** Imagine the ALL as a carpet being rolled up the front of your spine to bring you from spinal flexion to extension.

7. **Rebounding from the ligamentum flavum:** Flex your spine and imagine the ligamentum flavum being stretched like a rubber band. Imagine the ligamentum flavum powering your rebound into the upright position. Repeat the action and feel yourself rebounding with the help of the ligamentum flavum.

8. **Initiating from the front of the spine:** Imagine the power to move the spine coming from its anterior aspect. Initiating movement from the front relieves the dorsal muscles of excess effort.

9. **Spinal brushes:**

   a. **Supine, sitting, standing:** Imagine a brush moving up along the front of the spine and another brush moving down along the back. Try seeing the two brushes working in opposition, making several strokes before moving to the next level. Feel how the brush on the front of the spine imparts some lift to the front of the vertebral bodies. The brush in back helps the muscles near the spine and the spinous processes to release downward (figure 12.36).

   b. **Improvisation:** Visualize the brushes initiating spinal movement at different levels of the spine. Let the brushes interact in a variety of ways, working at the same level opposite each other or at different ends of the spine.

10. **Series of waterfalls:** Imagine a waterfall pouring down the back of the spine. Every spinous process is a ridge over which the waterfall cascades on its downward course. Imagine the water splashing between every crevice and ridge created by the transverse and spinous processes and the superior and inferior articulating processes.

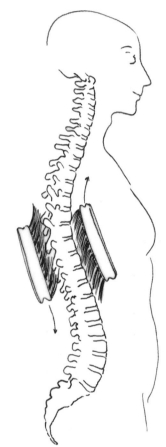

Figure 12.36 Imagine a brush moving up along the front of the spine and another brush moving down along the back.

MUSCULATURE OF THE ABDOMEN AND BACK

Often muscles seem to be running in discrete lines and directions, with insertions and origins being discernable. In reality, there are more interconnections between muscles through the fascial network than commonly depicted. Not only are muscles interrelated but also the layering of muscles down to the sarcomeres are in a complex

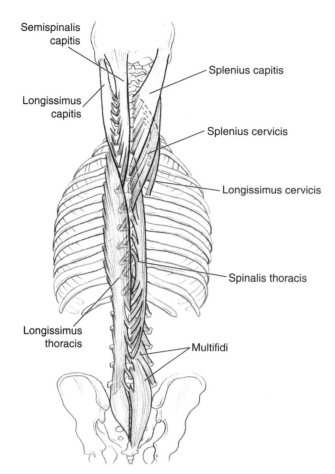

Semispinalis capitis

Splenius capitis

Longissimus capitis

Splenius cervicis

Longissimus cervicis

Spinalis thoracis

Longissimus thoracis

Multifidi

Figure 12.37 Erector spinae.

fascial dialogue. When you observe the muscles of the back, organizational principles are not apparent at first. It is therefore best to understand these muscles as patterns and relationships.

The long erector spinae muscles at the back of the torso—spinalis, longissimus, and iliocostalis (from the center out)—lie in three strands parallel to the vertebral column (figure 12.37). These muscles are involved in dynamic stabilization and movement of the spine, torso, and head as well as breathing. The lowest part arises from a strong aponeurosis that is attached to the sacrum and iliac crest. From here, discrete bands run up to the ribs (iliocostalis), transverse processes and ribs (longissimus), and spinous processes (spinalis). The longissimus is the most developed of the three and the iliocostalis the most lateral. All of these muscles can extend the spine, but the more lateral strand also can flex the spine to the side.

Below the erector muscles, several groups of short muscles lie deep within the gutter next to the spinous processes. These so-called transversospinalis muscles are the multifidi, semispinalis, and rotators. They all run from the transverse processes to spinous processes but at different angles. The most oblique are the rotators because they cross only one or two vertebrae. The multifidi cross two to four vertebrae and are therefore more angled upward. The semispinalis is the most oblique of all, crossing four to six vertebrae. Together, they look like layers of triangles with ever-larger and longer sides and narrower peaks. The semispinalis is the largest and most medial of the lumbar back muscles. It has wide attachments at the back of the pelvis and lower spine, such as the lumbosacral ligaments, posterior surface of the sacrum, posterior iliac spine, and the even sacrotuberous ligament. The deep fibers of the multifidi are in the perfect position to control shear and torsion and seem to have differing neural control from the superficial part. The deep layers play an important role in the dynamic stabilization of the low back and contract in anticipation of movement. The superficial layer is more able to extend the low back and control lordosis (Moseley, Hodges, and Gandevia 2002).

Imagery Exercises for the Erector Spinae

1. **Roll down, roll up from transversospinalis:** Imagine the erector spinae muscles. Lying deep to them are the transversospinalis muscles. Flex your spine and roll down slowly, focusing on the transversospinalis muscles. Roll up again, initiating from the transversospinalis. In rolling down, imagine the spinous processes stretching away from the lower-lying transverse processes. In rolling up, imagine the spinous processes being pulled downward toward the lower-lying transverse

processes. Repeat several times and notice the sensations arising from your spine and especially notice your posture. See if you can perform this exercise without moving at all as a mental simulation of movement with the previous anatomical imagery.

2. **Roll down, roll up from erectors:** Perform the same movement as previously, but focus on the more superficial erectors: spinalis, longissimus, and iliocostalis. Notice the difference in feeling between the two images.

3. **Activate the deep muscles:** Imagine the deep muscles of the spine, the transversospinalis muscles. Starting from an upright position, roll down the spine. As you roll up again, imagine the strength for this action residing in the deep spinal muscles while the superficial muscles remain soft and relaxed. You may imagine muscles sliding to focus your activation on the deep layers. Repeat rolling down and rolling up with this focus. Notice the improved alignment and feeling of centeredness in the spine after this imagery exercise. Also practice this as a mental simulation of movement combined with the previous image.

4. **Deep and superficial multifidi (standing):** Notice the state of your low back: How relaxed or tense does it feel? Move your low back by anteriorly and posteriorly rotating your pelvis. Now visualize the multifidi. Imagine that you are lifting your arms without actually doing it. Mentally simulate moving your torso. Imagine you are rapidly lifting and lowering your arms. Now lift and lower your arms actively several times and notice changes in your perception of lumbar spine movement. Has anything changed?

5. **Melting the superficial layer (standing position):** Place the fingertips of both hands on the multifidi just above the sacrum. See if you can find a position where the multifidi (at least the superficial layer) seem relaxed. Imagine the superficial layer is melting. It may be helpful to flex your legs and slightly rotate your pelvis to find this position. Once you have achieved some relaxation, see if you can maintain this superficial softness as you very slightly flex and extend your lumbar spine. Give it at least two minutes before you remove your fingers. You may now notice that your low back has relaxed significantly.

6. **Centered action of the abdominals (sitting, standing, supine):** Visualize four pairs of small spheres, or beads, on four common strings—one vertical, one horizontal, and two diagonal, all joining at the navel. As you exhale, watch the beads move toward each other and merge at the navel. As you inhale, the beads glide back to their original positions (figure 12.38).

7. **Pelvis suspended from the back of the neck (standing):** Imagine the front rim of the pelvis to be hanging from the back of the head on strands of muscles spiraling around to the front of the body like an apron hanging down in front and tied at the back

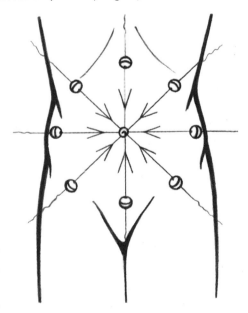

Figure 12.38 Imagine beads sliding away from and toward the navel as you breathe in and out.

of the neck. As the back of the head floats up, so does the front rim of the pelvis. Watch the sacrum drop as the front of the pelvis rises.

8. **Water releases the muscles (standing):** Imagine comfortably warm water flowing down along your spine and releasing muscular tension, melting it away wherever it can be found (figure 12.39). Be detailed about the image as you see the water flow around the transverse and spinous processes and relax the areas around all muscle insertions. Imagine also the muscles around your coccyx releasing. If you are successful in relaxing the muscles, you may feel more centered on your legs, and your shoulders will relax.

9. **River down the back (supine):** Imagine a river flowing down your back, expelling all muscular tension (figure 12.40). Visualize the tension points as little rocks and pieces of wood carried out with the flow. Imagine the murky water turning crystal clear. Watch the river flow down through the gutters between your spine and ribs to flush out all remaining tension.

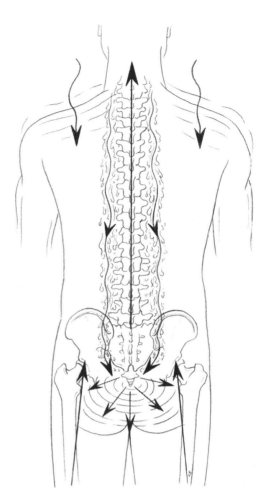

Figure 12.39 Comfortable flow of water releases all tension in the back.

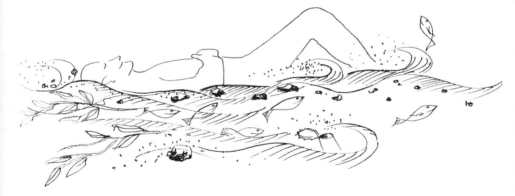

Figure 12.40 A river flows down your back, expelling all muscular tension.

10. **Stroking the cat's back (supine, sitting, standing):** Imagine your back to be covered with fluffy fur like a cat's back. Visualize the fur as ruffled and in disarray, and mentally stroke it from head to tail, untangling and smoothing it (figure 12.41). (Exercise adapted from Barbara Clark.)

Figure 12.41   Imagine your back is covered with fluffy fur, like a cat's back.

ABDOMINAL WALL AND FASCIA

Almost any sheet of connective tissue can be referred to as a fascia. The term is not precise and is currently undergoing much discussion and revision. There are basically three types of fascia:

- Areolar tissue, which is elastic and dynamic
- Deep fascia, which is inelastic and strong
- Visceral fascia, which relates to the organs

Connective tissue can be likened to the inner-tensegrity matrix that interconnects and separates the structures of the body and can fluidly respond to changes in posture and movement. The strength of fascia depends on the percentage of collagen it includes. Some deep fascia is almost entirely collagenous and is then called an aponeurosis. The superficial fascia lies deep to the dermis. It can move freely over the underlying bones and muscles. This is because it is very elastic and contains fat that is liquid at body temperature.

The body wall is made of concentric layers of skin, hypaxial muscle, and connective tissue. Hypaxial muscle lies in front of the transverse processes of the spine, which includes the psoas and abdominals. Epaxial muscles lie behind the transverse processes of the spine and include the erector spinae muscles. The function of the body wall is to protect the viscera from injury. It also includes structures involved in reproduction, respiration, and excretion and plays an important role in locomotion and dynamic stabilization of the trunk in all forms of movement. The abdominal fascia is known by a variety of names in various areas of the body, such as transversalis fascia, psoas fascia, and iliacus fascia. But it is one interconnected sheath. Think of all trunk-stabilizing muscles talking to each other through this fascia.

There are four layers of muscles in the body wall: a rectus series, which runs longitudinally along the front of the body from the pelvis to the rib cage, and three concentric layers on each side of the body. These layers create a complex latticework of muscles that are able to stabilize, balance, and move the trunk in myriad ways (figure 12.42).

The rectus abdominis muscle is contained within a sheath of connective tissue called an anterior and posterior lamina (thin plate). It is aptly called the rectus sheath.

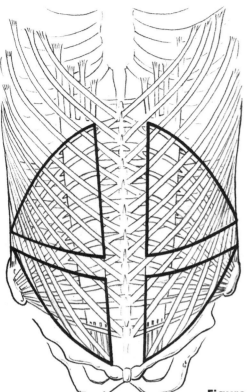

It is interesting to note that the dorsal aponeurosis of the rectus is not connected to the posterior lamina but slides on it to provide more freedom to the torso in movement. About 2 inches (5 cm) below the navel the posterior lamina ends in an archlike shape. At this point the aponeurosis extends into the anterior lamina. The sheath below is made up of only the transversalis fascia and the peritoneum.

The only body-wall muscles left in the neck are the scaleni: scalenus anterior, scalenus medius, and scalenus posterior. The scaleni run from cervical transverse processes to the first two ribs and help to lift the whole series of ribs when you inhale. The scaleni have the ability to slightly flex the neck and are an example of muscles that transfer the side load of the thorax to the center of the body. The most important part of the cervical body wall musculature is the diaphragm. It migrates from the neck into the thorax during fetal development (see chapter 15).

Figure 12.42 Latticework of abdominal muscles.

Imagery Exercises for the Fascia and Abdominal Wall

1. **Diving through the abdominal wall:** Imagine you could dive through the body wall. You will first encounter the skin, then superficial fascia and fat, muscle or associated tendons, abdominal fascia and fat, and finally peritoneum. If you dive deeper, you encounter the organs surrounded by visceral peritoneum.

2. **All is connected:** Imagine all connective tissue in the body as one interconnected system. Imagine this system communicating through the entire body. Every part can speak to every other part through this system. This is one of the explanations for the concurrent effects on seemingly unrelated and distant parts of the body when you work with imagery.

3. **Liquid wave:** Imagine a liquid wave running through the subcutaneous fascia.

4. **Surfing skin:** Imagine your skin surfing on the underlying fascia as you move your body in daily life, exercise, or dance.

5. **Initiating movement:** Feel the difference between initiating a movement while focusing on the muscles and initiating a movement while focusing on the deep fascia surrounding them.

6. **Muscle pulls on fascia:** When you contract a muscle to move a limb, it first pulls on the connective tissue, and this force is relayed to the bone. Flex your biceps and imagine it pulling on the connective tissue to pull on the bone. Compare this feeling to thinking it actually pulls on the bone directly.

7. **Breath and fascia:** Allow your breath to expand your fascia. Focus on the lumbar or abdominal fascia and notice the effects on your alignment.

ABDOMINAL MUSCLES AND THE CONCEPT OF CORE STABILITY

The rectus abdominis is the most powerful flexor of the torso and spine. It arises by a flat and narrow tendon from the front of the pelvis and runs up and attaches to the outside of the rib cage as far as the fifth costal cartilage. If your upper body is stable, it can lift the anterior rim of the pelvis. Because of their connection to the anterior lamina, segments of the rectus can contract individually. In primitive vertebrates, the rectus series extends all the way from the pelvis to the lower jaw. In mammals with well-developed sternums, the thoracic part of the rectus musculature is atrophied. What is left is mostly the rectus abdominis. Through the rectus series the pelvic floor communicates with the jaw and skull and vice versa. You may be able to move the jaw and notice the effect on the pelvic floor and vice versa.

The internal oblique (IO) muscle arises with most of its fibers from the crest of the ilium (pelvis) and flares fanlike upward and forward toward the midline of the belly. The IO forms the middle layer of the abdominals and is dorsally connected to the fascia thoracolumbalis. The middle part of the IO is a powerful ipsilateral rotator of the trunk.

The fibers that come from farthest back on the pelvis run to the lower edge of the rib cage. These lowest fibers of the IO function very much like the transversus abdominis (TA) to compress the lower abdomen to aid dynamic stabilization when lifting heavy weights or in birthing. Their contraction will cause a stretch in the pelvic floor. Pelvic floor and abdominal muscles should be balanced in their strength.

The outermost of the three lateral abdominal muscles is the external oblique (EO). It arises by fleshy slips from the sides of the lower eight ribs that interdigitate with the serratus anterior. These slips run diagonally downward toward the front of the belly where they blend into a single sheet of muscle and end as an aponeurosis that fuses to the front of the rectus sheath. Fascially this slip relates to the contralateral internal oblique in a diagonal and spiral fashion (figure 12.43).

The lowest part of the EO runs from the lowest ribs to the iliac crest. It is the only part of the EO that originates and inserts on bone. The uppermost part of the EO aids in exhalation and compression of the ribs and is important during the initiation of sit-up-type exercises.

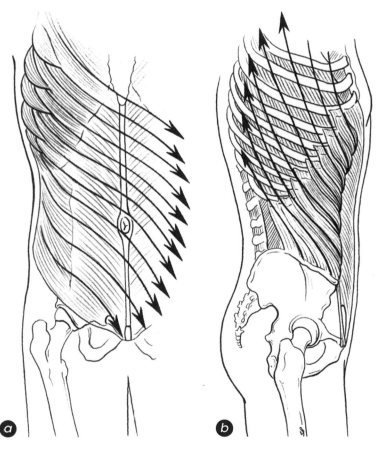

Figure 12.43 External oblique abdominals relating through aponeurosis of rectus to internal oblique of the opposite side: *(a)* anterior view and *(b)* lateral view.

The EO is a powerful contralateral rotator of the trunk. Synchronous contraction of the abdominals causes spinal flexion.

The band formed in the middle of the rectus abdominis is called the linea alba (white line). The linea alba is your anterior elastic spine. The linea alba separates the rectus abdominis into two halves from the rib cage all the way down to the pelvis.

The other two lateral abdominal muscles, the TA and EO, also become aponeurotic in front and fuse with the rectus sheath. The innermost is the TA. The middle part originates at the thoracolumbar fascia, which attaches to the transverse process of the lumbar vertebrae. From this tendinous sheath and from the lower edge of the rib cage and the upper edge of the pelvis, fleshy fibers arise and run horizontally around the abdomen toward the rectus sheath and fuse with the sheath's deep surface. The TA is therefore like a contractile tube around the whole abdominal viscera. Its function is to hold the viscera and aid in stabilizing the trunk. It is also an antagonist to the diaphragm for breathing.

The TA became famous because of a series of studies that relate it to back pain (Cholewicki and McGill 1996; Hodges and Richardson 1996). In the wake of these studies, the idea of core stability became popularized. It was postulated that increased stiffness was needed to protect the lumbar spine from injury, and this led to cues such as "hollowing" and pulling the abdominals "in and up" or even "sticking the navel to the spine." These images were welcomed by the fitness community striving to create the "six-pack" powerhouse and also by dancers' drive to become as flat as possible.

However, more recent research has demonstrated that true stabilization consists of an integration of many elements, including feedback from the nervous system and an adaptive response geared to the situation at hand. No single muscle alone is most important in stabilizing the lumbar spine. Hodges (2010) says, "Back pain rehabilitation is not about training a muscle, but about changing the function of the motor control system" and "it is clear that the deeper muscles do not provide the 'greatest' (sic) contribution to stability. These muscles are important in lumbopelvic motor control" (pp. 414-419). Stabilization is an integrated effort of bones, joints, muscles, and the nervous system and requires good coordination and adaptive activity of the musculature, including dynamic force absorption and increased or decreased stiffness of the system. But generally speaking, people with back pain already have muscles that are too stiff through muscular co-contraction, and this stiffening may actually lead to reduced control of posture.

Muscles that have survived the evolutionary process will be activated by daily movement, such as walking, running, climbing, and sitting. If you flex your legs in a standing position, the TA is concentrically activated to help with the self-bracing mechanism of the pelvis; when extending your legs the muscle contracts eccentrically. This happens every time you sit down and stand up. Through awareness and imagery, you can rehabilitate this muscle or train it as part of daily activities and chores. What counts in the end is how well you are moving and how you are feeling. What leads to this goal is a multimodal approach, which involves embodying better function emotionally, mentally, and physically.

A classic image that relates to the TA was developed long before the concept of core stability arose. It is the zipper image of Lulu Sweigard (1974). In this image the linea alba is imagined as a zipper and the TA as pants. You imagine running the zipper up the front of the pants (linea alba) and the pants (TA) tightening.

Imagery Exercises for the Abdominals

1. **Imagining the rectus series:** Touch your coccyx and the tip of the jaw and imagine the rectus series from top to bottom: geniohyoid, omohyoid, sternohyoid, rectus abdominis, pubococcygeus. Flex the spine and visualize all of these muscles sliding together. Extend the spine and visualize all of these muscles sliding apart. Flex the spine and imagine all these muscles sliding together. Imagine the rectus series and the erector spinae relating to each other in a flow up the front of the body and down the back.

2. **Intercostals and ribs suspended from scalenes:** Imagine the intercostals and ribs as the continuation of the scalenes. Imagine the rib cage suspended from the cervical spine via the scalenes like a tent (figure 12.44).

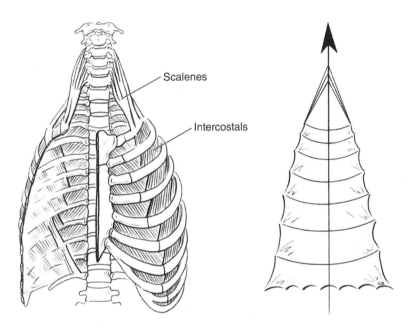

Figure 12.44 Ribs suspended from the scalenes.

3. **Internal oblique suspension:** Imagine the posterior crest of the ilium (pelvis) suspended from the anterior ribs via the internal oblique abdominals.

4. **Aligned linea alba:** Imagine the alignment of the linea alba in the standing position. Does it conform with the alignment of the spine? Is it located in the same median sagittal plane?

5. **Transversus tent:** The rectus sheath connects the pelvis to the sternum and ribs and consists of the aponeurosis of the transversus abdominis and oblique abdominals. Imagine the sheath as the top of a tent that suspends the transversus abdominis (figure 12.45). Posteriorly, the tent is anchored to the thoracolumbar fascia.

6. **Visualize and feel the internal oblique and external oblique in action:** Place your fingers in the muscles under the lateral ribs and rotate your spine to feel these muscles in action. They are synergistically involved in rotating the spine. To rotate the spine to the right, the right internal and left external obliques slide together. Imagine this interaction as one muscle. To rotate the spine to the left, the left internal and right external obliques slide together. Imagine this

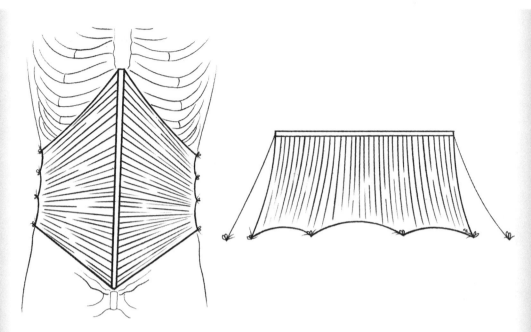

Figure 12.45 Transversus abdominis likened to a tent suspended from the aponeurosis of the rectus abdominis.

interaction as one muscle. To increase the force and range of motion, imagine the intercostals to be the continuation of the oblique abdominals.

7. **Muscle and bone interactions:** Imagine the coordination of the muscle and bone rhythms. As you flex the spine, imagine the facet joints sliding apart and the rectus series sliding together. As you extend the spine, imagine the facet joints sliding together and the rectus series sliding apart. As you rotate the spine, imagine the action of the facet joints and the oblique abdominals. When rotating to the left, for example, the left internal obliques as well as the left facets slide together. The right internal obliques as well as the right facets slide apart. As you rotate to the right, the right internal obliques as well as the right facets slide together. The left internal obliques as well as the left facet joints slide apart.

Thoracolumbar Fascia

The thoracolumbar fascia (TLF) is a broad and multilayered expanse of connective tissue located at the low back and covering the sacrum. It has been depicted in anatomy books for over 100 years, but not until recently has its function been unraveled and its importance for dynamic alignment begun to be revealed. It is an aponeurotic expanse, a flattened tendon resembling the central tendon of the diaphragm. The collagenous fibers crisscross in a variety of directions, and some of the layers of the fascia have the ability to slide on top of each other pulled by muscular forces arising from above and below, laterally and diagonally. The TLF is a relay station where forces from the lower body are transferred to the upper body and vice versa, and forces can transfer diagonally from one side of the body to the other. The TLF is the hub of the wheel that balances, relieves, and mediates forces though the posterior body (figure 12.46).

The latissimus dorsi arises at the top and front of the humerus and connects into the TLF via its aponeurosis, relating arm movements down the pelvis and legs. This aponeurosis forms the posterior layer of the TLF, which connects to a deeper layer of the erector spinae muscles (figure 12.47).

From the sides the thoracolumbar fascia is approached by the deepest abdominal muscle, the transversus abdominis. Its aponeurosis splits into layers, which involve the quadratus lumborum and relate to the psoas muscle. The middle layer, which is the thickest, attaches to the transverse processes of the lumbar spine. This muscle reaches laterally around from the front of the body to hold on to the transverse processes of the lumbar spine.

All three abdominal muscles, the transversus abdominis, internal obliques, and external obliques, form aponeurotic sheets that combine and then split to engulf the rectus abdominis muscles. This allows these muscles and especially the transversus abdominis to pull the anterior crests of the ilia inward, which is what happens in lower-limb flexion as part of the bone rhythms. This system works only if the back of the pelvis is stabilized, which happens with the help of the thickest portion of the thoracolumbar fascia at the back of the sacrum. This portion is made more taut with the help of the contracting multifidus muscle, which acts to stretch it like air pushing on the surface of a balloon (Willard and Carreiro 2010).

If you continue downward, following the path of the aponeurosis of the latissimus dorsi (the superficial thoracolumbar fascia), you find that in the middle lumbar the fibers cross over and connect on the other side of the body to the sacrum, posterior superior iliac spines (PSIS), and iliac crest. From there they continue into the fascia of the gluteus maximus (GM) and the fascia lata surrounding the thigh (figure 12.48). There is a thickening of this fascia referred to as the iliotibial tract (also known as the iliotibial band). The iliotibial tract is commonly depicted in isolation as if it were a lone strand of connective tissue.

The deeper layer of the TLF connects above to the tendons of the splenius cervicis and splenius capitis muscles (Barker and Briggs 1999). Above the sacrum the deep layer fuses with the superficial layer and is continuous with the sacrotuberous

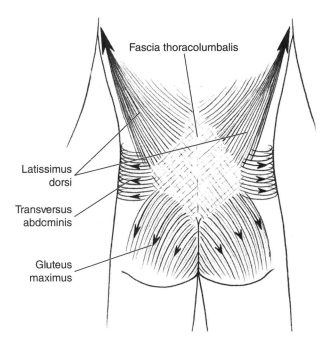

Figure 12.46 The thoracolumbar fascia as a relay station for muscles.

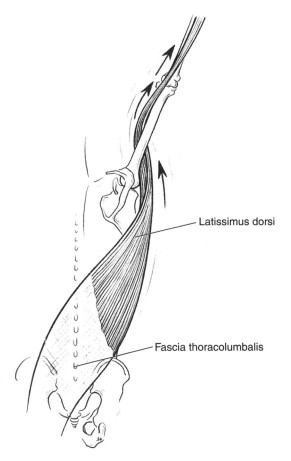

Figure 12.47 Diagonal connection from thoracolumbar fascia to latissimus dorsi to the arm.

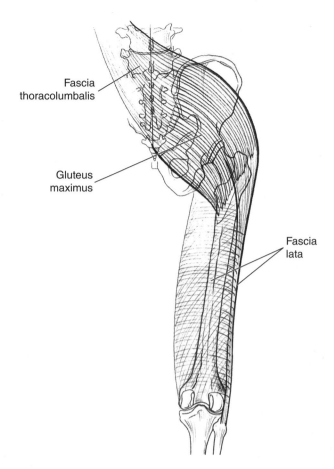

Figure 12.48 Thoracolumbar fascia connecting to the gluteus and fascia lata.

ligament, which in turn is connected to and relates to the biceps femoris. The deep lamina is also connected to the PSIS, iliac crests, and long dorsal ligament (see "Sacrum" in chapter 10).

Think also of organs talking to muscles and vice versa through thoracolumbar fascia. Moving or relaxing the kidneys, for example, influences the psoas fascia, to which it is connected, which in turn influences the abdominal fascia and the TLF. This may result in deeper hip flexion due to release in tension of the iliacus fascia or more flexibility in the arms due to the effect on the thoracolumbar fascia.

Muscle Slings and Spirals

Previously you encountered a posterior diagonal muscle sling running from the latissimus dorsi to the contralateral gluteus. In back pain, the muscles involved in these slings may become imbalanced (Mooney et al. 2001). The anterior sling runs from the oblique abdominals through the pubic area of the anterior pelvis to the contralateral adductors. Both slings relate to the pelvic floor and are important for the bracing of the pelvis and the dynamic stability of the spine (figure 12.49).

In the last century anatomist R.A. Dart (1950) proposed that a spiral line through the trunk of the body goes from the midline of the body, pubic symphysis, and iliac crest through the external obliques, external intercostals, ribs, and scalene musculature, to the transverse processes of the cervical vertebrae, and then through the deeper-lying sheet of the semispinalis to the cervical spinous processes and the occiput (back of the head).

The external obliques can be visualized as continuing across the ventral (front) midline of the body through the deeper-lying internal obliques. The superficial sacro-spinalis crosses the dorsal (back) midline, continuing the line of force of the deep multifidus (much-divided) sheet of muscles. "Thus, in a very real sense, the occiput and spines of the vertebrae suspend the body by means of two spiral sheets of muscle encircling the trunk" (Dart 1950, p. 268). These spiral movements continue into the muscles of the extremities. Besides creating dynamic interaction between the body halves, these spiral lines enable the body to perform rapid winding and unwinding movements, contractions, and twists (figure 12.50).

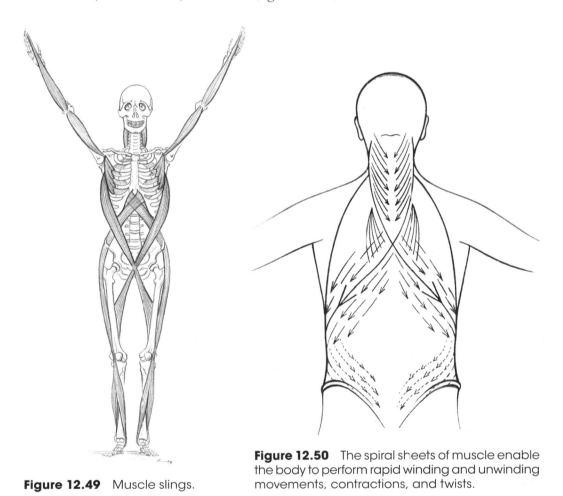

Figure 12.49 Muscle slings.

Figure 12.50 The spiral sheets of muscle enable the body to perform rapid winding and unwinding movements, contractions, and twists.

Imagery Exercises for Thoracolumbar Fascia and Slings

1. **Balanced thoracolumbar fascia and rectus sheath:** Imagine the rectus sheath and the thoracolumbar fascia in balanced alignment as you flex and extend the spine. Appreciate how the front and back wall of your body are linked via the fascia and muscles.

2. **Diagonal pull and slide of fascia in walking:** Place your hands on your low back, approximately where the thoracolumbar fascia is located. Now go for a slow walk and imagine the continuous change of pulls on the TLF. As your right leg swings forward and the left shoulder goes forward, imagine the top left to bottom right diagonal pull through the TLF. The top right to bottom left diagonal is slackened at this time. As your left leg swings forward and is balanced by the right shoulder going forward, imagine the top left and bottom right diagonal pull through the TLF. The opposing diagonal is being slackened. Walk and imagine the changes in diagonal pulls. Then remove your touch and notice the changes in your low back, posture, and sense of walking.

3. **Forward flexion and thoracolumbar fascia:** In a comfortable standing position, place your fingers on your TLF. Slide your fingers up and down with a gentle pressure to slide the skin and superficial fascia. Notice how far you can slide the fascia and notice whether the range of slide is the same on the left and right sides of the spinous processes. Now start flexing forward at your hips very slowly. Keep sliding your fingers up and down with some pressure and notice the speed at which your ability to slide the fascia is reduced as it comes under more tension. Return to the standing position and repeat the movement, and imagine that your finger sliding is affecting the deeper fascial layers, the ligamentum flavum, and the zygapophyseal joints. Now perform the same movement by flexing forward from your lumbar spine. Notice how fast the ability to slide your fingers up and down is reduced and if it is equal on both sides. In the upright position, release your touch and notice the changes in your alignment. You may notice a significant release of tension in your low back and a sense of spinal lengthening.

4. **Imagining posterior slings:** Have a partner slide a hand along the back sling from the latissimus dorsi to the contralateral gluteus maximus. Notice which sling feels stronger and clearer. Notice how your alignment changes once you can embody the slings.

5. **Tensing slings:** Lift your arms overhead and imagine all the slings tightening up just a bit to stabilize your body. Lower your arms and imagine the slings relaxing again. Imagine how the slings weave around the torso and pelvis to stabilize these structures to the perfect degree as you lift and lower your arms.

SUMMARY

Even though the human spine is uniquely adapted to verticality, this configuration comes at a price: Alignment and movement must be efficient for maintaining lifelong spinal health. The spine is not suspended horizontally as with a four-legged animal; rather, it is a stack of counterbalancing arches that improve its ability to move in three dimensions and absorb force. As the intermediary between the upper body and lower body, the spine carries the weight of the head, organs, and limbs and protects the spinal cord. The intervertebral discs increase the range of motion and disperse compressive forces. The spinal facet joints allow for smooth gliding motion. The ligaments provide dynamic stability and directionality.

The body wall is made of concentric layers of connective tissue and muscles. The function of the body wall is to protect the viscera from injury. These structures are involved in reproduction, respiration, and excretion and play an important role in locomotion and dynamic stabilization of the trunk in all forms of movement. There are four layers of muscles in the body wall: A rectus series runs longitudinally along the front of the body from the pelvis to the rib cage, and three concentric layers are on each side of the body. These layers create a complex latticework of muscles that are able to stabilize, balance, and move the trunk.

The thoracolumbar fascia is a broad expanse of connective tissue located at the low back. It is a relay station where forces from the lower body are transferred to the upper body and vice versa, and forces can transfer from one side of the body to the other. Diagonal slings create strong connections from the arms to the legs through the torso to provide stability and increased force generation over a wide range of motion. A throw, push, and pull are not isolated actions in the arms but are supported by slings reaching far into the lower limbs.

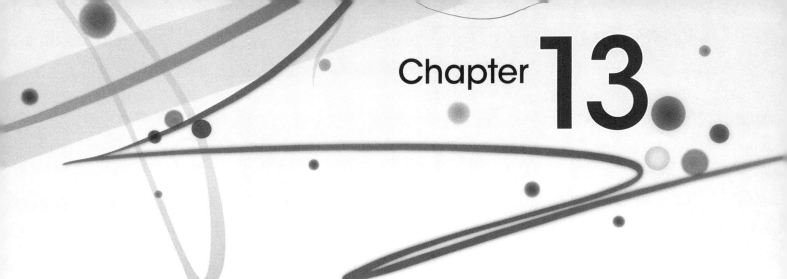

Chapter 13

Shoulders, Arms, and Hands

Attention is the beginning of change.

Our ancestors must have been avid pickers of fruit and berries, much of the fruit located at or above eye level. Although your body is comparatively short, you can reach very high with your arms. The mobility and specialized structure of the shoulder girdle permit you to hold your arms above your head for a fairly long time without tiring. The counterbalancing effect of the shoulder blades is especially helpful in arm elevation. Gymnasts and dancers or anyone reaching for coffee on the top shelf needs to be able to lift the arms without disturbing the center, losing balance, or increasing tension in the shoulders or back. If it weren't for our tree-picking and tree-swinging progenitors, we probably wouldn't have shoulders constructed to do so.

The main function of the shoulder girdle is to allow full mobility of the hand in space. The shoulder girdle complex also helps to protect the heart and lungs by maintaining the arms at a safe distance.

The shoulder girdle consists of two shoulder blades, or scapulae, and two collar-bones, or clavicles (small forks) (figure 13.1). In German, the clavicles are called the "keybones" because they resemble S-shaped keys (figure 13.2). They are indeed key to arm movement because, at their central ends, they connect the arms to the thorax in the only truly jointed connection of the shoulder girdle.

Many joints are involved in the shoulder girdle, both real joints containing a capsule, cartilage, and joint fluid and several virtual, or functional, joints. The functional joints do not have cartilage or a joint capsule but nevertheless are very important interfaces for movement. Arm movements involve all of these joints, forming a closed kinematic chain that increases shock absorption in the shoulder girdle. A blow to the arm is diverted to the scapula and clavicle and diffused before it can disturb the important functions of the heart and lungs within the rib cage. Like humans, birds and primates have

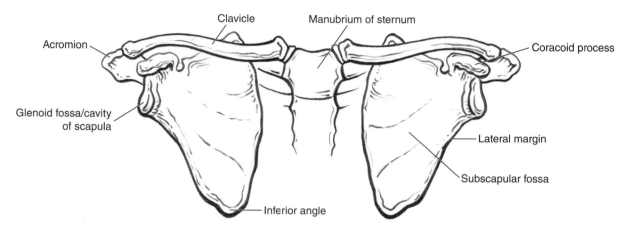

Figure 13.1 The shoulder girdle consists of two scapulae and two clavicles (anterior view).

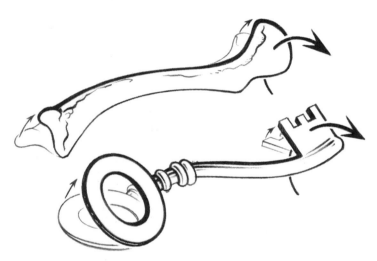

Figure 13.2 The S-shaped clavicle rotates to increase the elevation of its distal end to reduce the need for elevation where it joins with the sternum.

long clavicles, a distinct advantage if you want to fly or hang from a tree. Long clavicles free the arms from the sides, a distinct advantage if you want to climb, throw, or dance. Thanks to the clavicle, the arm can move in space with reduced muscular involvement. In its entirety, the shoulder girdle can be visualized as a tensegrity system that is able to absorb and direct force three-dimensionally.

The joint connecting the humerus to the scapula is called the glenohumeral joint. This is the most flexible joint in the human body. (For more information, see "Glenohumeral Joint" later in this chapter.)

The functional subacromial joint is located between the humeral head and the acromion. The joint space is filled with the subacromial bursa, a flat and fatty pouch that permits smooth gliding motions of the two joint surfaces. You can compare the motion to sliding two pieces of bread (the humeral head and the acromion) containing a thick layer of mayonnaise on top of each other. Without the bursa (mayo), you would have an uncomfortable amount of friction.

The humeroscapular motion interface (HMI) is the sliding surface between the deltoid muscles, coracoid process, coracoacromial arch, and muscles of the rotator cuff. The coracoacromial arch consists of the acromion, the coracoid, and a ligament connecting the two, aptly called the coracoacromial ligament. When you internally and externally rotate your arm, the two surfaces cover up to 3 centimeters of distance as they slide on top of each other.

The scapula is connected to the clavicle via the rather slight acromioclavicular joint. Both surfaces of the joint are slightly convex, not exactly a tight fit. A cartilaginous disc acts as a spacer to create better congruence. The joint permits movement in all directions: to the front and back, upward and downward, and some rotation. It is stabilized by the coracoclavicular and acromioclavicular ligaments. Small as it is, it is nevertheless essential for liberated arm movement.

The clavicle attaches to the manubrium of the sternum (see figure 13.1) at a saddlelike joint containing a disc. The disc acts as a pivot to increase the rotational mobility and stability of the joint, which can move in all planes: protraction, retraction, elevation, depression, and rotation. When the clavicle is elevated or depressed, the movement is a downward slide occurring between the clavicle and the disc. During protraction and retraction, the movement is primarily a swinging forward and backward action of the disc and clavicle around the sternum. The disc also serves to dampen forces, especially if the arm is reaching overhead. Visualizing arm gestures originating flexibly from the sternoclavicular joint increases their fullness.

The human clavicle displays both an outward and an inward curve, a trait shared with chimpanzees and orangutans. The action of the pectoralis major muscle is enhanced by the pronounced internal curvature that acts as a crank. If the bone were straight, the joints of the shoulder would need extra flexibility in arm flexion and elevation, which in turn would reduce joint stability. Because the sternum carries the weight of the shoulder girdle and the arms, it may be difficult to maintain a sense of openness and width in this area. A slouched or an arched posture impedes shoulder function and breathing patterns, which put strain on the spine. In Latin, the verb *sterno* means to widen or to smooth, a welcome notion for the top of the chest. The sternum transfers weight to the upper ribs, which in turn pass it on to the spine.

The scapulae (shoulder blades) are large triangular bones at the back of the rib cage. The scapulae function as an important attachment site for muscles and form a mobile base for the movements of the arms. The medial border is slightly convex and aligned at an angle of 3 to 5 degrees relative to the spine; the lateral border is slightly concave and oblique. The scapulae sit on the rib cage at an angle of 30 degrees to the frontal plane. Together, the clavicle and scapulae create an angle of 60 degrees. To reduce tension and create more space for the upper lung, visualize this area as wide and free, perhaps like a mouth opening (figure 13.3).

The scapulae span the area between the second and seventh ribs. There are four processes (glenoid, coracoid, acromion, and spinous) on the level of the third rib. The articular process, called the fossa glenoidalis, is pear shaped, or can be visualized as an

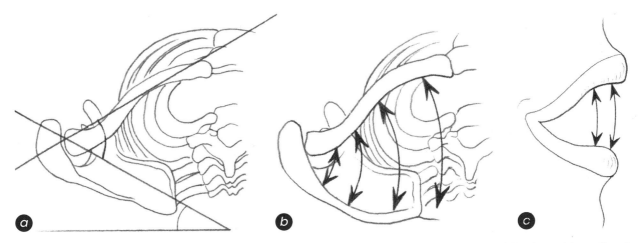

Figure 13.3 (a) Angle of the scapula to the clavicle; (b) imagining the angle widening; (c) angle of clavicle and scapulae opening like a mouth.

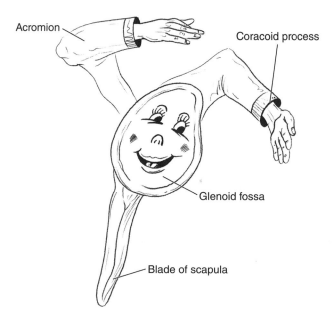

Acromion

Coracoid process

Glenoid fossa

Blade of scapula

Figure 13.4 Glenoid fossa as a face with coracoid and acromion.

inverted comma or even a face. Viewed laterally, the glenoid fossa with the acromion and coracoid can be seen as a figure with two arms (figure 13.4). This may help in committing the configuration to memory.

The inferior tip is one of the three angles and points toward the sit bones. The other angles are the medial and lateral located at opposing sides of the upper scapulae. The glenoid fossa is protected by the acromion (shoulder tip), which hovers atop the shoulder joint like an overhanging cliff. Throughout the ages, fashion designers have amplified this shape with shoulder pads. The fifth joint of the shoulder girdle is the scapulothoracic. The gliding mechanism of the scapula consists of two surfaces; the first is the subscapularis muscle, which in turn rests on the anterior serratus muscle and rib cage (figure 13.5).

The spine of the scapula extends behind the acromion like a miniature mountain range. The valleys above and below the spine are called fossa. Above the spine is the supraspinous fossa; below the spine is another groove called the infraspinous fossa. The scapula's coracoid process (from the Greek word *korax*, meaning raven; *Rabenschnabelfortsatz* in German, meaning crow's beak) actually reaches the front of the body. Here the short head of the biceps, the coracobrachialis, and pectoralis minor muscles attach, the latter of which is the only shoulder muscle not connected to the arm.

The shape of the axilla (armpit) is determined by the latissimus dorsi behind and the pectoralis major muscle in front. They shape the armpit like a pyramid, with its peak at the glenohumeral joint. The inside edge of the armpit is formed by ribs, the outside wall by the arm. Shoulder tension often manifests as a tightening in the armpits.

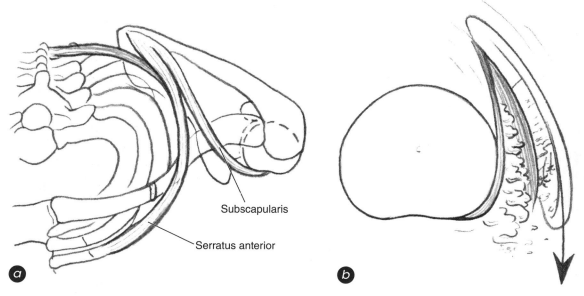

Subscapularis

Serratus anterior

a

b

Figure 13.5 (*a*) Scapula with subscapularis and serratus anterior; (*b*) scapula surfing on subscapularis and serratus anterior.

The brachial plexus of nerves as well as the subclavian vein and artery run underneath the clavicle and pectoralis minor muscles. In slouched, depressed, or retracted "military" posture, these spaces become tighter. Freeing the clavicle from the rib cage and making sure these spaces stay more available for the passage of nerves and vessels can be aided through imagery interventions (see "Guided Shoulder Girdle Tour").

Guided Shoulder Girdle Tour

1. **Touch exploration:** Walk your fingers up the outside of your upper arm. As you near the top of the arm, you will find a rounded area, which is the head of the humerus bone covered by the deltoid muscle. Just above this area, you can touch the bony process of the scapula, called the acromion. Tweeze the front and back edge of the acromion between your fingers to get a good image of its size and shape. Move your fingers medially and anteriorly to find a small crevice, which is the joint between the acromion and the clavicle. Another way to find the joint is to place your hand broadly on the shoulders and feel the angle between the clavicle and the spine of the scapula. Move your touch to the very corner of the angle, making sure to stay inside the bony edges. Once you are in the very corner, your finger is right behind the acromioclavicular joint, which can be readily felt if you move your elbow laterally and medially and upward and downward. If you glide your fingers to the posterior part of the acromion, you will find a bony edge. As your fingers move along this edge toward the center of your back, they are traveling across the spine of the scapula. In the groove above this spine, you can feel the trapezius and the supraspinatus, which lies beneath it. Below the spine of the scapula you can palpate the infraspinatus muscle, which you can feel in action when you externally rotate your arm.

   Continue your tactile voyage along the spine of the scapula, and depending on how flexible you are, you may be able to touch the medial border of the scapula. To touch the inferior tip of the scapula, reach under your arm and place your fingers on the dorsal surface of the scapula. From here, trace your fingers vertically downward, always remaining on the bony surface, until you reach the inferior tip of the scapula. The lateral border of the scapula may be difficult to palpate because it is partially covered by the latissimus dorsi musculature.

   Relocate your fingers back to the anterior tip of the acromion. Slide your fingers down from this point to feel the minor tubercle of the humerus. Laterally to it you may detect a groove, the intertubercular sulcus, which is the basin for the tendon of the biceps. If you bend and stretch your elbow, you may feel the movement of the long head of the biceps. Moving medially, you will feel a bony point, the coracoid process. Quite a few people experience this point as tender to the touch. Move slightly below it to feel the stringy tendons of the pectoralis minor, coracobrachialis, and short head of the biceps. Between the coracoid and the acromion stretches the coracoacromial ligament. The ligament is right above the coracoid and below the acromion. Palpate the two bones and the possibly tender area in between.

   Between the coracoid and the minor tubercle you can feel the subscapularis muscle, a sensation enhanced by externally and internally rotating the arm. Return to the acromioclavicular joint and from there follow along the clavicle until you reach a large, bony prominence that marks the medial end of the clavicle. This joint is easy to feel because the clavicular end of this joint is significantly larger than its counterpart, the manubrium. Drop your fingers over this ledge onto the bone medial to it, which is the manubrium of the sternum. Finally, glide your fingers down the sternum to its inferior tip, called the xiphoid process.

2. **Shoulder girdle on sternum:** Imagine the shoulder girdle resting on the manubrium of the sternum (figure 13.6). Embody this only bony connection of the shoulder girdle to the torso. Allow the weight of the shoulder girdle to be transferred through the sternum to the ribs, spine, pelvis, legs, feet, and ground.

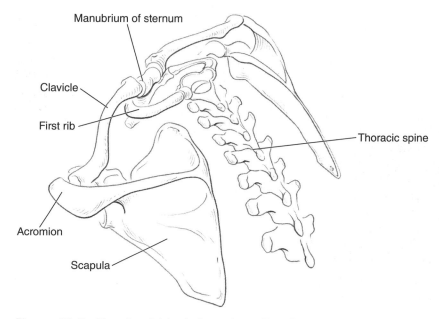

Manubrium of sternum

Clavicle

First rib

Thoracic spine

Acromion

Scapula

Figure 13.6 The shoulder girdle rests on the sternum.

3. **Coracoid spread (supine, sitting, standing):** Visualize the coracoid process and the surrounding area expanding. Touch the tip of the coracoid and perform slow widening circles with your fingertip. Visualize the area spreading like cake batter in an ever-widening circle. If you are not sure about being in the right place, lift your arm over your head. The bony point should then vanish and reemerge as you lower your arm back down. As the coracoid process reemerges, you can imagine it sliding forward under the clavicle like a finger sliding into a glove.

4. **Visualizing the glenoid fossa:** Visualize the shape and size of the glenoid fossa. It is shaped like a pear or an inverted comma. Notice how the acromion and coracoid relate to it. The acromion can be likened to a protective hand above and the coracoid to a protective hand in front (see figure 13.4).

5. **Scapular wax (sitting, standing):** Imagine the shoulder blade to be made of beeswax. Visualize the inferior tip of the shoulder blade melting downward. First it turns into soft drops of molten wax, and then the entire lower section melts. The drops fall down toward the sit bones. Smell the honeylike aroma of the wax as it glides down your back.

6. **Extended acromion (supine, sitting, standing):** Visualize the distance between the tip of the shoulder and the neck increasing as the acromion elongates sideways. Place your hand on the acromion and gently pull it to the side. Imagine the acromion to be made of infinitely stretchable taffy. A partner may

also help you visualize this image by sliding his or her hands out and away from the neck. This image gives you a sense of width in your shoulders and helps to release muscle tension.

7. **Clouds floating through the supraspinous fossa:** Imagine the supraspinous fossa as a valley filled with clouds (figure 13.7). These soft clouds gently flow through the fossa valley. Imagining soft, fluffy clouds in this area goes a long way toward releasing shoulder tension and improving the ease of elevating the arm.

Figure 13.7 Visualize the space contained within the supraspinous fossa filled with soft, fluffy clouds.

8. **Water flowing under acromion:** Visualize the space contained within the supraspinous fossa to contain a river flowing toward and under the acromion and coracoacromial ligament (figure 13.8). Imagining the coracoacromial ligament to be a flexible suspension bridge adds an additional touch of release to the muscles of the area.

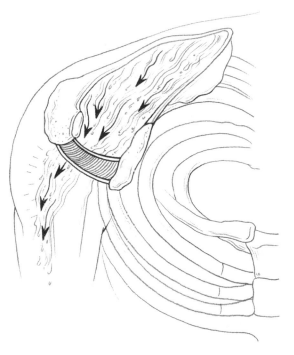

Figure 13.8 Imagine a river flowing under the acromion and coracoacromial ligament.

9. **Surfing clavicle:** Imagine the clavicle surfing on the first rib (figure 13.9). Feel the clavicle sliding on the first rib as you reach forward and backward with your arms.

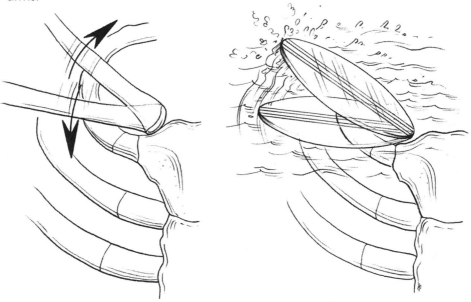

Figure 13.9   The clavicle surfing on the first rib.

10. **Bridge over nerves:** Imagine the brachial nerves flowing under the clavicle like a stream of water (figure 13.10). Imagine ample space for this flow. Imagine the clavicle also as a raft floating gently on a flowing stream.

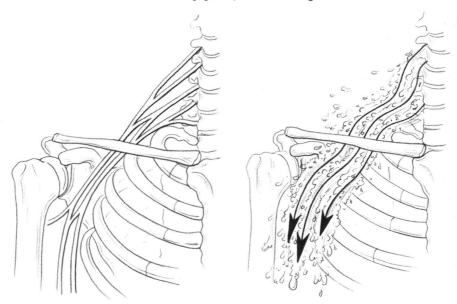

Figure 13.10   The brachial nerves flowing under the clavicle.

11. **Sagging nerves:** As you lift your arms, imagine the brachial nerves and vessels staying clear of the pectoralis minor muscle and clavicle by hanging down softly like overcooked spaghetti or festoons (figure 13.11). You can also stay with the direct anatomical imagery, in which case it is useful to imagine the nerves resting in their fatty covering of myelin.

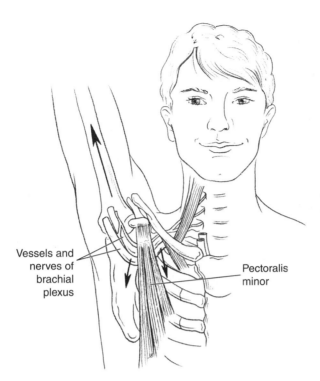

Figure 13.11   Imagine the nerves hanging down under the pectoralis minor.

12. **Hanging arms (standing, walking):** Imagine your arms detaching from your shoulders and sliding down the sides of your body. It might be helpful to imagine your hands trailing Neanderthal-like on the floor (figure 13.12).

13. **Watch your beautiful arms:** Watch yourself from the external perspective with positive self-talk. Admire your ability to lift your arms smoothly and with good coordination. If any negative thoughts try to enter your mind, pack them in a balloon and float them off.

14. **Differentiation of shoulder and rib cage:** Place your left hand on your sternum and upper-right ribs. Visualize your rib cage and shoulder girdle as separate entities. Move your shoulder girdle front and back and notice if you can keep the area you are touching still and relaxed. Notice any tendency to move the torso with the scapulae. Perfect the art of gliding your shoulder blades on your rib cage.

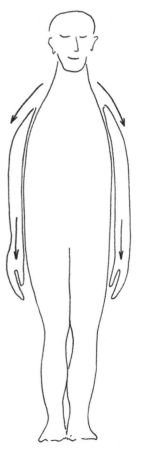

Figure 13.12   The arms detach from the shoulders and slide down the sides of the body.

15. **Relative opposite movement:** As you move your shoulder girdle to the front, focus on the rib cage going relatively back. As your shoulder girdle goes back, imagine the rib cage going relatively to the front.

16. **Three-layered surfing:** Visualize the three sliding surfaces for the scapulae: subscapularis, anterior serratus, and rib cage. As you reach forward, imagine the scapulae sliding on these layers one after one. Imagine the scapulae sliding on the subscapularis, which slides on the anterior serratus and finally on the thoracic fascia and rib cage. As you retract your arm, reverse the order: Anterior serratus slides on thoracic fascia, subscapularis slides on anterior serratus, and finally scapula on subscapularis (see figure 13.5).

17. **Arms as cords (standing):** Trace the bones of your left arm with your right hand. Touch the acromion above the shoulder socket. Trace your finger along the clavicle to the sternoclavicular joint. Lift your left shoulder and feel the movement of the clavicle on the sternum. Keep a finger on the sternoclavicular joint and bend your torso sideways to the left. Visualize the arm as a heavy cord attached at the top of the sternum (figure 13.13). As you swing your left arm front to back, imagine that you are initiating the arm swing from the clavicle. Let the arm swing higher, then decrease the swing, allowing gravity to pull on the cord. Let the arm come to a stop. Allow the manubrium to initiate the return to a vertical position as it pulls on your arm. Drop your right arm to your side. Stretch both arms forward and compare their lengths. Repeat the exercise on the other side. A partner can help you experience motion in the clavicle by manipulating it gently back and forth. Be careful, though, because the muscles around the clavicle may be tender. (Exercise adapted from André Bernard.)

18. **Deep armpits (supine, sitting, standing):** Imagine your armpits becoming deep and soft. Think of having tiny balloons in your armpits, inflating as you inhale and deflating as you exhale. Simultaneously, think of the back of your neck being soft and your jawbone heavy. Watch the balloons deflate as you exhale while making a hissing sound. Finally, imagine the balloons dropping out of your armpits on an exhalation, leaving a hollow, wide-open space behind (figure 13.14).

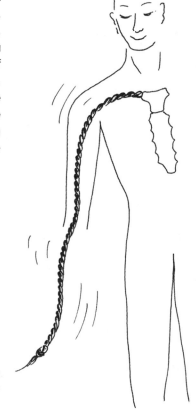

Figure 13.13 The arm as a heavy cord attached at the top of the sternum.

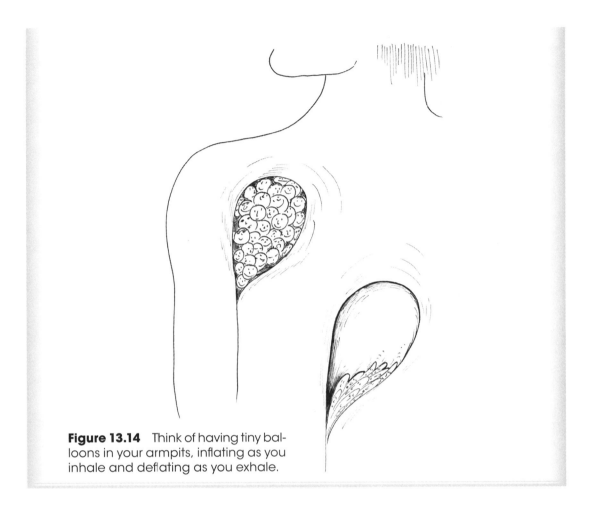

Figure 13.14   Think of having tiny balloons in your armpits, inflating as you inhale and deflating as you exhale.

SUSPENSION OF THE SHOULDER GIRDLE

Muscularly, the shoulder girdle is suspended from the neck and head like a sailing ship, in which the spine is the mast and the shoulder girdle a cross beam suspended from it (figure 13.15). Another way to visualize the design of the shoulder girdle is to see it as a tensegrity system that is able to distribute forces through a three-dimensional system of spacers and tensile elements. The hub of this system can be visualized as the scapulae, which have muscles radiating out in all directions. The scapulae are like the surface of a trampoline suspended between the surrounding springs (figure 13.16).

Efficient central suspension and tensegrity function depend on the proper alignment of the

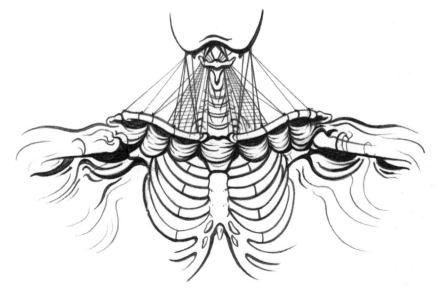

Figure 13.15   The shoulder girdle is suspended from the neck like sails from the mast of a ship.

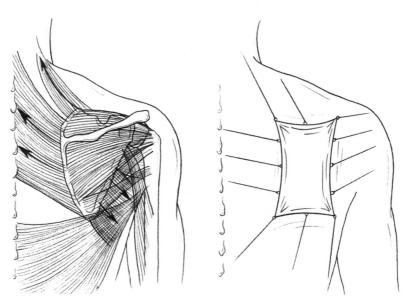

Figure 13.16 The scapula as a tensegrity system and trampoline.

spine. Habitual elevation of the entire girdle tends to cause it to move forward relative to your central axis, placing additional strains on the spine. In the reverse causality, a collapsed upper spine with the head and neck forward causes shoulder placement to suffer, reducing its flexibility and adding strain to the system. Because the muscles controlling the arm and shoulder girdle extend in all directions, head positioning has far-reaching consequences. For example, the latissimus (widest) dorsi muscles, familiarly known as the lats, create a connection between the top of the arms and the pelvis. Improving pelvic and spinal alignment greatly benefits the shoulder girdle as well.

Suspension of the Shoulder Girdle

1. **Flexibility test:** Lift your arms overhead and lower them again. Now slouch with your upper body, which will tend to bring your shoulder girdle forward. Repeat the lifting of the arms. In the slouched, rounded-shoulder position, you will have lost shoulder mobility. People with this habitual posture tend to compensate by thrusting the pelvis forward and arching the back. The lumbar spine especially will not be happy to compensate for lack of shoulder alignment.

2. **Suspended shoulder girdle (sitting, standing, walking):** Imagine the shoulder girdle suspended from the cervical spine and head. The primary muscle ties for the suspension are the trapezius and levator scapulae. The trapezius connects the skull to the clavicle and scapulae. The levator scapulae originates from the first four transverse processes of the cervical spine and attaches to the medial angle and upper border of the scapulae. Imagine the weight of the shoulder girdle and arms stretching these muscles. As stretching force is transferred to the central mast, the spine experiences compression and a simultaneous countering upward thrust. The more you can relax your bones into their muscular suspension, the more the spine lengthens upward. Take this experience into your exercise and daily life activities and enjoy a happy relationship between the spine and shoulder girdle.

3. **Tensegrity shoulder girdle (sitting, standing, walking, jumping):** Imagine the shoulder girdle to be a tensegrity system. With every movement, imagine the whole of the shoulder girdle participating, reacting, and absorbing the force. Thrust your arms in a variety of directions and imagine the shoulder girdle pulling your arms back again by rebounding elastically (figure 13.17). When walking or jumping, allow the shoulder girdle to react elastically to your movement.

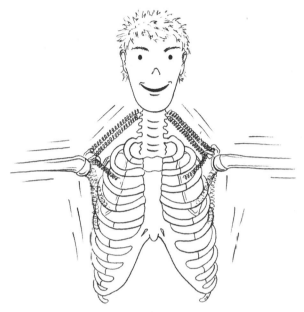

Figure 13.17 The shoulder girdle as a tensegrity system.

4. **Turtleneck shoulder girdle (sitting, standing, walking):** Think of the shoulder girdle as a turtleneck sweater covering your rib cage. Imagine the turtleneck being rolled down the sides of the thorax and the thorax emerging from the turtleneck. Visualize the sweater rolling down in increments. Watch it roll down on exhalation and widen on inhalation. Think of the sweater as being made of very wide mesh. As you inhale, imagine the mesh widening even more (figure 13.18).

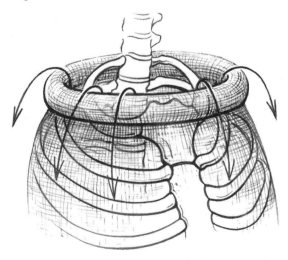

Figure 13.18 The shoulder girdle as a turtleneck sweater covering your rib cage.

5. **Dropping hoop (sitting, standing, walking):** Imagine the shoulder girdle as a hoop draped around your rib cage. Watch the hoop dropping to the level of the rib cage. Then imagine the reverse—thorax, neck, and head emerging from the hoop.

6. **Watershed (supine, improvisation):** Visualize a strong current of water moving up your central axis. As the water reaches the level of the shoulder girdle, it spreads sideways. The stronger the upward current, the greater the spreading of the current at the shoulder girdle (figure 13.19).

7. **Arm on trampoline:** Imagine the shoulder girdle to be a trampoline on which the arm can rest (figure 13.20). Reach your arm up and imagine this resilient support for the arm, which is expert at supporting, absorbing, and providing force for all movement. Reach your arm up and down and compare the kinesthetic response you are receiving from the trampoline metaphor to imagining the direct anatomy of the bones and joints.

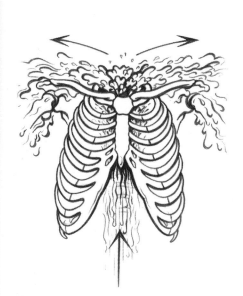

Figure 13.19 A strong current of water moving up your central axis.

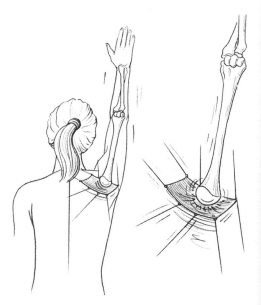

Figure 13.20 Trampoline shoulder support.

Muscles can act concentrically and eccentrically (see chapter 9). Eccentric action acts as a limit to movement, stabilizing and absorbing force. Eccentric contractions are more efficient than concentric. A muscle that is being lengthened at a certain speed is much stronger than a muscle that is being shortened at the same speed (Perry 1988). Shoulder tension is very common. Most of it is not related to an injury; in other words, it derives from stress, faulty posture, lack of movement, and inefficient movement patterns. For these reasons I emphasize the imagery of lengthening and dynamic force absorption of the shoulder.

The trapezius is an ancient muscle derived from a muscle sheet in fish that runs down the back of the head to the gill arch bones, functioning to lift the gills upward. In humans, it is the most superficial muscle of the back. The lower part was connected to the anterior limb bones the same as in humans today. When the neck and head developed, the trapezius remained stretched out between the skull and the forelimb bones. Its function remains to move the scapulae. Trapezius means diamond shaped. If the trapezius is tight, it is very difficult to properly align the spine. Because of its expanse, the proprioception of the trapezius is important for alignment. It is challenging to sense your spinal alignment if your trapezius is tight.

The upper part of the trapezius is called the pars descendens and pulls the shoulders up to the skull, called elevation. These fibers specifically pull the acromion craniomedially, which externally rotates the scapulae.

When the shoulder girdle is fixed, the trapezius is able to laterally flex the head and extend and rotate it to the opposite side. The lower part is called the pars ascendens and runs up to the scapulae from lower thoracic spinous processes and thoracolumbar fascia. It inserts on the medial end of the scapular spine. This part of the trapezius pulls the scapulae medially and downward, creating a fixed point around which the scapulae can swivel. The middle fibers are called the pars transversa. They pull the scapulae toward the spine. They are located above the rhomboids, which are synergists for this action.

Acting together, the upper, middle, and lower fibers of the trapezius create a torque (a turning force) that rotates the glenoid fossa upward without having to slide the whole scapula toward the head (figure 13.21). It is assisted in this action by the lower portions of the serratus anterior, creating a triple force that moves the scapula. The upward rotation of the scapula is initiated by the transverse part to help stabilize the scapula. Next the serratus anterior swings the inferior angle laterally. The ascending trapezius then pulls the scapula downward and outward. Finally the descending

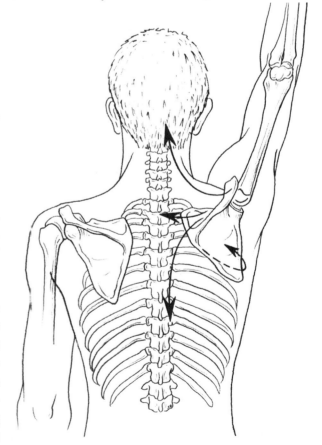

trapezius helps to lift the lateral part of the scapula. All these actions happen in a very coordinated fashion and almost simultaneously. Nevertheless, it is valuable to imagine these actions one by one in slow arm elevation. If you imagine the ascending trapezius initiating the movement, you will notice that the shoulder blade will tend to lift instead of drop as you elevate.

The horizontal part of the trapezius can be imagined in conjunction with the pectoralis minor. They tug on opposite ends of the scapulae, so to speak—an example of a muscle-bone-muscle chain. In general, the ascending fibers need more strength and tone (the "newer" ones, evolutionarily speaking), while the upper fibers (the "older" ones) tend to tighten up.

The scapulae are held against the thorax by the serratus anterior and rhomboids, a layer of the body-wall musculature attached to the medial edge of the scapulae and stretching away in both directions—forward beneath the scapulae to attach to the ribs and backward beneath to attach to the spinous processes. The serratus anterior arises along a zigzag line (*serratus* means sawtoothed) from the upper nine ribs by muscle slips that interdigitate with the origin of the external oblique, from which

Figure 13.21 Trapezius and serratus anterior rotating the scapula.

the serratus is an evolutionary derivative. The muscle runs around the rib cage and beneath the scapulae to attach all along the scapulae's medial border.

The rhomboids pick up where the serratus anterior leaves off and continue medially and headward from the scapulae to the spines of the upper thoracic vertebrae and C7. The serratus anterior and rhomboids are fascially connected, forming a mobile belt of muscle around the thorax, to which the scapulae are attached like a pair of shoulder holsters. This belt can contract to pull the scapulae forward or backward into abduction and adduction. The spiral around the body they are part of can be continued upward through the splenius muscles to the skull and downward into the external oblique abdominals to the pelvis and beyond.

The rhomboids run medially upward to their spinous process attachment sites. Their contraction therefore pulls the medial edge of the scapulae upward and depresses the glenoid downward. The middle and lower serratus anterior have the opposite effect and lift the glenoid fossa upward. They are antagonists for scapular rotation.

The original function of the serratus anterior is best understood in a four-footed mammal. The serratus anterior acts as a hammock slung between the two shoulder blades, cradling the thorax and supporting its weight (figure 13.22).

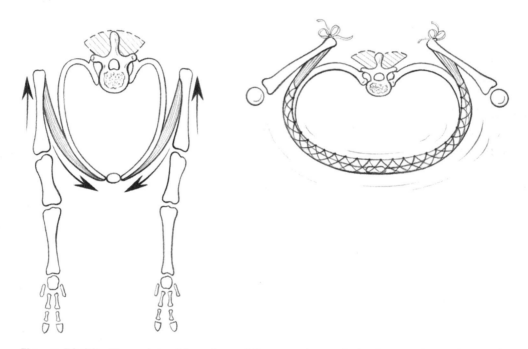

Figure 13.22 The original function of the serratus anterior in quadrupeds was to suspend the rib cage from the scapulae. In humans, it thrusts the scapulae forward.

In humans, the function of the serratus anterior is to thrust the scapulae forward or resist a backward push against the shoulders in, say, a punch or a shove. In anatomical terms, the serratus is destined to be the major protractor of the scapulae. (In Latin, *protraction* is *protrahere,* which means "forward puller.")

The levator scapulae is actually an isolated strip of the serratus anterior. It runs from what is left of the cervical ribs to the medial edge of the scapulae. Its function is similar to that of the rhomboids: to lift the scapula. Considering the levator scapulae, in a four-footed mammal the neck is literally suspended from the scapulae.

In a forward head, the levator scapulae is overstretched and tired. Liberally apply imagery to the levator scapulae. It is commonly tense and should melt into length for comfortable shoulders.

The latissimus dorsi (broadest muscle), teres major (big round muscle), and subscapularis are part of one family of muscles. The latissimus dorsi has several origins, from the scapulae, the lower thoracic vertebral spines, the thoracolumbar fascia overlying the erector spines, and even the ribs. Some slips run to the thoracolumbar fascia, forming an aponeurosis there and reaching the iliac crest. The latissimus dorsi can therefore be visualized as the muscle that connects the arms to the pelvis and low back. Its fibers run upward between the humerus and the rib cage and converge into a spiraled tendon, which inserts into the humerus high up in front of the ridge leading down from the lesser tubercle (figure 13.23). Press your elbow against the rib cage and palpate the tubercles at the top of the humerus.

The pectoralis major (from Latin *pectorem*, meaning chest) arises in three parts along a sweeping arc running from the medial part of the clavicle down onto the sternum and the upper six or so costal cartilages, giving it a fanlike appearance. The fibers of the pectoralis major insert on the greater tubercular crest on the front of the humerus. They do so in a very special way: The lowest fibers go to the upper end of this crest, and the highest fibers go to the lower end. The muscle fibers cross each other and spiral into their insertion.

This arrangement means that all parts of the muscle get stretched to about the same degree when the arm is abducted, making them equally efficient in pulling it back into the adducted position. No one set of fibers is overly stretched, while the others are slack, which would waste muscle power.

The deltoid can be visualized as an inverted triangle covering the shoulder joint. (Delta is a capital Greek letter shaped like a triangle.) Its fibers originate from the spine of the scapula and the lateral third or so of the clavicle. The deltoid is the most important abductor of the arm. It does this by closely interacting with the muscles of the rotator cuff. These center the humeral head in the glenoid fossa (pull down) because the impact of the deltoid is rather vertically upward at the onset of abduction. Visualize the middle part of the deltoid flowing downward and the edges flowing upward as you lift your arm. (The deltoid initially has a lot of vertical force on the humerus; this image helps to counteract that.)

The four short muscles running from the scapulae to the upper end of the humerus (the two spinatus, teres minor, and subscapularis) from the latissimus group are called the rotator cuff (figure 13.24).

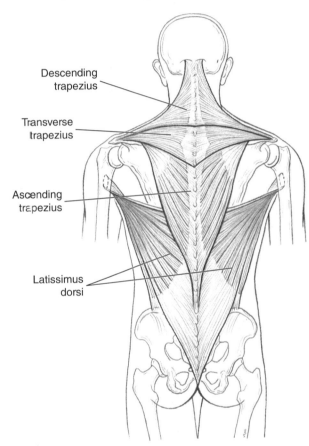

Figure 13.23 The latissimus dorsi.

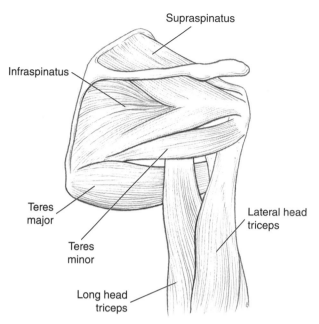

Figure 13.24 Muscles of the posterior shoulder.

Together, they constitute an active capsule for the shoulder joint, contracting en masse to pull the humerus and scapula more tightly together, whenever any dislocating forces threaten the joint's integrity. Infraspinatus attaches to a similar location as the teres minor and is the most powerful (90 percent) external rotator of the arm. The supraspinatus also inserts on the greater tubercle but has to run directly over the top of the glenohumeral joint to get there. It therefore rotates the humerus neither medially nor laterally but instead helps to depress the humeral head and then abduct the arm. If the supraspinatus is injured, initial arm lifting is a challenge.

The arteries supplying the supraspinatus are terminal. This explains the tendency for hypovascularity (lack of blood) in the zone near its tendinous attachment. Carrying a heavy load or doing certain arm movements can reduce blood flow to zero, explaining this muscle's tendency to rupture and inflame.

Imagery Exercises for the Shoulder Muscles

1. **Melting shoulders:** Visualize all the muscles of the shoulder melting like butter, ice cream, chocolate sauce, or any image that gives you a similar experience (figure 13.25). You may want to use a long exhalation to emphasize the release and melting of the muscles.

2. **Diamond trapezius:** Imagine the diamond shape of the trapezius muscles. Mentally compare it to a kite. Imagine the kite fluttering in the wind to release tension in this muscle.

3. **Flow through trapezius:** Imagine the descending trapezius and deltoid to be a stream of water flowing down from the back of the head to the shoulder.

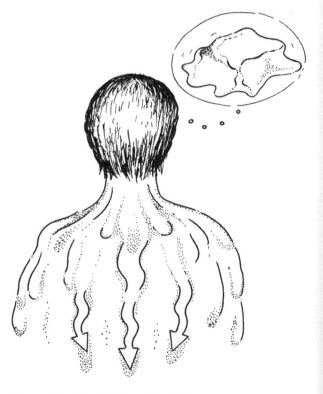

Figure 13.25 Melting shoulders.

Imagine the water cascading over the acromion and flowing down the side of the arm.

4. **Fluttering trapezius:** This is an external and global image. You are in a very windy spot. The wind is blowing in your face and over your shoulders. Now imagine the trapezius to be fluttering in the wind like a sail or a soft piece of cloth (figure 13.26).

Figure 13.26   Trapezius fluttering in the wind.

5. **Two triangles:** Visualize the trapezius as two triangles with touching base lines. The corners of the top triangle are at the acromia and the base of the skull. The corners of the bottom triangle are the spinous process of the scapulae and T12. As you shrug your shoulders, visualize the top triangle shrinking. Its base rises up and its surface area shrinks. The bottom triangle enlarges, the lateral sides elongate, and its surface area increases. As you lower your shoulders, the top triangle becomes larger, the sides lengthen, and the bottom triangle shrinks while its sides shorten. Notice whether the triangles are balanced in shape. Do the sides elongate and shorten harmoniously as you shrug your shoulders? Are the triangles lopsided, or are they balanced?

6. **Trapezius relaxing:** Focus on the layers of muscles that are on the top of your shoulders. This is mostly the trapezius, deltoid, and levator scapulae. Imagine that the deepest layer rests down like a hammock. Then go up through the layers and let one after the other rest and relax downward.

7. **Serratus-rhomboid belt:** Shrug your shoulders forward and backward and feel the mobile serratus-rhomboid belt in action. Perform the movement again, but focus the initiation on the rib cage. As your shoulders move forward, the rib cage swings back and vice versa.

8. **Suspended in a sling:** Imagine the scapulae suspended from the rib cage and spine via the rhombcids, levator scapulae, and serratus anterior. Imagine the scapulae resting in a hammock as it supports the arm.

9. **Lengthen and release rhomboids:** Lift your arms and imagine the rhomboids lengthening. Imagine the distance between the medial and spinal border of

the scapulae and the spinous processes increasing. Imagine the medial border of the scapulae melting, dripping with wax or ice cream. Embody this feeling as you elevate your arms.

10. **Serratus hammock:** In the quadruped position, practice the original function of the serratus, anteriorly lowering and lifting your shoulder blades. Sag your rib cage downward between the shoulder blades and feel the serratus lengthening. Engage the serratus anterior to pull the rib cage back up as if you were tightening up a hammock.

11. **Levator balancing:** In the quadruped position, focus on the levator scapulae connecting your neck to your scapulae. Lower your head, sag your neck downward, and imagine it lengthening. Lift your head up and imagine it shortening. Feel your neck being lifted back and up toward your scapulae. Move to the standing position while maintaining this imagery and notice the changes in posture.

12. **Spiraling lats and pecs:** Watch the pectoralis end unspiral as you elevate your arms. This contributes slightly to the lengthening of the muscle. As you lower your arms, the muscle spirals again. Imagine that the unspiraling of the muscle contributes to its ability to lift your arm (figure 13.27).

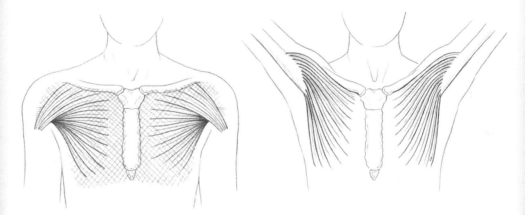

Figure 13.27 Spiraling pecs.

13. **Sponging lats:** At the back of the armpit it is possible to firmly engage the latissimus dorsi just before it inserts into the humerus. Hold this area and swing your arm forward and backward. Imagine the muscle you are holding to be a sponge. When the arm swings forward, gently squeeze the sponge; when the arm swings back, release the sponge. After the exercise, take a moment to compare your shoulders and the ease with which you can lift your arms overhead. Repeat on the other side.

14. **Sponging and sliding pectoralis:** The pectoralis muscle can be held at the front of the armpit. As in the previous exercise, imagine the pectoralis to be a sponge. As you swing the arm forward, gently squeeze the sponge; as you swing back, release it again. After repeating the action about 10 times, notice any difference between the two sides, then repeat on the other side.

15. **Sliding and sponging deltoid muscle:** Place one hand on the deltoid muscle. As you abduct your arm in the scapular angle (about 30 degrees anterior to the frontal plane), imagine the filaments to be sliding together. As you lower the arm, imagine the filaments to slide apart. After repeating this action several

times, give the muscle a gentle squeeze at the moment it arrives back down at the side of the body. Imagine you are squeezing a soft cloth or sponge. After repeating arm abduction about 10 times, compare sides and also the surprising ease with which you lift your arms overhead, then repeat with the other arm.

16. **Humeroscapular motion interface:** The deltoid forms the humeroscapular motion interface (HMI) with the rotator cuff muscles. The HMI can be considered a functional joint. Place your hand on your deltoid, rotate the arm internally and externally, and imagine the sliding between the rotator cuff and deltoid. Also imagine the HMI and the rotator cuff counterrotating. Notice the release of tension and the balancing of muscles.

17. **Relaxed supraspinatus:** Since this muscle is commonly overworked, it is very important to keep a relaxed, soft feeling in the supraspinatus as you lift your arm. Sense it being very soft and relaxed as you abduct your arm and repeat the imagery also with the other arm.

18. **Sliding latissimus:** Elevate your arms and imagine the fibers of the latissimus group sliding apart. Notice how this influences the quality of your movement. It will help you feel the shoulder drop down as you lift the arms.

19. **Latissimus cloak:** Imagine the latissimus as a large cloak swinging and moving with currents of air. Notice the deepening of the breath that results from releasing tension in the latissimus group.

20. **Balancing psoas and latissimus:** Visualize the relationship of the latissimus dorsi and psoas. The latissimus is the psoas of the upper body. They can be seen as continuations of each other's line of action. They both originate on the middle of the spine, but on opposite sides. Feel their pull balancing each other.

21. **Latissimus and gluteus spiral:** Visualize the spiral path created by the relationship between the gluteus maximus and the latissimus dorsi of opposite sides. They connect at the thoracolumbar fascia. Have your partner slide along this pathway with the fingertips. Notice how it feels if only one side has been touched.

22. **Pectoralis fan:** Imagine the pectoralis major as a fan. Imagine the fan widening at its area of origin from the ribs through the sternum and clavicle. Use your hands brushing from the upper humerus to reinforce this feeling.

23. **Sliding the rotators:** Bend your elbow. Internally rotate the arm, imagining the sliding apart of the posterior scapular muscles (teres major, infraspinatus). Externally rotate the arm and imagine the muscles on the anterior side of the scapulae sliding apart (subscapularis). Repeat several times and compare sides.

GLENOHUMERAL JOINT

Compared to the hip socket, which covers more than half of the head of the femur, the shoulder socket is extremely shallow. Thus, the glenohumeral joint is a relatively feeble structure. If it weren't for the strong muscles performing a constant balancing act to keep the heads of the humerus bones in their fossa, the arms would be in constant danger of dislocating. The trade-off for the potential instability is enhanced mobility—the glenohumeral joint can flex, extend, abduct, adduct, and rotate internally and externally. A superficial glance at the humeral head and fossa glenoidalis would make them seem like a very poor match. In fact, the surface area of the fossa is four times smaller than the opposing surface of the humeral head. If you mentally add the cartilage, the situation improves. The humeral head is angled at 45 degrees to its shaft and retroverted 30 to 40 degrees relative to the angle of the condyles at the distal humerus. Note that this is the opposite of the anteversion of the femur. The cartilage of the fossa is thin at the center and thick on the outside. The addition of a labrum (lip) on the circumferences makes it even more cuplike. The cartilage of the humeral head is arranged in the opposite fashion: thick at the center and thinner at the periphery. These arrangements combine to provide a better fit at the glenohumeral joint. The joint has a very lax capsule surrounding it, like a loose-fitting bedcover. This is necessary for allowing a large range of motion. Several muscles attach to all rims of the capsule to create a dynamic capsule. The muscles of the rotator cuff, subscapularis, supraspinatus, infraspinatus, and teres minor, all insert their tendons in the capsule and make the capsule come alive with adaptive tension.

When the arm is abducted (lifted to the side), the head of the humerus cannot simply roll upward on the glenoid fossa because it will collide with the acromial roof. Instead, the head of the humerus slides downward on the fossa while rolling upward, actually creating a relatively fixed center of rotation for itself. This dynamism is made possible by a complex muscular dance. Were the issue left to the deltoid, it would pull the humeral head up and over the fossa instead of keeping it in its socket. The infraspinatus and teres minor muscles pulling to opposite sides of the lower scapulae are key players in maintaining the humeral head in its socket. This action works best if the arm is abducted in the scapular plane, which is about 30 degrees anterior to the frontal plane. If you abduct the arm while it is straight to the side, the greater tubercle of the humeral head will impinge on the acromion unless you externally rotate the arm, which you will do instinctively. If you abduct your arms over the horizontal plane and lower them down again, you may notice that your arms are externally rotated, even if this was not your intention. This is called the Codman paradox. If you lift your arms again and try to maintain them in the same position or even internally rotate them, you will notice that your shoulder girdle will lift upward with your arms. Internal rotation of the humerus also spirals the joint capsule and pulls the humeral head more deeply into the socket, increasing stability. External rotation unspirals the capsule, making it easier to elevate the arm. The glenohumeral joint is aided by the negative pressure within the capsule, allowing the glenoid fossa to act as a suction cup for the humeral head, another useful anatomical image for increasing stability.

The bone rhythms of the arm extending forward reveal complex counterrotations. Flexing of the glenohumeral joint in the sagittal plane around a transverse axis involves a spinning of the humeral head on the glenoid fossa. There is a small amount of con-comitant internal rotation in the open chain (Palmer and Blakely 1986). You can feel this by placing your hand on your upper arm as you reach forward. First internally rotate the hand as you flex your glenohumeral joint (reach your arm to the front), then try again while attempting to externally rotate your arm. You may discover that external rotation at the glenohumeral joint will move the arm in the scapular plane instead of into a forward reach. The internal rotation compensates the slight abduc-tion at your elbow when you extend the arm forward. These bone rhythms reverse in the closed chain when you are supporting your body with your arms. Pushing down against the floor causes the humerus to externally rotate.

Imagery Exercises for the Glenohumeral Joint

1. **Humeral head drops:** As you elevate your arms, visualize the humeral heads rotating and gliding downward on the glenoid fossa. Exaggerate the image by visualizing the humeral heads gliding all the way down the sides of your body to the heads of the femurs, where they come to rest as you complete the elevation of your arms.

2. **Automatic rotation:** In the scapular plane, rapidly abduct your arms to 80 or so degrees of elevation. Imagine the underside of the arm swinging forward as you do this. If you imagine the arm externally rotating, even without any active movement, it will be easier to elevate the arm. If you lift your arm and keep it from rotating, you will create tension and your flexibility will be limited.

3. **Counterrotation:** Imagine the glenoid fossa moving in opposition to the humeral head. As you lift your arms and the humeral head spins and slides down, imagine the glenoid fossa sliding relatively upward. As you lower your arms, imagine the glenoid fossa gliding relatively downward.

4. **Head against a pillow:** To improve your kinesthetic imagery of the glenohumeral relationship, remember what it was like moving your head against a soft pillow. Imagine the humeral head to be resting against and moving within the glenoid fossa as if it were a soft pillow. Let the humeral head sink into the glenoid fossa as if it were a soft pillow.

5. **Humeral head suspended from the spine:** Imagine the humeral head to be suspended from the spine with coiled elastic springs. As you move, feel the relationship between the spine and the humeral head. Imagine the humeral head bobbing up and down relative to the spine.

6. **Humeroscapular counterrotation:** As you flex your glenohumeral joint (in other words, lift your arm forward from the shoulder), imagine the counterrotation of the humerus and scapula in the frontal plane. The humerus is rotating internally as the scapula relatively rotates externally (figure 13.28a). As you extend at the glenohumeral joint, the humerus will rotate externally while the scapula relatively rotates internally (figure 13.28b). Practice with a partner who places one hand on the scapula and the other on your humerus and counterrotates the two bones. The result will be a very lengthened and relaxed feeling in your shoulder and arm.

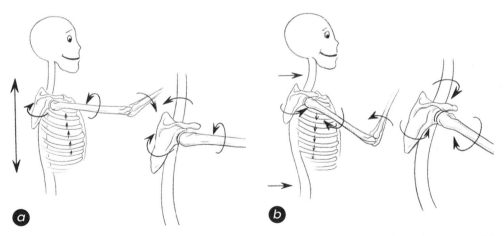

Figure 13.28 Bone rhythm of the humerus: *(a)* internal rotation on flexion; *(b)* external rotation on extension.

7. **Rotator cuff alive:** Imagine the muscles of the rotator cuff suspending the capsule of the glenohumeral joint. An instant before you lift your arms, imagine the rotator cuff muscles contracting to pull on the capsular covering and center the humeral head in its socket. Imagine the action as similar to tightening a shoe or a stocking.

8. **Subacromial:** As you move your arms, imagine a lot of space between the humeral heads and the acromion processes. Imagine a cushion of air or a soft pillow spreading within the space. As you move, feel air flowing between the acromion processes and humeral heads.

HUMEROSCAPULAR RHYTHM

The scapula (single shoulder blade) can glide up (elevation) and down (depression) on the back side of the rib cage (thorax); it can also move toward (adduction) and away (abduction) from the spine, and it can rotate upward and downward. However, the nature of scapular motions over the curved surface of the rib cage is more complex than these terms imply and also involves movements of the spine if full elevation is to be achieved. It may help to visualize the scapula as a surfboard on the crest of a rounded wave (the thorax). The surfboard can potentially dip and slide off the wave in four ways. If the surfboard (scapula) dips and glides sideways (horizontally) down the slope of the wave (thorax), it is called abduction (figure 13.29a) or adduction (figure 13.29b). These motions are not linear, but curved, with the surfboard (scapula) always in contact with the water (thorax). If the surfboard dips forward and glides off the wave in a superior direction, it elevates the shoulder blades (figure 13.29c). Once again, these are curved motions, with the surfboard (scapula) remaining in contact with the water (thorax). The reverse scapular glide in an inferior direction is called depression (figure 13.29d).

These movements are powered by pairs of synergistic muscle slings, comparable to a three-dimensional tug of war. When the levator scapulae pulls the scapula upward (as its name implies), the opposing muscle, in this case the ascending trapezius, is required to lengthen. To descend the scapula, the ascending trapezius shortens and the levator scapulae lengthens. Abduction and adduction are powered by the upper part of the serratus anterior and horizontal trapezius. When you adduct your shoulder blades (squeeze them together), the horizontal trapezius shortens; when you abduct your shoulder blades, the serratus anterior shortens and the horizontal trapezius lengthens. Anterior movement of the scapula is powered by the pectoralis minor while the ascending and horizontal

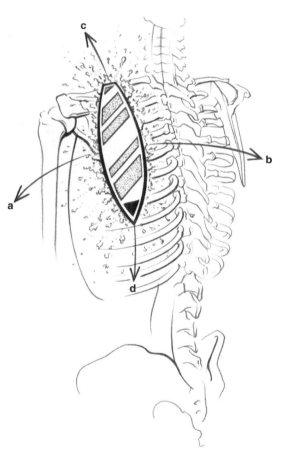

Figure 13.29 The scapula as a surfboard on the crest of a rounded wave: (a) abduction; (b) adduction; (c) elevation; (d) depression.

trapezius are lengthening. Upward rotation is managed by the trapezius in conjunction with the lower part of the serratus anterior. The antagonists in this case are the levator and upper part of the serratus anterior. It is important to realize that you can't just stretch a tense, gripped muscle by contracting its opposing muscle. You first must use a process to release the tension. Imagery and self-touch are an effective combination for this purpose.

When you abduct your arm, the humeral head rolls and slides in the glenoid fossa. However, the amount of elevation you can produce in this joint is limited. Starting at about 30 to 50 degrees, the scapula rotates, changing its position considerably relative to the rib cage and thorax. The purpose of scapular rotation is to position the glenoid fossa in an upward direction, allowing the scapula to form a base, albeit mobile for the arm. The coordinated movement of these joints, called the humeroscapular rhythm, is significantly greater in stability and range of arm motion than if it were only one joint. The glenohumeral-to-scapulothoracic movement ratio is about 2 to 1. The group effort allows the shallow glenoid fossa to remain in a good position relative to the head of the humerus in elevation and permits more balanced muscle action. The humeroscapular rhythm also enables the deltoid muscle to maintain its fibers at a good functional length and helps to avoid impingement of the muscles of the rotator cuff. If the scapula cannot rotate properly, you will not lift your arm very high or you will lift your shoulder girdle as you lift your arm. Other factors that play a part in allowing you to effortlessly lift your arm are a flexible joint capsule, automatic rotation of the humerus, flexibility of the spine and ribs, and coordinated movement of the clavicle.

As the arm is elevated, the scapula rotates first around an axis located at the base of the spine of the scapula and then around an axis located at the acromioclavicular joint. The S-shaped clavicle (see figure 13.2) rotates to increase the elevation of its distal end to reduce the need for elevation where it joins with the sternum. This is made possible by a small cartilaginous disc. Imagine holding a skeleton key in your hand with its teeth pointing downward, representing the distal end of the clavicle. If you rotate the key 180 degrees, the teeth point upward. The joint at this end has therefore gained height without actually lifting the shaft of the key. At its proximal end, the clavicle slides down and moves slightly back as the arm is elevated. When imagined, both of these design features help to maintain dynamic alignment during large arm movements.

A simple way to visualize the functioning of the humeroscapular rhythm is to think of it as a barrier at a train crossing. The barrier (arm) goes up as the heavy counterweight (scapula) arcs down and forward, saving a lot of mechanical energy (figure 13.30).

Without scapulae, you would need a very thick, muscular neck to pull up your arms with sheer force. Place one hand behind the lower part of your axle and lift your arm to feel

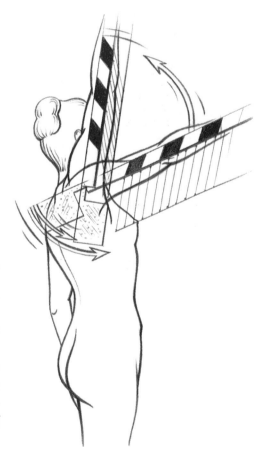

Figure 13.30 The functioning of the humeroscapular rhythm as a barrier at a train crossing.

the rotation of the scapula. The inferior part of the scapula can be sensed gliding forward under your fingers. Once the arm is elevated, the shoulder blade can also be considered a weighted ballast, a solid base for the arm, lowering the center of gravity (COG) and making it easy to keep the arms overhead as in fifth position. Freedom in the humeroscapular rhythm is critical for balance because it prevents arm gestures from disturbing the central axis. Mobility is achieved by allowing the scapulae to glide over the thorax and the clavicle to lift and rotate in an easy and unrestricted fashion.

Imagery Exercises for the Humeroscapular Rhythm

1. **Visualizing the humeroscapular rhythm:** Slowly abduct your arm in the scapular plane and visualize the coordinated action of the joints. First the humeral head rolls up into the glenoid fossa and slides down as it spins to maintain a centered action. At this time the scapula is relaxed. It should not be moving in these initial stages. As you keep elevating your arm, feel the scapula rotating. The inferior tip swings laterally and anteriorly. Finally, notice a slight amount of extension in your spine and elevation of your ribs. Keeping your ribs positioned will not allow for full elevation.

2. **Visualizing the clavicle:** Slowly abduct your arm in the scapular plane while imagining the movement of the clavicle. The distal end of the clavicle elevates at the proximal end and slides down on the sternum on the proximal end as the bone rotates like an upward swinging spiral (figure 13.31). Repeat the movement with the anatomical imagery of the humeral head spinning on the glenoid fossa and the scapula rotating upward. Imagine first the glenohumeral joint, then move to the scapulothoracic and finally the clavicular movement.

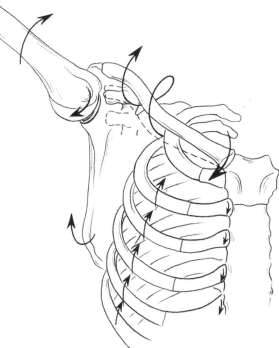

3. **Touching sternoclavicular joint:** Visualize the movement of the clavicle at the sternoclavicular joint as you elevate your right arm with the help of touch: Place a finger of your left hand on the joint and

Figure 13.31 Humeroscapular rhythm with the clavicle. The clavicle slides down on the sternum, the humeral head slides down on the glenoid fossa, and the cartilage of the ribs slide down on the sternum.

imagine the joint head of the clavicle sliding down on the manubrium. Gently push downward and backward with your finger. Repeat the action a few times and then compare the feeling between your right and left shoulders. Repeat the movement of the left.

4. **Clavicular pole vault:** Imagine the clavicle to be the pole of a pole vaulter. During the humeroscapular rhythm, imagine the clavicle pole pushing down on the sternum to lift the arm (figure 13.32).

5. **Scapular pendulum:** Imagine the inferior angle of the scapula lengthening downward and becoming a pendulum. As you lift your arm, imagine the pendulum swinging laterally; as you lower your arm, imagine the pendulum swinging medially. If you prefer the image of a bell, you can even add the auditory aspect of ringing.

6. **Clavicular movement (sitting, standing):** Visualize the movement of the clavicle as you elevate your arm. Imagine the clavicle lifting upward and then rotating. The left clavicle rotates clockwise, the right clavicle counterclockwise (looking out from your perspective). Imagine the rotation creating a spiral energy flow throughout the arm and hand. Watch the countering action of the manubrium at the sternoclavicular articulation. The top of the manubrium dips forward; the bottom dips backward. Simultaneously imagine the pubic rami rotating (as if rolling up toward you) and moving toward each other, creating an upward flow of energy to the xiphoid process (figure 13.33).

7. **Heavy and light:** Imagine the medial border of the scapula to be heavy while the lateral one is light. This image may help you align your scapula, but also practice the image while lifting your arm to create more effortless movement.

8. **Pouring out of supraspinous fossa:** Imagine water filling the supraspinous and infraspinous fossa. As you lift your arm, imagine the water pouring off the scapula

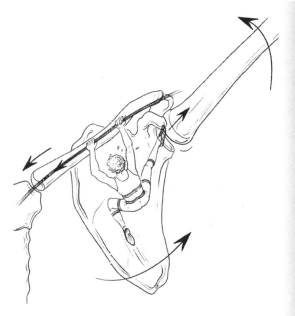

Figure 13.32 Clavicle pole-vaulting.

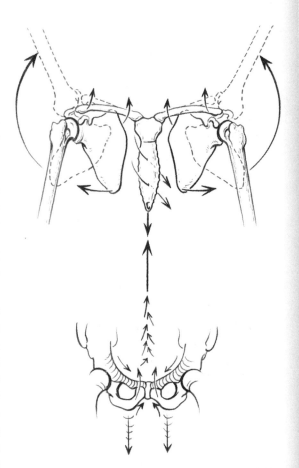

Figure 13.33 The rotational action of the clavicle as you elevate your arm.

and down your back (figure 13.34). If you hear the water flowing, the image may be more effective.

9. **Dropping the sandbags:** A passenger balloon releases sandbags to go up. Imagine your shoulder blades to be dropping down to release your arms to flight.

10. **Three-dimensional scapular swing:** The scapula swings in three dimensions during the humeroscapular rhythm. The top dips back slightly in the sagittal plane, descends and rotates in the frontal plane, and swings around the rib cage in the horizontal plane. The combined image is of the scapula swinging around a round ball. As you lift your arm, imagine the three-dimensional swinglike movement of the scapula (figure 13.35). You may use self-talk: *Drop down, rotate, and swing around.*

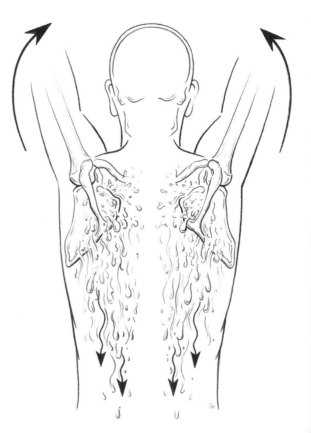

Figure 13.34 Water flowing off the scapulae and down the back.

11. **Train barrier (standing, sitting):** Maintain your central axis perpendicular to the floor when doing this exercise. Imagine your scapula to be the heavy counterweight of a train barrier (see figure 13.30). As the barrier lifts, the heavy counterweight arcs down and forward. With the help of a partner, you can feel the connection between the scapula, clavicle, and humerus. After placing fingers on the spine of the scapula and thumbs on the inside border of the scapula, your partner then pushes down with the fingers and out with the thumbs to help you elevate your arms. To feel scapular restriction, have your partner reverse this action, holding the lower part of both the medial and lateral border of the scapula between the thumb and fingers. To move under these circumstances, you must lift the entire shoulder girdle upward. Lifting the shoulders when elevating the arms is a common habit that can be corrected with the previous exercise. Be careful, though, when touching the area around the shoulder blades, because the muscles may be tender. Complete this tactile session with an assisted arm elevation.

12. **Scapular saucers (supine):** Visualize the shoulder blades as two teacup saucers floating on water. Watch them bank and bay under the rib cage. As water flows onto the saucers from the side closer to the spine, the saucers begin to dip downward on that side. Made heavy by the water, they sink downward, away from the rib cage (figure 13.36). Repeat this exercise two or three times.

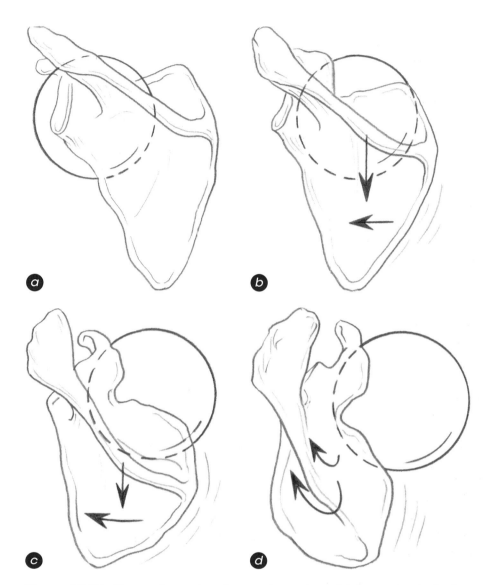

Figure 13.35 Three-dimensional scapular swing: *(a)* the scapula in the neutral position; *(b)* scapular rotation initiates, causing a slight drop of the medial scapula and an elevation of the glenoid fossa; *(c)* the medial drop and lift of the glenoid continues with an added rotation of the scapula in the horizontal plane as it slides around the rib cage; *(d)* in the final stage of the humeroscapular rhythm, the arm is fully elevated and the glenoid fossa faces nearly upward.

13. **Scapular sponges (supine):** Visualize the shoulder blades resting on the floor as if relaxing on the most comfortable bed imaginable. Feel a slippery sponge slide under one shoulder blade from the spinal side. As the sponge fills with water and expands, it moves the scapula down and away from the rib cage, increasing the distance between the shoulder blade and the rib cage. Repeat this exercise two or three times. (Exercise adapted from André Bernard.)

14. **Shoulder girdle as cape (standing, sitting):** To free the shoulder girdle from the rib cage, visualize it as a cape lightly draped around the rib cage, open in front

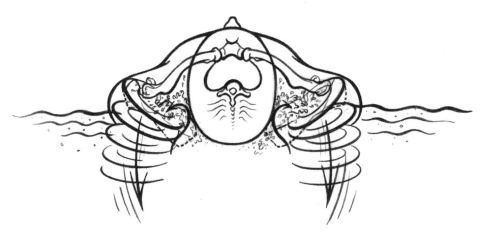

Figure 13.36 The shoulder blades as two teacup saucers floating on water, then sinking.

and attached to the top of the sternum with a sparkling diamond pin. Imagine a soothing wind blowing. As the wind sends ripples through the soft cloth, the cape (shoulder girdle) lifts, creating a space between the rib cage and the cape. As the wind dies down, the cape slowly settles against the rib cage (figure 13.37). Repeat this exercise two or three times. (Exercise adapted from André Bernard.)

Figure 13.37 The shoulder girdle as a cape lightly draped around the rib cage.

15. **Scapular fall (standing):** As you elevate your arms, picture the scapulae gliding down your back to your heels. Visualize the sit bones dropping with the scapulae. For tactile emphasis, have your partner slide her or his hands down your back to your heels.

16. Scapulae rotating in the flow of breath (standing, sitting): Exhale as you elevate your arms. Imagine your scapulae as pinwheels, and watch your breath set them into rotary motion. The right scapula moves counterclockwise, the left clockwise (from your point of view). The higher you lift your arms, the more effortlessly the pinwheels spin (figure 13.38).

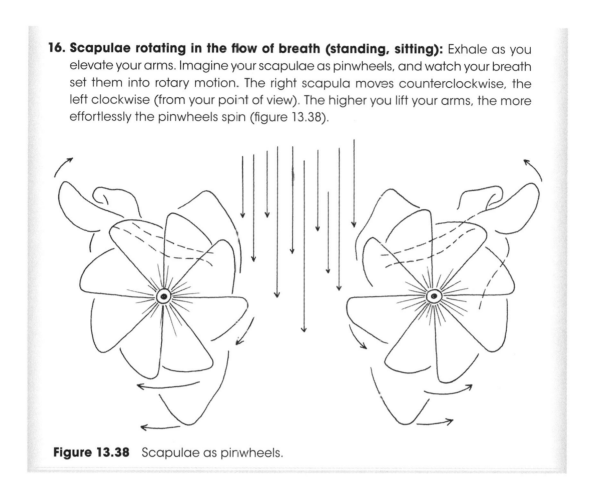

Figure 13.38 Scapulae as pinwheels.

ELBOW

The elbow consists of three joints contained in a single joint capsule: one between the humerus (upper arm bone) and the ulna (arm bone on the small finger side), one between the humerus and the radius (arm bone on the thumb side), and one between the upper ends of the radius and the ulna. The ulnar articulating surface consists of a concave half circle, the trochlear notch. The articulating surface of the radius is cup shaped. The ulna is larger at the elbow, whereas the radius is larger at the wrist. The humeroulnar and humeroradial joints of the elbow allow for flexion and extension. The axis of motion for elbow flexion and extension passes through the trochlea and capitulum, the articulating surfaces of the humerus, which together look like a chess pawn with its head pointing sideways. Another possible visual image is a champagne cork.

Touch the medial and lateral epicondyles of the humerus, two projections that can be easily palpated at the distal end of the humerus, and visualize the location of the axis just below these points (figure 13.39). The joints are situated ventrally, which facilitates many activities of daily life that require ventral movement of the hand and lower arm, such as lifting and eating. When the forearm is supinated (palm up), the long axis of the humerus and forearm form an angle (greater in women than in men) called the carrying, or cubital, angle (figure 13.40). It is about 10 degrees and is defined as the angle between the longitudinal axes of the humerus and the forearm when the elbow is fully extended and the forearm is fully supinated. The angled nature of the joint axis causes the ulna to adduct and abduct during flexion and extension.

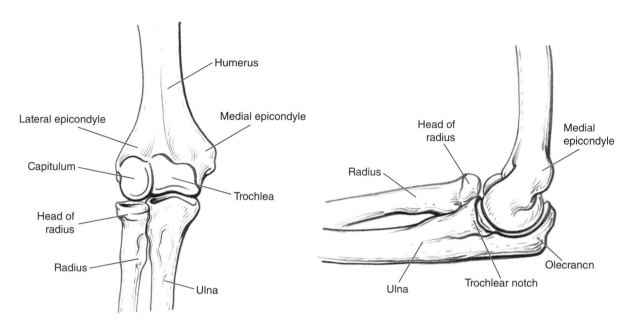

Figure 13.39 The elbow consists of three joints.

The trochlear groove itself displays a somewhat spiraled orientation, which is most prominently visible posteriorly, adding a slight amount of axial rotation to the ulna in flexion and extension.

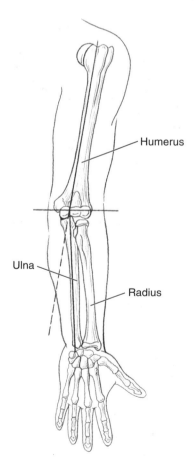

Figure 13.40 Carrying angle.

The carrying angle allows you to easily brace the humerus against the body when carrying a heavy load. This angle vanishes with flexion caused by the adduction of the ulna. When you reach straight forward with your arm with the palm of the hand facing up, the abduction (cubitus valgus) of the lower arm is visible. If you reach forward facing the palm of the hand down, which is called pronation, the radius crossing over the ulna masks the angle. Now the arm displays a nearly straight axis from the shoulder to the middle of the hand. If you are moving the arm forward in the sagittal plane, the humerus rotates slightly to the medial side and the ulna will abduct and rotate externally (figure 13.41*a*). The ulna and humerus are counterrotating as you stretch your arm forward. The radius is counterrotating as it crosses over the ulna (figure 13.41, *b-c*).

As you pull your arm back toward your body, the humerus rotates externally while the ulna abducts and rotates internally. The ulna and humerus are counterrotating, while the humerus and radius are moving in the same direction—inward during extension, outward during flexion.

When you are supporting your weight on your arms, such as when doing push-ups, the situation reverses. The radius has lost its mobility and is more firmly attached to the hand than the ulna. When pushing yourself off the floor with your arms, the humerus and ulna externally rotate (figure 13.41*d*). They are swinging around the fixed radius. When you bend your arm, the humerus and ulna rotate internally around the fixed radius (figure 13.41, *e-f*). In both cases, the humerus and radius are counterrotating.

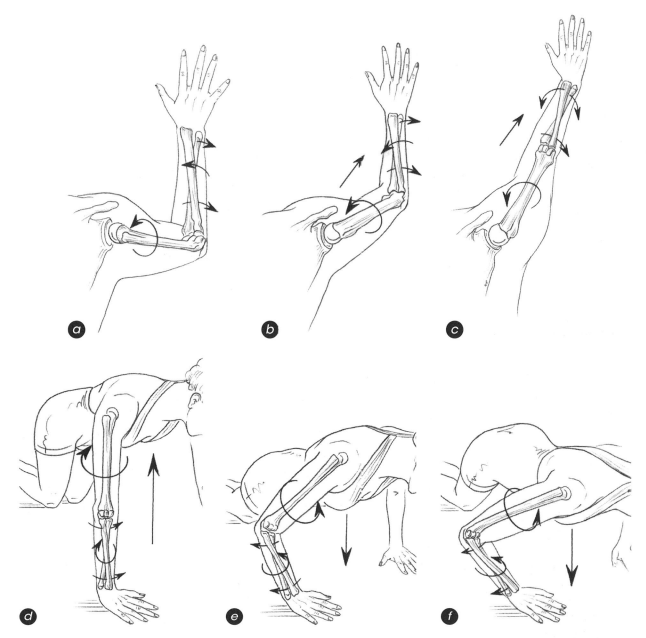

Figure 13.41 Bone rhythms of the arm *(a-c)* in open-chain movement and *(d-f)* in closed-chain movement.

The radioulnar joint allows supination (palm up) and pronation (palm down). Proximally, the annular ligament, which attaches to the ulna, forms a ring around the head of the radius within which the head can rotate. The ulna also has a concave notch to better accommodate the radius as it turns. Simultaneously, the head of the radius spins on the capitulum of the humerus. At the distal radioulnar joint, the radius pivots around the ulna during supination and pronation. The axis for supination and pronation runs through the head of the radius and the styloid process of the ulna.

The radioulnar joint is functionally linked to the wrist. Forces arising from the hand are transmitted first to the radius and then to the ulna via the interosseus membrane and ligaments (figure 13.42). When supporting the weight on your hands, the interosseus membrane also acts to absorb force.

In pronation, the radius crosses the ulna; in supination, the ulna and radius lie parallel to each other. You can distinguish between pronation and supination by visualizing spooning soup: You dip the spoon into the soup and rotate the spoon toward the body using your lower arm. This movement is called supination. Then you lift the spoon and flex at the elbow to bring the food to your mouth. If you watch a toddler trying to eat soup, you will see that supination and pronation combined with elbow flexion and extension is quite a complex movement. The way in which you use your arms, hands, and fingers to bring things to your mouth and to your eyes for close examination is uniquely human. Without supination and pronation, daily activities, dance, and sports would be a sorry-looking affair. The subtle and complex gestures of Indian and other Asian dance styles also require supination and pronation.

The head of the radius is slightly oval. As you supinate, the wider portion of the radial head faces the ulnar notch, causing the radius to be pushed laterally (figure 13.43a). This allows more space for the insertion of the biceps at the radial tuberosity. You may imagine the lower arm fanning open during supination (figure 13.43b).

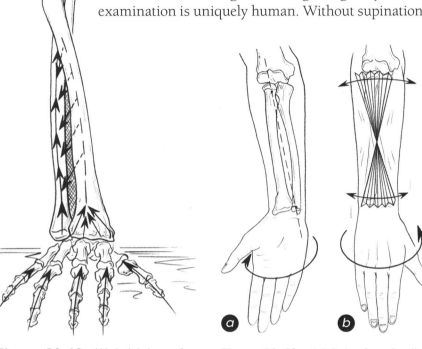

Figure 13.42 Weight transfer from radius to the interosseus membrane to the ulna.

Figure 13.43 (a) Axis of supination and pronation; (b) fanning the lower arm bones in supination.

Imagery Exercises for the Elbow

1. **Touching the elbow:** The parts of the elbow that can be easily palpated are the medial and lateral epicondyles of the humerus. What is normally considered the elbow is the olecranon of the ulnar bone (see figure 13.39). You can also touch the head of the radius just below the lateral epicondyle.

2. **Adduction and abduction:** Face the palm of your hand upward, which is the pronated position of the lower arm. Touch your ulna with your opposite hand as you extend your elbow. You can watch, feel, and imagine the ulna abducting. As you flex your elbow, watch, feel, and imagine the ulna adducting.

3. **Reaching and pulling gesture:**

   a. **With humeroulnar counterrotation:** As you stretch your arm forward with the palm of your hand facing downward and forward, imagine the humerus rotating internally and the ulna rotating externally. As you pull your arm back, imagine the humerus rotating externally and the ulna rotating internally.

b. **With humeroradial movement:** Place your hand on the radius. As you stretch your arm forward, feel and imagine it rotating internally as it crosses over the ulna. It is moving in tandem with the humerus. As you pull your arm backward, feel and imagine it rotating externally with the humerus.

c. **With forearm counterrotation:** As you reach with your palm facing forward and down, imagine the radius and ulna counterrotating. The ulna is rotating externally and the radius internally. As you pull your arm back, imagine the radius and ulna counterrotating, only now the ulna is rotating internally and the radius externally.

4. **Bone rhythm push-ups:** Practice this image with push-ups or modified push-ups from a kneeling position. Supination and pronation are mostly movements of the radius over the ulna, but this is not the case in the weight-bearing position. Now the radius is firmly attached to the wrist, which is in turn connected to the floor. The ulna will now move together with the humerus around a more stable radius. Start with the arms extended. As you flex the elbow and move your body downward, imagine the humerus and ulna rotating internally around the radius. As you push your body back upward, imagine the humerus and ulna rotating externally around the radius. Notice whether it is easier to perform push-ups while visualizing this bone rhythm as opposed to simply focusing on extending and flexing the elbows. As you go down, simply think *humerus and ulna swing in*; as you push up, think *humerus and ulna swing out*.

5. **Pronation and supination:** As you pronate, the radius crosses over the ulna, moving medially at the wrist while the proximal joint surface dips laterally. The ulna does the reverse. The distal end moves laterally while the proximal joint surface tilts medially. Imagine the two bones crossing and fanning away from each other at their distal ends. Compare the arms before repeating on the other side (see figure 13.43).

6. **Two spins:** Visualize the radial head spinning in the annular ligament and the ulnar head spinning in the radius as you supinate and pronate. The spins are in opposite directions.

7. **Forward motion of radius:** As you pronate, imagine the radius not only crossing over the ulna but also moving forward a bit. Place your hand on the outside of the elbow at the lateral epicondyle. As you pronate, slide your hand forward along the radius, wrist, and second finger. As you supinate, reverse the direction of your slide. Compare the arms before repeating on the other side. Also visualize the countermovement of the ulna.

8. **Centered supination and pronation:** Practice supinating your lower arm while allowing your lower arm to remain centered in space, like a jump rope swinging around the axis created by the two hands setting the rope in motion.

9. **Radioulnar counterrotation:** As you supinate and pronate, watch the radius rotate in the ulnar notch and the ulna glide in the opposite direction (figure 13.44a). To better understand this concept, compare it to the miniature merry-go-round in figure 13.44b. The child sets herself in motion in a counterclockwise direction by pulling on a center wheel in a clockwise direction. The outside observer sees the child rotating counterclockwise about a stable center wheel; the child sees the center wheel as rotating in a clockwise direction.

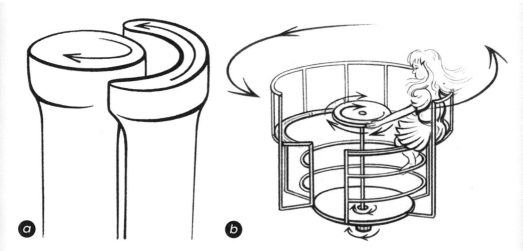

Figure 13.44 *(a)* The radius rotates in the ulnar notch while the ulna glides in the opposite direction. *(b)* The interaction is the same as a child operating a miniature merry-go-round.

10. **Radioulnar counterspiral:** As you supinate and pronate, imagine the radius and ulna counterrotating (figure 13.45). Imagine two opposing spirals traveling distally along the bones.

11. **Elbow buoy:** Imagine the elbow to be a buoy floating on water. Visualize the arms floating effortlessly in space with the aid of the elbow buoys (figure 13.46).

12. **Flow of weight (arms overhead):** Visualize the weight of the hand resting on the lower arm, the weight of the lower arm resting on the humerus, the weight of the humerus resting on the glenoid fossa of the scapula, the weight of the shoulder blades supported by the clavicles, and the weight of the clavicles supported by the sternum.

13. **Swing-dancing radius and ulna:** Imagine the radius and ulna connected via the interosseus membrane. During supination and pronation, imagine them to be swinging around each other like two partners in a dance (figure 13.47).

14. **Transferring of load from radius to ulna:** In the push-up position with the weight on your hands, imagine the

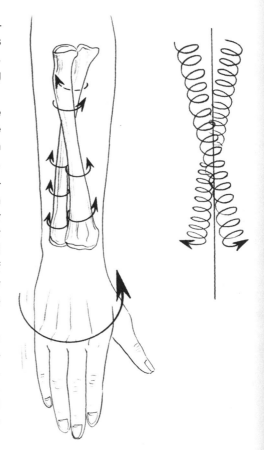

Figure 13.45 Counterrotating spirals of radius and ulna.

force traveling up through the radius, then traveling through the interosseus membrane to the ulna and from there to the elbow joint, humerus, and shoulder. Compare this image with the idea of the force traveling from the radius into the elbow (see figure 13.42).

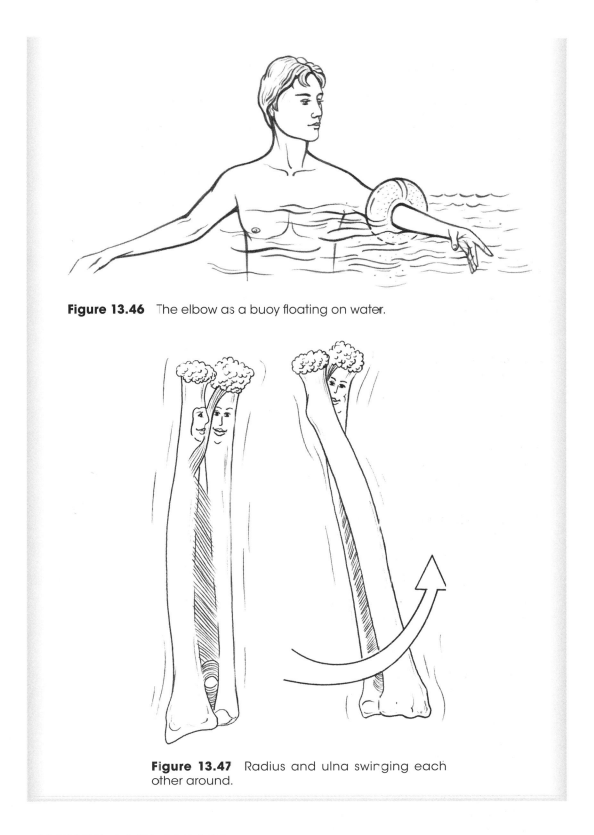

Figure 13.46 The elbow as a buoy floating on water.

Figure 13.47 Radius and ulna swinging each other around.

WRIST AND HAND

From the top down, the structure of the arm increases in complexity. The upper arm consists of one bone, the lower arm of two, the proximal (upper) carpals of three bones, the distal (lower) carpals of four, and the metacarpals and the fingers of five bones. Each unit supports the next, with the purpose of maximizing the movement possibilities of the hand in space. The myriad shapes the hand can assume can hardly be categorized. Immanuel Kant said that the hand is the brain turned to the outside (Shärli 1980). In many dance styles, the hands take center stage as the communicators of plot and meaning.

Wrist

The wrist is located between the radius and radioulnar disc (a fibrocartilage disc at the distal end of the ulna) on one end and the carpal bones on the other. The joint is ellipsoidal in shape. The joint permits flexion and extension as well as abduction, or radial deviation and adduction. The carpal bones of the wrist are very idiosyncratically shaped, as reflected in their names: The proximal row consists of the scaphoid (skiff form), lunate (moon), and triquetrum. With the radius and radioulnar disc, they compose the radiocarpal joint. The distal row consists of the trapezium, trapezoid, capitate (head), and hamate (hooked), which articulate with the proximal row to form the midcarpal joint and with the metacarpals to form the carpometacarpal joints. Although part of the proximal row, the pisiform (pea shaped) does not form part of the radiocarpal joint (figure 13.48).

The articular surface of the radius is concave; the surfaces of the proximal carpals are convex, like an egg, enabling the carpals to glide over the radius and radioulnar disc. The joint permits flexion, extension, adduction (ulnar deviation), and abduction (radial deviation). Touch the styloid process of the ulna and the radius to visualize the approximate axis for flexion and extension just below these two points. The proximal carpal row glides in opposition to the movement of the hand.

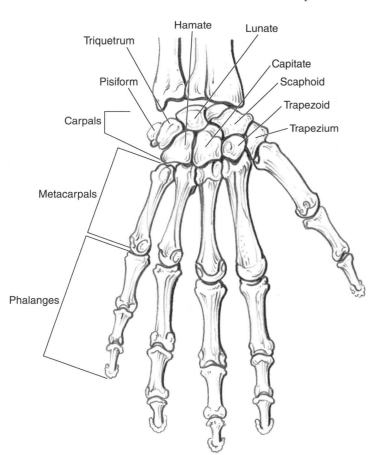

Figure 13.48 The hand and wrist.

Imagery Exercises for the Wrist

1. **Flexion and extension of the wrist:** Visualize the egg-shaped convexity of the proximal carpals sitting in the concavity formed by the radius and radioulnar disc. Extend your wrist and visualize the carpal dome sliding in the opposite direction of the fingers, toward the palm (figure 13.49a). Flex your wrist and visualize the carpal convexity sliding in the opposite direction of the fingers, toward the back of the hand (figure 13.49b).

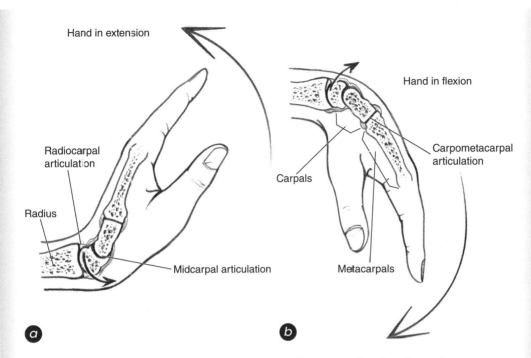

Figure 13.49 The carpal convexity slides in the opposite direction of the fingers: *(a)* extension, *(b)* flexion.

2. **Rotation in flexion:** The scaphoid slides more in extension than the other carpals do. This causes the wrist to perform a very slight rotation, which allows the smallest finger to move forward to initiate a grasp. Perform wrist extension and notice how the radial side of the wrist slides back farther.

3. **Bone rhythms of arm:** As you reach or push forward with your palm down, imagine the humerus rotating inward, the ulna abducting and rotating outward, and the wrist rotating medially. Note that the hand, radius, and humerus will rotate in the same direction while the ulna counterrotates.

4. **Radial and ulnar abduction:** Abduct and adduct your hand at the wrist and imagine the curved surface of the proximal carpals sliding back and forth on the distal radius, ulna, and disc (figure 13.50).

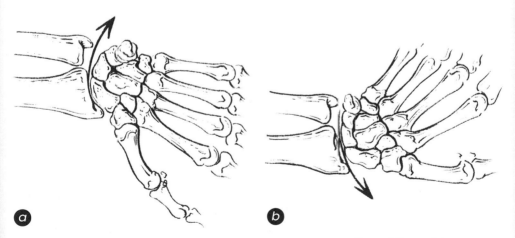

Figure 13.50 *(a)* Radial abduction and *(b)* ulnar abduction at the wrist.

5. **Visualize the spaces between your carpal bones:** Imagine fog or mist flowing through these spaces (figure 13.51).

6. **Disc trampoline:** Imagine that the disc between the ulna and the lunate of the wrist is a trampoline. In all hand movements and especially when supporting your weight on your hands, imagine the trampoline-like resilience at the ulnar side of the wrist (figure 13.52). Rebound the ulna off your disc.

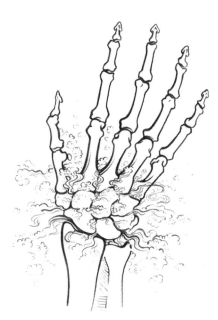

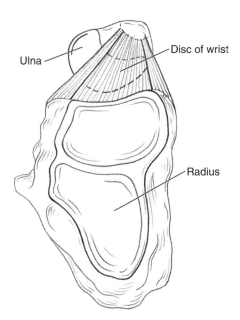

Figure 13.51 Visualize fog or mist flowing through the spaces between your carpal bones.

Figure 13.52 Imagine that the disc between the ulna and lunate is a trampoline.

Hand

The human hand is highly complex, and the imagery presented here is only a fraction of the possibilities inherent in this uniquely human part of the body. The hand is a sensory organ for holding a tool or an instrument, and it serves communication as well. The hand consists of 19 bones with 36 joints that are moved by 39 muscles.

The digits (fingers) of the hand consist of 5 metacarpal bones and 14 phalanges, 2 in the thumb and 3 in each of the other fingers. The digits articulate with the carpals at the carpometacarpal (CMC) joints. The CMC joints can flex or extend, except for the thumb CMC joint and the 5th finger CMC joint, which are both saddle joints. The thumb can flex, extend, circle, and move in and out to touch the tip of every other finger—the thumb opposition so beloved by evolutionary scientists. The 5th finger CMC joint is somewhat less flexible than the thumb and can flex and extend and adduct and abduct. Eight intrinsic (originating in the hand) and extrinsic (originating outside of the hand) muscles control the intricate movements of the thumb. A baby's ability to grasp tiny objects (often a piece of dust an adult can hardly see) using thumb opposition is an important developmental landmark.

The hand has several arches: a longitudinal and a proximal and distal transverse. The CMC joints help the hand create a cup shape when holding an object. The shape of the carpals, enhanced by ligaments, creates the carpal arch, which remains even if the hand is extended. With the fingers slightly flexed, the hand serves as a miniature pouch, shovel, or watertight bowl that can carry small amounts of water to the mouth. Basically, the hand can imitate every tool made by humans. Perhaps the statement should be reversed: Humans conceive of tools that are inherent in the design of the hand.

The lumbricals, found in the hands and feet, are the only muscles of the body that attach to the tendons of other muscles on both ends—to both flexors and extensors. They flex the joints between the metacarpals and phalanges and strongly extend the joints within the phalanges, making them the muscles of choice for creating the cup-shaped hands of the Graham technique in dance. The lumbricals are also important for any pushing action initiated from the tips of the fingers or toes. Well-trained lumbricals improve a dancer's jumping ability.

Imagery Exercises for the Hand

1. **Arm-hand axis:** Visualize the axis of the hand passing through the third finger, third metacarpal, capitate (second row of carpals), lunate (first row of carpals), between the radius and ulna, and through the center of the arm and into the glenoid fossa. Rotate the arm and hand around this axis. Let the axis support the entire length of the arm (figure 13.53).

2. **Beam of light through the axis of the arm and hand:** Visualize an arrow or a beam of light emerging from the center of the glenoid fossa and shooting out through the arm, hand, and third finger. Practice initiating arm and hand movements from the arm's central axis.

3. **Joint lubrication:** Move your wrist and fingers in a variety of ways and imagine the most slippery and well-nourished joints possible. Imagine all the joint surfaces gliding on top of each other effortlessly moved by a perfectly orchestrated synchrony of muscles.

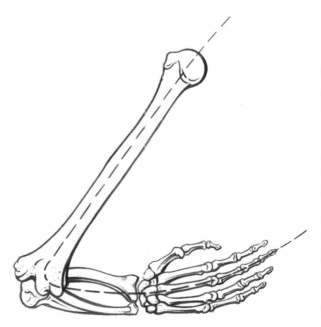

Figure 13.53 Visualize the central axis of the arm.

4. **Hand self-image:** Imagine an activity that you perform often. It could be writing, dancing, or some other activity that involves the hands. Watch yourself using your hands from an external perspective. Notice what it feels like to visualize your hands that have done so many things for you and will do so in the future.

5. **Finger stretch (touch):** With the fingers of your left hand, hold the lower end of the right thumb's metacarpal (knuckle). To locate this point, slide your fingers

down the thumb to a thicker area. Circle the thumb with your left hand and then slide your fingers out over the thumb. Imagine the thumb lengthening, as if it were made of clay. Repeat the following procedure with every right-hand finger: Slide the fingers of the left hand over the finger phalanges, continuing over the metacarpals on the back side of the hand until you reach the lower end of the metacarpal. Imagine that your fingers actually begin here. Slide your fingers outward over the metacarpal and finger bones, giving each fingertip a little tug. Feel each finger lengthening. When you finish with all the fingers, compare the sensations arising from the hand you have exercised with those of the other hand. You may notice differences all the way up to the shoulder. Repeat for the other hand.

6. **Initiation from fingers:** Imagine that each finger leads you into space, perhaps via a string attached to the fingertip. After you have explored individual finger strings, imagine that strings are attached to every finger simultaneously. Visualize all the finger strings in unison leading your hand and body into space.

7. **Hand sponges (improvisation):** Imagine that your hand can fill with air like a sponge fills with water. Stretch your hand and watch the air flow into your hand. Make a fist and feel the air being expelled. Imagine that you can also fill your hands with colors, scents, and sounds.

8. **Hand centering (sitting):** Grasp the second finger of your right hand with the palm of your left hand, as if trying to pull or inhale the finger into the center of your left hand. Alternate hands.

9. **Finger rhythms:** As you stretch out your hand, imagine the fingers counterrotating on opposite sides of the middle ray. The finger bones on the thumb side rotate inward while the finger bones on the small-finger side rotate outward. Imagine also the wrist widening. Reverse the imagery for hand flexion. Stretch your arm and imagine the bone rhythms. The humerus rotates inward, the radius and ulna counterrotate, the wrist widens, and the fingers counterrotate on opposite sides of the midline of the hand. Imagine the action also as counterrotating spirals (figure 13.54).

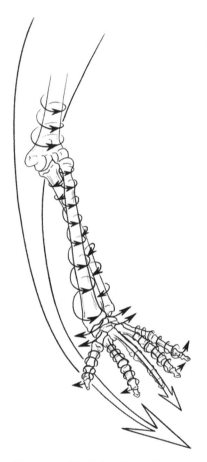

Figure 13.54 Arm-finger rhythms.

SUMMARY

The main function of the shoulder girdle is to allow full mobility of the hand in space. Its unique design helps to protect the heart and lungs and dampen forces that arrive at any point on the arm. It consists of two shoulder blades, or scapulae, and two collarbones, or clavicles.

A novel way to visualize the design of the shoulder girdle is to imagine it distributing forces three-dimensionally through a system of tensegrity-like spacers and tensile elements. The hub of this system can be visualized as the scapula, which has muscles radiating out in all directions. The humeroscapular rhythm describes the one-third to two-third ratio of thoracoscapular to glenohumeral motion in arm elevation. This design allows you to reach above your head with ease.

The trapezius is the most superficial muscle of the back and key driver of the humeroscapular rhythm together with the latissimus dorsi. If the trapezius is tight, it is very difficult to properly align the spine. Because of its expanse, the proprioception of the trapezius is important for balance.

The elbow consists of three joints: one between the humerus and the ulna, one between the humerus and the radius, and one between the upper ends of the radius and the ulna. The joints of the elbow and wrist allow for flexion and extension, and supination and pronation of the lower arm.

The human hand is a highly complex and uniquely human part of the body. The hand is an important sensory organ that can diligently manipulate objects and instruments, write eloquently, and express artistically.

Chapter 14

Head and Neck

Flexibility is an image.

Having the head perched at the top of the spinal column offers many advantages. Ancient humans could see much farther over the plain to evaluate food sources and potential dangers while they were still at a distance. Rapid surveying of the surrounding area and fast directional changes demanded a nonrigid, easily balanced structure. Watching children learning to walk, you witness this head-on-spine balancing act. A toddler is rather top-heavy, her head large in relation to her body as compared to an adult. The child's first steps resemble a fledgling circus aerialist making his way across a tightrope (figure 14.1). This balancing act can also be witnessed at the level of pelvis on femur heads. The head rests on the most mobile part of the spine, its considerable weight balancing on this small base, rather like a large ball sitting precariously on a seal's nose. The seal keeps the ball on the nose through its strong muscular base and rapid but delicate adjustments (figure 14.2).

Because of the head's high center of gravity (COG) relative to the rest of the body, any deviations from optimal head alignment have a great impact on the entire body. The vestibular system, located in the inner ear, measures the position and acceleration of the head. The neck's receptors and reflexes indirectly measure the position of the head in comparison to the rest of the body. Thus cooperation between head and neck is essential for good alignment and movement control (Hotz and Weineck 1983). The relatively small cervical vertebrae of the neck have a shape designed

Figure 14.1 Watching children learning to walk, you witness this head-on-spine balancing act.

Figure 14.2 The head rests on the most mobile part of the spine; its considerable weight sits on a small base.

to increase their stability. Cervicals 3 through 5 are slightly curved upward at their outer rims, like shallow cups. These rims are called the uncinate processes. Most people use the uncinate processes the way football players use their massive neck muscles.

As the result of overzealous attempts to straighten the spine or hours spent stooped over books or a computer, many people have poor neck and head alignment. Imagine that you have to learn all over again how to balance your head on your spine (many people do). It is much like learning how to balance a bottle on top of your head. I speak from experience, since I once danced in *Fiddler on the Roof*, where such balancing acts were required. I admit to also witnessing a bottle (my own) break into a thousand pieces during a rehearsal.

Head Balances on the Neck

1. Head as a balloon:

a. Sitting, standing: Imagine the head to be a balloon filled with helium. Remember that it is the helium that provides the lift (the space within the head); the surface of the balloon rests on the helium inside it. The neck and central axis are the string attached to the balloon that follows it as it floats upward. Imagine this string to be as soft as wool, especially in the neck area. From the balloon's vantage point, the shoulders recede rapidly, much as the earth recedes from an astronaut as he catapults into the sky (figure 14.3).

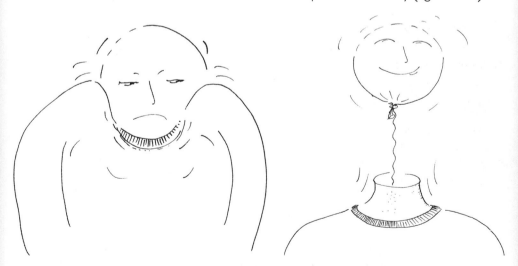

Figure 14.3 The head floating upward like a balloon filled with helium.

Adapted from L.E. Sweigard, 1974, *Human movement potential: Its ideokinetic facilitation* (New York: Dodd, Mead), 233.

b. Initiation: Your new balloon-head initiates your movement in space. Use the sensory memory of letting go of an untied balloon and watching it deflate with a hissing sound as it flies off into space.

2. **Head on geyser (sitting, standing):** Imagine your central axis to be a waterspout or a geyser. Picture your head floating effortlessly atop this gurgling column of water, which flows back to the floor in the form of your shoulders and body surface. As the geyser becomes stronger, your relaxed head is pushed upward, causing it to bob up and down. Find the place where the force of the waterspout creates the best alignment. (Also see chapter 17, figure 17.7.)

3. **Sliding layers of neck muscles:** Imagine the many layers of the muscles of the neck being able to slide on top of each other as you move the head and neck.

Figure 14.4   Fluttering neck muscles like soft cloth in the wind.

4. **Wind blows layers of neck muscles:** Imagine the neck muscles being fluttered like flags by a gentle gust of wind (figure 14.4).

5. **Core support for the neck:** Imagine the neck to be the base of a long, narrow cone with its point rooted between the sit bones in the pelvic floor. (Instead of being a conehead, you're a conebody!) Watch the axis of the cone merge with your central axis (figure 14.5).

6. **Equal volume in neck:** Visualize your cervical spine. Begin to appreciate the space between your bony cervical spine and the outer surfaces of your neck. Imagine that there is equal space between the bodies of the vertebrae and the front, back, and side surfaces of your neck. Imagine this space to be open and uncluttered (figure 14.6).

Figure 14.5   The neck as the base of a long, narrow cone with its point rooted between the sit bones.

7. Focus on thyroid: The thyroid gland is located at the bottom of the voice box approximately in the middle front of the neck. The thyroid hormones relate to growth and cellular metabolism. By focusing on the thyroid and keeping a balanced image of the structure in mind, you can help to align your cervical spine and release muscular tension. The image also balances the often-overemphasized focus on the back of the neck, where tension mostly resides. Touch your thyroid and imagine it is supporting the front of the neck.

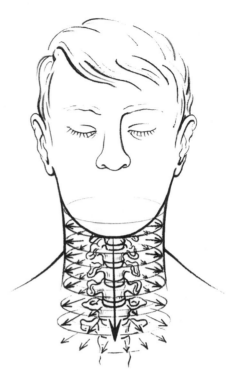

Figure 14.6 The equality of space between the cervical spine and the surfaces of your neck.

ATLAS AND AXIS

The ring-shaped topmost vertebra, the atlas (named after the mythological Atlas who carries the earth), has no body or spinous process. The superior facets are slightly concave and articulate with the convex surfaces of the occipital condyles (see figure 8.2).

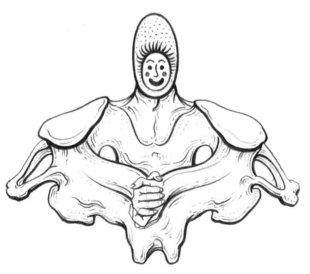

Figure 14.7 Imagine the axis is a person with the arms held in a circular position to support weight from above.

The axis, the second cervical vertebra, has a dens (Latin for tooth) protruding from its front surface. The axis has a very long transverse process, which is the origin of many muscles, including the levator scapulae and the semispinalis cervicis. These muscles must be balanced for good head alignment.

The axis and atlas articulate at three points: two lateral joints between the upper facets of the axis and the lower facets of the atlas, and the atlanto-odontoid, a pivot joint where the dens of the axis rotates within a ring formed by the front arch of the atlas and the transverse ligament. The axis looks like a human being with arms held in a circular position, ready to support the load above (figure 14.7). The dens of the axis is the slender head, the face is the posterior articular facet for the transverse ligament of the atlas, and the arms are the lateral mass (figure 14.8). The

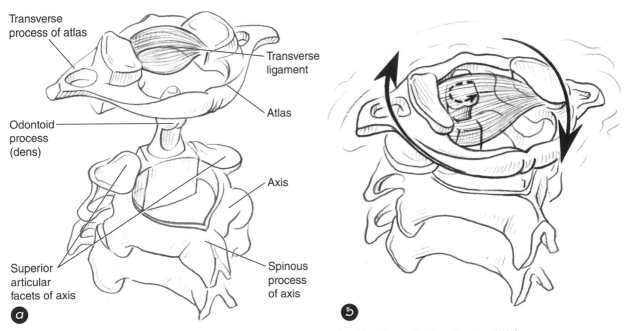

Transverse
process of atlas

Transverse
ligament

Atlas

Odontoid
process
(dens)

Axis

Superior
articular
facets of axis

Spinous
process
of axis

a

b

Figure 14.8   *(a)* Atlas and axis with transverse ligament; *(b)* atlas rotating to the right.

superior articular facets even look like shoulder pads, which come in handy for carrying the atlas and the head.

The pivot joint between dens and atlas enables the head to rotate quickly and economically in the horizontal plane with little involvement of the rest of the neck. The lateral atlanto-occipital joints permit flexion and extension, a nodding of the head, and a small amount of sideways flexion and rotation. Half of the rotational ability of the neck resides in the atlantoaxial joint. Rotational movement involves a sliding of the atlas on the convexly slanted shoulders of the axis, which tightens certain ligaments. As the head rotates to the right, for example, the left alar ligament will pull the left occipital condyle slightly downward. The reverse happens when the head is rotated to the left. This means that rotating your head involves a lateral flexion but on the opposite side you are moving toward (i.e., a contralateral lateral flexion; figure 14.9).

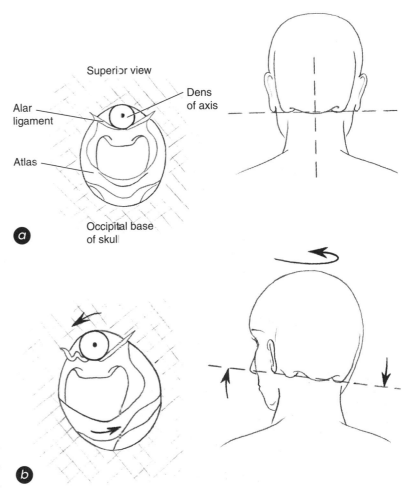

Superior view

Alar
ligament

Dens
of axis

Atlas

a

Occipital base
of skull

b

Figure 14.9   Rotation of the head involves a slight contralateral lateral flexion due to the tightening of the alar ligament: *(a)* neutral position and *(b)* rotation to the left.

The movement can be imagined as a subtle figure-eight or banking movement in repeated head rotation to the right and left. Because of the convex nature of the shoulders of the axis, the atlas will also move slightly downward during rotation. This action helps to prevent shear on the spinal cord. The common cue in dance and exercise of "lengthen your neck in rotation" is therefore not truly functional in nature. Rather, the head lowers down and banks. This action compensates for the ipsilateral flexion of the neck in rotation, keeping the head perfectly aligned. The seemingly level position of the head during rotation is achieved by a complex three-dimensional movement that is easier on the muscles and joints while simultaneously increasing the strength of the movement.

Imagery Exercises for the Atlas and Axis

1. **Visualizing the atlanto-occipital joint:** Place the fingers on the mastoid process, the bony prominence behind the earlobes. You may be able to feel the transverse processes of the atlas just below as well. It is located under quite a few muscular layers, so be careful, because this area may be tender to the touch. A line connecting the anterior of the two mastoid processes will traverse the atlanto-occipital joint and the dens of the axis. Rock your head on top of the spine and imagine the action happening in this area. Commonly you may rock the head from farther down. Find the highest rocking you can.

2. **Aligning the occipital condyles with the sit bones (standing, sitting):** Visualize the occipital condyles and the rounded inferior portion of the pelvic sit bones. Imagine the occipital condyles extending downward to become aligned with the pelvic sit bones in the same frontal plane. Visualize the central axis located between the pelvic sit bones and occipital condyles (see chapter 17, figure 17.4).

3. **Relating upper and lower sit bones (sitting):** Think of the occipital condyles as miniature sit bones. It may be helpful to rock on the pelvic sit bones and notice the sensations of sitting equally on these bones and transferring weight from sit bones to the chair. Once you have established these sensations, project them up to the less accessible (through touch) occipital condyles sitting in their facets of the atlas. Visualize the shallow cups of the facets and allow the occipital sit bones to sink into them. Now rock gently both on your pelvic and occipital sit bones.

4. **Counterslide of condyles:** Imagine the condyles of the occiput slide back as the head rocks forward. As the head rocks back, the condyles of the occiput slide forward. The top of the head and the condyles are moving in opposite directions (figure 14.10). It may help to realize that the same is happening when you rock on your sit bones. As the pelvis rocks forward, the sit bones swing back. This imagery will help you center the head on top of the spine and release peripheral tension in the neck and jaw.

5. **Atlanto-occipital moving in opposite directions (sitting, standing):** Imagine balancing your occipital condyles equally on both superior articular facets of the atlas. Nod your head to the front and back and watch the occipital condyles (convex) glide in the superior facets of the atlas (concave). Now visualize the facets and condyles countersliding. The facets of the atlas glide forward under the condyles of the occiput in flexion (forward nod). The facets of the atlas glide posteriorly under the occipital condyles in extension (nod to the rear). Reduce

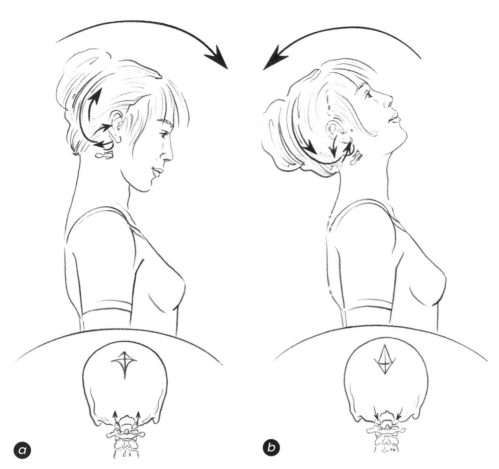

Figure 14.10 *(a)* Head rocks forward and condyles of the occiput slide back; *(b)* head rocks back and condyles of the occiput slide forward.

this rocking motion until you are just imagining the movement. This image will leave you with a centered postural experience.

6. **Atlas as a lifesaving ring (sitting, standing, dance improvisation):** Imagine the atlas to be a circular lifesaving flotation ring. Visualize the head floating easily on this ring. As the water level rises, the ring floats upward, carrying the head up. Experiment with initiating side bending, rotation, and other movements from the flotation ring (see chapter 8, figure 8.2). Be sure not to use any voluntary effort. Let the image create the changes.

7. **Atlas rotates around axis:** Rotate the head to the side and visualize the atlas rotating around the dens. As you rotate, imagine the dens extending upward, creating an axis about which the entire head can revolve.

8. **Initiate movement from atlas:** Imagine movement initiating from the atlas as you perform a variety of whole-body movements.

9. **Down the slope:** As the atlas rotates on the axis, imagine it to be sliding down the convex slope of the axis' shoulders but in opposite directions. In a rotation to the right, the left shoulder slides down and forward and the right one down and back. Imagine how this is allowing the skull to move downward just a bit. This is not a collapse but simply a slight descent along the vertical axis of the body to protect the spinal cord. When returning to center, the head and atlas ride up again on the axis' shoulders. It may be valuable to try the opposite

image (the one more commonly used but not functional). As you rotate the head, the head and atlas go up; as you rotate back to center, the head comes back down again. You may notice that this functionally incorrect image feels awkward unless you have practiced so much that nothing else can possibly enter your mind. The idea that the head goes up in rotation and then up again as it comes to center is also not an option because that would mean you can extend your neck upward, higher and higher, by rotating it back and forth.

10. **Figure eight:** As you rotate your head to the right, visualize the left side of your head descending a bit. As your head rotates to the left, visualize the right side of your head descending slightly. Move your head back and forth and notice how it is performing a subtle figure eight.

11. **Odontoid counterrotation (head rotation, pirouette):** As you rotate your head to the right, visualize the odontoid process rotating in the opposite direction (counterclockwise from above). As your head rotates to the left, visualize the odontoid rotating clockwise. In your mind's eye, picture the odontoid becoming very slippery and spinning rapidly in the opposite direction.

12. **Odontoid determining the plumb line (standing, relevé):** Visualize an axis extending upward and downward through the odontoid process being made perfectly perpendicular by the downward pull of an attached ballast. This plumb line should be identical with your central axis (see chapter 17, figure 17.5).

SKULL

A strong protective cover for the brain, the skull provides a safe and advantageous position for the olfactory, auditory, visual, and balancing organs. Its one large opening below the foramen magnum, an exit for the spinal cord, lies in the horizontal plane, enabling the human head to perch on top of the spine, unlike that of our gorilla cousins, who need powerful neck muscles to hold on to the head because this angle is slanted obliquely forward. At birth, the bones of the skull are widely separated by sutures (fibrous joints) to allow the slight overriding necessary for compression as this largest part of the baby's body passes through the birth canal. Located at the top of the head, the largest suture, called the anterior fontanelle, is an area of softness and relative weakness.

The adult skull has a dome-shaped brain case and several flat bones: the frontal bones over the forehead, the parietals and temporals at the sides, and the occipital bone at the back. There are also several facial bones in a variety of shapes: the nasal bone and zygomatic bones, among others, and the maxilla, which forms the upper part of the jaw. The base of the skull and the containers for the sensory organs are the most ancient parts of the skull; the face, mandible, and dome are its more recent additions. The last bones of the skull to connect firmly do not do so until the age of 18. Even then, the skull retains a certain amount of flexibility because of its sutures. We benefit from thinking of the skull as a flexible structure. Remember, the skull's weight (8 pounds, or 3.6 kg) and the crucial role in movement initiation make its alignment critical in all forms of movement.

If you move with the idea of your head held high, or up, you may be blocking your proprioception and reducing flexibility. If you allow natural function, your head will be naturally up without effort.

Imagery Exercises for the Skull

1. **Touch:** Touch the forehead, called the frontal bone, and glide your fingers over the top of the head (which consists of the two parietal bones) to the back of the head, the occipital bone. The occipital bone extends under the head to areas you cannot touch and forms the back part of the base of the skull. Return to the front of the head and touch the frontal bone over your eyes. If you move your fingers down the sides of your eyes and to the rear, you will discover a ledge called the zygomatic bone. Above the zygomatic bone you will find the sphenoid bone, and if you continue along the zygomatic to the rear, you will reach the temporal bone, which extends above and behind this area. Now touch the top part of the nose, or the nasal bone; the lower part of the nose consists of cartilage. Below the nose is the maxilla, the upper jaw. You will explore the jaw later.

2. **Breathe into the skull:** As you inhale, visualize your breath filling the skull, making it soft and malleable. Watch the skull fill and expand on inhalation and empty and relax on exhalation.

3. **Subtle balance:** To preview the subsequent imagery exercises, you may start with the sensation of the head resting on the spine and the spine conversely supporting the head in a compression-tensile manner, but the relationship is more subtle. Even the slightest shift of the considerable weight of the head causes a change in the balance of the spinal column. Sense the movement of the head directing your spine and whole body from the top down, so to speak. The head may then be perceived as the guiding instrument, not just a static object perched on the top or held on the top of a column. Start by feeling how flexion, lateral flexion, and extension affect the spine. Then feel the interaction of the head with the whole body.

4. **Head as a ball (supine, improvisation):** Imagine the skull to be round and soft like a ball. Explore all the surfaces of the skull in your mind's eye and see them become round. Find the center point of this ball. Practice initiating head movement from this point.

5. **Empty head (supine):** Imagine the head to be empty and spacious. Move around inside your head, clearing its interior of all obstructions. Dispel the clutter in your head as if you were doing spring cleaning.

6. **Floating skull bones (supine):** Imagine the flat bones of the skull floating on cerebrospinal fluid (which surrounds the brain) like tectonic plates floating on the earth's mantle.

7. **Widening the base:** Focus on the base of your skull, the skull's belly. Feel this area expanding and releasing tension from the foramen magnum outward. Imagine the facets of the atlas supporting the skull but the remaining underside of the skull to feel free and wide (figure 14.11).

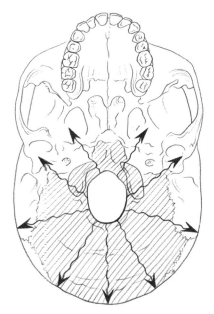

Figure 14.11 Widening the base of the skull.

8. **Widening the pelvic floor and the base of the skull:** Now relate the skull to the pelvic floor. Bend your legs and feel the pelvic floor widening along with a sense of the base of the skull widening. Notice how these two images support each other. As you stretch your legs, reverse the image but with a subtle difference: Feel the pelvic floor narrowing and integrating while you imagine more lift under the center of the skull.

9. **Mastoid lifting:** Place your fingertips under each of the mastoids. Push gently against them and then upward. Imagine the neck lengthening without any voluntary effort whatsoever. Experience the shoulders dropping at the same time. When you release your touch, enjoy the feeling of more length with less muscle activation.

10. **Line of support:** Focus on the occipital bone as the interface between the spine and the rest of the skull. Feel the atlas supporting the occiput and the occiput supporting the other bones of the skull.

11. **Pulling the ears:** This is probably one of the most humorous alignment exercises, but it works! The innominate bone of the pelvis and the temporal bone of the skull relate to each other though the bone rhythms. Stand in a comfortable position and hold your ears. As you flex your legs, the iliac crest inflares; when you extend your legs, the iliac bones outflare, mirroring the temporal bones. When you stretch your legs, pull on your ears and think of the temporal bones flaring out. When you bend your legs, relax your pull. Repeat three times and notice how the pull on the ears helps in giving you a feeling of width and lift in the pelvis. Remove your grip and notice your posture. Even after a few repetitions you may feel more aligned and lifted in your pelvis.

SUBOCCIPITALS

The atlas and axis together with the muscles that cross the area from the skull to the neck provide dynamic alignment and subtle movement for this key area of the body. The sensory organs and specifically the eyes must be maintained at a functional level in a variety of body positions, and the safety of the spinal cord must be maintained at all times. The many muscles of the neck function as dynamic guy-wires and can be visualized as the complex system of ropes and pulleys sustaining the mast of a ship even in the stormiest weather. Without these muscles, the neck bones and discs would buckle under the weight of the head. The system is maintained by the complex interactions between your muscles, bones, ligaments, and joints.

If you imagine diving through the muscular layers of the neck, you will encounter the trapezius, splenius, semispinalis capitis, and finally suboccipitals. These muscles and specifically the suboccipitals form a force-absorbing tensegrity system similar to and complementary to the pelvic floor. The suboccipitals, both the anterior and posterior, are located, as the name implies, beneath the occipital bone and produce subtle movements of the skull (figure 14.12). Tension here will disrupt movement coordination and impede the flow of blood and nerve conduction. They are the deepest muscles of the upper neck. As you move your body and specifically the spine, this system responds in a dynamic manner. When you walk or jump, the suboccipitals subtly lengthen and shorten as they adjust the position of the head. They are absorbing force and reacting to the changes in posture and the spinal curves. Actively making a long neck will tend to reduce force absorption and negatively affect your whole spine and body. You can best achieve a long neck by moving with imagery based on function. This will prevent movement restrictions. Initially it may be a challenge to visualize the suboccipitals because they are short and closely packed together. This is a worthwhile endeavor because the imagery will greatly improve the clarity and ease of balance of your head on the spine and benefit the whole body's alignment.

The splenius muscle (from Greek *splenion*, meaning bandage) arises from the lower half of the ligamentum nuchae and the spinous processes of T6 to C7. The splenius capitis attaches to the base of the skull while the splenius cervicis attaches to the transverse processes of C1 to C3.

The rectus capitis posterior major (RCMA) connects the spinous process of the axis (C2) to the occiput. The rectus capitis posterior minor (RCMI) connects the spinous process of the atlas to the occiput close to the sagittal midline. Both muscles are able to extend the atlanto-occipital joint. Unilateral (one-sided) contraction of the rectus capitis posterior major and minor laterally flexes the skull to the same side (ipsilateral flexion). A posterior view of these muscles reveals two downward-pointing triangles that are placed within each other.

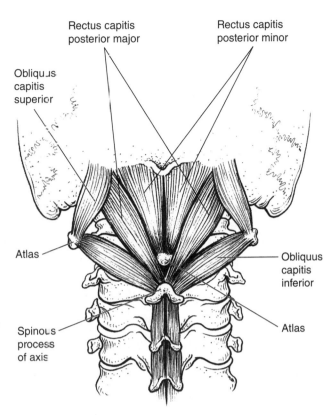

Figure 14.12 The suboccipitals, which include the rectus capitis major and minor and the obliquus capitis superior and inferior.

From E. Franklin, 2002, *Relax your neck, liberate your shoulders* (Hightstown, NJ: Princeton Book Company). Reprinted by permission of the author.

The other pair of suboccipitals are the obliquus capitis inferior and superior. They both attach to the long transverse process of the atlas. The superior oblique runs upward and backward (dorsally) from the transverse process of the atlas to the occiput. The contraction of both superior obliques rocks the head backward (extends the atlanto-occipital joints). The contraction of one superior oblique contralaterally rotates the skull. The inferior oblique is an ipsilateral rotator. In other words, the contraction of the left inferior oblique rotates the skull (via its support, the atlas) to the left, and the contraction of the right inferior oblique rotates the skull (and atlas) to the right.

Imagery Exercises for the Suboccipitals

1. **Imagining the layers:** Touch the upper part of the neck and imagine the layers: trapezius attaching to the very tip of the spinous processes and deep to it the splenius and semispinalis capitis. Below these muscles lie the suboccipitals. Imagine these muscular layers to be resting softly on each other like many layers of soft cloth. As you move your head, imagine the muscle bellies sliding on each other.

2. **Splenius lengthening:** Visualize the splenius capitis connecting the ligamentum nuchae and spinous processes of the upper back to the base of the skull. Imagine the ligamentum nuchae and spinous processes melting down while the base of the skull floats up in the other direction to lengthen the splenius.

3. **Splenius spiraling:** The two splenius capitis muscles spiral as they course up the back of the neck to reach the skull. Imagine these spirals extending up beyond the skull.

4. **Scalene tie-rods (supine, sitting, standing):** Visualize the scalene musculature extending from the uppermost ribs to the transverse processes of the second through seventh cervical vertebrae. Imagine these muscles to be tie-rods, maintaining the cervical spine in an equal, upright balance. Feel these tie-rods vibrating. Imagine this vibration eliciting the same sound on both sides of the neck (figure 14.13).

5. **Imagining the recti:** Run your fingers up, back, and slightly diagonally outward from the neck pit to visualize the minor rectus. Run your fingers steeply up and diagonally outward from the spinous process of the axis to visualize the major rectus. Imagine the differing obliquities of the two recti. Glide your fingertips along the muscles repeatedly. Think *up and back* through the rectus capitis posterior major (RCMA) and *down and forward* through the rectus capitis posterior minor (RCMI). Notice changes in your neck and spinal alignment. You will probably have achieved a sense of increased length without actively lengthening.

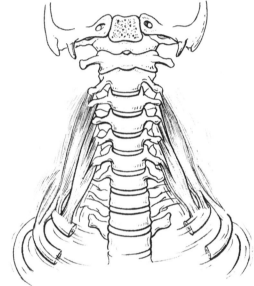

Figure 14.13 The scalene muscles as tie-rods vibrating equally on both sides of the neck.

6. **Minor melt:** Visualize the minor rectus resting or melting inside the major triangle. Visualize an upward flow along the minor triangle and down along the inner triangle. Imagine both triangles expanding, their sides lengthening to create more openness and space at the base of the skull. Slide your fingertips along the base of the skull to support this image.

7. **Muscle sliding:** The contraction of the recti and superior oblique rocks the skull backward (extension). Imagine muscle sliding as you perform this action. Is the action happening equally on the left and the right sides? Use your fingers to reflect the action of the muscles. Place your pointing finger on the spinous process of the axis and the neighboring middle finger on the base of the skull. Flex your head forward while spreading your fingers apart. Think of the muscles sliding apart. Bring the fingers together and think of the muscles sliding together. Repeat a dozen times and enjoy the feeling.

8. **Recti fountains:** Imagine the two rectus capitis muscles as little water fountains or waterspouts, their water gushing against the base of the skull, creating a sense of soft support.

9. **Lateral flexion slide:** Laterally flex your skull and imagine the muscle sliding of the left and right rectus capitis muscles. Practice with the following self-talk as you flex to the right: *Slide together on right, slide apart on left.* As you flex to the left: *Slide together on left, slide apart on right.* Use your fingers on the base of the skull and the spinous process of the axis to help embody the movement. In this case, one set of fingers will be spreading apart as the other set comes closer together. Notice also how the imagery affects your shoulders and whole sense of dynamic alignment.

10. **Tensegrity suboccipitals:** As you walk, imagine the elastic rebound of the suboccipitals lengthening and shorting to absorb force and give your skull and brain a soft and smooth ride (figure 14.14).

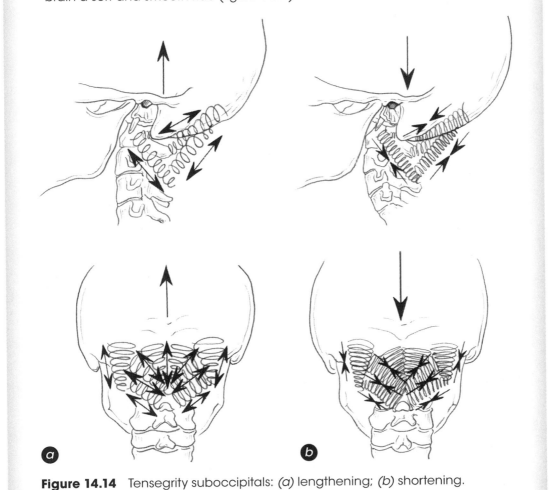

Figure 14.14 Tensegrity suboccipitals: *(a)* lengthening; *(b)* shortening.

MANDIBLE

The mandible, or jawbone, a horseshoe-shaped bone that attaches to the temporal bones at each end, consists of the body in front, the rami on the sides, and two upward-facing projections called the mandibular condyle and the coronoid process (figure 14.15). A small disc separates the temporomandibular joint (TMJ) into a large upper and a small lower joint. The hingelike lower TMJ consists of the condyle of the mandible and the lower surface of the dividing disc. The disc freely rotates on the condyle and vice versa. The upper TMJ is formed by the articular eminence (joint protrusion) of the temporal bone and the upper surface of the disc, allowing the disc to glide on the temporal bone. A very strong joint with a variety of movement possibilities, the TMJ can open, close, slide sideways, jut forward, and move backward. Attached at the coronoid process, the temporalis muscle, which elevates the mandible, passes beneath the zygomatic arch (figure 14.16). The TMJ is constantly in use when you speak, eat, drink, and swallow. Therefore, telltale tension patterns readily manifest in the temporalis muscle, located in front of and above the ears and seen in action during chewing.

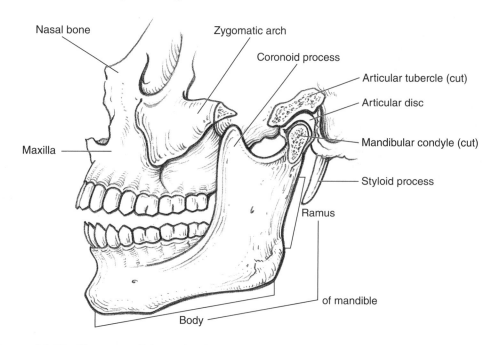

Figure 14.15   The mandible, or jawbone.

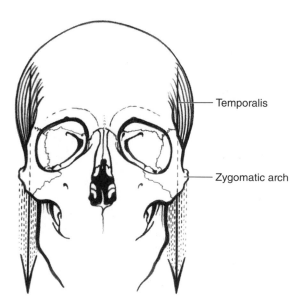

Figure 14.16   The temporalis muscle melts downward and passes under the zygomatic arch.

In the back of the cheek, you can touch another powerful muscle of mastication, the masseter, which is involved in clenching the teeth. It is quite common for people to clench their jaws during great effort, but this habit inhibits the free flow of movement and constricts the breath. Try clenching your jaw for a minute and notice that when you unclench your jaw, you instinctively take a deep breath. Changes in jaw position will manifest also in spinal alignment. Releasing the jaw also helps consolidate the experience of the central axis.

Opening the mouth is a two-phase process. First, the condyle rotates on the disk, and then, to open the mouth wider, the disc slides forward and down along the articular eminence. Closing the mouth reverses these actions: First, the disc slides back and up on the articular eminence, then the condyle rotates on the disc. Thus, the opening action occurs first in the lower then the upper TMJ. Conversely, the closing action occurs first in the upper then the lower TMJ. Jutting of the jaw requires a forward-and-backward sliding of the condyle and disc. No rotation is involved, and thus the action is limited to the upper TMJ.

Sideways motion of the jaw requires a forward movement of the condyle on one side and a rotation of the condyle on the other side. If you move your jaw to the right, the right condyle rotates around a more vertical axis while the left condyle moves forward. If you move your jaw to the left, the left condyle rotates around a vertical axis while the right condyle moves forward (figure 14.17).

The floor of the jaw consists of several muscles, including the mylohyoid. The jaw floor and pelvic floor relate to each other through the rectus series of muscles (figure 14.18).

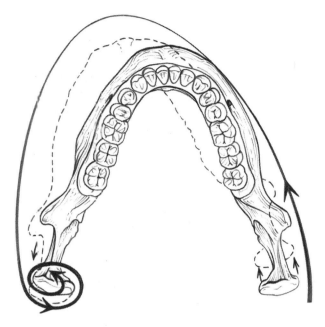

Figure 14.17 If you move your jaw to the left, the left condyle rotates around a vertical axis while the right condyle moves forward.

Adapted from P.K. Levangie and C.C. Norkin, 2001, *Joint structure and function: A comprehensive analysis*, 3rd ed. (Philadelphia: F.A. Davis), 191.

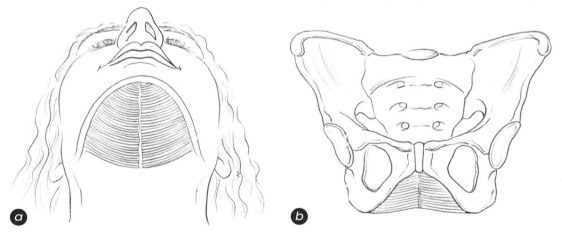

Figure 14.18 Comparing (*a*) the jaw floor (mylohyoid) and (*b*) the anterior pelvic floor.

Imagery Exercises for the Mandible

1. Touch: Begin at the front of the jaw, called the body of the mandible. Use both hands to follow along the sides of this body while performing a gentle circling massage. As you move back, your fingers will glide around a corner called the angle of the mandible and will begin moving up the rami of the mandible to the joint between the skull and mandible. You can feel the activity at this joint as you open and close your jaw. Just behind this area and beyond the earlobe, you will discover the thick protrusion called the mastoid process. Just above the joint between the mandible and the skull, you will detect a bony ledge, called the zygomatic arch. The temporalis muscle passes beneath this arch. Open and close your jaw and feel the temporalis muscle in action above this arch.

Move your fingers about an inch forward along the zygomatic arch and slide them downward another inch. You are now massaging your masseter.

2. **Temporalis release (sitting, standing):** Visualize the temporalis muscle melting downward as it passes under the zygomatic arch. Watch it flow and hang perpendicularly down the side of the skull. See the flow of both temporalis muscles being vertically aligned with each other (see figure 14.16).

3. **Masseter release (supine, sitting, standing):** Palpate the masseter muscle at the back of the cheek and imagine it softening. Move your fingers to various places on this muscle and watch these points melt. Begin to move the jaw in various directions while continuing to see the points you are touching melt away (figure 14.19).

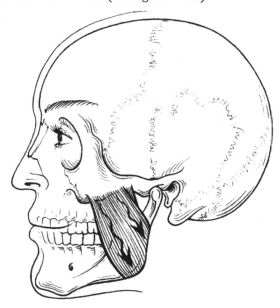

4. **Widening the back "arms" of the joints (supine, sitting, standing):** Visualize the mandibular rami floating sideways from each other. Visualize the space between the left and right TMJ becoming larger, widening, opening up (figure 14.20).

Figure 14.19 Melting masseter.

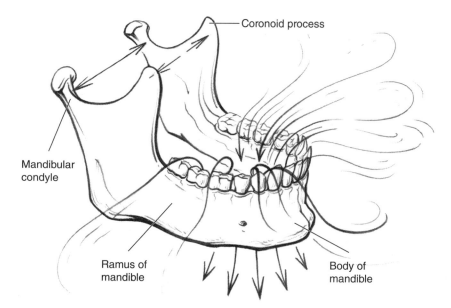

Coronoid process

Mandibular condyle

Ramus of mandible

Body of mandible

Figure 14.20 The mandibular rami float sideways from each other; air pours down the inner surface of your jaw.

5. **Widening the back "arms" with the pelvis:** Touch the back of the mandibular rami at the posterior angle. Gently pull these points apart and notice how it affects your neck and shoulders. Bend and stretch your legs and coordinate

the widening of the mandible with your downward movement and the sit bones moving apart.

6. **Releasing the inner jaw space (supine, sitting, standing):** Let air flow into the mouth. Watch this air pour down the inner surface of the jaw and back out into space through the bottom of the chin (see figure 14.20).

7. **Softening the floor of the mouth (supine):** Visualize the area beneath your tongue, between the rami of the mandible, becoming soft and malleable. This is the floor of the jaw. Using your fingers, you can gently move your tongue from underneath to facilitate this. Allow this area to stay relaxed as you rock your head on the atlas.

8. **Jaw on cloud (standing, sitting):** Imagine the mandible floating on a cloud just beneath it. Don't tighten your jaw; let the cloud support it like a cushion. This will result in a subtle lengthening of the neck.

9. **Jaw drawer (sitting, standing):** Imagine your jaw to be a sliding drawer that fits very loosely on well-oiled runners. Lean your head forward and imagine the drawer sliding forward easily. Lean your head back and watch the drawer slide back just as easily. Repeat this image a few times.

10. **Disc gliding:** As you open your mouth, visualize the condyles rotating forward. Now open your mouth wider and imagine the discs sliding along the articular eminence. The motion is wavy, downward, and forward. Compare the feeling to going down a wavy slide. It may be helpful to sigh while performing this action. Finally, close your mouth and watch the discs glide back and the condyles rotate to the rear (figure 14.21).

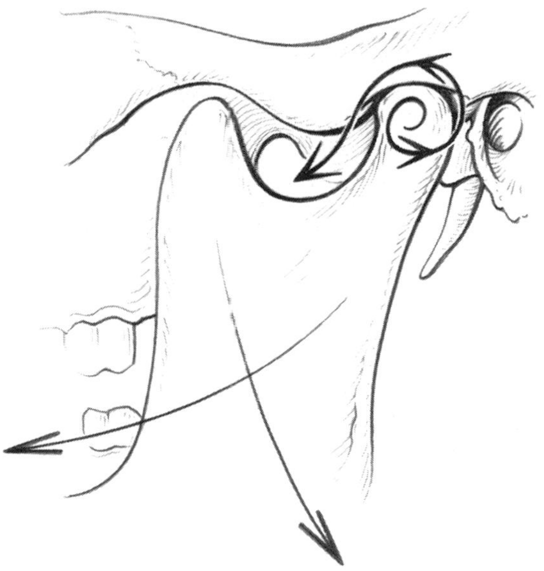

11. **Fluffing up your discs:** Place your fingertips on your TMJ and imagine your disc. Gently massage the area as you imagine you are fluffing up the disc as if it were a pillow. Think of fluffy light discs and notice how this affects your neck and whole posture.

Figure 14.21 As you open your mouth, the condyles rotate forward. As you open your mouth wide, the discs slide along the articular eminence.

12. **TMJ and legs:** Imagine the TMJ to be soft and balanced as you perform movement with your legs. You may notice that a balanced sense of the TMJ will create a balanced feeling in the hip joints and legs.

13. **TMJ and clavicle:** Feel the TMJ and clavicle in a moveable relationship. If the TMJ is free, then the clavicle will be so as well and vice versa.

14. **Massage jaw with balls:** Perform circular massage movements with two smooth balls on the masseter while you imagine it melting.

HYOID AND TONGUE

The hyoid, a free-floating bone shaped like a boomerang, lies at an angle between the floor of the mouth and the front of the neck. It is believed to have evolved from the second and third gill arches. The hyoid has a multitude of muscular and ligamentous attachments but no bony connections to the rest of the body. It is literally a floating way station for muscles attached to the mandible, cervical spine, sternum, and clavicles (figure 14.22). The tongue is muscularly rooted to the hyoid. Breathing is adversely influenced by tension in the tongue via the hyoid and the upper-accessory breathing musculature. Tension in the tongue (bunching or sticking the tongue out of the mouth) is common. An off-center tongue influences alignment of the hyoid and neck.

Hyoid placement influences the alignment of the cervical spine, head, and shoulders. If you experience your tongue resting on its supportive base, the hyoid, as well as balanced support for the hyoid by the surrounding musculature, you will experience dynamic alignment of your neck (figure 14.23).

Hyoid imagery can improve forward head positions and release concomitant neck tension. To appreciate how pelvic activities can influence the neck, and vice versa, visualize a circular chain of bony and muscular links running down the spine to the tail, across the pelvic floor to the pubic symphysis, up the rectus abdominis, through the sternum to the hyoid and cervical spine and the occiput of the skull (figure 14.24).

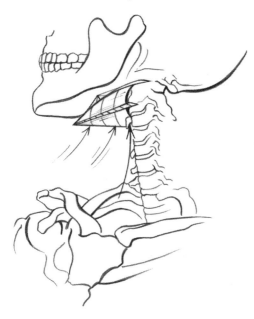

Figure 14.22 The hyoid bone as a hang glider.

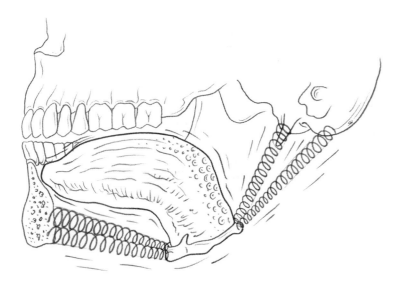

Figure 14.23 Tongue resting on the hyoid.

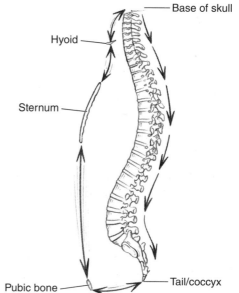

Figure 14.24 A circular chain of bony and muscular links running down the spine to the tail and back up the front of the torso.

Imagery Exercises for the Hyoid Bone

1. **Visualize the shape and location of the hyoid:** Put your fingers on the thyroid cartilage (Adam's apple), which can easily be found protruding slightly from the neck (more so in men than in women). Just above this cartilage is a small space that delineates the area just below the hyoid bone. You can readily touch the front and sides of the hyoid.

2. **Tongue sits, hyoid hangs:** Imagine the tongue resting, sitting on a well-balanced hyoid. At the same time, think of the hyoid as suspended, hanging down from long attachments to your central axis. Compare this image to resting on the seat of a swing. You rest your weight on the seat, which is suspended from above.

3. **Hyoid suspension:** Imagine the muscles that suspend the hyoid to be flexible and elastic (figure 14.25). These include the stylohyoid, digastric, mylohyoid, geniohyoid, sternohyoid, and omohyoid. Imagine the hyoid as the way station between the back of the skull, jaw, sternum, and shoulder blade to where the aforementioned muscles connect. In your mind's eye, run through the lengths of the muscle bellies and appreciate these three-dimensional pathways. Imagine the digastric connecting the mastoid to the tip of the jaw, the geniohyoid and omohyoid connecting the jaw to the scapulae, or the sternohyoid relating the jaw and hyoid to the sternum.

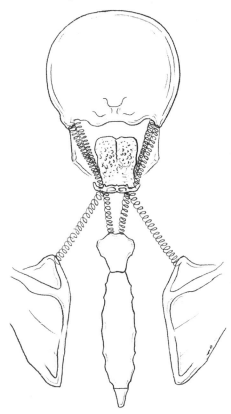

Figure 14.25   Hyoid suspended from flexible muscles.

4. **Tongue relaxes, neck lengthens:** Imagine your tongue being very free and relaxed, especially at its root area just above the hyoid. Allow the tongue to sit back and feel supported. Notice how this allows your neck to naturally lengthen and center in your axis (figure 14.26). Notice also the opposite: What happens to your neck and sense of center if you tense or bunch up your tongue?

5. **Contract and release tongue:** Another way to relax your tongue is to first tense it. Grip your

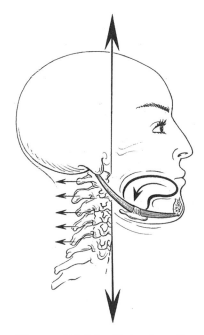

Figure 14.26   Relaxing the tongue on the hyoid lengthens the neck.

tongue, bunch it up for a moment, and then let it go. Notice what happens to your neck when you bunch it and also when you relax it. Move your head with a gripped tongue, then with a relaxed tongue. Tongue tension is obviously not beneficial for movement of the whole spine.

6. **Hyoid hang glider (supine, sitting, standing):** Imagine the hyoid bone to be a hang glider. Visualize a strong wind current gusting up the front of the spine, lifting the hyoid. Emphasize the lifting of the wings rather than the tip of the hyoid. Watch the glider (hyoid) hanging in the air, wafting upward on gentle and consistent breezes. Watch the glider dip and bank in the air currents (see figure 14.22).

7. **Tongue over clothes hanger (sitting, standing):** This image does for the tongue and neck what the Sweigardian clothes-hanger image does for the legs and back. Imagine the tongue hanging over a clothes hanger as if it were a soft and fluffy blanket. The clothes hanger is positioned under the back center of the tongue. Imagine the tongue resting on and drooping over this hanger.

8. **Tongue centering (supine, sitting, standing):** Visualize the sagittal plane that divides the tongue into two equal halves. Think of the two halves of the tongue sliding down equally along this plane. Imagine a line of movement from the front tip of the tongue around the sides to the back. Let the rim of the tongue flow back toward this central axis (figure 14.27).

9. **Neck, mouth, and top of head release (supine, sitting, standing):** Imagine the dome-shaped top of the mouth expanding toward the top of the skull. Watch from the inside as the dome becomes larger, as if you are standing inside an expanding balloon. Imagine your whole body hanging from the top of your mouth. Let the top of the skull and the neck soften and the tongue melt. You may also think of the tongue deflating, as if filled with air that is now escaping from the edges of your tongue (figure 14.28).

10. **Cotton tongue (supine):** Imagine the tongue becoming permeable like cotton. Let your breath float around and through your tongue.

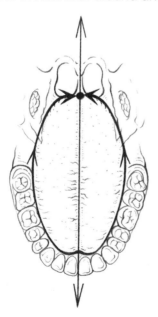 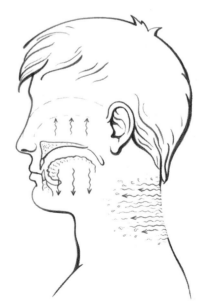

Figure 14.27 Imagine a line of movement from the front tip of the tongue around the sides to the back.

Figure 14.28 The dome-shaped top of the mouth expanding toward the top of the skull.

EYES

Set deep in their cone-shaped sockets, the eyes face forward and slightly outward, creating an overlap of visual fields and binocular vision. A relatively small snout and nose area accentuate this overlap of visual field. In the embryonic state, the eyes are not connected to the brain. An axon, or nerve, grows out from the back of the eye and searches for the brain. Chopra (1990a) writes the following:

> Structurally, the retina is just a pool of nerve endings fanning out like the frayed end of a rope, the rope being the optic nerve, which gathers a million separate fibers into one bundled cord. Even though they are located deeper inside you than the nerve endings under your skin, the eye's sensory cells are also "touching" the outside world. (p. 200)

The eyes are very revealing. A baby's eyes sparkle, wide and excited. A clouded visual channel diminishes expressivity. Said to be the mirrors of the soul, the eyes are a visible part of the brain. Kükelhaus (1988) points out that developmentally the eyes are connected to the "master gland," the pituitary (in the brain). Sight directly influences the hormones of the body. As organs of reception, the eyes get filled with incoming reflected light. People usually think of looking in an active context, but the opposite notion of drinking with the eyes and allowing a visual impression to fall into the body and create a mood or an image through its transformation within is most valuable (Kükelhaus 1978).

Tatsumi Hijikata, considered the father of Japanese butoh dance, once said that whatever he saw, he absorbed into his body. Even his neighbor's dog lives in his body. All these things float inside him like rafts on a river, Hijikata said in a lecture at the first Butoh festival in Japan in 1985 (Haerdter and Kawai 1988). Studies have shown that sightless people may learn to see with their bodies—to transform tactile stimulation into a visual image, creating a substitute sensation. They can learn how to "see sound" via tactile stimulation patterns produced by hundreds of small points on the skin.

The eyes also aid balance through the optical righting reflexes. Try doing a balance exercise with your eyes closed to see how much more difficult it is to balance without them. I often take off my glasses when practicing movement (and regular wearing of contact lenses irritates my eyes), so I have become rather aware of these changes in balance control. With my glasses on, everything appears sparkling clear and balancing is easier. When performing without glasses or contact lenses, I have found myself well prepared for the impaired vision from glaring stage lights when dancing because I am accustomed to imperfect vision in dance classes. Training balance organs other than the optical organs greatly improves the overall ability to maintain balance.

Imagery Exercises for the Eyes

1. **Space around eyes:** Imagine plentiful space around your eyeballs. Imagine the eyes to be floating gently in this space (figure 14.29).
2. **Deep light:** Feel the light coming into your eye arriving at the back of the eyeball rather than the front. This will give you a sense of depth and centering in your alignment. You can even imagine the brain areas at the back of the skull to be reacting to the incoming light, to create a whole-skull feeling for vision.

3. **Deep space:** Imagine the deep conical space provided for the eyes. Imagine a lot of space behind the eyes as well.

4. **Eyes suspended:**

   a. **Central axis (standing, sitting):** Imagine that your eyes are suspended from your central axis.

   b. **Eyes suspended from optic nerve:** Imagine your eyes are suspended from the optic nerve.

   c. **Eyes suspended from muscles:** Lean forward and imagine the eyes are suspended from the eye muscles, dangling from them. Allow them to stretch like chewing gum.

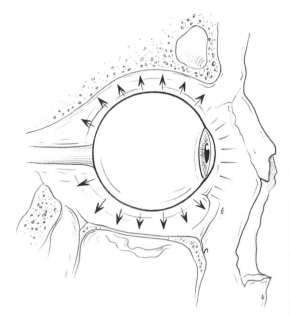

Figure 14.29 Space around the eyeballs.

5. **Eyes gliding (eye movements):** Visualize the eyes sitting in their spherical sockets. As you move your eyes, allow the sockets to become very slippery so that the eyes glide effortlessly as you shift your gaze.

6. **Resting on the horizon (sitting, standing):** The horizontal plane beneath the eyes supports their weight. Imagine them resting on the horizon created by this plane.

7. **Eyes as ponds (supine):** Imagine your eyes as ponds of fresh, clear spring water. See the water welling up from below through the optic nerve, slowly replenishing the pond in the cavity of the eye with the clearest, purest crystalline water. See the eyelids as lily pads floating on the pond, moving very slowly and with infinite ease, propelled by a warm summer breeze (figure 14.30). Now try imagining the area

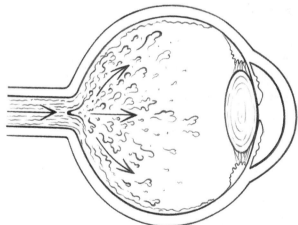

Figure 14.30 The eyes as ponds of fresh, clear spring water.

around the eyes as a pond and the eyes as round balls floating in this pond.

8. **Rolling eyes (improvisation):** Let the eyeballs dance gently in their sockets. Try using music that suggests the motion. Bach sonatas for the flute or Scarlatti sonatas for the piano may be suitable classical music selections. Let the eyes respond to the music; they are part of the total-body feeling.

9. **Swing the eyes:** Sit comfortably and rest your closed eyes in your hands. Imagine your eyes moving gently in their sockets. Front to back, side to side, and

diagonally; front to back, side to side, and then the other direction diagonally. Repeat five times. Then actively perform the movement. Repeat the imagined movement one more time and return to upright sitting. Notice changes in your alignment.

10. **Initiate movement from the eyes:** Now let the eyes initiate the body's motion. Experiment with letting the right, then the left, then both eyes lead the body into space. Now imagine that you can see up, down, to the front, back, and both sides simultaneously. How does this three-dimensional vision change your movement?

11. **Sphincter eyes:** Imagine the orbicular muscles of the eyes relating to the other circular muscles of the body. Notice how tensing your eyes affects your mouth and pelvic floor. Also notice the reverse. Can you relax your mouth while you tense your eyes? Can you do the reverse? Notice how your body feels once you have released strain from your orbicular muscle. Imagine it widening out into space, releasing the eyes.

12. **Light drops into the eyes (improvisation):** Imagine the light coming from the scenery around you falling into your eyes without any effort on your part whatsoever. They soak up all the visual information surrounding you as you move.

13. **Whole-body seeing (improvisation):** Imagine that every cell on the surface of your skin is sighted. Your sight has thousands of possibilities, thousands of angles from which to look out into space. What is it like to be the sighted cells on the soles of your feet? What is it like to be the sighted cells on the top of your head?

NOSE AND MOUTH

What you see of the nose is largely a cartilaginous projection, not part of the skull. The actual nasal cavities, which generally are buried in the skull, are separated by a partition called the septum. A thick mucous membrane covers the inner walls of the nose to warm the incoming air and remove dust particles. The flow of air through the nasal passages creates resistance that trains the diaphragm and other breathing muscles.

The center of the baby's world, the mouth and lips, serve as a powerful built-in suction pump for mother's milk. Feeding from mother's breast is one of humans' first coordinated acts, involving locating the breast and nipple, reaching for it, connecting to it, correcting the whole-body position, activating the suction pump, and maintaining the vacuum connection. An extremely sensitive area of the body, the lips provide your first experience of shape. A baby sucks on a wooden ring and experiences roundness; he takes a wooden block into his mouth and experiences squareness. This presymbolic awareness becomes the basis for language and, later, imagery.

The mouth is related to the pelvic floor and anus because they are the opposite ends of the long digestive tube. Tension in the mouth indicates tension in the pelvic floor, which inhibits the breathing process and does not allow for resilient support of the pelvic organs.

The sense of taste and the sense of smell are intimately connected. What you consider as taste is largely a matter of adding the information gathered through smell to the findings of meagerly distributed taste receptors on the tongue. You can discover how much the sense of smell contributes to the sense of taste by holding your nose while eating—you will find that much of the taste is lost.

Imagery Exercises for the Nose and Mouth

1. **Nasal airflow:** As you inhale, imagine the air flowing up the center of the nose. As you exhale, imagine the air flowing down along the sides of the nose.

2. **Soft nostrils:** Imagine your nostrils to be very soft. As the air passes through them, they billow like the sides of a tent in the wind.

3. **Soft center:** As you inhale and exhale through your nose, imagine the air creating a subtle vibration in the septum between the two nostrils. The front part is cartilaginous, and the back part consists of the ethmoid bone.

4. **Nostrils and occipital condyles:** As you inhale and exhale, the air flows at about the level of your occipital condyles. Imagining backward from the flow of air aids you in imagining the location of the spinal support for your skull.

5. **Swirling air:** As you inhale and exhale through the nostrils, imagine the air to be swirling and spiraling. Compare this sensation to the air going in straight. You may notice that the swirling image is easier because it corresponds to the physics of flow. You can extend the image to the air swirling in the bronchi as well, even to the blood swirling in the arteries.

6. **Sucking on a straw (improvisation):** After you have been moving for a few minutes, imagine that you are sucking water up through a straw. Notice how this affects your movement.

7. **Space in lips (standing):** Visualize the space contained within your lips. Appreciate their inner volume. Notice how this affects your neck as well as your whole standing posture.

8. **Smell and alignment (standing):** If you think this exercise is humorous, it is. To discover how smell can affect your body tone and alignment, try the following experiment: Imagine the smell of cow manure, or any other smell that does not appeal to you, and notice any changes in body tone or posture. Now imagine the smell of your favorite perfume, or any other scent that appeals to you, and again notice any changes in body tone or posture.

SUMMARY

Although some animals occasionally make an attempt at upright walking, only humans have reached perfection, or at least they have the potential to do so by being dynamically aligned.

The head is perched on top of a long mobile spine and pelvis, its considerable weight supported only by the hind legs. Because of the head's high center of gravity relative to the rest of the body, any deviations from optimal head alignment have a great impact on the entire body. Cooperation between head and neck is essential for good alignment and movement control. The relatively small cervical vertebrae of the neck have a shape designed to increase their stability. The cervical lordosis allows the head to be more over the center of the body, just as the lumbar lordosis enables this for the thorax.

The ring-shaped topmost vertebra, the atlas, carries the weight of the head and has no body or spinous process to mention. The most inferior bone of the skull, called the occiput, has two condyles that can glide on the facets of the atlas to produce nodding of the head. The axis, the second cervical vertebra, has a dens protruding from its front surface around which the head and atlas can rotate. The axis has a very long transverse process, which is the origin of many muscles, such as the levator scapulae and the semispinalis cervicis. These muscles must be well organized for good head alignment.

The skull is a strong protective cover for the brain and provides advantageous positioning for the olfactory, auditory, visual, and balancing organs. The foramen magnum, the exit for the spinal cord from the skull, lies in the horizontal plane, enabling the human head to perch on top of the spine. At birth, the bones of the skull are widely separated by sutures to allow the slight overriding necessary for compression as the largest part of the baby's body passes through the birth canal.

The many muscles of the neck function as dynamic guy-wires, without which the bones and discs of the neck would buckle under the weight of the head. The system is maintained by complex interactions between muscles, bones, ligament, joints, and the nervous system.

The mandible is a horseshoe-shaped bone that attaches to the temporal bones at each end. It consists of the body in front, the rami on the sides, and two upward-facing projections called the mandibular condyle and the coronoid process. The temporomandibular joint contains a disc dividing the joint into an upper and a lower compartment.

Opening the mouth is a two-phase process. First, the condyle rotates on the disc, and then the disc slides forward and down along the articular eminence. Closing the mouth reverses these actions: First, the disc slides back and up on the articular eminence, then the condyle rotates on the disc.

Set deep in their sockets, the eyes face forward and slightly outward, creating an overlap of visual fields necessary for binocular vision. A relatively small nose accentuates this overlap of visual field.

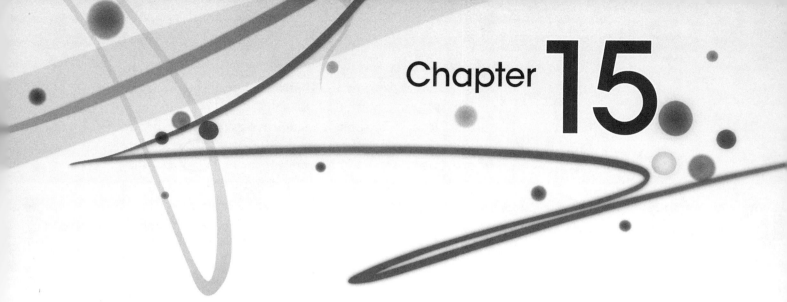

Chapter 15

Rib Cage, Breath, and Organs

If you improve your breathing you have become better at something you do 20,000 times a day.

Breathing is perhaps the most important function of the body and involves ventilation and respiration. Ventilation is the transport of oxygen and carbon dioxide in and out of the body. This involves the movement of the diaphragm, rib cage, joints, muscles, and organs. The two kinds of respiration are external and internal. In the external phase, O_2 and CO_2 are brought through the thin walls of the lungs into the bloodstream. Internal respiration describes how the gases arrive in the cells to produce the energy that drives the functions of the body from muscle contraction to nerve conduction. In this chapter you will be concerned mostly with ventilation and the mobility of the organs and rib cage to create dynamic alignment and efficient coordination of movement and breathing.

RIB CAGE

The rib cage, or thorax, consists of 12 ribs, the thoracic spine, the sternum, joints, muscles, and ligaments. The function of the rib cage is to protect vital organs such as the heart and lungs, allow for respiration, and serve as an origin of many muscles and connective tissue structures that relate to the head, arms, and pelvis. The rib cage also dissipates forces. This is useful imagery for an athlete or dancer when rebounding from a jump or responding to impact. The damping of forces will allow for more dynamic stability and safety of the spine and organs by reducing excess vibration.

The sternum, spine, pelvis, and rib cage must be balanced in relation to each other for the spine to support the head efficiently, releasing excess tension in the neck and shoulders. The head can then move freely in a high and erect alignment. Good alignment of these two adjoining structures helps create optimal freedom of motion for both.

The rib cage makes the thoracic spine the most stable but least flexible portion of the spine. The lower ribs slant upward toward the spine at an increasing angle. Each pair of ribs braces the spine from either side, lifting it and actively supporting it. The lower ribs are approximately three times as wide as the first rib, creating a conical shape resembling a birdcage (figure 15.1).

Since the rib cage has such an intricate relationship to the spine, a misaligned or tense rib cage will influence the whole body. As soon as your rib cage is freely centered and balanced on the spine, you will notice that the joints of the body free up, including the hip joint, knees, and joints of the feet. These relationships are mediated through the spine and sacrum to the pelvic bone rhythms. The names of the joints you need to consider in order to understand the design and movement of the rib cage sound like vocabulary words in an ancient language: manubriosternal, xiphisternal, chondrosternal, costochondral, costovertebral, costotransverse, and interchondral articulations.

The sternum is composed of three bones: manubrium, body, and xiphoid process. The manubriosternal joint is a synchondrosis (in other words, a joint with a fibrocartilaginous disc in between the bony endings covered with hyaline cartilage). The manubriosternal joint is similar in structure to the pubic symphysis. It does at times ossify, a process that may be accelerated by lack of movement and slouched posture. The xiphisternal joint is a synchondrosis and ossifies starting as early as age 40 if you do not keep it active.

By imagining and moving these joints, you can keep them mobile, which allows for more freedom in breathing and greater flexibility in the upper spine. The xiphoid process (lower edge of the sternum) must swing in and out in breathing. Ideally the manubrium (top of the sternum) is high to allow space for the upper ribs and upper-thoracic organs (figure 15.2).

The first to seventh ribs connect to the cartilage around the sternum, which connects to the sternum itself. The costochondral joints are synchondroses surrounded by periosteum. The chondrosternal joints are true synovial joints. The articulation of the first rib to the sternum has the hardest cartilage, by far, and is a synchondrosis. This means that the move-

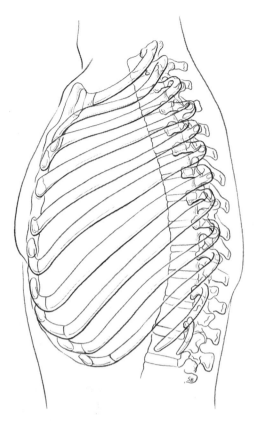

Figure 15.1 Lateral view of the rib cage.

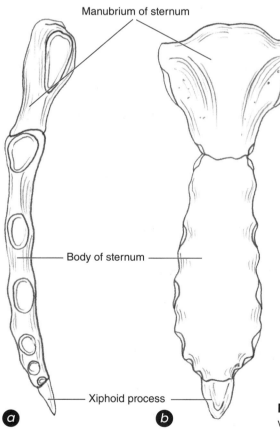

Manubrium of sternum

Body of sternum

Xiphoid process

a *b*

Figure 15.2 The sternum: (*a*) lateral view with joint facets and (*b*) anterior view.

ments of the top of the sternum and the first rib are linked. The 8th to 10th ribs are connected to the adjacent above-lying cartilage. They are synovial and reinforced by ligaments.

Most of the elliptically shaped ribs connect to the spine at two points. The 1st through 10th ribs connect to a socket created half by the upper vertebra and half by the lower vertebra. These costovertebral joints are flattish, oval synovial joints. Ribs 11 and 12 articulate with one vertebra only and are not connected to the sternum in front. Note that most of the ribs are spiraled along their length (figure 15.3).

The 1st through 10th ribs also articulate with the transverse process of the vertebrae. The costovertebral joints are flattish, oval synovial joints between the rounded head of the rib and the two demi-facets (half sockets) formed by adjacent vertebrae. The costotransverse articulations connect the articular tubercle of the ribs to the transverse processes of the 1st to 10th thoracic vertebrae (figure 15.4). It is interesting to note that most of these ribs have a relationship to the spinal intervertebral discs via the intra-articular ligament of the head of the rib.

The joint axes through the costovertebral and costotransverse joints are closer to the frontal plane (35 degrees) in the upper spine and closer to the sagittal (35 degrees) plane in the lower spine. This will cause the upper ribs to move more up and down in the sagittal plane and the lower ribs to move more up and down in the frontal plane during breathing. These movements have been described as a bucket handle for the lower ribs and a pump handle for the upper ribs (Norkin and Levangie 1992). Ribs 11 and 12 simply move rearward during inhalation. If you imagine the breathing movement from the bottom to the top of the ribs, you will get a movement to the back, then to the side, and finally to the front. In other words, the ribs form a spiral path in response to breathing.

The movement in the costovertebral and costotransverse articulations is a sliding action as well as a rotation around the costal intra-articular ligament of the head of the rib.

Figure 15.3 Ribs are spiraled.

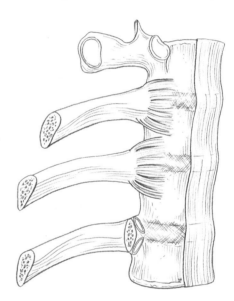

Figure 15.4 The costovertebral and costotransverse joints.

Imagery Exercises for the Rib Cage and Spine

1. **Centered and free rib cage:** Imagine the right and left side of the rib cage to be balanced and affecting the spine in a harmonious manner. Imagine that the rib cage can respond in a synchronized way to the actions of the lower and upper limbs. Notice the relationship between the organization of the rib cage and the pelvis and hip joints especially.

2. **Moving the xiphisternal articulation:** Touch the bottom of the sternum and slide your fingers up. You will notice a ridge at the beginning of the body of the

sternum. This is where your xiphisternal joint is located. As you inhale, allow it to swing slightly forward; as you exhale, allow it to swing back. This is a key point for breath. Gently massage the area around the xiphoid process to free your breathing. Deep to your touch is the solar plexus (also known as the celiac plexus), a hub for your autonomic nervous system.

3. **Hanging lower sternum (standing, sitting):** Visualize the xiphoid process hanging down. Imagine it swinging just slightly to the front and to the back like a pendulum until it comes to rest perpendicularly over the pubic symphysis.

4. **Superelastic sternum:** Imagine your sternum to be very elastic, like rubber. Flex and extend your spine and notice how your ease of motion increases if you think of the sternum being stretchy like chewing gum. The same holds true for lateral flexion. Alternately, you may think of the sternum as soft and billowy like a piece of silk.

5. **Supported sternum:** Imagine the sternum to be carried by the ribs from both sides. Relax your sternum into its many supporting ribs.

6. **Tugging the sternum:** Imagine the relationship between the ribs and the sternum to be like tugboats and a larger vessel. Visualize several tugboats (ribs) nudging the large vessel (the sternum) from both sides. Watch the sternum react to the gentle pushes and shoves of the adjoining ribs until it is aligned in the same median sagittal plane as the spine. Once they are aligned, subtle adjustments of the tugboats allow it to maintain alignment (figure 15.5).

7. **Suspended sternum:** The sternum is not connected directly to the bony part of the ribs, but it relates to cartilage, which is more elastic and resilient than bone. Imagine your sternum to be suspended from the ribs by this elastic suspension system (figure 15.6). As you

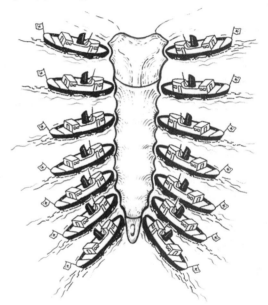

Figure 15.5 Imagine the relationship between the ribs and the sternum to be like tugboats and a larger vessel.

move, sense the sternum rebounding and reacting elastically. Notice how the whole rib cage is a damping system as you move. Relate the movement of the sternum to the movement of the intervertebral discs. Think of the two systems acting as force absorbers in movement, jumping, and leaping.

8. **Spiraling sternum:** As you rotate or laterally flex the spine, the sternum adapts in a spiral fashion. Place one hand on the top of your sternum and the other on the bottom. Rotate your spine and you will notice how the top part rotates more than the lower, causing the sternum to spiral.

9. **Sternum as a cork (sitting, standing):** Imagine the sternum to be a cork floating on water. Watch the water level rise and the cork float upward. Let the sit bones and coccyx drop downward as the cork is buoyed upward. Notice how this image spontaneously lengthens your spine.

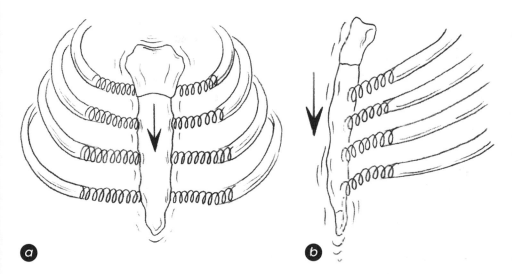

Figure 15.6   Elastically suspended sternum: *(a)* front view; *(b)* side view.

10. **Wavelike sternum:** As you perform spinal flexion, imagine the sternum to be very flexible as well. In a deep spinal curl you may imagine the sternum rolling up like a carpet, and in spinal extension you can imagine the sternum to be a cresting wave moving up toward the head.

11. **Imagining chondrosternal movement:** Touch the joints on the left and right sides of the sternum. They may feel a bit tender. Flex and extend the spine and imagine sliding and rotating at these joints.

12. **First rib:** Focus on your first rib. It is the flattest and smallest of them all. Imagine it to be horizontal. Feel it to be the counterpoint to your pelvic floor, the "roof" of the rib cage. As you move, imagine it floating through space like a hovering cloud or Frisbee. Imagine the air lifting it from underneath as you walk.

13. **Spacious first rib:** Feel your first rib to be very expansive and spacious. Imagine space contained within it. Imagine it gently floating on top of the second rib and under the clavicle. Imagine it gliding freely under the clavicle as you move your arms.

14. **Rib tassels:** Imagine the ribs to be tassels or colorful ribbons suspended from your sternum.

15. **Ribs sink into the spine (supine):** Imagine the ribs to be free floating, and watch as they approach the spine. Visualize each rib contacting the spine in two places: the costal articular facet of the transverse process and the costal articular facet of the body of the vertebrae. Imagine the ribs sinking into the latter facet as if it were made of clay. Begin with the 12th rib and imagine your way up to the first.

16. **Spine attracts the ribs:** Repeat the previous exercise, this time imagining that the spine actively attracts the ribs. Visualize the spine's articular facet and transverse process pulling on the head of the rib like a vacuum cleaner. Adjust the spine's suction so that the ribs are held in place freely, without rigidity (figure 15.7). (If you would like to save mental electricity, you may visualize magnetic attraction or simply energy rather than a vacuum cleaner.)

17. **Ribs gently nudge the spine:** Compare the previous image with the rib heads gently nudging the spine like soft gusts of wind pushing a cloud. Imagine the spine to be a long, slender scarf and the rib heads to be as soft as cotton and pushing a scarf into the desired alignment. Use the image also in all kinds of

spinal movements, such as flexion, extension, rotation, and lateral flexion to create a soft, velvety quality of movement.

18. **Spiral ribs:** Imagine the ribs, which are spiraled, spiraling into the spine (figure 15.8). Imagine the spirals to be supporting the spine.

19. **Space between ribs:** Imagine the space between ribs to be soft and resilient.

20. **Clouds of ribs:** Imagine each rib to be a curved cloud. Perform a variety of exercises and notice how this image informs your movement. Alternatively, imagine each rib to be supported by a small cloud (figure 15.9).

21. **Melting ribs:** Imagine your ribs to have a melting quality, especially in lateral flexion, where the upper ribs will melt toward the spine.

22. **Cascading water:** Imagine water gushing out of your first rib circle and flowing down your ribs to relax them (figure 15.10). Make the water just perfect in temperature and hear the water, too.

23. **Resting ribs equally:** Imagine your ribs resting equally against the sternum in front and the spine in back. Imagine the weight of the ribs perfectly balancing your torso from both sides. Perform a variety of movements and imagine the ribs remaining in this embodiment of ease and rest. This image may even improve your hip flexibility.

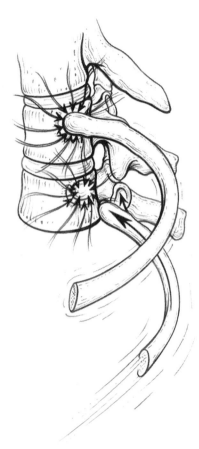

Figure 15.7 The spine's articular facet and transverse process pull on the head of the rib like a vacuum cleaner.

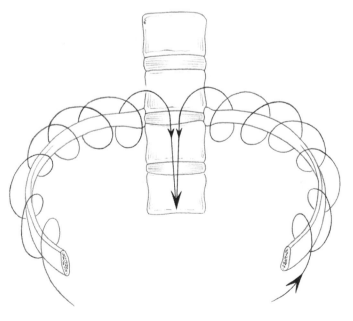

Figure 15.8 Ribs spiraling into the spine.

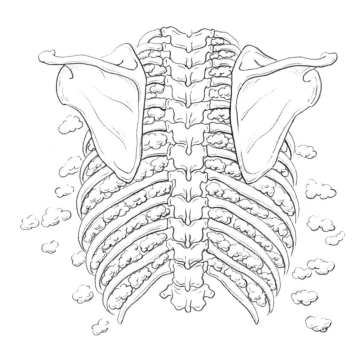

Figure 15.9   Ribs supported by clouds.

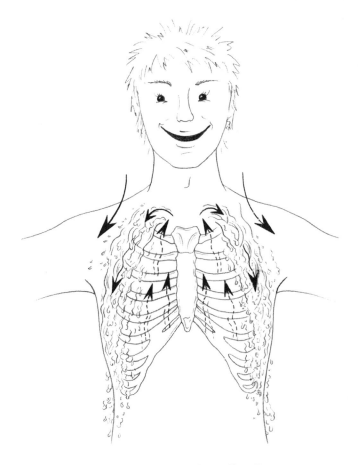

Figure 15.10   Water flowing down the ribs.

24. **Lateral flexion and bucket handles:** Laterally flex the spine and watch the ribs on the flexing side lower down like bucket handles and the ones on the extending side lift up like bucket handles.

25. **Lateral flexion and centering:** Laterally flex the spine. Watch the ribs on the flexing side center into the spine and the ones on the extending side rest and center in to the sternum (figure 15.11).

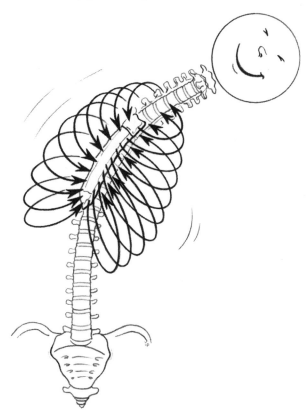

Figure 15.11 Lateral flexion with ribs.

26. **Rib accordion:** Imagine the rib cage to be folding up like an accordion on the flexing side. Imagine the ribs to be stretching like an accordion on the extending side.

27. **Flexible ribs in rotation:** Think of the ribs as very flexible as you rotate the spine. Compare this to rotation while feeling the ribs as part of a rigid rib cage. Teaching a correct position for the rib cage will tend to cause a rigid concept and reduce the ability to move, which means less exercise for the body.

28. **Ribs slide in rotation:** As you rotate the spine, imagine the individual ribs can slide over each other. Imagine them to be very slippery on top of each other, like layers of a multilayered sandwich. Notice how the image of slippery ribs can increase your spinal flexibility. This image also enhances lateral rotation.

29. **Spirals in rotation:** As you rotate the spine, imagine the ribs spiraling. The ribs on the ipsilateral side (the one you are rotating toward) spiral outward and the ribs on the contralateral side spiral inward (figure 15.12).

30. Rotation and approximation: As you rotate, the ribs move relative to each other, causing the intercostals to be stretched and finally pulled closer together. This means that the rib cage becomes slightly shorter in rotation, mirroring the same action happening in the intervertebral discs (see figure 12.28). Use the metaphor of a sponge being slightly compressed as you rotate your rib cage. When you come back to center, the sponge will rebound to its full height.

31. Rib power (sitting): Place a band over your head and sit on the other end, making the band slightly taut. Flex your spine and imagine the ribs

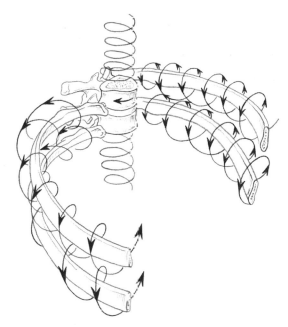

Figure 15.12　Ribs spiral in rotation (figure shows rotation to the right).

dropping or rolling down, then extend your spine and imagine your ribs floating and rolling up to extend your spine (figure 15.13). Repeat five times and remove the band to notice your naturally elevated alignment.

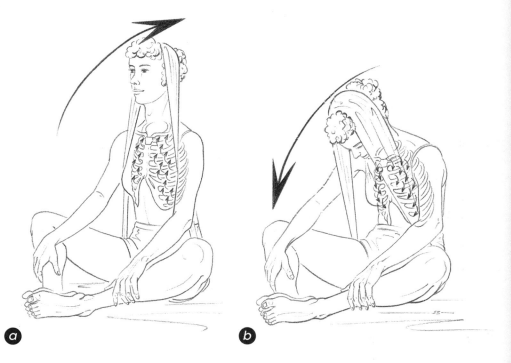

Figure 15.13　(a) Ribs lift in extension; (b) ribs lower in flexion.

Imagery Exercises for the Rib Cage in Breathing

1. **Breathing ribs:** Imagine your inhalation floating out in between your individual ribs, imparting a feeling of lift and lightness.

2. **Elastic intercostals:** Imagine your inhalation expanding the muscles between your ribs, the intercostals. As you exhale, imagine these muscles releasing. Notice how an elastic image for the intercostals affects your breathing.

3. **Float and drop:** As you inhale, imagine the bodies of the ribs being lifted while the joint heads slide down on the spinal and transverse facets. Since the joints are located at or near the spine, the feeling is up in front and on the side of the body and down in back near the spine during inhalation.

4. **Light and heavy rib heads:** Imagine the rib heads sliding down on inhalation, making the rib bodies float up in counterpoint. Enhance the rib heads with some extra imaginary weight while the rib bodies become lighter. Imagine light rib heads and heavy bodies during exhalation.

5. **Balloon-supported ribs:** On inhalation, imagine the rib bodies to be lifted upward by balloons while the rib heads slide down (figure 15.14). On exhalation, the rib bodies lower down and the rib heads slide up.

6. **Exhaling seesaw lift:** During exhalation and as the ribs drop downward, feel them providing the spine with a sense of lift. You can use the image of the seesaw. As the ribs go down, the other end, the spine, is lifted.

7. **Spiral lift:** The facet of the rib facing the transverse articulation is concave; the head of the rib facing the spine, however, is more convex. This causes the rib to perform a slight spiral action as it moves up and down.

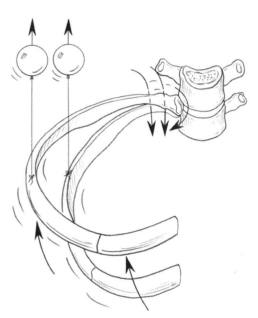

Figure 15.14 Ribs supported by balloons on inhalation.

8. **Rib cage as an umbrella (supine, standing):** Visualize the rib cage as an umbrella. The handle of the umbrella is in the pelvis, and the point is the top of the spine. The shaft of the umbrella is aligned with the central axis. As you inhale, the umbrella opens and widens all around—front, back, up, down, and sideways. As you exhale, the umbrella closes toward the central axis. Practice this image three or four times, accompanying an exhalation with a sibilant hiss. (Exercise adapted from Lulu Sweigard.)

9. **Rib oars (supine):** Imagine the interaction between the ribs and the spine to be like a rowing team propelling a slender boat through the water. The oars move in the opposite direction of the boat as the blades push though the water and transfer their leverage to the boat. On exhalation, the oars (ribs) move downward through the water's resistance, imparting upward force to the boat

(spine); on inhalation, the spine is embraced by the inflating lungs. In this way the ribs and lungs combine to create an upward push and expansion (exhalation and inhalation) against the spine (figure 15 15).

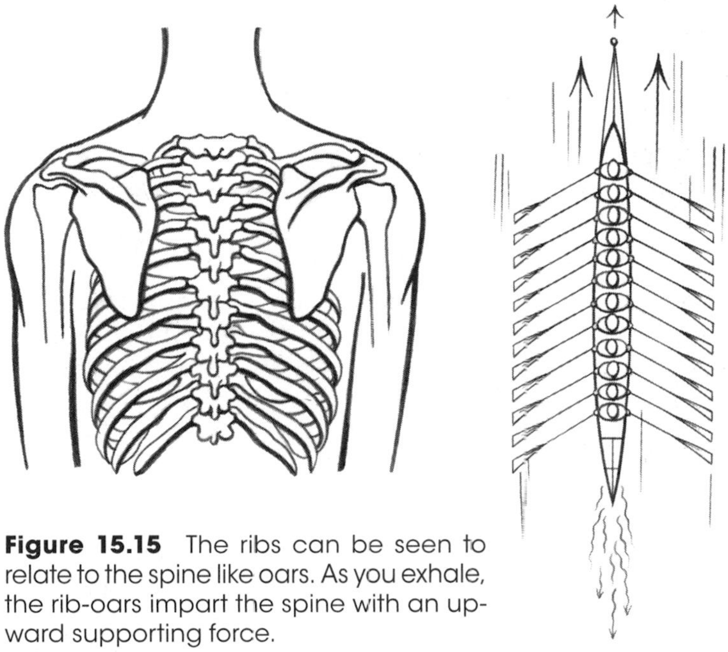

Figure 15.15 The ribs can be seen to relate to the spine like oars. As you exhale, the rib-oars impart the spine with an upward supporting force.

BREATH

The breath is a great teacher, leading you to new experiences and telling much about your current physical and psychological state. Any improvement in your alignment and movement patterns will improve your breathing patterns, and vice versa. You can survive without water for three days and without food for much longer, but within minutes the brain will starve from lack of oxygen. You breathe approximately 20,000 times a day. A small improvement in your breathing organization brings much improvement to your movement, energy, and life.

Lungs

You absorb oxygen into the body through the inner surface of the lungs, an extremely large contact area between the air and the body surrounded by the airtight pleura. The human breathing apparatus is quite different than that of a fish. A land-breathing system was a great evolutionary step and most likely occurred as a way to avoid predation and find food above water. There were challenges. Air is too thin for gills to work on land. You would most likely have to run around at 150 miles an hour to create sufficient air pressure for gills to work—not a very handy option. In addition, it is easier to extract oxygen from water than from air. A fish can take 90 percent of the oxygen out of water; humans take only 50 percent out of air. The solution was a bellows system that would actively take the air into the body and a very large surface for the oxygen transfer, the lungs.

In the beginning, the lungs were just air sacks. The lungs are passive in breathing in the sense that they do not muscularly contract or lengthen when you breathe.

Figure 15.16 A tree is a fractal structure, and the lungs can be likened to an inverted one.

Robert Lambiase/Phototake

The lungs are expanded and contracted by the movement of the diaphragm and ribs. To create the bellows system, the ribs were made mobile. As they moved out, the lungs were expanded; as they moved in, the lungs were contracted. This early system was inefficient, because the vacuum created by the expanding ribs sucked the organs up from below into the space that was meant for air. A membrane, the remnant of which is the diaphragm's central tendon, was created to separate the upper and lower cavities. This prevented the upward movement of organs during inhalation. Later this membrane was fitted with muscle fibers to actively push the organs down and increase the amount of expansion afforded to the lungs.

Such delicate organs as the lungs need to be well protected. The trachea and bronchi are the large passageways that guide the air to the alveoli, small bubblelike structures where the exchange of gases takes place. The basic shape of the lungs can be visualized as a hollow, upside-down tree. The trunk is the trachea in the upper chest; the first large branches are the bronchi, subdividing further into smaller and smaller branches, which eventually reach the spherical leaves, the alveoli. This tree is fractal in design, which means it bifurcates (subdivides) in a continuously similar way into ever smaller branches (figure 15.16). Even when you look very close, it still looks similar. The aforementioned connective tissue network, the circulatory system and neuronal branches, are fractal structures as well. Fractality allows the lung maximal use of available space.

Alveoli have a combined surface area of more than 100 square meters, and there are approximately 500 million alveoli in the lungs. Here oxygen molecules pass through the thin surface into the bloodstream where they are transported to the billions of cells contained within the body. This is where the actual breathing takes place, at the level of the cell. The exhalation of the cells, carbon dioxide, is then transported back to the lungs where it is expelled.

The right, larger lung is divided into three lobes; the left, smaller lung is divided into two lobes, leaving additional space for the heart (see chapter 10, figure 10.63). If this inverted tree is distorted, the alveoli are compressed and the alignment of the upper body will suffer. Inefficient alignment hinders deep breathing. Try the following experiment: Bend over into a hunched position and try to take a few deep breaths. Your breathing will be shallow and forced, which increases tension throughout the body. On the other hand, elastic, well-aerated lungs support good alignment. The lungs need to fill the entire space allotted to them if they are to function optimally.

Deep, calm, and rhythmic breathing creates balanced muscle tone, which favors ease of motion and dynamic alignment.

Breathing patterns are greatly influenced by your psychological state and vice versa. You breathe differently when you hear good news than when you hear bad news. You breathe differently when you watch a romantic movie as opposed to a comedy or drama. Your breathing patterns, as well as your alignment, are always being influenced by the environment and the people around you. When you're around a shallow breather, your breathing will tend to become shallow. If someone you're with has hunched shoulders, you tend to hunch your shoulders. Around someone whose breathing is deep and rhythmic, you gravitate toward that pattern. Breathing, alignment, and psychological factors are interdependent.

Breathing Exercises With a Partner

1. **Breathing with a partner:** Stand opposite a friend. Focus on each other's breathing. Do this for two or three minutes and notice how your breathing changes and perhaps adapts to your partner's. Take a moment to discuss your experiences.

2. **Movement and breathing with a partner:** Face your partner again. This time, as you exhale, bend your legs and as you inhale, stretch your legs. Notice how long it takes for both of you to breathe in the same rhythm. Then one of you should change your breathing rhythms on purpose. Notice how it may be more difficult to stay synchronized with your partner.

3. **Influencing each other's breathing:** Stand opposite a friend and repeat the previous exercise. Then have your friend deliberately go into a slouched posture with shallow breathing. Notice how your friend's breathing and posture affect your own breathing and alignment.

Imagery Exercises for the Lungs

1. **Lungs and shoulder alignment:** The lungs extend from the diaphragm, which ranges from the bottom six ribs all the way up to the space within the topmost ribs. It is important to allow the lungs their space; when you hunch your shoulders, the upper lung becomes cramped and is pushed downward.

2. **Massaging lungs:** Place your hand on one shoulder. Imagine the tip of your lungs below your touch. Slowly circle your shoulders and visualize the surrounding bones and muscles massaging your lungs. Imagine that this massage allows the lungs to regain their flexibility and shape. Circle the shoulders in the opposite direction as you continue to think of the internal massage. Rest your shoulders for a moment and focus on the lungs expanding. Imagine your breath flowing into this area. Compare the sensation between your two shoulders and repeat on the other side.

3. **Flexible alveoli:** Imagine your alveoli to be very flexible and stretchy as you breathe in. Imagine them to be like millions of flexible, elastic bubbles (figure 15.17).

4. **Spiral the air:** Imagine the air spiraling and swirling as it enters the nose and bronchi. Compare this to imagining the air moving linearly through these structures. You may notice that the spiraling and swirling imagery, which is more biologically appropriate, is easier to perform. Fluids naturally move in swirls, spirals, and eddies, not linearly.

5. **Breathing through the lobes:** Visualize the lobes of your lung: three on the right lung, two on the left lung. Imagine breathing into the lowest lobes. Now imagine breathing into the middle lobes. Now breathe into the upper lobes. Notice changes in postural sense as you do this. Now breathe into all the lobes of the lungs at the same time.

Figure 15.17 Elastic alveoli bubbles.

6. **Lung expansion:** As you inhale, the lungs expand in all directions, some of which may be more perceptible than others. Place your hands on the lower and lateral ribs. As you inhale, you will feel the ribs move laterally but you may also notice that your hands are moving slightly to the back. As you exhale, your hands will come inward but also move slightly to the front. Allow this rotary motion (side and to the back) to take place on inhalation. On exhalation, allow the inward and to-the-front motion to take place. If you allow only a lateral expansion of the ribs and lungs, you may feel restricted in your breathing.

Diaphragm

The most important muscle for breathing is the diaphragm (figure 15.18). Dividing the body into the abdominal and thoracic cavities, the diaphragm can be visualized as a lopsided mushroom with two small stems called crura. The right side of the mushroom is higher to accommodate the liver, which is significantly larger than the stomach (the stomach is situated on the left side). The diaphragm's central tendon is fused to the pericardium, the covering of the heart, via the ligamentum fibrosum. The pericardial sack is suspended superiorly via the thoracopericardial ligaments and anteriorly by the sternopericardial ligaments. Therefore, posture and breathing influence the position and movement of the heart. In other words, the pericardium, which contains the heart, is suspended like a three-point hammock from the spine, sternum, and diaphragm (figure 15.19). Additional support to the heart is provided by the aorta from above. The heart can be visualized as riding up and down on the diaphragm during exhalation and inhalation, receiving continuous movement therapy.

Various muscular parts of the diaphragm radiate from its central tendon. The costal part of the diaphragm attaches to the inner surface of the xiphoid process and to

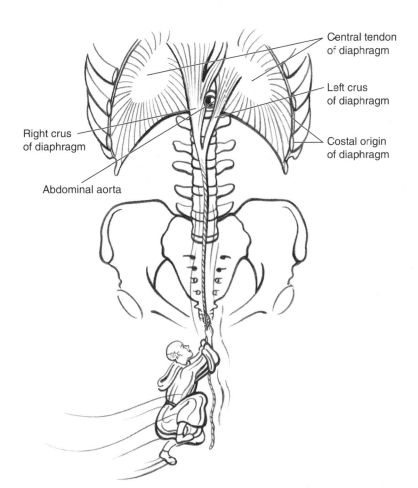

Central tendon
of diaphragm

Left crus
of diaphragm

Costal origin
of diaphragm

Right crus
of diaphragm

Abdominal aorta

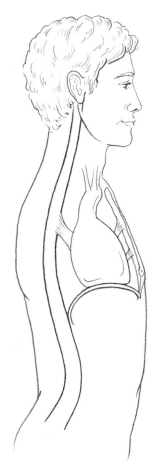

Figure 15.18   The left and right crura of the diaphragm as imaginary cords extending all the way down to the coccyx.

Figure 15.19   The heart sits on the diaphragm and is suspended by ligaments from the spine and sternum.

the lower six ribs and costal cartilage. The crural portion of the diaphragm attaches to the first, second, and third lumbar vertebrae on the right side and the first and second lumbar vertebrae on the left. The crura extend downward from the diaphragm next to the psoas and the quadratus lumborum, suggesting an intimate connection between breathing and locomotion. The medial and lateral arcuate ligaments are suspended above the psoas and quadratus lumborum and are fascially connected to these muscles. Because the iliopsoas is the most powerful hip flexor and lumbar stabilizer, restricted breathing adversely affects dynamic alignment.

Inhalation

As the diaphragm contracts on inhalation, its central tendon moves down relative to the ribs along the body's central axis. In deep breathing, the distance covered is 5 centimeters. In this sense, breathing is an axial (vertical) activity. Imagining axial movement of the diaphragm is a tool for improving dynamic alignment. Commonly the movement of the diaphragm needs to be more fully experienced at the sides and back of the body. Since the diaphragm moves down over a very large surface, it creates more space for the lungs than is apparent. Once the organs are fully compressed and moved inferiorly, the diaphragm continues to contract for a moment without moving farther down; it helps pull the ribs out to the side and up. The diaphragm first contracts to lower the central tendon and subsequently contracts to lift the ribs. During exhalation these actions reverse. The crura (Latin for lower leg) of the diaphragm can be visualized as muscular strings that help descend the dome of the diaphragm (see figure 15.18). Expansion of the rib cage during inhalation does not take place in the same direction and at the same time throughout the rib cage. When the central tendon stops moving down, the lower ribs are pulled upward and outward along an arc as mentioned previously. This expands the rib cage sideways; the much smaller upper ribs rotate forward and lift the sternum (minimally in quiet breathing). The external intercostals and other accessory breathing muscles aid in lifting the ribs.

The diaphragm pushing down on the organs during inhalation increases intra-abdominal pressure. Initially the organs resist in a springlike fashion and provide elastic recoil, which increases the contractile power of the diaphragm.

In the next stage, the organs are displaced downward. Since the lumbar spine blocks any path to the back, they move forward. The abdominal muscles lengthen and the abdominal wall expands to afford the organs more room. The downward displacement of the diaphragm is now relating to a horizontal forward movement of the abdominals.

Efficient breathing involves the abdominals and diaphragm in a constant interplay; they are antagonists in breathing yet may be synergists for dynamic lumbar stabilization. These two relationships need to be synchronized for good alignment.

Hollowing your abdominal muscles as a postural strategy prevents the organs from moving down and forward properly, impeding the diaphragm. In the first phase of breathing, a certain amount of abdominal tension may augment the pull of the diaphragm on the ribs, helping them elevate. Constant gripping of the abdominals creates compensatory actions such as lifting the shoulder girdle in an effort to increase the space within the lungs. This in turn raises the center of gravity (COG), making the body less stable and hindering balance and turns in dance.

The way to keep the abdomen from bulging is to ensure efficient interaction between the diaphragm, abdominals, and iliopsoas and create good organ tone. Holding in the abdominal muscles may weaken the abdominals in the long run by reducing (axial) movement of the (antagonistic) diaphragm. Good breathing organization means 24-hour conditioning for the abdominals and diaphragm, a feat that is hard to beat with an exercise system. A certain natural hollowing of the abdominal area follows good breathing patterns without requiring gripping or holding.

The muscles of the pelvic floor respond to inhalation by lengthening slightly. Contract your pelvic floor and notice the effect on your breathing. Release your pelvic floor and notice the effect on breathing. When you inhale, both the dome of the diaphragm and the pelvic floor move downward, but the muscle fibers of the diaphragm shorten while the fibers of the pelvic floor lengthen.

Exhalation

As you exhale, the muscle fibers of the diaphragm lengthen to allow its central dome to go up. The abdominal muscles assist by contracting to help push the organs back against the upward-bound diaphragm. The elastic recoil of the organs is an assistive factor. The ribs drop and move inward with the aid of gravity, expelling air from the lungs. Muscle release, gravity, and elasticity combine to make exhalation the easier of the two respiratory phases. The intercostals release tension built up during inhalation and aid the recoil of the ribs.

As mentioned earlier, the smaller the up-and-down motion of the diaphragm, the shallower the breathing. A complete exhalation stimulates a deep inhalation. Exhaling with a sibilant hiss between the teeth and tongue encourages the abdominal muscles to push in the organs and close the angle of the ribs. Hissed breath, a type of forced exhalation, lengthens expiration, teaching the abdominals complete expiration. Generally, lengthening your expiration is calming, whereas shortening your expiration will tend to create nervous activation.

Movement influences your ability to breathe. If you extend your spine, you are aiding the ability of your rib cage to bring air into the body. If you flex your spine, this movement will naturally aid the expelling of air. Running patterns in quadrupeds are favorably coordinated with breathing (figure 15.20). Spinal flexion will tend to push the organs up against the diaphragm, and spinal extension will tend to move the organs away from it.

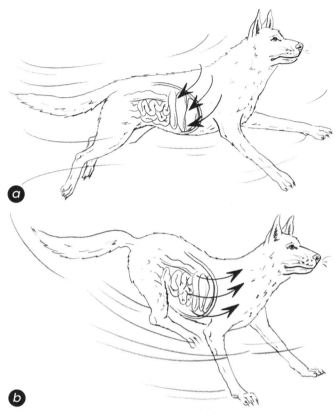

Figure 15.20 Dog running and diaphragm movement: *(a)* spinal extension favors organs moving down and away from the diaphragm; *(b)* spinal flexion favors the organs being pushed up against the diaphragm.

Summary of Breath

Nature designed breathing to be as effortless as possible. You do not need to suck air into the lungs. If you empty a bucket of water, you hear and see the water flowing out, but you don't notice the air flowing in to fill the vacuum. The motion of the rib cage and diaphragm and the lungs' encasing pleura create a vacuum that air flows in to fill. It could be said that the lungs are suspended within the rib cage through the negative atmospheric pressure of the vacuum. On inhalation, the air freely flows into the lungs through the nose or mouth, down the trachea, and into the bronchi and alveoli. If the airtight pleura is pierced, the lungs may collapse because the vacuum is impaired.

Breathing Exercises for the Diaphragm, Abdominals, and Pelvic Floor

1. **Exhaling through a straw (sitting):** Exhale through a straw. Do not take an extra-deep breath before you exhale. Do not push the air through the straw beyond your normal exhalation, and do not keep the straw clenched between your teeth as you exhale. Practice for about five minutes and notice how your breathing becomes calmer and longer. Repeat the exercise with an imaginary straw.

2. **Axial movement of diaphragm (supine, sitting, standing):** Imagine the diaphragm moving up on inhalation and down on exhalation. Visualize this

motion in line with your central axis. Place your hands horizontally at the front of your rib cage at the level of the diaphragmatic dome. Move your hands down with the inhalation and up with your exhalation to better visualize the movement.

3. **Diaphragmatic elevator (supine, sitting, standing):** Imagine the diaphragm to be an elevator moving up and down in its shaft (the ribs). As you inhale, the elevator moves down; as you exhale, it moves up.

4. **Diaphragm as soft cloth:** Imagine the diaphragm to be a soft cloth or scarf. As you inhale, imagine the cloth floating down and draping over the organs (figure 15.21).

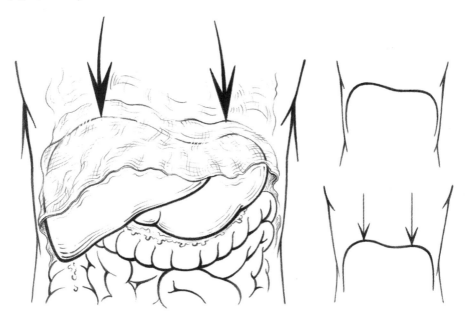

Figure 15.21 Diaphragm as a soft cloth draping over the organs.

5. **Diaphragm stretch:** The muscle fibers of the diaphragm shorten when you inhale and lengthen when you exhale. They are muscles like any other, but you rarely consciously stretch them. Place your right hand on the left side of your rib cage in the zone of opposition between the ribs and the diaphragm. Your left arm is stretched up over your head. Laterally flex your torso to the right as you exhale and watch the diaphragmatic fibers lengthening both as the result of your movement and breathing. As you return to the upright position, inhale and watch the fibers shorten. Repeat this action seven times. Then notice how different it feels to breathe into your left lung and your right lung. The left lung and rib cage have more freedom to move, causing the breath to deepen. Repeat on the other side.

6. **Abdominals and diaphragm:** Use one hand to model the movement of the diaphragm and the other hand to model the movement of your abdominals. The hand in front of the belly is vertical in orientation, and the hand modeling the diaphragm is horizontal. As you inhale, move the diaphragmatic hand down and the abdominal hand forward. As you exhale, reverse the direction. Notice the interaction of these two movements. Now imagine the organs being moved between the diaphragm and the abdominal wall. Imagine the movement to be beneficial to the blood circulation through the organs.

Notice also what happens if you do not allow the abdominals to move. The organ-piston will push against the diaphragm, making breathing more challenging.

7. **Downward reach of crura (supine, sitting, standing):** Visualize the left and right crura of the diaphragm as imaginary cords extending all the way down to the coccyx. Visualize someone pulling these cords as you inhale and releasing them as you exhale (see figure 15.18).

8. **Spiraling diaphragm and lungs:** Focus on the two lungs and the two sides of the body. As you inhale, imagine two opposing columns of outwardly rotating spirals through your diaphragm and lungs and down into the pelvis (figure 15.22). As you exhale, the direction of the spiral reverses and goes inward.

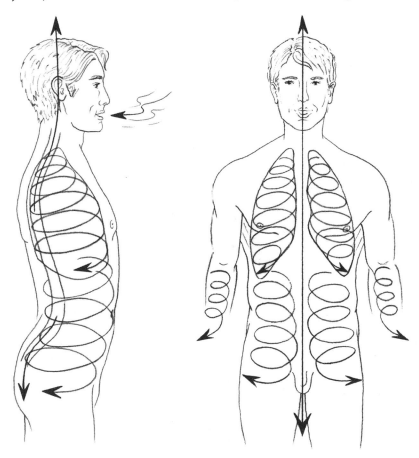

Figure 15.22   Spiraled breathing during inhalation.

9. **Diaphragmatic parachute (sitting, standing):** Imagine the diaphragm to be a parachute. As you inhale, the center of the parachute drops downward, the sides billow, and the strings loosen (figure 15.23*a*). As you exhale, the parachute expands its dome upward as the strings become taut and stretch down toward the pelvic floor (figure 15.23*b*).

10. **Pelvic balloon (supine):** Imagine a balloon situated in the pelvis. As you inhale, the balloon expands equally in all directions. The balloon pushes against the inner borders of the pelvis, spreading the arms of the pubic bones and somewhat releasing the pressure of the two arms pushing against each other at the pubic symphysis. As you exhale, the balloon collapses toward the center. The

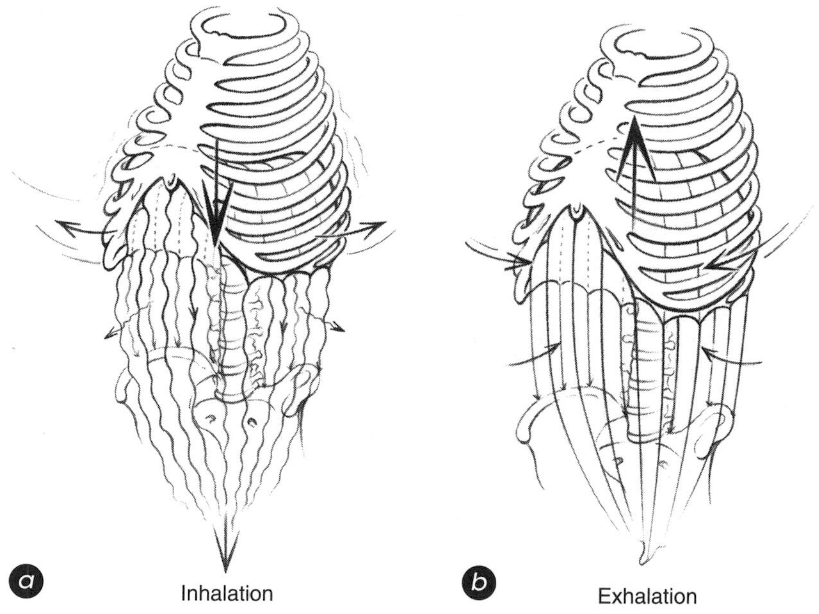

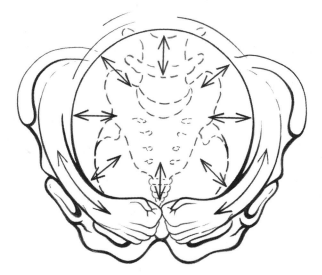

Figure 15.23   The diaphragm as a parachute.

arms of the pubic bones move inward and push more solidly against each other at the pubic symphysis. Visualize the balloon from the inside as well as the outside. Be sure to visualize all sides of the balloon expanding equally (figure 15.24). Repeat the exercise 10 to 12 times, intermittently using a sibilant "sss" on exhalation. (Exercise adapted from André Bernard.)

Figure 15.24   A balloon situated in the pelvis.

11. **Navel flower petal (supine):** Imagine the navel to be a pretty flower petal. As you exhale, visualize the flower petal falling through your body to the ground. As you inhale, rest your mind or create a new flower petal. Repeat the exercise three or four times.

12. **Belly water rings (supine):** As you inhale, imagine circular waves expanding away from your navel. Watch these rings expand into space throughout the length of your inhalation. Rest your mind while you exhale.

13. **Body balloon (supine):** Picture your whole body as a large inflatable balloon. As you inhale, fill your body from the center outward, expanding the balloon. In the pause before you exhale, fill your arms and legs. As you exhale, watch the air flow out of the shriveling balloon. Pause in the collapsed position before the next inhalation. (Exercise adapted from *Zen Imagery Exercises* [1991] by Shizuto Masunaga.)

14. **Cell lungs (supine):** Imagine each cell of your body to be a small lung in its own right. As you inhale, imagine millions of cells inhaling, taking in oxygen. As you exhale, visualize millions of cells exhaling.

15. **Exhaling tension (supine):** As you inhale, imagine your body releasing its tension into the incoming air. All tension leaves your body with your exhalation. Let your breath discover all the areas in your body that are tense. Think of your breath as an explorer, capable of discovering hidden tension. As soon as a tense spot is detected, breath flows into the area, collects the tension, and transports it out of your body with your next exhalation.

SUPPORT FOR ABDOMINAL ORGANS

In addition to the ribs, the spine has help from other areas in supporting the weight of the upper body both upright and in bending. The organs of the abdominal cavity provide help in the form of hydrostatic lift when they are restrained by a surrounding muscular wall. Like water-filled balloons in a tin can, if compressed from any direction, the organs generate equal, load-supporting hydrostatic pressure in all directions (Radin et al. 1992). The way you breathe influences the efficiency of upper-body motion because the abdominal muscles are in constant interplay with the diaphragm. Insufficient muscular tone in the abdominals and diaphragm impairs the hydrostatic system. On inhalation, the lungs more actively support the spine like air-filled balloons. On exhalation, the deflated lungs are least supportive and the abdominal muscles and walls of the abdominal cavity are most active.

Breathing also causes complex movement of the abdominal organs, such as the stomach, liver, and intestines. Initially these organs are compressed similar to a sponge. The organs react by storing elastic energy similar to a coiled spring, which can be used to aid the following exhalation. Organ compression during inhalation also stimulates nerves and vessels of the area and supports balanced muscle tone of the abdominal wall. The compression also stimulates the glands in the surface of the organs to produce a fluid secretion, which keeps them mobile in relation to each other. This is very important for dynamic alignment and movement.

Relaxed and deep inhalation also maintains normal tone in the organs, which enables them to remain autonomous as opposed to sagging down and pulling on their attachment sites, which in turn puts more strain into the musculoskeletal system. Organs that lack tone and blood circulation often cause tension and stiffness in the back and other areas of the body. The increased circulation caused by deep, relaxed breathing also improves digestion, which is very important for feeling energetic and for rapid regeneration. The amount of blood flowing back upward through the vena cava doubles during inhalation and supports the venous flow of blood to the right atrium of the heart. Full, functional breathing relieves the heart and allows you to be more concentrated and energetic throughout the day.

It is advisable to follow a strategy of relaxed and complete breathing. It is not advisable to constantly hold the abdominals. This may create momentary cosmetic improvement of the contour, but all the previously mentioned functions are impeded, leading to lower muscle tone, poor posture and circulation, and weakened muscles of the abdominal wall.

Imagery Exercises for the Organs and Breath

1. **Elastic recoil:** With each inhalation, imagine the organs being elastically compressed by the diaphragm (figure 15.25); with each exhalation, imagine the organs recoiling elastically to push the diaphragm back up.

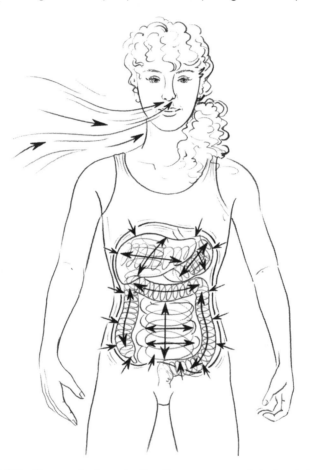

Figure 15.25 Organs being elastically compressed during inhalation.

2. **Compressing a sponge:** Use the image of a sponge being compressed on inhalation and expanding on exhalation. The recoil action of the organs is the opposite movement of what you are experiencing in the rib cage, which expands on inhalation and shrinks on exhalation.

3. **Organ-lung counterbalancing:** As the lungs enlarge on inhalation, the organs are compressed; as the lungs shrink during exhalation, the organs expand.

4. **Return of blood:** Imagine that your breathing is assisting the return of blood to the heart, helping your heart to relax and regenerate. Then focus on the fact

that your breathing is increasing the lubrication of the organs, allowing them to support greater ease of movement of the spine, pelvis, and thorax.

5. **Resting on the abdominal balloon:** Imagine your abdominal cavity to be filled with a large balloon. Visualize your diaphragm and upper torso resting on this balloon. Exhale and imagine the balloon shrinking to initiate a forward flexing of the spine. Let your upper body be carried downward on the deflating balloon. Once you have exhaled completely, reinflate the balloon on inhalation. Watch as the increasing pressure created by the expanding balloon pushes the upper torso back up to vertical. Try this exercise at various speeds.

6. **Lungs and heart sliding:** To liberate your upper spine and create a feeling of mobility and flexibility within your chest and whole upper body, imagine the lungs swinging and sliding around your heart as you flex and extend your spine. You alternately imagine the lungs rolling softly around the heart. As you extend your spine, imagine the heart moving forward between your lungs; as you flex your spine, imagine the heart swinging back between your lungs (figure 15.26).

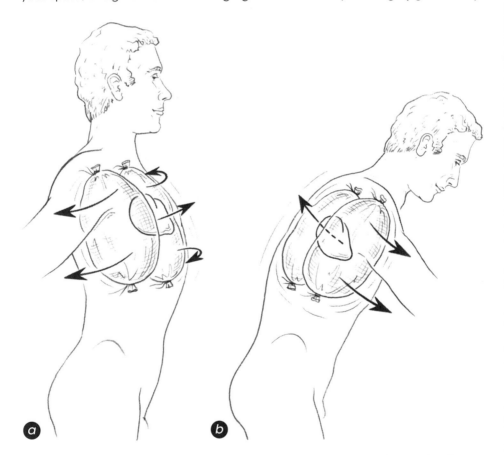

Figure 15.26 *(a)* Extending the spine and swinging your heart forward between the lungs that are rolling back; *(b)* flexing your spine and rolling the lungs forward around the heart.

7. **Feeling the kidneys:** Put your hands on your lower back and visualize the kidneys sliding up and down on the psoas and the quadratus lumborum as you breathe. As you inhale, the kidneys move down; as you exhale, they float back up. Make the image as fluid as possible and repeat for 12 breaths. Perform

circular movements with the palms of your hands, imagining that you are massaging the kidneys. Remove your hands and notice the effect on your pelvic posture and spine.

8. **Lateral flexion with lungs and organs:** Lift your arms overhead. Flex your spine to the left and imagine the lungs and organs on the right side stretching and expanding like a sponge (figure 15.27). The organs on the left side are being compressed like a sponge. Allow the kinesthetic imagery of the organ-sponges on the left side expanding to bring you back to the upright position. Now practice assisting lateral flexion with the organs on the other side. Repeat the action several times and notice the newfound sensation of internal support when you return to a neutral position.

9. **Lung and organ initiation:** Rotate your upper body and imagine you are initiating the movement from the organs (figure 15.28). Feel the lungs and colon swinging around the spine. What does it feel like to move from the inside as opposed to thinking of a muscular movement initiation? Notice what movement qualities are inherent when focusing on the organs.

Figure 15.27 Lungs and organs as sponges in lateral flexion.

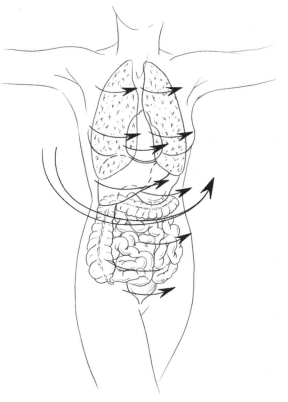

Figure 15.28 Initiating movement from the organs.

SKIN AS AN ORGAN

The skin, the body's protective cover, is a large, delicate sensory organ. Lungs are a comparatively recent evolutionary development, so primitive animals breathed through their skin. Humans retain some of this primitive ability to exchange gases through the surface of the skin, which is able to absorb, excrete, and respire. Surprisingly, the skin is practically waterproof.

Varying in thickness from one millimeter on the eyelids to three or more millimeters on the palms of the hands and soles of the feet, the skin has many functions. Sweat glands and sensory nerves in the skin keep the mind informed of the relationship between the body and its immediate surroundings, tactile stimulation, temperature changes, and sources of pain. The skin can even perceive sound waves (Kükelhaus 1978). If you have ever been near a large gong when it was sounded, you have experienced this. The pressure changes in the air can be felt all over the body.

Imagery Exercises for the Skin

1. **Sensing sound through the skin (movement improvisation):** Imagine that you are perceiving a sound such as music with the entire surface of your body. Feel the sound reaching remote parts of the skin—the back of the neck and knees, the soles of the feet, the space between the fingers, and the heels. Then imagine the music soaking into your skin. Absorb the music with the entire surface of your body.

2. **Breathing through the skin (supine):** Imagine yourself breathing through your skin. Concentrate on specific areas. Breathe in and out through the soles of your feet . . . through your knees . . . through the back of your neck . . . through your lower back . . . through your face . . . through your shoulders. Experiment with other body parts. Notice where it seems easy to breathe and where your pores seem to be constricted.

SUMMARY

If you improve something that you are doing all the time, such as breathing, your alignment, movement, and whole life benefit. Since the lungs are passive organs, efficient breathing requires a flexible and mobile rib cage and diaphragm. The rib cage consists of 12 ribs, thoracic spine, sternum, joints, muscles, and ligaments. Besides aiding in breathing, the rib cage protects vital organs and serves as an origin of many muscles that relate to the head, arms, and pelvis. An astonishing 760 square feet or 6,000 miles of capillaries are contained in the lungs, allowing for a large surface for gas exchange.

The diaphragm below the lungs is made of muscular tissue with a large central tendon. When you inhale, the diaphragm moves down, expanding the lungs and compressing and moving the organs below. The abdominals serve as a mobile body wall to accommodate the movement of the organs in breathing. An increase in abdominal pressure caused by co-contraction of the abdominals and diaphragm can assist in childbirth but should not be used as a general postural strategy because it greatly increases capillary pressure in the upper body. When you exhale, the situation reverses: The lungs recoil and the organs move up and back. The organs greatly benefit from a constant movement and massage between the pelvic floor and diaphragm.

PART IV

Returning to Holistic Alignment

In chapter 2, you took a macroview, discovering the principles and unifying theories of posture and alignment. The chapters in part III focused on the microaspects—detail and subtle adjustment of anatomy. The microview creates a deeper understanding of the macroview. But lest you lose sight of the spine for the vertebrae, you will return for a final macroview, or holistic view.

Holistic alignment is dynamic in the sense that it is an expression of the whole body in motion, in a unified state of being, rather than a conglomerate of contradicting actions within the body. The way I was originally taught alignment sounded like this: "Hold this in, tighten that, push that down, lift that up!" The body seemed to be one contradiction on top of another. This was the question in my head: *How can I lift this up when I am supposed to push that down?* Needless to say, it was not a very happy state of affairs. In holistic alignment, the whole body, every cell, is working toward the same goal. When your alignment is holistic, it is effortless, because you have not suppressed one of the body's needs in favor of another.

Chapter 16 discusses the plumb line, defines ideal alignment, increases your clarity about dynamic alignment (versus static alignment), and helps you understand the nature of joint stability. You will also look at why "pulling up" might not be an advisable alignment strategy. Finally, the imagery presented in chapter 17 is specific to creating an understanding of alignment both from a cognitive and experiential standpoint.

Chapter 16

Definitions of Dynamic Alignment

Don't just solve problems; experience solutions.

Armed with essential knowledge in biomechanics and anatomy, we can return to the discussion of dynamic alignment begun in chapter 2. This will bring you to a deeper level of understanding and experience.

Dynamic alignment allows you to have the maximum amount of resources available to move your body efficiently because they are not being wasted in an effort to statically align or maintain an ineffective alignment. To state this biomechanically, ideal posture or body alignment should engender minimal torques and stresses throughout the kinematic chain (Norkin and Levangie 1992). Torque, or moment, is the tendency of a force to rotate an object around the axis. The ground reaction force (GRF) vector and line of gravity (LOG) create a line through the body that determines the torque in each body segment. If the LOG passes in front of the axis of a joint between two segments, the top segment will receive a forward gravitational moment. In figure 16.1, you can see a slight forward moment in the tibia because the ankle joint is behind the LOG. The femur receives a slight forward moment as well because the LOG passes just in front of the center of the knee. The LOG passes just behind the center of the hip socket, creating a backward rotational moment of the pelvis.

Anatomists disagree about the path of the LOG through the spine. In chapter 12, figure 12.1, I have depicted the LOG passing through the bodies of the lumbar and cervical vertebrae (see Kendall 1983). Other anatomists show the line passing farther to the rear, behind the bodies of the lumbar and cervical vertebrae and in front of the bodies

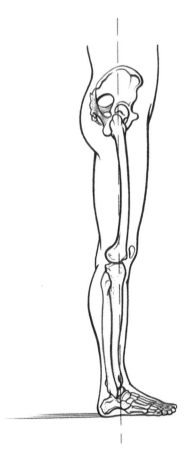

Figure 16.1 The plumb line of the leg.

of the thoracic vertebrae. In this scenario, gravity is more likely to increase the spinal curves. The LOG is generally seen as passing through the odontoid process of the axis.

PLUMB LINE

It is easy to visualize the relationship between body segments and the LOG using a plumb line of the type that builders use to ensure that a wall is being built perpendicularly to the ground. As mentioned earlier, there are differing opinions on the ideal plumb line. The following is a widely accepted version of the "correct" plumb line as viewed sagittally: The plumb line passes just in front of the outside anklebone, just in front of the midline of the knee, through the greater trochanter (round protrusion) of the femur, through the shoulder girdle, and through the earlobe (see figure 16.1).

Because humans are bilaterally symmetrical, it is much easier to define the ideal plumb line from the front or back. From the front, it ideally passes through the tip of the nose, the center of the sternum, and the pubic symphysis and touches the floor equidistant from both feet. Figure 16.2 shows this plumb line for a one-legged stance, where it passes through the foot of the standing leg.

Each leg can be further examined from the front. A plumb line passes through the second toe, between the malleoli (anklebones), through the center of the knee, and through the center of the hip joint (see figure 10.61). In genu valgum (knock knees), the knees are more central than the plumb line, causing compression stress on the outside and tensile stress on the inside of the knees. In genu varum (bow legs), the knees are farther outside than the plumb line, causing tensile stress on the outside and compression stress on the inside of the knees.

Viewed from behind, the plumb line ideally passes through the center of the back of the head and the spine and touches the floor equidistant from both feet. As mentioned, sideways deviations of the spine from the plumb line are called scoliosis. Ideally, from front or back, the eyes, ears, shoulders, crests of the ilia, knees, and inner borders of the feet should be on the same level (see figure 16.2). Although generally caused by postural imbalance, some deviations, especially those in the eyes and ears, are due to genetic differences. Discrepancies in the levels of the iliac crests may result from differing leg lengths or postural inequalities.

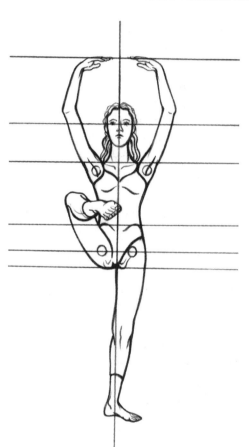

Figure 16.2 The plumb line for a one-legged stance.

MEDIAN ALIGNMENT

There is a certain amount of postural sway in the upright position, which means that you are never perfectly motionless when standing. Your body is losing and regaining balance most of the time. Alignment is truly median, the peak of a bell-shaped curve representing the sum of all your alignment states over time. In practical terms, this means that you must observe your alignment at various times of the day to gain a functional understanding of it. Photographs with a plumb line in place can help you evaluate posture, enabling you to compare your self-image of alignment with the outward reality over time.

DEFINING IDEAL ALIGNMENT

Sweigard (1974) defines the upright posture as follows:

> *the consistent and persistent alignment of the skeletal structure in relation to the line of gravity when the subject assumes an easy standing position with the weight evenly distributed—according to his or her own judgment—on the feet, with the ankles in the sagittal plane of the femoral joints and with the arms hanging freely at the sides. (p. 173)*

André Bernard used to define ideal alignment along these lines: Ideal alignment in the standing position can be found when you allow the parts of the structure to balance as close to the central axis as the individual structure permits.

The second part of the definition discusses the COG: A low COG will make the body more stable. This should be achieved without jeopardizing the principles of biomechanical alignment discussed previously. The body's central axis should be as long as the person's individual build allows for without the addition of any tension-producing lengthening effort. Derived from Sweigard, this definition emphasizes the biomechanics of reducing harmful torque and the kinetic nature of the never-static body segments. Energy is saved by decreasing the effort required for balancing the first-class levers throughout body (head rests on spine, vertebrae rest on top of each other, pelvis balances on femur heads).

This brings us back to the building-block model—align the major centers of mass above each other and you create ideal alignment. It is important to remember that this alone will not create good movement if the major centers of mass are above each other because they were forced to be there. Just as important as the mass relationships of the individual parts are their functional relationships. (How does my leg movement affect my pelvis? How does a change in my head position influence my spine?) As mentioned previously, a "well-placed" person may not move as successfully as one who is a master at sensing and adjusting the relationships among his body parts. Obviously, a dancer's poor alignment does not predict this skill. Ideally a dancer combines a good sense of how the centers of mass balance on top of each other with a high awareness of the functional relationships throughout the body. In the final analysis, both skills are reverse sides of the same coin.

DYNAMIC VERSUS STATIC ALIGNMENT

A human being is a biological system that is inherently complex and cannot be explained by reductionism—that is, by putting a human being in a fixed schemata and judging the person relative to that. It is important not to evaluate someone's alignment based on rigid geometric criteria only. A dancer, for example, may henceforth be focused on her "bad posture," constantly imagining that her posture is not good enough, which will have a deleterious effect on coordination. To this day I remember my dance teacher declaring, "Your back looks crooked like a banana!"

Figure 16.3 The Eiffel Tower's alignment is static and unchanging; a person's alignment should be dynamic and variable.

Human alignment is part of a biological system that involves variability and even chance. Your alignment of today is not exactly the same as it was yesterday. Your alignment changes throughout the day and will be changing throughout your life. Awareness of how to maximize postural potential on a given day is much more useful than using a fixed set of postural rules. Experiential understanding of the problem is key. The image that worked for you yesterday may not help today. The dancer who imagines his central axis as a magnet pulling his body parts close as he spins may experience great success on day 1, but on day 2 the image does not help. This does not make the dancer or the image wrong. Change and variability are biology, and once this is accepted, they lead to a variable approach to imagery. The dancer then has the tools to come up with the image that makes today's spins work. You are not like the Eiffel Tower, which has stood with just about the same alignment for over 100 years and will hopefully do so for another 100 years (figure 16.3).

Many factors go into the mix that determines good alignment, such as limberness, reactivity, balance, muscle tone, mood state, motivation, and imagery ability. The test of alignment is movement. Does your improved alignment improve movement coordination? Good alignment should also contribute to the long-term health of your musculoskeletal system.

A fixed sense of alignment does not necessarily correlate with better coordination. On the flip side, even if a dancer is not well aligned, but his functional awareness of posture is superior to that of a well-aligned dancer, he will be more skilled at moving. If the first dancer improved his dynamic sense of alignment, the liberated biomechanical relationships among body segments would further improve his dancing. Alignment and movement are interdependent only insofar as your definition of alignment is dynamic.

DYNAMIC AND STATIC STABILITY

Dynamic stability is the ability to maintain or to return to a position after a disturbance. A common cue in exercise is to "stack your bones" and to "stack your vertebrae." The human body, however, does not simply function as a stack that stabilizes by being placed properly. In fact, the weight of the head is enough to topple the bones of the neck, and the weight of the torso would collapse the lumbar spine were it not for muscles increasing stiffness and a nervous system adding control. The human body is dynamically stabilized. Dynamic stabilization can be defined as the ability of a system to maintain its trajectory despite some outside disturbance. To be able to do this, the system needs to have a certain stiffness or resistance to change, but it also needs something that observes the system (proprioception) and controls it (the brain) based on these observations (Cholewicki 2010). Observation and control need to be in constant dialogue with each other.

If you want to make a building more stable, you could reinforce its walls and make a more solid foundation. This does not apply to the human design that deals with constantly changing forces. Human alignment is adaptive. A strategy involving relying entirely on stiffening the system by co-contracting muscles actually would make the body less dynamically stable. Alignment that is dynamic requires a counterbalancing or inertial strategy, force absorption (damping), and a proprioceptive rather than simple strength-based model. Healthy human alignment also requires constant minute changes of posture-maintaining muscles to make sure that no one muscle is overly exerted and that no joint, bone, or tissue is constantly compressed in the same fashion.

Look at the example of lifting one leg forward and off the floor. The moment you think of doing this, your muscles are already responding and preparing the trunk and whole body for the upcoming change. Some muscles in the support leg start increasing their recruitment; they become stiffer to ready themselves to carry the whole weight of the body while some of the muscles of the leg that will lift off the floor start relaxing. Muscles of the trunk are changing their activation to prepare for the slightly altered position as the pelvis and torso will be moving to counterbalance the forward and upward moving leg (Belenkii, Gurfinkel, and Paltsev 1967). In addition, breathing patterns will adjust as the rib cage moves and oxygen requirements change. These changes are highly complex and function mostly at a level beyond your consciousness. This is a good thing, because otherwise moving would be near impossible—the number of perceptions would be overwhelming.

The static strategy of voluntary co-contraction of certain muscles does not suffice as a form of postural training and mostly leads to gripping. Under these circumstances the body will try to change activation patterns as you move and counterbalance and dampen forces, but this is impeded by the voluntary contraction of muscles, resulting in tension.

According to Vleeming and colleagues (2008), joint stability is defined as follows:

> Static and dynamic stability throughout the body is achieved when the active, passive and neuromotor control systems work together to transfer load. Adequate compression of the joint surfaces must be the result of reaction forces acting at the joint, if stability is to be insured. Adequate means ideally tailored to the existing situation, using the least amount of compression to guarantee stability: In fact, efficient neuromuscular control.

The definition states that the least amount of compression should be used to achieve stability, while common postural strategies revolve around adding more compression. Neither a prescribed amount of designated muscle contraction nor the positional model of alignment, in other words placing someone in a position that is deemed correct, can be reconciled with that required of a constant adaption and updating of the level of stiffness and the amount of effort required.

Different people use different strategies of motor control to achieve the same movement goals and postures. Even if the movement seems exactly the same, each person will use muscles with slightly different timing and force. The same person will use unique strategies when performing the same movement repeatedly caused by variability in the motor control system. Variability reduces strain on the neuromuscular system and joints as loads are constantly redistributed (Van Beers 2004).

The strategies reflected in this book mirror the individualistic nature of alignment and movement. The same imagery may be used by many people with differing results, and dynamic alignment can be created through a great variety of imagery. If you consider the fact that the body is composed of many interacting systems such as organs, fluids, and connective tissue, all of which contribute to erect alignment, the definition of ideal alignment can be expanded to encompass all its components:

> *In ideal alignment, the sum effort of all tissues allows for minimal waste of energy in the upright standing posture and maximum use of the resources available for motion in accordance with the individual's structure.*

And by emphasizing dampening and oscillation, we find the following definitions of dynamic alignment emerge:

> *Dynamic alignment allows counterbalancing movements and oscillations to dampen the effect of movement, gravity, and muscular forces.*

By allowing variability and oscillation, your body will be elastically aligned. And finally:

> *Dynamic alignment is the ability of the body to react adaptively through force absorption, counterbalancing, and oscillation to create the most economical physical state in all positions.*

How, then, do you teach alignment if not by placement or telling which muscle to contract? The answer is to teach alignment through variable imagery and movement. Dynamic alignment will result from good movement organization, which is based on embodied anatomical function. When teaching alignment, it is key to allow students to try new strategies of alignment and discover what works best for them. The following sections contain many exercises that can be applied toward this aim. The more proprioceptive ability is trained, the better the students will become at controlling their alignment in movement.

A strategy that I propose and has been shown to be effective is the following (Rieman and Franklin 2010): Perform simple movements that involve balancing tasks and gradually increase the challenges while using imagery that remains efficient and free of tension. As the challenges increase, the brain will be implementing more efficient solutions to meet the increasing demands on dynamic alignment. When such a sequence is performed, you are left with a feeling of alignment that is dynamic. You can use the exercises in this book to achieve this aim and lead you through the process of embodying anatomical function. Changes in a single muscle, muscle group, or joint must be integrated into an adaptive whole to be useful for the dynamic whole.

Imagery Exercises for Dynamic Alignment

1. **Postural sway:** Close your eyes and notice your postural sway. Notice how the sway is constantly changing and never the same.
2. **Relationship to center (standing, walking, leaping):** In the standing position, focus on the center of your body. Think of the relationship between the parts of

your body and this center. Notice how this relationship changes as you inhale and exhale. Take a few steps and notice how the relationship changes. Jump up and down a few times and notice any changes in the relationship of the parts to the perceived center.

3. **Counterbalancing:** Close your eyes and notice your alignment. Now imagine lifting your leg forward and up. Notice whether this already causes your body to move, if only very slightly. Now actually lift your leg and notice what parts of your body are counterbalancing to make this possible. Notice also what happens to your torso and pelvis when you lift one or both arms. Move back to standing on both legs with your arms at your sides. Notice your position. See if you can keep your body exactly as it is when you lift your leg. Do not let your pelvis or torso move even in the slightest bit. Notice how this may cause tension and limit the degree to which you can lift your leg.

4. **Static image, counterbalancing image:** Start in the standing position. You shall again lift your leg in this exercise. First try a strategy of static imagery. Think of your spine and standing leg as immobile poles: Perhaps the leg pole is stuck in the ground and quite rigid. Notice how high you can lift your leg with this image. Now imagine that your lifting leg is a pendulum swinging forward and your supporting leg is a pendulum swinging backward in the opposite direction as a counterbalancing measure. Notice that it is now easier to lift your leg.

5. **Breathing through layers (standing, sitting, supine):** Focus on the layers of your body. Think of your inhalation originating at your center. As you inhale, watch your breath spread radially out through the consecutive layers to the final layer, your skin. As you exhale, watch your breath fall back toward your center.

6. **Variability:** Close your eyes and notice your postural sway. Now lift your arms over your head and notice how your alignment adapts. Lower your arms again. Record the way you just performed this action. Now repeat it again in exactly the same fashion. If you are sensing acutely, you will notice that the second time and the third and so forth are always slightly different.

PULLING UP AND IDEAL ALIGNMENT

This is a rather controversial subject. Dancers and Pilates and yoga teachers sometimes try to "pull up," or lift the pelvis or other areas of the body, in an effort to "improve alignment." When pulling up, you maintain your alignment by holding body parts high and under firm control. After a review of the science and principles already covered, you can safely conclude that this causes more problems than it solves. As Mabel Todd (1972) writes, it is desirable to have a naturally high chest where "the curve of the dorsal aspect of the sternum and the curve of the ventral aspect of the spine are symmetrical in their design" (p. 166). At the same time, she points out the following: "It is futile to attempt to lengthen the axis of the spine by expanding or pulling up the chest" (p. 185).

A dropped chest or anteriorly rotated pelvis obviously fails to conform to dance or fitness aesthetics or alignment and disturbs organs and breathing mechanisms. In particular, dancers who started training later in life, having adopted "cool" postural habits, may not have time to go through the lengthy process of changing postural patterns to achieve a natural "high chest." As Sweigard (1974) says, *"All voluntary contribution to a movement must be reduced to a minimum to lessen interference by established neuromuscular habits*" (p. 6, italics in original). Sweigard continues, "The idea, the concept of movement, is the voluntary act and the sole voluntary component of all movement. Any further voluntary control only interferes with the process of movement and inhibits rather than promotes efficient performance" (p. 7).

When pulling up, you add plenty of voluntary control, lifting the ribs, holding the abdomen, and tucking the buttocks. In dance class I have been told to "suck my stomach back and up to my spine," which would keep "the weight out of my legs and make me become lighter." I always respectfully listen to every statement, but this kind of instruction invariably caused me to become very rigid when I was supposed to become lighter. I could not breathe properly and the chance of fluid, centered movement, with full spatial awareness happening under these circumstances seemed minimal.

Unless you can drop a few sandbags like a hot-air balloonist, you will not become lighter by sucking up your abdomen. From the standpoint of physics, the only way to become lighter is to lose mass or to move to a planet with less gravitational pull. The intention behind pulling up is, of course, a very good one: You are trying to defy gravity, improve your alignment, and be up on your legs, and so on. New York-based ballet teacher and choreographer Zvi Gotheiner said the following to me:

> *Pulling up is a cultural notion, originating in the effort at the French courts to ennoble oneself with high postural carriage. There is also an instinctual aspect; you gain a certain power by looking at the world from above. Pulling up in no way benefits alignment and efficient movement.*

In my opinion, the aim of creating strong abdominals, or a "honeybee" waist, by artificially pulling in the abdominals is self-defeating. Holding in the abdomen reduces the amount of motion available to the diaphragm and spine. Since the abdominals oppose the action of the diaphragm and organize the organs toward the center of the body on exhalation, their activity and intrinsic training are reduced. Also, the organs receive less of a massaging effect since their motion within the abdominal cavity is restricted. This reduces their tone and makes the abdomen bulge out even more. Often dancers ask me this question: "How is it possible that my belly is sticking out when I do so many sit-ups?" The answer is that there is no better training for the abdominals and the organs than deep breathing, which is not possible with your belly voluntarily compressed toward the spine. I will mention, however, that in many cases nutritional factors also play a role in such abdominal imbalances.

If your placement is good and your abdominal muscles are well conditioned, you should be able to forget about them when moving. The abdominal muscles, however, are often insufficiently conditioned. Daily exercises, including breath and sound, are required for increasing the tone of the abdominals as well as the underlying organs.

The aim is to achieve an energized rather than a tight feeling in the abdominal area. If you join with gravity, you will be much more successful in the end. According to physical principles, you need to use the ground reaction force as efficiently as possible. Guide this force up through your body (primarily through the bones). Liberated from their tasks of superfluous gripping, the muscles begin to create optimal alignment and lift. The nervous system becomes more alert, the reflexes more nimble. Freeing the muscles eliminates any uncontrolled precipitation of weight down into the knees and feet. When you feel your weight, you gain control. Kevin Poe, who danced the part of Mephistopheles in the musical *Cats* in New York, Zurich, and Vienna, related the following in a conversation with me in 1994:

> *I was standing in the wings one day during the ballet Raymonda, when I noticed how completely exhausted I was from the last dance. At this point, I realized that I was not breathing correctly. As soon as I relearned how to breathe in movement, I did not feel exhausted anymore from dancing. Singing helped a lot in this respect. I imagine that I can sing while dancing, or at least speak. One should be free enough to sing the song of one's movement out loud. This will also greatly benefit your phrasing. If you habitually grip your stomach muscles, you cannot breathe, certainly not sing. Intentional contraction of these muscles needs to be reserved for power moves.*

The lifted position also raises the center of gravity, making you less stable, necessitating even more holding and tightening to maintain position. The problem is that the way to achieve lightness is perhaps counterintuitive. To be lighter, you need to appreciate your weight, to explore how the limbs lever against the ground to move the body's weight and use the ground reaction force. This requires practice because body weight and limbs are not commonly experienced as levers for movement. When you lift a sandwich weighing one-20th the weight of your arm, do you feel the weight of the sandwich or the weight of your arm? You feel the weight of the sandwich, although the arm is much heavier. Although feeling 15 pounds of arm every time you lift a mouthful of food would probably be an effective dieting strategy, the brain will not allow you to be overly occupied with how heavy a limb feels when moving because this unnecessary distraction would endanger your survival. As mentioned in part I of this book, you peer through a rather small peephole at incoming sensations, getting only the information you need for the immediate tasks at hand. To include differentiated experience of weight, you must widen this peephole.

SUMMARY

In this chapter you learned dynamic alignment and discussed muscular co-contraction, force absorption, and counterbalancing in light of alignment. Ideal body alignment should cause minimal torques and stresses throughout the kinematic chain. The pressure on joints during movement should be adequate and ideally tailored to the existing situation, using the least amount of compression to guarantee stability.

Dynamic stability is the ability to maintain or to return to a position after a disturbance. Dynamic stabilization can be defined as the ability of a system to maintain its trajectory despite some outside disturbance. To be able to do this, the body needs force absorption, counterbalance, and something that observes the system and controls it based on the observations. Observation and control need to be in constant dialogue with each other; this is the job of the brain and nervous system.

If you want to make a building more stable, you could reinforce its walls and make a more solid foundation. This does not apply to the human design, which deals with constantly changing forces. Human alignment is adaptive. A strategy that relies entirely on stiffening the system by co-contracting muscles actually would make the body less dynamically stable.

Finally, you found that the strategy of lifting to improve alignment makes you less stable, necessitating holding and tightening to maintain position. However, the goal of dynamic alignment is to allow you to have the maximum amount of resources available to move your body efficiently.

Chapter 17

Integrating Dynamic Alignment Exercises

The closer your body image relates to your actual design, the better your function.

The study of alignment includes the in-depth evaluation of the relationships among the body segments as itemized in part III. Improving one relationship improves the whole. You may also improve your alignment by consciously or unconsciously imitating people with good alignment or through bodywork, somatic therapies, and psychological insight. However, and I cannot emphasize this enough, *for any improvement in alignment to be permanent, the changes need to become part of your body image. The new alignment pattern needs to become part of your identity, or you will always slip back into old habits.* Because your body image is based largely on how you see and feel yourself, using imagery is a very direct way to repattern your alignment.

The exercises in this chapter focus on increasing your sense of center, which in turn facilitates a cohesive energy and biomechanical optimization in erect posture—always in a dynamic sense. You can practice the imagery individually or during a class to remind you of principles of alignment. The subdivisions simply yield emphasis for each image. To gain maximum benefit, visualize those that appeal to you.

ALIGNMENT IN SUPINE POSITIONS

The following exercises should be done in the constructive rest position or supine lying positions and aided by a clear horizontal sense of the floor.

The Floor Is Your Guide to Verticality

Heighten your awareness of the floor beneath you. Notice which parts of the body rest on the floor and which do not. Notice differences between the right and left halves of your body. Do not force any segment onto the floor; just allow each one to rest on the supporting surface. Notice the difference in sensation in your body parts as you inhale and exhale. Notice the areas that seem a bit achy or tense. Notice those that feel good.

Flying Carpet

Imagine that you are resting on a flying carpet. Watch the carpet slowly lift you off the ground, supporting every part of your body equally. As the carpet floats back to the ground, see the body segments—head, torso, and pelvis—arrive at the same time.

Spheres

One at a time, visualize the pelvis, torso, and head as individual spheres. Allow the three spheres to line up on top of each other. Visualize the center point of each sphere from pelvis to head. Imagine a line connecting them. Begin by connecting only two spheres at a time: Connect the center of the pelvic sphere to the center of the thoracic sphere. Then connect the center of the thoracic sphere to the center of the head sphere. Finally, connect all three spheres. Watch them float off and settle on the ground while you maintain the connection among them.

Meeting of Planes

Imagine the median frontal plane. Does it pass through the earlobes, acromion (shoulder tip), and greater trochanter? Which of these bony landmarks are in front of this plane, and which are behind it? Is the plane parallel to the floor?

Now imagine the median sagittal plane. Does it pass through the centers of the nose, chin, breastbone, navel, and pubic symphysis? Which of these landmarks are to the left of the plane, and which are to the right?

Now imagine both the sagittal and frontal planes at the same time. Locate the line where the two planes meet. This is your central axis. Is your central axis parallel to the floor? Can you visualize the entire length of the axis, or are some parts easier to see than others?

ALIGNMENT IN SITTING POSITIONS

Sitting is a good position for practicing alignment because you can work from a strong pelvic base—more specifically, from your pelvic floor and sit bones, which provide a clear guideline for the previously mentioned structures. Also, you can address many problems in alignment by becoming more aware of pelvic placement.

Balanced Sitting

1. **Balancing weight on sit bones:** Place your weight equally on both sit bones. Notice whether you feel the weight more on the front or the back of them. Try to place your weight on the center of the sit bones. (If you have the tendency to slouch, to tilt the top of the pelvis to the rear, you will feel as if you are hollowing your back.) Imagine the midline of the body passing through the dens of the second cervical vertebra and equidistant from both sit bones. Visualize the midline grazing the lumbar vertebrae and passing through the superior cervical vertebrae. The median sagittal plane passes through the earlobes and the acromion (figure 17.1).

2. **Tailbone jingling:** If you release the muscles around your coccyx (tailbone), it may help you to feel more centered and grounded on your sit bones. For example, imagine your tailbone to be a chain of ringing bells—a nice auditory image (figure 17.2).

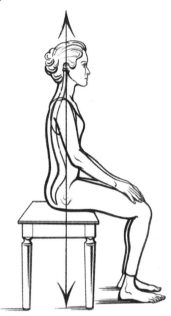

Figure 17.1   Sitting alignment.

Figure 17.2   Tailbone as a jingling chain of bells.

3. **Shifting weight on sit bones:** Place your weight equally on both sit bones. Shift your weight to the right sit bone and push it down into the chair. Shift your weight to the left sit bone and push it down into the chair. Notice which sit bone

feels stronger. This sensation will provide information on your pelvic alignment. Repeat the action several times, then return to centered sitting.

4. **Walking on sit bones:** Imagine your sit bones to be little feet. Walk forward to the front edge of the chair and back on your sit bones (figure 17.3). Repeat the sit-bone walking several times. Then return to balance on both sit bones and notice your alignment. (Exercise from Franklin [2006], *Inner Focus, Outer Strength*.)

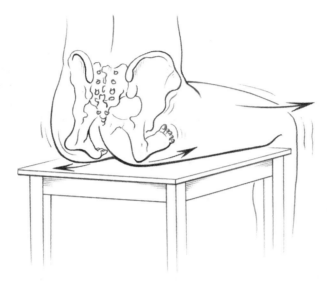

Figure 17.3   Imagine walking on the sit bones.

5. **Regaining good sitting posture:** Starting from your head, roll your spine forward and down until your head is hanging over your legs. Now bring your head back up until you feel you have found good alignment. Roll down your spine once again and try an image to help you regain your upright sitting posture: Think of the pelvic floor dropping down through the chair toward the floor as you bring your head back up. How does this method compare to the original way of coming up? Now try again, only push the pelvic floor down to bring you up. Practice visualizing the pelvic floor dropping and pushing down on an exhalation or an inhalation to bring you back up.

STANDING AND WALKING ALIGNMENT

Compared to body size, human beings' center of gravity (COG) is relatively high, making standing a challenge. Walking is easier because the continuous momentum of moving forward has a certain stabilizing effect. Except for the first of the following exercises, which you should do only while standing, I recommend doing the exercises first while standing and then while walking.

Noticing Reflexes

Stand with your eyes closed and become aware of your whole body. You may notice continuous tiny adjustments in your posture taking place automatically. Your body is constantly falling and regaining its center. This helps the body to balance the work of standing between many muscles and joints, increasing efficiency. Your reflexes operating at a subconscious level are keeping you from falling over. Notice also that this allows a constantly changing combination of muscles to maintain your upright posture.

Spheres on a String

Picture yourself as a series of spheres on a string: The string is your central axis, the spheres your body segments. An imaginary force is pulling both ends of the string in opposite directions, aligning the spheres on top of each other. See and hear them (as they touch) in perfect alignment, with their centers of gravity directly above each other. Allow the image to have movement, which is in the nature of an oscillating string. (See figure 2.4.)

Magical Planes

Visualize the median sagittal plane passing through the nose, center of the chin, sternum, and pubic symphysis. Visualize several parallel horizontal planes passing through the body, as though the plates of a magician have sliced painlessly through it. One touches the bottom of the sit bones, one passes through the hip sockets, one grazes the superior crests of the hips, and one passes through the left and right acromion. The eyeballs rest on another one, and the arms, which are held overhead, as in figure 16.2, touch still another one. (Figure 16.2 shows a modern dancer. Even without perfect balletic turnout, the previous instructions hold true.)

Imagining Your Central Axis

1. **Sit bones and condyles melt:** Imagine the convexities of the occipital condyles (projections at the bottom of the back of the head) and the sit bones lengthening downward until they are aligned in the same frontal plane. Visualize the central axis located between the sit bones and the occipital condyles (figure 17.4).

2. **Odontoid determines the plumb line:** Visualize an axis through the odontoid process extending upward and downward and made perfectly perpendicular by the downward pull of a ballast. The ballast is aligned in the same frontal plane as the talus (figure 17.5).

3. **Oscillating spine in walking:** As you walk, imagine the oscillations of the spine. With each step you take, allow the spine to reverberate just slightly, like the string of a bass guitar being plucked. Notice how easy it is to swing your legs. Now imagine your spine to be a rod with no oscillations. Notice how this affects your walking.

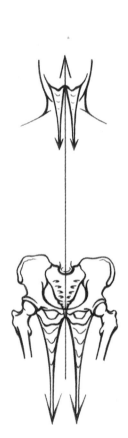

Figure 17.4 Convexities of the occipital condyles and the sit bones lengthening downward.

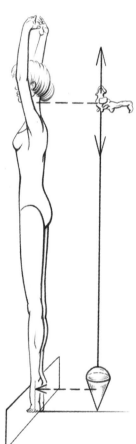

Figure 17.5 An axis through the odontoid process extends upward and downward, made perfectly perpendicular by the downward pull of a ballast.

RELEASING EXCESS TENSION

Obviously, one of our main goals is to create alignment that is dynamic and as effortless as possible—ready to meet any challenge. Tension is not a good state of readiness because it exhausts the muscles and other tissues of the body. If your muscles are tense, they are overly contracted. Needless to say, when you move, you need to contract your muscles, which is less feasible if they are already contracted. Therefore, tension defeats your purpose of readiness and ease.

Releasing Around a Pole

Visualize your central axis as a round elastic pole. Surrounding this axis is your body, which is composed of layers of soft cloth draped over the top. Watch the cloth fall toward the central axis.

Central Axis and Fluffy Clouds

Like clouds surrounding a mountain peak, your body surrounds your central axis. As you move, the fluffy layers of clouds move with you. Experiment with the image in movement. Start with sitting, then walking and running (figure 17.6).

Figure 17.6 Imagine your body consisting of soft clouds that hover around your central axis.

Hanging From a String

Imagine your body hanging easily from an elastic string attached to the top of your head and dangling into perfect alignment. Experiment with this image in movement—start sitting, then walk and run. Allow the string to initiate your motion. Don't focus on the fact that the string is pulling you upward, but concentrate on the feeling of suspension. (Of course, the string pulls you upward or you could not hang from it, but direct your attention to the fact that you are hanging from it.) (Exercise adapted from Stephanie Skura.)

Experiencing Centrifugal Force

Imagine that your body is attached to the center of the Earth via your line of gravity (LOG) and that the centrifugal force created by Earth's rotation extends your axis, making it point away from the core, perpendicular to the Earth's surface. You can visualize this image more easily by comparing it to swinging an object around on a string held in your hand; in this case, you are the object and the earth is your hand. If you swing the object quickly enough, the string becomes taut.

Hanging Upright

As you stand, think of yourself hanging from the ceiling. Your shoes are glued to the ceiling and you are hanging from them (you can't fall out of them, of course). You are now being pulled upward. In this position, gravity (coming from above your head) pulls you into perfect alignment.

Intensifying the Experience of the Central Axis

1. **Head on geyser:** Imagine your central axis to be a waterspout or geyser. Your head floats effortlessly on top of this column. Visualize your shoulders and the surface of your body as the water falling back down to the ground. Allow your head to bob on top of the column of water. As the geyser becomes stronger, your head is buoyed upward; as it weakens, your head bobs back and forth. Let the power of the water increase the height of your head (figure 17.7).

2. **Ice cream pop:** Imagine your body to be an ice cream pop. As the ice cream (shoulders) melts, the stick (central axis) emerges (figure 17.8).

3. **Flowing water:** Stand with your feet on a small wedge of wood so that the front of your feet is higher than your heels, or lean against a wall with your hands. This position will stretch the back of your calves. Maintain this position for a minute while visualizing water flowing down your back, carrying all tension down over your heels and into the ground. Get off the incline and stand upright. You may

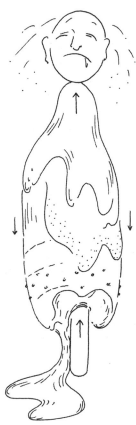

Figure 17.7 The central axis as a waterspout or geyser that your head floats effortlessly on.

Figure 17.8 Melting like an ice cream pop.

immediately notice a floating, lifted feeling. (To simulate the flowing of the water, a partner can brush her hands down your back and the back of your legs.)

4. **Tiny bubbles:** Imagine your central axis to consist of a stream of tiny bubbles like those found in champagne or mineral water. The bubbles surge upward between the sit bones, through the thorax and neck, and out the top of the head. They come from an inexhaustible source located between your feet. Hear the crackle and pop of the bubbles; feel them gliding up the front of the spine, perhaps tickling it on their way. You may imagine the bubbles to have a color, such as red (as in raspberry syrup) or green (as in peppermint syrup). How do the different colors affect you?

5. **Volcano erupts (standing):** Visualize a volcano shooting its fiery missiles into the air up along your central axis.

6. **Spiraling plant (standing):** Visualize a plant spiraling up around a wooden shaft. The shaft is your central axis. Watch as the plant grows ever taller, its leaves reaching toward the sky.

Leg Alignment

1. **Creating equal footprints:** Imagine yourself standing on sand. Look at the impressions your feet are making to see if they are equal in shape and depth. If not, imagine a smooth patch of sand and create equal footprints.

2. **Melting greater trochanter:** Visualize the leg axes. Imagine the outside of your legs melting downward. Specifically, imagine the greater trochanter melting down the sides of your legs (figure 17.9).

3. **Waterspouts:** Visualize water shooting up through both legs, as if fire hoses are located under your feet. The waterspouts are perpendicular to the floor and shoot straight up into the acetabulae (hip sockets) (figure 17.10). These water columns can support the weight of the pelvis. The returning water flows back down the outside of the legs. Have your partner place his hands around your ankle as both of you visualize the force of water shooting up through the area being touched. Repeat the procedure several times with your partner's hands around your lower leg, your knee, the middle of your thigh, and finally, over your hip socket. To complete the exercise, your partner should glide his hands down the sides of your legs, then glide one hand out over the toes and the other down over the heels.

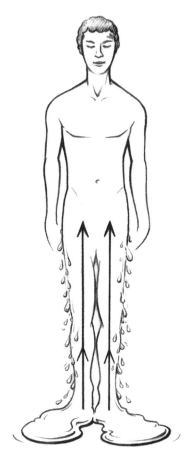

Figure 17.9 The outside of your legs melting downward.

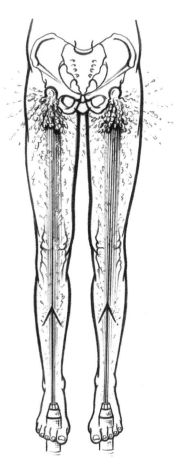

Figure 17.10 Water shooting up through each leg.

CONTINUING IMAGERY EXERCISES

Although you were born with the natural ability to use imagery, many of your imagery skills may have dissipated in adolescence and adulthood, when exposing your fantasy life becomes an aberration outside of psychotherapy or personal development workshops. The inner eye often becomes dark and shrouded as the immense influx of visual information from every direction saturates your senses. Television, computer screens, video games, and smart phones deliver a stream of captivating prefabricated visions. Turning on the inner screen may initially seem rather unexciting by comparison. But once you have discovered this treasure trove of fabulous insights and well-being, you will gain the ability to transform your body, mind, and life with help from the most sophisticated circuitry: your brain and nervous system. Every invention in existence today was born from this inner source, and it is ready to provide your alignment, movement, and life with a continual flow of inspiration.

Bibliography

Achterberg, J. 1985. *Imagery in healing.* Boston: Shambhala.

Alexander, G. 1976. *Eutonie.* Munich, Germany: Kösel.

Alfassa, M. 1982a. *A diary for all times.* Pondicherry, India: All India Press.

Alfassa, M. 1982b. *The great adventure.* Pondicherry, India: All India Press.

Angier, N. November 10, 2010. Bodies are as good as nature allows. *New York Times.*

Aurobindo, S. 1996. *The synthesis of yoga.* Pondicherry, India: Aurobindo Ashram Press.

Barba, E., and N. Savarese. 1991. *A dictionary of theatre anthropology.* London: Routledge.

Barker, J., and C.A. Briggs. 1999. Attachments of the posterior layer of the lumbar fascia. *Spine* 24(17): 1757-1764.

Bäumlein-Schurter, M. 1966. *Übungen zur Konzentration. (Exercises for concentration).* Zurich: Origo.

Bayés, A., L.N. van de Lagemaat, M.O. Collins, M.D.R. Croning, I.R. Whittle, J.S. Choudary, and S.G.N. Grant. December 19, 2010. Characterization of the proteome, diseases and evolution of the human postsynaptic density. *Nature Neuroscience* 14: 19-21.

Belenkii, V., V.S. Gurfinkel, and Y. Paltsev. 1967. Elements of control of voluntary movements. *Biofizika* 12: 135-141.

Bogduk, N. 1997. *Clinical anatomy of the lumbar spine and sacrum.* London: Elsevier.

Brumagne, S. 2010. The complexity of sensory function in spinal control and low back pain. Proceedings of the 7th Interdisciplinary Congress on Low Back and Pelvic Pain, Los Angeles.

Brumagne, S., P. Cordo, and S. Verschueren. 2004. Proprioceptive weighting changes in persons with low back pain and elderly persons during upright standing. *Neuroscience Letters* 386: 53-65.

Carey, T.S., A.T. Evans, N.M. Hadler, G. Lieberman, W.D. Kalsbeek, A.M. Jackman, J.G. Fryer, and R.A. McNutt. 1996. Acute severe low back pain. A population-based study of prevalence and care-seeking. *Spine* 21(3): 339-344.

Carpenter, C.B. 1894. *The principles of mental physiology* (4th ed.). New York: Appleton.

Chiao, R.Y., P.G. Kwiat, and A.M. Steinberg. 1993. Faster than light? *Scientific American* 269: 38-46.

Cholewicki, J. 2010. Spine stability and low back pain: What can the models contribute? Proceedings of the 7th Interdisciplinary Congress on Low Back and Pelvic Pain, Los Angeles.

Cholewicki, J., and S.M. McGill. 1996. Mechanical stability of the in vivo lumbar spine: Implications for injury and chronic low back pain. *Clinical Biomechanics* 11: 1-15.

Chopra, D. 1990a. *Magical mind, magical body.* Chicago: Nightingale-Conant.

Chopra, D. 1990b. *Quantum healing.* New York: Bantam.

Clark, B. 1963. *Let's enjoy sitting-standing-walking.* Port Washington, NY: Author.

Clark, B. 1968. *How to live in your axis—your vertical line.* New York: Author.

Clark, B. 1975. *Body proportion needs depth—front to back.* Champaign, IL: Author.

Cohen, B. 1993. *Dynamic rotation of foreleg.* Amherst, MA: Author.

Cohen, B. 1994. *Sensing, feeling, and action: The experiential anatomy of body-mind centering.* Northampton, MA: Contact Editions.

Cohen, B., and M. Mills. 1979. *Developmental movement therapy.* Amherst, MA: Authors.

Crommert, H. 1998. Neural control of locomotion: Sensory control of the central pattern generator and its relation to treadmill training. *Gait and Posture* 7: 251-263.

Daprati, E., D. Nico, S. Duval, and F. Lacquaniti. 2010. Different motor imagery modes following brain damage. *Cortex* 46(8): 1016.

Dardik, I., and D. Waitley. 1984. *Quantum fitness.* New York: Pocket Books.

Dart, R.A. 1950. Voluntary musculature in the human body: The double spiral arrangement. *The British Journal of Physical Medicine* 13(12): 265-268.

Debarnot, U., T. Creveaux, C. Collet, A. Gemignani, R. Massarelli, J. Doyon, and A. Guillot. 2009. Sleep related improvements in motor learning following mental practice. *Brain and Cognition* 69: 389-405.

Dossey, L. 1985. *Recovering the soul.* New York: Bantam.

Dowd, I. 1990. *Taking root to fly.* Northampton, MA: Contact Editions.

Dror, I.E., and S.M. Kosslyn. 1994. Mental imagery and aging. *Psychology and Aging* 9(1): 90-102.

Durkheim, K.F.G. 1992. *Hara, the vital center of man.* London: Allen & Unwin. (Original German edition).

Epstein, G. 1989. *Healing visualizations.* New York: Bantam Books.

Feldenkrais, M. 1972. *Awareness through movement.* New York: Harper Collins.

Feuerstein, G. 1996. *The Shambhala guide to yoga.* Boston: Shambhala.

Fick, L.J., E.V. Lang, H.L. Logan, S. Lutgendorf, and E.G. Benotsch. 1999. Imagery content during nonpharmacologic analgesia in the procedure suite: Where your patients would rather be. *Academic Radiology* 6(8): 457-463.

Flanagan, O. 1991. *The science of mind.* Cambridge, MA: MIT Press.

Franklin, E. 1996. *Dance imagery for technique and performance.* Champaign, IL: Human Kinetics.

Franklin, E. 2004. *Conditioning for dance.* Champaign, IL: Human Kinetics.

Franklin, E. 2006. *Inner focus, outer strength.* Hightstown, NJ: Princeton Books.

Franklin, E. 2009. *Beautiful body, beautiful mind.* Hightstown, NJ: Princeton Books.

Freeman, L.W., and D. Welton. 2005. Effects of imagery, critical thinking, and asthma education on symptoms and mood state in adult asthma patients: A pilot study. *Journal of Alternative Complementary Medicine* 11(1): 57-68.

Fritz, R. 1984. *The path of least resistance.* Salem, MA: DMA.

Fuchs, M. 1984. *Funktionelle Entspannung. (Functional relaxation).* Stuttgart: Hyppokrates.

Fuller, B. 1975. *Synergetics.* New York: Macmillan.

Gandevia, S.C. 1996. Kinaesthesia: Role for afferent signals and motor commands. In L.B. Rowell and J.T. Shepherd (Eds.), *Handbook of physiology, section 12. Exercise: Regulation and integration of multiple systems* (pp. 128-172). New York: Oxford University Press.

Gandevia, S.C., D.I. McCloskey, and D. Burke. 1992. Kinaesthetic signals and muscle contractions. *Trends in Neuroscience* 15(2): 62-65.

Ganis, G., W.L. Thompson, and S.M. Kosslyn. July 2004. Brain areas underlying visual mental imagery and visual perception: An fMRI study. *Cognitive Brain Research* 20(2): 226-241.

Gelman, D., D. Rosenberg, P. Krandell, and R. Crandall. 1992. Is the mind an illusion? *Newsweek* 116 (April 29): 46.

Gibbons, S. 2010. Primitive reflex inhibition and sensory motor training improves cognitive learning function and outcomes in chronic disabling low back pain: A case series with follow-up. Proceedings of the 7th Interdisciplinary Congress on Low Back and Pelvic Pain, Los Angeles.

Gottlieb, D. 1988. GABAergic neurons. *Scientific American* 258(2): 38-45.

Guillot, A., and C. Collet. 2005. Duration of mentally simulated movement: A review. *Journal of Motor Behavior* 37(1): 10-20.

Haerdter, M., and S. Kawai. (Eds.). 1988. *Butoh.* Berlin: Alexander.

Hall, C.R. 1998. Imagery use by athletes: Development of the sport imagery questionnaire. *International Journal of Sport Psychology* 29: 73-89.

Hall, C.R. 2001. Imagery in sport and exercise. In R. Singer, H. Hausenblas, and C. Janelle (Eds.), *Handbook of sport psychology* (2nd ed., pp. 529-549). New York: Wiley.

Hawkins, A. 1991. *Moving from within.* Pennington, NJ: A Capella Books.

Heiland, T., E. Franklin, and E. Rovetti. 2010. Do metaphorical, metaphorical-anatomical, and global images support increased jump height among university dancers? 20th Annual Meeting of the International Association for Dance Medicine and Science, Birmingham.

Hodges, P. 2010. Strategies for motor control of the spine and changes in pain: The deep vs. superficial muscle debate. In Proceedings of the 7th Interdisciplinary Congress on Low Back and Pelvic Pain, Los Angeles.

Hodges, P.W., and C.A. Richardson. 1996. Inefficient muscular stabilization of the lumbar spine associated with low back pain: A motor control evaluation of transversus abdominis. *Spine* 21: 2640-2650.

Holmes, P.S., and D.J. Collins. 2001. The PETTLEP approach to motor imagery: A functional equivalence model for sport psychologists. *Journal of Applied Sport Psychology* 113: 60-83.

Hölzer, B.K., J. Carmody, K.C. Evans, E.A. Hoge, J.A. Dusek, L. Morgan, R.K. Pitman, and S.W. Lazar. 2010. Stress reduction correlates with structural changes in the amygdala. *Social Cognitive and Affective Neuroscience* 5(1): 11-17.

Hotz, A., and J. Weineck. 1983. *Optimales Bewegungslernen. (Optimal kinesiology)*. Erlangen, Germany: Perimed.

Jacobson, E. 1930. Electrical measurements of neuromuscular states during mental activities: Imagination of movement involving skeletal muscle. *American Journal of Physiology* 91: 597-608.

Juhan, D. 1987. *Job's body*. Barrytown, NY: Station Hill Press.

Kapandji, I.A. 1986. *The physiology of the joints, volume 2: The lower limb* New York: Churchill Livingstone.

Kavner, R.S. 1985. *Your child's vision: A parent's guide to seeing, growing and developing*. New York: Simon & Schuster.

Keleman, S. 1985. *Emotional anatomy*. Berkeley, CA: Center Press.

Kendall, F.P. 1983. *Muscle testing and function*. Baltimore: Lippincott Williams & Wilkins.

Kingmann, L. 1953. *Peter's long walk*. New York: Doubleday.

Klein-Vogelbach, S. 1990. *Funktionelle Bewegungslehre. (Functional kinetics)*. Berlin: Springer.

Kosnick, H. 1927. *Lebensteigerung. (Life enhancement)*. Munich: Delphin.

Kosnick, H. 1971. *Busoni: Gestaltung durch Gestalt. (Shaping through form)*. Regensburg, Germany: Bosse.

Krauss, R. 1950. *I can fly*. (Little Golden Book Series). New York: Simon & Schuster.

Kükelhaus, H. 1978. *Hören und Sehen in Tätigkeit. (Hearing and seeing in action)*. Zug, Switzerland: Klett und Balmer.

Kükelhaus, H. 1984. *Urzahl und Gebärde. (Primal number and gesture)*. Zug, Switzerland: Klett und Balmer. (Original edition Frankfurt am Main, Germany: Alfred Metzner, 1934).

Kükelhaus, H. 1988. *Unmenschliche Architektur. (Inhuman architecture)*. Cologne, Germany: Gaia.

Larsson, M. 2010. The management of lower back pain: Whose responsibility? Proceedings of the 7th Interdisciplinary Congress on Low Back and Pelvic Pain, Los Angeles.

Linton, S. 2000. A review of psychological risk factors in back and neck pain. *Spine* 25: 1148-1156.

Lips, J.E. 1956. *The origin of things*. New York: Fawcett.

Lloyd, R., B. Parr, S. Davies, and C. Cooke. 2010. No "free ride" for African women: A comparison of head-loading versus back-loading among Xhosa women. *South African Journal of Science* 106(3/4). Available at www.sajs.co.za.

Lotze, M., G. Scheler, H-RM Tan, C. Braun, and N. Birbaumer. 2003. The musician's brain: Functional imaging of amateurs and professionals during performance and imagery. *Neuroimage* 20: 1817-1829.

Lovett, A.W. 1903. A contribution to the study of the mechanics of the spine. *American Journal of Anatomy* 2: 457-462.

MacPherson, A., D. Collins, and S. Obhi. 2009. The importance of temporal structure and rhythm for the optimum performance of motor skills: A new focus for practitioners of sport psychology. *Journal of Applied Sport Psychology*: S48-S61.

Masunaga, S. 1991. *Zen imagery exercises*. Tokyo: Japan Publications.

Matt, P. 1993. *A kinesthetic legacy: The life and works of Barbara Clark*. Tempe, AZ: CMT Press.

Maxwell, M. 1984. *Human evolution*. Sidney: Croom Helm.

Mechelen, W. 1996. Subject-related risk factors for sports injuries: A 1-yr prospective study in young adults. *Medicine & Science in Sports & Exercise* 28(9): 1171-1179.

Mees, L.F.C. 1981. *Das menschliche skelett. (Form and metamorphose)*. Stuttgart: Urachhaus.

Merlau-Ponty, M. 1962. *Phenomenology of perception*. London: Routledge.

Meyer, H. 1853. Die Mechanik des Kniegelenks. (The mechanics of the knee.) *Archiv für Anatomie und Physiologie*: 497-547.

Miller, J. 1982. *The body in question.* New York: Random House.

Mooney, V., R. Pozos, A. Vleeming, J. Gulick, and D. Swenski. 2001. Exercise treatment for sacroiliac joint pain. *Orthopedics* 24(1): 29-32.

Moseley, G.L., P.W. Hodges, and S.C. Gandevia. 2002. Deep and superficial fibers of the lumbar multifidus muscle are differentially active during voluntary arm movements. *Spine* 27: E29-E36.

Munroe, K.J., P.R. Giacobbi, C. Hall, and R. Weinberg. 2000. The four W's of imagery use: Where, when, why and what. *The Sport Psychologist* 14: 119-137.

Murphy, S. 2002. Athletic imagery. In T. Horn (Ed.), *Advances in sport psychology* (2nd ed., pp. 405-440). Champaign, IL: Human Kinetics.

Naville, S. 1992. Class notes. Institute for Psychomotor Therapy, Department of Special Education, Postgraduate Studies, Zurich, Switzerland.

Noh, Y.E., T. Morris, and M.B. Andersen. 2007. Psychological intervention programs for reduction of injury in ballet dancers. *Research in Sports Medicine* 15(1): 13-32.

Norkin, C.C., and P.K. Levangie. 1992. *Joint structure and function.* Philadelphia: Davis.

Ohashi, W. 1991. *Reading the body.* New York: Penguin Books.

Olsen, A., and C. McHose. 1991. *Body stories: A guide to experiential anatomy.* Barrytown, NY: Station Hill Press.

Ornish, D. 1990. Can lifestyle changes reverse coronary heart disease? The Lifestyle Heart Trial. *Lancet* 336(8708): 129-133.

Overby, L.Y. 1990. The use of imagery by dance teachers: Development and implementation of two research instruments. *Journal of Physical Education, Recreation and Dance* 61: 24-27.

Palmer, M.L., and R.L. Blakely. 1986. Documentation of medial rotation accompanying shoulder flexion. *Physical Therapy* 66: 55-58.

Panjabi, M., and A. White. 1995. *Clinical biomechanics of the spine* (2nd ed.). Philadelphia: Lippincott Williams & Wilkins.

Parivzi, J., and A. Damasio. April 2001. Consciousness and the brainstem. *Cognition* 79(1-2): 135-160.

Pavio, A. 1985. Cognitive and motivational functions of imagery in human performance. *Canadian Journal of Applied Sport Sciences* 10: 22-28.

Perry, J. 1988. Muscle control of the shoulder. In C.R. Rowe (Ed.), *The shoulder* (pp. 17-34). New York: Churchill.

Piaget, J. 1993. *Der Zeitfaktor in Der Kindlichen Entwicklung: Aus Probleme der Entwicklungspsychologie.* (*The time factor in child development: A problem in developmental psychology*). Hamburg, Germany: Europäische Verlagsanstalt.

Pierce, A., and R. Pierce. 1989. *Expressive movement: Posture and action in daily life, sports, and the performing arts.* New York: Plenum Press.

Radin, E.L., R.M. Rose, J.D. Blaha, and A.S. Litsky. 1992. *Practical biomechanics for the orthopedic surgeon.* New York: Churchill Livingstone.

Reeves, N.P., K.S. Narendra, and J. Cholewicki. 2007. Spine stability: The six blind men and the elephant. *Clinical Biomechanics* 22(3): 266-274.

Rieman, K., and E. Franklin. 2010. *Gemeinsame und einheitliche Evaluationsverfahren zu Par 20 und Par 20a SGB der Spitzenverbände der Krankenkassen: Evaluation der Franklin-Methode.* (*Common and uniform evaluation procedures for Par 20 and Par 20a SGB of the central associations of the health insurance companies: Evaluation of the Franklin method*). Freiburg, Germany: Gesomed.

Rishabhchand. 1953. *The integral yoga of Sri Aurobindo.* Pondicherry, India: Sri Aurobindo Ashram.

Robin, N. 2007. Effects of motor imagery training on returning serve accuracy in tennis: The role of imagery ability. *International Journal of Sport and Exercise Psychology* 2: 177-188.

Rolf, I.P. 1977. *Rolfing: The integration of human structures.* Santa Monica, CA: Dennis Landman.

Rolf, I.P. 1989. *Rolfing.* Rochester, VT: Healing Arts Press.

Rolland, J. 1984. *Inside motion: An ideokinetic basis for movement education.* Northampton, MA: Contact Editions.

Rossi, E. 1986. *The psychobiology of mind-body healing: New concepts of therapeutic hypnosis.* New York: Norton.

Samuels, M., and N. Samuels. 1975. *Seeing with the mind's eye.* New York: Random House.

Schrader, C. 1993. *Geo.* Hamburg: Gruner und Jahr.

Schultz, I.H. 1982. *Das Autogene Training. (Autogenic training).* Stuttgart: Georg Thieme.

Schwartz, S. 1988. *Wie Pawlow auf den Hund kam. Die 15 klassischen Experimente der Psychologie. (How Pavlov got the idea of the dog: 15 classic experiments in psychology).* Weinheim, Germany: Beltz.

Selver, C., and C. Brooks. 1981. Sensory awareness. In G. Kogan (Ed.), *Your body works* (pp. 122-123). Berkeley, CA: And/Or Press.

Serrebrenikov, N., and J. Lawson. 1978. *The art of pas de deux.* London: Dance Books Ltd.

Shah, U. 2004. Heart and mind: (1) relationship between cardiovascular and psychiatric conditions. *Postgraduate Medical Journal* 80(950): 683-689.

Shärli, O. 1980. Leib, Bewegung und Bau. (Body, movement and structure) (p. 5). *Resonanzen.* Aarau, Switzerland: AT.

Sherrington, C. 1964. *Man on his nature.* New York: Mentor Books.

Skura, S. 1990. Releasing dance: An interview with Joan Skinner. *Contact Quarterly* 15(3): 11-18.

Snijders, C.J., A. Vleeming, and R. Stoeckart. 1993. Transfer of lumbosacral load to iliac bones and legs, part 1: Biomechanics of self-bracing of the sacroiliac joints and its significance for treatment and exercise. *Clinical Biomechanics* 8(6): 285-294.

Sohier, R. 1991. *Grundlage der biomechanischen Reharmonisation und Therapie der osteopathischen Gelenkläsionen als Einführung in das analytische Konzept. (Foundations of biomechanical reharmonization and therapy of osteopathic joint lesions as an introduction to the analytic concept).* La Louviere, Belgium: Kin-Science.

Stewart, D. February/March 1997. Is the octopus really the invertebrate intellect of the sea? *National Wildlife* 35(2).

Sullivan, M.J., K. Reesor, S. Mikail, and R. Fischer. 1992. The treatment of depression in chronic low back pain: Review and recommendations. *Pain* 50: 5-13.

Suzuki, S. 1970. *Zen mind, beginner's mind.* New York: Weatherhill.

Sweigard, L. 1961. The dancer and his posture. *Annual of Contemporary Dance.* (Reprinted from *Impulse.*)

Sweigard, L. 1974. *Human movement potential: Its ideokinetic facilitation.* New York: Dodd, Mead.

Todd, M. 1953. *The hidden you.* New York: Dance Horizons.

Todd, M. 1972. *The thinking body.* New York: Dance Horizons.

Todd, M. 1977. *Early writings: 1920-1934.* New York: Dance Horizons.

Topf, N. 1994. John Rolland remembered. *Contact Quarterly* 19(2): 13-17.

Van Beers, R. 2004. The role of execution noise in movement variability. *Journal of Neurophysiology* 91: 1050-1063.

Verin, L. 1980. The teaching of Moshe Feldenkrais. In G. Kogan (Ed.), *Your body works* (pp. 83-86). Berkeley, CA: And/Or Press.

Vitruv. 1993. De architectura (E. Franklin, Trans.). *Tages Anzeiger Magazin* 50: 39. (Original work published 33-14 BC).

Vleeming, A., H.B. Albert, H.C. Östgaard, B. Sturesson, and B. Stuge. 2008. European guidelines for the diagnosis and treatment of pelvic girdle pain. *European Spine Journal* 17(6): 794-819.

Vleeming, A., H.B. Albert, F.C.T. van der Helm, D. Lee, H.C. Östgaard, B. Stuge, and B. Sturesson. 2004. A definition of joint stability. In *European guidelines on the diagnosis and treatment of pelvic girdle pain. Cost Action B13: Low back pain: Guidelines for its management.* Working group 4.

Vleeming, A., A.C.W. Volkers, C.J. Snijders, and R. Stoeckart. 1990. Relation between form and function in the sacroiliac joint, part II: Biomechanical aspects. *Spine* 15(2): 133-136.

Vojta, V. 1992. *Das Vojta-Prinzip. (Vojta principle).* Berlin: Springer.

Weed, D. 1990. *What you think is what you get.* Langnau am Albis, Switzerland: 1445 Publications.

Weinert, C., J.H. McMaster, and R.J. Ferguson. 1973. Dynamic function of the human fibula. *American Journal of Anatomy* 138(2): 145-149.

Werner, H. (Ed.). 1965. *The body percept.* New York: Random House.

White, R. 1989. Visual thinking in the Ice Age. *Scientific American* 26(1): 74.

Willard, F.H., and J.E Carreiro. 2010. The aponeurotic roots of the thoracolumbar fascia. Proceedings of the 7th Interdisciplinary Congress on Low Back and Pelvic Pain, Los Angeles.

Willems, J.M., G.A. Jull, and J-KF Ng. 1996. An in vivo study of the primary and coupled rotations of the thoracic spine. *Clinical Biomechanics* 11(6): 311-316.

Woby, S., P. Watson, N. Roach, and M. Urmston. 2004. Are changes in fear avoidance beliefs, catastrophizing and appraisal of control predictive of changes in chronic low back pain and disability? *European Journal of Pain* 8(3): 201-210.

Zuckerman, J.D., and F.A. Matsen. 1989. Biomechanics of the shoulder. In M. Nordin and V.H. Frankel (Eds.), *Basic biomechanics of the musculoskeletal system* (2nd ed., pp. 225-247). Philadelphia: Lea & Febiger.

Index

Note: The italicized *f* or *t* following page numbers refers to figures and tables, respectively.

About the Author

Eric Franklin is director and founder of the Franklin Method Institute in Wetzikon, Switzerland. He has more than 35 years' experience as a dancer and movement educator, and he has shared imagery techniques in his teaching since 1986.

Franklin has taught extensively throughout the United States and Europe at the Royal Ballet School and Trinity Laban Conservatory in London, the Royal Danish Ballet in Copenhagen, the American Dance Festival, the Dance Academy of Rome, La Scala in Milan, and the Institute for Psychomotor Therapy in Zurich; he is also a guest faculty member at the University of Vienna and the Julliard School in New York. He has provided training to Olympic and world-champion athletes and professional dance troupes such as Cirque du Soleil and the Forum de Dance in Monte Carlo.

Franklin earned a BFA from New York University's Tisch School of the Arts and a BS from the University of Zurich. He has been on the faculty of the American Dance Festival since 1991.

Franklin is coauthor of the bestselling book *Breakdance*, which received a New York City Public Library Prize in 1984, and author of 18 books in 12 languages, among them *Dance Imagery for Technique and Performance* and *Conditioning for Dance* (both books about imagery in dance and movement); *Pelvic Power; Relax Your Neck, Liberate Your Shoulders*; and *Inner Focus, Outer Strength*. He is a member of the International Association of Dance Medicine and Science.

Franklin lives near Zurich, Switzerland.

LEARN MORE ABOUT DYNAMIC ALIGNMENT.
ACCELERATE YOUR TEACHING SKILLS.
CONTINUE YOUR TRANSFORMATION.

Go to franklinmethod.com and experience free imagery exercises on video. Plus, when you sign up for our newsletter, you will receive regular imagery inspirations from Eric Franklin and the Franklin Method. To sign-up: email books@franklin-methode.ch with subject "join mailing list"

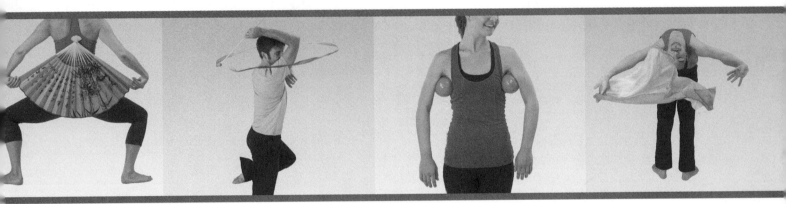

EXPERIENCE A FRANKLIN METHOD WORKSHOP:

Workshops are taught all around the globe by Eric Franklin as well as the other Franklin Method teachers.

Topics include Pelvic Power; Imagery for a Healthy Spine; Relax Your Neck, Liberate Your Shoulders; Fluid and Powerful: Introduction to Muscle Imagery; Psoas: Activate Your Inner Core; and Fabulous Feet, Dynamic Base.

Visit FranklinMethod.com to find an upcoming workshop!

BECOME A FRANKLIN METHOD TEACHER:

In LEVEL 1, you will learn about the basics of imagery, bone rhythms of the body, biomechanics, posture, and breathing.

In LEVEL 2, you will deepen your knowledge of the muscular system. You will learn how to use imagery to facilitate muscles, how to use touch to change muscle tension, and all the ins and outs of strength, stretching, and endurance training.

In LEVEL 3, you will cover the nervous, cardiovascular, immune, and lymphatic systems of the body. You will learn how to use imagery to create a positive change and experience full organic support. You will combine the information of all three levels into a whole.

For more information on teacher training, email: books@franklin-methode.ch

FRANKLIN
METHOD®

FranklinMethod.com   **f** facebook.com/FranklinMethod   **t** @FranklinMethod

You'll find other outstanding
dance resources at

www.HumanKinetics.com

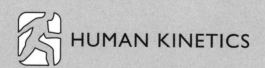